Postwar

Negotiations for

Arms Control

BERNHARD G. BECHHOEFER

Postwar

Negotiations for

Arms Control

The Brookings Institution

Washington, D.C.

© 1961 BY

THE BROOKINGS INSTITUTION

Published July 1961

Library of Congress Catalogue Card Number 61-14923

Printed in the United States of America
George Banta Company, Inc.

THE BROOKINGS INSTITUTION is an independent organization engaged in research and education in the social sciences. Its principal purposes are to aid in the development of sound public policies and to provide advanced training for students in the social sciences.

The Institution was founded December 8, 1927, as a consolidation of three antecedent organizations: the Institute for Government Research, 1916; the Institute of Economics, 1922; and the Robert Brookings Graduate School of Economics and Government, 1924.

The general administration of the Institution is the responsibility of a self-perpetuating Board of Trustees. In addition to this general responsibility the By-Laws provide that, "It is the function of the Trustees to make possible the conduct of scientific research and publication, under the most favorable conditions, and to safeguard the independence of the research staff in the pursuit of their studies and in the publication of the results of such studies. It is not a part of their function to determine, control, or influence the conduct of particular investigations or the conclusions reached." The immediate direction of the policies, program, and staff of the Institution is vested in the President, who is assisted by an advisory council, chosen from the professional staff of the Institution.

In publishing a study, the Institution presents it as a competent treatment of a subject worthy of public consideration. The interpretations and conclusions in such publications are those of the author or authors and do not necessarily reflect the views of other members of the Brookings staff or of the administrative officers of the Institution.

Foreword

THE search for effective international regulation of armaments has been a matter of widespread concern for over a generation. Although the peace plans of World War II, especially the Charter of the United Nations, emphasized arms control less than it was stressed after World War I, the effort devoted to the problem since 1945 has been greater than ever before, largely due to the awesome implications of nuclear weapons. Yet no significant progress has yet been made in achieving any substantial degree of international arms regulation.

Still the people of the world urge that the quest go on, and there are redoubled efforts currently to seek out new trails to the cherished goal. The Brookings Institution feels, therefore, that it is useful at this juncture—fifteen years and several administrations since the latest effort began—to present a study that reviews the record of the past, sorting out the threads of major continuing issues, as a basis for thinking about the future.

The author, Bernhard G. Bechhoefer, has had extensive experience in the field, having served as a senior officer of the Department of State on the armaments control question for twelve years, from 1946 to 1958. During this time he participated in most of the major arms policy discussions, both domestically and internationally. Since resigning from the Department of State in 1958, for the practice of law in Washington, he has written several articles and monographs on the problem in addition to the present book, which he began in March 1959.

The study is organized both chronologically and functionally. The historical treatment is divided into the five major phases of the armaments deliberations: (1) the first period of United Nations negotiations, 1946-48; (2) complete frustration, 1948-51; (3) comprehensive proposals, 1952-54; (4) search for partial disarmament, 1955-57; and (5) recent negotiations, 1958-60. Within each of these periods, the author traces the development of the main issues that run through the fabric of the whole experience.

In accordance with its usual practice, the Institution appointed an advisory committee, composed of individuals who had had extensive and authoritative experience in the field, to consult with the author at various stages during the course of the study. The members of the committee were: Harding F. Bancroft, Benjamin V. Cohen, Joseph E. Johnson, Morehead Patterson, Thomas R. Phillips, George M. Weil and Arnold O. Wolfers. To all of these individuals the author and the Institution are deeply indebted.

Thanks are due to others who were of special assistance to the author. These include Gordon Arneson, Herbert Dinerstein, John C. Elliott, Paul Fine, Edmund A. Gullion, John D. Hickerson, Jules Moch, Howard Meyers, David Popper, Harold Stassen, Lewis Strauss, David Wainhouse and Lawrence D. Weiler. The Disarmament Staff of the Department of State and the Subcommittee on Disarmament of the Senate Committee on Foreign Relations were particularly helpful.

Frances A. Gulick served as the author's research assistant from March to July 1959, and her knowledge of the negotiations from 1955 through 1957 played an important role in developing the analysis of that period. When Mrs. Gulick was compelled to relinquish the task, the author's wife, Estelle S. Bechhoefer, generously agreed to assist him in bringing the work to a successful conclusion. Evelyn Breck, the Brookings editor; Esther K. Austern, who checked the proof; Pauline Manning, the indexer; and Gladys M. Fyffe, the author's secretary, deserve special thanks for their skilled assistance. Ernst Reichl produced the design for the book and its jacket. *The New York Times* furnished some of the illustrations and helped the author to obtain the remaining illustrations elsewhere.

The study was conducted under the general supervision of H. Field Haviland, Jr., Director of Foreign Policy Studies, and was financed out of funds contributed for general support of the Institution by the Rockefeller Foundation and the Ford Foundation. The findings and conclusions are solely those of the author and should not be interpreted as necessarily reflecting the views of the Brookings trustees, officers, other staff members, members of the advisory committee, or of the foundations providing financial support.

May 1961   ROBERT D. CALKINS
                                              PRESIDENT

Contents

PART ONE

Prologue

I

Highway Without Signs

DISARMAMENT, or at least some measure of arms control, has been a heavily traveled road toward the destination of world peace. Yet on the surface, little if any progress is evident. Despite the absence of progress, however, the international negotiations on arms control will certainly continue. At the change of administration, both President Eisenhower and President Kennedy indicated their concern.

President Eisenhower in his farewell address to the nation on the completion of his two terms as President noted both the need for some measure of disarmament and his disappointment with the past. Referring to the conference table, he said: "That table, though scarred by many past frustrations, cannot be abandoned for the certain agony of the battlefield.

"Disarmament with mutual honor and confidence is a continuing imperative."[1]

President Kennedy in his inaugural address, hopefully called for fresh negotiations: "Let us never negotiate out of fear. But let us never fear to negotiate.

"Let both sides, for the first time, formulate serious and precise proposals for the inspection and control of arms—and bring the abso-

[1] U.S. Department of State *Bulletin*, Vol. 44 (Feb. 6, 1961), p. 181.

3

lute power to destroy other nations under the absolute control of all nations."[2]

Since World War II, the problem of arms control has posed one of the dilemmas of this era. In the United States, the public demand for progress toward disarmament is equaled only by the pressures for re-armament to provide the country with the great and costly military power needed to ensure its national survival and that of its allies and friends.

Increasing armaments may be symptoms rather than causes of conflict. It remains true, nonetheless, that the present nuclear arms race has become a cause not only of vast expenditure and increasing government control over the national economy but also of exacerbation of the East-West struggle. Each side fears technical advances that might give supremacy in deadly striking power to the other. Both sides have ample reason to want to find some way out of the unbridled race of armaments. Yet this race is compelling each side to forge ahead and to try at least to remain abreast of its opponent.

On the occasion of a recent failure of arms control negotiations—the walkout of the Soviet bloc delegations in June 1960 from the Geneva meeting of the Ten Nation Committee—one American periodical condemned the entire procedure of arms control negotiations: "Having lacked the courage to denounce disarmament from the beginning as the surest road to war, the West must now seek ways and means to escape international censure for being reluctant to commit suicide."[3]

This raises a fundamental issue. Does arms control (which only too often is identified with "disarmament" though they are not the same) in fact lead to peace or to security? In the period since World War II, the negotiations certainly have not led to the biblical dream of turning swords into plowshares. Nor have they led to the nuclear holocaust that the entire world dreads. It is most difficult to delineate both their past and their present direction. The arms control negotiations have truly been a highway without signs.

One reason for this is that the volume of material is so vast that it is difficult to separate the essential from the nonessential. The subject has

[2] *Ibid.*, p. 176.
[3] *Barron's National Business and Financial Weekly*, Vol. 40 (July 4, 1960), p. 7.

appeared on the agenda of every United Nations General Assembly commencing with 1946. A series of commissions, committees, and sub-committees either established or recommended by the United Nations have dealt in each year with some phase of the problem.

Linked to the direct negotiations on armaments within the United Nations are a vast number of collateral discussions, within and outside the Organization, which bear on the subject. Within the United Nations these include such matters as the establishment of the International Atomic Energy Agency, the establishment of United Nations armed forces under the aegis of the Organization, the broad Soviet proposals for lessening world tensions, which appear every year at the annual session of the General Assembly, and the linking of efforts to establish funds to assist underdeveloped areas with the savings that might be realized through an agreed arms control program.

Developments outside the United Nations include several propaganda campaigns by the Soviet Union—the Stockholm Appeal, the demands for immediate elimination of nuclear weapons testing, and the accusations that the United States waged bacteriological warfare in Korea. Likewise the Summit Conference in Geneva, the various meetings of the Foreign Ministers of the great powers, the meeting between President Eisenhower and Premier Khrushchev at Camp David, and indeed practically all top level international discussions over the past fourteen years have had implications in this field. The sum total of such developments creates a vast amorphous mass of material that is confusing and difficult to interpret.

A second set of circumstances has compounded this confusion. The Soviet approach during all this period has seldom shown promise but has occasionally held out suggestions that seemed to open attractive vistas for genuine negotiations and ultimate agreement. One possible interpretation of this approach is that the Soviet Union has no genuine interest either in disarmament or in arms control. Under this interpretation, all Soviet moves have been directed toward securing through international pressures the unilateral disarmament of the West. The Soviet Union had witnessed the headlong Western disarmament after World War I, which contributed to the temporary success of Hitler. Soviet leaders wished to repeat the process after World War II, with

Soviet imperialism reaping the benefits. Unquestionably such a Soviet motivation is one element in the arms control negotiations.

The Soviet leaders, while invariably alert to the propaganda implications of their moves, may have motives in the negotiations beyond that of securing the unilateral disarmament and ultimate destruction of the West. They may be looking forward to an extended period of "peaceful coexistence"—to use their phrase—which might be nothing more than holding the line militarily while resorting to other means to expand their influence. This posture would be consistent with some reduction of tensions and with understandings or agreements for lower levels of some armaments. If this is a correct interpretation of Soviet motivation, and if in the judgment of the West, the "peaceful coexistence" program might in fact lead to a more secure world rather than to the destruction of the West, then a study of the negotiations may usefully separate the roads that are blind alleys from those that could move in the ultimate direction of greater security.

A third factor leading to confusion has been the fact that the Western approach, particularly during the period of weakness of conventional forces prior to 1951, could not be entirely forthright because it was necessary to avoid a situation in which Soviet distortions of the Western position might destroy the essential program for strengthening the military posture of the West. It is not possible, therefore, to take at face value all of the Western statements of position. The Western positions as well as the Soviet positions require much interpretation to make them meaningful. The evidence, however, overwhelmingly shows Western support of feasible arms control.

Common to all negotiations with the Soviet Union is the Soviet practice of inextricably linking procedures and substance. This is another element of confusion. The Soviet representatives during the fifteen years of arms control negotiations have generally sought initially to achieve their desired substantive result through a procedural decision, such as the adoption of an agenda that precludes the submission of any other than the Soviet proposals. As a result of this practice, the substantive issues in the negotiations are frequently incomprehensible except when narrated within the framework of complicated procedures.

In the past the veil of security precautions at times greatly restricted general debates on many of the issues and has added to the confusion. This is no longer a seriously inhibiting factor.

These circumstances have created a situation in which it has been most difficult for all but a small corps of specialists to keep abreast of arms control developments, much less to understand them. Meanwhile, the entire world is watching these developments with a keener interest than ever before.

The terminology in this narrative presents problems. The Soviet Union during practically the entire fifteen-year period has used the single word "disarmament" to describe the negotiations even though many of the specific proposals over the years have not called for disarmament or even reduction of armaments. The Western powers with greater caution have preferred to use the term "limitation, regulation, and control of arms" or since 1958 its shorter variant "arms control." They have thereby subjected themselves to the Soviet charge that the West is not interested in disarmament or reduction of armaments but is concerned solely with control and the resulting penetration of the Soviet iron curtain, which in turn is vaguely linked to espionage. The United States uses the terms "disarmament" and "arms control" or any variants interchangeably in the recognition that the popular meaning of neither term accurately describes the subject matter of the negotiations.[4] In describing the past negotiations, this study will follow the United States official practice of using the terms interchangeably. The conclusions, however, will seek greater precision.

Beginning in 1955, the negotiations moved in a direction giving rise to even greater confusion in terminology. Ever since 1955, there has been considerable stress on partial measures of disarmament intended to build confidence, reduce international tensions, lessen the dangers of

[4] Francis O. Wilcox, *The Search for Disarmament*, Department of State Publication 6398 (1956). Prior to 1958, the West generally used the term "regulation of armaments" in lieu of "arms control" or "disarmament." The historical background of Western avoidance of the term "disarmament" is set forth in Chapter 3. Years of negotiations resulted in the association of the term "regulation of armaments" with a program precisely defined in a United Nations General Assembly resolution adopted on November 28, 1953 (see Chap. 13). The Western proposals commencing in 1956 were only remotely related to these earlier programs. The term "arms control" is perhaps no more descriptive of recent Western programs than "regulation of armaments," but avoids the close historical association with the earlier programs.

war, and lead to more drastic future reductions of armaments. Inherent in the language of this approach are a number of doubtful assumptions:

First, that partial disarmament will reduce international tensions. The specific measures might have the reverse effect.

Second, that the various measures of partial disarmament will reduce armaments. Some proposals for partial disarmament not only do not reduce armaments but may even increase them.

Third, that partial disarmament measures will lessen the danger of war. For example, the United States consistently assumes that "open skies" and disclosure by both the Soviet Union and the West of their missile-launching sites and the bases for their long-range aircraft will reduce the danger of war.

The Soviet representatives have on occasions contended that such measures would increase the danger of war by enhancing the possibility that a first nuclear strike would destroy the capability of the victim to retaliate. Therefore, the pressures for a pre-emptive strike would increase along with the corresponding danger of the outbreak of nuclear war. Yet the "open-sky" proposals are described as partial measures to build confidence and reduce the danger of war.[5]

These are but a few examples of the lack of precision in the terminology of the negotiations. To use a different terminology in the narrative, however, would merely create an added source of confusion. Therefore, where one or both of the negotiating parties describe a proposal as a confidence-building measure, it will be so described in the narrative portion of this study, even though its effects may be the reverse. Similarly, the proposals for cessation of tests and for detection of surprise attack will be described as parts of the package of partial measures of disarmament, though they may not result in any reductions of armaments.

The nature of the basic material that must be explored to obtain an

---

[5] The problems of the goals of arms control and the suitability of the most important approaches followed in the arms control negotiations for achieving these goals are dealt with in three papers in the special issue of *Daedalus*, Vol. 89, No. 4, on Arms Control published in the fall of 1960: Donald G. Brennan, "Setting and Goals of Arms Control," p. 681; Thomas C. Schelling, "Reciprocal Measures for Arms Stabilization," p. 892; Jerome B. Wiesner, "Comprehensive Arms-Limitation System," p. 915.

understanding of arms control developments has dictated the method of approach in this study. A detailed chronological narrative of the chief events of the arms control negotiations would be lengthy, disjointed, and as confusing as the amorphous mass of original materials. Since the objective of the study is to relate the past to the present and future, to consider arms control developments in the perspective of broader international developments, and, if possible, to point the way to some international accord on arms control, it becomes necessary in all periods of the negotiations to select from the vast mass of materials those ideas and events that have been significant and continuing themes in the negotiations. The negotiators themselves were usually thoroughly aware of such ideas and events although in the official records they were frequently submerged in torrents of rhetoric directed toward considerations other than the advancement of the negotiations. After the selection of the important ideas and events in the various periods of the negotiations, it becomes necessary to relate these ideas and events to the main course of the negotiations and to the stream of international developments of the period. Many of the most significant international events must receive scant mention because they are remote from the arms control negotiations, while other less important events must receive extended treatment. Moreover, many of the most publicized positions on arms control were pure froth.

The arms control negotiations since World War II can be divided into five phases:

1. The period from the First General Assembly of the United Nations in 1946 until the final Soviet rejection of the United Nations plan for control of atomic energy in the fall of 1948.

2. The period of minimum activity from 1948 until the convening of the General Assembly in the fall of 1951.

3. The period of maximum Soviet intransigence from the fall of 1951 until the conclusion of the General Assembly of 1954.

4. The period of the development of new policies by both the Soviet Union and the West, commencing late in 1954, until the refusal of the Soviet Union in December 1957 to participate further in the Disarmament Commission negotiations.

5. The most recent negotiations beginning in 1958.

In all these periods, certain ideas and proposals appear regularly like leitmotivs throughout the negotiations. Yet there is a progression that differentiates seemingly identical proposals when viewed in relation to changing circumstances.

In each period, this study will present the important events, relating them to the broader international currents, and in particular to United States policy, and will then seek to appraise their significance. The selection of important events as well as the evaluation of their significance must inevitably reflect the author's personal participation in the vast majority of the negotiations, tempered by his revisiting them years later through study of the records and discussions with participants in the negotiations, with the further aid of the extensive comments and interpretations that have appeared publicly over the years.

Foreshadowing the conclusions, the author believes that arms control negotiations could be—and indeed may have been during the past fifteen years—a road toward peace and security. It is not a smooth, straight throughway, moving directly to its ultimate destination; it is not the only road, and may not even be the best road, the world may pursue. Yet it is sufficiently important to call for signs which will avoid the detours and dead ends that in the past have obstructed forward motion. This study will have amply fulfilled its purpose, if it can provide some of the signs.

II

Framework for World Peace

IN MARCH 1952, Jacob Malik, the representative of the Soviet Union in the newly organized United Nations Disarmament Commission, in a dramatic address bristling with invective, accused the United States of resorting to bacteriological warfare in Korea, in violation of the Geneva Protocol of June 17, 1925, which prohibited the use of poison gas and of bacterial warfare.[1] This was apparently the first official reference, other than vague general statements, to the vast disarmament efforts that took place between the two world wars. Since most of the delegates were unfamiliar with the earlier efforts, the Secretariat was requested to prepare a background paper outlining the negotiations prior to World War II and continuing the narrative up to the formation of the Disarmament Commission. This study was published as a United Nations document in February 1953.[2] The narrative of all the events preceding the formation of the United Nations occupied nine pages, and satisfied the requirements of the commission.

This incident illustrates graphically the complete break between the United Nations discussions of regulation of armaments and all the preceding negotiations. During the first six years of United Nations

[1] U.N. Disarmament Commission, *Official Records*, Special Supplement No. 1, Doc. DC/20 (Oct. 13, 1952), p. 5.
[2] Background Paper No. 75, Disarmament, U.N. Doc. ST/DPI/SER. A/75 (Feb. 20, 1953).

11

negotiations—except for some Soviet propaganda blasts against the Western powers[3]—there had never been any occasion to refer to the earlier negotiations.

The reasons for this break with the past are fairly obvious. First the efforts to disarm between the wars ended in World War II. Hitler had flouted the Versailles Treaty obligations limiting German rearmament. Japan had evaded the naval limitation treaty of 1922. Article 8, paragraph 1 of the Covenant of the League of Nations had provided: "The Members of the League recognize that the maintenance of Peace requires the reduction of national armaments to the lowest point consistent with national safety and the enforcement by common action of international obligations."[4] The negotiations to carry out this provision of the Covenant had gone forward until the eve of World War II, with vast debates but with a minimum of achievement. The new United Nations did not contemplate world disarmament.

A second reason for a new approach to the subject of regulation of armaments after World War II was that the chief protagonists were changed. The United States and the Soviet Union, which had emerged from World War II as the two most powerful states, had comparatively minor roles in the League of Nations negotiations, with the United States participating merely as an observer. Before World War II, Great Britain and France had played the major roles. The decision to make a new approach to this problem paralleled the decision to replace the League of Nations with a stronger and more effective United Nations because of the failure of the League to maintain world peace.

Despite this almost complete break with the past, many of the problems of the negotiations following World War II echoed the past. Perhaps the most controversial issue in the League of Nations discussions was whether disarmament agreements must await the establishment of more friendly relations among nations, or alternatively, whether disarmament agreements in and of themselves would succeed in reducing tension. In the League of Nations, Great Britain was the chief proponent of immediate disarmament agreements, while France

[3] For example, see speech of Vyshinsky in the First Committee of the General Assembly. U.N. General Assembly, Third Session, *Official Records*, 153rd Meeting (Oct. 7, 1948), p. 96.
[4] Ruth B. Russell assisted by Jeannette E. Muther, *A History of the United Nations Charter: The Role of the United States 1940-1945* (1958), App. E, p. 978.

called for an improvement of relations among nations and greater security prior to any disarmament. This same situation constantly emerges in the United Nations discussions.

Another problem that arose in the period between the wars was the value, if any, of pacts unaccompanied by machinery to ensure their observance. The most publicized United States contribution in the period between the wars was the Kellogg-Briand Pact outlawing war but containing no enforcement machinery.[5] This pact did not prevent Japanese aggression in Manchuria, the Italian wars against Ethiopia, or the belligerent moves of Hitler and the Soviet Union, which led directly to World War II. The Soviet Union in the period between the wars had at one time suggested the complete abolition of armaments and percentage reductions in armed forces and armaments, also without machinery to ensure enforcement of the commitments.

The Geneva Protocol of 1925, prohibiting bacterial and chemical warfare,[6] is cited as an example of a successful pact even though it was unaccompanied by machinery to ensure observance of the pact because during World War II the antagonists did not resort to bacterial or chemical warfare.[7] The question arises whether the existence of the pact or the exigencies of warfare should receive the credit.

The most important question that has confronted negotiators since World War II also made its appearance in the earlier period—the problem of inspection and other safeguards to ensure observance of a disarmament treaty. After the emergence of Hitler, Maxim Litvinov, the Soviet representative, became the chief proponent of rigorous supervision, without, however, outlining any details of the supervision. In contrast to its insistence since World War II on adequate inspection and safeguards, the United States in the period between the wars had looked with skepticism on the development of an international inspection system. Frank Kellogg, the Secretary of State during the Coolidge administration, stated in 1926 that the country "should not be

[5] *Ibid.*, p. 208, note: "The General Treaty for the Renunciation of War (1928) obligated sixty-three states to renounce war as an instrument of national policy and to settle conflicts only by peaceful means."
[6] "Protocol for the Prohibition of the Use in War of Asphyxiating, Poisonous or Other Gases, and of Bacteriological Methods of Warfare," Geneva, June 17, 1925, 94 League of Nations Series (1929), p. 65.
[7] The protocol apparently did not prevent Italy from using chemical warfare against Ethiopia.

subject to inspection or control by foreign agencies. Limitation must depend upon good faith."[8] A logical outcome of this attitude was the Kellogg-Briand Pact. The Roosevelt administration, however, reversed this earlier attitude in 1933 through its support of a disarmament convention requiring international supervision of the execution of the convention.[9]

The arms control negotiators after 1945 referred only rarely to these parallels. Jules Moch, the French delegate during most of the negotiations since 1951, with his broad approach to the entire problem of world peace, was aware of the earlier history and occasionally referred to it. The Soviet delegates sometimes used Litvinov's name to demonstrate Soviet devotion to disarmament. John Foster Dulles, the late Secretary of State of the United States, had participated in certain activities of the League of Nations. His skepticism of the League of Nations approach, generated by this past experience,[10] undoubtedly played a significant role in several vital United States decisions in 1957.

While in retrospect it is possible to find parallels between these two sets of negotiations, and even a few points of contact, the emphasis must be on the complete break from the earlier period. The parallel developments arise solely because certain problems are inherent in any disarmament negotiations and are bound to emerge.

PLANNING A UNITED NATIONS

ORGANIZATION

During World War II, the United States and its chief allies gradually developed plans for the new and better world that would follow the defeat of Germany, Japan, and Italy. From the outset this planning

[8] *New York Times*, Aug. 19, 1926.
[9] "Draft Disarmament Convention: Provisional text prepared in the light of the modifications adopted in the first reading on June 8, 1933, Geneva, September 22, 1933," in *Disarmament and Security*, a collection of documents (1919-1955) prepared by Subcommittee on Disarmament, for use of Senate Committee on Foreign Relations, 84 Cong. 2 sess., p. 118. Supervisory machinery is provided in pt. 5, p. 141.
[10] John Foster Dulles, *War, Peace and Change* (1939).

called for a reduction in the burden on mankind of excessive armaments.

President Roosevelt in his annual message to Congress on January 6, 1941, which became known as the "Four Freedoms Address" defined the objective: "In the future days, which we seek to make secure, we look forward to a world founded upon four essential human freedoms." [The first three freedoms were freedom of speech, freedom of worship, and freedom from want.]

"The fourth is freedom from fear—which, translated into world terms, means a world-wide reduction of armaments to such a point and in such a thorough fashion that no nation will be in a position to commit an act of physical aggression against any neighbor—anywhere in the world."[11]

The first indication of the nature of the planning for the postwar framework to achieve this objective was in the joint declaration of Roosevelt and Winston Churchill on August 14, 1941, known as the Atlantic Charter. This joint declaration noted that Roosevelt and Churchill "being met together, deem it right to make known certain common principles in the national policies of their respective countries on which they base their hopes for a better future for the world."[12] The eighth and last of these principles was as follows:

> Eighth, they believe that all of the nations of the world, for realistic as well as spiritual reasons must come to the abandonment of the use of force. Since no future peace can be maintained if land, sea or air armaments continue to be employed by nations which threaten, or may threaten, aggression outside of their frontiers, they believe, pending the establishment of a wider and permanent system of general security, that the disarmament of such nations is essential. They will likewise aid and encourage all other practicable measures which will lighten for peace-loving peoples the crushing burden of armaments.[13]

This paragraph, based on a United States draft, was welcomed by

[11] *Public Papers and Addresses of Franklin D. Roosevelt: War—And Aid to Democracies* (1941), p. 672.
[12] U.S. Department of State, *Cooperative War Effort*, Publication 1732 (1942), p. 4.
[13] *Ibid.*

Churchill, who described it as "most remarkable for its realism."[14]

The Soviet Union and China considerably later, in the Declaration of Four Nations on General Security, in effect endorsed the Atlantic Charter.[15]

The Atlantic Charter added a tangible first step to the original objective of lightening the burden of armaments—the disarmament of aggressor nations. Perhaps more important than any positive declaration of policy in the Atlantic Charter was the omission of all reference to the League of Nations as the framework for the maintenance of future world peace.

By March 1943 United States planning had progressed somewhat further. Harry Hopkins reports a meeting of President Roosevelt, British Foreign Minister Eden, Cordell Hull, the United States Secretary of State, Sumner Welles, the Undersecretary, Lord Halifax, the British Ambassador, and William Strang of the British Foreign Office, in which there was a general discussion of international organization after the war.

> The President and Welles were very emphatic that the United States could not be a member of any independent regional body such as a European Council; they felt that all the United Nations should be members of one body for the purposes of recommending policy; that this body should be world-wide in scope; that there would be under this body regional councils with similar advisory powers made up of the nations geographically located in the regions; but finally, that the real decisions should be made by the United States, Great Britain, Russia and China, who would be the powers for many years to come that would have to police the world.[16]

This was the first appearance of the doctrine of the Four Policemen, which foreshadowed the role and organization of the Security Council of the United Nations.

[14] Sumner Welles, *Where Are We Heading?* (1946), p. 11.
[15] The text of the declaration is given in U.S. Department of State, *Toward the Peace Documents,* Publication 2298 (1945), p. 6.
[16] Robert E. Sherwood, *Roosevelt and Hopkins, An Intimate History* (1948), p. 717.

Stalin's comment on the Four Policemen proposal was that it would not be favorably received by the small nations of Europe.[17] Furthermore, he did not believe that China would be very powerful when the war ended. He therefore suggested alternative arrangements. However, he raised no strong objections.

The Declaration of Four Nations

The Four Policemen concept, in somewhat modified form, was contained in the Declaration of Four Nations on General Security made by the representatives of the United States, the United Kingdom, the Soviet Union, and China in November 1943. The portions of this historic declaration relevant to the subject of arms regulations are:

The Governments of the United States of America, the United Kingdom, the Soviet Union and China: . . .
jointly declare:
1. That their united action, pledged for the prosecution of the war against their respective enemies, will be continued for the organization and maintenance of peace and security.
2. That those of them at war with a common enemy will act together in all matters relating to the surrender and disarmament of that enemy. . . .
4. That they recognise the necessity of establishing at the earliest practicable date a general international organization, based on the principle of the sovereign equality of all peace-loving states, and open to membership by all such states, large and small, for the maintenance of international peace and security.
5. That for the purpose of maintaining international peace and security pending the re-establishment of law and order and the inauguration of a system of general security, they will consult with one another and as occasion requires with other members of the United Nations with a view to joint action on behalf of the community of nations. . . .

[17] *Ibid.*, p. 786.

7. That they will confer and co-operate with one another and with other members of the United Nations to bring about a practicable general agreement with respect to the regulation of armaments in the post-war period.[18]

The declaration added considerably to the planning for the postwar world by providing for a general international organization to maintain world peace and outlining the transition from war to peace.

The Declaration of Four Nations nowhere contemplates general world disarmament. Stated in blunt terms, the policy enunciated in the declaration had two main poles: (1) the negative pole of the doctrine was that the four great powers should forcibly disarm Germany and Japan and also assure that no other states should develop sufficient armaments to threaten world peace. (2) The second and positive pole that is implicit in the Atlantic Charter but explicit in the Declaration of Four Nations was that the four powers after the war must remain militarily strong. The four powers would police the world until the establishment of an international system of security, which would take over the task.

Despite Stalin's initial reservations, the Soviet Union gave its full endorsement to this doctrine. Commenting on the Atlantic Charter, a Soviet author, Judge S. B. Krylov, states:

> The Declaration indicated that such states threatening aggression should be disarmed pending the creation of a broader and more reliable system of general security. The signers of the Declaration declared that they would also encourage the development of all other practicable means which might facilitate the liberation of peace-loving peoples from the burden of armaments.[19]

Krylov further points out that the Atlantic Charter was incomplete in that it said nothing of an international armed force for preservation of peace or of an international security organization, a difficulty that

[18] U.S. Department of State, *Toward the Peace Documents*, p. 6.
[19] S. B. Krylov, *Materials for the History of the United Nations*, Vol. 1, "Framing of the Text of the Charter of the United Nations," unpublished translation by H. Bartlett Wells (undated), p. 12.

was later remedied in the Declaration of Four Nations and in the proposals for a United Nations.

He concludes: "The adherence of the U.S.S.R. to the Atlantic Charter conferred upon it the character of an international document of World significance."[20]

THE CHARTER OF THE

UNITED NATIONS

It was inevitable that the doctrine of the Four Policemen should receive considerable modification before it became embodied in formal proposals for a United Nations. As Stalin had pointed out, the doctrine ran roughshod over the role of smaller states in international deliberations. It excluded France from the realm of great powers. The Declaration of Four Nations went no further in the direction of sketching the structure for an international organization than to point out that there should be an international organization based on the principle of the sovereign equality of states.

Even prior to the Atlantic Charter, the planning of a new international organization had commenced within the United States Department of State. In 1943, as the prospects for an Allied victory improved, the planning accelerated its pace; draft papers were prepared to translate the doctrine of the Four Policemen into a statute for an international organization.[21]

As early as December 1943, the planners in the State Department had realized the fundamental truth that the contemplated structure for the maintenance of world peace in the era after the war depended on the West retaining its military strength.

By the time of the Yalta Conference in February 1945, the planning had gone a long distance toward defining the roles of the smaller states in the postwar international organization. Despite Stalin's pre-

[20] *Ibid.*, p. 15.
[21] A full description of the steps starting with the Atlantic Charter and ending in the completed Charter of the United Nations is contained in *A History of the United Nations Charter*, by Ruth B. Russell, Chap. 10.

vious comments on the Atlantic Charter that it would be unwelcome to the smaller European states, he had considerable reservations concerning the role of states other than the great powers in the new international organization. He made it quite clear that he agreed with Churchill and Roosevelt that the three great powers that had borne the brunt of the war should be the ones to preserve the peace. It was ridiculous to believe that a small country like Albania should have an equal voice with the big three. He was prepared to join with the United States and Great Britain to protect the rights of the small powers, but he would never agree to having action of any of the great powers submitted to the judgment of small powers.[22]

The proposals emerging from the Dumbarton Oaks Conference on October 9, 1944, with one addition made at Yalta on the question of voting in the Security Council,[23] became the basis for the Charter of the United Nations, adopted at the San Francisco Conference in June 1945.[24] The United Nations Charter secured the necessary number of ratifications in October 1945, and the first meetings of the Security Council and General Assembly took place in January 1946. Since the Charter of the United Nations furnished the framework for substantially all of the international conferences on regulation of armaments from January 1946 until December 1957, it is appropriate to consider in some detail the provisions of the Charter dealing with regulation of armaments and the ideas underlying these provisions.

The Members of the United Nations conferred on the Security Council "primary responsibility for the maintenance of international peace and security," and agreed that "in carrying out its duties under this responsibility, the Security Council acts on their behalf." (Article 24) The Security Council was to consist of eleven members—five permanent and six elected members. The five permanent members were the United States, the United Kingdom, the Soviet Union, and China (the Four Policemen) and France, which between the time of the

[22] See Edward R. Stettinius, Jr., *Roosevelt and the Russians: The Yalta Conference* (1949), pp. 149-50.
[23] Russell, *op. cit.*, pp. 417, 502-04, 714.
[24] U.S. Department of State, *Charter of the United Nations and Statute of the International Court of Justice*, Publication 2368 (1945), pp. 1-20.

Dumbarton Oaks Conference and the adoption of the Charter had become the fifth policeman. (Article 23) Decisions of the Security Council on all except procedural matters required the affirmative votes of the permanent members. In other words, each of the permanent members had a right of veto. (Article 27) An immediate task of the Security Council and the Military Staff Committee was to work out agreements under which all Members of the United Nations would undertake to make available to the Security Council on its call armed forces assistance and facilities. (Article 43) Until sufficient of these agreements had come into being to permit the Security Council to exercise its responsibilities for maintenance of world peace:

> . . . the parties to the Four Nations Declaration signed at Moscow, October 30th, 1943, and France, shall in accordance with the provisions of paragraph 5 of that Declaration consult with one another and, as occasion requires, with other Members of the United Nations with a view to such joint action on behalf of the Organization as may be necessary for the purpose of maintaining international peace and security. (Article 106)

By the time the San Francisco Conference had convened, Germany had surrendered and the four great powers of the West were engaged in disarming Germany. In the regulation of armaments, the Security Council was given the following specific authority.

> In order to promote the establishment and maintenance of international peace and security with the least diversion for armaments of the world's human and economic resources, the Security Council shall be responsible for formulating, with the assistance of the Military Staff Committee referred to in Article 47, plans to be submitted to the Members of the United Nations for the establishment of a system for the regulation of armaments. (Article 26)

The Charter goes on (Article 107) to provide that "nothing in the present Charter shall invalidate or preclude action in relation to any state which during the Second World War has been an enemy of any signatory to the present Charter, taken or authorized as a result of that war by the Governments having responsibility for such action."

The General Assembly, consisting of representatives of all Members of the United Nations, was given authority to "consider the general principles of cooperation in the maintenance of international peace and security, including the principles governing disarmament and the regulation of armaments, and may make recommendations with regard to such principles to the Members or to the Security Council or to both." (Article 11)

Through these provisions, the Charter of the United Nations, in effect, set up a system of priorities for dealing with postwar problems relating to the regulation of armaments. The task with the greatest urgency was to disarm the Axis nations. This was already being performed by the Western policemen with Charter sanction for their actions.

The first task of the Security Council, with its primary responsibility for the maintenance of world peace, was to secure through agreements with Member states the forces required for the United Nations to maintain international peace. The Military Staff Committee consisting only of the representatives of the policemen, now become five, had the responsibility for working out these agreements. (Article 47)

A much less urgent task was for the Security Council with the assistance of the Military Staff Committee to prepare the plans to be submitted to the Members of the United Nations for the establishment of a system for the regulation of armaments. Finally, the least urgent task was for the General Assembly as a long-range planning organization, making recommendations but taking no action, to consider "the principles governing disarmament and the regulation of armaments," and to "make recommendations with regard to such principles to the Members or to the Security Council or to both." (Article 11)

It is clear that the United Nations was not intended to repeat the fruitless debates on disarmament that occupied the League of Nations during almost the entire period between World War I and World War II. Therefore, it was no accident that in the Charter of the United Nations the word "disarmament" appears only twice: in Article 11 permitting the General Assembly to "consider the principles governing disarmament and the regulation of armaments" and in Article 47 authorizing the Military Staff Committee to advise the Security Council on "the regulation of armaments and *possible* disarmament."[25] The basic United States thinking underlying the Charter was that the five great powers should not disarm after the war, but should continue to be in a position to maintain international peace against any aggressor until the United Nations itself had the military strength to take over the task.

That this was likewise the Soviet concept is plain from the comment of Judge Krylov on Article 26: "One cannot fail to note that this refers to regulation of armaments which of course includes their possible reduction. On the other hand, it is plain that the limit of such reduction is represented by that contingent which is necessary for collective action prescribed by the Security Council."[26]

This wartime thinking on the subject of the regulation of armaments persisted for many years in the peacetime negotiations under the United Nations and is a factor in placing in proper perspective the later proposals both of the Soviet Union and of the West. Not until 1952 did the United Nations create a committee, the title of which contained the word disarmament (and even at that time the use of the word disarmament met considerable opposition).

In commenting on the Yalta discussions for meeting aggression after the war and for maintaining world peace, Harry Hopkins, the man closest to Roosevelt, points out: "There seems to be no evidence of any discussion of the possibility that the offending aggressor might be one of the Four Policemen.[27] Certainly the entire concept of the "Four Policemen" depended on the assumption "that their united action, pledged for the prosecution of the war against their respective enemies, will be continued for the organization and maintenance of peace and security."[28]

The San Francisco Conference took a number of steps, initially opposed by the Soviet Union, to provide in the United Nations Char-

[25] Italics added.
[26] Krylov, *op. cit.*, p. 56.
[27] Sherwood, *op. cit.*, p. 786.
[28] "Declaration of Four Nations on General Security," U.S. Department of State, *Toward the Peace Documents*, p. 6.

ter for contingencies that might arise in the event of a disagreement of the great powers. One of these steps was described by Krylov as a "tendency to broaden the rights of the General Assembly."[29] The amendments adopted at San Francisco did not, however, directly affect the problem of regulation of armaments where the General Assembly already had adequate authority to deal with the problem in the event of an impasse in the Security Council. The greater role visualized at San Francisco for the General Assembly in maintaining world peace carried over into the field of regulation of armaments, and after 1948, the Security Council played only a minor part in the negotiations.

[29] Krylov, *op. cit.*, p. 171. Amendments of Article 11 of the Charter.

The First Period of United Nations Negotiations 1946-1948

PART TWO

The First Period
of United Nations
Negotiations
1946-1948

III

Aftermath of Hiroshima

On June 25, 1945, the San Francisco Conference unanimously adopted the Charter of the United Nations, and the delegates of all states participating in the Conference affixed their signatures to the document. Less than a month later, the successful explosion of a nuclear device at Alamogordo, New Mexico[1] set off a chain reaction in the field of international negotiations and initiated a pattern differing radically from the previous planning.

Aware of the successful explosion in New Mexico, the heads of governments of the United States, the United Kingdom, and China on July 26, 1945, issued the Potsdam Declaration calling for Japanese surrender and threatening "the complete destruction of the Japanese armed forces and just as inevitably the utter devastation of the Japanese homeland."[2] Two days later the Premier of Japan rejected the Potsdam ultimatum as "unworthy of public notice."[3] Hiroshima was bombed on August 6, and on the same day the President announced: "The force from which the sun draws its power has been loosed against those who brought war to the Far East."[4]

[1] Henry D. Smyth, *Atomic Energy for Military Purposes* (1945), p. 247.
[2] U.S. Department of State, *The International Control of Atomic Energy: Growth of a Policy*, Publication 2702 (1946), p. 8. Cited hereafter as *Growth of a Policy*.
[3] Henry L. Stimson, "The Decision to Use the Atomic Bomb," *Harper's Magazine* (February 1947).
[4] *Growth of a Policy*, p. 95.

The next few days witnessed momentous international developments. The President signed the formal document of ratification of
the Charter of the United Nations on August 8. A plutonium bomb
destroyed Nagasaki on August 9. The next day the Emperor of Japan
offered to surrender. Agreement was reached on the terms of surrender
on August 14.[5]

Eight years later, John Foster Dulles, during his first year as Secretary of State, called the provisions of the Charter on regulation of
armaments obsolete before the Charter came into force.

> The United Nations Charter now reflects serious inadequacies.
> One inadequacy sprang from ignorance. When we were in San
> Francisco in the Spring of 1945, none of us knew of the atomic
> bomb which was to fall on Hiroshima on August 6, 1945. The
> Charter is thus a pre-Atomic Age Charter. In this sense it was
> obsolete before it actually came into force. As one who was at San
> Francisco, I can say with confidence that if the delegates there
> had known that the mysterious and immeasurable power of the
> atom would be available as a means of mass destruction, the pro-
> visions of the Charter dealing with disarmament and the regulation
> of armaments would have been far more emphatic and realistic.[6]

Dulles' statement that the delegates at San Francisco knew nothing
of the bomb is not literally correct. Although the final decision to use
the bomb was made after the San Francisco Conference, Secretary of
State Stettinius, Assistant Secretary of War John J. McCloy, Assistant
Secretary of the Navy Artemus Gates, Assistant Secretary of State
Clement Dunn, and perhaps other members of the United States delegation knew that atomic weapons were being developed. Lord Halifax,
the British Ambassador, also knew of the bomb.

The work on the bomb, however, was a closely guarded secret.

[5] *Ibid.*, p. 10.
[6] Address by Secretary of State John Foster Dulles before the American Bar Association, August 26, 1953. Secretary Dulles referred again to the Charter as "pre-
atomic" in his address before the U.N. General Assembly, September 22, 1955,
Department of State Press Release 558.

President Truman first learned of the bomb on April 25, after the death of Roosevelt who had made the early decisions to develop the bomb.[7] Churchill complained that the United States military kept its information out of the hands of Great Britain,[8] and Prime Minister Mackenzie King of Canada stated: "The Americans alone were active in large-scale work."[9]

We now know that the Soviet leaders through espionage had learned a great deal about the bomb,[10] but they certainly would not have admitted their knowledge.

The members of the United States delegation who knew of the work on the atomic bomb did not realize the impact atomic weapons would have on military strategy; and even if they had foreseen in part the later developments, this probably would not have changed their views on the United Nations Charter. The basic objective of the Charter was to prevent future wars. A new and terrible weapon reinforced the validity of that objective.

UNITED STATES INITIATIVE

After Hiroshima, President Truman moved rapidly toward national and international control of atomic energy. On August 9 in reporting to the country on the Berlin Conference, he devoted a major portion of his speech to the international consequences of nuclear weapons:

> The atomic bomb is too dangerous to be loose in a lawless world. That is why Great Britain and the United States, who have the secret of its production, do not intend to reveal the secret until means have been found to control the bomb so as to protect our-

[7] Harry S. Truman, *Memoirs*, Vol. One (1955), pp. 10-11, 87, 417-19.
[8] Robert E. Sherwood, *Roosevelt and Hopkins, An Intimate History* (1948), pp. 703-04.
[9] *Growth of a Policy*, p. 8.
[10] Dominion of Canada, "The Report of the Royal Commission to Investigate the Facts Relating to the Circumstances Surrounding the Communication by Public Officials and Other Persons in Positions of Trust, of Secret and Confidential Information to Agents of a Foreign Power" (1946).

selves and the rest of the world from the danger of total destruction. . . .

We must constitute ourselves trustees of this new force—to prevent its misuse, and to turn it into the channels of service to mankind. It is an awful responsibility which has come to us. . . .[11]

On August 16, 1945, the War Department issued the so-called Smyth report, "A General Account of the Development of Methods of Using Atomic Energy for Military Purposes,"[12] which for the next several years was the textbook in atomic energy discussions.

In his message to the Congress on October 3, the President asked for immediate action along both the domestic and international fronts.[13] On the domestic front, Congress passed the McMahon Bill, which became effective on August 1, 1946, and furnished the basis for domestic regulation until August 1954. This bill created the United States Atomic Energy Commission and the Joint Committee of the Congress on Atomic Energy. The bill sought to ensure that certain technical data on the design and construction of the bomb would remain secret "until effective and reciprocal international safeguards could be designed."[14]

In the international field, despite the fact that the United Nations Charter had never contemplated dealing with this problem, the President sought to use the machinery provided by the Charter. Immediate action was essential:

In international relations as in domestic affairs, the release of atomic energy constitutes a new force too revolutionary to consider in the framework of old ideas. We can no longer rely on the slow progress of time to develop a program of control among nations. . . .

The hope of civilization lies in international arrangements looking, if possible, to the renunciation of the use and development of the atomic bomb, and directing and encouraging the use of atomic energy and all future scientific information toward peaceful and

[11] *Growth of a Policy*, p. 108.
[12] Published as Henry D. Smyth, *Atomic Energy for Military Purposes*.
[13] *Growth of a Policy*, pp. 108-12.
[14] *Ibid.*, p. 19.

humanitarian ends. The difficulties in working out such arrangements are great. The alternative to overcoming these difficulties, however, may be a desperate armament race which might well end in disaster. . . .[15]

This was a call to nip in the bud an atomic arms race.

We have seen that, in creating the Charter, the anticipation was that the initial activities of the United Nations would be confined to disarming the enemy states, Germany and Japan, and thereafter creating a security force under the direction of the United Nations. A second and lower priority would be the regulation of armaments of states other than the great powers "in order to promote the establishment and maintenance of international peace and security with the least diversion for armaments of the world's human and economic resources."[16] The determination of "the principles governing disarmament"[17] by the United Nations General Assembly had a still lower priority, and the development of any detailed program for disarmament was never mentioned in the Charter. In view of the immediate United States decision to seek to eliminate nuclear weapons, this latter idea, that of "principles of disarmament," the least immediate of the three basic concepts considered at San Francisco, was nevertheless the one possible point of contact with the newly arising problem of the threat of nuclear power in war.

The Charter of the United Nations specified no exact procedures for dealing with "a disarmament problem." Therefore the President, in the spirit of the Charter, in general followed the provisions for transitional security arrangements contained in Article 106. This article provided that, pending the creation of a United Nations military force to enable the Security Council to carry out its responsibilities for peace, the parties to the Four Nation Declaration signed at Moscow on October 30, 1943 (United States, United Kingdom, China, Soviet Union), and France, should "consult with one another and, as occasion

[15] *Ibid.*, "Message from the President of the United States to Congress . . . October 3, 1945," pp. 109-12.
[16] Art. 26.
[17] Art. 11.

requires, with other Members of the United Nations with a view to such joint action on behalf of the Organization, as may be necessary for the purpose of maintaining international peace and security." President Truman proceeded promptly and expeditiously to institute consultative processes.

The consultative procedures commenced on November 15 with a meeting in Washington of Clement Attlee, the British Prime Minister, W. L. Mackenzie King, the Canadian Prime Minister, and President Truman.[18] The United States position in this meeting had emerged from studies undertaken before the explosion of the bomb. As early as May 1945, President Truman had requested Secretary of War Stimson to appoint a high-level committee to consider means of control. The measure of importance of this committee can be seen in the quality of its members: Secretary Stimson; James F. Byrnes, who had resigned from the Office of War Mobilization and Reconversion and was a private citizen, not yet nominated to be Secretary of State; William L. Clayton, Assistant Secretary of State for Economic Affairs; Ralph Bard, Undersecretary of the Navy; George Harrison, President of the New York Life Insurance Company and Special Assistant to the Secretary of War; Dr. Vannevar Bush, Chairman of the Office of Scientific Research and Development; Dr. Karl Compton, President of Massachusetts Institute of Technology; and Dr. James Conant, President of Harvard University. Four eminent scientists who had been associated with the atomic bomb development were appointed to assist the committee. This panel of scientists was made up of Dr. J. R. Oppenheimer, Dr. E. O. Lawrence, Dr. A. H. Compton, and Dr. Enrico Fermi. A group of representative industrialists, also prominently enlisted in the bomb project, worked with the committee.[19]

As a result of intensive efforts, the committee brought in a report definite in its recommendations. The five basic concepts first made public by President Truman in his Navy Day address October 27, 1945 were distilled from the findings of scientists, statesmen, and the military:

[18] *Growth of a Policy*, p. 120.
[19] *Ibid.*, pp. 3-4.

1. No nation can long maintain a monopoly of atomic weapons.
2. No nation could long maintain or morally defend a monopoly of the peaceful benefits of atomic energy.
3. For the foreseeable future there can be no adequate military defense against atomic weapons.
4. All the initial processes in the production of fissionable materials and certain subsequent processes are identical whether their intended use or purpose is peaceful or military.
5. The nuclear chain reaction required for the release of atomic energy is now based upon uranium or uranium and thorium as the only suitable raw materials occurring in nature. Ores containing these materials are only relatively rare. Although rich deposits are not numerous, the lower concentrations of the ores have a wide geographical distribution.[20]

The deliberations of the three chiefs of government resulted on November 15, 1945, in the Three Nation Agreed Declaration on Atomic Energy. This declaration enlarged considerably on the five basic concepts presented by Truman in his Navy Day address. In addition, the three countries, which were the only ones at that time to possess "the knowledge essential to the use of Atomic Energy," declared their willingness "to proceed with the exchange of fundamental scientific literature for peaceful ends with any nation that will fully reciprocate." Spreading this information, however, could not take place without great peril until "it is possible to devise effective reciprocal and enforceable safeguards acceptable to all nations," which "would contribute to a constructive solution of the problem of the atomic bomb."[21] The three countries therefore suggested the setting up of a commission under the United Nations to prepare recommendations for submission to the United Nations.

The Three Nation Declaration ripened quickly, with a minimum of friction and discussion, into one paragraph of the Soviet Anglo-American communiqué of December 27, 1945, popularly known as the

[20] *Ibid.*, pp. 1-2.
[21] *Ibid.*, pp. 118-20.

Moscow Declaration. This communiqué stated that the three governments "agreed to recommend for the consideration of the General Assembly of the United Nations, the establishment by the United Nations of a Commission to consider problems arising from the discovery of atomic energy and related matters."[22] They agreed to invite France and Canada to join in sponsoring at the first session of the General Assembly of the United Nations in January 1946, a resolution contained in the declaration. This resolution would establish a commission consisting of the members of the Security Council, and in addition, Canada when that state was not a member of the Security Council. The terms of reference of the commission were to

> inquire into all phases of the problem, and make such recommendations from time to time with respect to them as it finds possible. In particular the Commission shall make specific proposals:
> (a) For extending between all nations the exchange of basic scientific information for peaceful ends;
> (b) For control of atomic energy to the extent necessary to ensure its use only for peaceful purposes;
> (c) For the elimination from national armaments of atomic and of all other major weapons adaptable to mass destruction;
> (d) For effective safeguards by way of inspection and other means to protect complying states against the hazards of violations and evasions.
>
> The work of the Commission should proceed by separate stages the successful completion of each of which will develop the necessary confidence of the world before the next stage is undertaken.[23]

On the insistence of the Soviet Union, the resolution provided:

> In view of the Security Council's primary responsibility under the Charter of the United Nations for the maintenance of inter-

[22] *Ibid.*, pp. 125-27.
[23] *Ibid.*, p. 127.

United Nations, New York. Bernard Baruch talking with Jacob Malik (U.S.S.R.).

United Nations Disarmament Commission 1952, New York. *From left to right:* Elim Sarper (Turkey); Jacob Malik (U.S.S.R.); Sir Gladwyn Jebb (U.K.); Benjamin V. Cohen (U.S.). The author is seated behind Cohen.

Photo by New York Times

Atoms for Peace. President Eisenhower addresses the United Nations December 8, 1953. *Seated above the rostrum are:* Dag Hammarskjold, Secretary General of the United Nations; Mme. Pandit (India), President of the General Assembly; Andrew Cordier, Assistant Secretary General.

Photo by Leo Rosenthal

United Nations Disarmament Commission 1954, New York. *Front row:* Semyon Tsarapkin (U.S.S.R.); Sir Pearson Dixon (U.K.); Morehead Patterson (U.S.); *U.S. Advisers, left to right are:* Col. William Bailey, Bernhard Bechhoefer, Gordon Arneson.

Photo from European

The Disarmament Subcommittee, Lancaster House, London 1956. *Left to right:* Sir Anthony Nutting (U.K.); Jules Moch (France); Norman Robertson (Canada); Andrei Gromyko (U.S.S.R.); Harold Stassen (U.S.); Dragon Protich (U.N. Secretariat).

Photo from European

The Disarmament Subcommittee, London, August 2, 1957. John Foster Dulles bids farewell to Harold Stassen at London Airport.

Photo by New York Times

The Security Council votes to resume disarmament discussions, May 1960. Henry Cabot Lodge (U.S.) and Sir Pearson Dixon (U.K.) vote affirmatively. Andrei Gromyko (U.S.S.R.) abstains.

national peace and security, the Security Council shall issue directions to the Commission in matters affecting security. On these matters the Commission shall be accountable for its work to the Security Council.[24]

The debate in the United Nations General Assembly on the resolution was brief, and on January 24 it was approved with no dissenting votes,[25] indeed without debate until after its approval. Thus the United Nations in its first month embarked on a consideration of not only the regulation of armaments but also atomic disarmament, contrary to the expectations of its founding fathers.

BIRTH OF THE BARUCH PLAN

The *Forrestal Diaries* describe vividly a United States cabinet meeting on September 21, 1945, "occupied entirely with a discussion of the atomic bomb." The question before the meeting was the policy the United States should follow in making available to other nations the information in its possession. Henry Wallace, Secretary of Commerce, was in favor of giving the information immediately to the Russians. "Failure to give them our knowledge would make an embittered and sour people."

No one else in the meeting held these views. Forrestal himself suggested that "we could exercise a trusteeship over the bomb on behalf of the United Nations and agree that we would limit its manufacture for use on such missions as the United Nations should designate." Forrestal somewhat overstated the significance of the meeting when he wrote that it "laid the foundations upon which there were erected, in turn, the Lilienthal-Acheson Report, the Baruch Plan and the United Nations majority program."[26]

The President's message to the Congress less than two weeks later[27]

[24] *Ibid.*, p. 128.
[25] *Ibid.*, pp. 132-33.
[26] Walter Millis, ed., *The Forrestal Diaries* (1951), pp. 94-96.
[27] *Growth of a Policy*, pp. 109-12.

dealt with both domestic and international aspects of atomic energy and proposed the procedures that resulted in the creation of the United Nations Atomic Energy Commission. In December, Secretary of State Byrnes, in anticipation of the adoption by the United Nations of the proposed resolution, appointed a committee consisting of Dean Acheson, John J. McCloy, Dr. Vannevar Bush, Dr. Conant, and General Groves, to begin work on plans to be presented to the United Nations Atomic Energy Commission when it was organized.[28] In January 1946, the committee appointed a board of consultants with David E. Lilienthal as chairman and including Chester L. Barnard, president of New Jersey Telephone Company; Dr. J. Robert Oppenheimer; Dr. Charles Allen Thomas, vice president of Monsanto Chemical Company; and Harry A. Winne, vice president of General Electric Company. This latter group, with the addition of Carroll Wilson as secretary of the board, and later Herbert S. Marks, a brilliant attorney who was Dean Acheson's assistant on atomic energy matters, produced on March 28, 1946, the Acheson-Lilienthal Report from which emerged the Baruch Plan.[29]

An interview with Marks describes the preparation of the report:

> Last winter, a group of seven men made a strong bid for an endurance record of a very special sort when they spent two months talking about nothing but atomic energy and how to control it. . . . The study was a peculiar one because the consultants had little idea of where to start and were even more uncertain about where they were going. . . . The consultants talked atomic energy in Pullman compartments and aloft in an Army plane. Sometimes they deliberated for as long as eighteen hours a day.[30]

The Acheson-Lilienthal Report contained practically all of the essential basic decisions of the Baruch Plan: the decision that inspection

---

[28] James F. Byrnes, *Speaking Frankly* (1947), p. 268.
[29] *Growth of a Policy*, p. 35.
[30] Daniel Lang, "A Reporter at Large," *The New Yorker Magazine* (Aug. 17, 1946), p. 45.

of nuclear facilities would be insufficient protection to assure the peaceful use of atomic energy; the necessity for strict accountability to an international organization for past as well as future production of fissionable material, with the organization knowing at all times the location and use of all materials; the requirement of internationalization of thorium and uranium deposits and of all plants producing fissionable materials; provisions for "denaturing" fissionable material, which would make possible with minimum risk the peaceful uses of the atom.

Bernard Baruch was appointed United States representative on the United Nations Atomic Energy Commission in March 1946. He always acknowledged that the Acheson-Lilienthal Report "which laid the basis for a system of international control of atomic energy proved indispensable in formulating specific plans. But it was in Acheson's words 'a rough sketch,' 'a sort of working paper.' It did not pretend to offer a definitive program. For example, it did not deal with the problem of enforcement—a problem which I considered crucial."[31]

Baruch objected strenuously to the publication of the Acheson-Lilienthal Report almost simultaneously with his appointment, on the ground that it created the impression that United States policy had already been determined prior to his appointment.[32] His significant addition to the report, as he had suggested, dealt with the problem of enforcement. He was responsible for the proposal that the provisions of the United Nations Charter calling for unanimity of the great powers in most decisions of the United Nations Security Council affecting world peace should not apply to international control of atomic energy.[33]

Baruch's contribution did not stem primarily from new ideas or changes in the Acheson-Lilienthal proposals. Rather it arose from his great prestige, particularly in the United States, and from his genius in gauging and responding to currents of world public opinion. It was

---

[31] Bernard M. Baruch, *The Public Years* (1960), p. 361.

[32] *Ibid.*, p. 361. See also Margaret L. Coit, *Mr. Baruch* (1957), p. 565. Baruch's personal relations with Acheson at that time were far from cordial. *Ibid.*, p. 576.

[33] *Ibid.*, p. 566. Margaret Coit cites further differences on the problem of the timing of the United States disclosure of atomic secrets (p. 567). It later developed that neither the Acheson-Lilienthal Report nor the Baruch Plan contained a schedule of the timing and phasing of the program.

Baruch's decision that the United States, at the outset of the negotiations, should present a full plan providing answers for any anticipated questions rather than merely a framework for future negotiators.[34] It was he who set the tone of almost religious fervor that prevented the negotiations from degenerating immediately into vituperative propaganda. Baruch could convincingly call on Americans, despite past isolationist sentiment, "to start freeing ourselves from the fetish of national sovereignty." At the same time, he played the major role in counteracting the harm to United States prestige that might have arisen from Henry Wallace's attacks—from the vantage point of a position in the Cabinet— on United States policy toward the Soviet Union and specifically on the Baruch Plan.[35]

Baruch chose as his associates a group of high-caliber individuals drawn from varied segments of American life, in the main other than the diplomatic world. Baruch, as well as most of the group, had access to the White House and entree into top level government officialdom. In this group was John Hancock, a New York banker, co-author of the Baruch-Hancock Report on postwar economic problems. Another was Ferdinand Eberstadt, investment banker, lawyer, and former vice-chairman of the War Production Board. There was the journalist and publisher, Herbert Bayard Swope, and Fred Searls, a mining engineer with service on several important government agencies during the war. Major General Leslie Groves, head of the atomic bomb development project, and later his former deputy, Thomas F. Farrell, were named to serve. Richard Tolman, Dean of the Graduate School of California Institute of Technology, and scientific adviser to the Manhattan Project during the war, became an associate. Dr. Tolman had an assisting scientific panel consisting of such eminent men of science as Drs. R. F. Bacher, A. H. Compton, J. R. Oppenheimer, C. A. Thomas, and H. C. Urey. In addition to this group there was a distinguished lawyer, John Parks Davis, as executive officer, and three legal advisers to the delegation, all drawn from the Department of State.[36]

A delegation of this caliber had both advantages and disadvantages.

[34] *Ibid.*, pp. 564, 571.
[35] Baruch, *op. cit.*, pp. 373, 375. Coit, *op. cit.*, p. 597.
[36] *Ibid.*, pp. 33, 48-49.

Foremost among the advantages was that the prestige of Baruch assured to as great a degree as is possible under our form of government that he would speak for the nation and that any agreements he might negotiate would have the full support of the Executive Branch of the government and a favorable reception in Congress. His prestige made it easy to secure adequate personnel and budgetary support for a difficult negotiation with the Soviet Union. Negotiating with the Russians is a gruelling experience that exhausts the participants. Between the Baruch operation and the appointment of Harold E. Stassen a decade later, the delegations were never sufficiently staffed to conduct, if the opportunity had arisen, the type of detailed negotiations essential to achieve an international convention.

There were, however, disadvantages in a delegation of this nature. Baruch was too eminent and independent a figure to meld his position into the general framework of United States foreign policy. Rather United States policy had to transform itself into the pattern of the Baruch Plan. This caused problems both then and later.

In spite of the high seriousness of purpose of this first United States delegation and its strong leadership, none of these men remained very long in the service of the United States. In this respect there is a notable difference in the personnel of the other powers' representation. The delegations of the United Kingdom, Canada, France, China, and the Soviet Union, the representatives and their associates, were also of high caliber, and even now some of these men continue to represent their respective countries. Their tremendous accumulation of knowledge of the subject has proved valuable to them; at times, lack of continuity of personnel has proved detrimental to the United States.

The entire world focused on Baruch when the United Nations Atomic Energy Commission convened on June 14, 1946. Baruch addressed his audience with this solemn salutation:

My Fellow-Members of the United Nations Atomic Energy Commission, and my Fellow-Citizens of the World,
We are here to make a choice between the quick and the dead. That is our business.
Behind the black portent of the new atomic age lies a hope

which, seized upon with faith, can work our salvation. Let us not deceive ourselves. We must elect World Peace or World Destruction.[37]

The United States was in truth ready with much more than a "working-paper"; as its answer it had prepared specific proposals, known from that time forward as the "Baruch Plan."

[37] Compare Deuteronomy 30:19 "I call heaven and earth to record this day against you, that I have set before you life and death, blessing and cursing, therefore choose life that both thou and thy seed shall live."

IV

The Baruch Plan

Baruch in his first statement to the United Nations Atomic Energy Commission on June 14, 1946, outlined the main features of the United States proposals for international control of atomic energy. Most of the details of the program were blocked out in three memoranda submitted between July 2 and July 12. While two years of feverish discussion produced some additional details and a few modifications, the crux of the United States proposals—which from this point on became known as the Baruch Plan—can nevertheless be found in the first Baruch statement and the three memoranda.[1]

The details of the plan have had far less influence than its broad enunciation of policy and are today overtaken and outdated by the progress of science. Likewise, the day-to-day narrative of the extensive negotiations concerns itself mainly with issues and events that are no longer of consequence. However, the plan itself in broad outline was

[1] Detailed and objective descriptions of the plan itself and of the discouraging negotiations within the commission, its committees, and subcommittees are readily available. The official State Department record of the negotiations is contained in two publications of the U.S. Department of State, *The International Control of Atomic Energy: Growth of a Policy*, Publication 2702 (1946), cited hereafter as *Growth of a Policy*; and *The International Control of Atomic Energy: Policy at the Crossroads*, Publication 3161 (1948), cited hereafter as *Policy at the Crossroads*. An authoritative and detailed narrative of the negotiations may be found in an unpublished Yale University dissertation, 1958, entitled "Soviet Policy Toward International Control of Atomic Energy 1945-1953," by Joseph Lippman Nogee.

the keystone of Western policy toward arms control for nine years and is the source of much current thinking. The negotiations, in their broader aspects, may be historically more important than the plan because of their disclosure of Soviet attitudes and techniques.

A description of the most important features of the plan and a chronicle of the highlights of the negotiations throw light on the basic problems and mysteries of dealing with the Soviet Union, which continue to arouse public interest and debate. Was the United States offer to eliminate atomic weapons the generous gesture we and our friends claim or was this generosity a fraud or at least a deception as claimed by the Russians? Why did the United States offer to give up the only weapon in which it was superior without provision for reduction of mass armies where the Soviet bloc had superiority? Would the United States Senate have ratified a treaty incorporating the Baruch Plan with its massive interference with the national sovereignty of all states? Was the Soviet rejection of the plan attributable to defects that might have been remedied without destroying the effectiveness of the plan, or, alternatively, was such a rejection an inevitable part of a broader Soviet policy?

The central thought of the Baruch Plan was its provision for complete international control of the entire process of producing atomic weapons from the uranium and thorium mines to the completed weapons. This immediately raised the question whether effective control of atomic energy was possible—whether any system of control could ensure the use of atomic energy solely for purposes of peace. The Acheson-Lilienthal Report and the Baruch Plan both gave an affirmative answer to this question through their stress on complete accountability from mines to weapons.

In 1946 complete accountability appeared to be a realizable objective. Only the United States and the United Kingdom had a knowledge of the technique of producing fissionable materials and weapons. The United States War Department estimated that our monopoly would last for a period of about five years.[2] Natural uranium in concentrations

---

[2] "War Department Thinking on the Atomic Bomb," *Bulletin of the Atomic Scientists,* reprinting "The Effects of the Atomic Bomb on National Security (An Expression of War Department Thinking)," as submitted to Congress and as reprinted in the *Army-Navy Journal* (April 12, 1947).

of sufficient richness to justify its extraction was considered a scarce material.[3] Substantially all of the uranium used up to that time had come either from Canada or the Belgian Congo. Our government believed that it could purchase all uranium that might be produced anywhere in the world. Gigantic plants and tremendous expenditure were deemed essential to separate the fissionable U-235 from natural uranium as at Oak Ridge, Tennessee or to produce plutonium, as at Hanford, Washington.[4]

The Scientific and Technical Committee of the United Nations Atomic Energy Commission made a study of these and other factors, and on September 26, 1946, reported unanimously:

> With regard to the question . . . "whether effective control of atomic energy is possible," we do not find any basis in the available scientific facts for supposing that effective control is not technologically feasible. Whether or not it is politically feasible is not discussed nor implied in this report, nor is there any recommendation of the particular system or systems by which effective control can be achieved.[5]

For the first and almost the last time, the Soviet delegation had agreed with the United States. Even today, when both the Soviet Union and the United States have recognized that changed conditions have destroyed the possibility of complete accountability for nuclear materials, the principle of accountability still forms the basis of the most important proposals to lessen the dangers of nuclear war.

The second basic feature of the Baruch Plan was not only "to prevent the use of atomic energy for destructive purposes," but also "to promote the use of recent and future advances in scientific knowledge, particularly in the utilization of atomic energy for peaceful and humanitarian ends."[6] This language of the "Three Nation Agreed Declaration on Atomic Energy" was carried into the General Assembly resolu-

---

[3] *Growth of a Policy*, p. 37.
[4] *Ibid.*, pp. 265-67.
[5] *Ibid.*, p. 278.
[6] "The Three Nation Agreed Declaration on Atomic Energy . . . November 15, 1945," *ibid.*, p. 118. The declaration was signed by the President of the United States, the Prime Minister of the United Kingdom, and the Prime Minister of Canada.

tion creating the United Nations Atomic Energy Commission and into the Baruch Plan. It was not inevitable that the Baruch Plan take this path. There were at least two alternatives. The United States might have taken the position that the dangers of atomic energy so greatly outweighed the possible benefits that all development of this new force—whether for peace or war—should if possible be suppressed. Another alternative was to disclose all the secrets immediately. The middle path of the Baruch Plan has until this time been followed consistently by both the Soviet Union and the United States.[7] On the two fundamental ideas, the United States and the Soviet Union were in agreement and remained in agreement. On all other fundamental features of the Baruch Plan, divergences between the United States and the Soviet Union developed at the outset. In some if not the majority of instances, the divergences narrowed as the negotiations proceeded.

Before dealing with the features of the Baruch Plan in which divergences developed, it is appropriate to review the chief developments during the negotiations from which the divergences emerged.

THE FIRST YEAR OF

NEGOTIATIONS

At the second meeting of the Atomic Energy Commission on June 19, 1946, only five days after the initial meeting, Andrei Gromyko presented the Soviet plan, which called for an international convention "prohibiting the production and employment of weapons based on the use of atomic energy." For this purpose, the parties to the convention would assume obligations:

a. not to use atomic weapons in any circumstances whatsoever;
b. to prohibit the production and storing of weapons based on the use of atomic energy;

[7] The peaceful benefits of the atom have developed much more slowly than either the United States or the Soviet Union anticipated in 1946. The illusion of immediate economic benefits led to some unnecessary difficulties in the negotiations, which will be described in Chap. 11.

c. to destroy, within a period of three months from the day of the entry into force of the present convention, all stocks of atomic energy weapons whether in a finished or unfinished condition.

The only suggestion to assure enforcement of these commitments was a provision that the parties to the convention would, within six months, pass legislation providing severe penalties for violations.[8]

At the same time, Gromyko presented another resolution "concerning the organization of the work of the Atomic Energy Commission." The commission would have two main committees: one would work out practical measures for organizing the exchange of scientific information; the other would have as its objective "the prevention of the use of atomic energy to the detriment of mankind."[9]

Gromyko's proposals raised the chief issue of all the subsequent disarmament negotiations. Which come first: the commitments to disarm or the measures to ensure the observance of commitments? The Baruch Plan called for the elimination of atomic weapons only after the establishment of machinery to ensure that the weapons would certainly be eliminated. The Soviet Union called for the prohibition and "destruction" of weapons at the outset, with the machinery to ensure observance set up at a later date. In submitting his plan, Gromyko did not even mention the Baruch Plan. Therefore, he did not need to reject it. Unfortunately, in the speed of the following negotiations and in the network of details, the fundamental difference in the goals of the United States and Soviet plans became hazy and obscured.

The negotiations moved swiftly. By the end of the third meeting on June 25, almost all of the states represented on the commission, except Poland and the Soviet Union, had endorsed the Baruch Plan. The Netherlands made no specific choice. Poland approved the Soviet plan. Shortly thereafter the United States filed three memoranda amplifying its original position.[10]

[8] *Growth of a Policy*, p. 213.
[9] *Ibid.*, pp. 214, 215.
[10] *Ibid.*, "United States Memorandum No. 1 . . . July 2, 1946," p. 148; "United States Memorandum No. 2 . . . July 5, 1946," p. 152; "United States Memorandum No. 3 . . . July 12, 1946," p. 160.

All along the line the debates were moderate in tone, leaving ample room for genuine negotiation. By July 8, the chairman of the commission, Herbert V. Evatt of Australia, was already attempting to find a middle road between the United States and Soviet proposals.

During this period the commission set up a complicated committee structure to carry on detailed discussions of the most important issues.[11] The extensive committee discussions which lasted from July through October produced three main events:

1. The statement of John Hancock of the United States delegation that

... We propose making more and more information available to the [Atomic] Authority in step with the progressive establishment of workable safeguards proven in operation, to protect ourselves and the world from the misuse of such information by any nation. . . . National security is not going to be impaired while we seek—but have no firm assurance of securing—an effective treaty.[12]

This statement crystallized one of the main divergences between the Soviet Union and the West.

2. Gromyko's statements of July 31 and August 6 of his attitude toward controls. On July 31, he repeated his original suggestion that each state a party to the convention should enact legislation to ensure the observance of the convention. Beyond that, the only possibility was through international cooperation.[13] On August 6, he supplemented this position by contending for the first time that the inspection proposed under the Baruch Plan was not reconcilable with the principle of sovereignty of states. He agreed, however, that the Security Council of the United Nations (where the Soviet Union had a veto) could take action against a violation.[14]

3. The report of the Scientific and Technical Committee agreeing that international control of atomic energy was feasible.[15] This was an

[11] *Ibid.*, p. 55.
[12] "Address by Mr. John Hancock . . . July 15, 1946," *ibid.*, p. 171.
[13] *Ibid.*, p. 232.
[14] *Ibid.*, p. 242.
[15] *Ibid.*, pp. 261-78.

encouraging omen, giving rise to the hope that further negotiations might lead to further agreements.

Gromyko's negative reaction to the control features of the Baruch Plan seemed less discouraging at the time than they do today. It must be remembered that during the first year after Hiroshima, there were only a few official Soviet pronouncements concerning the bomb. In the fall of 1945 a series of articles in the Soviet periodical *New Times* tended to minimize the importance of the bomb, and at the same time accused the United States of atomic blackmail. Col. M. Tolchenov, the correspondent for *New Times* quoted a British scientist, Professor Oliphant, who had worked in America on the development of the bomb: "There is no way of preventing nations from producing this bomb except by political agreement and international control. There is no question of keeping it as a military secret." The article ends: "To attempt to re-fashion the world with the help of 'atomic diplomacy' can lead to no good, least of all for those who attempt it."[16] On November 7, 1945, Molotov stated: "It is not possible . . . for a technical secret of any great size to remain the exclusive possession of some one country. . . . We will have atomic energy and many other things too."[17]

These statements *preceded* the Moscow Declaration with its agreement on procedures in the United Nations. After Gromyko's short speeches in the United Nations, endorsing the establishment of the United Nations Atomic Energy Commission, a complete silence prevailed in the Soviet Union on atomic energy until Gromyko's first speech to the Atomic Energy Commission in June 1946.[18] Therefore, the hope remained that the Soviet positions were incomplete and subject to modification—a hope buttressed by the successful outcome of the technical discussions on the feasibility of international control. Indeed, within less than three months, the Soviet Union had modified its position and for the first time had suggested an international control system.

[16] "The Atomic Bomb Discussion in the Foreign Press," *New Times* (Nov. 1, 1945), pp. 14-17.
[17] *New York Times*, Nov. 7, 1945, p. 14, text of Foreign Commissar Molotoff's address, broadcast by Moscow and recorded by the Soviet Monitor. See also M. Rubenstein, "The Foreign Press on the Atomic Bomb," published in the journal of *Trud* (Moscow), Sept. 1, 1945.
[18] *Growth of a Policy*, pp. 209-16.

On October 29, 1946, Soviet Foreign Minister Molotov introduced in the General Assembly a resolution covering the entire field
of arms control, atomic and conventional. In this resolution, the Soviet
Union moved a short distance toward recognizing the necessity of international control of atomic energy. Molotov, in presenting the plan
to the Assembly, again called for a convention prohibiting the production and use of atomic weapons: "only by taking such a decision, shall
we create suitable conditions for a free and fruitful expression of the
questions relating to the establishment of control for atomic energy in
all countries."[19]

As a result of much negotiation in the General Assembly, a resolution entitled "Principles Governing the General Regulation and Reduction of Armaments" was worked out that received the approval of
both the Soviet Union and the United States. The fifth and sixth paragraphs of this resolution explicitly recognized the necessity of an international system of safeguards to ensure observance not only of the commitments relating to atomic energy but also of the limitations of armed
forces and international armaments.[20] Thus, the Soviet Union, for the
first time, endorsed the principle of an international system of control.

The Soviet Union's proposals for control were not presented to the
Atomic Energy Commission until June 11, 1947.[21] When they finally
appeared, they turned out to be far more detailed than any previous
Soviet proposals. Indeed, not until May 10, 1955, did the Soviet Union
present proposals even comparable, in their detailed elaboration, to
these. The Soviet decision to support at least nominally an international control system was apparently a part of a much broader Soviet
decision emerging from the meetings of Foreign Ministers, which took
place in New York in September and October 1946 simultaneously
with the session of the General Assembly. At that time, the Soviet

[19] *Journal of the United Nations*, No. 18, Supplement A-A/P.V./42, pp. 167-68,
175-80.
[20] *United States Participation in the United Nations, Report by the President to the
Congress for the Year 1946*, Department of State Publication 2735 (1947), pp. 96-
97. Cited hereafter as *U.S. Participation in the U.N., Report* (with year).
[21] U.N. Atomic Energy Commission, *The International Control of Atomic Energy*,
The Second Report to the Security Council, Department of State Publication 2932
(December 1947), p. 88. Cited hereafter as U.N. Atomic Energy Commission, *International Control of Atomic Energy* (with report number).

Union agreed to conditions outside the field of arms control, which permitted the negotiations of peace treaties with Hungary, Finland, Rumania, Bulgaria, and Italy.[22] Apparently, the Soviet leaders had reached the conclusion that the political and economic collapse of Europe and the triumph of communism in Europe was unlikely to take place immediately. Therefore, *modus vivendi* could be established to bridge the short interval until the postwar economic crisis of capitalism would ensure the victory of communism. It should be recalled that at this time E. S. Varga, a leading Soviet economist, found himself in disgrace because of his prediction that the economic crisis leading to the downfall of capitalism might be delayed as much as 25 years.[23]

The implications in the field of arms control of this new Soviet position can more properly be considered in a later chapter dealing with the establishment of the United Nations Commission for Conventional Armaments. In the atomic field, however, the changed policy had one specific implication that almost immediately became apparent —the slowing down of the tempo of negotiations.

Perhaps the most remarkable feature of the early negotiations in the United Nations Atomic Energy Commission was their fast pace. Baruch at the opening meeting wasted no time on procedural matters or agenda but on that day presented the outline of a complete plan. The Soviet proposals appeared five days later. By June 19, 1946, all members of the commission had expressed their views concerning both sets of proposals. The United States had elaborated its position by July 14. A committee structure was in full operation before the end of July. The report of the Scientific and Technical Committee on the technical feasibility of control was complete on September 26.[24] While the pace slowed down a little between October and December, the "Report on Safeguards"[25]—the safeguards required at each stage of the production

---

[22] William Reitzel, Morton A. Kaplan, and Constance G. Coblenz, *United States Foreign Policy, 1945-1955* (1956), p. 86.
[23] Georg von Rauch, *History of Soviet Russia*, Translated by Peter and Annette Jacobsohn (1957), p. 402.
[24] *Growth of a Policy*, pp. 49-87.
[25] U.N. Atomic Energy Commission, *International Control of Atomic Energy*, First Report, Department of State Publication 2737 (1947), pp. 14-19. See also Pt. 5, "First Report on Safeguards Required to Ensure the Use of Atomic Energy Only for Peaceful Purposes," pp. 45-71.

and use of atomic energy to prevent the possibilities of misuse—was a splendid achievement. This speed reflected both the urgency of the problem and the drive and energy of Baruch and his team.

If Gromyko had adhered to his earlier view rejecting all international control systems, the same speedy procedures would have led to the collapse of the entire negotiations within a short time. The issue causing the collapse would have been clear-cut: the Soviet Union rejected international control with the accompanying destruction of its secrecy.

The immediate effect in the commission of the Soviet change of front was to slow down and prolong the negotiations. Molotov's original proposal would have had that result by linking with the control of atomic energy such matters as a general reduction of armaments and by scrapping the United Nations Atomic Energy Commission. His acceptance of a resolution of the General Assembly sponsored by the United States, endorsing in principle international control, achieved the same result.[26] It now became necessary to examine in detail the divergences between the United States and Soviet control proposals.

It seems clear that the Soviet Union was deliberately slowing down the tempo of negotiations. The first Soviet request for delays came in December during the discussion of the commission's first report to the Security Council.[27] Baruch resisted these delays and secured commission approval of the report and its submission to the Security Council on December 31. The Soviet Union and Poland were not yet ready to oppose the point and abstained.[28] They accomplished the objective of further delays through the new Soviet position.

Frederick H. Osborn, Baruch's successor in the Atomic Energy Commission, dwells at considerable length on the Soviet tactics of delay. He describes graphically one revealing incident:

By the end of May most of the sub groups had brought their papers in for informal discussion by the New York group, after

[26] *Policy at the Crossroads,* sec. 5: "Regulation and Reduction of Armaments: The Debate in the General Assembly, October 29 to December 14, 1946," pp. 58-60.
[27] *Ibid.,* pp. 54-55.
[28] Frederick Osborn, "Negotiating on Atomic Energy," Chap. 8 in *Negotiating with the Russians,* Raymond Dennett and Joseph E. Johnson, eds. (1951), pp. 209-36.

which the respective chairmen were to give them a final redrafting prior to their going to Lake Success for presentation and formal discussion by the Committee. At an informal meeting held in New York a number of these papers were presented in fairly complete form and for the first time it was evident that the Commission was going to be in a position to put out a Second Report which would contain sound and carefully written specific proposals. Dr. Skobeltzyn was sitting in, in his position as observer, flanked by the two younger members of the Soviet staff who usually accompanied him wherever he went. As the discussion developed, one of these young men handed Dr. Skobeltzyn a paper. When he opened and read it, he became highly excited and interrupted with the demand that he be given the floor at once. The Chairman suggested that the delegate then speaking might complete his remarks, but Dr. Skobeltzyn insisted he be given the floor. The other delegate withdrew and Dr. Skobeltzyn then spoke quite excitedly. He demanded, first, that a verbatim record be made of what he was about to say. When this was arranged (fortunately a stenographer-interpreter was present, although no record was being made of any other talks) Dr. Skobeltzyn launched into an extraordinarily bitter attack on the meetings and the people taking part in them. He said that the meetings were illegal, conducted according to unauthorized procedures, and represented a treacherous attempt of the tools of the ruling clique to develop their sinister purposes, secretly and without participation of the Soviet Union, and that he, for one, repudiated any part in the proceedings; all of this delivered with much vehemence. When he was through he handed to the men sitting behind him the paper they had given him. None of the other delegates who were present at this outburst made any reply. The procedures we were following had been approved in great detail in the formal meetings of the committee at Lake Success. Dr. Skobeltzyn had been urged in the strongest possible terms to take part in the work of the sub groups and had been present in all the meetings of the group as a whole. It was the feeling of the other delegates that this outburst was due to Skobeltzyn's sudden realization that the work had advanced further than anything he had reported to Moscow, and his fear that he would be criticized for having permitted so much of a constructive nature to be done.

Dr. Skobeltzyn's outburst was the beginning, and, in a sense, the end of Soviet participation in the constructive work of the Commission.[29]

The Soviet Union did not stand alone in its desire to slow down the discussions. During the consideration of the first report, Alexandre Parodi of France and Col. Mohamed Bey Khalifa of Egypt had stated that the conclusions were getting ahead of the discussions.[30] After the approval of the first report, the Atomic Energy Commission adjourned until March. In January and February, the United Nations Security Council had before it not only the first report of the Atomic Energy Commission but the General Assembly resolution dealing with conventional armaments and other phases of arms control, which will be considered later.

When the Atomic Energy Commission resumed its work on March 19, the procedures and the pace were more characteristic of international negotiations with a proliferation of committees and subcommittees, proposals and amendments, and of procedural debates. The negotiations had not yet deteriorated to pure propaganda and name calling. However, it had become clear that an immediate and radical resolution of the atomic energy problem, separate from other international issues, was no longer possible.

The first casualty of the new approach was Baruch himself. On January 4, 1947, Baruch recognized the changed situation in his letter of resignation to the President:

The active undertaking of the problem of General Disarmament by the Security Council, expressed in the Resolution of the United Nations General Assembly on December 14, 1946, has created a new situation in which our hand would be strengthened by an identic representation on the Security Council and the Atomic

---

[29] Ibid., pp. 225-26.
[30] *Growth of a Policy*, pp. 181-87, 194.

Energy Commission. This country is one of the few whose Atomic Energy Commission representative is not the same as the representative on the Security Council.

Former Senator Warren Austin, our member in that body, is thoroughly equipped to handle this business as it develops from now on. In fact, he would be handicapped by divided authority. . . .

So, because of my belief that the work of my American associates and myself is over, and because I am convinced that the job now should be taken over by Senator Austin, I submit my resignation and those of the men who have worked with me. . . .[31]

Senator Warren Austin, the United States representative in the United Nations, became the representative on the commission. The new deputy representative, Frederick H. Osborn, formerly Director of the Information and Education Division of the United States Army, was responsible for the day-to-day work. The senior members of Baruch's staff resigned with their chief. The celebrated nuclear scientists such as Oppenheimer, Bacher, and Tolman continued as advisers, but were consulted less frequently. The negotiations were conducted by a small and able group from official level. This had some advantages. It was now possible to coordinate the policy toward control of atomic energy and the general foreign policy of the United States. This prevented the emergence of positions, such as that on the veto, which were inconsistent with the broader United States policies. The assignment of permanent government officials at the negotiating levels should have facilitated continuity of United States representation.[32] Until the appointment of Stassen in 1957, however, none of the United States arms control negotiators after Baruch had direct and easy access to the White House with the accompanying assurance of thorough consideration of arms control problems and speedy decisions.

[31] U.N. Atomic Energy Commission, *International Control of Atomic Energy*, First Report, pp. 95-96.
[32] Gordon Arneson from Baruch's staff joined the State Department and continued in this field until 1954, and Dr. Paul Fine of the Atomic Energy Commission participated in negotiations as late as 1956. Both are outstanding officers.

DIVERGENCES

There were 122 meetings of the commission and its committees and working groups between March 19, 1947, when the commission reconvened after the Security Council consideration of its first report, and the commission approval of its second report on September 11, 1947.[33] It would be profitless to attempt a detailed chronicle of the proceedings during that period. The bulk of the second report is devoted to the divergences between the Soviet position and that of the rest of the commission, and the significance of the meetings rests almost entirely in these divergences. The small degree of agreement attained after 1946 was purely a narrowing of differences on a few specific points and is a part of the description of the divergences. In dealing with the divergences, this study covers much of the same ground as the second and third reports of the commission and the State Department publication *Policy at the Crossroads*. The justification for going over this ground once again is that the previous treatments date from 1948. Much has happened since then that places the negotiations in a different focus. The fact to be stressed is that these meetings were serious negotiations where both sides presented detailed plans generally with a minimum of attention to the propaganda aspects of their views. This pattern was not repeated in the international negotiations for arms control between 1947 and 1955.

The President of the United States in his report to the Congress on the United Nations indicated the United States view of the chief divergences.[34] The Soviet Union in substance recognized the same divergences but described them differently.[35]

[33] *Policy at the Crossroads*, pp. 187-90.
[34] Ownership of source material; ownership, management, and operation of dangerous facilities; research; inspection; elimination of atomic weapons; and enforcement (the "veto"). See *U.S. Participation in the U.N., Report 1947*, Department of State Publication 3024 (1948), pp. 102-03.
[35] The veto; safeguards; whether the international control of atomic energy, including prohibition of atomic weapons, is to be established by one treaty or by several, and, in the latter case, the question of priorities; stages of transition from existing conditions to international control; the right of the international control agency to conduct research. See U.N. Atomic Energy Commission, *International Control of Atomic Energy*, Second Report, p. 87.

The Veto

The divergence between the Soviet proposals and the United States proposals that created the greatest attention at the time, and that perhaps was substantively the least important, concerned the principle of the unanimity of the great powers in the Security Council of the United Nations—the so-called "veto." Under the Charter of the United Nations, the Security Council is primarily responsible for the maintenance of international peace and security. Article 27 of the Charter provides a voting formula under which nonprocedural decisions can be made only with the concurrence of each of the five great powers, the United States, the United Kingdom, the Soviet Union, China, and France. This meant that in practice all major decisions in connection with world peace would necessarily rest on the principle of unanimity of the five permanent members of the Security Council. Any permanent member could veto any action that it did not approve.

Baruch in his first statement to the Atomic Energy Commission said:

> It would be a deception, to which I am unwilling to lend myself, were I not to say to you and to our peoples, that the matter of punishment lies at the very heart of our present security system. It might as well be admitted, here and now, that the subject goes straight to the veto power contained in the Charter of the United Nations so far as it relates to the field of atomic energy. The Charter permits penalization only by concurrence of each of the five great powers—Union of Soviet Socialist Republics, the United Kingdom, China, France, and the United States.

> I want to make very plain that I am concerned here with the veto power only as it affects this particular problem. There must be no veto to protect those who violate their solemn agreements not to develop or use atomic energy for destructive purposes.[36]

Baruch elaborated these general ideas in the third United States memorandum dated July 12, 1946, dealing with the relations between

[36] *Growth of a Policy*, p. 142.

the atomic development authority and the organs of the United Nations.[37] He made two main points: The first was that none of the organs of the United Nations was constituted in a manner to make it competent to deal with the matters coming before the authority. Therefore the authority should be an autonomous body making its own decisions on all matters not of sufficient gravity to constitute a threat to peace. The authority would act by a majority vote. In other words, there would be no veto.

Baruch's second point dealt with the role of the United Nations Security Council. Serious breaches of the treaty would constitute a threat to peace and would require action by the United Nations Security Council. Baruch stated, "The controls established by the treaty would be wholly ineffectual if, in any such situations, to be defined in the treaty, the enforcement of security provisions could be prevented by the vote of a state which has signed the treaty. Any other conception would render the whole principle of veto ridiculous." Baruch went on to point out,

> This in no way impairs the doctrine of unanimity. No state need be an unwilling party to the treaty. But every state which freely and willingly becomes a party to the treaty, by this act, solemnly and formally binds itself to abide by its undertakings. Such undertakings would become illusory, if the guarantee against their breach resided solely in the conscience of the one who commits the breach.[38]

From the strictly legal standpoint, this proposal did not run counter to the Charter of the United Nations. Baruch was requesting that the states party to the treaty, should through a treaty modify the voting formula in the Security Council of the United Nations on matters arising as a result of breaches of the treaty. There are legal precedents in the United Nations for such a procedure although the precedents arose subsequent to the Baruch proposals.[39] However, this proposal

[37] *Ibid.*, pp. 160-65.
[38] *Ibid.*, p. 163.
[39] The Italian Peace Treaty procedures, and the procedure in connection with the Palestine settlement.

ran counter to the basic concept of the continued unity of the great powers as embodied in the Charter. The United Nations was to have available the military forces adequate to deal with threats to the peace by small states. Unanimity among the great powers would be required in order to utilize those forces. Roosevelt, Churchill, and Stalin all recognized that the United Nations would be practically powerless to deal with a threat to the peace by a great power. Only a world war could eliminate a serious breach of the peace by a great power, and the United Nations could not conduct a world war.

At the San Francisco Conference in 1945, the most serious friction had concerned the problem of the veto. The smaller states led by Dr. Evatt of Australia had reserved their most violent protests for this issue. Ultimately the Soviet Union acquiesced in changes and interpretations of the Charter, which made it possible for the United Nations General Assembly to appeal to world opinion in case of a threat to peace by a great power, and which greatly broadened the scope of permitted self-defense without any United Nations authority in resistance to armed attack. However, it was conceded that the United Nations itself could not conduct a military operation in the absence of unanimity among the permanent members of the Security Council.[40]

During the first six months of the United Nations, the Soviet Union had embarked on a policy of abundant use of the veto in the Security Council.[41] Simultaneously with the discussions in the Atomic Energy Commission, several of the smaller states had placed on the agenda of the General Assembly an item calling for an investigation of Soviet abuse of the veto. The Soviet Union had always considered the smaller states as satellites of the great powers, which would undertake no action except at the suggestion of the great powers. Therefore the Soviet leaders unquestionably concluded that both the Baruch proposals on the veto and the initiative of the smaller states in raising

[40] See Charter of the United Nations, Arts. 10, 12, 14, and 51; Four Power Statement of June 7, 1945 quoted in U.S. Department of State, *Report to the President on the Results of the San Francisco Conference by the Chairman of the United States Delegation,* Publication 2349 (June 26, 1945), pp. 73-76; for Soviet views, see S. B. Krylov, *Materials for the History of the United Nations,* Vol. 1, "Framing of the Text of the Charter of the United Nations," unpublished translation by H. Bartlett Wells (undated), pp. 171-73, 223, 225.
[41] *U.S. Participation in the U.N., Report 1946,* pp. 8-11.

the question before the General Assembly were evidences of a United States decision to attack the underlying basis of postwar settlements. Thus, at a minimum, this proposal tended to poison the atmosphere of the negotiations and to diminish the chance of a successful outcome.

As the discussions of the veto in the General Assembly of the United Nations and in the commission began to generate more heat, Baruch sought to soften the impact of his position. In October 1946 he stated: "Our proposal is concerned with the veto power only as it affects this particular problem, and not with the general veto written into the structure of the United Nations."[42]

The most unfortunate feature of this position was that most of the friction which it stirred up was probably unnecessary. It was reasonable to contend that there should be no veto in the atomic authority. Gromyko accepted this position in one of the amendments and additions to the first report, which he proposed in the United Nations Security Council on February 18, 1947:

Sixth Amendment:

Make the following alterations in paragraph 3:

In place of the introductory sentence: "The treaty or convention should include, among others, provisions for:" substitute the following sentence: "The convention should include, among others, provisions for:"

Paragraph 3 (a) should read as follows:

(a) Establishing within the framework of the Security Council an international control commission possessing powers and charged with responsibility necessary for the effective implementation of the terms of the convention and for the prompt discharge of its day-to-day duties. Its rights, powers, and responsibilities should be clearly established and defined by the convention. Such powers should be sufficiently broad and flexible to enable the commission to deal with the situation that may arise in the field of atomic energy in connexion with new

[42] Speech by Bernard M. Baruch, "The International Control of Atomic Energy" (Oct. 8, 1946), Department of State Publication 2681, p. 2.

discoveries. In particular, the commission shall assist in every way in promoting among all nations the exchange of basic scientific information on the use of atomic energy for peaceful purposes, shall be responsible for preventing the use of atomic energy for military purposes and for stimulating its uses for the benefit of the peoples of all countries. The control organs and the organs of inspection should carry out their control and inspection functions, *acting on the basis of their own rules, which should provide for the adoption of decisions, in appropriate cases, by the majority vote.*[43]

This amendment is full of weasel words. The delegation of responsibility to the control commission was vague and would have to be spelled out. The decisions of the control commission would be by majority vote only "in appropriate cases." Nevertheless, the amendment should have shifted the discussion from the problem of a veto to the issue of the authority of the control commission, which was politically far less sensitive. If the Soviet position was that the international authority should receive sufficient powers to deal by majority vote with all matters except major violations of the convention leading to a threat to world peace, then the divergence over the veto should have disappeared. Such a position, however, was not sufficient for Baruch, who insisted that the United Nations action to punish the violator, even by military force, should not be subject to the veto. It was unrealistic for Baruch to assume United Nations military force of sufficient strength to wage successful war against a major power. Even Evatt, the chief opponent of the Security Council veto, recognized the distinction between the decisions of the commission and the decisions of the Security Council.[44]

The basic weakness of Baruch's veto position was that it permitted the Soviet Union to reject the Baruch Plan for the wrong reason. If agreement could not be reached on international control of atomic

[43] *Policy at the Crossroads,* p. 75. Italics added.
[44] "Tentative Proposals by Chairman of the Atomic Energy Commission, Herbert V. Evatt, representative of Australia, New York, July 1, 1946," *Growth of a Policy,* pp. 202-03.

energy, it was desirable that failure to agree should rest firmly on Soviet unwillingness to permit sufficient penetration of its iron curtain to ensure observance of its commitments. This was an issue on which the entire world outside of the Soviet orbit would support fully the position of the United States and of the West. The veto approach of the Baruch Plan introduced an extraneous and unnecessary element into the negotiating picture, and permitted the Soviet Union to take a position on which it had substantial support outside its own bloc.

Baruch's veto position is the extreme example of his isolation from the general currents of United States foreign policy. It was the only place where his program moved away from the recommendations of the Acheson-Lilienthal Report. He had had no contact with the Department of State officials working on this problem until approximately a week before his original statement. The only contribution to his position arising outside his immediate staff was the attempt to construct a bridge, however flimsy, between his position and the provisions of the United Nations Charter. In short, this divergence on the subject of the veto was of considerably less substantive importance than some of the more technical differences that received much less publicity, but went to the heart of the problem of breaching the iron curtain.

International Ownership

Another feature of the Baruch Plan that attracted great attention when the plan was originally presented and that led to some of the most violent Soviet attacks on the plan, was its insistence on international ownership of practically all materials and facilities concerned with nuclear fission. Baruch had initially proposed:

> . . . the creation of an International Atomic Development Authority, to which should be entrusted all phases of the development and use of atomic energy, starting with the raw material and including:
> 1. Managerial control or ownership of all atomic-energy activities potentially dangerous to world security.

2. Power to control, inspect, and license all other atomic activities.
3. The duty of fostering the beneficial uses of atomic energy.
4. Research and development responsibilities of an affirmative character intended to put the Authority in the forefront of atomic knowledge and thus to enable it to comprehend, and therefore to detect, misuse of atomic energy. To be effective, the Authority must itself be the world's leader in the field of atomic knowledge and development and thus supplement its legal authority with the great power inherent in possession of leadership in knowledge.[45]

In his elaboration of the plan, Baruch had gone into considerable detail in specifying the objects of international ownership. The Soviet Union in 1947, when it finally reached the point of admitting the necessity of an international safeguards system, rejected the concept of ownership and advocated merely a system of international inspection. Actually, the positions of the United States and of the Soviet Union on the general problem of international ownership versus inspection—though not on the degree of inspection and supervision that might be required—were far closer together than was apparent during the negotiations. Much later, in 1952, without any change in United States policy, Ambassador Benjamin Cohen in the United Nations Disarmament Commission restated the Baruch proposals without any reference to the concept of ownership.[46] Part of this restatement follows almost verbatim the section of the second report of the Atomic Energy Commission dealing with "ownership," the only changes being the substitution of words such as "authority over" and "operational control" for the word "ownership."[47]

Still later, in 1957, when the veil of secrecy had been lifted from problems associated with fission, apparently conflicting positions

[45] Growth of a Policy, p. 141.
[46] On May 14, 1952, in Committee One of the United Nations Disarmament Commission. Text in U.S. Department of State, Documents on Disarmament, Vol. 1, Publication 7008 (August 1960), pp. 358-64.
[47] U.N. Atomic Energy Commission, International Control of Atomic Energy, Second Report, pp. 18-21.

turned out to be much closer to each other. Most of the instrumentation and automation associated with safeguards to prevent diversion of fissionable materials from peaceful purposes were also essential to the operation of the nuclear facilities.[48] Therefore, unless there was to be a complete duplication of staffs, the individuals responsible for inspection would also have functions in connection with the operation of the installations. In essence, this divergence also reduced itself to a question of the extent of penetration of its iron curtain that the Soviet Union was willing to admit.

The substance of the Baruch position calling for international controls beyond the ordinary definition of an inspection system continues not only as a part of the Western position but has even been incorporated into some Soviet proposals. The terminology of the proposal permitted and encouraged Soviet propaganda attacks only remotely related to the substantive issue. Gromyko on March 5, 1947, made a long speech to the Security Council, lasting the entire meeting, which has been described as the linking of the Soviet objections to the atomic energy proposals with the entire ideological conflict between East and West.[49] This provision furnished the materials to construct the link.

We are still being told that atomic weapons cannot be prohibited until the Soviet Union accepts the United States proposals on the question of the control of atomic energy. Such a statement of the question, at the basis of which lies a desire to dictate to other Member States of the United Nations the terms which one country is trying to impose with the purpose of strengthening its monopoly position in the field of atomic energy, cannot conform with the interests of an urgent and successful solution of the problems of the establishment of atomic energy control. It is necessary to pay tribute to the frankness of the authors and

[48] See statement of Richard I. Kirk (May 14, 1957), *Statute of the International Atomic Energy Agency*, Hearings before the Senate Committee on Foreign Relations and Senate Members of Joint Committee on Atomic Energy, 85 Cong. 1 sess., p. 93.

[49] Nogee, *op. cit.*, p. 141.

advocates of such a plan, who do not conceal that they identify the interests of the United Nations in this field with the interests of one country, by subordinating the interests of other countries to the narrowly understood national interests of this one country.[50]

The position of the Soviet Union on this question has already been stated more than once. If it is necessary, I am prepared to repeat that such an organ must have the right to take decisions by majority vote in appropriate cases. Does this mean, however, that it is possible, by invoking the principle of international control, to agree in reality to grant the right of interference in the economic life of a country even through the decision of the majority in the control organ? The Soviet Union does not wish to and cannot allow such a situation. The Soviet Union is aware that there will be a majority in the control organ which may take one-sided decisions, a majority on whose benevolent attitude toward the Soviet Union the Soviet people cannot count. Therefore, the Soviet Union, and probably not only the Soviet Union, cannot allow that the fate of its national economy be handed over to this organ.[51]

It is, of course, impossible to determine whether Gromyko's position at the time was pure propaganda or rested in part on genuine fear that the United States intended to use the international authority to secure for itself a world monopoly of the industrial uses of the atom. Two circumstances tend to support the latter view:

First, the statements of the United States and the details of the plan were over-optimistic in their ideas for the rapid development of peaceful uses of the atom.[52] The Soviet leaders could easily have assumed that the United States had already made great scientific advances in

[50] U.N. Security Council, Second Year, *Official Records*, No. 22, 115th Meeting (March 5, 1947), p. 445.
[51] *Ibid.*, p. 453.
[52] For example, the glowing Baruch statement: "In our success lies the promise of a new life, freed from the heart-stopping fears that now beset the world. The beginning of victory for the great ideals for which millions have bled and died lies in building a workable plan. Now we approach fulfilment of the aspirations of mankind. At the end of the road lies the fairer, better, surer life we crave and mean to have." *Growth of a Policy*, p. 139.

the peacetime uses, which it intended to conceal until the acceptance of the Baruch Plan and thereafter to exploit commercially.

Second, the Baruch Plan originally gave to the atomic development authority complete and unrestricted control over the peaceful use of atomic energy including the ownership of all uranium and thorium, and the right to decide where atomic power plants would be located.[53] The negotiations leading to the second report modified the original position, which might have been as objectionable to the United States Senate as to the Soviet Union. The second report no longer recommended international agency ownership or management of the mines, but the establishment by the agency of world minimum quotas, national mining quotas and prescribed rates of production to ensure effective use of the world's resources of uranium and thorium. The most equitable basis on which to establish such quotas would be the principle that comparable national deposits throughout the world should be depleted proportionately.[54] The international agency would have the duty to make the necessary decisions to implement the quotas, but the principles governing the quotas would be laid down by the initial treaty.[55] The Soviet qualified approval of a quota system was practically the only progress achieved in 1947 in narrowing the differences between the Soviet Union and the United States.

It will be obvious that Soviet approval of a quota system ran counter to their propaganda themes directed against United States monopolists. The later Soviet repudiation of the quota system was a signal of the deterioration of the negotiations into pure propaganda exercises.

In short, here again, the terminology of the Baruch proposals tended to play into Soviet propaganda themes and to divert attention from the main issue—whether the Soviet Union was willing to permit sufficient penetration of its iron curtain to make possible an effective

[53] *Ibid.*, pp. 153, 156, 157.
[54] U.N. Atomic Energy Commission, *International Control of Atomic Energy*, Second Report, p. 33.
[55] *Ibid.*, p. 49.

international control system. In contrast to the position on the veto, it is difficult to imagine how Baruch could have foreseen this turn of events.

Safeguards

The remaining major differences between the Soviet proposals and the Baruch Plan, while probably attracting less public attention, were more fundamental and were carried into all future arms control negotiations.

This leads to the third and fundamental divergence, the extent of safeguards to ensure observance of commitments. As soon as the Soviet Union recognized the necessity of an international control system, two separate aspects of the safeguards problem arose. The first was the degree of international control over declared facilities. The second was the authority of the international agency to seek out clandestine facilities.

The Soviet Union, to use their terminology, had accepted the concept of "strict international control." Even this phrase contained two ambiguities. "Strict" control in English did not necessarily mean "adequate" control, though the Soviet representatives contended that in Russian, the words were synonymous. Furthermore, "control" in Russian (and in French) apparently referred to an accounting process comparable to the duties of a controller rather than to operational direction. "Control" in the later Soviet proposals generally went no further than submission to an international authority of statistical data that the authority would study, with possible spot checks to verify the authenticity of the statistics.

On inspection of declared activities, the first report of the United Nations Atomic Energy Commission had gone into some detail in specifying the types of safeguards.[56] The second report had gone much further in elaborating the methods and functions of the agency. On

---

[56] U.N. Atomic Energy Commission, *International Control of Atomic Energy*, First Report, Pt. 2, "Findings," p. 13; Pt. 4, "A First Report on the Scientific and Technical Aspects of the Problem of Control," p. 23.

this subject, the Soviet Union had also made proposals that, until 1955, went into greater detail than any Soviet proposals in the entire field of arms control. After a thorough consideration, all of the commission membership except the Soviet Union and Poland supported a resolution declaring "that these proposals as they now stand and the explanations given thereon do not provide an adequate basis for the development by the committee of specific proposals for an effective system of international control of atomic energy."[57]

With respect to inspection of declared facilities, the impasse was reached on the unwillingness of the Soviet Union to permit any controls beyond "periodic inspections," inspections "carried out at definite intervals." The Soviet system would not permit the permanent stationing of inspectors at nuclear facilities.[58]

The difference between the Soviet position and the majority position on clandestine facilities is succinctly summarized as follows:

> While it is generally agreed that there should be some system of international inspection, the majority have concluded that there must be comprehensive inspection, particularly in unreported areas where clandestine activities might be carried on. The minority considers that inspection should be limited to those atomic facilities reported by states; inspection as to clandestine or unreported facilities is virtually ignored.[59]

On this subject there was no narrowing of differences between the Soviet Union and the West during the entire life of the commission or for many years afterward. In later years, the problem of the extent of inspection to discover hidden facilities played less of a role in the discussions than other problems for the reason that, between 1947 and 1955, the Soviet proposals were too vague to permit discussion of specific safeguards machinery.

[57] *Policy at the Crossroads,* p. 115.
[58] *Proposals and Recommendations of the United Nations Atomic Energy Commission,* Sec. 2, "Report and Recommendations of the Third Report of the United Nations Atomic Energy Commission, adopted 17 May 1948," pp. 77-78.
[59] *U.S. Participation in the U.N., Report 1947,* p. 103.

International Research

The fourth divergence, recognized by both the Soviet Union and the United States concerned the respective roles of the international authority and national governments in nuclear research. The President's report to the Congress in 1947 summarized this difference in the following terms:

The majority declare that positive research and developmental responsibilities for all dangerous activity should be assigned exclusively to the international agency and that atomic research on nondangerous activities may be carried on in national states subject to licensing by the international agency. While the Soviet Union agrees in principle that the international agency would itself conduct research and development activities, the Soviet Union would permit national research and development of a dangerous character to be carried on in national states. In addition, the Soviet Union would make no provision for the control of national research or development activities of a nondangerous character.[60]

This Soviet position reflected its determination to have its own nuclear program as soon as possible. Molotov made this point in the only Soviet official statement on the general problem of atomic energy prior to the middle of 1946.[61] After a long official silence Modesto Rubenstein, a well-known Soviet columnist, reiterated the Molotov position in his comments on the Baruch Plan: "This Plan is an attempt to consolidate the monopoly of the United States in the manufacture of atomic weapons and to make it possible to continue research in atomic explosives on a still wider scale."[62]

This difference, though fundamental, did not carry into the negoti-

[60] *Ibid.*, pp. 102-03.
[61] See above, p. 47.
[62] "Monopoly Trusts Control Atomic Energy," *New Times* (July 15, 1946), pp. 6-10.

ations after 1948. In the arms control negotiations the question of international control of research did not arise until 1955, since the later negotiations never became sufficiently detailed to require a review of the problem of research.[63]

Phasing and Timing

Perhaps the most fundamental divergence between the Soviet position and that of the West is described by the United States under the heading "Elimination of Atomic Weapons from National Armaments."[64] The Soviet Union dealt with this divergence under two related headings: (1) the question whether the international control of atomic energy including the prohibition of atomic weapons is to be established by one treaty or convention or by several, and, in the latter case, the question of priorities; (2) the question of the stages of transition from existing conditions to international control.[65] The President's report to the Congress describes this divergence in the following over-simplified terms:

While it is generally agreed that atomic weapons must be eliminated from national armaments, the majority have concluded that such elimination should come at that stage in the development of the international control system which would clearly signify to the world that the safeguards then in operation provided security for all participating states. The Soviet Union, on the other hand, has insisted that atomic weapons be destroyed at once and

[63] During the discussions in the Preparatory Commission for the International Atomic Energy Agency in 1956, the Soviet Union initially opposed the establishment of a research laboratory by the agency. A number of the Western governments, among them France, Belgium, and the Union of South Africa, for a variety of reasons took the same position. Ultimately the Soviet Union, perhaps less reluctantly than some of the Western governments, agreed to the United States proposal for a laboratory. The Soviet Union, in the nuclear test cessation negotiations in 1960, approved in principle some international research.

[64] U.S. Participation in the U.N., Report 1947, p. 103.

[65] U.N. Atomic Energy Commission, International Control of Atomic Energy, Third Report, Department of State Publication 3179 (July 1948), p. 37.

that international control including safeguards should be worked out and established later.[66]

This divergence raised the two basic issues that have continued throughout the arms control negotiations:

1. Will the Soviet Union agree to international control machinery within its borders, adequate to give the rest of the world assurance that the Soviet Union is observing its commitments?

2. What will the West give up in return for what it regards as an essential part of effective control—a greater knowledge of events within the Soviet Union, including military developments?

These issues arise since the installation of any extensive control systems on both sides of the iron curtain deprives the Soviet Union of part of its secrecy, which it regards as one of its greatest elements of strength. Since secrecy is not a significant element of Western strength, the West in a truly symmetrical program must make some concessions to compensate for Soviet loss of secrecy. While these were the issues in substance, the manner of their presentation completely fogged the results.

The Soviet contention that the international control of atomic energy should be established through two treaties rather than one attempted to use a procedural device to decide the substantive question of penetration of the iron curtain in favor of the Soviet view. This latter became a familiar Soviet negotiating technique.

The first Soviet treaty in its first article, called for the prohibition of the production and employment of atomic weapons and the destruction of all existing weapons within three months.[67] The agreement outlawing nuclear weapons "must be complemented by the establishment of a comprehensive system of international control, including inspection, to ensure the carrying out of the terms of the convention and 'to protect complying states against the hazards of violations and evasions.' "[68]

---

[66] U.S. Participation in the U.N., Report 1947, p. 103.
[67] Growth of a Policy, p. 213.
[68] U.N. Atomic Energy Commission, International Control of Atomic Energy, Second Report, Revised text of Amendment 3 to the First Report, introduced by the representative of the Soviet Union, pp. 77-78.

The Soviet representative made his position clear in answer to a question propounded by the United Kingdom representative on August 11, 1947. The United Kingdom representative asked: "Would the Soviet representative be ready to modify his position to the extent of saying that the first convention (on prohibition) shall only come into force following satisfactory implementation of the second convention?" Answer:

The Soviet Government has considered and continues to consider the prohibition of atomic weapons and the conclusion of appropriate convention to this end as a foremost and urgent task in the establishment of international control of atomic energy. After the conclusion of convention on prohibition of atomic weapons, another convention can and must be concluded, to provide for the creation of an international control commission and for the establishment of other measures of control and inspection, ensuring the fulfilment of convention on the prohibition of atomic weapons.[69]

Since Gromyko had eliminated the possibility of the first convention not coming into effect until the implementation of the second convention, the Chinese representative determined to carry the question further and to learn the consequences of failure to agree on a second convention after completion of the first convention. The exchange between Gromyko and the Chinese representative, Dr. Wei, was as follows:

Mr. Wei (China): The answer of the representative of the Soviet Union to the Canadian question is definite and absolute. I understood him to say that this first convention on prohibition would not make any sense unless it was concluded, ratified and carried out before the conclusion of the second convention on control. I wish to raise the question whether this sentence, "After the conclusion of a convention on the prohibition of atomic weapons, another convention can and must be concluded . . ." makes any sense, unless there is some assurance.

[69] *Policy at the Crossroads*, p. 113.

Let us imagine further that we have a majority and minority proposal on measures of control. Will the minority go along with the majority? Can any compromise or reconciliation be proposed which will furnish some assurance that the second convention will be concluded? . . .

Mr. Gromyko (USSR): It is difficult for me to understand what the Chinese representative has in mind. He speaks about guarantees. I think he understands very well that it is impossible to speak in such terms in connection with the second convention, on which agreement has not yet been reached. I may ask the same question: whether the other members will guarantee that they will agree with our point of view on this subject. The second convention—the establishment of a system of control and inspection—and any other convention should be formulated as a result of negotiations. It would be wrong to speak in terms of guarantees given in advance of negotiations. I think this point is so simple to understand that it is not desirable to dwell on it at length.

The second convention should come about as the result of our negotiations in the Atomic Energy Commission and in the Security Council, under which the Atomic Energy Commission carried out its work. If we reach an agreement as a result of such negotiations, then the convention will be concluded. If there is found to be no basis for agreement, then naturally the convention cannot be concluded, whether it be the second convention or any other convention.[70]

The Soviet Union had thus taken the extreme position that the bomb must be prohibited and all weapons destroyed even though a convention to ensure enforcement might never materialize—even though there might never be any penetration of the iron curtain.

Conversely, the Soviet Union contended that the purpose of the Baruch Plan was to set up an international authority, dominated by the United States, in the Soviet Union and everywhere else in the world. The Soviet claim was that after this international authority

[70] *Ibid.*, p. 154.

had been set up, there would be no assurance that the United States would in fact eliminate the bomb. For this reason, the Soviet Union did considerable probing into the stages of transition from existing conditions to international control. The probing process was not very successful. Neither the first nor the third report of the Atomic Energy Commission to the Security Council went further than to recommend that the treaty

> ... should provide a schedule for the completion of the transitional process over a period of time, step by step, in an orderly and agreed sequence leading to the full and effective establishment of international control of atomic energy. In order that the transition may be accomplished as rapidly as possible, and with safety and equity to all, the United Nations Atomic Energy Commission should supervise the transitional process, as prescribed in the treaty, and should be empowered to determine when a particular stage or stages have been completed and subsequent ones are to commence.[71]

The best indication of the indecisive nature of the discussion is found in the second report of the Atomic Energy Commission. The Soviet Union had injected a bogus issue into the discussion through an amendment calling for "the destruction of stocks of manufactured atomic weapons and of unfinished atomic weapons."[72] The original text of the first report had provided "for the disposal of any existing stocks of atomic weapons and for the proper use of nuclear fuel adaptable for use in weapons." The second report describes in some detail the discussion of these texts.

The principal point at issue was whether destruction of atomic weapons was intended to include the destruction of nuclear fuel. A majority agreed that the word "disposal" in paragraph 3 (d) of the recommendations of the first report should be interpreted to mean that the mechanisms of atomic weapons would be destroyed and that

[71] U.N. Atomic Energy Commission, *International Control of Atomic Energy*, Third Report, p. 18. See also First Report, p. 22.
[72] *Ibid.*, Second Report, p. 83.

the nuclear fuel contained therein would be used for peaceful purposes only. The representative of the United States stated that he was not prepared at that time to express a final attitude on this point on the ground that this question could not be considered effectively apart from the question of stages and that the really significant problem here was not "disposal" or "destruction" of atomic weapons but effective control over nuclear fuel, which is only a short way from being an atomic weapon. The representative of the Soviet Union considered, however, that it was impossible to imagine the establishment of control of atomic energy without the destruction of atomic weapons. The delegation of the Soviet Union was ready to discuss at any time the question regarding the time of carrying out such measures.

Attempts to express the consensus in the form of a resolution led to a discussion of the stage at which the destruction of weapons should take place. Disagreement on this factor made it impossible to find an acceptable formula for expressing the agreement as to the meaning of "destruction" as all the drafts proposed made reference to the time element and the element of stages. It was, therefore, agreed that the record of the debates should constitute the evidence of the extent of agreement. The representative of the Soviet Union thought that it was insufficient to confine oneself to writing the agreement down in the record, but considered it necessary to take a decision.[73]

The argumentation is admirably summarized by Frederick Osborn's comment:

"Destruction" of atomic weapons was an almost meaningless phrase, because it was understood throughout the debate that the destruction applied only to the bomb casings or detonating mechanisms. All of the delegates, including those of the Soviet Union, agreed that the nuclear fuel which was the actual explosive should not be destroyed, because it had, potentially, too great a value for peaceful purposes. But, of course, it was the nuclear fuel which was expensive and took a long time to make, and constituted the unique danger. The bomb mechanisms could be recreated in a

[73] Ibid., Pt. 3, "Proceedings of the Working Committee in Connection With the Amendments," pp. 75-87.

short time, at a relatively small expense, and in secrecy, no matter how strict the control, which would not be the case with the elaborate processes necessary to the production of nuclear fuel. It would be in a very real sense a fraud on the public to say that the bombs had been destroyed, when actually the explosive was available and the mechanism could be made almost overnight.[74]

While the debates resulted in slightly more precision in defining the stages leading to the elimination of nuclear weapons, the United States at this time went no further than the following concise statement:

> While it is generally agreed that atomic weapons must be eliminated from national armaments, the majority have concluded that such elimination should come at that stage in the development of the international control system which would clearly signify to the world that the safeguards then in operation provided security for all participating states.[75]

In the latter part of 1947 and early 1948 all Soviet statements placed the greatest emphasis on this problem. The following examples are taken from the statement of the Soviet representative on March 29, 1948, which is an annex to the third report. The same theme was reiterated time and again.

> For instance, all the Soviet Union delegation's attempts to clarify even approximately or in general terms, the question of when the prohibition of atomic weapons should take effect have been resolutely opposed by the delegation of the United States. As a result, we have such a situation that the Atomic Energy Commission has made no progress in settling this problem. . . .
>
> All atomic weapons should be destroyed and their nuclear fuel used for peaceful purposes! [Statement quoted from representative of the United Kingdom.]

[74] Frederick Osborn, *op. cit.*, pp. 221-22.
[75] *U.S. Participation in the U.N., Report 1947*, p. 103.

The representatives of Canada, Brazil, and China immediately associated themselves with the United Kingdom representative's statement. It was clear that, with the exception of the United States, the overwhelming majority of the members of the Atomic Energy Commission shared this view. Nevertheless, when a resolution was introduced summarizing the statements which members of the Committee had made on this question, it was rejected. It was rejected because the United States representative disagreed with the opinion of the majority, to which the representatives of the United States are so fond of referring.

May I remind you all of the draft resolution which was then put forward:

The Committee agreed that the treaty or treaties or convention or conventions should provide for the destruction of stocks of manufactured atomic weapons and of unfinished atomic weapons and for the use of the nuclear fuel contained therein for peaceful purposes only. As to the question of time when the destruction of atomic weapons must be carried out, this should be discussed at a later date. . . .

With regard to the date for introducing atomic control, the United States representatives side-step whenever the Soviet Union representatives so much as touch on this question in the discussion. They prefer to speak in general terms of stages of control, since they do not want this general formula about stages to contain any concrete provisions providing the dates for the introduction of measures for the control and inspection of atomic plants and sources of raw materials.[76]

By the end of 1947, the cold war had proceeded so far that the Soviet statements were cluttered with blatant propaganda. Therefore any genuine issue tended to get lost in the argumentation.

The true importance of this issue is emphasized by two events that took place long after the period in the negotiations which we are here discussing. On June 15, 1949, when the atomic discussions had ceased to

[76] U.N. Atomic Energy Commission, *International Control of Atomic Energy*, Third Report, pp. 48-50.

have any substantive content, there was one day of serious discussion that stands out like an island of sense in a sea of propagandistic nonsense. On that day the Soviet representative Tsarapkin, asked three questions.

The second question was the crucial one: "Is the U.S. ready to agree to simultaneous extension of controls to all atomic facilities from mines to production plants?"

This question implied a major Soviet change of position. Never before had the Soviet Union conceded the possibility of controls *preceding* prohibition.

The answer was:

The plan states that the treaty should provide a schedule for the completion of the transitional process over a period of time, step by step in an orderly and agreed sequence.

The AEC in its Third Report stated that until agreement on the basic principles of control had been reached, the elaboration of many topics would serve no useful purposes. The words "remaining topics" include stages.

The other questions were:

"Is the U.S. ready to agree to immediate prohibition of atomic weapons?" The answer, of course, was "No."

"Is the U.S. ready to abandon the idea of international ownership of mines, raw materials, and the production of atomic materials and atomic energy?" The answer was lengthy and conceded the possibility of modifications of the United States position.[77] Tsarapkin of course rejected this response.

Five years later, after the development of the hydrogen bomb and after the United States had all but abandoned the Baruch Plan, during the first London meeting of the subcommittee of five of the Disarmament Commission, the Soviet representative, Jacob Malik, asked approximately the same question and got the same answer from the United States representative, Morehead Patterson. Within less than two months thereafter, the Anglo-French memorandum changed the

[77] U.N. Atomic Energy Commission, Committee 1, *Official Records*, 47th Meeting (June 7, 1949), pp. 32, 33.

position and by coincidence or otherwise almost immediately the United States delegation at the official level had a clear indication of a forthcoming Soviet change of policy.[78]

On this important divergence, it may be concluded that at this time (1946-1948)

1. The Soviet Union insisted that "prohibition" must precede "controls" and was unwilling to give any assurance that given "prohibition," "controls" would follow.

2. The United States insisted that "controls" must precede "prohibition" and in 1946 and 1947 was unwilling to submit a detailed program of installation of controls leading to "prohibition."

These themes from this time on ran through the negotiations like leitmotivs in a Wagnerian opera. No progress toward agreement on arms control was possible until a formula could be devised to solve this impasse.

One clear conclusion emerges from a study of these divergences. The issues separating the Soviet Union and the majority of the commission were substantive. The discussions were in the main serious and to the point, though they tended to deteriorate as the cold war gained in intensity.

IMPASSE

The circumstances of the collapse of the negotiations in the Atomic Energy Commission shed sufficient light on later developments on the international scene to justify detailed study.

As we have seen, from the first meeting of the Atomic Energy Commission in June 1946 until the end of the year, the commission moved with great speed to analyze the Baruch Plan and the outlines of a Soviet plan. On a few important issues agreement was attained, and on others, differences were narrowed. After the resignation of Baruch and his chief deputies in January 1947, the tempo became slower. The Security Council consideration of the first report of the commission lasted from January until the middle of March when the Security Council unanimously transmitted the record of its discussions to the

[78] See Chap. 10.

commission and called on the commission to continue its deliberations, prepare a draft treaty, and submit a second report to the Security Council before the second session of the General Assembly in the fall of 1947.

During the Security Council discussions, the Soviet Union had considerably elaborated its initial proposals. This process continued in the commission culminating in the detailed Soviet proposals of June 11, spelling out the facilities and tasks of the international control commission. The cheerfulness of Gromyko was obvious when he submitted the proposals, and his increasing bitterness emerged as criticism of the proposals developed.[79]

The commission and its committees were extremely active from April until September 11, when in accordance with its instructions from the Security Council, it submitted its second report. This report went no further than to outline the discussions in the commission mainly on the operational and developmental functions of the international control agency and the various Soviet proposals. The closest approach to a conclusion was the statement that "until unanimous agreement is reached on the functions and powers of the international agency, there will be limitations on the extent to which proposals on other topics in the Summary of Principal Subjects can be worked out in detail."[80]

This statement might conceivably be construed to support the majority view that the establishment of the agency must precede the prohibition of weapons. It is also recognized, however, that no progress was possible without the approval of the Soviet Union. Despite the interim nature of the report, the Soviet Union voted against it and Poland abstained.[81]

The commission adjourned in September 1947 to await the Security Council and General Assembly consideration of its second report, and, with the exception of a meeting of its Working Committee in December 1947 to determine a plan of work, it did not reconvene until January 16, 1948. Between January 16 and May 17 when the commission sub-

[79] Osborn, op. cit., pp. 222-25.
[80] U.N. Atomic Energy Commission, International Control of Atomic Energy, Second Report, p. 3.
[81] U.S. Participation in the U.N., Report 1947, p. 101.

mitted its third report, 17 commission or committee meetings took place in contrast to the 122 meetings in 1947. Ten of the 17 meetings were devoted to the Soviet proposals, resulting in a joint statement of Canada, China, and France analyzing the proposals and finding

> . . . that the Soviet Union proposals ignore the existing technical knowledge of the problem of atomic energy control, do not provide an adequate basis for the effective international control of atomic energy and the elimination from national armaments of atomic weapons and, therefore, do not conform to the terms of reference of the Atomic Energy Commission.[82]

Of the remaining seven meetings, five were devoted to a futile effort to elaborate on the organizational structure of the international control agency and two to the consideration of the commission's third report.

The atmosphere of irreconcilability prevailing in this desolate period is described by Jules Moch.[83] Mr. Anthony Nutting believes that the Soviet Union was using this period for purposes of international stalemate, "playing for time to develop its own atomic weapons programme."[84]

The third report contains the following conclusions and recommendations:

> The failure to achieve agreement on the international control of atomic energy arises from a situation that is beyond the competence of this Commission. In this situation, the Commission concludes that no useful purpose can be served by carrying on negotiations at the Commission level.
>
> The Atomic Energy Commission, therefore
>
> Recommends that, until such time as the General Assembly finds that this situation no longer exists, or until such time as the

[82] U.N. Atomic Energy Commission, International Control of Atomic Energy, Third Report, p. 45.
[83] "Elle fournit un effort considérable, mais ne peut concilier les deux théses en présence. Nous ne suivrons pas le detail de ces debats, fort longs et souvent fastidieux." La Folie des Hommes (1954), pp. 223-24.
[84] Disarmament (1959), p. 5.

sponsors of the General Assembly resolution of 24 January 1946, who are the permanent members of the Atomic Energy Commission [Canada, China, France, the Union of Soviet Socialist Republics, the United Kingdom, and the United States of America] find, through prior consultation, that there exists a basis for agreement on the international control of atomic energy, negotiations in the Atomic Energy Commission be suspended.

In accordance with its terms of reference, the Atomic Energy Commission submits this report and recommendation to the Security Council for consideration, and

Recommends that they be transmitted, along with the two previous reports of the Commission, to the next regular session of the General Assembly as a matter of special concern.[85]

The commission adopted the third report on May 17, 1948, by a vote of 9 to 2 with the Soviet Union and Ukraine voting against it.[86] In the Security Council a United States proposal in June calling for the approval of the findings and recommendations of the three commission reports failed to carry because of a Soviet veto. The reports were then submitted to the third session of the General Assembly.[87]

Gromyko strongly protested sending the reports to the General Assembly. "There is . . . no sense in sending the matter back from the Security Council to the General Assembly. It is obvious to all that this can lead nowhere; that nothing positive or useful can come out of it."[88] Gromyko's protest was an early example of the proposition that no measures for arms control can be of value without the support of both the Soviet Union and the United States. Gromyko could not veto the Security Council decision to send the reports to the General Assembly since it was a procedural matter where the veto did not apply.

[85] U.N. Atomic Energy Commission, *International Control of Atomic Energy,* Third Report, p. 5.
[86] *U.S. Participation in the U.N., Report 1948,* Department of State Publication 3437 (April 1949), p. 29.
[87] U.N. General Assembly, Third Session, Plenary, *Official Records,* Pt. 1, 155th Meeting (Nov. 3, 1948).
[88] U.N. Security Council, Third Year, *Official Records,* No. 88, 325th Meeting (June 22, 1948), p. 14.

The General Assembly, despite the opposition of the Soviet Union, approved the "general findings" of the first report and decided that those findings along with the specific proposals of the second report concerning the functions of the international agency constituted "the necessary basis for establishing an effective system of international control."[89] Thus a part of the Baruch Plan became the "United Nations Plan" and thereafter was so described by the Western powers, but not by the Soviet bloc.

The General Assembly, however, did not go along with the recommendation of the third report that negotiations in the commission be suspended, but suggested meetings of the five permanent members of the Security Council and Canada to determine "if there exists a basis for agreement on the international control of atomic energy."[90] This was the first but not the last occasion when the smaller states declined to accept the verdict of the greater powers that an impasse in the negotiations for arms control justified the abandonment of the negotiations. It showed the universal concern over the problem and the universal insistence that channels of negotiation remain open.

The second and more sinister significance of the General Assembly action was the majority approval of an arms control program over Soviet opposition. As pointed out, this was a futile act with import only in the field of propaganda. One result, however, was a new Soviet propaganda line concerning United Nations majorities exemplified in the following:

Vassili Tarasenko of the Ukraine made a statement to the commission on March 18, 1948 that was probably the earliest example of bringing into the open the idea that the "capitalistic" governments did not represent the peoples of the country, an idea that if carried to an extreme might have led to the Soviet recognition of "governments in exile":

We often hear in the Atomic Energy Commission that the Soviet Union insists stubbornly or stubbornly does not want to agree with

[89] U.N. General Assembly, Third Session, *Official Records,* 157th Meeting (Nov. 4, 1948), Res. 191(III).
[90] *Ibid.*

the views of the majority concerning this question. But I do not see quite clearly what majority is meant here. Is it the majority of the members of the Atomic Energy Commission which is meant? Or is it the majority of public opinion of the world and of each country separately? If it is the majority among the members of the Atomic Energy Commission, that is one matter. If, however, it is the majority of the public opinion of each country separately, then it is quite a different matter. They are two completely different things.

As an example, the representative of the United Kingdom in the Atomic Energy Commission belongs, as stated, to the majority which shares the United States delegation's conception of control. But I shall take the liberty of expressing a certain doubt that the majority of British public opinion shares the view of the British representative on this question. . . ."[91]

The same ideas appeared in the General Assembly where Andrei Vyshinsky, the Soviet delegate, stated:

The minority was systematically over-ridden by a closely knit majority which ignored, not only the views of the minority, but also of that increasing majority throughout the World which stood behind the minority in the United Nations. The minority in the United Nations represented, in fact, the majority of the public opinion; the majority of the peoples who wanted peace at all costs, who were against war mongers, and who demanded measures to ensure peace throughout the World. In the United Nations, however, there existed a majority which ignored the views of the minority. It was the latter's duty, therefore, to state its case so that the people outside the precincts of the General Assembly hall should hear the voice of truth.[92]

The stage was set for the Soviet propaganda techniques that completely stultified the arms control negotiations from 1948 to 1955.

[91] *Policy at the Crossroads*, p. 160.
[92] U.N. General Assembly, Third Session, *Official Records*, 156th Meeting (Nov. 4, 1948), Pt. 1, p. 408.

V

The Commission for Conventional Armaments

On October 29, 1946, shortly after the opening of the second part of the first United Nations General Assembly, Soviet Foreign Minister Molotov introduced into the Assembly a resolution calling for the general reduction of armaments—an initiative that ultimately resulted in the birth of the United Nations Commission for Conventional Armaments. The birth of this commission was much more remarkable than its later life.

As we have seen, a general reduction of armaments was originally intended to be a deferred, nonurgent task of the United Nations. The priority objectives were to disarm the axis powers, to create armed forces for the United Nations, and to establish general principles for the regulation of armaments. When the United States decided to depart from the predetermined pattern for the United Nations because of the urgent new problem presented by the atomic bomb, it took great pains to consult and reach agreement with the Soviet Union before acting in the United Nations.[1] The Soviet Union, on the other hand, introduced its resolution on general disarmament with no advance consultation and practically no notice to the other great powers, there-

[1] The United States followed the procedures prescribed in Article 106 of the United Nations Charter relating to "Transitional Security Arrangements."

by signaling its abandonment of the idea of great power agreement in the field of arms control.

The draft resolution read as follows:

1. In the interests of consolidating international peace and security and in conformity with the purposes and principles of the United Nations Organization, the General Assembly considers a general reduction of armaments necessary.

2. The implementation of the decision on the reduction of armaments should include as a primary objective the prohibition of the production and use of atomic energy for military purposes.

3. The General Assembly recommends to the Security Council that it provide for the practical achievement of the objectives set forth in paragraphs 1 and 2 above.

4. The General Assembly calls upon the Governments of all States to render all possible assistance to the Security Council in this responsible undertaking, the accomplishment of which accords with the task of establishing lasting peace and international security, and also serves the interests of the peoples by lightening the heavy economic burden imposed on them by excessive expenditure on armaments, which is not in keeping with peaceful postwar conditions.[2]

The resolution disregarded the United Nations Atomic Energy Commission, which had already received authority from the General Assembly to deal with the control of atomic energy and its elimination from national armaments. This would have the effect of discarding the comparatively substantial achievements of the commission discussions and starting all over again.

The resolution also was an early example of a typical Soviet negotiating technique: the attempt to use a procedural device to decide a substantive issue. In the Atomic Energy Commission, the Soviet Union had insisted that prohibition of nuclear weapons must precede

[2] U.N. General Assembly, First Session, *Official Records*, Pt. 2, 42nd Meeting (Oct. 29, 1946), p. 847.

the establishment of an international control system. This resolution would have decided that substantive question in favor of the Soviet Union through establishing a new negotiating body to deal with only the prohibition of atomic weapons.

The resolution must be considered in conjunction with an earlier effort in the Security Council where the Soviet Union requested all Members of the United Nations to report to the Council the number and location of their armed forces in foreign states except in former enemy territories. The Security Council resolution reinforced the Communist agitation to hasten the process of "bringing the boys home." It may have foreshadowed the Communist efforts a year later to establish a Communist regime in Greece and to isolate Turkey, objectives that would be difficult to achieve while substantial United States forces remained in Europe. The Soviet Union did not include in the proposal troops stationed in former enemy territory since all the Soviet troops stationed outside its borders were located in former enemy territory.[3]

While the Soviet Union did not incorporate this proposal in its original resolution in the General Assembly, it raised the issue at a later stage of the discussions in the Assembly of the disarmament problem. Here again, the Soviet Union was abandoning the basic concept of great power agreement.

On the specific issue of the census of troops stationed abroad, the United Kingdom took the position that the survey should cover all forces wherever located and should provide for an inspection system to verify the reported information. The United States took the position that such information should be supplied only in connection with a comprehensive inspection and control system to monitor reductions in armaments.

Molotov's speech in the General Assembly introducing his resolution was loaded with bitter attacks on the motives of the United States in general, and in particular, on the performance of Baruch. Neverthe-

[3] *United States Participation in the United Nations, Report by the President to the Congress for the Year 1947*, Department of State Publication 3024 (1948), p. 105. Cited hereafter as *U.S. Participation in the U.N., Report* (with year).

less, Senator Warren Austin, the United States representative in the United Nations, although he had no advance notice of this new Soviet line, replied within twenty-four hours in a moderate tone, contenting himself with the comment that "The initiative of the Soviet Union in this matter is appropriate, because of its mighty armies; just as the initiative of the United States was appropriate in proposing measures to prevent the manufacture and use of atom weapons."[4]

The United States and the United Kingdom then set out diligently and laboriously to obtain a resolution on the subject of arms control that would meet with the approval of both the Soviet Union and the West. The effort was successful partly because of an improvement in the general atmosphere accompanying the decision of the meeting of Foreign Ministers to go forward with peace treaties. The moderate United States position opposing the more intemperate attacks on the voting formula in the Security Council may have contributed to this result.

Finally, by dint of persistent negotiation, a drafting group whittled out a lengthy omnibus resolution entitled "Principles Governing the General Regulation and Reduction of Armaments," which received the unanimous approval of the General Assembly on December 14, 1946.[5]

This resolution, as its lengthy name suggests, attempted to deal with all phases of the arms control problem. In the field of atomic energy, it specifically reaffirmed the resolution of January 24, 1946, establishing the Atomic Energy Commission. In addition, the commission should proceed both to draft a convention outlawing nuclear weapons (the Soviet approach) and to establish a practical and effective safeguards system (Baruch's approach.) The resolution recognized the close connection between arms reduction and the establishment of United Nations military forces, and requested the Security Council to accelerate the agreements placing such forces at the disposal of the United Nations.

The resolution further recommended the progressive withdrawal of forces stationed in former enemy territory and the immediate with-

---

[4] U.N. General Assembly, First Session, Plenary, *Official Records,* Pt. 2, 44th Meeting (Oct. 30, 1946), p. 894.
[5] *Ibid.,* 63rd Meeting (Dec. 14, 1946), pp. 1310-20.

drawal of forces stationed in territories of Members of the United Nations without their consent freely and publicly expressed in treaties or agreements.

On the main subject of reduction in conventional armaments, the resolution set up the framework for a second set of arms control negotiations.[6]

CHIEF EVENTS, 1947-1948

To comply with this resolution, the Security Council on February 13, 1947, created the Commission for Conventional Armaments composed of the Members of the Security Council.[7] Ralph A. Bard, formerly Undersecretary of the Navy, was named in March as Deputy United States representative in the United Nations Commission for Conventional Armaments. Bard served from March 28, 1947, to January 19, 1948.

[6] The resolution states that: *"The General Assembly, Recommends* that the Security Council give prompt consideration to formulating the practical measures, according to their priority, which are essential to provide for the general regulation and reduction of armaments and armed forces and to assure that such regulation and reduction of armaments and armed forces will be generally observed by all participants and not unilaterally by only some of the participants. The plans formulated by the Security Council shall be submitted by the Secretary-General to the Members of the United Nations for consideration at a special session of the General Assembly. The treaties or conventions approved by the General Assembly shall be submitted to the signatory for ratification in accordance with Article 26 of the Charter. . . .

"The General Assembly

"Further recognizes that essential to the general regulation and reduction of armaments and armed forces is the provision of practical and effective safeguards by way of inspection and other means to protect complying States against the hazards of violations and evasions.

"Accordingly,

"The General Assembly

"Recommends to the Security Council that it give prompt consideration to the working out of proposals to provide such practical and effective safeguards in connexion with the control of atomic energy and the general regulation and reduction of armaments. . . ." Res. 41 (I).

[7] U.S. Department of State, *The International Control of Atomic Energy: Policy at the Crossroads*, Publication 3161 (1948), p. 69. Cited hereafter as *Policy at the Crossroads*. Text of resolution in U.N. Security Council, Second Year, *Official Records*, No. 13, 105th Meeting (Feb. 13, 1947).

When the commission convened on March 26, its first step was to prepare a plan of work.[8] Despite the decision of the General Assembly to the contrary, the Soviet Union sought to include the prohibition of atomic weapons in the work plan of the commission. When the commission accepted the United States draft of a plan of work and submitted it for approval to the Security Council, Gromyko stated that despite the adoption of the United States draft, he would proceed in the commission along the lines expressed in the Soviet plan. During the remainder of 1947, the commission got no further than to define its jurisdiction to cover all armaments and armed forces except atomic weapons and weapons of mass destruction.[9]

When the commission reconvened in 1948 after the General Assembly of 1947, it proceeded to discuss the second item of its agenda: principles relating to the regulation and reduction of conventional armaments and armed forces. This discussion led to the adoption over the opposition of the Soviet Union of six principles as follows:

. . . (1) a system for the regulation and reduction of conventional armaments and armed forces should provide for the adherence of all states and initially should include all states having substantial military resources; (2) it can only be put into effect in an atmosphere of international confidence and security; (3) examples of conditions essential to such confidence and security are (a) the establishment of an adequate system of agreements under article 43 of the Charter, (b) the international control of atomic energy and (c) the conclusion of the peace settlements with Germany and Japan; (4) a system for the regulation and reduction of armaments and armed forces should provide for the least possible diversion for armaments of the world's human and economic resources; (5) it must include an adequate system of safeguards which functions under international supervision to insure the observance of the provisions of the treaty or convention and which (a) is technically feasible and practical, (b) is capable of detecting promptly the oc-

[8] U.N. Commission on Conventional Armaments, Doc. S/C.3/SR 1 (March 26, 1947), p. 5.
[9] U.S. Participation in the U.N., Report 1947, p. 110.

currence of violations, and (c) causes minimum interference with the economic and industrial life of individual nations; and (6) provision must be made for effective enforcement action in the event of violations.[10]

The first principle was obvious and noncontroversial. The fourth principle was merely a repetition of language of the United Nations Charter. The fifth and sixth principles diverged only slightly from the general principles for a safeguards system as presented by both the Soviet Union and the West in the Atomic Energy Commission. In short, except for paragraphs 2 and 3, this resolution contained nothing but generalities.

The second and third principles expressed the view that an atmosphere of international confidence must precede arms reductions. This view was difficult to reconcile with the United States position in the Atomic Energy Commission calling for immediate international control *prior* to any improvement in the international atmosphere.[11] The resolution then proceeded to list international control of atomic energy as one of the "conditions essential to confidence" that must be established prior to conventional arms reductions.

This created the strange result that under the United States contentions, atomic energy could be controlled and atomic weapons eliminated without an improvement in the international atmosphere, but reduction of conventional weapons and armed forces had to wait for the improvement in international affairs. Furthermore, reduction in conventional weapons had to await agreement on the control of atomic energy.

The best descriptions of the circumstances within the United States Government leading to these decisions are found in *The Forrestal Diaries*. Forrestal and a large part of the military establishment apparently had opposed all discussion of disarmament in the United Nations.

[10] U.S. *Participation in the U.N., Report 1948*, Department of State Publication 3437 (April 1949), pp. 34-35.
[11] A possible differentiation would be that the Commission for Conventional Armaments was dealing with existing armaments while the Atomic Energy Commission was mainly concerned with prospective armaments.

To Ralph A. Bard, 11 July 1947

. . . The thing that I think we have to hammer home is the fact that there is practically *no* basis for any realistic talk about disarmament until the Russians have made it manifest and clear that they want the substance and not merely the sham of peace in the world. By this I mean cooperation in a swift conclusion of treaties with Germany and Japan, and real cooperation in the economic and social reconstruction of Europe. If they don't mean business along these lines, I know you will agree that even the talk of disarmament is highly dangerous, because of the American tendency always to take for granted that other nations have the same objectives as ourselves. . . .

I am most apprehensive of our people's mistaking the *discussion* of disarmament for the fact. There is plenty of evidence that this tendency is already underway. (Did you know that Mike Robertson was teamed up with Jo Davidson in a group to prevent World War III?!!!). . .[12]

General Marshall, the Secretary of State, took a less extreme position and was apparently responsible for the decision that the commission should discuss *how* and *when* to regulate armaments rather than *what* to regulate.[13] This accounted for the second item on the United States plan of work. Marshall made it clear that a position in opposition to disarmament discussions could not be taken publicly.

29 January 1947   State-War-Navy

. . . General Marshall explained that the other members of the Security Council were unanimous in the belief that the Council should go ahead with the discussion of the general problem of disarmament. He believed that other nations would take a solid vote against us should we propose otherwise. He said Senator Austin and Mr. Baruch shared the view that it would be unwise for us to eliminate the atomic bomb until other matters in the field of regulation of armaments were well along. Admiral Nimitz suggested that

[12] Walter Millis, ed., *The Forrestal Diaries* (1951), pp. 290-91.
[13] *Ibid.*, p. 241.

in view of present circumstances U.S. position should be that committee discussions should be directed toward the problem of *how* and *when* to regulate armaments rather than *what* to regulate. He said that the important thing was to establish methods of inspection and control, and also to establish criteria of world conditions, such as conclusion of peace treaties and establishment of forces under the Security Council as prerequisite to undertaking general disarmament. There was complete acceptance of these views after considerable discussion. . . .

I pointed out that there was imperative need for informing the public of the vital issues involved in considering regulation of armaments. I suggested that once discussion in the Security Council appeared to hold out a plan for a disarmed utopia there would perhaps be irresistible public pressure to adopt such a plan forthwith, regardless of world conditions which for some time will require existence of force to accomplish stability. There was general agreement with these views.[14]

This policy made any agreement on reduction of conventional armaments, even though accompanied by satisfactory safeguards, contingent on prior agreement on atomic energy. The United States was now following the example set by the Soviet Union in the Atomic Energy Commission and other negotiations of refusing to go on to a later agenda item until agreement on the prior item. The result was that even discussion of reduction of armaments or safeguards could not proceed until agreement had been reached on the control of atomic energy.

This policy was most embarrassing to the United States and to Ralph Bard, who requested a change. Eisenhower, then Chief of Staff of the Army, rejected Bard's suggestion.

The extent to which the atomic bomb was slowly emerging as a pivotal point in American politico-strategic thought is indicated by an entry a few days later on a meeting with Ralph Bard—who represented the United States in the U.N. negotiations over conven-

---

[14] *Ibid.,* p. 241.

tional armaments—Lovett, Eisenhower and Gruenther. Bard felt himself hampered by the Joint Chiefs of Staff position that there should be no further discussion of conventional armaments until atomic weapons had been dealt with. "Eisenhower made the point, which Bard had apparently not heard before, that it would be dangerous" to proceed with conventional armaments "until the Russians had agreed to a workable plan of inspection," since if we agreed to a plan for conventional weapons without rigid inspection requirements the Russians could move for the application of the same formula to atomic weapons. In Eisenhower's opinion, "any agreement about atomic weapons without enforceable methods of inspection would be most dangerous for the U.S. Bard saw the point." It is interesting that he had not already seen a point which a year or two later would appear obvious to everyone.[15]

The logic of Eisenhower's response leaves much to be desired. Certainly the United States could not accept either reductions in conventional armaments or international control of atomic energy without safeguards to ensure that all states would observe their commitments. Why should not the United States call for sufficient safeguards to assure conventional disarmament as well as effective international control of atomic energy, instead of making the conventional armaments discussions contingent on agreement in the field of control of atomic energy?

The position of the United States Joint Chiefs of Staff is understandable in the light of both the domestic and international atmosphere. The United States was experiencing the greatest difficulty in meeting the increasing menace of Soviet imperialism with its existing military establishment. Henry Wallace was spearheading an attack on the entire political and military policy, described later as "containment" of the Soviet Union. Limitation of military budgets went hand in hand with agitation for disarmament. The immediate emergency called for the rapid development of an adequate military establishment both in the United States and in Western Europe, and any-

[15] *Ibid.*, pp. 327-28.

thing interfering with that objective should be opposed. Furthermore, the discussions on atomic energy had revealed that the Soviet Union had little real interest in a safeguarded disarmament program.

In later years these justifiable fears almost certainly would not have expressed themselves in a position opposing all international discussion of disarmament. However, as time went on, certain educational institutions such as the National War College of the Armed Forces, and joint political-military programs such as NATO, and the United Nations operations in Korea, all had produced a cross-fertilization of ideas between the diplomats and the soldiers and a realization that political and security objectives were identical. In 1946 and 1947 this *expertise* was lacking, with the result that the United States took a position that in later years it could not justify, and which it had to revise.

Thus, by the fall of 1948, when the General Assembly convened, the United States and the West in general had done nothing of any consequence in the Conventional Armaments Commission either to advance an agreement on reduction of conventional armaments or even to create an attractive position vis-à-vis world public opinion. The only factor to minimize possible Western loss of prestige was that the Soviet position was even worse. Soviet bloc representatives confined themselves to personal attacks on the West and propaganda speeches devoting much more time to atomic energy than to conventional weapons. A possible explanation might be that during this period Soviet military leaders tended to downgrade the atom bomb and emphasize huge armies. They apparently had no interest at that time in reduction of conventional weapons, which were essential to their program of spreading communism.[16]

We have chosen to end the study of the earliest period of United Nations arms control negotiations with the convening of the Third General Assembly in September 1948. This is a logical dividing point in negotiations in the Atomic Energy Commission, in the Military Staff Committee, and to a certain extent in the progress of the cold war. In the Commission for Conventional Armaments, however, 1949 was no

[16] Raymond L. Garthoff, *Soviet Strategy in the Nuclear Age* (1958), pp. 71-76.

different from 1948. The 1947-1948 meetings had most of the characteristics of the intensified cold war that emerged in full vigor at later dates in the Atomic Energy Commission and in Military Staff Committee meetings. Even though the separation of periods is somewhat artificial, it seems desirable to postpone the consideration of the later developments in the Conventional Armaments Commission until we deal with parallel events in and outside of the United Nations negotiations.

STALEMATE IN THE MILITARY

STAFF COMMITTEE

An immediate task of the United Nations after its establishment was to arrange for agreements between the Security Council and United Nations Members under which the Members would make available to the Security Council "armed forces, assistance, and facilities, including rights of passage, necessary for the purpose of maintaining international peace and security."[17]

The Military Staff Committee, consisting of military representatives of the five permanent members of the Security Council, had the responsibility "to advise and assist the Security Council on all questions relating to the Security Council's military requirements for the maintenance of international peace and security."[18] The initial discussions of United Nations forces took place in that committee, which was extremely active throughout 1946 and in the early part of 1947.

The General Assembly resolution of December 14, 1946, on regulation of armaments, reaffirmed the original concept of the Charter that the existence of United Nations forces was an essential part of any system of arms control.[19]

[17] Charter of the United Nations, Art. 43.
[18] Ibid., Art. 47.
[19] "The General Assembly, regarding the problem of security as closely connected with that of disarmament,
"Recommends the Security Council to accelerate as much as possible the placing at its disposal of the armed forces mentioned in Article 43 of the Charter." See Res. 41 (I), Dec. 14, 1946.

Accordingly, the Security Council on February 16, 1947, requested the Military Staff Committee to submit as a matter of urgency a report on this problem, and, as a first step, to submit to the Council not later than April 30, 1947, its recommendation concerning the basic principles that should govern the organization of the armed forces to be made available to the Security Council.[20]

The report showed much labor and considerable agreement in the Military Staff Committee, but at the same time, substantial areas of disagreement between the Soviet Union and the other four members. The discussions of this report in the Security Council raised the issue of the relationship of the United Nations forces to the entire problem of disarmament.

The most important divergence in the Military Staff Committee arose from the Soviet insistence that *each* permanent member of the Security Council make identical contributions of each component of the armed forces—in other words, that no permanent member make available any component larger than or different in composition from the weakest component of the same type made available by any of the other permanent members. The majority of the committee opposed this Soviet position on the ground that it assured a weak United Nations force.

Probably the underlying reason for the position of the Russians was their fear that the air force would play the largest role in the United Nations police force. The Soviet military position at the time was such that its main contribution would have been ground forces while the main United States contribution would have been naval and air forces.[21]

In the Security Council, however, Gromyko justified his demand for exact equality in the contributions of each permanent member for each component on the ground that a strong United Nations force was unnecessary.[22]

[20] *U.S. Participation in the U.N., Report 1948*, p. 38.
[21] William Reitzel, Morton A. Kaplan, and Constance G. Coblenz, *United States Foreign Policy 1945-1955* (1956), p. 239.
[22] "I drew attention to the U.N. decision on the question of the general reduction of armaments and armed forces in connection with the USSR proposal, and pointed

As a result of this Soviet position, the United States suggested that the Military Staff Committee, in order to facilitate the discussions in the Security Council, estimate the size of the forces that would be required. This request was transmitted to the committee despite Gromyko's objection. The committee reported that agreement had not been reached on the size of the forces, but transmitted the estimates of the delegates of the United States, the United Kingdom, France, and China. The Soviet delegate refused to make an estimate. The estimates of the other four members showed wide variations. The United Kingdom and France estimated that the United Nations would require 1,200 planes. The United States suggested 3,800. The United Kingdom and France suggested 12 submarines, the United States, 90. The United Kingdom figure for destroyers was 24, the United States figure 84.[23]

In short, the United States alone was calling for large United Nations forces. The United Kingdom, France, and China were in general agreement with the Soviet view that the United Nations forces should be small, even though they did not go along with some Soviet conclusions based on a small United Nations force.

Up to this point, no one had questioned during the Security Council deliberations, the general principle that the effectiveness of United Nations military forces depended on a relatively disarmed world. No one had suggested a United Nations military arm that could fight a major war, even one not directly involving the great powers. The Western powers as well as the Communist states had recognized the close

---

out that the USSR proposal is based on the U.N. decision on general disarmament. I pointed out that, if effect is to be given to the U.N. decision on reduction of armaments, the U.N. will not need to have an army, fleet and air force of excessive numerical strength. What can be inferred from this? The inference can be drawn that, if this is so, it will not be necessary for the Security Council to have large armed forces at its disposal under special agreements since the various U.N. members will not have excessively numerous armed forces. From this it follows that, since the armed forces made available to the Security Council will be comparatively small, even one of the comparatively weaker among the five Powers would have no serious difficulty in making armed forces available to the Security Council in accordance with agreements, on the basis of the principle of equal contributions." Statement by Gromyko (USSR), U.N. Security Council, Second Year, *Official Records*, No. 50, 146th Meeting (June 25, 1947), p. 1109.
[23] *Ibid.*, No. 52, 149th Meeting (June 30, 1947), p. 1177.

link between the problems of arms control and United Nations forces.[24] With this background, the United States representative in the Security Council found himself hard pressed to maintain the United States position calling for large United Nations forces. The logic was unassailable that progress toward disarmament would make large United Nations forces unnecessary. The United States representative sought to rescue his position with the following statement:

My delegation's view is that we should not allow the work we are doing now to become entangled with the disarmament question. If we do, we shall certainly make our present task infinitely more difficult. In our view we should agree that the contributions of the Members of the United Nations in the form of armed forces, assistance and facilities should not in any way provide a criterion at some future date for disarmament.[25]

The effect of this statement was amazing. After about fifteen minutes of discussion, which can best be characterized by the word bewilderment, the meeting adjourned, and the Security Council never afterward resumed discussion of United Nations forces.

The Military Staff Committee went through the motions of dis-

[24] Statement by Parodi (France):
"We should have no illusions. Since it has been submitted, the Military Staff Committee's report has occupied a central position in relation to our current work. The whole work of disarmament depends upon it, and certain delegations have deliberately reserved their positions with regard to Disarmament until Article 43 of the Charter is implemented." *Ibid.*, No. 46, 141st meeting (June 16, 1947), p. 1007:
Statement by Lange (Poland):
"Obviously, if we should have no disarmament, or if we should ever have the reverse—an increase in national armaments—the Security Council, in order to be effective, would need very large armed forces, or otherwise those forces would be too small to have any military and, consequently, any political effect.
"Therefore, we should consider a speedy solution of the problem of disarmament—a very necessary step in order to make the armed forces which are to be put at the disposal of the Security Council a really effective tool in the hands of our Organization." *Ibid.*, pp. 1010-11.
[25] U.N. Security Council, Second Year, *Official Records*, No. 58, 157th and 158th Meetings (July 15, 1947), pp. 1297-98.

cussions for several months, but gradually the committee sank into oblivion. To this day, it meets at regular intervals. The military delegates all don their dress uniforms and attend a meeting with two agenda items: "Adoption of Agenda" and "Minutes of Previous Meeting." After ten minutes, largely devoted to translations, the meeting adjourns.

To the Soviet Union, the United States representative had torpedoed the basic United Nations doctrine of the responsibility of the great powers acting through the Security Council for maintaining world peace, and was visualizing a world of large national forces with an independent large United Nations force.[26] Such a picture, when coupled with attacks on the principle of unanimity in the Security Council almost certainly raised in the minds of the Soviet Union the bogey that the United States might seek to evade the veto in the Security Council and use the United Nations force against a permanent member.

The unfortunate United States statement probably arose from conflicting channels of instructions to the United States representative. Instructions on Military Staff Committee matters at that time proceeded directly from the Joint Chiefs of Staff to the United States delegate on the Military Staff Committee, and from him to the representative on the Security Council. On too many occasions, scant attention was paid to officers in the State Department with responsibility for United States policies in the United Nations who would have realized the implications of such a statement. The negotiations themselves were the chief victims of the bureaucratic shortcomings of the United States Government.

It is of course impossible to correlate directly this breakup of the Military Staff Committee discussions with the deterioration of the atomic energy discussions. The two situations came about almost simultaneously. It was apparent as early as 1947 that the Charter provisions for a United Nations military force were unrealistic. Within a short time, the Military Staff Committee would have become dormant. This

[26] For one among many Soviet references to this episode, see statement by Manuilsky in Political Committee of the Third General Assembly (Oct. 11, 1948), p. 115.

episode permitted the Soviet Union, with some show of reason, to blame the United States for the collapse of the negotiations.

THE VANDENBERG RESOLUTION

By the summer of 1948, United States policy on the entire subject of arms control had reached a state of poverty never thereafter duplicated. In the Conventional Armaments Commission the United States was clinging to the position that no reductions could take place prior to an improvement in the international atmosphere, and one of the conditions necessary to improvement was Soviet acceptance of the Baruch Plan. The efforts to reach agreement on a program of armed forces for the United Nations had virtually ceased. The concept of the great powers preventing war until such time as the United Nations itself could act had disappeared with Western demobilization and increasing East-West friction. In the Atomic Energy Commission the United States still adhered to its one really constructive contribution toward arms control, the Baruch Plan, but declined to elaborate on the conditions under which control of atomic energy would lead to the elimination of nuclear weapons.

The Soviet position was even more devoid of substantive content than that of the United States. In the Atomic Energy Commission, the Soviet Union refused to admit the possibility of the slightest variance from proposals the commission had already found inadequate. In the Conventional Armaments Commission, the Soviet Union had not gone beyond the stage of propaganda slogans largely dealing with atomic armaments, which were beyond the jurisdiction of the commission.

The United States made the first move to fill the policy vacuum. The Executive branch of the government developed certain views which became the official doctrine of the United States with the passage by the Senate of the Vandenberg Resolution of June 11, 1948. The ideas set forth in this resolution became the starting point for much of the future policy in the entire field of arms control and is therefore quoted in its entirety:

Whereas peace with justice and the defense of human rights and fundamental freedoms require international cooperation through more effective use of the United Nations: Therefore be it

RESOLVED, That the Senate reaffirm the policy of the United States to achieve international peace and security through the United Nations so that armed force shall not be used except in the common interest, and that the President be advised of the sense of the Senate that this Government, by constitutional process, should particularly pursue the following objectives within the United Nations Charter:

(1) Voluntary agreement to remove the veto from all questions involving pacific settlements of international disputes and situations, and from the admission of new members.

(2) Progressive development of regional and other collective arrangements for individual and collective self-defense in accordance with the purposes, principles, and provisions of the Charter.

(3) Association of the United States, by constitutional process, with such regional and other collective arrangements as are based on continuous and effective self-help and mutual aid, and as affect its national security.

(4) Contributing to the maintenance of peace by making clear its determination to exercise the right of individual or collective self-defense under article 51 should any armed attack occur affecting its national security.

(5) Maximum efforts to obtain agreements to provide the United Nations with armed forces as provided by the Charter, and to obtain agreement among member nations upon universal regulation and reduction of armaments under adequate and dependable guaranty against violation.

(6) If necessary, after adequate effort toward strengthening the United Nations, review of the charter at an appropriate time by a General Conference called under article 109 or by the General Assembly.[27]

[27] S. Res. 239, 80 Cong. 2 sess. (June 11, 1948).

The Vandenberg Resolution made it clear that despite the frustrations of the cold war, the United States Government was not to return to the isolation of the 1920's. The preamble reiterated that the United States would continue to support, and act through, the United Nations. The most important paragraphs were the second, third, and fourth, which spelled out the United States determination to support regional and collective self-defense arrangements to maintain the security of the non-Communist world. The resolution also specifically reversed the United States position in the Commission for Conventional Armaments, that reductions in armaments could be discussed only after Soviet acceptance of the Baruch Plan and also the United States statement in the Security Council disassociating the problems of the United Nations armed forces and reduction of armaments. It took more than a year for President Truman and the Executive branch of the government to transform the general statement of policy into an arms control program. The Vandenberg Resolution became the firm base on which the United States in 1949 constructed a more meaningful policy toward arms control.

VI

Appraisal of the Period

IN A GENERAL AND BROAD SENSE, during the period we have been discussing, 1946-1947 and the first nine months of 1948, arms control negotiations followed the pattern of political events. As the cold war mounted in intensity, negotiations deteriorated, with the Soviet Union resorting to abusive propaganda and refusing to face the issues. During the short periods of narrowing political differences, there was roughly equivalent progress, or rather relaxation, in the field of arms control.

It is not possible to sketch in sharp outlines the ebb and flow of the cold war during this period. Agreements resulting in progress toward the reconstruction of the postwar world frequently overlapped actions exacerbating the relations of the Soviet Union and its wartime allies. The first phase extended from January 1946 until the third meeting of the Council of Foreign Ministers in New York in October and November of that year. This period was characterized by the gradual disappearance of the wartime collaboration between the Soviet Union and its allies, arising largely from the hostile and aggressive policies and actions of the Soviet leaders, and their unwillingness to cooperate in the rehabilitation of Europe. The second short period commenced with the decision of the Council of Foreign Ministers to proceed immediately with the negotiation of peace treaties and lasted until March 1947. The characteristic of this period was the valiant effort of the

102

United States, the United Kingdom, and France to eliminate outstanding differences with the Soviet Union through patient negotiations. Its most tangible accomplishment was agreement on the treaties of peace with Italy, Bulgaria, Hungary, Rumania, and Finland. It came to an end as a result of the convincing evidence of Soviet plans to proceed rapidly toward the Sovietization of all Eastern Europe and, at the same time, to spread anarchy and disorder in Western Europe with the ultimate objective of the Soviet Union taking over the entire continent. After the spring of 1947, relations with the Soviet Union consistently deteriorated.

Without attempting to sketch the lines too sharply, the chief events in the arms control negotiations seemed to follow the pattern of outside political events. This was particularly true in the Military Staff Committee and the Atomic Energy Commission. The parallel is not too exact as the Commission for Conventional Armaments never had a period of sensible discussion and of relative freedom from Soviet propaganda and invective. The parallelism of international developments and arms control negotiations can be most graphically portrayed by listing in columns some of the most important international events and the developments in the arms control negotiations taking place simultaneously.

Important International Events	*Developments in Arms Control*
March 1946: Russia refuses to withdraw its troops from Iran.	January 1946: Unanimous agreement on establishment of U.N. Atomic Energy Commission.
March 1946: Stalin calls Churchill the "war monger of the Third World War."	
May 1946: Agreement on administration of Austria and Vienna.	
May 1946: Soviet troops leave Iran.	
June 1946: Churchill coins term "Iron Curtain."	June 1946: Baruch presents plan for control of atomic energy.
January-August 1946: Soviet "ve-	August 1946: Gromyko rejects in-

Important International Events

toes" in United Nations Security Council.

September 1946: Zhdanov's ideological declaration of war against the West.

October 1946: Third meeting of Council of Foreign Ministers reaches agreement on peace treaty negotiations with European allies of Germany.

January 1947: Polish elections end hope of Polish independence.

February 1947: Agreement on peace treaties with Italy, Finland, Hungary, Rumania, Bulgaria.

March 1947: Soviet decree forbidding marriages between Soviet citizens and foreigners.

March 1947: Crisis in Greece because of Communist subversion. Announcement of Truman doctrine and aid to Greece and Turkey.

May 1947: Fall of last non-Communist government in Hungary.

June 1947: Marshall Plan for economic aid with offers of aid to Soviet bloc.

July 1947: Soviet bloc rejects Mar-

Developments in Arms Control

ternational control system.

September 1946: Soviet Union introduces disarmament resolution in United Nations discarding Atomic Energy Commission.

October 1946: Russians agree to Report of Scientific and Technical Committee of Atomic Energy Commission.

December 1946: Unanimous agreement on General Assembly resolution for reduction of armaments.

January 1947: Resignation of Baruch.

February 1947: Establishment of Commission for Conventional Armaments.

February 1947: Gromyko submits Soviet proposals for international atomic control agency in form of amendments to first report of commission.

April 1947: Military Staff Committee report to Security Council showing areas of agreement and disagreement.

June 11, 1947: Gromyko makes detailed proposals for international agency to control atomic energy.

July 1947: Breakup of Security

Important International Events

Developments in Arms Control

shall Plan aid on eve of negotiations with United States.
July 1947: "Mr. X," George Kennan, publishes article in *Foreign Affairs*, advocating policy of "containment" of Soviet Union.
September 1947: At Communist Conference in Upper Silesia, Zhdanov declares world split into two hostile camps. Communists create the Cominform.
September 1947: Arrest of opposition leaders in Bulgaria and Rumania.
November 1947: Communist-organized general strikes in France and Italy.
December 1947: Overthrow of Monarchy in Rumania.
December 1947: Arrest of opposition leaders in Poland and Hungary.
February 1948: Communist "putsch" in Prague. Masaryk's death.
March 1948: End of Allied Control Commission in Berlin.

Council discussions of Military Staff Committee report.

September 1947: Second report of Atomic Energy Commission records impasse in commission.

April 1948: Atomic Energy Commission finds Soviet proposal inadequate.
May 1948: Third report of Atomic Energy Commission finds no basis for agreement on international control of atomic energy and rec-

Important International Events	Developments in Arms Control
	ommends suspension of negotiations.
June 1948: Soviet break with Tito. August 1948: Commencement of Berlin blockade. August 31, 1948: Death of Zhdanov.	June 1948: Soviet Union vetoes Security Council resolution to approve reports of Atomic Energy Commission. November 1948: U. N. General Assembly approves report of Atomic Energy Commission over Soviet objections.

This table is far too imprecise to permit definitive conclusions as to cause and effect. For example, it would be hazardous to assert that the program of United States aid to Greece and Turkey had as one of its results the increasing rigidity of the Soviet position in the atomic energy negotiations. Nor would it be safe to conclude that the debacle in the Military Staff Committee negotiations had any direct relations to contemporaneous events such as the Soviet revival of the Cominform. The table does show, however, that the arms control negotiations cannot be viewed apart from the broader historical developments. It also shows that in this period, world events outside the field of arms control were overwhelmingly more important than the arms control negotiations. The Soviet leaders wished to develop an atomic weapon, but doubted that United States possession of atomic weapons would be decisive in a war. The Soviet leaders had not yet realized and informed their own citizens that a nuclear holocaust would result in the destruction of both the Soviet Union and the West. It was only at a later time that reduction of international tensions through agreement on arms control became a prime stated objective of Soviet policy. At this time the Soviet policy toward arms control seemed to have two main goals: (1) to delay the atomic energy negotiations until the Soviet Union itself had a bomb; (2) to use all possible means to achieve the unilateral disarmament of the West to hasten the ultimate victory of communism.

QUESTIONS

With this brief discussion of the contemporaneous events in the international scene, it now becomes possible to attempt to answer some of the questions concerning United States policy during this period, and to attempt an appraisal both of the policy and of the period.

The first question is: Why did the United States offer to give up the atomic bomb, the one weapon where it had superiority, and at the same time resist even a discussion of reduction of conventional armaments where the Soviet Union had superiority? The same question can be posed in slightly different terms. The constant military answer of the United States to the mass armies of the Communist nations is Detroit as the symbol of United States industrial power. Why did the United States in 1946 offer to abandon atomic warfare—the type of warfare in which its industrial superiority could be most effective—and at the same time resist Soviet efforts to reduce mass armies?

Dr. Harvey A. DeWeerd of the Rand Corporation discusses this question in the article, "The Case for Weapons Limitation," in *Army* in February 1957. He points out that

. . . since we did not accompany the Baruch proposals with a demand for concurrent reductions in Soviet Ground-Force strength, we might have withdrawn from ourselves and our Allies whatever deterrent force our Air-Atomic capability exerted during the years 1946-55. The fact that it took our Government five years to recognize these facts and add a demand for reduction in conventional forces as a *sine qua non* for nuclear disarmament or limitations— will be difficult to explain to future generations. They will not understand why we offered to surrender our nuclear weapons to international control at a time when we were systematically divesting ourselves of ground force strength and when we depended almost entirely on nuclear weapons to prevent the Soviet Union from overrunning Western Europe.

Dr. DeWeerd gives two answers to this question. The first is the absence of any effective long-range planning of military political problems facing the United States in 1946. He points out that there was not even a policy planning staff in the State Department until after World War II. His second explanation is that the Baruch proposals are another example of the United States penchant for attempting total and immediate solutions to long-standing problems in international relations.

We are not satisfied with small gains; we want to solve all the big problems at once. The Kellogg Pact of 1928 which typified an American belief that the proper way to do away with war was simply to get the nations of the world to denounce war as an instrument of national policy is an example. This famous "drunkard's oath" which no one outside the United States took seriously, did not reduce the number of wars; it merely reduced the number of declared wars.

While these answers contain elements of truth, it is suggested that they do not come even close to expressing the entire truth. The Baruch Plan might have had different provisions if, in 1946, the State and Defense Departments had developed some effective long-range planning. We have already pointed out the apparent inconsistency between the acquiescence of the military services in the Baruch Plan and their opposition even to international discussion of conventional disarmament. Perhaps one explanation of this inconsistency may be that the decision on conventional armaments came one year later—after some long-range military planning had commenced. The Acheson-Lilienthal Report and the Baruch Plan had been developed by relatively insulated groups and may have become fixed United States policy without complete consideration by the Defense Department and the military services. In the latter part of 1945, when the committees headed by Acheson and Lilienthal were developing what later became the Acheson-Lilienthal Report and the Baruch Plan, the original concept of the great powers maintaining the peace of the world was still officially the United States policy. This concept envisioned that the United States would remain strong and would not repeat the headlong disarmament following World

War I. In the context of a world in which the United States and its Western allies retained strong conventional armed forces, the Baruch Plan would not have created an imbalance of power favoring the Soviet Union. Indeed the acceptance by the Soviet Union of an international control authority with the vast powers envisioned by Baruch, as the Soviet leaders clearly recognized, would have destroyed that secrecy which the Soviet Union has always regarded as one of its prime elements of strength. It might well have resulted in the triumph of the ideal of "One World," which was current in the wartime thinking of both United States political parties.

The *Forrestal Diaries* trace the rapid progress of United States demobilization after World War II. The first alarms came in October 1945, almost simultaneously with the initiation of the serious studies that led to the Baruch Plan.

Demobilization: It was agreed by all present that the point of this discussion was . . . that it was most inadvisable for this country to continue accelerating the demobilization of our Armed Forces at the present rate. Mr. Forrestal pointed out that at this rate there will necessarily come a point between the present time and the time when the Army and Navy reach their planned postwar strength at which neither the Army nor the Navy will have sufficient trained men to be able to operate efficiently. Mr. Forrestal stated that this was a situation of such gravity that in his view the President ought to acquaint the people with the details of our dealings with the Russians and with the attitude which the Russians have manifested throughout. Mr. Byrnes demurred somewhat on this point, however. He stated that he was a little dubious about the advisability of such a procedure as it would give the Russians an excuse for claiming that we had furnished provocation which justified their actions.[1]

Several months elapsed before an awareness developed in the United States Government of the adverse effects of demobilization on our foreign policy.

[1] Walter Millis, ed., *The Forrestal Diaries* (1951), p. 102.

11 January 1946   Cabinet

The President expressed concern over the events of the last ten days; said he had gone into the system and method of demobilization and was satisfied that with some gaps it had been done efficiently and thoroughly. The Under Secretary of State (Acheson), representing the State Department, said it was a matter of great embarrassment and concern to his own Department in their conduct of our foreign affairs.

I said that I thought the President should get the heads of the important news services and the leading newspapers—particularly Mr. Sulzberger of the *New York Times*, Roy Roberts, Palmer Hoyt, the Cowles brothers, John Knight, plus Roy Howard and Bob Mc-Lean of the AP—and state to them the seriousness of the present situation and the need for making the country aware of its implications abroad. I said these were all reasonable and patriotic men and that I was confident that if the facts were presented we would have their support in the presentation of the case. The President agreed to do so.[2]

By this time, Baruch had been asked to represent the United States, and the terms of reference had been established in the United Nations, which required some United States initiative along the lines of the Baruch Plan.

Although Forrestal implied that the President had agreed to the seriousness of the situation as early as January, he notes that even in August 1946, the President ordered the services to make drastic reductions, not in their future budget estimates but in their current spending, despite the opposition of both the Secretary of Defense and the Secretary of State.[3] In short, by the time the United States Government realized the effects on our foreign policy of rapid demobilization, the preparations for the Baruch Plan had gone too far to permit a reversal.

Even if it had been possible to reverse the United States policy and the bureaucratic processes leading to the Baruch Plan during the early

[2] *Ibid.*, p. 128.
[3] *Ibid.*, p. 197.

months of 1946, it is doubtful whether such a step would have been advisable. The Acheson-Lilienthal report assumed that the terrible mathematics of the nuclear weapon together with the technical requirements for immediate control would result in a universal reaction calling for international control.[4] To expect Soviet acquiescence in such a project may have been naive. However, it was easy to predict that a Soviet rejection of the Baruch Plan would result in political gains to the United States. It is clear that Baruch himself was aware of the dilemma that might arise from the elimination of nuclear weapons without any reduction of conventional weapons.[5]

By January 1947, when Baruch resigned, it had been ascertained that the Soviet Union would not accept the Baruch Plan and also that United States demobilization had reached a stage where Soviet acceptance would leave the United States naked. This probably accounts for the unwillingness of the United States to go into any detailed explanation of the stages of implementation of the plan, leading ultimately to the elimination of the bomb. The Soviet proposals on June 11, 1947, in the Atomic Energy Commission for a system of safeguards, indicating the maximum degree to which the Soviet Union would permit a breach of its iron curtain did not change the situation. The safeguards the Soviet Union was willing to accept were insufficient to permit the United States to give up the bomb in view of its weakened military position.

In this background the United States decision not to discuss reductions in conventional armaments regardless of the wisdom of such action becomes understandable. The weak military posture of the United States made the leaders of armed forces reluctant even to enter into discussions that might create public sentiment for further weakening of our military establishment. The military were never impressed with the idea that safeguards might be devised so that reductions in armed forces and conventional weapons would not weaken the United States vis-à-vis the Soviet Union. Undoubtedly a factor in this attitude was the Berlin situation, already becoming acute. The United States

[4] Joseph Lippman Nogee, "Soviet Policy toward International Control of Atomic Energy 1945-1953," unpublished Yale University dissertation, 1958, p. 40.
[5] Bernard Baruch, *The Public Years* (1960), p. 384.

Government thought it had a corridor to Berlin as a result of the Potsdam negotiations, but this turned out to be an illusion. A disarmament agreement might likewise result in the United States thinking that it had safeguards, but not having them.

A second and related question is whether the United States Senate would ever have ratified a treaty to bring into effect the Baruch Plan. It is of course impossible to give a categoric answer to this question. The strong support in later years in the Senate for the Bricker Amendment, which would have prevented the United States from entering into any agreement in the field of international arms control, indicates how difficult it would have been to obtain support for as drastic an agreement as the Baruch Plan. Moreover, years later several senators voted against United States entry into the International Atomic Energy Agency, largely influenced by the almost nonexistent possibility that some international inspector might have access to the United States. Nevertheless the prestige of Bernard Baruch as our outstanding elder statesman might well have overcome these difficulties if a treaty had been formulated in 1946 when he was the United States representative. An additional favorable factor was the role of Senator Vandenberg. While the Senator had initial doubts concerning the Baruch Plan, he later supported it. It is therefore suggested that the critics of United States policy are making rash assumptions when they suggest that the United States would never have ratified a treaty based on the Baruch Plan even though the Soviet Union had accepted it.

The third question is the crucial one. Was there any real chance between 1946 and 1948 that an agreement could have been reached between the Soviet Union and the West for the international control of atomic energy? At that time, many individuals in all walks of life took the position that a middle ground existed between the Soviet position and the United States position, on which agreement might have been reached if a proper spirit of compromise prevailed. The thought was that if the United States had changed its position on the veto, had modified and reduced the types of installations over which international control would be required, and, most important, furnished a time schedule for permitting disclosure of nuclear secrets and elimination of nuclear weapons prior to the final stages of the Baruch Plan—if the United States had made these concessions—perhaps an agreement could have been reached. In the greater perspective of today, this does not seem to be a correct view. The attack on United States policy by Henry Wallace apparently had as its primary aim the development of such a middle ground between the United States and Soviet positions on international control of atomic energy.[6]

The more thoughtful critics based their conclusions on analysis and comparison of the two plans. The Soviet rejection of the Baruch Plan, however, did not rest to any great degree on technical considerations or even military considerations. The Soviet response was intermingled with the Soviet theory of dialectical materialism. To quote a prominent Soviet military writer, Major General G. I. Pokrovsky:

Military science itself can develop successfully only when the achievements of all other fields of knowledge, from which it gleans materials to solve its own practical problems, are utilized to the maximum degree. . . . Dialectical materialism arms scientists with the correct philosophical view of the world. . . . In contrast with metaphysics dialectical materialism considers the inter-relationships of all social phenomena, their movement and their change, and their constant development. Dialectical materialism provides the necessary foundation for an objective scientific foresight into the circumstances on which future warfare may hinge.[7]

The key to the Soviet position on arms control is therefore found in following the zig-zag course of successive Russian interpretations of dialectical materialism.

In the period from 1946 through 1948 the Soviet ideology was frequently given the label "Zhdanovschina"—the policies of Zhdanov, who at that time was apparently the most influential adviser to Stalin. Zhdanov's program predicted the immediate collapse of capitalism in Western Europe and the triumph of communism. The leading Soviet economist, E. S. Varga, was severely censured for doubting that an

[6] Margaret L. Coit, *Mr. Baruch* (1957), p. 599.
[7] G. I. Pokrovsky, *Science and Technology in Contemporary War*, translated from the Russian by Raymond L. Garthoff (1959), p. 17.

immediate postwar economic crisis would destroy the power of the United States.[8]

This same trend in the ideological field led to the view that the economic laws that required the imminent collapse of capitalism were immutable and could not be altered by "planning." The most important writer on Soviet ideology, N. A. Voznesensky, who in 1947 had been awarded the Stalin prize, had emphasized the role of the state in planning the development of communism. This ran contrary to the new theory of immutable economic laws and Voznesensky was executed.[9]

In this atmosphere it was impossible for the Soviet Union to respond favorably to the Marshall Plan, which offered economic aid without any strings attached to it to rehabilitate all of Europe including the Soviet Union. In the summer of 1947, Molotov had arrived in Paris with some eighty experts to attend a conference on Marshall Plan aid. Suddenly, his delegation was recalled to Moscow, and the negotiating terminated.[10]

At the same time, Poland and Czechoslovakia, which had given some indications of an intention to cooperate, refused to participate in the conference.[11] If the minimum amount of cooperation that would have been required for an agreement on Marshall Plan aid to the Soviet Union was impossible, the vast cooperation required for successful implementation of the Baruch Plan would have been out of the question. In fact, any cooperation or collaboration between the Soviet Union and the West was inconsistent with a policy that called for an immediate spontaneous Communist revolution in Germany, the overthrow of the Italian and French regimes through general strikes, armed rebellion in Greece, and, in general, all possible sabotage of capitalistic economies in Western Europe during the period of postwar weakness to prevent any postwar revival of the European economy.

Another facet of "Zhdanovschina," which became even more notorious, was the attempt to lower the "iron curtain," which had been

[8] Georg von Rauch, A History of Soviet Russia (1957), p. 402.
[9] Ibid., p. 422.
[10] Ibid., p. 390.
[11] William Reitzel, Morton A. Kaplan, and Constance G. Coblenz, United States Foreign Policy 1945-1955 (1956), p. 119.

partially lifted as a result of the collaboration of the wartime allies. Zhdanov had insisted on the complete elimination of all bourgeois influences from Soviet culture and on the glorification of all that was Russian. There was a strict centrally dictated Communist line in art, in music, in agriculture, in philology, and in genetics. "Cosmopolitanism"—influence by foreign cultures—became the gravest term of reproach. It was at this time that the Soviet Union forbade the marriage of its nationals to foreigners and claimed Russian invention of everything from airplanes to baseball. In this atmosphere, the Baruch Plan opening up the entire Soviet Union to international inspectors and controllers was anathema. It was indeed amazing that Gromyko was permitted to go so far as to introduce his detailed safeguards proposals on June 11, 1947. His jubilance was understandable.[12] It may well have represented a victory in a hot skirmish against the Zhdanov influence. In this atmosphere any adequate plan for the international control of atomic energy was inconceivable.

Even the strategic situation militated against Soviet acceptance of the Baruch Plan. The Russian representatives constantly accused the United States representatives of attempting nuclear blackmail because of their monopoly of the bomb. The Soviet Union itself was making rapid progress in producing its own nuclear weapons aided by information gathered through espionage. It is reasonable to believe that the Soviet leaders felt that they would be in a better position to bargain after they had successfully tested a nuclear weapon.

Nevertheless, in the Atomic Energy Commission negotiations, the Soviet Union was much more specific and in fact went a much greater distance toward meeting the Western position than ever took place in the negotiations for reductions in conventional armaments. One reason may have been that the Baruch Plan was specific and precise. Another reason may have been that Soviet strategic thinking at this time placed much less stress on nuclear weapons than on large armies.[13] This may have merely reflected the fact that the Soviet

[12] Frederick Osborn, "Negotiating on Atomic Energy," in Raymond Dennett and Joseph E. Johnson, eds., *Negotiating with the Russians* (1951), p. 229.
[13] Raymond L. Garthoff, *Soviet Strategy in the Nuclear Age* (1958), pp. 71-76.

Union had no nuclear weapons and therefore, in public statements, sought to downgrade them. However, the same attitude persisted long after the Soviet Union had developed its own arsenal of nuclear weapons. General Pokrovsky in 1957 stressed that "As Soviet military science teaches, only an expedient combination of different forms of military technology can ensure the successful achievement of victory in contemporary armed conflict."[14] In other words, the idea of an "absolute weapon" never had much currency in Soviet thinking. This factor rather than any genuine desire to lessen international tensions may have explained the Soviet willingness to make a few concessions in the field of international control of atomic energy. There was no evidence in the atomic energy negotiations of any genuine Soviet desire to lessen tensions and reach an agreement with the West.

However, the basic Soviet objection to the Baruch Plan was the requirement of an international control authority operating within the borders of the Soviet Union. The Soviet leaders had only with reluctance consented to even the slight penetration of the iron curtain involved in the establishing of UNRRA missions in the Soviet Union, although this was the only way to obtain relief from hunger in the desperate postwar period.[15]

Even if the Soviet Union could have gained early economic benefits by accepting the Baruch Plan, or the United States secrets could have been disclosed at an early stage in the plan, it is inconceivable that the Soviet Union of the last years of Stalin could have consented to the vast penetration of its secrecy essential to the establishment of an effective international control plan. This was especially true prior to the death of Zhdanov, when the central authority attempted to dictate the music of Shostakovitch and to impose the aberrations of Lysenko as a Communist theory of genetics. The shortcomings of United States policy during this period may have obscured the basic fact that the failure to secure an agreement for the international control of atomic energy rested on the refusal of the Soviet Union to lift its iron curtain. But even if the shortcomings could have been re-

[14] Pokrovsky, *op. cit.*, p. 180.
[15] Robert W. Frase, "International Control of Atomic Energy," *Annals of the American Academy of Political and Social Science* (November 1955), p. 17.

moved, this would not have altered the ultimate result. The question, which no one can answer, is whether the entire East-West situation would have been different if the United States had not demobilized so rapidly at the end of the war and had remained militarily strong as President Roosevelt had so often advised.

ORGANIZATION

This period witnessed the birth of both the United States organization and the United States policies that carried on into the later arms control negotiations. It also exposed the United Nations negotiators for the first time in the postwar period to the negotiating techniques of the Soviet Union. It is appropriate to conclude the discussion of this period with a brief analysis of these subjects.

The chief characteristics of Baruch's organization stemmed from the position and character of the man himself. As the United States representative in the United Nations Atomic Energy Commission, Baruch reported directly to the President of the United States. In all except major policy decisions, he was relatively independent of any control from other branches of the government. He had an ample budget and staff, and attracted to his staff individuals of outstanding ability from all walks of life.

This organizational pattern had many advantages—Baruch's prestige ensured broad national support for his policies. His direct contact with the President made it easy to secure speedy decisions at the top level of the United States Government. This eliminated much of the frustration arising from the tortoise-like pace of bureaucracy and greatly facilitated Baruch's efforts to secure outstanding personnel.

The Baruch pattern of organization, however, had its disadvantages. In the first place, the outstanding leaders in the business, professional, and academic worlds were unlikely to remain permanently in the government. This fact made the Baruch organizational pattern more suitable for a speedy action than for the long drawn-out negotiations so characteristic of United States relations with the Soviet Union. In addition, Baruch himself was isolated from the general policy-making processes of the government, and this unquestionably adversely affected his performance. His proposals, without sacrificing any substance, might well have been more attractive both to the Soviet Union and to some of our allies if Baruch had had on his staff officers experienced in international political negotiations. As an example of his isolation from policy-making, there is reason to believe that Mr. Baruch's veto proposal was made over the disapproval of the State Department and without consideration by the military authorities.

Baruch's personal characteristics added materially to the detachment of his position. His associates report that he would frequently switch off his hearing aid for long periods when the argumentation displeased him or failed to interest him. As a negotiator, Baruch lacked flexibility. His infrequent statements never moved far from the Messianic tone of his initial effective address to the Atomic Energy Commission in June 1946. Thus the exchange of views never contained the quality of give-and-take so essential to successful international negotiations. In the main, the statements of Baruch as well as those of Gromyko were largely reiterations of past broad decisions with the addition of some details.

Baruch recognized that his organizational pattern was unsuitable for an extended negotiation, and in his letter of resignation, supported a new organizational pattern, which with comparatively minor variations continued until the appearance of Governor Stassen in 1955. After Baruch's resignation, Senator Warren Austin, the United States representative to the United Nations, became the United States representative on both the Atomic Energy Commission and the Conventional Armaments Commission. The active negotiations in these commissions were carried on by deputy representatives—Frederick Osborn in the Atomic Energy Commission and Ralph Bard and later Frederick Osborn in the Commission for Conventional Armaments. Senator Austin received his instructions from the Secretary of State. Within the Department of State a section was set up in the Office of United Nations Affairs to deal with arms control problems. Because of classified data in the field of atomic energy, a much smaller group, cleared for atomic secrets, was established in the office of the Secretary of State. The atomic energy group and the section in the Office of United Nations Affairs maintained close personal liaison. In the latter part of 1946 and early 1947, interdepartmental consideration of positions on the subject of arms control took place, at least in theory, through a general committee dealing with all types of problems concerning both the State Department and the armed services. The letters of this interdepartmental committee, State-War-Navy Committee, on arms control work became a synonym for excessive paper work and ineffectiveness.

This group was replaced in the middle of 1947 by an interdepartmental committee organized specifically to deal with the problems coming before the Conventional Armaments Commission. This committee, known as the Regulation of Armaments Committee, continued with some changes in structure until shortly before the appointment of Governor Stassen in 1955. In 1947-1948 this committee had ready access to the top levels of the State Department, the Defense Department and the armed services. However, differences in viewpoint among the members of the committee were great and during this period were not resolved. After the resolution of the main differences through presidential decisions and after the reorganization of the committee in 1951, this organizational pattern was adequate to ensure fairly rapid decision-making (so long as the decisions were unimportant), and efficient communication of these decisions to the United States representatives in the United Nations. The problems in the later period arose, not from the structure of the organization but from the low governmental level at which it operated. The top officer in the Department of State devoting full time to the field of conventional arms control was three stages removed from the Secretary of State. Since the officers in the intervening bureaucratic layers generally had no comprehension of the problems of arms control, it was very difficult to obtain intelligent top-level consideration of the necessary problems.

As long as the United Nations Atomic Energy Commission continued as a separate body, the responsibility in the State Department for back-stopping the United States representative in the United Nations continued in the assistant to the Secretary of State on atomic energy matters. Since this officer was already in the office of the Secretary of

State, the problem of quick access to the top levels of the State Department never existed.

The organizational pattern in the Military Staff Committee, despite Senator Austin's vehement protests, continued anomalous, with the United States representative receiving his instructions direct from the Chairman of the Joint Chiefs of Staff. This might have resulted in unmitigated confusion had it not been for the fact that the Military Staff Committee was practically dormant after June 1947.

Baruch had alluded in his letter of resignation to the necessity of turning over the work to permanent government personnel.[16] In 1946 and 1947, five or six officers in the Office of United Nations Affairs in the Department of State devoted their full time to this work and another half-dozen spent substantial time on these problems. These could have been the basis for a permanent staff. However, by 1952 when for the first time after the Baruch Plan the negotiations became really active, only two of the officers remained in the work.[17] The chief reason for the failure of the Department of State to develop a permanent staff in the field of arms control at this time was lack of support within the United States Government for the activity. Each year the appropriation for personnel for this activity became less, and the number of personnel became fewer. One reason for the lack of support was that the activity was located in the Office of United Nations Affairs, which unfortunately during this period received little administrative support. The personnel situation in the Pentagon was even less satisfactory. A number of highly talented officers from time to time worked on arms control problems, but their association with the activity was generally short-lived. It then became necessary to indoctrinate a successor who usually came to the job reluctantly and with preconceived views largely divorced from political realities. The United States Atomic Energy Commission, however, did develop a

[16] U.N. Atomic Energy Commission, *The International Control of Atomic Energy,* The First Report to the Security Council, Department of State Publication 2737 (1947), pp. 95-99.
[17] The author and Gordon Arneson, formerly assistant to the Secretary of State on atomic energy matters.

group of scientists with great technical competence, who stayed with the work for years.

The United States organizational pattern was in sharp contrast to that of the Soviet Union. In the Soviet Union six of the most prominent officials engaged in the conduct of foreign affairs became thoroughly versed in the problems of arms control. These were Vyshinsky, Gromyko, Malik, Sobolev, Zorin, and Tsarapkin. These six have conducted substantially all of the negotiations in this field on behalf of the Russians from 1946 until today. They were the top officials of the Soviet Foreign Office. Vyshinsky was the Foreign Minister until his death. After a short interval, he was succeeded by Gromyko, who is the present Foreign Minister. Zorin, one of the Deputy-Foreign Ministers, had to his credit (in Soviet eyes) the achieving of the destruction of the non-Communist government in Czechoslovakia in 1948. Sobolev was the top Soviet official assigned to the Secretariat of the United Nations in the early years of its existence and for many years has served as Soviet representative to the United Nations. Malik was a Soviet representative in the United Nations succeeding Gromyko, and was later Ambassador to the United Kingdom. He is still a Deputy-Foreign Minister. He dropped out of the active negotiations apparently after a heart attack in 1954. Tsarapkin, of slightly lower rank, was second to Gromyko in the Atomic Energy Commission negotiations in 1946 through 1948 and is still the Soviet representative in the test cessation negotiations.

While it is more difficult to trace the Soviet personnel at the official level, it is nevertheless a fact that Usachev and Roschin, two of the more prominent advisors, have been appearing and reappearing in the negotiations year after year. Their knowledge of the subject is encyclopedic.

The British and French representation was in general at this time confined to the members of their delegations to the United Nations. Not until a later date did the British and French attempt to build up permanent staffs dealing with this subject. General MacNaughton was the first of a long line of brilliant Canadian representatives who, because of their ability and knowledgeability, wielded an influence out of proportion to the military strength of Canada.

SUBSTANTIVE ISSUES AND

NEGOTIATING TECHNIQUES

The substantive issues and negotiating techniques—it is often difficult to distinguish one from the other—which emerged during these years, and which continued into the future negotiations, may be summarized as follows:

The first major issue, which has been the dominant issue in all subsequent arms control negotiations, was the relationship of arms limitations and reductions to the establishment of safeguards to ensure the observance of the limitations and reductions. The United States, when it submitted the Baruch Plan, took the straightforward position that the installation of the safeguards system must precede the implementation of the measures for arms limitation. The Soviet Union in response to the Baruch Plan initially took the opposite position that the prohibition of nuclear weapons must take place immediately with no international safeguards system. Subsequently, the Soviet Union modified this position to permit the establishment of an international safeguards system, but insisted that the prohibition of nuclear weapons and their elimination from national armaments must precede the establishment of the safeguards system. At this stage of the negotiations, the Soviet Union sought to accomplish this result through the procedural device of having two separate treaties. The first in time would provide for the elimination of nuclear weapons. The second and later treaty would establish the safeguards system.

The second substantive issue that emerged from the negotiations was the relation of arms limitation agreements to political settlements. The United States position in the Baruch Plan was that the international control of atomic energy should take place regardless of political settlements and therefore could precede the political settlements. The Baruch Plan was presented at a time when a modicum of goodwill still remained between the Soviet Union and the United States as a result of the alliance to defeat Hitler. Eight months later, in the winter of 1947, the United States position was not only that reductions of conventional armaments could not take place until an improvement in the international atmosphere but also that discussions of such reductions could not proceed until then. This was diametrically the opposite position from that taken on atomic energy.

The Soviet Union evaded the issue whether political settlements must precede arms reduction. In the negotiations on atomic energy and conventional armaments the Soviet Union was willing that atomic weapons be prohibited and conventional armaments be reduced at the outset. The establishment of a safeguards system to ensure the observance of the commitments, however, would come at a later date, if ever. This position was obviously advantageous to the Soviet Union since it could readily ascertain whether the Western powers were observing their commitments while the iron curtain would prevent the Western powers from determining the extent of Soviet observance.

By the end of this period of the negotiations, the United States had ample evidence that it would have great difficulty in holding to its position in the Conventional Armaments Commission that political settlements must precede disarmament discussions. The world response to the Soviet resolution in 1946 calling for discussions of reduction of conventional armaments had been overwhelmingly favorable. Furthermore in 1948, despite the recommendation of all of the members of the Atomic Energy Commission, excepting the Soviet Union and the Ukraine, that further talks on the international control of atomic energy were useless, the General Assembly insisted that the talks continue and in effect overruled the positions of the United States and its allies. This established a principle that has been confirmed over the years that, regardless of how discouraging the arms control negotiations may become, world public opinion will not accept their discontinuance. Yet every time negotiations with the Russians on arms control reach an impasse, the cry arises in the United States, first within the government and then outside: Why should we continue to negotiate? The negotiations must stop until the international political atmosphere has improved.[18]

[18] Two outstanding recent examples: (1) Francis Vivian Drake, "What Would Total Disarmament *Really* Mean?" in *Reader's Digest* (January 1960); (2) E. B. White, "Disarmament," *New Yorker Magazine*, reprinted in the *Washington Post*, June 26, 1960, entitled "Letter from the West."

The third issue that arose during this period was the battle for world public opinion. It is not nearly as well defined in terms of substance as the two other issues. The United States scored an initial major triumph in the Baruch Plan. The world-wide favorable response proved that world opinion overwhelmingly wanted arms control—generally described as disarmament. The Baruch Plan discussions created the broad image that the United States also wished arms control and the Soviet Union opposed it. Unfortunately, the United States negative position in the Conventional Armaments Commission tended to offset partially the political advantages the United States had achieved through proposing the Baruch Plan. The damage might have been much more serious if the Soviet Union had had its own positive program for reduction of conventional armaments. However, the Soviet posture of talking mainly about atomic energy in a commission that had no jurisdiction over the subject matter had little appeal within the United Nations.

In short, during this period, the United States in both the atomic energy and the conventional armaments negotiations was relying on positions it considered sound, but was paying little attention to world public opinion either within the United Nations or outside. The Soviet Union during this period obviously considered the negotiations relatively unimportant and used them to advance specific tactical aims such as the unilateral disarmament of the West ("Bring the Boys Home"). Only in the next period of the negotiations did the subject of arms control become a major field for Soviet propaganda outside the United Nations.

A fourth issue that arose was whether the negotiations for arms control should be relatively specific or general. The United States at first made specific proposals both in the Atomic Energy Commission and in the Military Staff Committee, and the Soviet replies, while more general, were more specific than any later proposals until 1955. While the Soviet Union had thus initially acquiesced in relatively specific discussions, by the fall of 1946 it had changed its position. This apparently accounts for the Soviet General Assembly resolution of October 1946[19] which would have discarded the Atomic

[19] U.N. General Assembly, First Session, *Official Records*, 42nd Meeting (Oct. 29, 1946), p. 847.

Energy Commission where the negotiations were specific. Even though the resolution failed, the Soviet approach became increasingly vague with the exception of the June 11, 1947 proposals on safeguards for the international control of atomic energy,[20] which represent the high point of Soviet concessions to the desire of the United States and the Western governments to have specific discussions rather than to indulge in broad generalities.

The fifth issue of importance that arose during this stage of the negotiations came at the very end: the question whether the Western powers, with the support of the majority of votes in the General Assembly, should seek decisions by the Assembly regardless of Soviet opposition. The initial reaction of the West was to secure such decisions. Thus, over Soviet opposition, the three reports of the Atomic Energy Commission were transferred from the Security Council, where a Soviet veto had prevented their approval, to the General Assembly. In the General Assembly, the reports received virtually unanimous approval except from the Soviet bloc, with the result that the major portion of the Baruch Plan became known as the United Nations Plan. The adverse effects of this policy became apparent in the next stage of the negotiations. Nevertheless, the issue re-appeared in 1957.

The sixth issue (which may not properly be describable as an issue) related to Soviet negotiating techniques, which were entangled with the substance. In this early period the Soviet Union developed a number of negotiating techniques that have persisted: (1) The Soviet Union made a practice of attempting to use arms control proposals to obtain specific strategic or tactical military advantages. For example, the Soviet Union had proposed in the United Nations General Assembly and in the Security Council that all countries withdraw their troops stationed outside their borders, except those stationed in former enemy territory. The bulk of Soviet troops stationed outside its territories were in former enemy territory, while the United States and United Kingdom had stationed their troops in other states with the full agreement of the states where the troops were stationed. (2) A second Soviet tactic can be described as follows: "You (the Western

[20] U.N. Atomic Energy Commission, *The International Control of Atomic Energy,* The Second Report of the Security Council, Department of State Publication 2932 (December 1947), pp. 88-91.

powers) take action involving a concession to us (the Soviet Union), and in return, we shall agree to talk." The best example of this technique in this period was the Soviet atomic energy proposals, which in essence provided that if the United States and the Western powers agreed to eliminate their nuclear weapons, the Soviet Union would talk about a treaty for international controls to assure the observance of commitments.

In summary, while the negotiations during this period from the beginning of the United Nations in January 1946 to the autumn of 1948 achieved no substantial result in terms of an agreement, they nevertheless set certain patterns—of organization, of negotiating techniques, as well as the outlines of substantive issues—which furnished a framework for the later negotiations.

PART THREE

The Period of Complete Frustration 1948-1951

VII

Stalemate

THE GENERAL ASSEMBLY OF 1948 marked the beginning of a basic change in the nature of the arms control negotiations. The United Nations Atomic Energy Commission in its Third Report had found "that no useful purpose can be served by carrying on negotiations at the Commission level."[1] While the majority of the General Assembly refused to accept this verdict and insisted that discussions continue, the renewed discussions never got past the stage of statements of broad generalities and could scarcely be considered as negotiations. During the early part of 1948, the Military Staff Committee had continued to deal with the question of the over-all strength and composition by types of the forces that states might make available to the Security Council. In July, however, the committee came to the conclusion, and informed the Security Council, that it could go no further until the Security Council had acted on the 1947 report of the Military Staff Committee on the basic principles that should govern the organization of the armed forces to be made available to the Security Council. The Security Council had adjourned its

[1] U.N. Atomic Energy Commission, *The International Control of Atomic Energy*, The Third Report to the Security Council, Department of State Publication 3179 (July 1948), p. 5.

discussion of this issue in July 1947 and never resumed the discussion. After July 1948 the Military Staff Committee ceased all activities although it continued to meet on a purely formal basis.

The change from serious negotiation to pure propaganda did not particularly affect the Commission for Conventional Armaments since there never had been any serious negotiation in that committee.

Outside the United Nations, the death of Zhdanov coincided with a shift in Soviet tactics, the full significance of which was not realized until many years later. Once again the change in Soviet attitudes in the arms control negotiations generally paralleled the broader shift in Soviet tactics.

THE 1948 GENERAL ASSEMBLY

Vyshinsky opened the 1948 session of the General Assembly in September with a proposal which, in varying forms, was to become the theme song of the Soviet Union for the entire period from 1948 until the close of 1954. In his address Vyshinsky accused the United States and the United Kingdom of preparing for aggressive war against the Soviet Union and introduced a resolution calling for

. . . the prohibition of atomic weapons, the reduction of the armaments of Armed Forces of China, France, the United Kingdom, the United States and the Soviet Union by one-third within one year's time, and the establishment within the framework of the Security Council of a Control Commission to supervise the carrying out of these proposals.[2]

The chief characteristic of this position was its ready adaptability to propaganda uses. It could be summarized for propaganda blasts in about ten words: ban the bomb; reduce conventional weapons by

[2] "Soviet Draft Resolution Introduced in the General Assembly: Reduction of Armaments and Prohibition of Atomic Weapons," U.N. Doc. A/658 (Sept. 25, 1948). The revised version of this proposal was rejected by the General Assembly on November 19, 1948.

one third; international control. No equally glib rejoinder could demonstrate the unsoundness of this type of proposal.

As a general rule, this type of proposal would appear not once but twice in each session of the General Assembly. The Soviet Union would propose it in connection with the General Assembly agenda item dealing with the reports of the Atomic Energy Commission and the Conventional Armaments Commission, and a second time as a separate item with some appealing title such as "Measures to Remove Menace of a New War."

The significance of the period from the standpoint of Soviet actions rests neither in the Soviet proposals nor in the Western responses, but rather in the relationship of the Soviet negotiating positions and techniques to the broader aspects of Soviet policy.

From the standpoint of the West, the Soviet rejection of the Baruch Plan left practically a policy vacuum. The chief significance of this period was the gradual emergence of a new policy which was given full expression only after the establishment of the United Nations Disarmament Commission in 1952.

ATOMIC ENERGY NEGOTIATIONS,

1948-1949

The General Assembly resolution of November 4, 1948, called on the United Nations Atomic Energy Commission to resume its sessions, to survey its program of work, and to proceed to the further study of such subjects remaining in the program of work as it considered to be practicable and useful. In addition, the resolution requested the permanent members of the Atomic Energy Commission (the United Kingdom, the Soviet Union, the United States, China, France, and Canada)

. . . to meet together and consult in order to determine if there exists a basis for agreement on the international control of atomic energy to ensure its use only for peaceful purposes and for the elimination from national armaments of atomic weapons, and to report to the General Assembly the results of their consultation not later than its next regular session.[3]

In the United Nations Atomic Energy Commission, the Soviet Union slightly modified its previous proposals. In earlier years, the Soviet Union had called for two conventions, the first in point of time to prohibit nuclear weapons and the second to provide a control system. The Soviet Union now suggested that the two conventions should go into effect simultaneously or that there should be one convention with two parts. This raised the issue of the meaning of coming "into force simultaneously."[4] Prohibition of atomic weapons is a single act which could be effectuated by a single declaration. On the other hand, international control contemplates a long series of acts to establish an international control authority in all areas in the world with the necessary powers to ensure that it could carry out its duties. This substantive issue was raised in the debates in the Political Committee of the General Assembly by the British delegate (Hector McNeil) who asked: "Did the USSR delegation agree that a fully effective international control system should come into operation before the other convention on prohibition and destruction of atomic weapons was brought into effect? That was the crucial point and the question of the number of conventions was of secondary importance."[5]

Malik in his reply failed to answer this question.[6] Until May 10, 1955, the Soviet Union consistently avoided the issue whether the prohibition of nuclear weapons would take place on the signing of

[3] U.N. General Assembly, Third Session, Plenary, *Official Records*, Pt. 1, 157th Meeting (Nov. 4, 1948), p. 17.
[4] U.N. General Assembly, Fourth Session, *Official Records*, Supplement No. 2, pp. 74-75. The resolution referred to is entitled "Soviet Draft Resolution introduced in the Security Council: Prohibition of the Atomic Weapon and a One-Third Reduction of Great-Power Forces" (Feb. 8, 1949).
[5] U.N. General Assembly, Third Session, First Committee, *Summary Records*, Pt. 1 (Oct. 6, 1948), p. 78.
[6] *Ibid.*, p. 80.

the treaty for international control or at a later period when the control authority had come into existence with the necessary powers to ensure observance of the commitment to eliminate nuclear weapons.

The 1949 discussions in the United Nations Atomic Energy Commission broke down when it became apparent that by "control," the Soviet Union meant its own proposals of June 1947, already found to be inadequate, which it declined to enlarge or modify. In July 1949, the commission adopted resolutions concluding that "no useful purpose can be served by further discussions in the Atomic Energy Commission of those proposals which have already been considered and rejected by the appropriate organs of the United Nations," and that no useful purpose could be served by continuing the discussions in the commission until the great powers had found a basis for agreement.[7]

The consultations among the great powers requested by the General Assembly resolution took place in August, September, and October of 1949. A statement by the representatives of all of the great powers except the Soviet Union summarized the divergences and differences of viewpoint which were discussed in these consultations.

The Soviet Union proposes that nations should continue to own explosive atomic materials.

The other five powers feel that under such conditions there would be no effective protection against the sudden use of these materials as atomic weapons.

The Soviet Union proposes that nations continue, as at present, to own, operate and manage facilities making or using dangerous quantities of such materials.

The other five powers believe that, under such conditions, it would be impossible to detect or prevent the diversion of such materials for use in atomic weapons.

The Soviet Union proposes a system of control depending on periodic inspection of facilities the existence of which the national

[7] U.N. General Assembly, Fifth Session, *Official Records*, Supplement No. 2, pp. 32-34.

government concerned reports to the international agency, supplemented by special investigations on suspicion of treaty violations. The other five powers believe that periodic inspection would not prevent the diversion of dangerous materials and that the special investigations envisaged would be wholly insufficient to prevent clandestine activities. . . .

It is apparent that there is a fundamental difference not only on methods but also on aims. All of the Sponsoring Powers other than the U.S.S.R. put world security first and are prepared to accept innovations in traditional concepts of international cooperation, national sovereignty and economic organization where these are necessary for security. The Government of the U.S.S.R. puts its sovereignty first and is unwilling to accept measures which may impinge upon or interfere with its rigid exercise of unimpeded state sovereignty.[8]

On the eve of the General Assembly, President Truman announced that evidence had been received of an atomic explosion in the Soviet Union and therefore that there was a greater need than before for effective international control of atomic energy.[9] TASS conceded the accuracy of President Truman's statement two days later.[10]

During the 1949 General Assembly, in referring to the Soviet nuclear explosion, Vyshinsky made one of the most nonsensical statements ever perpetrated on an international organization. He claimed that the Soviet nuclear explosions, in contrast to the nuclear explosions of capitalist countries, were peaceful, that they were being used to level mountains and move rivers. The United States representative, John Hickerson, promptly replied that the same atomic explosives could be used to destroy cities, and therefore could not safely be allowed to remain in national hands.[11]

[8] United States Participation in the United Nations, Report by the President to the Congress for the Year 1949, Department of State Publication 3765 (May 1950), pp. 74-75. Cited hereafter as U.S. Participation in the U.N., Report (with year).
[9] Ibid., p. 76.
[10] U.N. General Assembly, Fourth Session, Plenary, Official Records, 254th Meeting (Nov. 23, 1949), pp. 355, 356.
[11] U.N. General Assembly, Fourth Session, First Committee, Official Records, 334th Meeting (Nov. 23, 1949).

On October 24, 1949, the President of the United States at the laying of the cornerstone of the permanent headquarters of the United Nations in New York, restated the United States position toward the United Nations plan for control of atomic energy.

This is a good plan, it is a plan that can work and more important it is a plan that can be effective in accomplishing its purpose. It is the only plan so far developed that would meet the technical requirements of control, that would make the prohibition of atomic weapons effective, and at the same time promote the peaceful development of atomic energy on a cooperative basis.

We support this plan and will continue to support it unless and until a better and more effective plan is put forward.[12]

This remained the official United States position on international control of atomic energy until 1955 when the development of thermonuclear weapons and the inability to account for past production of fissionable materials made it necessary to develop new programs in the field of arms control.

In the 1949 General Assembly, the Western powers did not make the political mistake they had made in 1948 of suggesting the suspension of further negotiations on atomic energy. The Secretary of State in his opening address emphasized that discussions among the great powers should continue and expressed the view that the forum of informal conferences among the permanent members of the Atomic Energy Commission offered the best prospect for progress.[13] The General Assembly resolution calling for the continuance of the consultations among the permanent members of the Atomic Energy Commission received 49 supporting votes, and only the Soviet bloc voted against it.[14]

At the first meeting of the permanent members of the Atomic Energy Commission subsequent to the General Assembly, on January

[12] *U. S. Participation in the U.N., Report 1949*, p. 76. See also, U.N. General Assembly, Fourth Session, Plenary, *Official Records*, 237th Meeting (Oct. 24, 1949), p. 171.
[13] *U.S. Participation in the U.N., Report 1949*, p. 75.
[14] U.N. General Assembly, Fourth Session, Plenary, *Official Records*, 254th Meeting (Nov. 23, 1949), p. 358.

19, 1950, the Soviet Union, as in all other United Nations organs and committees, demanded the seating of the representatives of Communist China, and on the rejection of this demand, walked out of the meeting.[15] This brought to an end the discussions of the international control of atomic energy, since any discussions would have been futile without Soviet participation. The problem received no further consideration in United Nations commissions until the General Assembly of 1951 abolished the Atomic Energy Commission and the Commission for Conventional Armaments and created in its place the United Nations Disarmament Commission.[16]

NEGOTIATIONS ON CONVENTIONAL ARMAMENTS, 1948-1949

In the fall of 1948, the Soviet Union had introduced in the General Assembly a proposal calling for "The Prohibition of the Atomic Weapon and the Reduction by One-Third of the Armaments and Armed Forces of the Permanent Members of the Security Council."[17] The Soviet Union introduced this same proposal in the Commission for Conventional Armaments, the only substantive proposal the Soviet Union ever introduced in that body.[18]

This proposal was debated on its merits in the Political Committee of the General Assembly of 1948, and subsequent discussion in the Commission for Conventional Armaments added nothing to the substance of that early debate. The British delegate (Hector McNeil), summarized the Western objections to the Soviet proposal:

. . . While the U.S.S.R. knew exactly how much was spent on armaments by the United Kingdom, for instance, how many men

[15] *U.S. Participation in the U.N., Report 1950*, Department of State Publication 4178 (July 1951), p. 112.
[16] *U.S. Participation in the U.N., Report 1951*, Department of State Publication 4583 (July 1952), p. 59.
[17] U.N. Doc. A/658 (Sept. 25, 1948), p. 2.
[18] *U.S. Participation in the U.N., Report 1948*, Department of State Publication 3437 (1949), pp. 34-35.

it had under arms, and how they were equipped and disposed, no one, not even the Representatives of countries most closely associated with the U.S.S.R. knew the full data in respect of that country.

Moreover, the method of disarmament proposed by the U.S.S.R. gave a premium to those who had disarmed least. Unlike the U.S.S.R., the United Kingdom, in common with most of the other countries of Western Europe, had, since the last war, committed itself to drastic disarmament, and its defence forces were now down to a minimum.[19]

Vyshinsky answered McNeil the next day with a propaganda blast. The closest he came to meeting the issues was the following: "The fear of being tricked by one's partner was always felt by those who regarded every international conference as an excuse for trickery." After alluding to the fact that the Soviet Union was willing to accept international controls, Vyshinsky stated:

But if it was requested to entrust the entire atomic industry of the world to a trust, and to allow the agents of that trust to take aerial pictures of U.S.S.R. territory, the U.S.S.R. would never accept such a control system. The only acceptable control system was one based on common interests, and every effort should be made to set up such a system.[20]

The next day, Malik added one additional element to the debate.

Mr. Vyshinsky had stated that the U.S.S.R. would give full and complete information on its armed forces if a reduction of armaments by one-third and the prohibition of atomic weapons were

[19] U.N. General Assembly, Third Session, First Committee, *Summary Records,* Pt. 1, 153rd Meeting (Oct. 7, 1948), pp. 101-02.
[20] *Ibid.,* p. 139. Even at this early date the Soviet antipathy to any proposal for aerial photography over the Soviet Union is significant in view of the violent Soviet initial reaction to President Eisenhower's proposals for aerial overflight in 1955 and to the U-2 incident in 1960.

agreed upon. What more could it do? It would be folly for the U.S.S.R. to disclose everything and then have the others invent more conditions as a pretext for dropping the whole question of the reduction of armaments after they had found out everything they wished to know.[21]

In effect, the Soviet Union had taken the position: "You accept our proposal and we shall then tell you what it means." The General Assembly overwhelmingly rejected the Soviet resolution.

The debate on the Soviet resolution had shown the obvious fact that agreement on a percentage reduction of armed forces and conventional armaments was impossible unless both sides could know the starting point for the reduction. Accordingly, the French introduced a resolution calling for verified data on the conventional armaments and armed forces of all states. In its study on the regulation and reduction of armaments and armed forces, the Conventional Armaments Commission should give first attention to formulating proposals for the receipt, checking, and verification by an international agency of information concerning conventional armaments and armed forces.[22] The General Assembly accepted this resolution with only the Soviet bloc voting against it.[23]

When the Commission for Conventional Armaments convened in May 1949, and again in July, the French representative introduced into the commission a working paper providing for a census of conventional armaments and armed forces and for the verification of the reported data by a control organ established by the Security Council.[24]

The Soviet Union objected strongly to the French proposal on the ground that it must be preceded by an agreement for the reduction of conventional armaments and armed forces and for the prohibition of atomic weapons. The Soviet Union made the additional objection that the proposed census, if it took place, should include atomic weapons

[21] *Ibid.*, p. 150.
[22] *U.S. Participation in the U.N., Report 1948*, pp. 37-38.
[23] U.N. General Assembly, Third Session, *Official Records*, Pt. 1, *Resolutions*, pp. 17-18.
[24] *U.S. Participation in the U.N., Report 1949*, p. 79.

as well as conventional weapons. Egypt joined the Soviet Union and the Ukraine in supporting the latter proposition.[25]

The French proposal was a logical response to the Soviet suggestion for a one-third reduction of armed forces and conventional armaments, and, at least, went a short distance toward eliminating the policy vacuum of the Western powers on this subject. The paper defined the types of "effectives" and "conventional armaments" which would be subject to census, and in an even vaguer manner made recommendations on methods of verifying the census. The one significant sentence required that "the complete order of battle should be made avaliable to the control organ." The third section outlined the functions and structure of the international organ of control.[26]

The study was a commendable effort to bring the arms control negotiations back to specifics and away from sweeping generalities. However, it played little part in later negotiations. In the first place, the study called for only a one-time operation. The organizational requirements for a one-time operation were quite different from those of a permanent supervisory authority. Also the definitions of effectives and of conventional armaments were too vague to be of much assistance when the identical issue arose in the negotiations during the summer of 1957.

The Commission for Conventional Armaments (over Soviet objection) approved a report to the Security Council containing the French proposal, which was vetoed in the Security Council by the Soviet Union.[27]

The Soviet Union then introduced its own resolution reading as follows: "The Security Council recognizes as essential the submission by states both of information on armed forces and conventional armaments and of information on atomic weapons." The representative of France thereupon amended the Soviet resolution to call for a verification of the information submitted on conventional armaments

[25] *Ibid.*
[26] U.N. Doc. S/1372 (Aug. 9, 1949): "Working Paper of the Commission for Conventional Armaments: Collection and Verification of Information on the Armaments and Armed Forces of United Nations Members, Aug. 1, 1949."
[27] *U.S. Participation in the U.N., Report 1949*, p. 80.

and armed forces and to point out that the submission of information on atomic weapons was part of the United Nations plan for the international control of atomic energy. The Soviet Union also vetoed this resolution as amended. The French thereupon produced a draft resolution transmitting both of the vetoed resolutions to the United Nations General Assembly. This resolution being procedural was not subject to the Soviet veto.[28]

The General Assembly approved the French resolution for an international census and verification of conventional armaments and armed forces with only the Soviet bloc in opposition. Thus for the second time, the Western powers had secured the General Assembly endorsement of a proposal in the field of disarmament even though the Soviet Union was in opposition.[29]

To reiterate, no action in the field of arms control can be carried out over the objection of the Soviet Union. Therefore, the approval of this resolution was a futile act. It did not create the unfavorable repercussions of the General Assembly approval of the plan for control of atomic energy, partly because the subject was less important and partly because the plan itself specified that its implementation required its acceptance by all the permanent members of the Security Council including the Soviet Union. From this time until the fall of 1957 the Western powers never sought to secure General Assembly approval of a substantive proposal in the field of arms control when the Soviet Union objected.

The 1949 General Assembly resolution also recommended to the Security Council that the Commission for Conventional Armaments continue studying the general problem of regulation and reduction of conventional armaments and armed forces in accordance with the commission's plan of work. The next two items of the plan of work were: "Consideration of practical and effective safeguards by means of an international system of control operating through special organs (and by other means) to protect complying States against the hazards

[28] *Ibid.*, pp. 81-82.
[29] The first occasion was the General Assembly approval of the Baruch Plan for the international control of atomic energy.

of violations and evasions" and "Formulate practical proposals for the regulation and reduction of armaments and armed forces."[30]

"ESSENTIALS OF PEACE," 1949

In the General Assembly of 1949 the Soviet Union, following the precedent of 1948, introduced a broad general item dealing with the essentials of peace. Vyshinsky called on the Assembly to condemn "the preparations for a new war being conducted in a number of countries and particularly in the United States and in the United Kingdom." He requested the five great powers "to conclude among themselves a pact for the strengthening of peace."[31] Only the concluding portion of the Soviet essentials of peace proposals related to arms control—the usual Soviet demand for the unconditional prohibition of atomic weapons and the establishment of appropriate strict international control.[32] This resolution marked a further step of the Soviet Union away from specifics and toward broad generalities and propaganda. Its brevity was equaled only by the brevity of the Soviet resolution made originally in the Security Council and re-introduced in the General Assembly to secure information both on conventional armaments and nuclear weapons.

The Soviet Union insisted that this resolution be considered as a separate agenda item independently of the reports of the Atomic Energy Commission or of the Commission for Conventional Armaments. The Western powers thereupon produced their own resolution on essentials of peace, which was adopted by an overwhelming majority of the General Assembly in place of the Soviet resolution. This resolution among other things called upon every nation to

   . . . cooperate to attain the effective international regulation of conventional armaments; and to agree to the exercise of national

[30] U.S. Participation in the U.N., Report 1949, p. 83.
[31] Ibid., p. 23.
[32] U.N. General Assembly, Fourth Session, Official Records, Resolutions, p. 13.

sovereignty jointly with other nations to the extent necessary to attain international control of atomic energy which would make effective the prohibition of atomic weapons and assure the use of atomic energy for peaceful purposes only.[33]

CONVENTIONAL ARMAMENTS

NEGOTIATIONS, 1950

After the 1949 General Assembly the Commission for Conventional Armaments did not meet again until April 27, 1950. On that occasion the Soviet representative walked out of the meeting after the commission refused his request to seat the representative of the Chinese Communists.[34]

Despite the fact that the Soviet Union did not participate, the commission held several meetings at which the United States introduced three working papers. The first presented the views of the United States on the general subject of safeguards. The second dealt with the nature and scope of military safeguards together with information on the military and quasi-military establishments to be reported, inspected and verified. The schedules attached to this paper went into considerably greater detail than the French census proposals a year earlier in elaborating on the information that would be required in the event of a census of armaments and armed forces and also in detailing the methods of verification. The information in these schedules turned out to be quite useful in the negotiations both in 1952 and in 1957. The third paper, entitled "Industrial safeguards—Safeguards through Industrial Information,"[35] contained the germ of an idea—that clandestine preparations for an important war could be detected by checking certain key industrial installations. This paper led to a thorough study within the United States Govern-

[33] U.S. Participation in the U.N., Report 1949, p. 26.
[34] U. N. General Assembly, Fifth Session, Official Records, Supplement No. 2, p. 41.
[35] U.N. Doc. S/C3/43 (Aug. 9, 1950), pp. 6-9, 14-23, 24. This idea was strongly endorsed several years later by President Eisenhower in an address entitled The Chance for Peace, Department of State Publication 5042 (April 16, 1953).

ment of the iron and steel industry and its relation to armaments, some of the material of which entered into later negotiations. However, the paper was only a half-page long.

It can be assumed that these papers represented the entire effort of the United States up to that point to develop a program of arms control—certainly a meager effort. The progress from the complete vacuum in United States policy that followed the Soviet rejection of the Baruch Plan was barely perceptible.

The Soviet Union never returned to the Commission for Conventional Armaments. Its brief 1950 report consisting chiefly of the United States studies was its last gasp. The 1950 General Assembly witnessed a new approach to the entire subject.

THE COLD WAR

The events that had the greatest effect on the course of the arms control negotiations from 1948 on transpired outside the negotiations and in the main outside the United Nations. These events were the so-called Stockholm Appeal and the Communist attack on South Korea, with the chain of consequences resulting therefrom. In the United Nations negotiations, the Soviet positions during the entire period had moved steadily away from substance and toward propaganda. The audience for the Soviet statements was no longer the delegates assembled in the United Nations, but rather those who are swayed by mass media of communication.

In the United Nations, the switch from substance to propaganda resulted in progressively shorter and more general Soviet proposals. As the proposals grew shorter, the Soviet speeches grew longer. Invective and personal slander substituted for discussion of the issues. Frederick Osborn refers to a statistical study of the General Assembly Arms Control debates in 1947 and in 1949, by Dr. Lillian Wald Kay, of the Psychology Department of New York University, which confirms this judgment. Among other statistics, Dr. Kay shows that in 1947 the meetings produced fifteen attacks on motives of other delegates. The Soviet Union was responsible for twelve of these fifteen attacks. The 1949 meetings produced sixty-five such attacks on motives with the Soviet Union responsible for fifty-three out of sixty-five. Most of the other attacks were contributed by other members of the Soviet bloc.[36] The speeches of Malik and Vyshinsky in 1949 bristled with attacks on the United States warmongers and fascists, the Marshallized lackeys of the United States, the Marshallization of Free People etc.[37]

As a part of this movement away from substance, the Soviet Union adopted a negotiating technique, which became almost routine in the period from 1952 to 1955—the technique of seeking a substantive decision through a procedural device. The Soviet resolution on disarmament introduced into the General Assembly in 1948 had the title "The Prohibition of the Atomic Weapon and the Reduction by One-Third of the Armaments and Armed Forces of the Permanent Members of the Security Council."[38] The Soviet Union had insisted on a separate agenda item to deal with this proposal, and the agenda item had a title identical with the title of the proposal. This was logical enough. At the Commission for Conventional Armaments, Malik made the startling claim that the General Assembly by admitting an agenda item with this title had in effect adopted the Soviet proposal.[39]

Along the same lines, Malik contended in the Political Committee of the General Assembly of 1949, that the title of the agenda item foreclosed the committee from adopting any proposal except the Soviet proposal. The committee responded by voting to change the title of the item despite the protests of Malik.

This Soviet propaganda campaign within the United Nations had little appeal to its delegates. As the crescendo of Soviet attacks increased, more and more delegates expressed their opposition to the Soviet proposals and their displeasure with the Soviet attitude. In the

[36] Frederick Osborn, "Negotiating on Atomic Energy," in Raymond Dennett and Joseph E. Johnson, eds., *Negotiating with the Russians* (1951), pp. 231-33.
[37] U.N. General Assembly, Fourth Session, Plenary, *Official Records*, 226th Meeting (Sept. 23, 1949), p. 39; 268th Meeting (Dec. 5, 1949), pp. 513 ff. Soviet speeches frequently contained blatant absurdities such as Malik's denunciation of the United States for preventing disarmament agreements in the League of Nations even though the United States was neither a member of the League nor a participant in the negotiations. See *ibid.*, p. 513.
[38] U.N. Doc. A/658 (Sept. 25, 1948).
[39] U.N. Doc. S/C.3/SR.17 (July 26, 1948), p. 2.

discussions in the Security Council and the General Assembly in 1949, with one minor exception, the Soviet Union received no support for its proposals except from the Soviet bloc. A year earlier, when the United Nations had overwhelmingly approved the Baruch Plan, Vyshinsky had sought to draw a distinction between the views of the United Nations and the views of the peoples of the world. In the Security Council in August 1949, Malik shouted that "the people of the world demanded from the United Nations not empty declarations but concrete and effective measures for strengthening peace."[40] In his opening statement to the United Nations General Assembly on September 23, 1949, Vyshinsky stated: "A powerful movement for peace was spreading and growing ceaselessly among the masses in all the countries of the world. The forces of democracy and peace were growing a hundred times faster than the sinister ranks of the warmongers."[41] It was only a short step from utterances of this nature to complete Soviet rejection of the United Nations as a forum for international negotiations. Beginning in January 1950, the Soviet Union withdrew its representatives from participation in all United Nations organs and committees because of the failure of the United Nations to seat the Communists as the representatives of China.

The Stockholm Appeal

The next logical step in manufacturing history in true Orwellian fashion was for the powerful movements for peace to rise among the masses of the world in accordance with Vyshinsky's predictions. Accordingly in March 1950, the Communist-sponsored "World Congress of Partisans of Peace" convened in Stockholm, Sweden, and adopted the so-called Stockholm Appeal. This appeal read as follows:

We demand the absolute banning of the atom weapon, arm of terror and mass extermination of populations.

[40] U.N. Doc. S/C.3/SR.19 (Aug. 4, 1949).
[41] U.N. General Assembly, Fourth Session, Plenary, *Official Records*, 226th Meeting (Sept. 23, 1949), p. 39.

We demand the establishment of strict international control to ensure the implementation of this banning measure.

We consider that any government which would be first to use the atom weapon against any country whatsoever would be committing a crime against humanity and should be dealt with as a war criminal.

We call on all men of good will throughout the world to sign this Appeal.[42]

The so-called "partisans of peace" thereupon proceeded to secure literally millions of signatures from all countries of the world to this appeal. Additional congresses were held in Warsaw and in Mexico to increase the number of signatures. The most thorough analysis of the Stockholm Appeal concludes that it was without precedent in world history. "These propositions could move men of goodwill but they were an integral part of an extremely aggressive diplomatic campaign, the motivations of which were properly suspect when one recalled the recent actions of the Soviet Union, especially the forceful seizure of Prague."[43] The Stockholm Appeal fooled many individuals of talent and goodwill. Many outstanding Americans, including scientists and scholars who were horrified by some of the Communist excesses, nevertheless joined in the appeal.

The fervor of the partisans of peace was certainly genuine. For example, despite the Communist orientation of the movement, the partisans started to align organized religion on their side. The Assembly of the Cardinals and Archbishops of France found it necessary to point out in June 1950 that in the atmosphere of panic arising from popular realization of the means of destruction which modern science has placed at the disposition of belligerents, "the Stockholm Appeal against the use of the atomic weapon has misguided many generous spirits."[44] One of the most amazing examples of Communist

[42] "Stockholm Appeal of the World Peace Council, March 19, 1950," in U.S. Department of State, Documents on Disarmament, Vol. I (1945-1956), Publication 7008 (August 1960), p. 252.
[43] Translated from L'Atome pour ou contre l'Homme, Éditions Pax Christi, Paris (1958), p. 83.
[44] Ibid., p. 83.

effrontery was a letter from the scientist, Joliot Curie to the Vatican calling on the Holy Father to support the Stockholm Appeal. In replying on February 16, 1951, the secretary of the Vatican noted with satisfaction that Joliot Curie had recognized that the Holy Father had always take a position in favor of peace. He noted that this was a point which, in recent years, had frequently been denied or misconstrued. In his Christmas message in 1951, His Holiness sought to place the problem of disarmament in a proper perspective. He pointed out the distinction between true and false disarmament, stating that the simultaneous and reciprocal reduction of armaments is hardly a firm guarantee of durable peace if it is not accompanied by the elimination of hate, of cupidity and of the uncontrolled desire for prestige. He characterized as superficial sentimentalism an approach that deals with the problem of peace solely or principally from the standpoint of the existence, or the threat, of certain types of arms.[45]

These examples of the magnitude of the Soviet propaganda effort could be multiplied many times. A next logical step in the pursuit of this type of propaganda campaign might have been the establishment of a new international organization as a rival to the United Nations where the partisans of peace would have determined national representation. In other words, the Stockholm Congress and the Warsaw Congress might have been expanded into a permanent international body. It is impossible to determine whether the Soviet Union had any such plan in mind. However, it is clear that the Stockholm Appeal had little attraction for the great majority of the United Nations delegates; and the fact that the Soviet Union was no longer participating in the United Nations activities is further evidence that the appeal was not directed primarily to the United Nations.

Korea

The Communist attack on South Korea at the end of June 1950, initiated a chain of events that led to the return of the Soviet Union

[45] *Ibid.*, p. 84.

to the United Nations in August 1950. When the Communists moved across the 38th parallel boundary line and attacked South Korea, apparently to the considerable surprise of the Soviet Union, the United States and other Western powers provided military support including ground troops to the South Koreans. The United Nations Security Council was in a position to sanction this military assistance and to develop a framework for a United Nations military effort to defend South Korea against aggression because of the absence of the Soviet Union from the Security Council. The Soviet Union, if it had been present in the Security Council, would certainly have vetoed the three Security Council resolutions establishing the United Nations Command over the Korean operation. The successful organization of a United Nations military effort apparently convinced the Soviet Union that more was to be gained from returning to the United Nations organs than from remaining aloof. Accordingly on August 1, Malik appeared at the Security Council Meeting and assumed his place as president for that month of the Security Council. Shortly thereafter, the Soviet representatives returned to the other organs, sub-organs, and committees of the United Nations pursuing the same policies and tactics that had characterized their performance during the latter half of 1949. The propaganda blasts directed against the Western powers and particularly the United States increased in intensity.

During the Security Council debate in the month of August, when Malik presided over its meetings, the Soviet Union again sought to differentiate between the peoples of the states Members of the United Nations and their governments. Malik spoke of "the ruling circles of the United States" rather than of the government of the United States.[46] Perhaps the high point of this effort to separate the governments of the Western powers from their populations was Malik's speech in the meeting of August 22nd. At one point he explained "Even the inhabitants of the United States, deafened by the daily thunder of monopolistic, military propaganda, no longer believe the

[46] U.N. Security Council, Fifth Year, *Official Records,* 482nd Meeting (Aug. 3, 1950), p. 8; 486th Meeting (Aug. 11, 1950), p. 22; 489th Meeting (Aug. 22, 1950), p. 3.

assurances of President Truman that the war in Korea . . . is not a war but a sort of 'police action in support of the United Nations.' " A little further on, he amended slightly his description of the United States Government which now became "the ruling circles of the United States and Wall Street." He referred to the allies of the United States as "colonial slaves and 'Marshallized' lackeys of the United States."[47]

Despite these outbursts, the Soviet Union never took the final step of establishing a rival international organization with national representatives elected by the partisans of peace. The Stockholm Appeal was presented to the United Nations and became merely one additional document in the huge Soviet propaganda campaign conducted within the organization.

The Changed Soviet Timetable

During this period, the belief was quite general in the West that the Soviet propaganda was the prelude to military action by the Soviet Union to take over Western Europe.[48] Such military action, however, never materialized and in perspective it is apparent that the "ban the bomb" campaign had a different explanation.

Zhdanov during his lifetime was known to favor military action in Western Europe before the Western powers would be in a position to re-establish their peacetime economies.[49] After his death in 1949, a coalition of Malenkov, Beria, and Molotov took over his role as chief advisers of Stalin. Apparently, some time toward the end of 1949, the Soviet Union changed its timetable for the destruction of the capitalist nations of Western Europe. The economist, Varga, who had been disgraced because of his prediction that the economic crisis that would destroy the United States might be delayed, returned to Moscow, and early in 1950, was permitted to publish in Pravda

---

[47] Ibid., pp. 5, 6, and 9.
[48] This conclusion received support from the known Soviet build-up of forces near its western frontiers and of Atlantic-based submarines.
[49] Georg von Rauch, A History of Soviet Russia, Translated by Peter and Annette Jacobsohn (1957), p. 410. See also Hugh Seton-Watson, From Lenin to Khrushchev (1960), p. 383.

his doubts about the imminence of an economic crisis in the United States.[50] Von Rauch points out that in the field of foreign policy "the change from Zhdanov's policy to that of Molotov and Vyshinsky, simply meant that a strategy of annihilation was replaced by one of attrition."[51]

As a part of this new policy, the Soviet Union paid more attention to the Far East than to Western Europe. In March 1949, the Soviet Government created a new satellite state in North Korea and a year later concluded a Pact of Friendship, Alliance and Mutual Aid with the Chinese Communists, who had by this time expelled Chiang Kai-shek from the continent of Asia.

A second manifestation of this new policy was the purge of the Communist parties in the Eastern European satellites.[52] In this purge, the Soviet Union removed from office any Eastern European Communist leader, such as Gomulka in Poland and Dimitrov in Bulgaria, who had shown the slightest nationalist leanings. Generally, these leaders were arrested and in some instances executed. Such a policy ran counter to the Zhdanov demand for immediate military action in Europe since it created discontent and hatred of the Soviet Union in the very territories over which the military action would have to take place.

A third manifestation of this policy was the constant deterioration of relations between the Soviet Union and Tito, the one Communist leader who had defied the Kremlin.

A fourth manifestation of the deferred Soviet timetable to take over Western Europe is found in the indications of Soviet willingness to end the blockade of Berlin.

The Soviet propaganda campaign for disarmament apparently fitted very well into this pattern. The excesses of the propaganda campaign disgusted and antagonized the leaders of even the left-wing non-Communist parties in Western Europe—even those who had joined with the Communist party in popular front governments immediately after the war. However, the Soviet Union had no longer wished to cultivate

---

[50] von Rauch, op. cit., p. 414.
[51] Ibid., p. 410.
[52] For general discussion see Seton-Watson. op. cit., pp. 263-66.

popular fronts, but rather preferred to create discontented minorities in the capitalist countries of Western Europe, wholly dependent on Soviet leadership. The partisans of peace were an ideal vehicle for such a program.

Whatever the cause, with the sole exception of the Communist attack on South Korea, during the entire period from the end of 1948 to the end of 1951, the Communists, contrary to expectations, took no military action against the West. Even in Korea, the Soviet Union took no steps to enlarge and expand the Korean operation into a world war, though this would have been not only possible but feasible. Thus, the intensification of the cold war did not lead to a world-wide hot war.

PRELUDE TO THE DISARMAMENT

COMMISSION

In 1949 and 1950, slowly but steadily the United States Government began to fill the policy vacuum that had existed in the field of arms control since the Soviet rejection of the Baruch Plan.

The first step was the passage of the Vandenberg Resolution of June 11, 1948, which called for "maximum efforts . . . to obtain agreement to provide the United Nations with armed forces as provided by the Charter, and to obtain agreement among member nations upon universal regulation and reduction of armaments under adequate and dependable guarantee against violation."[53] This in effect repudiated two unsound positions: first, that the existence of United Nations military forces and the level of world armaments were unrelated; second, and more important, that conventional disarmament even if safeguarded must await Soviet acceptance of the Baruch Plan. More than a year elapsed, however, before the Executive branch of the United States Government developed specific proposals to implement the policy of the Vandenberg Resolution.

The French took the second step in establishing a more realistic policy on arms control through proposing a census and verification of

[53] S. Res. 239, 80 Cong. 2 sess. (June 11, 1948).

conventional armaments and armed forces. This was an independent and separate action in no way tied to the atomic energy proposals of the West. The United States, by supporting this proposal, conceded that safeguards to ensure the observance of commitments to reduce conventional armaments and armed forces could be studied even prior to agreement on a plan for international control of atomic energy.

The gradual development of a new policy in the field of arms control coincided in time with a change in the leadership of the Department of State. President Truman after his re-election as President in November 1948, appointed Dean Acheson as his Secretary of State. In the spring of 1949, Frederick Osborn resigned as United States deputy representative on the Commission for Conventional Armaments and the Atomic Energy Commission. He was replaced by Frank Nash, who was a young Washington attorney of outstanding ability and energy, but with no past experience in the field of arms control. Nash began his task with enthusiasm and with a genuine conviction that progress toward safeguarded arms control would lessen the threat of a third world war. Under his direction, a United States policy began to emerge.

The first evidence in the Executive branch of the United States Government of a change of policy appeared in President Truman's speech, previously quoted, wherein the President promised support of the United Nations Plan until such time as a better and more effective plan could be put forward.

By the opening of the General Assembly of 1950, the United States had gone much further toward establishing a new policy. On October 24, 1950, the President of the United States in person addressed the General Assembly and enumerated three principles essential to any successful disarmament plan.

First, the plan must include all kinds of weapons. Outlawing any particular kind of weapon is not enough. The conflict in Korea bears tragic witness to the fact that aggression, whatever the weapons used, brings frightful destruction.

Second, the plan must be based on unanimous agreement. A majority of nations is not enough. No plan of disarmament can work unless it includes every nation having substantial armed forces. One-sided disarmament is a sure invitation to aggression.

Third, the plan must be fool-proof. Paper promises are not enough. Disarmament must be based on safeguards which will insure the compliance of all nations. The safeguards must be adequate to give immediate warning of any threatened violation. Disarmament must be policed continuously and thoroughly. It must be founded upon free and open interchange of information across national borders.[54]

This pronouncement represented at least two mammoth strides toward an improved position on arms control. In the first place the United States was recognizing that any arms control plan must be based on unanimous agreement. The United States was conceding that the General Assembly approval of the Baruch Plan, even by an overwhelming vote, was a futile gesture. The United States never again called for Assembly approval of a substantive proposal to which the Soviet Union had objected until John Foster Dulles broke that precedent in the General Assembly of 1957. Genuine negotiation between the Soviet Union and the West unquestionably became much easier as the Soviet Union realized that a proposal that it had rejected would not be put to a vote, with adverse propaganda stemming from an unfavorable vote.

The second and more important step was the recognition by the United States Government that any disarmament plan must include all kinds of weapons. Progress toward reduction of conventional armaments and armed forces was no longer dependent on prior agreement on the international control of atomic energy.

This changed position made it apparent that the two commissions of the United Nations, the Atomic Energy Commission and the Commission for Conventional Armaments, had outlived their usefulness and should either be combined or replaced by a single commission to deal with both phases of arms control. The President's proposal on that matter was as follows:

[54] *U.S. Participation in the U.N., Report 1950,* pp. 113-14.

Much valuable work has already been done by the two disarmament commissions on the different technical problems confronting them. I believe it would be useful to explore ways in which the work of the commissions could now be more closely brought together. One possibility to be considered is whether their work might be revitalized if carried forward in the future through a new and consolidated disarmament commission."[55]

The General Assembly in December 1950, adopted a resolution establishing a Committee of Twelve, consisting of representatives of the members of the Security Council as of January 1951, together with Canada "to consider and report to the next regular session of the General Assembly on ways and means whereby the work of the Atomic Energy Commission and the Commission for Conventional Armaments may be co-ordinated and on the advisability of their functions being merged and placed under a new and consolidated disarmament commission."[56] While the Soviet Union and its satellites voted against this proposal, the Soviet Union participated in the work of the Committee of Twelve, which in 1951 produced the report recommending the establishment of the United Nations Disarmament Commission.[57]

ESTIMATE OF THE PERIOD

The period from the General Assembly of 1948 to the General Assembly of 1951 in the field of arms control resulted in maximum frustration and minimum achievement.

The vast number of meetings of United Nations bodies—the Security Council, the General Assembly and its political committees, the Atomic Energy Commission, the Commission for Conventional Armaments, the Committee of Twelve—paid little attention to substance. The Soviet Union in no way altered its earlier positions. Toward the

[55] *Ibid.*, p. 114.
[56] U.N. General Assembly, Fifth Session, *Official Records*, Supplement No. 20 (Dec. 13, 1950), p. 80.
[57] U.N. General Assembly, Sixth Session, *Official Records*, Annexes, "Report of the Committee of Twelve" (Oct. 23, 1951), pp. 2-3.

end of the period, some United States positions, mainly reflected in President Truman's speech to the United Nations in 1950, became more flexible.

To be more specific, the United States now recognized that any arms control agreement to be effective required the adherence of all the great powers. Presumably, the United States in 1950 would not have sought to secure the General Assembly approval of the Baruch Plan over Soviet objection.

The United States now recognized that any disarmament plan to be effective must cover all weapons—nuclear and conventional. The United States no longer supported an atomic energy plan standing alone and unrelated to an agreement concerning armed forces and conventional armaments. This coincided with the Soviet position. Furthermore, the United States no longer insisted on acceptance of the plan for international control of atomic energy prior to any plan for reducing conventional armaments. This also came closer to the Soviet position. Moreover, the United States had shown some flexibility in its advocacy of the United Nations Plan for international control of atomic energy. It would now accept as an alternative to the United Nations Plan any plan that was better and no less effective. However, the United States still insisted that arms control agreements must await an improvement in the international atmosphere. No progress had been made in narrowing the major divergence between the Soviet Union and the West on the timing of the establishment of international control.

On the question whether negotiations should be relatively specific or general, the Soviet Union and the West were further apart. Each year, the Soviet proposals became shorter and more vague. The West continued to call for more detailed proposals, but did not attempt to revise the Baruch Plan to conform to technological and other changes or to produce the equivalent of a Baruch Plan for armed forces and conventional armaments.

The Soviet Union had by this time realized the political profits arising from the twin advocacy of "peace" and "disarmament." Within the United Nations, the Soviet propaganda campaign backfired for a combination of reasons—the inadequacy of the Soviet proposals, the violence of the Soviet speeches, and the contrast between words of peace and acts of aggression. Outside the United Nations, the Soviet Union had launched its major propaganda effort in this field.

Within the United Nations, the West had apparently learned the lesson that its proposals for arms control must not only be sound but must also be politically attractive. The West had shown great ingenuity in stalemating the Soviet propaganda moves in the United Nations. The Western positions, however, still had little appeal to the masses. The Soviet Union might have scored a heavy propaganda victory through the Stockholm Appeal, if the Korean aggression had not turned world opinion against the Communists.

While the United States had started moving toward a more positive substantive position on arms control, the organizational support for the activity had actually become less. From 1948 to 1952, only three officers in the State Department devoted their full time to the work and only one officer in the Department of Defense. Several officers in both the State and Defense Departments spent a part of their time on this work. However, from 1949 until 1955 there were few personnel changes among State Department officers devoting either full or part time to the activity, and the governmental performance began to reap some of the benefits arising from experience and continuity of service.

The other states members of the Atomic Energy Commission and Conventional Armaments Commission continued to be represented almost entirely by their permanent representatives to the United Nations. France was the only state other than the United States and the Soviet Union that during this period took the initiative of making a substantive proposal.

The relative inactivity in arms control negotiations ended with the convening of the United Nations General Assembly in 1951.

The Period of Comprehensive Disarmament Proposals 1952-1954

VIII

The Disarmament Commission

WHEN THE Sixth United Nations General Assembly convened in November 1951 in Paris, it had before it the report of the Committee of Twelve recommending the establishment of a new commission for regulation of armaments, which would coordinate plans for international control in both the nonatomic and atomic fields.[1]

THE TRIPARTITE PROPOSALS

On November 7, on the eve of the General Assembly, France, the United Kingdom, and the United States submitted to the General Assembly a brief tripartite proposal for reduction of armaments. The main features of this proposal were: (1) "The three governments . . . are unshakeably determined to continue their efforts to develop the strength required for their security and that of the free world, because without security there can be no peace with justice" (Par. 2). (2) The

[1] U.N. General Assembly, Sixth Session, *Official Records*, Annexes, Agenda Items 66 and 16, p. 3. The Soviet Union, in the Committee of Twelve, had sought to confine the jurisdiction of the new commission to consideration of the Soviet proposals and had opposed the report when its suggestions were turned down, even though the report stressed that the commission should receive and consider any and all proposals that might be made in connection with arms control.

159

three governments indicated their intention of submitting proposals for a system of safeguards to ensure observance of all commitments—conventional and atomic (Par. 3). (3) The objective of the proposal for the reduction of armaments would be "regulation, limitation and balanced reduction of all armed forces and armaments to a level which would decrease substantially the possibility of a successful aggression and thereby decrease the chance that armed aggression would be used to further national objectives" (Par. 4). (4) A workable program would include provisions for reduction of the size of all armed forces and limitations of the portion of national production which could be used for military purposes. In the field of atomic energy, the United Nations plan "should continue to serve as the basis for the atomic energy aspects of any general program . . . unless and until a better and more effective plan can be devised" (Par. 5). (5) While the program could not be put into effect while United Nations forces were resisting aggression in Korea, "the three Governments believe that discussion of the program should begin now" (Par. 6).[2]

This proposal represented for the United States a considerable expansion of the positions which President Truman had enunciated in his speech to the United Nations a year earlier. Indeed, in certain respects, the tripartite proposal reversed previous United States positions. It was therefore appropriate and necessary for President Truman simultaneously with the release of the tripartite proposals to deliver a radio address describing the plan. The high-lights of President Truman's speech, which in general corresponded to the high-lights of the tripartite proposal, were as follows:

1. President Truman recognized the relationship between the continued military strength of the Western allies and any successful arms control negotiation.

This build-up of the defenses of the free world is one way to security and peace. As things now stand it is the only way open to us. But there is another way to security and peace—a way we

---

[2] "Tripartite Proposal for Reduction of Armaments," U.N. General Assembly, Sixth Session, Doc. A/1943 (Nov. 8, 1951), pp. 4-5.

would much prefer to take. We would prefer to see the nations cut down their armed forces on a balanced basis that would be fair to all. . . . It may seem strange to talk about reducing armed forces and armaments when we are working so hard to build up our military strength. But there is nothing inconsistent about these two things. Both have the same aim—the aim of security and peace. If we can't get security and peace one way, we must get it the other way.[3]

This represented a vast change from the headlong demobilization into which the United States and its Western allies had plunged in 1946. A position of this nature had become possible only after the Western powers had increased their strength vis-à-vis the Soviet Union, through the organization of the North Atlantic Treaty Organization and the program of rearmament following the Communist aggression in Korea.

2. President Truman recognized the necessity of the West taking the lead in the advocacy of world peace thus countering the Soviet propaganda campaigns.

We make this proposal because it is the right thing to do. We are not making it in any sudden spurt of optimism. We are not making it as a last gesture of despair. We are making it because we share, with all the members of the United Nations, the responsibility of trying to bring about conditions which will assure international peace and security. The people of the world want peace. To work in every possible way for peace is a duty which we owe not only to ourselves, but to the whole human race.

3. Coupled with this appeal for peace, was a new position on the relationship of arms control negotiations and international tensions.

While aggression and fighting continue—as in Korea—and while the major political issues that divide the nations remain unsettled,

[3] U.S. Department of State *Bulletin*, Vol. 25 (Nov. 19, 1951), pp. 799-803.

real progress towards reducing armaments may not be possible. But we cannot fail to bring before the world the problem of growing armaments, which presses so heavily on all mankind. We believe deeply that discussions of this question in the United Nations can and should begin now, even though tensions are high. Indeed, one way to reduce these tensions is to start work on such proposals as the one we are now making.

This was a far cry from Secretary of State Marshall's position four years earlier that we should not even discuss the terms of a disarmament program until an improvement in international tensions occurred. It was an equally far cry from the 1948 position of the West suggesting the suspension of all negotiations for the international control of atomic energy.

4. President Truman in his speech elaborated, in considerably greater detail than the proposals themselves, the United States views on a system of safeguards. The safeguards system would depend primarily on a "continuing inventory of all armed forces and armaments" including atomic. "The fact finding must, therefore, be continuous. It cannot be a one-shot affair. The fact finders must know not only what the state of armament is on any given date, but how it is proceeding—whether the armed forces of the country concerned are increasing or diminishing."

Such an inventory would proceed by stages, disclosing the least vital information first and then proceeding to more sensitive areas. This was an answer to the Soviet contention that after the Soviet Union had laid bare all its secrets and eliminated its iron curtain, the West might refuse to eliminate nuclear weapons.

An inspection system would be provided to verify the inventory. While this process of inventory and inspection was taking place, the nations would work out specific arrangements for the actual reduction of armed strength. "Let me stress that each stage of this program for reducing armaments would be entered upon only after the previous one had been completed. And each stage would be continuously policed by inspectors, who would report any breach of faith."[4]

[4] *Ibid.*, pp. 800-01.

This proposal for disarmament in stages was the beginning of an attempt to meet what was perhaps the most important Soviet objection to the Baruch Plan—the fact that under the Baruch Plan the United States gave no assurance that any steps would be taken to eliminate nuclear weapons prior to complete installation of international control. The one major arms control proposal of the West previous to this— the Baruch Plan—was sponsored only by the United States, and the only other substantive Western proposal—for a one-time census and verification of armed forces and armaments—was solely a French proposal. This tripartite proposal stemmed from the cooperation of the United States and the free nations of Europe.

Secretary of State Acheson, the day after President Truman's speech from Washington, elaborated on the proposals in an address to the General Assembly and placed in perspective their relationship to the foreign policy of the United States.[5]

The 1951 General Assembly marked the first appearance in the arms control debates of a number of Western leaders who for many years thereafter played the major roles as negotiators.

A Conservative Government had replaced the Labour Government in England, and Britain was represented in the negotiations by its newly appointed Minister of State, Selwyn Lloyd—an eminent jurist with little previous experience in diplomatic negotiations. His judicial experience served him in good stead in the highly technical field of arms control, and he immediately assumed a role of leadership in the negotiations. Even after he succeeded Anthony Eden as Foreign Minister and of necessity had to concern himself with the entire field of foreign affairs, he continued his participation in the arms control negotiations at their most critical periods.

For the first time, Jules Moch appeared as the French representative in the arms control negotiations. Moch had ably served many French governments in the highest positions. From this time on, he became M. Désarmément in France. He continued to serve France in this capacity through many and diverse cabinets with policies covering almost the entire spectrum of French politics. Even the constitu-

[5] U.N. General Assembly, Sixth Session, *Official Records*, Plenary, 335th Meeting, (Nov. 8, 1951), pp. 13-17.

tional changes accompanying the De Gaulle regime, which left his own party without a single representative in the Chamber of Deputies, only briefly interrupted his tenure as M. Désarmément. He continues to represent France in all arms control negotiations.

The United States representatives in the Paris disarmament discussions were Dean Acheson and Philip Jessup. The latter was an eminent student of international law, with a record of great practical achievements in diplomatic negotiation in the United Nations. Jessup's association with arms control activities lasted only through this General Assembly.

Vyshinsky's first reaction to the Western proposals was to scoff at them, stating that he had hardly been able to sleep because of his laughter when he read them. He likened them to a still-born mouse.[6] However, after hearing the reactions of other United Nations delegates and realizing that the presentation at long last of a positive Western position covering the entire field of arms control negotiations had undermined the Soviet propaganda position, Vyshinsky had second thoughts. These were to present to the General Assembly roughly the same position that the Soviet Union had taken in the Committee of Twelve during the summer. The Soviet Union would agree to a new commission to deal with both atomic energy and conventional armaments.[7] However, the frame of reference of the commission would permit discussion of only the Soviet proposals.

All of this was highly confusing to the vast majority of the delegates who had never had experience in negotiating with the Soviet Union, particularly in the field of arms control. On the surface, both the Soviet Union and the West were calling for elimination of nuclear weapons, for reduction of conventional armaments and armed forces, and for establishment of international control. Yet there was no area of agreement.

During the discussions in the Political Committee, many smaller states in the Middle East, in Asia, and in Latin America expressed the belief that the only way to secure agreement on disarmament would be through direct negotiations among the great powers, and that de-

[6] *Ibid.*, 336th Plenary Meeting (Nov. 8, 1951), pp. 25-28.
[7] *Ibid.*, 348th Plenary Meeting (Nov. 16, 1951), pp. 188-95.

bates in a committee of sixty states on technical matters of this nature would be unlikely to produce tangible results. One propitious circumstance facilitated discussions of disarmament by the great powers during this Assembly. The President of the General Assembly was Dr. Luis Padilla Nervo, the Foreign Minister of Mexico who had the highest reputation among all Members of the General Assembly for fairness and objectivity, and who also had shown great interest in and knowledgeability on the problems of arms control. The Political Committee of the General Assembly therefore established a subcommittee consisting of the representatives of the Soviet Union, France, the United Kingdom, and the United States, with the President of the General Assembly acting as chairman, to seek by private discussion proposals acceptable to all four great powers. The talents of the members of this subcommittee (in addition to Padilla Nervo, Jules Moch, Selwyn Lloyd, Philip Jessup and Andrei Vyshinsky) assured an interesting discussion.

During the week from December 3 to December 10, 1951, the subcommittee blocked out areas of agreement and disagreement between the East and the West. These discussions served two main purposes: (1) Since the discussions were in private, there was little incentive for the Soviet Union to indulge in excessive propaganda. The report of the subcommittee, by disclosing the technical nature of the issues, helped to unmask the propaganda of the Stockholm Appeal. All of the United Nations delegates were now convinced that the solution of arms control problems would come through technical negotiations rather than through the adoption of slogans. (2) The exchange of views clarified the thinking sufficiently so that the Western powers were able to prepare a resolution that not only established the new Disarmament Commission but furnished the framework for its deliberations for the next five years.

On December 19, the United States, the United Kingdom, and France presented in the Political Committee a revised resolution, which, with certain amendments, was adopted by the General Assembly on January 11, 1952, after the Christmas recess.[8] This resolution, after certain findings concerning the dangers of the arms race, established

[8] Res. 502(VI), Jan. 11, 1952.

under the Security Council a "Disarmament Commission" with the same membership as the former Atomic Energy Commission and Commission for Conventional Armaments (the Members of the Security Council plus Canada when it is not a member of the Security Council). The resolution recommended the dissolution of the Atomic Energy Commission and the Commission for Conventional Armaments and directed the Disarmament Commission to prepare

. . . proposals to be embodied in a draft treaty (or treaties) for the regulation, limitation and balanced reduction of all armed forces and all armaments, for the elimination of all major weapons adaptable to mass destruction, and for the effective international control of atomic energy to ensure the prohibition of atomic weapons and the use of atomic energy for peaceful purposes only.

The resolution further provided that "there must be an adequate system of safeguards to ensure observance of the disarmament programme, so as to provide for the prompt detection of violations while at the same time causing the minimum degree of interference in the internal life of each country."

The resolution had thus recognized four separate subjects for discussion: (1) regulation, limitation, and balanced reduction of all armed forces and all armaments; (2) elimination of all weapons adaptable to mass destruction; (3) effective international control of atomic energy; (4) establishment of an adequate system of safeguards. All proposals in the Disarmament Commission until 1955 were directed to one or more of these items.

If the resolution had gone no further, the Soviet Union might conceivably have voted for it. However, it went on to indicate certain substantive principles that would govern the commission. It provided that in a system of guaranteed disarmament, there must be progressive disclosure and verification on a continuing basis of all armed forces and all armaments including atomic, and that the commission in preparing proposals should consider from the outset plans for progressive and continuing disclosure and verification, "the implementation of which is recognized as a first and indispensable step in carrying out the disarmament programme envisaged in the present resolution." In view of Soviet negotiating tactics, a provision of this kind was probably essential. Logically enough, the resolution referred to the reduction of armaments prior to mentioning the safeguards to ensure the observance of the reductions. Unless the resolution had specifically provided as it did that the discussion of safeguards should proceed from the outset, the Soviet Union would unquestionably have contended that no discussions could take place on safeguards until agreement had been reached on the reductions since the earlier reference in the resolution was to the reductions.

The resolution also followed the language of President Truman in stating: "Unless a better or no less effective system is devised, the United Nations plan for the international control of atomic energy and the prohibition of atomic weapons should continue to serve as a basis for the international control of atomic energy."

THE SOVIET PROPOSALS

The Soviet Union strenuously objected to both of these provisions even though it was fairly clear that they in no way limited the type of resolutions or proposals that the Soviet Union could submit to the Disarmament Commission.

On the day the General Assembly adopted the disarmament resolution, Vyshinsky announced that the Soviet Union was planning to submit to the United Nations a new omnibus proposal entitled "Measures to Combat the Threat of a New World War and to Strengthen Peace and Friendship among the Nations."[9] This proposal would deal with the Korean situation as well as disarmament and would include some important modifications of previous Soviet proposals. The "new" proposals turned out to be, with one exception, the same old Soviet proposals that the General Assembly had rejected on many occasions. The Soviet draft resolution contained one new paragraph:

[9] U.N. Doc. A/C.1/698 (Jan. 12, 1952), pp. 2-3.

With a view to the establishment of an appropriate system of guarantees for the observance of the General Assembly's decisions on the prohibition of atomic weapons and the reduction of armaments, the international control organ shall have the right to conduct inspection on a continuing basis; but it shall not be entitled to interfere in the domestic affairs of States.

When the Baruch Plan was being discussed in the United Nations, one of the major divergences had centered around the fact that the plan called for continuous inspection of certain installations, while the Soviet Plan provided only for periodic inspections. Vyshinsky hailed this new language as a tremendous concession to the Western position, since the Soviet Union was now accepting "continuous inspection." However, he declined to elaborate on the meaning of "inspection on a continuing basis" that would not "interfere in the domestic affairs of States." He described all efforts to determine the meaning of his proposal as "playing at questions and answers." He flatly declared that unless the United Nations Atomic Energy Plan were withdrawn "there is no need for me to give any details."[10]

A year later this so-called Soviet concession turned out to be a complete sham. A new Soviet representative in the disarmament negotiations, Valerian Zorin, apparently got his signals mixed and denied the United States contention that the Soviet Union had refused to explain the meaning of its proposals for inspection. He said that the proposals had been explained in great detail as early as June 1947, and then repeated the substance of the Soviet proposals made on June 11, 1947 in the United Nations Atomic Energy Commission.[11]

These were the same proposals the Soviet Union itself had described as providing for periodic inspection. Therefore, the Soviet proposals for inspection on a continuing basis were identical with the proposals for periodic inspections. The United States representative in

[10] For description of this discussion see Statement of Ernest A. Gross, United States Representative in Committee I of the General Assembly on March 18, 1953. U.N. General Assembly, Seventh Session, First Committee, *Official Records,* 577th Meeting (March 18, 1953), pp. 465-67.

[11] U.N. Doc. AEC/24 (June 11, 1947).

the Political Committee, Ernest A. Gross, pointed this out on March 18, 1953.[12]

The General Assembly referred to the Disarmament Commission the paragraphs of the Soviet omnibus proposal relating to disarmament, thus clearing any doubts that might have existed that the Disarmament Commission would consider any and all proposals relating to disarmament.

The Disarmament Commission held an organizational meeting in Paris on February 4, 1952, with the Soviet Union participating. After adopting rules of procedure and disposing of certain other procedural matters, it decided to adjourn and to continue its work in New York.[13]

BUILDING THE WESTERN

POSITION

In February 1952, shortly after the General Assembly resolution establishing the Disarmament Commission, President Truman appointed Benjamin V. Cohen as the United States representative on the Disarmament Commission. As the close adviser to President Roosevelt during the early days of the New Deal, Cohen had not only developed many of the basic ideas that underlay the New Deal, but had also drafted the legislation to implement these ideas. Additionally, six years of service in the field of international relations, first as counselor of the State Department and then as an alternate or delegate on many United States delegations to the General Assembly of the United Nations, had exposed him to the problems of disarmament, so that he was in a position to move quickly into the negotiations without a lengthy period of training. Cohen's close association with Franklin Roosevelt was likewise a favorable omen, since during all the years when the Soviet leaders were heaping insults on the American leadership, they had carefully avoided statements deprecatory to Roosevelt.

[12] U.N. General Assembly, Seventh Session, First Committee, *Official Records*, 577th Meeting (March 18, 1953), pp. 465-67.
[13] U.N. Disarmament Commission, *Official Records*, Special Supplement No. 1, p. 3.

Two months later the Secretary of State established a panel of well-known scientists, educators, and officials "charged with the task of working out comprehensive plans for the regulation, limitation, and balanced reduction of all armed forces and armaments including atomic." This panel[14] consisted of scientists J. Robert Oppenheimer and Vannevar Bush, John Dickey, the President of Dartmouth College, Joseph Johnson, President of the Carnegie Endowment for International Peace, and Allen Dulles, Deputy Director of the Central Intelligence Agency, and at present its director. One of the duties of the panel was to review the positions Cohen planned to present to the Disarmament Commission and to advise concerning these positions. The bulk of the work of the panel was classified top secret and its contents were never communicated even to Cohen.[15] Some of the panel's conclusions, however, very likely coincided with Oppenheimer's public statements and writings.

Oppenheimer, in an article in *Foreign Affairs* (July 1953), emphasized the gravity of the situation arising from the multiplication of nuclear weapons. "We may anticipate a state of affairs in which two Great Powers will each be in a position to put an end to the civilization and life of the other, though not without risking its own. We may be likened to two scorpions in a bottle, each capable of killing the other, but only at the risk of his own life." He expressed the opinion "that we should all have a good idea of how rapidly the situation has changed, and of where we may stand, let us say, three, four, or five years ahead, which is about as far as one can see. I shall revert to the reasons why I think it is important that we all know of these matters. I cannot write of them."[16]

Oppenheimer called for candor—on the part of the officials of the United States Government to the people of their country and on the

---

[14] U.S. Department of State, Press Release 325, April 28, 1952.
[15] U.S. Atomic Energy Commission, *In the Matter of J. Robert Oppenheimer,* Transcript of Hearing before Personnel Security Board, April 12, 1954 through May 6, 1954, p. 95. It should be noted that a great portion of this phase of the work of the panel became available to the public as a result of the Oppenheimer hearings. Its chief significance relates to the reappraisal of United States policy that took place after 1954, and is dealt with in Chap. 11.
[16] J. Robert Oppenheimer, "Atomic Weapons and American Foreign Policy," *Foreign Affairs,* Vol. 31 (July 1953), pp. 529, 527.

part of the United States in dealing with its major allies. This was an endorsement of "Operation Candor" within the United States Government, which a few months later resulted in President Eisenhower's "Atoms for Peace" address to the United Nations. However, in 1952 the panel's recommendations did not materially affect the United States position in the arms control negotiations.

It was obvious from the speeches of President Truman and Dean Acheson as well as from the Tripartite Proposal, that extensive preparations had already taken place within the governments of the United States, the United Kingdom, and France toward presenting new proposals to the Disarmament Commission. Cohen discussed these proposals with the members of the panel and received some helpful suggestions. Oppenheimer in particular believed that while the program did not reflect the anticipated technological weapons developments, it was as satisfactory as any that could be presented in the existing circumstances. Cohen, however, felt strongly that progress toward arms control would be greatly facilitated if the Western powers could submit some small proposal where agreement with the Soviet Union might readily be obtained. A small agreement might clear the air and furnish a foundation for larger agreements in the future. Cohen was thus anticipating the United States approach after 1955. The problem of discovering such an area of agreement quickly reduced itself to a search for some measure under which the system of inspection could be effective without resulting in a major breach of the iron curtain. The panel was unable to find any area with such characteristics.

Dr. Vannevar Bush at one time suggested an agreement not to produce or to use nerve gases in warfare. The inspection system to ensure observance of such an agreement would be less onerous than other inspection systems because of the large size of the plants required to produce nerve gas. However, further study showed that even such an inspection system would have been too extensive to interest the Soviet leaders. This search for a suitable subject for immediate agreement with the Soviet Union led directly to the suggestion (also by Dr. Bush) that the United States approach the Soviet leaders and propose an understanding that neither side would detonate a thermonuclear weapon. Such an accord would need no safeguard system since the detonation of a thermonuclear weapon could not be concealed. The panel, whether rightly or wrongly, in the light of future developments, rejected this approach.[17]

The First Month

The first substantive meeting of the commission took place on March 14, 1952, in New York. Ambassador Cohen attempted to set the tone of the meeting with a conciliatory address calling for world peace through disarmament.

We are met here to consider how peace may be made more secure and the general welfare advanced by disarmament. We have been given a broad mandate by the General Assembly because the peoples of the world want a world free from the burden and fear of armaments. It is no accident that President Roosevelt translated the fourth freedom—freedom from fear—into world terms to mean "a world-wide reduction of armaments to such a point and in such a thorough fashion that no nation will be in a position to commit an act of physical aggression against any neighbor—anywhere in the world." . . .

Our goal is freedom from fear. The goal can be reached by reducing armaments to such a point, in such a thorough fashion and with such fool-proof safeguards that no nation is in a position to wage successful war. That means the elimination of mass armies and other instruments of mass destruction. That means an open world with no secret armies, no secret weapons, and no secret war plans.

Toward the end of his statement he introduced into the commission a draft plan of work with the remarks that: "The language was deliberately designed to cover the essential elements of any balanced disarmament system without prejudging the details of those elements.

[17] This will be considered in greater detail in Chapter 11 dealing with the reappraisal of U.S. policy commencing in 1955.

We believe that any proposals any government may wish to advance can be considered under the appropriate headings of the plan." He closed his statement with an eloquent appeal:

Our desire is to proceed as rapidly as possible to the goal of an open world where national armaments will be reduced drastically, and mass armies and other instruments of mass destruction completely eliminated, so that no state need stand in fear of aggression from any other state. Let us resolve to work together, determined, with God's help, to carry out our mandate: to lift from the peoples of this world the burden and fear of armaments and thus to liberate new energies and resources for positive programs of reconstruction and development.[18]

Malik immediately replied to Cohen by accusing the American forces in Korea and China of using bacterial weapons intended to bring about the mass annihilation of the civilian population. He called upon the Disarmament Commission immediately and without delay to consider the "question of the violation of the prohibition of bacterial warfare—a shameful and dishonourable method of warfare, intolerable to the conscience of honourable people and civilized nations—so as to prevent further use of bacterial weapons and to call to account those who had violated the prohibition of bacterial warfare."[19] Thus Malik introduced to the world the second major Soviet propaganda effort relating to arms control. His blast destroyed all hopes that the Soviet Union might be ready to negotiate sincerely at this time for some form of limitation of armaments and arms control.

Cohen pointed out immediately that the investigation of any charges that the United States had waged bacterial warfare in Korea was beyond the scope of the work of the Disarmament Commission. He stated that the charges were false, unwarranted, and uncorroborated and pointed out that an impartial investigation by the Inter-

[18] U.S. Mission to the United Nations, Press Release 1442, "Statement by Ambassador Benjamin V. Cohen, Deputy United States Representative, at Meeting of the Disarmament Commission," March 14, 1954, pp. 1-5.
[19] U.N. Disarmament Commission, *Official Records*, Special Supplement No. 1, p. 5.

national Committee of the Red Cross had been requested by the United States. The separate question of the prohibition of bacterial warfare was covered under one of the items of the United States work plan.[20]

At the next meeting of the commission on March 19, the representative of the Soviet Union submitted the Soviet plan of work. He followed the now familiar tactic of seeking a substantive result through a procedural decision. For example, the agenda item on reduction of armed forces read in part as follows: "Preparation of agreed recommendations on the reduction by the Five Powers . . . of the armaments and armed forces in their possession by one-third within a year."[21] This agenda item would have permitted the Disarmament Commission to consider only the Soviet proposals.

Another item read: "Consideration of the question of violation of the prohibition of bacterial warfare, the question of the impermissibility of the use of bacterial weapons and the question of calling to account those who violate the prohibition of bacterial warfare."[22]

A work plan of this kind would prevent the Disarmament Commission from getting into substantive discussions but would permit the Soviet Union to use the commission as a sounding board for its propaganda blasts. The Soviet Union never submitted any substantive proposal to the commission beyond this plan of work, which purportedly at least was merely an agenda.

The Soviet representative used most of the next five meetings to speak on a wide variety of subjects unrelated to the commission's future work plan: the Baruch Plan, United States collaboration with Japanese and German war criminals, and particularly all aspects of bacterial warfare. It was not until March 28 at its eighth meeting that the commission finally adopted a simple work plan submitted by the French, with the Soviet Union in opposition. The French plan of work contained three items: "(A) Disclosures and verification of all armaments, including atomic armaments, and of all armed forces. (B) Regulation of all armaments and armed forces" with sub-paragraphs refer-

[20] Ibid., p. 6.
[21] Ibid., pp. 6-7.
[22] Ibid., p. 7.

ring to atomic weapons, other weapons of mass destruction and all other armaments and armed forces. "(C) Procedure and timetable for giving effect to the disarmament programme." The plan of work went on to state, "Points (A) and (B) to be studied concurrently in the first stage of the Commission's work."[23]

The Later Events

On the adoption of this program of work, two committees were created, the first to deal with disclosure and verification and the second to deal with the reductions of armaments, the committees to meet on alternate days.[24] Between April 2, when the substantive discussions commenced, and August 29, the commission and its two committees met twenty-nine times. The vast majority of the meetings were devoted to consideration of a series of papers introduced by the United States alone or in conjunction with the British and French, and covering in outline most of the features of a comprehensive disarmament plan. The individual papers were as follows:

1. "Proposals for a Progressive and Continuing Disclosure and Verification of Armed Forces and Armaments," submitted by the United States on April 5.

2. "Essential Principles for a Disarmament Programme," submitted by the United States on April 24.

3. "Working Paper Setting Forth Proposals for Fixing Numerical Limitation of all Armed Forces," submitted by France, the United Kingdom, and the United States on May 28.

4. "Supplement to Tripartite Working Paper Setting Forth Proposals for Fixing Numerical Limitation of all Armed Forces," submitted by France, the United Kingdom, and the United States on August 12.

5. Working paper setting forth a summary of proposals made by the United States representative in the Disarmament Commission on August 15, 1952, for "elimination of bacterial weapons in connection

[23] *Ibid.*, p. 17.
[24] *Ibid.*, p. 22.

with the elimination of all major weapons adaptable to mass destruction," submitted by the United States on September 4.[25] In addition, Cohen on May 14 restated in some detail and with slight modifications the United States position on the international control of atomic energy.[26] As previously stated, the Soviet Union made no proposals beyond its plan of work. After August 29, the only business transacted by the commission was the approval of its report.

[25] *Ibid.*, pp. 22-30, 63-64, 99-102, 130-31, 154-55.
[26] U.N. Doc. DC/C.1/PV.6 (May 14, 1952), pp. 32-33.

IX

The Western Program 1952

THE FRAMEWORK for the 1952 Western program is described as follows by Ambassador Cohen:

Disarmament must be viewed as a means of carrying out the obligations under the Charter not to use force or the threat of force for settling disputes among nations.

In its efforts toward disarmament, the United States has concentrated single-mindedly on the root problem, the prevention of war itself. When men fight to kill it is hard to regulate the manner of killing. True humanitarianism as well as realism supports the view that the only practical way to eliminate the horror of war is to eliminate war itself.[1]

The most solemn promise in the history of international relationships is that contained in the Charter against the threat or use of force of any kind in any way in international relations contrary to the purposes of the Charter. A disarmament program should provide the safeguards necessary to assure that no state will be in a position to break this solemn promise. No lesser promise can be relied upon if that most solemn promise is broken. A state which

[1] Almost the same as the language of Baruch.

177

would flout the Charter to make war cannot be relied upon to honor any lesser promise as to how it will wage war.

This is the framework within which we have undertaken in the Disarmament Commission our Charter responsibility for formulating . . . plans . . . for the establishment of a system for the regulation of armaments.[2]

ESSENTIAL PRINCIPLES OF

DISARMAMENT

Logically, the Western program commences with the paper on "Essential Principles for a Disarmament Program," which the United States presented in the Disarmament Commission on April 24. The sole author of this proposal was United States representative Benjamin Cohen. In this respect, it is almost unique among international documents. Ordinarily, even where an individual is responsible for the initial draft of a proposal, in the course of clearance within the government, it is changed beyond recognition.

The philosophy of this paper and indeed some of the language harks back to President Roosevelt's Four Freedoms speech during World War II. President Truman's address to the nation on November 7, 1951, and Secretary Acheson's opening statement to the United Nations a day later reflected the same general philosophy of disarmament. Cohen himself presented practically all of the ideas contained in this paper in his initial statement to the Disarmament Commission. Therefore the paper contained no surprises. Its introduction as a formal document in the proceedings was essential because of Soviet unwillingness at that time even to discuss ideas contained only in addresses and not formalized in proposals. The Soviet Union has carried this idea to such an extreme that it frequently introduced as its proposals the verbatim speech of its representative without changes even though the

[2] U.S. Department of State, *United States Efforts Toward Disarmament*, Report to the President by the Deputy U.S. Representative on the United Nations Disarmament Commission, Publication 4902 (February 1953), pp. 5-6.

speech in form was totally unsuitable as a proposal. This sharp differentiation between statements and official proposals undoubtedly reflected the characteristic of Soviet representatives of ranging far and wide in their speeches. The Soviet Union certainly never intended that its broad propaganda outbursts be considered and refuted in detail. Therefore the more serious portions of their statements were reintroduced as official documents in the negotiations.

The brief United States proposal is as follows:

The Disarmament Commission accepts as a guide for its future work the following principles as the essentials of a disarmament programme:

1. The goal of disarmament is not to regulate but to prevent war by relaxing the tensions and fears created by armaments and by making war inherently, as it is constitutionally under the Charter, impossible as a means of settling disputes between nations.

2. To achieve this goal, all states must co-operate to establish an open and substantially disarmed world:

(a) In which armed forces and armaments will be reduced to such a point and in such a thorough fashion that no State will be in a condition of armed preparedness to start a war, and

(b) In which no State will be in a position to undertake preparations for war without other States having knowledge of such preparations long before an offending State could start a war.

3. To reach and keep this goal, international agreements must be entered into by which all States would reduce their armed forces to levels, and restrict their armaments to types and quantities, necessary for:

(a) The maintenance of internal security,

(b) Fulfillment of obligations of States to maintain peace and security in accordance with the United Nations Charter.

4. Such international agreements must ensure by a comprehensive and co-ordinated programme both:

(a) The progressive reduction of armed forces and permitted armaments to fixed maximum levels, radically less than present levels and balanced throughout the process of reduction, thereby eliminating mass armies and preventing any disequilibrium of power dangerous to peace, and

(b) The elimination of all instruments adaptable to mass destruction.

5. Such international agreements must provide effective safeguards to ensure that all phases of the disarmament programme are carried out. In particular, the elimination of atomic weapons must be accomplished by an effective system of international control of atomic energy to ensure that atomic energy is used for peaceful purposes only.

6. Such international agreements must provide an effective system of progressive and continuing disclosure and verification of all armed forces and armaments, including atomic, to achieve the open world in which alone there can be effective disarmament.[3]

Cohen expressed the basic philosophy of the proposal in his statement introducing the proposal in the Disarmament Commission.

Excessive armaments aggravate, if they do not create, tensions and fears among nations. Disarmament by relaxing tensions and fears should facilitate peaceful settlement of political differences. . . . To achieve this goal all states must cooperate to establish an open and substantially disarmed world. . . . The principle of an open and substantially disarmed world is the Fourth Freedom—Freedom from Fear, which President Roosevelt proclaimed in 1941. It was President Roosevelt himself who translated freedom from fear in world terms to mean "a world-wide reduction of armaments to such a point and in such a thorough fashion that no nation will be in a position to commit an act of physical aggression against any neighbour—anywhere in the world."

To reach this goal, however, nations would not completely disarm but would "restrict their armaments to types and quantities, necessary for

³ U.N. Doc. DC/C.1/1 (April 24, 1952), pp. 8-9.

(a) the maintenance of international security, (b) fulfillment of obligations of states to maintain peace and security in accordance with the United Nations Charter."

An essential feature of any disarmament program is that the reductions must be

> . . . balanced throughout the process of reduction, thereby eliminating mass armies and preventing any disequilibrium of power dangerous to peace. . . . This principle in plain and no uncertain terms makes clear that a comprehensive and coordinated disarmament programme must relieve the world not only from the terror of all weapons of total destruction, including atomic and bacteriological, but from the threat of mass armies, without which no aggressor can carry through his evil designs.

Cohen thus made it plain that the elimination of nuclear weapons in which the United States had superiority must be accompanied by the elimination of mass armies in which the Communist powers had superiority.

Finally, "Disarmament without effective and fool-proof safeguards is a snare and a delusion—a cruel deception. There must be effective safeguards to protect complying states against the hazards of violations and evasions."[4]

This effective paper presented the basic philosophy underlying all the Western proposals for arms control until 1955. Even in 1955 the Western philosophy did not change. However, the development of thermonuclear weapons, coupled with the vast increase in quantities of fissionable materials, made it impossible to devise a safeguards system that could assure a relatively disarmed world.

All members of the Disarmament Commission except the Soviet Union heartily endorsed this United States proposal. In particular, Jules Moch pointed out that the principles contained in the United States declaration reflected the principles of the Charter.[5] He recog-

---

[4] U.S. Mission to the United Nations, Press Release 1464, April 23, 1952.
[5] U.N. Disarmament Commission, *Official Records,* Special Supplement No. 1, p. 65.

nized that even unanimous approval of these principles would not relieve the commission of the necessity of going into more complex questions of detail, nor would any fundamental problem be resolved. However, he appealed to the representative of the Soviet Union to accept these principles and not to link them to other and more controversial features of the Western program.

Nevertheless, the Soviet representative rejected the proposal in a long, rambling speech.[6] Two lines of argumentation emerged. First, the Soviet Union wanted "concrete practical decisions" and not decisions in principle. The concrete practical decisions, of course, were the Soviet proposal for an immediate prohibition of atomic weapons and a one-third reduction of armed forces and conventional armaments. The second line of argumentation was one that the Soviet Union followed throughout the remainder of the negotiations in the Disarmament Commission. The Soviet Union rejected the statement of principles because it did not provide a program for prohibition of atomic weapons and for the reduction of armed forces and conventional armaments, and because it did not provide for an international control system. When, at a subsequent date, the Western powers introduced proposals for the reduction of armed forces, the Soviet delegate, following a similar line of reasoning, rejected these proposals because they did not provide for the prohibition of atomic weapons or for the reduction of conventional armaments. When the United States presented its position supporting an inspection system, it was unsatisfactory because it did not provide for the prohibition of nuclear weapons, and it did not provide for the reduction of armaments and of armed forces. No Western proposal was satisfactory unless it combined in one package the entire field of arms control.

The Soviet position during these talks was to reject anything the Western powers might propose. The Soviet Union was waging its propaganda campaign outside the Disarmament Commission and was using the Disarmament Commission merely as one sector of its broader propaganda battle.

[6] *Ibid.,* pp. 66-68.

The paper on essential principles produced favorable reactions throughout the free world. It helped immeasurably to create a world image of the Western powers as the true supporters of peace despite the vast propaganda appeals of the Soviet Union. Several years later, in September 1959, Khrushchev paid the greatest compliment to this paper. When he appeared in person to address the United Nations and called for total world disarmament, he appropriated almost literally but without attribution large portions of it. Four years earlier, Stassen had disassociated the United States from all previous positions including this paper. Years later Khrushchev picked it up even though it had been discarded by the West.

DISCLOSURE AND VERIFICATION

The first paper introduced into the Disarmament Commission called for progressive disclosure and verification of armed forces and armaments. The Disarmament Commission received this paper sponsored by the United States on April 5 at its first meeting following the adoption of a plan of work.[7]

Logically, it would have been preferable for the Western powers to commence the presentation of their position with the proposals dealing with essential principles, which appeared three weeks later. Since the paper on essential principles was basically noncontroversial, theoretically its early introduction might have created a better atmosphere in the commission.

However, there was one compelling reason for introducing the disclosure and verification paper at the earliest possible moment. The paper represented a considerable policy shift on the part of the United States. While Secretary Acheson had foreshadowed the general nature of the shift during the General Assembly, its extent could be measured only by a close study of the paper itself. Any serious Soviet reaction to the paper must follow both a thorough study in Moscow and the mysterious and time-consuming Soviet bureaucratic decision-making

[7] *Ibid.*, pp. 22-27.

processes. The Western powers hoped that an early presentation of this paper could conceivably result in a favorable reaction by the Soviet Union prior to the 1953 Assembly.

This proposal contained the following significant innovations in the Western position.

1. It provided for disclosure in each stage of both nuclear and conventional armaments. This represented a concession in the direction of the Soviet resolution of 1949 introduced into both the Security Council and the General Assembly calling for submission by states of information on armed forces and conventional armaments and of information on atomic weapons.

2. President Truman had previously indicated United States flexibility on international control of atomic energy and support of the United Nations plan only until a better and no less effective plan is devised. The disclosure and verification paper carried this one step further by providing an inspection system that supplemented and could be construed to modify the United Nations plan through setting up a different system of stages.

3. The most important new idea in the proposal was the provision for stages. This was at least an effort to respond to the most important unanswered Soviet question in connection with the Baruch Plan: How would the imposition of an international control system lead to the elimination of nuclear weapons? While the disclosure and verification proposal did not give an answer, it established a principle that the international control system would deal first with the least sensitive areas of control.

The best description of the rationale of the stages as well as of the stages themselves is contained in Cohen's report to the President made at the time of his resignation on Jan. 12, 1953.

We suggested that disclosure and verification should be carried out progressively, step by step. We suggested the system should proceed by stages not because we wanted to proceed at a snail's pace but because we know that in the present state of world tension no state would tear the veil of secrecy from its most carefully guarded security arrangements unless it could be satisfied that all states are proceeding with the same good faith and the same understanding and at the same pace. The concept of stages is introduced not to delay and obstruct, but to facilitate and expedite progress and to establish confidence.

Our paper suggested five stages in all, each stage to follow when the previous stage has been satisfactorily completed. This concept of stages was intended to protect all states in the event of a serious violation or collapse of the program by providing a check on the good faith of other states. The disclosure and verification system, we believe, should proceed from the less secret to the more secret information, both to prevent premature disclosure of more secret information until substantial cooperation and good faith had been demonstrated through the working of the previous stage, and also because the less secret information can be more readily verified. We sought to provide that the information disclosed in the atomic field at successive stages should be approximately parallel to the information disclosed in the non-atomic field.

We have tried to make the first step in both fields a meaningful stride toward the goal of confidence. The first stage would disclose in breadth, although not in depth, the general contours of the military establishments of all nations. And the first stage includes so much information of a quantitative nature that the disclosures in the atomic field, for example, would give a clear indication of existing atomic strength—our own and that of other countries. That first stage calls for a verified report on the existing strength of all armed forces as well as on the location of installations and facilities required for the production of armaments of all types, including atomic. The successful completion of this first stage would do more to inspire international confidence and reduce tensions than any amount of words could ever accomplish.

The second stage would provide detailed information on the organization of armed forces and on the installations and facilities supplying the basic materials required to produce all armaments, including atomic. The third stage would give detailed information on armaments (except novel armaments which were not in general use by the end of World War II but are in volume production today), as well as detailed disclosure of kinds and amounts of fissionable material, and full data on the operation of installations and facilities which produce armaments and fissionable material. The fourth stage would give information in detail concerning the installations and facilities used to produce novel armaments, including atomic weapons. And the fifth stage would provide detailed disclosure of the novel armaments themselves and of atomic weapons.[8]

The disclosure and verification paper contained other suggestions—particularly in relation to the type of inspection that might be required to verify the information presented including aerial inspection, which might have been useful if the Soviet Union had not rejected the proposal from the outset. These details never entered into the discussions in the Disarmament Commission.

The favorable response to these proposals by all members of the Disarmament Commission except the Soviet Union reflected the opinion that the United States was making a genuine effort to come to grips with the problems involved, the problems of arms control. The general concepts of this paper showed flexibility on the part of the United States, and a willingness to modify its position to meet some of the chief Soviet objections to the Baruch Plan. The same favorable characterization would certainly not apply to the annexes, which elaborated in some detail the objects to be disclosed and the methods of verification in each stage.[9] The annexes were weighted in favor of the West and against the Soviet Union.

For example, it is difficult to criticize the general position set forth in the paper that the disclosure and verification system should proceed from the less secret to the more secret information. However, the least secret information in the United States and in the West might well be the most secret information in the Soviet Union. The first stage in the disclosure of atomic information covered the "location of all installations directly concerned with production of atomic energy or the

[8] U.S. Department of State, United States Efforts Toward Disarmament, Report, pp. 15-17.
[9] U.N. Disarmament Commission, Official Records, Special Supplement No. 1, pp. 27-30.

product of which is primarily useful in the production of atomic energy; also man-power employed, physical dimensions, and power input of each installation (excluding weapons storage sites)." This certainly would be the least sensitive information in the United States since the Smyth report had already disclosed the existence of Hanford and Oak Ridge. In order to verify this information "inspectors will have access to the entire national territory to the extent necessary to determine through such means as aerial survey, inspection of water and railways and power lines, that all atomic installations have been declared."[10] The aerial survey would of necessity disclose the most secret information in the Soviet Union.

Another example of weighting the scales against the Soviet Union was the division of the process of disclosure and verification into five stages, which seemed to delay interminably the disclosure and verification of the most important piece of information the Soviet Union desired—the quantities and design characteristics of nuclear weapons. Jules Moch objected to having five stages, and suggested that the number be reduced to three.[11]

This might have been a serious indictment of the United States proposals had it not been for the specific language used by Cohen in introducing them:

These proposals are intended only to provide the basis for discussion. They are not intended to express a definite or inflexible position of my Government, and my Government itself may wish to suggest changes and revisions as our discussions proceed.

We welcome suggestions and constructive criticism. The United States does not commit itself or ask others to commit themselves to the working paper as it is submitted. It is intended only to provide a basis on which we can intelligently undertake an exchange of views on the procedures necessary to provide progressive disclosure and effective verification of our arms strength.[12]

[10] *Ibid.,* p. 29.
[11] *Ibid.,* p. 44.
[12] U.S. Mission to the United Nations, Press Release 1459, April 5, 1952.

This was not lost on the Soviet representative. When Jules Moch suggested reducing the number of stages from five to three, Malik replied that "the French proposals merely showed the division of labour between the United States and French representatives, the former presenting the maximum, the latter the minimum programme: The French compromise was thus really only an abridged United States plan."[13]

The Soviet Union denounced the entire proposal as a gigantic intelligence and espionage operation bearing no relation to disarmament. The Soviet representative declined to suggest amendments to the United States proposal for the reason that amendments and modifications could be made only to proposals that could serve as a basis for the solution of the question. He insisted that the United States proposal must be turned down in its entirety.

The annexes, in fact, were nothing more than a belated recognition by the United States of the fact that any negotiation with the Soviet Union involves give and take and that a state cannot give if its initial position is its final position.

In 1955, when the positions of the Soviet Union became less rigid, it accepted a number of the basic ideas that appeared for the first time in this paper—the concept of stages and a progression in inspection from less sensitive to more sensitive areas.

LIMITATION OF ARMED FORCES

AND AMENDMENTS

The Western position on the limitation of armed forces and armaments was contained in two papers submitted jointly by France, the United Kingdom, and the United States, the first on May 28, and the second on August 12. The first of these papers dealt solely with the question of fixing numerical ceilings for armed forces. This paper suggested the following working formula as a basis of discussion:

[13] U.N. Disarmament Commission, *Official Records,* Special Supplement No. 1, pp. 44-47, particularly par. 150.

. . . there should be fixed numerical ceilings for China, France, the Union of Soviet Socialist Republics, the United Kingdom and the United States of America. A ceiling between 1,000,000 and 1,500,000 is suggested for the Union of Soviet Socialist Republics, the United States of America and China, while a ceiling between 700,000 and 800,000 is suggested for the United Kingdom and France.

For all other states "having substantial armed forces" agreed maximum ceilings should

. . . be fixed in relation to the ceilings agreed upon for the five Powers. Such ceilings should be fixed with a view to avoiding a disequilibrium of power dangerous to international peace and security in any area of the world, thus reducing the danger of war. The ceilings would normally be less than 1 per cent of the population and should be less than current levels, except in very special circumstances.[14]

The paper went on to point out that a nation's armed forces are not the only measure of its armed strength and further elements of strength would have to be considered in any comprehensive program for reduction of armed forces and armaments. However, since all armament programs depend on man power and must be affected by limitations on permitted armed forces, a substantial reduction of armed forces would tend to reduce the likelihood of successful aggressive warfare.

The paper added a few ideas on the implementation of the proposals including the general statement that there should be adequate safeguards throughout the process of reduction to ensure that the limitations are put into effect and observed.

The British representative in introducing the paper stressed that this proposal dealt with only one element of the disarmament problem and that any final plan must cover all armaments and armed forces

[14] *Ibid.*, p. 100.

and also must cover atomic weapons.[15] Cohen made the same point
and in addition stressed that

. . . adequate provision would have to be made to ensure that all
kinds of armed forces are embraced within the limitations, including para-military and security forces. Provision would have to be
made to ensure that the limitations are not circumvented through
the building up of large forces of trained reserves or militarily
trained police.[16]

Despite these statements, the Soviet representative declared that
so long as the promised proposals on the reduction of armaments and
prohibition of atomic weapons had not been submitted to the commission, it was appropriate to conclude that the sponsors of the three-
power proposal were seeking to bring about a reduction of armed
forces while ignoring the question of prohibition of atomic weapons
and the reduction of armaments. The three-power proposal therefore
merely aimed at setting ceilings on the armed forces of states and
relegated the other questions to some indeterminate future.[17] Along
the same line, the Soviet representative assumed that the use of the
word forces referred only to land forces and did not include air and
naval forces.

The Soviet representative also criticized the proposals for reduction of armed forces because they "passed over in silence the question
of bacterial warfare," and because the proposals did not call for the
liquidation of the more than four hundred military bases that the
United States had in foreign territory.[18]

The Western powers met most of this Soviet line of argumentation
through submitting on August 12 a supplement to their original tripartite working paper, which dealt with the relation of limitations on
armed forces to the balance of a comprehensive program. The first
paragraph of this paper pointed out that any agreement for limitation

[15] *Ibid.*, p. 103.
[16] U.S. Mission to the United Nations, Press Release 1483, May 28, 1952, p. 4.
[17] U.N. Disarmament Commission, *Official Records*, Special Supplement No. 1,
pp. 112-13.
[18] *Ibid.*, pp. 115, 117.

of armed forces would necessarily comprehend "(a) provisions to ensure that production of armaments and quantities of armaments bear a direct relation to the amounts needed for permitted armed forces; (b) provisions for composition of permitted armed forces and armaments in order to prevent undue concentration of total permitted armed forces in a manner which might prejudice a balanced reduction"; and (c) procedures for the negotiation of an over-all program of reduction of armed forces and armaments. The second paragraph outlined "one possible procedure, advanced for the purpose of initiating discussions." The third paragraph confirmed certain principles governing the relationship of the various parts of a comprehensive disarmament program:

The timing and coordination of the reductions, prohibitions and eliminations should ensure the balanced reduction of over-all armed strength and should avoid creating or continuing any disequilibrium of power dangerous to international peace and security during the period that the reductions, prohibitions and eliminations are being put into effect. In particular, the initial limitations or reductions in armed forces and permitted armaments and the initial steps towards the elimination of prohibited armaments should commence at the same time. Subsequent limitations and reductions should be synchronized with subsequent progress in the elimination of prohibited armaments. An international control authority should be established at the commencement of the programme and it should be in a position to assume progressively its functions in order to ensure the carrying out of such limitations, reductions, curtailments and prohibitions. Thus, when the limitations and reductions in armed forces and permitted armaments provided by the treaty or treaties are completed, production of prohibited armaments will have ceased, existing stockpiles of prohibited armaments and facilities for their production will have been disposed of, atomic energy will be utilized for peaceful purposes only, and the international control authority will have assumed its full functions.[19]

[19] *Ibid.*, pp. 130-31.

In introducing this paper, Cohen pointed out that the sponsors of the original tripartite working paper on reduction of armed forces

. . . attached great importance to this paper and hoped that it might be an opening wedge to a serious discussion and substantial progress in the field of disarmament. We were disappointed when the Soviet Union indicated its unwillingness to give consideration to our proposals even as a basis for discussion. The Soviet Representative explained to us that the Soviet Union regarded the tripartite paper as fatally deficient because, in its opinion, it did not deal with the distribution of the armed forces among the land, sea and air services, and did not limit or restrict the armaments which might be available to support permitted armed forces.

Cohen indicated that he had covered in his statements to the commission much of the material in the supplementary paper.

The sponsors of the Tripartite Working Paper and its Supplement have tried hard to break ground in order to make it possible for the Commission to progress in its work. The Tripartite Paper with its Supplement is a working paper. It is not in final or definitive form. It is submitted for discussion. The Sponsors, as well as other members, may have changes to suggest as a result of further thought and discussion. But the sponsors of the paper do believe that the procedures suggested constitute a constructive approach and are entitled to serious consideration.[20]

The representative of the Soviet Union waited twelve days before giving "his considered position respecting the supplementary proposals of the three Powers." On August 29, the Soviet Union rejected the supplementary proposals because they did not call for a decision on the control of atomic weapons, and because they did not deal with bacterial warfare.[21] This ended the 1952 discussions of disarmament,

[20] U.S. Mission to the United Nations, Press Release 1526, Aug. 11, 1952, pp. 1, 4.
[21] U.N. Disarmament Commission, *Official Records*, Special Supplement No. 1, pp. 139-41.

the remaining meetings of the commission being devoted solely to consideration of the commission's report to the General Assembly.

ATOMIC ENERGY

During this series of meetings, the Western powers made no specific proposals on the subject of international control of atomic energy and the elimination of nuclear weapons. The General Assembly resolution creating the Disarmament Commission had specifically provided that the commission should be

. . . ready to consider any proposals or plans for control that may be put forward involving either conventional armaments or atomic energy. Unless a better or no less effective system is devised, the United Nations Plan for the International Control of Atomic Energy and the Prohibition of Atomic Weapons should continue to serve as a basis for the international control of atomic energy to ensure the prohibition of atomic weapons and the use of atomic energy for peaceful purposes only.[22]

Two developments, however, indicated increasing United States flexibility on the subject of atomic energy.

The proposal for disclosure and verification of all armed forces and armaments had included atomic weapons. This was a clear invitation to the Soviet representatives to renew the discussions on the time relationship between the installation of international controls over atomic energy and the prohibition and elimination of nuclear weapons. While the specific provisions of the annexes to this paper relating to nuclear weapons unquestionably favored the United States, Cohen had made it clear that these represented only the opening positions and could be modified. The Soviet representative declined to enter into a discussion of this matter unless the United States completely abandoned the United Nations Plan for control of atomic energy.[23]

[22] Res. 502(VI), Jan. 11, 1952, pp. 1-2.
[23] U.N. Disarmament Commission, *Official Records*, Special Supplement No. 1, pp. 160-61, 83-84.

On May 14, Cohen made a second move to indicate United States flexibility in the form of a lengthy statement concerning the United Nations Plan for the international control of atomic energy. At the beginning of the speech, Cohen said: "The term 'ownership' as used in the United Nations Plan for the control of atomic energy does not contemplate any super-monopoly on a commercial basis. It has nothing to do with private profits. It does not contemplate strict control by United States capitalists."[24] Cohen then proceeded to restate the entire United States position toward the international control of atomic energy without once using the word "ownership," which heretofore had been an essential part of the Baruch Plan. In general he substituted for the term "ownership" "operational control." The United States thus eliminated one of the two initial divergences between it and the Soviet Union on the subject of international control of atomic energy, which had created the greatest controversy in the 1946 discussions. There was still no agreement between the United States and the Soviet Union on the extent of international control that would be necessary. However, this statement eliminated a bogus issue—that the United States was proposing international ownership of nuclear facilities in order to create a capitalistic monopoly that would levy a tribute in the shape of vast profits from the rest of the world. It thus served to focus world attention on the real divergence between the Soviet position and the Western position—the fact that the Soviet Union was unwilling to permit a sufficient breach of its iron curtain to make possible an adequate system of international control.

BACTERIOLOGICAL WARFARE

The General Assembly resolution of January 11, 1952, recognized that one of the essential parts of a program for the regulation, limitation, and balanced reduction of all armed forces and all armaments would be "the elimination of all major weapons adaptable to mass destruction."[25] Both the program of work submitted by the United States to the Disarmament Commission and the French program,

[24] U.S. Mission to the United Nations, Press Release 1472, May 14, 1952, p. 1.
[25] Res. 502 (VI), Jan. 11, 1952.

which the commission actually adopted, included as an agenda item a paragraph dealing with this portion of the program. The item as finally adopted by the commission read as follows: "Elimination of weapons of mass destruction and control with a view to ensuring their elimination."[26]

The subject of bacteriological warfare occupied a large proportion of the time of the Disarmament Commission because of its association with the vast propaganda campaign that the Soviet Union was at that time carrying on against the United States.

As Cohen described the situation:

Beginning with the very first meeting of the Disarmament Commission in New York, the Soviet Union sought to poison the atmosphere of the Commission and obscure the clear and unequivocal position of the United States on this subject by making false and sensational charges that U.S. troops were conducting germ warfare in Korea and China. The Soviet Union sought to leave the false impression that the United States was opposing any effort in the United Nations to devise ways and means of eliminating bacteriological weapons as a part of a disarmament program.[27]

This Soviet propaganda campaign had two main facets. First, the Soviet Union was using all means of propaganda available to it to charge the United States with the use of bacteriological warfare in Korea. This vast campaign emerged as the number one theme of world Communist propaganda in February 1952, just a month before the convening of the Disarmament Commission. It raged with increasing fury until its obliteration in the General Assembly in 1953.[28]

This first aspect of the campaign had no relation to disarmament

[26] U.N. Disarmament Commission, *Official Records*, Special Supplement No. 1, p. 17. This paragraph (B, 2) was amended on Aug. 27, 1952, to read as follows: "Elimination of weapons of mass destruction *including bacterial weapons* and control with a view to ensuring their elimination." *Ibid.*, p. 20. (Italics added.)
[27] U.S. Department of State, *United States Efforts Toward Disarmament*, Report, pp. 26-27.
[28] For the best discussion of this campaign see statement by the Hon. Charles W. Mayo, Alternate U.S. Delegate to the General Assembly, to the Political Committee of the General Assembly: U. S. Mission to the United Nations, Press Release 1786, Oct. 26, 1953.

although Gromyko in his effort to spread confusion, had demanded that the Disarmament Commission investigate the charge that bacteriological warfare had been used in Korea.

The second and more subtle facet of the campaign was directly related to disarmament. This was the Soviet effort to secure resolutions from various United Nations organs, calling on all states to ratify the Geneva Protocol of 1925 prohibiting chemical and bacteriological warfare. The United States had taken an active role in drafting the Geneva Protocol. However, even though 42 states had ratified the protocol, the United States Senate had refused to take any action. Cohen discussed the circumstances surrounding America's failure to ratify the protocol as follows:

When the Geneva Protocol was submitted to the Senate for ratification, America was retreating rapidly into isolationism and neutralism and feared any involvement with the League and any treaties originating from Geneva. It is ridiculous and absurd for Mr. Malik to think that the nation which a few years later was to attempt to ban any shipments of arms to any belligerent failed to ratify the Geneva Protocol because of the profit motives of its ruling classes.[29]

Malik sought constantly to associate the failure of the United States to ratify the Geneva Protocol with the Soviet charge that the United States had used bacteriological warfare in Korea.[30] In addition to the obvious motive of striking out wildly in all directions to support the Soviet charges, Malik had the more subtle motive of eventually securing a decision from some organ of the United Nations calling on all states to ratify the Geneva Protocol. Since the Geneva Protocol did not provide safeguards to ensure the observance of the commitments not to use bacteriological warfare or chemical warfare, a recommendation that states ratify it would be an opening wedge toward the greater objective of obtaining a United Nations decision calling for the prohibition of nuclear weapons without safeguards.

[29] U.S. Department of State *Bulletin*, Vol. 27 (Aug. 25, 1952), pp. 294-97.
[30] U.N. Disarmament Commission, *Official Records*, Special Supplement No. 1 (1952), p. 15.

It therefore became necessary for the Western powers to establish in the Disarmament Commission a program to prevent the use of bacteriological warfare as part of the general program of comprehensive disarmament that the Western states were outlining. This was the objective of Cohen's statement of May 27.[31] Cohen pointed out:

The United States as a member of the United Nations has committed itself, as have all other members, to refrain from not only the use of poisonous gas and the use of germ warfare but the use of force of any kind contrary to the law of the Charter. . . . We must approach the problem of disarmament from the point of view of preventing war and not from the point of view of regulating the armaments to be used in war. . . . We believe, as the Soviet Delegation maintained in 1932, that paramount importance should be attached "not to the prohibition of chemical weapons in war-time, but to the prohibition of chemical warfare in peacetime" and that "efforts should be directed not so much to the framing of laws and usages of war as to the prohibition of as many lethal substances . . . as possible. But we do not intend, before such measures as safeguards have been agreed upon, to invite aggression . . . by committing ourselves to would-be aggressors and Charter-breakers that we will not use certain weapons to suppress aggression. To do so in exchange for mere paper promises would be to give would-be aggressors their own choice of weapons." . . .

The Soviet Representative has suggested that there are no effective safeguards to ensure the elimination of bacteriological warfare and contends in effect that it is therefore necessary for us to rely on the moral force of paper promises prohibiting its use in war. We do not agree. Nor did the Soviet Delegation agree with that position in 1928 or in 1932, as we have shown. It may be true that there are no theoretically fool-proof safeguards which would prevent the concoction of some deadly germs in an apothecary's shop in the dark hours of the night. But when the United States proposes the establishment of safeguards to ensure the elimination of germ warfare along with the elimination of mass

[31] U.S. Mission to the United Nations, Press Release 1482, May 12, 1952.

armed forces and all weapons adaptable to mass destruction, it demands what is possible and practical, not the impossible. . . . Bacteriological weapons to be effective in modern warfare require more than the dropping at random of a few infected spiders, flies or fleas. They require industrial establishments, facilities for maintaining the agents, transport containers and disseminating appliances. Such arrangements and facilities will not readily escape detection under an effective and continuous system of disclosure and verification of all armed forces and armaments which the General Assembly has declared to be a necessary prerequisite of any comprehensive disarmament program. . . . The United States proposes that, at appropriate stages in such an effective system of disclosure and verification, agreed measures should become effective providing for the progressive curtailment of production, the progressive dismantling of plants, and the progressive destruction of stockpiles of bacteriological weapons and related appliances. Under this proposal with good faith cooperation by the principal states concerned, all bacteriological weapons, and all facilities connected therewith, could be completely eliminated from national armaments and their use prohibited.[32]

Because of the Soviet refusal to pay any attention to proposals set forth merely as speeches, the United States on September 4 submitted a short memorandum entitled "Working Paper Setting Forth a Summary of Proposals made by the United States Representative in the Disarmament Commission on August 15th, 1952 for elimination of bacterial weapons, in connection with the elimination of all major weapons adaptable to mass destruction."[33]

The Disarmament Commission had already on September 4 ceased its discussion of substantive issues and was engaged in preparing its report to the General Assembly.

While bacteriological warfare as an issue in the disarmament discussions died down with the adjournment of the Disarmament Com-

[32] U.S. Mission to the United Nations, Press Release 1527, May 27, 1952, pp. 4-5.
[33] U.N. Disarmament Commission, Official Records, Special Supplement No. 1, pp. 154-55.

mission in the fall of 1952, the main propaganda campaign charging the United States with waging bacteriological warfare in Korea, continued with increasing vigor. On October 20, 1952, the United States requested the General Assembly to place on its agenda an item calling for an impartial investigation by the United Nations of these charges.[34]

In the meantime the Communists sought to support the charges of bacteriological warfare in Korea by the so-called confessions of six American fliers that they had dropped germs over North Korea. The Communists created "the International Scientific Commission for the investigation of the Facts concerning Bacterial Warfare in Korea and China," which filed a lengthy report in the United Nations on October 8, 1952.[35]

The United States item calling for investigation of the charges of use by the United Nations forces of bacteriological warfare in Korea did not come before the General Assembly until April 1953. With only the Soviet bloc in opposition the General Assembly created an "impartial investigatory commission" consisting of Brazil, Egypt, Pakistan, Sweden, and Uruguay and requested that they be given "the right to travel freely throughout such areas of North and South Korea, the Chinese Mainland and Japan as it deemed necessary to perform its tasks and with full freedom of access to persons, places and relevant documents."[36] The Chinese Communists and the North Korean Communists refused to allow the commission access to their territories.

Shortly afterwards, the Korean armistice resulted in the release of all the captured American fliers, including the six whose confessions of waging bacteriological warfare in North Korea had been published by the Soviet Union. The United States Air Force and the United States Marine Corps immediately discovered, as they had previously suspected, that the Communists had extracted the confessions of use of bacteriological warfare through threats and tortures almost beyond belief in the twentieth century.

[34] U.N. General Assembly, Seventh Session, "Question of Impartial Investigation of Charges of Use by United Nations Forces of Bacteriological Warfare," Doc. A/2231 (Oct. 20, 1952).

[35] U.N. Doc. S/2802 (Oct. 8, 1952).

[36] U.N. General Assembly, Seventh Session, Plenary, *Official Records*, 428th Meeting (April 23, 1953).

The noted American surgeon, Dr. Charles W. Mayo of Rochester, Minnesota, alternate United States representative to the General Assembly in 1953, disclosed the story in a magnificent address to the Political Committee of the General Assembly on October 26, 1953.[37]

It is not a pretty story that confronts us. It is a story of terrible physical and moral degradation. It concerns men shaken loose from their foundations of moral value—men beaten down by the conditioning which the science of Pavlov reserves for dogs and rats—all in a vicious attempt to make them accomplices to a frightful lie. In an even deeper sense, the story we have to tell reflects a Communist system which deliberately flouts every principle of morality and truth, devoting itself to one sole object, the progress of Communism by any effective means, no matter how evil. . . .

Dr. Mayo then went on to deal with the circumstances of the six confessions which the Soviet Union had publicized in the reports of its so-called "scientific commission."

We know that the Communists accused at least 107 of our captured fliers of engaging in bacteriological warfare. Of these we know that 40 refused to sign any confession. Of the 36 that did sign, all under duress, some 20 were subjected to what can fairly be called extreme and prolonged physical and mental torture.

Dr. Mayo discussed the treatment of some of the captured fliers who had not confessed and others who had confessed but whose confessions were not publicized by the Communists. He then discussed the methods of extracting the confessions, suggesting that:

. . . The Communists were deliberately perverting to their ends essentially the same techniques which the famous Soviet biologist, Pavlov, used in experiments on dogs and rats. This technique, as

[37] U.S. Mission to the United Nations, Press Release 1786, Oct. 26, 1953: "Part 1 of Three Parts: The Question of Impartial Investigation of Charges of Use by United Nations Forces of Bacteriological Warfare," pp. 1-8.

you all know, is called the "conditioned reflex." when a rat goes through the wrong door he gets an electric shock. When he goes through the right door, he gets a bit of cheese. Before long, you can dispense with the shock and the cheese because the rat has been conditioned to enter the door you want him to enter. The Soviet regime has used this same technique against its own people in efforts to dislodge them from their traditional reverence to the Almighty and from their aspirations towards freedom; and to force them willy-nilly into the Communist slave pattern. . . . Consider the evidence of those who did not yield. A prisoner whom the Communists assume is already acting like an animal is offered in sharp terms a purely animal stimulus; food or death. The obvious animal response is expected. Yet in one case, a man was sentenced to death twelve times, and he refused to yield. Another man was made to dig his own grave, was taken before a firing squad, heard the command to fire, and heard the pistols click on empty chambers; and he refused to yield. Such testimony as this seems to teach us that the spirit of man can run deeper than the reflexes of Pavlov.

Dr. Mayo's address and the devastating testimony that he submitted to the General Assembly in the form of sworn statements by returned United States fliers, completely obliterated this second major Soviet propaganda campaign. Never thereafter were the Soviet statements in the disarmament discussions so completely devoid of substantive content and so totally subordinate to the rabble-rousing outpourings of the Communist propaganda machine. The complete Soviet propaganda defeat signaled by the enthusiastic endorsement of the United States position, even by states that were becoming increasingly critical of other United States actions, played a considerable role in setting the pattern of future arms control negotiations. It was, however, only one of a number of factors, since the period from the end of the Disarmament Commission discussions in September 1952 until the convening of the next set of serious discussions in May 1954 included some of the most significant events of recent world history.

X

Thaw

The General Assembly of 1952 convened in the midst of the political campaign that resulted in the election of General Dwight D. Eisenhower as President of the United States. Cohen resigned as United States representative in January 1953, and no successor was named for more than a year. The report of the Disarmament Commission was one of the last items on the agenda of the Political Committee and was not reached until late in March 1953 after a long Christmas recess. Unquestionably, one of the reasons for deferring consideration of this item was to permit the new administration to decide whether there should be modifications of the United States position.

In a general way, the new President confirmed in his inaugural address the objectives that the United States had carried into the arms control negotiations since 1951. He stated:

> In pleading our just cause before the bar of history and in pressing our labor for world peace, we shall be guided by certain fixed principles. These principles are: 1. Abhoring war as a chosen way to balk the purposes of those who threaten us, we hold it to be the first task of statesmanship to develop the strength that will deter the forces of aggression and promote the conditions of peace. . . .
> In the light of this principle, we stand ready to engage with

any and all others in joint effort to remove the causes of mutual fear and distrust among nations, so as to make possible drastic reduction of armaments. The sole requisites for undertaking such effort are that, in their purpose, they be aimed logically toward secure peace for all; and that—in their result—they provide methods by which every participating nation will prove good faith in carrying out its pledge.[1]

Within ten days after the General Assembly consideration of the report of the Disarmament Commission, the President had confirmed and indeed strengthened the previous United States positions on arms control. On April 16, 1953, in an address entitled "The Chance for Peace," the President reviewed the international situation pointing out the necessity of "the re-birth of trust among nations and the specific steps which might lead to such a re-birth of trust. . . . The first great step along this way must be the conclusion of an honorable armistice in Korea." The President then outlined other barriers requiring "just political settlements." Coming to the subject of disarmament, he stated:

As progress in all these areas strengthens world trust, we could proceed concurrently with the next great work—the reduction of the burden of armaments now weighing upon the world. To this end we would welcome and enter into the most solemn agreements. These could properly include:

1. The limitation, by absolute numbers or by an agreed international ratio, of the sizes of the military and security forces of all nations.

2. A commitment by all nations to set an agreed limit upon that proportion of total production of certain strategic materials to be devoted to military purposes.

3. International control of atomic energy to promote its use for peaceful purposes only and to insure the prohibition of atomic weapons.

[1] "Inaugural Address of Dwight D. Eisenhower," S. Doc. 9, 83 Cong. 1 sess. (Jan. 20, 1953).

4. A limitation or prohibition of other categories of weapons of great destructiveness.

5. The enforcement of all these agreed limitations and prohibitions by adequate safeguards, including a practical system of inspection under the United Nations.

The details of such disarmament programs are manifestly critical and complex. Neither the United States nor any other nation can properly claim to possess a perfect, immutable formula. But the formula matters less than the faith—the good faith without which no formula can work justly and effectively.

The fruit of success in all these tasks would present the world with the greatest task, and the greatest opportunity, of all. It is this: the dedication of the energies, the resources, and the imaginations of all peaceful nations to a new kind of war. This would be a declared total war, not upon any human enemy but upon the brute forces of poverty and need.[2]

While the United States was in a position to discuss disarmament in this General Assembly, the same could not be said of the Soviet Union. Stalin died less than two weeks before the commencement of the discussion, and the only public hint of the policy of his successors was found in two short sentences uttered by Georgi Malenkov, the new chairman of the Council of Ministers. "In the field of foreign policy, our main concern is to avert a new war and to live in peace with all countries. . . . States interested in the maintenance of peace can rest assured in the present as in the future of the solid peaceful policy of the Soviet Union."[3] Valerian Zorin, the Deputy Foreign Minister of the Soviet Union, had the difficult task of translating these words into a position in the General Assembly.

In his opening statement to the Political Committee of the General Assembly, Ernest Gross, the United States deputy representative to the United Nations, asked Zorin two questions:

[2] *The Chance for Peace,* address by President Eisenhower delivered before the American Society of Newspaper Editors, April 16, 1953, Department of State Publication 5042 (April 1953), pp. 6-8.
[3] "Statement of the Delegate of the U.S.S.R.," U.N. Doc. A/C.1/2563 (March 20, 1953), p. 1.

1. Is this a time when the Soviet Government is willing to discuss constructively the subject of disarmament which the Charter recognizes is so important for the attainment of conditions of peace? 2. Is this a forum in which the Soviet Representative will negotiate with his colleagues in order to give tangible form in this particular field to what the Soviet Rulers claim is their "tried and tested policy of peace?"[4]

Zorin did not answer these questions, but on March 19 delivered one of the longest speeches on disarmament ever presented to the United Nations, supplemented by a shorter speech on March 21. These statements reviewed in minute detail all of the Soviet objections to the Baruch Plan. The military budgets of the United States and its NATO allies received full coverage. Zorin analyzed in detail and rejected all of the papers the West had introduced into the Disarmament Commission. It is particularly interesting that he contended that

The United States proposal on the so-called essential principles of the disarmament programme had nothing in common with true disarmament or with any reduction of armaments or armed forces, nor did it have in mind the prohibition of the atomic weapons. It was quite clear that the whole proposal of the United States under the grandiloquent title of "Essential Principles for a Disarmament Programme" was mere empty phraseology, designed to delude public opinion.[5]

This was ironical in view of Khrushchev's later approval of these principles.[6]

Zorin's lengthy speeches did have one significance. However one-sided his presentation, he was dealing with the issues under consideration in the Disarmament Commission. The Soviet propaganda posi-

[4] U.N. General Assembly, Seventh Session, First Committee, *Official Records,* 577th Meeting (Mar. 18, 1953), p. 465, par. 4.
[5] *Ibid.,* 578th Meeting (Mar. 19, 1953), pp. 477-80 and 581st Meeting (Mar. 21, 1953), pp. 498-99.
[6] See Chap. 9, p. 183.

tions were all present in this speech, but they were subordinate to the discussion of the issues. This was a change for the better.

The Soviet draft resolution reprimanded the Disarmament Commission for not directing its efforts to approving the Soviet program and required the commission to proceed without delay to "decide the question of the unconditional prohibition of atomic weapons, bacterial weapons and other types of weapons of mass destruction, and of the establishment of strict international control in compliance with these decisions." The Soviet resolution had one innovation—in the field of conventional armaments, it called merely for "practical measures for achieving armaments reduction" instead of a one-third reduction of all armed forces and armaments.[7]

The United States co-sponsored a draft resolution that merely took note of the Disarmament Commission's report, commended the commission for its efforts, and reaffirmed the General Assembly resolution that had established the Disarmament Commission redefining its terms of reference in slightly simplified terms.[8]

In accordance with their usual custom, the Communists raised the issue of disarmament a second time through a Polish omnibus resolution dealing with a vast variety of political questions in addition to disarmament. There was nothing new in the Polish approach, and the Poles did not press their resolution to a vote after its sharp criticism by other delegations. The report by the President of the United States to the Congress on United States participation in the United Nations for the year 1953 concluded that "despite the fact that the Soviet statements in the disarmament discussions were less inflammatory than formerly, there was no indication at the Seventh General Assembly of any basic change in the Soviet position."[9]

The resolution of the seventh General Assembly, calling on the Disarmament Commission to continue its work, was dated April 8, 1953.[10]

[7] U.N. General Assembly, Seventh Session, First Committee, *Official Records,* Agenda Item 17 (March 19, 1953).
[8] Res. 704 (VII), April 8, 1953.
[9] *United States Participation in the United Nations, Report by the President to the Congress for the Year 1953,* Department of State Publication 5459 (August 1954), p. 56.
[10] Res. 704 (VII), April 8, 1953.

The eighth General Assembly was slated to convene early in September of the same year. The Disarmament Commission met only once between April and September for the purpose of adopting a report to the Assembly explaining why it had not met. The only statement at that meeting, by the Canadian representative, was to the effect that the commission "saw no useful purpose in meeting before the protracted and difficult armistice negotiations in Korea had been successfully concluded. . . . As the report indicates, we look to the future with greater hope that recent international events will indeed create a more propitious atmosphere for the resumption of our work." Vyshinsky moved the adoption of the report containing this explanation.[11]

THE SUBCOMMITTEE OF THE DISARMAMENT COMMISSION

In the eighth General Assembly the report of the Disarmament Commission came before the Political Committee during the first week of November. By that time, the new administration in the United States had been in office for ten months, and seven months had elapsed since the death of Stalin. Beria's bid for supreme power resulted in his execution in July, and the collaboration of Malenkov and Khrushchev was an apparent signal for a more moderate Soviet international policy.

The meetings of the Political Committee reflected an overwhelming world-wide sentiment that the Disarmament Commission should get back to work. The successful tests of hydrogen devices by the United States and by the Soviet Union on the very eve of the General Assembly accentuated the fears of the delegates. A large number of states other than the great powers participated actively in the discussions in the Political Committee and made suggestions, some of which were later incorporated into the resolution that the General Assembly adopted. In particular, Yugoslavia, India, and Australia participated actively.

[11] U.N. Disarmament Commission, *Official Records*, Doc. DC/PV.31 (Aug. 20, 1953), pp. 1-2.

The discussions in the Political Committee produced no substantive proposals but were devoted almost entirely to the dual purpose of expressing in the General Assembly resolution the world-wide concern arising from the increasing destructiveness of weapons and of perfecting the procedural framework of the Disarmament Commission in order to facilitate the negotiations. The Political Committee was partially successful in its efforts since its final resolution of November 28, 1953, was adopted with no negative votes and only the five abstentions of the Soviet bloc.[12] Without going into the many technical and procedural discussions that occupied twelve meetings of the Political Committee, the resolution itself was significant in two respects: (1) The Soviet Union was acquiescing in a definition of the problem of disarmament, which affirmed

the need of providing for: (a) The regulation, limitation and balanced reduction of all armed forces and all armaments, (b) The elimination and prohibition of atomic, hydrogen and other types of weapons of mass destruction, (c) The effective international control of atomic energy to ensure the prohibition of atomic weapons and the use of atomic energy for peaceful purposes only, the whole programme to be carried out under effective international control and in such a way that no State would have cause to fear that its security was endangered.

This statement of the problem was contained in the first paragraph of the preamble. (2) The Soviet Union was acquiescing in further talks among the great powers in an effort to secure agreement.

The sixth and seventh operating paragraphs of the resolution were extremely important.

The sixth paragraph suggested that the Disarmament Commission study the desirability of establishing a sub-committee consisting of representatives of the Powers principally involved, which should

[12] Res. 715 (VIII), Nov. 28, 1953.

seek in private an acceptable solution and report to the Disarmament Commission as soon as possible, in order that the Commission may study and report on such a solution to the General Assembly and to the Security Council not later than September 1, 1954. . . .

The seventh paragraph further suggested to the Disarmament Commission "in order to facilitate the progress of its work, to arrange for the sub-committee, when established, to hold its private meetings as appropriate in the different countries most concerned with the problem."[13] This was the origin of the Subcommittee of Five, which became the forum for all of the disarmament negotiations through 1957.

In international negotiations, it is ordinarily difficult to give credit for an idea or a suggestion to one individual or even one country. In this particular instance, however, Jules Moch correctly claimed and deserved credit for the suggestion.[14] Moch observed that the meetings of the representatives of the great powers in Paris in 1951 under the chairmanship of the President of the Assembly, Luis Padilla Nervo, compelled the Soviet leaders to concentrate on the main issues and to avoid ranging far and wide in presenting the entire Communist line on every issue even remotely related to disarmament. He sincerely believed that a renewed effort along the same lines—private informal meetings by the representatives of a few great powers—was the best method of bridging divergences and coming to agreed conclusions.

The resolution did not specify the composition of the subcommittee —"representatives of the powers principally involved." The Western powers suggested a Committee of Five: the Soviet Union, the United States, the United Kingdom, France, and Canada. The Soviet Union suggested three additional members, Czechoslovakia, India, and the Chinese Communists. Obviously, the United States could not accept Chinese Communists as participants in the discussions, and the Soviet Union would have found difficulty in accepting India without the Chinese Communists, since both are Asian powers. It was a favorable

---

[13] *Ibid.*

[14] U.N. Disarmament Commission, Subcommittee of the Disarmament Commission, Third Meeting, *Verbatim Record*, Doc. DC/SC.1/PV.3 (May 14, 1954) p. 18. (Cited hereafter by document number and date.)

omen that the Soviet representative, while objecting for record purposes to the omission of the Chinese Communists, nevertheless acquiesced in the Western proposal to limit the subcommittee to five.[15]

After an organization meeting in New York on April 23, 1954, the subcommittee decided to commence its sessions in London in the middle of May. Thus, for the first time since August 1952, the great powers were again engaging in substantive discussions of arms control problems.

The most important event of the 1953 General Assembly had occurred at the very end of the session, the December 8, 1953 address of President Eisenhower to the Assembly on the peaceful uses of the atom.[16] This eloquent statement of the increasing perils of nuclear warfare, coupled with the hope of a better world inherent in the peaceful utilization of the atom, created an atmosphere of enthusiasm and hope in the General Assembly.

The President's address was directed primarily to the new conditions stemming from the development of thermonuclear weapons, which were to require a complete reappraisal of United States policies toward arms control. This reappraisal had scarcely started in December 1953, and neither the President's speech nor the forthcoming reappraisal of policy greatly affected the 1954 disarmament negotiations. Therefore, the President's address can more readily be considered as a part of the later United States reappraisal of its policies.

THE FIRST SESSION OF THE

SUBCOMMITTEE

The first session of the subcommittee was not a "Summit Meeting" in that the delegates were several layers removed from chiefs of states. However, the high caliber of the representation of all states assured that if the Soviet Union were willing to enter into serious negotiations,

[15] U.N. Doc. DC./SC.1/PV.1/Rev. 1 (May 3, 1954), p. 3.
[16] *Atomic Power for Peace*, address by President Eisenhower before the General Assembly of the United Nations Dec. 8, 1953, Department of State Publication 5314 (December 1953).

the Western powers could respond. The United Kingdom was represented by its Minister of State, Selwyn Lloyd, who had been dealing with the problems of arms control ever since his initial appearance in the General Assembly of 1951. Jules Moch, the great statesman in all disarmament negotiations, continued to represent the French. Canada was represented by its two highest ranking diplomats, initially Lester Pearson, its Foreign Minister, and, later, Norman Robertson, its High Commissioner in London, who had been dealing with the problem of disarmament ever since the end of World War I. The United States representative, Morehead Patterson, in contrast had no experience in the field of disarmament and had never before represented the United States in a major diplomatic assignment. Indeed, he had received his assignment less than a month prior to the commencement of the London discussions. Nevertheless, Patterson was generally qualified both by temperament and background for an assignment of this nature. Malik was delighted to deal with an American businessman whom he considered to be the true representative of the American capitalistic system. Patterson acquired rapidly the necessary *expertise* in connection with this highly technical subject, and by the middle of the series of meetings, participated successfully in even the most technical debates. The Soviet representative was Malik, the Soviet Ambassador in London.

Between May 13 and June 22, when the subcommittee recessed, it met nineteen times.[17] All of the meetings were in private followed by uninformative joint communiqués to the press. None of the delegates gave either interviews or informal briefings to the press. The secrecy of the meetings was carried to such a point that *Punch* magazine wrote a highly amusing article about the conference that was "so secret" that everyone forgot about it. This policy of extreme secrecy went some distance toward eliminating from the discussions the Soviet propaganda statements that had become almost routine on this subject. However, as the meetings developed without agreement, the representatives began to realize that ultimately their statements would become public property. To a large extent, this neutralized the benefits of private

[17] U.S. Department of State, *The Record on Disarmament*, Publication 5581 (1954), p. 1.

meetings. While the meetings of the subcommittee in subsequent years theoretically continued to be private, in fact both the United States and Soviet delegates disclosed the contents of the meetings to the press in private briefings immediately following the meetings. The meetings had no agenda or plan of work. At the first meeting in London on May 17, Selwyn Lloyd outlined three groups of problems and suggested that the discussions commence with the first group and proceed to the second and third groups.[18] None of the delegates in practice adhered to this suggestion. The three groups of problems overlapped, and the vast majority of the statements of the delegates tended to cover the entire field of arms control.

Jules Moch in his first statement to the subcommittee suggested the procedural device that three years later became fundamental to the negotiations. He said: "Our meetings will be either private like today's, or secret, as we may appoint. In both cases we shall be able to follow the procedure which I may call that of 'agreements subject to reservation,' for which public meetings are unsuitable."[19]

Moch went on to point out that the Soviet Union was certain to call for the unconditional prohibition of the atomic weapon and that the Western powers could not consent to that in the form in which it was proposed, prior to agreement on other points. In a private meeting, however, it would be possible to agree to the unconditional prohibition of the atomic weapon provided agreement could be reached on the subject of control. The subcommittee could then proceed to the discussion of the problem of control.

. . . But as we cannot discuss them simultaneously we have no alternative but to take them one by one, a method that the private nature of our Sub-committee and the procedure of agreements "subject to reservation" will allow us to adopt. This first method, indeed, will enable us to agree to discuss unconditional prohibition and to concur perhaps in a provisional formula which will only become final in the event of agreement being reached on the other controversial points. . . .

If we are all ready to accept some such method of work, as I

[18] U.N. Doc. DC/SC.1/PV.2 (May 13, 1954), p. 18.
[19] U.N. Doc. DC/SC.1/PV.3 (May 14, 1954), p. 18 et seq.

earnestly hope we are, we may have good ground for hope, since all progress made in one direction in the shape of agreements subject to reservation, will lead to further progress in other fields and perhaps on the same lines. Then, when we have completed our work, we shall find—at least I hope so—that all reservations put forward on one side or another will cancel each other out and the only remaining text will be one without reservations that can be submitted unanimously to the Disarmament Commission.[20]

This statesmanlike suggestion facilitated the negotiations even during these meetings and to a much greater degree three years later. Nevertheless, it somewhat increased the tendency of the delegates to skip from one group of problems to another and greatly increased the problem of describing the negotiations. The most important discussions can be described under three headings: (1) the fundamental issue of control of atomic energy; (2) the Soviet proposal to prohibit the use of nuclear weapons; and (3) timing and phasing (the relation of limitations and safeguards). This grouping of problems is only to facilitate their presentation and in no way corresponded to any plan of work, explicit or implicit, in the subcommittee.

The Fundamental Issue: Control of Atomic Energy

Malik in his first statement to the subcommittee immediately after placing in the record his official unhappiness about the absence of the Chinese Communists from the discussions, came directly to the main point.

What have the Western Powers brought with them to the Subcommittee, in particular the United States, Britain and France? Have they again brought to this Sub-committee the long outdated and defunct Baruch Plan, or are they here with the serious intention of finding a solution to the problem of prohibiting atomic and

[20] *Ibid.*, p. 20.

hydrogen weapons and bringing about a considerable reduction in armaments?

These were Malik's opening words. He then went on with excessive verbiage to the climax of his talk, his main objection to the Baruch Plan.

As regards the control of atomic-energy plants, the United States continues to object to the immediate establishment of control over such undertakings. At the same time reference is made to the need for such control to be considered in remote and indeterminate successive stages of some sort. That is the fundamental difference between the Soviet Union position and that of the United States, supported by the United Kingdom and France.

We are for immediate prohibition and control; they are against prohibition and only in favour of control over atomic raw materials as a "first stage."[21]

Malik pointed out that the disclosure of nuclear secrets and with it the prohibition and elimination of nuclear weapons, came only at the end of the program proposed in the Baruch Plan. The disclosure and verification proposals likewise relegated the disclosure of important atomic secrets to the fifth and last stage. He expressed this thought with considerable humor in his second statement to the subcommittee.

Gentlemen, I must frankly say that, reflecting on the idea of a fifth stage, I draw the following conclusions. The ancient Greeks and Romans devised a very humourous proverb. If they knew that something would never happen, they used to say it would be put off till the Greek Kalends—ad Kalendas Graecas. I think the Americans have invented their own version of the Greek Kalends, summed up in the two words "fifth stage." . . . I mean to say, if something is never going to happen, then we can say it will happen at the fifth stage.[22]

[21] *Ibid.*, pp. 26, 34.
[22] U.N. Doc. DC/SC.1/PV.4 (May 19, 1954), p. 31.

In his first statement to the subcommittee, Malik reintroduced the identical proposals the Soviet Union had made in the previous General Assembly and that had been rejected. This was disappointing since the objective of forming a subcommittee was to move away from the old formula that had failed to achieve any agreement. This disappointment, however, was more than counterbalanced by the other factors. In the first place, Malik had seized directly on the main substantive issue which had separated the Soviet position and the Western position since 1946. This was a complete change from the Soviet tactics pursued since 1947, of delaying the discussions and seeking to obscure the issues. The second favorable factor was that Malik was inserting some humor into the discussions, a quality completely absent from all previous negotiations on arms control.

The Western powers had come to the meetings with two positions that modified the Baruch proposals—the United States control organ paper and certain proposals for phasing and timing of both safeguards and limitations and reductions of armaments (the Anglo-French memorandum). The time was not ripe to introduce these papers. The Western powers had learned that introduction of a paper on safeguards would serve no purpose except in the framework of limitations and reductions. Similarly these powers wished to launch the phasing and timing paper in circumstances most propitious for a favorable Soviet response. This required several weeks of constant probing and adjustments of the paper to come as close as the basic position would permit to the Soviet views.

Therefore, Patterson at this time had no choice but to give the inevitable answer to Malik's question on the United States attitude toward the Baruch Plan.

They [the Baruch proposals] were good proposals when they were made and, so far as I know, none better have been devised since. There have been changes in detail but, so far as the broad outlines and basic philosophy are concerned, these proposals still stand in our judgment as comprehensive and excellent approaches to the general problem. . . .

The United States continues to be flexible in its views on the regulation and control of atomic energy. The position of the United Nations, which is also the position of the United States, is that the United Nations Plan shall continue to be a basis of control until, and only until, a better or no less effective plan is put forward.[23]

Malik said that the United States reiteration of its position of support for the Baruch Plan, unless and until a better and no less effective plan could be devised, set his teeth on edge. He persisted in asking whether anything in the Western position would permit either the disclosure of nuclear weapons or their elimination from national armaments prior to the last stage of the plan for international control of atomic energy.

The initial United States indication of a flexible position was linked to the presentation to the subcommittee of the paper dealing with an international control organ. Patterson submitted this paper to the subcommittee at its ninth meeting on May 25. At the start of his statement he said:

Before I comment on that working paper, I should like to say for the record and in order to clear the air, temporarily at least, that the United States does not insist that the United Nations Plan referred to this morning is the only way to carry into effect the prohibition of atomic weapons and the use of atomic energy for peaceful purposes only. We are ready to examine in a constructive spirit any other proposals that will bring about an effective prohibition. I bring that in now as an earnest of the fact that at the end of our remarks on the control paper, I will refer to it again at greater length![24]

The control paper itself both in its terms and in the spirit in which it was submitted to the subcommittee, was the answer to Malik's question. Patterson emphasized that the paper "is not a final unalterable position of the United States Government." The United States wished

[23] U.N. Doc. DC/SC.1/PV.5 (May 22, 1954), pp. 3 and 4.
[24] U.N. Doc. DC/SC.1/PV.9 (May 25, 1954), p. 4.

. . . the view of the United Kingdom, France, Canada and the Soviet Union. Ambassador Lodge emphasized in the Disarmament Commission that "an acceptable solution" as is called for by the General Assembly Resolution of last November means a solution acceptable to all of us who are sitting here in the Subcommittee. This holds for the general subject of disarmament and it holds for the specific topic with which this paper deals.

Patterson continued:

Mr. Malik has forcibly pointed out to us that there is no point in discussing the details of a control organ until we know what the organ is going to control. I find this reasonable enough. Accordingly, the second paragraph of our paper states briefly, but in our opinion adequately, the objectives of the control organ. Make no mistake about this: the first and one of the most important objectives of the control organ is to see to it that if atomic weapons are prohibited they remain prohibited forever. This objective of the control organ—and I quote from the paper—is "to provide international control of atomic energy, so as to enforce observance of prohibition and elimination of atomic and hydrogen weapons, and to ensure use of nuclear materials for peaceful purposes."[25]

Patterson went on to concede that the control organ "would be an infringement on the sovereignty of States accepting the authority of the control organ if we use the term 'sovereignty' in the strict sense in which it was used during, say, the nineteenth century." The paper "sought to reduce to a minimum all such interference through granting to the control organ only the minimum powers which are required to carry out its functions." Patterson next pointed out in the strongest terms the flexibility of this United States position.

The control organ as we envisage it in this paper is even consistent with the Soviet Union disarmament proposals. I do not mean to infer that if we should add this paper to the Soviet Union

[25] *Ibid.*, pp. 5-6.

proposals, we should then have a program acceptable to us in its entirety for the regulation of armaments. We definitely would not. There are flaws and gaps in the Soviet proposals beyond their failure to elaborate on the control organ. The only point I want to make is that the control organ as we have drawn it up here would be as applicable to a program based upon the Soviet Union concepts, as sketched over the past seven years, as it is to the United States program.[26]

After elaborating only slightly on the details of the paper, Patterson gave his answer to Malik's question as to whether the United States continued to insist on the Baruch Plan for the control of atomic energy.

Well, being here at this meeting is the best earnest that we can offer of the fact that we have not—and I repeat "not"—a fixed position on the United Nations Plan. We have continually stated that we are not standing on any plan. We are actively seeking new and advanced and up-to-date plans. We hope that such a plan may appear from Mr. Lloyd's efforts. So much for that particular question.[27]

The control organ paper itself in two respects moved away from the United Nations Plan. In the first place, as Patterson had pointed out, the structure and authority of the control organ in no way depended on the adoption of the Baruch Plan. It could apply even in the event of the adoption of the Soviet plan.

In the second place, the control organ was given four specific powers in connection with violations of the treaty establishing the system for the control of atomic energy.

a. Calling upon the offending state to remedy within a reasonable time the violations or other infractions; b. bringing about the suspension of the supply of nuclear materials to the offending state; c. closing of plants utilizing nuclear materials in the offending state;

[26] *Ibid.,* pp. 6-8.
[27] *Ibid.,* p. 12.

d. reporting to the Security Council, to the General Assembly and to all States the violation or other infractions in order to permit appropriate action by the United Nations or by individual states in connection with the international convention establishing the control organ.[28]

The first three powers were appropriate for remedying minor violations. Clearly, the only way to remedy a major violation was contained in d., "reporting to the United Nations." Military action by the United Nations to remedy the violation could come only from the Security Council in which the Soviet Union had its veto. Thus paragraph 41 d. of this paper marked the end of United States adherence to the original Baruch position that all states should give up their veto in the Security Council in connection with measures to punish violations of the treaty for the control of atomic energy.

Philip Noel-Baker concludes that the Soviet change of policy, which made possible the negotiations from 1955 through 1957, stemmed from the statements of Selwyn Lloyd and Patterson virtually abandoning the United Nations Plan for atomic energy control.[29] While Patterson and his advisers did not at the time foresee any such far-reaching result, in perspective there is much to be said for the soundness of this conclusion.

The paper itself played no great role in subsequent arms control negotiations. Patterson correctly commented: "It is true that a great deal of effort and thought has gone into the production of this paper, which certainly reflects the best judgment of the individuals who worked on it."[30] The paper was in fact little more than a check list of some of the problems that would be encountered when states got around to establishing a control organ. Stassen made no use of the paper during the later discussions. It was of help when the Preparatory Commission of the International Atomic Energy Agency began planning the structure of the agency, largely because by a coincidence the chief authors of the paper also worked on the structure of the

[28] U.N. Doc. DC/SC.1/5 (May 25, 1954), p. 11.
[29] Philip Noel-Baker, *The Arms Race* (1958), p. 225.
[30] U.N. Doc. DC/SC.1/PV.9 (May 25, 1954), p. 5.

agency. However, when the disarmament negotiations themselves came to the specifics of forming an organization to monitor a treaty prohibiting nuclear tests, there was no resemblance to the organ envisaged in this paper.

In the discussion of the control organ paper, Malik never got beyond the first paragraph, which referred to the General Assembly resolution of January 11, 1952, that the Soviet Union had opposed. All efforts to secure a paragraph by paragraph consideration failed on the ostensible ground that the Soviet Union could not accept the first paragraph.[31] In effect, however, Malik rejected the paper by repeating previous Soviet positions that would make it impossible for the control organ to detect clandestine activities contrary to the disarmament treaty.[32]

Ban the Bomb

The Soviet Union made three proposals during the session. The first introduced at the first London meeting was the same Soviet proposal that the General Assembly had consistently rejected year after year. The third Soviet proposal introduced almost at the end of the meetings, on June 11, 1954, added to the first proposal the Soviet suggestions for an international control organ presented to the United Nations Atomic Energy Commission on June 11, 1947, seven years earlier to the day.[33] The only significance of this third proposal was that it marked a reversal of the Soviet trend toward substituting short slogans for detailed plans. The Soviet Union once again was as specific as in 1947, a change for the better.

The second Soviet proposal, introduced on June 1, was considerably more significant. It read as follows:

The Disarmament Commission deems it essential that, as an important step towards achieving complete elimination from the arma-

---

[31] U.N. Doc. DC/SC.1/PV.13 (June 3, 1954), p. 39.
[32] U.S. Department of State, The Record on Disarmament, pp. 7-8.
[33] Ibid., p. 10.

ments of all States of atomic, hydrogen and other types of weapons of mass destruction, together with the simultaneous establishment of strict international control securing the observance of an agreement to prohibit the use of atomic energy for military purposes, the States concerned should assume a solemn and unconditional obligation not to employ atomic, hydrogen or other weapons of mass destruction.[34]

This was in essence the Stockholm Appeal. The logical and foreseeable outcome of both of the major Soviet propaganda campaigns over the past several years, the Stockholm Appeal and the bacteriological warfare campaign with its corollary of the United Nations endorsing the Geneva Protocol of 1925, was this exact resolution. In the atmosphere of 1949 and 1950, however, this resolution would have been offered to the General Assembly itself with the greatest publicity with partisans of peace marching in the streets, with twenty-four hour strikes all over the world to ensure its passage, with the Soviet radio blasting away about the demands of the peoples of the world for action. In contrast, it was offered in a meeting that was secret not only in theory but in fact. This probably reflected the collapse of the Soviet propaganda campaigns.

The second novelty of Malik's approach was that he carefully explained that this resolution should be deemed "as a first step towards the realization of this great and noble aim (the broader Soviet programme)."[35]

For the first time, the Soviet Union had suggested something less than a complete package calling for decisions on prohibition of nuclear weapons and extensive reductions of other weapons in advance of the establishment of a control system. Jules Moch was ready for this development. Instantly, he pointed out the resemblance between this protocol and the Geneva protocols prohibiting the use of gas, chemical, and bacterial weapons. In ratifying the Geneva Protocol, the Soviet Union had made the specific reservation, "That the said Protocol shall

[34] Ibid., p. 11.
[35] U.N. Doc. DC/SC.1/PV.12 (June 1, 1954), p. 23.

cease to be binding on the Government of the Union of Soviet Socialist Republics in regard to all enemy States whose armed forces or whose allies *de jure* or in fact do not respect restrictions which are the object of this Protocol." Moch inferred "that if the Soviet Union were attacked by an enemy using gas and atomic bombs at the same time it would regard itself as entitled to counter a gas attack with gas but not to use atomic bombs. We have here a pretty glaring discrepancy."[36] At an earlier date Moch had asked whether:

> If a country is attacked either by an incursion of armed forces which have not received permission to be stationed on its territory, or by an atomic bombardment of any sort, the Government of that country must regard itself as still bound by the ban on the use of the atomic weapon, or whether the attack which it has suffered—either from armed forces or from the bombardment—will entitle it to defend itself by all the means which may remain available to it during the period preceding, of course, the destruction or conversion to peaceful purposes of all stocks.

Malik immediately asked Moch "whether these are your questions alone or whether the United States delegation associates itself with them, too."[37]

Malik was somewhat embarrassed by Moch's inquiry, since a concession that atomic bombs might be used in retaliation would cast doubt on one of the arguments to support the earlier and broader Soviet position calling for a decision on the prohibition of atomic weapons. After much verbiage, Malik finally reached the following conclusion:

> Mr. Moch cannot deny that atomic and hydrogen weapons are a special type of weapons. On that account, to make a reservation concerning the use of these weapons in the declaration on renunciation of their use would mean to start towards sanctioning them,

[36] *Ibid.*, pp. 32, 33-35.
[37] U.N. Doc. DC/SC.1/PV.8 (May 25, 1954), pp. 52-53.

and legalizing the use of atomic weapons of mass destruction. The Soviet Union and its people cannot follow such a road. The policy of the Soviet Union is abstinence from the use of atomic and hydrogen weapons—that is, that these weapons as weapons of mass destruction should never be used for military purposes.[38]

The Western answer to this Soviet proposal was summarized as follows by Patterson in his report to the Secretary of State:

. . . In 1950 world communism made its greatest propaganda campaign since the Second World War when it launched the Stockholm Appeal. Radio, mass meetings, petitions, parades—all known media of information—were used to support the Stockholm Appeal which among other things called for an unconditional declaration prohibiting the use of atomic weapons and declaring the first government to use atomic weapons a war criminal. The Soviet Union introduced a resolution incorporating the Stockholm Appeal in the 1950 General Assembly—a resolution which was overwhelmingly rejected. Last fall in the Eighth General Assembly the Soviet Union submitted a similar proposal which was again rejected.

It was therefore apparent that there was nothing new in substance about the Soviet proposal of June 1. However, this proposal had some interesting implications which we had not fully discussed in previous General Assemblies, and therefore we dealt with the proposal at considerable length. The United States made a number of points in the Subcommittee which I shall summarize.

First, the Soviet representative was careful to explain that this pledge was merely to be the first step to lead to a comprehensive disarmament program. We pointed out that during this first stage and until we have a comprehensive disarmament program, we would have nothing more than the solemn pledges of the Great Powers not to use atomic weapons. We have those pledges already, subject to one and only one condition—that condition being the

[38] U.N. Doc. DC/SC.1/PV.12 (June 1, 1954), pp. 64, 65-70. See also U.N. Doc. DC/SC.1/PV.13 (June 3, 1954), p. 39.

equally sacred pledge under the Charter of the United Nations not to commit aggression.

Second, during this first stage of the Soviet program, there would be no safeguards of any nature to insure the observance of the pledges. We pointed out that the nature of *our* democratic institutions and way of life would preclude any violation of our pledge even if we wanted to. Unfortunately, we had no such assurance with respect to the Soviet Union. While the Iron Curtain, which Mr. Malik described as a capitalistic myth, has its cracks, the amount that can be observed through those cracks was small indeed. It would be entirely possible that preparations could be made to annihilate the West without our having any advance knowledge of Soviet actions or intentions. The past record of the Soviet Union was such that we could not sleep comfortably so long as our security was dependent upon a bare, naked, unsafeguarded pledge.[39]

The Anglo-French Memorandum

During the 1952 sessions of the Disarmament Commission, Jules Moch made the point that any treaty for arms limitation would of necessity have to include a series of decisions on limitations and prohibitions. It would also include control mechanisms to ensure the observance of the limitations and prohibitions. Presumably these control mechanisms would be based on the continuing disclosure and verification of all required information. The Western powers submitted papers calling for certain prohibitions and limitations, and also a paper requiring the disclosure and verification of all information concerning both conventional and atomic weapons in stages. But the Western position nowhere suggested a synchronization of the prohibitions and limitations into the stages of disclosure and verification. Moch even suggested a method of synchronization.

(1) Each limitation or prohibition should be undertaken only after

[39] U.S. Department of State, *The Record on Disarmament*, pp. 11-12.

the previous one had been achieved and so certified by a designated international organ; (2) each limitation or prohibition should be subject to the establishment and functioning of the corresponding control mechanism. Once the qualified organ has found that its specific achievement had been properly carried out and that the control scheme was capable of verifying compliance with the following one, the matter should be undertaken automatically.

Malik did not wish to discuss Moch's suggestions without further study and the suggestion went no further during the 1952 discussions.[40]

Selwyn Lloyd brought the matter before the subcommittee in his first statement.

The Disarmament Commission already has before it a working paper submitted by the United States Representative in April 1952. This proposed five stages for disclosure and verification. Perhaps we might look at this paper again and see whether it offers today a better chance of agreement than it did in 1952. We shall have to consider at what point in any programme of disclosure the first steps in disarmament and the first steps towards the elimination of prohibited armaments should commence. We shall have to consider, I suggest, whether we can draw up the complete programme or timetable which we envisage for the completion of an agreed programme covering disclosure and verification and the abolition of the use, possession and manufacture of atomic and hydrogen or other weapons of mass destruction and the major reductions in conventional armaments and armed forces which we consider must come into force simultaneously.[41]

The memorandum of the British and French to establish such a timetable of disarmament did not appear until practically the end of the sessions. It was first discussed informally with the Soviet repre-

[40] U.N. Disarmament Commission, *Official Records*, Special Supplement No. 1, "Second Report of the Disarmament Commission," pp. 123, 126.
[41] U.N. Doc. DC/SC.1/PV.2 (May 17, 1954), p. 23.

sentative at two private meetings in the second week of June, when the sole participants were the delegates themselves, each accompanied by one adviser. The United Nations was represented by one interpreter. No minutes were taken of these meetings, and any private reports from the delegations themselves to their Foreign Offices remained classified. Some changes were made in the paper as a result of the meetings, and it was formally submitted to the subcommittee at its seventeenth meeting on June 14.[42] This highly significant document has continued as a basis for Western positions on arms control.[43] The memorandum was properly described as a "possible basis for compromise" between the Soviet position, that the decisions to prohibit nuclear weapons and to limit conventional weapons must precede the establishment of the international control system, and the Western position, that until the establishment of the control system, the prohibitions and limitations could not come into effect.

The main points of this memorandum may be summarized as follows:

The first numbered paragraph was the Western answer to the Soviet proposal for an initial renunciation of the use of nuclear weapons. It referred to the provision of the United Nations Charter under which all Members of the United Nations have assumed the obligation to refrain in their international relations from the threat or use of force against the territorial integrity or political independence of any state. The paragraph called on all states signatory to a disarmament treaty to pledge themselves to refrain "from the use of nuclear weapons except in defence against aggression."

The second paragraph stated the objectives of the disarmament treaty—prohibition of nuclear weapons, major reductions in all armed forces and conventional armaments, and the establishment of a control organ.

The first clause of the fifth paragraph provided the formula for synchronizing controls with the proposed limitations and prohibitions:

[42] U.S. Department of State, *The Record on Disarmament*, p. 1. The author was present at these meetings.
[43] U.N. Doc. DC/SC.1/10 (June 11, 1954), pp. 21-22.

"After the constitution and positioning of the control organ, which shall be carried out within a specified time, and as soon as the control organ reports it is able effectively to enforce them, the following measures shall enter into effect." The remainder of paragraph five and paragraphs six and seven described in general terms the stages of disarmament now reduced to three. The first stage would be a freeze on military man power and military expenditure both atomic and non-atomic as of December 31, 1953. In the second stage, half of the agreed reductions of conventional armaments and armed forces would take effect, and on the completion of these reductions, the manufacture of all kinds of nuclear weapons and all other prohibited weapons would cease. In the third stage, the second half of the agreed reductions of conventional armaments and armed forces would take effect, and on the completion of this second half of the reductions, the total prohibition and elimination of nuclear weapons and the conversion of existing stocks of nuclear materials to peaceful purposes would be carried out. Likewise the total prohibition and elimination of all other prohibited weapons would be carried out. The eighth paragraph provided:

It is hoped that when all the measures enumerated above have been carried out, the armaments and armed forces of the Powers will be further reduced to the level strictly necessary for the maintenance of international security and the fulfillment of the obligations of signatory states under the terms of the United Nations Charter.

Immediately after Selwyn Lloyd and Jules Moch had presented the proposal to the seventeenth meeting of the subcommittee, Malik stated that the Soviet delegation had not sufficient time and opportunity to make a careful study of the proposals. After thus qualifying his entire position, he rejected them.[44] Malik's statement was somewhat more vituperative than his other statements, probably for the purpose of making a record. At that time all the delegates realized that the full minutes of the meetings would inevitably be submitted

[44] U.N. Doc. DC/SC.1/PV.17 (June 14, 1954), pp. 36-43.

to the Disarmament Commission and to the United Nations General Assembly.

Moch's comment on Malik's analysis (using a figure of speech that Patterson had placed in the record) was:

> I felt as if I were looking into one of those distorting mirrors which make the thinnest people appear fat or shapeless and give immense pleasure to children and, sometimes, even to grown-ups. To-day, however, I can take no pleasure in such systematic distortion. I deplore it, since I see postponed, perhaps *sine die,* hopes to which we had clung, to which I had clung despite the warnings of many skeptical spirits and also practical measures the need for which we believe is daily becoming more imperative.[45]

At the end of the meeting, Patterson spoke briefly concerning the proposal.

> We find the suggestions made in the French-United Kingdom memorandum in general not inconsistent with basic United States concepts, and we give the memorandum as interpreted by Mr. Lloyd our support. We believe that when sufficient progress has been made to enable a specific treaty to be drafted, with a description of each particular step, the scheme will turn out to be considerably more complicated than would appear from the outline in the memorandum. That, however, is a matter of detail.
>
> At the same time, we are not inflexible and do not take the position that this is the only plan of phasing of the various elements of a disarmament program which would conform to United States views.[46]

The United States had participated in all stages of drafting the paper, which fully accorded with United States policy. Patterson's statement of caution that a specific treaty would turn out to be considerably more complicated than would appear from the outline was

---

[45] *Ibid.,* p. 59.
[46] *Ibid.,* p. 76.

the first intimation in the disarmament negotiations that the hydrogen blast at Eniwetok was forcing a reappraisal of all past arms control positions. While all the representatives on occasions recognized the greater urgency arising from the development of thermonuclear weapons, there was no specific suggestion of a changed approach.

Malik's rejection of the Anglo-French memorandum was anticipated. The memorandum was submitted at far too late a date in the proceedings to permit a thorough Soviet study. However, submission at an earlier date would have assured an unsatisfactory Soviet reaction. Moch optimistically predicted that the favorable response might come when the Disarmament Commission would meet to consider the report of its subcommittee.[47]

The remaining three meetings of the subcommittee were devoted largely to completing the record for submission to the Disarmament Commission. Patterson emphatically rejected the Soviet proposals in the eighteenth meeting and, as anticipated, in the nineteenth meeting, Malik attacked Patterson personally, accusing him among other things of being the representative of Wall Street and having eighteen Latin American states under his thumb.[48] The twentieth and final meeting of the subcommittee on June 22 was devoted entirely to approval of the subcommittee report.[49]

SIGNS OF A THAW

The substantive record of the subcommittee gave little indication of any intention of the Soviet Union to attempt to accommodate itself to the Western viewpoint. The one possible sign of flexibility was Malik's emphasis and reiteration that the Soviet proposal for renunciation of use of nuclear weapons prior to any action on the broader proposals for nuclear and conventional disarmament was a new approach. This statement turned out to be of major importance when in later years the Soviet Union suggested other and less controversial measures that could precede the adoption of its general program of disarmament.

[47] *Ibid.*, p. 71.
[48] U.N. Doc. DC/SC.1/PV.18 (June 15, 1954), pp. 1-31. U.N. Doc. DC/SC.1/PV.19 (June 17, 1954), p. 31.
[49] U.S. Department of State, *The Record on Disarmament*, p. 14.

Apart from the substance of the discussions, however, the atmosphere of the negotiations was far more relaxed than any previous negotiation. The personal relationships of the Western negotiators almost approached cordiality. Much of the credit for this goes to Patterson. During the earlier part of the negotiations, the United States was the target for most of the Soviet propaganda thrusts. It was apparent that the initial tactic of the Soviet Union was to drive a wedge between the United States, on the one hand, and the United Kingdom, France, and Canada, on the other.[50] Patterson's geniality and goodwill went a long distance in preventing the deterioration of the meetings into pure propaganda contests.

For the first time in the arms control negotiations, the seriousness of the negotiations was occasionally lightened by humor. Some of this appeared in the verbatim records. On May 20, when Patterson was acting as chairman of the meeting, a pigeon kept smashing its head against the huge plate glass window in the beautiful room in Lancaster House where the meetings took place. Patterson observed: "I should just like to observe that the dove of peace has just made an unsuccessful attempt to enter this room through the window. Perhaps we should consider that as a good omen, and during our future discussions, should leave the window slightly ajar." Malik, always anxious to score a debating point, smilingly replied:

> After to-day's speech by Mr. Patterson, the United States Representative, I think that I should not be in error if I summed up the situation by saying that the United States Representative has emptied a cup of cold water over the whole work of the Subcommittee.
>
> Precisely for this reason the dove of peace has taken alarm and has not flown into our room but, after hearing about Mr. Patterson's speech, has flown off again.[51]

Among symptoms of an improving atmosphere was the Soviet willingness, indeed insistence, on discussing the major points of divergence

[50] Ibid., pp. 3, 4.
[51] U.N. Doc. DC/SC.1/PV.5 (May 22, 1954), pp. 35, 36.

between the East and West; and the Soviet return to considerably more detailed proposals than those made between 1948 and this meeting.

Outside the meetings, the improvement in the negotiating atmosphere was even more noticeable. For the first time since 1947, the Western representatives at the official level became socially acquainted with their Soviet counterparts. The series of cocktail parties initiated by the United States delegation included all of the Soviet advisers. On all procedural problems, such as the timing of meetings and the preparation of the subcommittee report, the relationships between the Soviet delegation and the Western delegations were highly satisfactory, and at times, even cordial.

At the end of the session, a senior adviser of Malik suggested to his opposite numbers in the British and United States delegations that the Western delegations should study carefully the second proposal of the Soviet Union for the renunciation of the use of nuclear weapons, together with Malik's statement introducing this proposal, inferring that it presaged a Soviet change of position. The British adviser then suggested that the Soviet Union should study carefully the Anglo-French memorandum, which also presaged a change of position. The Soviet adviser agreed and stated that such a study was being made. He would not predict when the results would emerge but described the new and unannounced Soviet decisions to encourage close cultural and economic relationships with the West. The Soviet Union hoped that Western musicians would appear in Moscow and Soviet musicians in New York and London. The Soviet Union hoped for increasing trade. Two large new hotels were under construction in Moscow to encourage tourism in the Soviet Union. The Soviet adviser went on to point out that a policy for broader international contacts was extremely difficult to achieve in the Soviet Union since the vast majority of Soviet officials had practically no interest in international matters. He likened them to the isolationists in the United States.

These predictions turned out to be accurate. Increasing cultural and economic contacts between the East and West became the policy of both Malenkov and Khrushchev. The Soviet Union announced with great fanfare, that it was making a major change in its position toward arms control three months later when the 1954 General Assembly convened.

THE THAW BECOMES OFFICIAL

In the Disarmament Commission discussion of the report of the first session of the subcommittee, neither the West nor the Soviet Union went any further than to restate their positions with unaccustomed brevity. At the opening of the General Assembly, however, on September 30, the Soviet representative introduced a proposal, the most significant feature of which was to suggest that the British-French memorandum be used as a basis for an international disarmament treaty.[52] The Soviet representative, Mr. Vyshinsky, set forth his proposal in such a manner as to create the impression that the Soviet Union had accepted practically the entire Western position and that with little difficulty it would be possible to reach agreement between the Soviet Union and the West. As a result of detailed discussions, which were far more precise than any disarmament discussions since the rejection of the Baruch Plan in 1948, it became clear that the differences between the Soviet Union and the West had narrowed, but not to the extent claimed by Mr. Vyshinsky. In the field of conventional armaments, the Soviet Union was accepting the Western position that the approach should be through establishing fixed ceilings for the armed forces and reducing armed forces from the present levels to those fixed ceilings. Likewise, the Soviet Union accepted the Western position that the reductions should take place in stages rather than all at one time.

On the fundamental problem of the relationship in time between the prohibition of atomic weapons and the installation of controls to ensure the observance of the prohibition, the Soviet Union at least indicated its willingness to negotiate. The traditional Soviet line had

[52] U.N. General Assembly, Ninth Session, "Conclusion of an International Convention (Treaty) on the Reduction of Armaments and the Prohibition of Atomic, Hydrogen and Other Weapons of Mass Destruction," Doc. A/2742 (Sept. 30, 1954).

been that the prohibition of atomic weapons and the institution of controls should be simultaneous. As the United States representative, Ambassador Wadsworth, pointed out

> ... "Simultaneous" is a pretty word, but ... in this context, it is literally meaningless. ... The prohibition of atomic weapons is a single act. The institution of controls is a long series of acts. The real question, therefore, is this: at what point during the development of the control organ would prohibition of atomic weapons take place?[53]

The debate in the General Assembly indicated that the Soviet Union and the West were as far apart as ever on the question of inspection. Vyshinsky, in an exchange with Wadsworth, rejected the Western proposals for inspectors with broad powers. He said:

> ... During the last world war even button factories—at least in my country—began to make weapons to fight Germans, and they did so successfully. Do you suggest that with a view to the reduction of armed forces and armaments we have to supervise every factory making buttons for ladies' suits and men's trousers?[54]

Ambassador Wadsworth replied:

> Mr. Vyshinsky pointed out yesterday that during the war certain button factories in the Soviet Union manufactured munitions. This, I can assure him, is quite parallel to the history of United States industry during the war—and indeed that of most of the countries in the war. The international control commission must therefore, in our view, have the right to inspect button factories in order to determine whether or not they are manufacturing munitions. That is precisely what the Soviet Union representative denied to us during the London talks. ... If ... we correctly interpret Mr. Vyshinsky's

[53] U.N. General Assembly, Ninth Session, First Committee, *Official Records*, 687th Meeting (Oct. 12, 1954), p. 34.
[54] *Ibid.*, 686th Meeting (Oct. 11, 1954), p. 28.

statement yesterday, any country can frustrate the international inspection simply by posting on a munitions factory a sign reading: "Keep out. This factory is making buttons."[55]

Vyshinsky stated that the Soviet Union was at least willing to negotiate on a basis whereby the prohibition of nuclear weapons and the institution of international controls have to be completed within the same period.[56] This might be interpreted as an acceptance in principle of the most fundamental idea in the British-French memorandum— that the prohibitions and reductions should not take place until a control organ was organized and in a position to ensure observance of commitments.

All of this was unquestionably a marked change in the Soviet position, but was far short of Soviet agreement to the Western positions. The Soviet Union still confined itself to a discussion of general principles. On many previous occasions, the Soviet concessions proved to be nonexistent when attempts were made to translate the general principles into specific provisions.

The chief significance of the new Soviet approach was that it opened a vast area for future detailed discussions. Both Vyshinsky and Wadsworth recognized that the General Assembly was not an appropriate organ for such discussions. Since the 1954 meetings of the subcommittee had apparently succeeded in narrowing the differences between the West and the Soviet Union, the General Assembly unanimously and enthusiastically welcomed further sessions of the subcommittee.[57]

Immediately after the General Assembly consideration of the disarmament problem, Morehead Patterson resigned and was appointed the United States representative in the conduct of the International Atomic Energy Agency negotiations. Shortly thereafter, Harold Stassen was appointed White House Adviser on Disarmament.

[55] *Ibid.*, 687th Meeting (Oct. 12, 1954), p. 34.
[56] U.N. General Assembly, Ninth Session, First Committee, *Official Records,* 686th Meeting (Oct. 11, 1954).
[57] Res. 808 (IX), Nov. 4, 1954, pp. 3-4.

APPRAISAL

During the entire period from 1952 through 1954, the Western powers maintained the initiative in the arms control negotiations. The United States altered its main earlier positions, which had exposed the United States to some criticism from unbiased sources.

1. The United States no longer insisted on an improvement in the international political atmosphere as a precondition to arms control negotiations.

2. The Western powers recognized that any measures of arms control to be effective, must be acceptable to the Soviet Union and abandoned their previous practice of seeking United Nations endorsement of proposals the Soviet Union found objectionable.

3. The United States indicated its flexibility on international control of atomic energy, and actually made proposals that modified two of the most controversial parts of the Baruch Plan: international ownership of nuclear facilities and waiver of the "veto" in the United Nations Security Council.

On the positive side, the Western powers produced a fairly complete outline for a balanced reduction of armaments under international control. This Western initiative created the most favorable reaction of world opinion. Within the United Nations, the Western powers had virtually unanimous support for their proposals, and the Soviet Union had difficulty in mustering a single vote outside its satellites. This unanimity of support for the Western position was attributable partly to the Soviet tactics of framing its speeches and proposals within the United Nations primarily for use through its mass media of propaganda.

The two major Soviet propaganda campaigns, the Stockholm Appeal and the bacteriological warfare charges, both were unsuccessful even as propaganda. The Stockholm Appeal failed largely because the Communist attack in Korea was an action that spoke louder than the words of peace in the Stockholm Appeal. The bacteriological warfare charges were overshadowed and discredited by the story of the forced confessions extracted from captured United States fliers.

The failure of the Soviet propaganda campaigns outside the United Nations and the Western success in securing support for its arms control proposals within the United Nations seem closely related. The United Nations delegates resented the Soviet speeches within the United Nations directed primarily to audiences outside, and this contributed to their support of Western positions within the United Nations. The overwhelming votes for the Western proposals in the United Nations and against the Soviet proposals tended to discredit the Soviet propaganda campaigns outside the United Nations, since the most important moulders of public opinion in many countries were the United Nations delegates from those countries.

During this period, the Western position became associated with the world desire for peace to a greater extent than before or since. To repeat, this arose as much from the intransigence of the Soviet position as from the merits of the Western position, and the Soviet intransigence was closely linked to the rigidity of the last years of Stalin.

This period also produced some improvement in the Western governmental machinery dealing with the arms control negotiations. For the first time, the United Kingdom and France had continuity of representation largely in the persons of Selwyn Lloyd and Jules Moch, who developed the highest skills and knowledgeability in this field.

The United States also achieved greater continuity of representation during this period than at any time before or since, even though none of its three chief negotiators—Nash, Cohen, or Patterson—served for long. Cohen was in close touch with Nash; and Patterson, who succeeded Cohen after the change of administration, received valuable advice and assistance from Cohen and also from Baruch.

More important, the basic United States policy that began to develop in 1949 continued without fundamental change until the end of 1954. The number of individuals dealing with arms control at the official level in the State Department, Defense Department, and the Atomic Energy Commission never increased during the period and actually declined after the election of Eisenhower. However, the officers remaining had to their credit years of experience.

In the fall of 1951, immediately prior to the establishment of the Disarmament Commission, the interdepartmental apparatus in the

United States Government for dealing with these problems, the Committee on Regulation of Armaments (RAC), set up a subsidiary group, which became known as DAC. DAC consisted of individuals of the official level in the State and Defense Departments, the three military services, and the Atomic Energy Commission, chaired by an officer from the State Department's Bureau of United Nations Affairs. This committee was assigned the task of developing the United States Government positions, which later emerged as the program submitted to the United Nations Disarmament Commission. The individual officers were expected to participate in the meetings not as representatives of their respective departments and services, but as individuals with specialized knowledge and skills. During this entire period, despite conflicting viewpoints among the interested departments, DAC secured agreed positions on all problems except one, without referring the matters to its parent committee (RAC).

Governor Stassen, on a much larger scale, carried this concept of individuals from the various services and departments participating in the work as individuals rather than as representatives of their departments and services into the organization of his staff in 1955.

Despite these organizational improvements and their apparent success, the United States at no time during this period was in a position to conduct a serious and prolonged negotiation. Neither Cohen nor Patterson had ready access to the White House or even to the Secretary of State. This was not lost on the Soviet representatives. Gromyko once remarked to one of the Indian representatives that he was convinced that Cohen was a sincere believer in disarmament but had no influence in his government.

Patterson had serious doubts whether the legislative branch of the United States Government would support the control organ paper, even though it represented the approved position of the Executive branch. With the support for the Bricker Amendment and Senator McCarthy, any agreement calling for international inspection would have had hard sledding in the United States Senate. Patterson's more immediate fear stemmed from his realization that literally nothing had transpired in the United States Government in the direction of transforming the outlines of the United States position into a detailed plan.

The available personnel would have been swamped by a negotiation such as that which transpired in 1957. New personnel would require months and even years of training.

From the standpoint of the West, these years were fruitful in developing attractive and flexible positions commanding broad world support. Soviet inflexibility prevented agreement or even any genuine negotiation. The experience in this period should have helped to chart the course of the Western governments in the more difficult period ahead when the dynamism of Khrushchev replaced the static rigidity of Stalin.

PART FIVE

The Search for
Partial Disarmament
1955-1957

XI

The Western Reappraisal

THE GENERAL ASSEMBLY OF 1954 is a convenient terminal point for the phase of disarmament negotiations that commenced with the establishment of the United Nations Disarmament Commission in 1951. It is true that the procedural framework for the negotiations within the United Nations—the Disarmament Commission and its subcommittee, reporting to the General Assembly—remained the same until the end of 1957. However, world developments changed the entire substance and spirit of the negotiations. The development of thermonuclear weapons forced both the Soviet Union and the West to reappraise their positions in the light of the new technology. The death of Stalin, followed by a gradual thaw of frozen attitudes, made possible a shift in the Soviet position to accommodate itself to the changed international situations.

Neither in the West nor in the Soviet Union did the changed positions emerge suddenly and fully mature. Therefore January 1955 is not a landmark in time completely separating and isolating eras. Practically all of the events leading to the changed environment of the negotiations and the changed positions of both sides, took place prior to January 1955. Likewise, some proposals were made in 1955 and 1956, mainly by the British and French, which looked backward rather than forward. Nevertheless, the date of January 1955 remains significant. Prior thereto, the negotiations had proceeded with scant heed to the in-

241

creased destructiveness of weapons and had therefore become un-realistic. The subcommittee reconvened in February 1955, and by May had moved into new ground. It took two more years, however, until the spring of 1957, for the changed viewpoints of both the Soviet Union and the West to crystallize and to approach each other sufficiently to permit a genuine negotiation—with give and take on both sides and with some promise of ultimate agreement.

The key to an understanding of the three-year period from 1955 to 1957 is the reappraisal of positions by both the Soviet Union and the United States, the discussion of which must necessarily precede any chronicle of the three years.

THE H-BOMB

Over the years since the final Soviet rejection of the Baruch Plan in 1948, the arms control concepts and proposals of both East and West had undergone some evolution, some accommodation to political reali-ties, some adjustment to technological change.

The political terms of reference of 1945 had changed first. The "cold war" had replaced the wartime concept of great power postwar cooperation to maintain world peace. A decade of unchecked nuclear production had augmented stockpiles of fissionable materials in both East and West. Uranium was no longer a scarce commodity. It had long been known that fissionable material once produced could readily be concealed.[1] The impossibility of accounting for all past production would mean that a significant amount of material could escape detec-tion and be used for clandestine production of weapons. This explained the urgency of the original Baruch proposals, which provided controls that were destined to become less effective with each year that delayed their installation, as stockpiles of fissionable materials grew. The United Kingdom began production of atomic weapons in 1952, and France was soon to have a significant plutonium production capability. By 1955,

---

[1] U.S. Department of State, *The International Control of Atomic Energy: Growth of a Policy*, Publication 2702 (1946), p. 1. Paraphrase of President Truman's Navy Day Speech of Oct. 27, 1945.

the United States and presumably also the Soviet Union had greatly increased the production of fissionable materials.[2]

Nevertheless the United States continued to follow the Baruch approach, which was based on a situation in which total weapons stocks remained low and were mainly in United States hands. The modifications of the Baruch Plan that had been suggested up to and during 1954 were attempts to adjust to these encroaching technological changes. But until 1955, the official United States position continued to be that even in the atomic age, the task of controlled limitation and reduction of armaments could be effectively accomplished by the old proposals for elimination of nuclear weapons under appropriate controls, with adjustments made in their details to conform to technological advances.

The Disarmament Commission and its subcommittee, despite heavy going, continued to meet, and negotiations toward a comprehensive arms control agreement ground on with difficulty. A number of factors accounted for this delayed reaction, one being the generally lethargic pace of policy making. A more cogent factor was that the Soviet Union had actually made certain concessions in the negotiations on the Baruch Plan that could be valid in future negotiations. To abandon the Baruch Plan would have made it necessary to repeat, with further obstacles, the arduous negotiating process.

This situation changed completely with the development of thermonuclear weapons. On November 1, 1952, at Eniwetok, the United States detonated the first hydrogen device. Less than a year later, on August 20, 1953, Radio Moscow announced the successful explosion of the Soviet Union's first thermonuclear device. With the March 1, 1954 explosion at Bikini, and the consequent radiation exposure to the Japanese fishermen on the "Lucky Dragon" nearly one hundred miles downwind,[3] the public began to realize that the thermonuclear revolution had destroyed the remaining technological assumptions of the Baruch proposals.

As a result of this single explosion, "about 7,000 square miles of

[2] Howard Simons, "World-Wide Capabilities for Production and Control of Nuclear Weapons," in *Daedalus*, Vol. 88, No. 3 (Summer 1959), p. 400.

[3] Ralph E. Lapp, *The Voyage of the Lucky Dragon* (1958), pp. 44-45.

territory downwind from the point of burst was so contaminated that survival might have depended upon prompt evacuation of the area or upon taking shelter and other protective measures."[4] The direction of the fall-out depended on meteorological conditions.

The "tenuous ties with the past were threatened when it became known that thermonuclear bombs were not only feasible, but also inexpensive enough to justify their manufacture in substantial numbers."[5] Time and technology had brought the world to a point at which the predictable margin of error in accounting for nuclear materials represented not a debatable margin of risk to national security, but potential catastrophe.

Churchill, then Prime Minister, described this new and great divide in the first full debate in the House of Commons following the revelation of the 1954 explosion.

> We must realize that the gulf between the conventional high explosive bomb in use at the end of the war with Germany on the one hand, and the atomic bomb as used against Japan on the other, is smaller than the gulf developing between that bomb and the hydrogen bomb. . . . With all its horrors the atomic bomb did not seem unmanageable as an instrument of war, and the fact that the Americans have such an immense preponderance over Russia has given us passage through eight anxious and troublous years. But the hydrogen bomb carries us into dimensions which have never confronted practical human thought. . . .[6]

And a year later:

> It is now the fact that a quantity of plutonium, probably less than would fill this box on the table—it is quite a safe thing to store —would suffice to produce weapons which would give indisputable

[4] Statement by Lewis L. Strauss, *The Nature of Radioactive Fall-out and its Effects on Man,* Hearings before the Joint Committee on Atomic Energy, 85 Cong. 1 sess., Pt. 2, p. 1947.
[5] Bernard Brodie, *Strategy in the Missile Age* (1959), p. 154. For cost of production as well as capabilities of other nations to produce bombs, see evaluation given in Simons, *op. cit.* pp. 385-409.
[6] Address delivered Apr. 5, 1954, Great Britain, *Parliamentary Debates,* Commons, Vol. 526, Col. 48.

world domination to any great power which was the only one to have it. There is no absolute defence against the hydrogen bomb, nor is any method in sight by which any nation or any country can be completely guaranteed against the devastating injury which even a score of them might inflict on wide regions.[7]

The extreme secrecy established to preserve such scientific advantages as the United States still held in a nuclear race with an opponent fast gaining from behind delayed the initial impact on the arms control negotiations. But the profound reappraisal of positions which it set in motion, in both the West and in the Soviet Union, produced major changes that by 1957 revealed themselves in new programs.[8]

THE UNITED STATES REVIEWS

ITS POSITIONS

As early as 1952, before Ambassador Cohen had presented any portion of the United States program for comprehensive disarmament, discussions had taken place within the United States Government on a highly classified basis concerning the possible effects of thermonuclear weapons and other technological developments on such a program. As we have pointed out, in the spring of 1952 the Secretary of State had appointed a panel to advise Cohen, and this panel made a study of the entire question of the regulation of armaments.[9] Its findings and its report were highly classified and remained so until the hearing of the charges against Dr. Oppenheimer before a personnel security board in April and May 1954.

At that hearing, Oppenheimer testified:

But there was clearly not much reality to the discussions of dis-

[7] *Ibid.,* Vol. 537, Col. 1899.
[8] Maxwell D. Taylor, *The Uncertain Trumpet* (1959-60), Chap. 4, and Gordon B. Turner, "The Influence of Modern Weapons on Strategy," *National Security in the Nuclear Age,* Gordon B. Turner and Richard O. Challener, Eds. (1960), p. 59.
[9] See Chap. 8. See also U.S. Atomic Energy Commission, *In the Matter of J. Robert Oppenheimer,* Transcript of Hearing before Personnel Security Board, April 12, 1954 through May 6, 1954, p. 95.

armament in the United Nations, and the most we could do was make a few helpful suggestions which would encourage our friends as to our good faith and interest. . . . We took a look at the armaments situation, getting some estimates of the growth of Russian capability and some estimates of our own as a measure for where they might be some time in the future. I think as always we thought we were being careful, but we were a little too conservative in estimating the speed and success of the Soviet program. We became very vividly painfully aware of what an unregulated arms race would lead to in the course of years. We tended to think in the course of five or ten years, but probably the time was shorter. Our report was of course classified.

As a result of this gloomy prospect, we now know that Dr. Enrico Fermi, Dr. Vannevar Bush, and others believed "that one should try to outlaw the thing before it was born."[10] The specific measure would have been announcements by the United States and the Soviet Union that neither would attempt to detonate a thermonuclear device. No such proposal ever reached the Disarmament Commission or even became the subject of public discussion.

Cohen and one or two members of his staff[11] were aware of Dr. Bush's suggestion and were also aware that in the future, technological developments might require a reappraisal of all basic positions. However, even the scientists vastly underestimated the time required for those developments.

In the United States Government, the formal reappraisal of past disarmament positions began in 1954 in the Policy Planning Staff of the Department of State and was continued, after March 1955, through intensive studies conducted by a new office—that of the Special Assistant to the President on Disarmament—with review at cabinet level in the National Security Council. At the end of 1956 the President, writing to Bulganin, stated that the United States would make further proposals in the United Nations; Ambassador Lodge made the proposals in

[10] *Ibid.*, p. 395. Testimony of Dr. Fermi.
[11] Including the author, who was a member of Cohen's staff.

the Political Committee of the United Nations General Assembly on January 14, 1957.[12] Well in advance of these formal full-scale interdepartmental conclusions, however, the basic change can be traced in the President's growing personal concern, which in turn gave rise to a new approach in formulating his key policy decisions.

ATOMS FOR PEACE

Even before the March 1954 explosion, the probability of some kind of nuclear stalemate was becoming apparent. In December 1953, only eight months after the President had reaffirmed United States policy as seeking "international control of atomic energy" and "prohibition of atomic weapons" under a "practical system of inspection"[13] and four months after the Soviet Union had exploded its first thermonuclear device, the President acknowledged the impact of the emerging thermonuclear impasse in his famous address of December 8, 1953, to the United Nations.[14] The main objective of this address was to inaugurate an international program to develop the peaceful uses of the atom. We know today, however, that the President had originally planned to concentrate solely on the materials developed in "Operation Candor"[15] showing the increased destructive potential of nuclear weapons. The President himself had decided on the shift of emphasis to the peaceful uses of the atom.[16]

Despite the main preoccupation with the peaceful use of the atom,

[12] U.N. General Assembly, Eleventh Session, First Committee, *Official Records*, 821st Meeting (Jan. 14, 1957).
[13] *The Chance for Peace*, address by President Eisenhower delivered before the American Society of Newspaper Editors, April 16, 1953, Department of State, Publication 5042 (April 1953), p. 8.
[14] *Atomic Power for Peace*, address by President Eisenhower before the General Assembly of the United Nations, Dec. 8, 1953, Department of State, Publication 5314 (December 1953), pp. 1-14.
[15] See Chap. 8.
[16] Laurin L. Henry, *Presidential Transitions* (1960), p. 636. See also U.S. Atomic Energy Commission, Press Release, April 19, 1954: "Remarks of Lewis L. Strauss to the Los Angeles World Affairs Council."

the President's address clearly foreshadowed a shift in the United States approach toward regulation of armaments. One of the main objectives of the President was stated as follows: to "open up a new channel for peaceful discussion, and initiate at least a new approach to the many difficult problems that must be solved in both private and public conversations, if the world is to shake off the inertia imposed by fear, and is to make positive progress toward peace." The positive progress which he specifically visualized as a result of his program to develop the peaceful atom, was a start toward diminishing "the potential destructive power of the world's atomic stockpiles."[17] The President in his speech gave a clear indication that this objective of attempting to create some measure of understanding with the Soviet Union should receive the closest emphasis in the early stages of negotiation. "The United States would be more than willing—it would be proud to take up with others 'principally involved' the development of plans whereby such peaceful use of atomic energy would be expedited. Of those 'principally involved,' the Soviet Union must, of course, be one."[18] The phrase "principally involved" referred to the General Assembly resolution calling for private talks on disarmament among the states "principally involved," which led to the creation of the Subcommittee of Five of the Disarmament Commission.

"We shall carry into these private or diplomatic talks a new conception," he said. "To hasten the day when fear of the atom will begin to disappear from the minds of people, and the governments of the East and West," and as a step toward the reversal of the "fearful trend of atomic military buildup," he proposed that the

> Governments principally involved . . . begin now and continue to make joint contributions from their stockpiles of normal uranium and fissionable materials to an International Atomic Energy Agency. . . . The ratios of contributions, the procedures and other details would properly be within the scope of the "private conversations" I have referred to earlier.
>
> Undoubtedly initial and early contributions to this plan would

[17] Eisenhower, *Atomic Power for Peace*, pp. 13-14.
[18] *Ibid.*, p. 13.

be small in quantity. However, the proposal has the great virtue that it can be undertaken without the irritations and mutual suspicions incident to any attempt to set up a completely acceptable system of world-wide inspection and control.[19]

In view of these statements by the President, it was hardly surprising that the Soviet representative in the subcommittee during its first session in the spring of 1954 dealt in some detail with the President's proposals concerning the peaceful atom. The United States representative took the position that the December 8 proposals were not disarmament proposals and should not be considered in the subcommittee.[20] Thus the three years of successful negotiations leading to the creation of the International Atomic Energy Agency were conducted outside the Disarmament Commission and its subcommittee.

As we have seen during the 1954 subcommittee session, the United States in the main merely carried forward and developed its previous policies calling for comprehensive disarmament with effective safeguards. The reappraisal of United States policy was proceeding in secret within the United States Government and with little, if any, apparent contact between the planners and the United States negotiators. The sole indication during the discussions in London in the spring of 1954 of any pending reappraisal of policy may be found in the failure of the United States to co-sponsor, even though it approved, the Anglo-French memorandum of June 11, 1954.[21]

---

[19] *Ibid.*, pp. 10-12.
[20] U.N. Disarmament Commission, Subcommittee of the Disarmament Commission, Third Meeting, *Verbatim Record*. Doc. DC/SC.1/PV.3 (May 14, 1954), p. 61. (Cited hereafter by document number and date.)
[21] U.N. Doc. DC/SC.1/10 (June 11, 1954), pp. 76-80.
Mr. Patterson: "Mr. Malik is indeed clairvoyant; he stated on three different occasions that the United States gives its general approval to the memorandum submitted by the Representative of France and the United Kingdom. The United States is now about to give its approval, as stated.
"We find the suggestions made in the French-United Kingdom memorandum in general not inconsistent with basic United States concepts, and we give the memorandum as interpreted by Mr. Lloyd our support. We believe that when sufficient progress has been made to enable a specific treaty to be drafted, with a description of each particular step, the scheme will turn out to be considerably more complicated than would appear from the outline in the memorandum. . . ."

IMPACT ON THE THEORY

OF DETERRENCE

The theory of deterrence through massive retaliation was not new to the thermonuclear age. The elaborate structure of interlocking collective security alliances built up since 1945 had been founded on the theory of the creation of collective military capabilities to "deter armed aggression and *to cope with it* if it should occur."[22] Well before the advent of the H-bomb, the threat of massive atomic retaliation via the Strategic Air Command of the United States had been incorporated into Western military strategy to shore up the deterrent value of conventional ground forces, increasingly outnumbered by Soviet and satellite divisions.

In December 1950, the man who was to become the Secretary of State in the thermonuclear age stated that as against the possibility of full-scale attack by the Soviet Union itself there is only one effective defense, for us and for others. That is "the capacity to counter-attack. That is the ultimate deterrent. . . . The arsenal of retaliation should include all forms of counter-attack with a maximum flexibility. . . ."[23]

In his address of December 8, 1953, to the United Nations the President first laid down the dimensions of the emerging thermonuclear impasse. This was four months before the Bikini explosion publicized the bomb's destructive potential.

Atomic bombs today are more than 25 times as powerful as the weapons with which the atomic age dawned, while hydrogen weapons are in the ranges of millions of tons of TNT equivalent. . . . The knowledge now possessed by several nations will eventually be shared by others—possibly all others. . . . [and] even a vast superiority in numbers of weapons, and a consequent capability of dev-

[22] John Foster Dulles, "Challenge and Response in U.S. Policy," *Foreign Affairs* (October 1957), p. 6.
[23] John Foster Dulles, "Where Are We: A Five-Year Record of America's Response to the Challenge of Communism," Department of State *Bulletin*, Vol. 24 (Jan. 15, 1951).

astating retaliation, is no preventive, of itself, against the fearful material damage and toll of human lives that would be inflicted by surprise aggression.

The free world, at least dimly aware of these facts, has naturally embarked on a large program of warning and defense systems. . . . But let no one think that the expenditure of vast sums for weapons and systems of defense can guarantee absolute safety for the cities and citizens of any nation. The awful arithmetic of the atomic bomb does not permit of any such easy solution. Even against the most powerful defense, an aggressor in possession of the effective minimum number of atomic bombs for a surprise attack could probably place a sufficient number of his bombs on the chosen targets to cause hideous damage . . . the probability of civilization destroyed —the annihilation of the irreplaceable heritage of mankind. . . .[24]

The President had stated in his "atoms for peace" speech that if an aggressor should launch an "atomic" attack against the United States, "our reactions would be swift and resolute . . . the defense capabilities of the United States are such that they could inflict terrible losses upon an aggressor . . . the retaliation capabilities of the United States are so great that such an aggressor's land would be laid waste." He went on to say that "all this, while fact, is not the true expression of the purpose and the hope of the United States,"[25] but he made clear that the United States held and would, if need be, use this strength.

Secretary Dulles spelled out the application of the doctrine to the conflict in Indochina: "I have said, in relation to Indochina, that if there were open Red Chinese aggression there, that would have 'grave consequences which might not be confined to Indochina.' "[26]

Thus, before the Bikini test in March 1954, the United States had extended the doctrine of massive retaliation to cover an increasing

[24] Eisenhower, *Atomic Power for Peace*, pp. 4-6. For discussion of development of doctrine of massive retaliation, from December 1950 to December 1953, see General Maxwell D. Taylor, *op. cit.*, Chap. 2.
[25] Eisenhower, *Atomic Power for Peace*, p. 6.
[26] "The Evolution of Foreign Policy," address delivered before the Council on Foreign Relations, Jan. 12, 1954, Department of State *Bulletin*, Vol. 30 (Jan. 25, 1954), p. 108.

number of specific situations. The United States response even to local aggressions would be through massive retaliation against the aggressor. An aggressor might be deterred from employing massive surprise thermonuclear attack by the prospect of lethal fallout drifting back across his own territory from his own attack, but a retaliator would be himself strongly deterred from employing these "massive" weapons as a means of meeting a non-nuclear attack on Western Europe, say, knowing that the outcome would be the destruction of Western Europe.

This new thermonuclear development, coupled with the realization that the Soviet Union also had thermonuclear weapons, required —and achieved—a drastic shift in the doctrine of deterrence to adjust to a nuclear stalemate. In his first public comment on the March 1954 H-bomb explosion, the President said it was quite clear that this time something must have happened that we had never experienced before, and that must have surprised and astonished the scientists.[27] On April 5, the President stated flatly that the H-bomb would not be used on the initiative of the United States.[28] His personal concern over the destructive potential now at large was expressed in language the more impressive because he was recognized to be one of the few men to whom the full facts of the thermonuclear weapon were known.

Since the advent of nuclear weapons, it seems clear that there is no longer any alternative to peace, if there is to be a happy and well world. . . . The soldier can no longer regain a peace that is usable to the world. I believe that the best he could do would be to retain some semblance of a tattered nation in a world that was very greatly in ashes and relics of destruction.[29]

[27] New York Times, Mar. 25, 1954, p. 12. Press Conference, Mar. 24, 1954, unofficial transcript. The President's remarks are quoted in indirect discourse as required by conference rules prevailing at this time.

[28] "Multiplicity of Fears," address to the nation, April 5, 1954, New York Times, April 6, 1954, p. 16.

[29] "Fifth Annual Awards Ceremony," Department of State Bulletin, Vol. 31 (Nov. 1, 1954), p. 636. See also President Eisenhower's address at Trinity College, Hartford, Connecticut, Oct. 20, 1954, New York Times, Oct. 21, 1954; text of President Eisenhower's address for delivery at the American Jewish Tercentenary Dinner, Oct. 21, 1954, ibid.; Our Quest for Peace and Freedom, address at the Annual Dinner of the American Society of Newspaper Editors, April 21, 1956, Department of State Publication 6337 (May 1956).

In September 1956 Eisenhower described the world situation in emphatic terms:

We witness today in the power of nuclear weapons a new and deadly dimension to the ancient horror of war. Humanity has now achieved, for the first time in its history, the power to end its history. This truth must guide our every deed. It makes world disarmament a necessity of world life. For I repeat again this simple declaration: The only way to win World War III is to prevent it.[30]

The President's statement might well have been the prelude to a unilateral renunciation of first use of nuclear weapons or in the alternative of unlimited nuclear warfare, if our military establishment had been modified to permit resistance to aggression through other means.[31] In the absence of such a capability the President's statement signified little more than an earnest personal expression of hope.

Secretary Dulles became the earliest articulator of a necessarily revised strategy for a theory of effective deterrence. On March 19, 1954, the Secretary reiterated the original basis for deterrence—"an aggressor must not be able to count upon a sanctuary status for those resources which he does not use in committing aggression," but now introduced the revised concepts of "selective" retaliation and "tactical" atomic weapons:

To apply this deterrent principle the free world must maintain and be prepared to use effective means to make aggression too costly to be tempting. It must have the mobility and flexibility to bring collective power to bear against an enemy on a selective or massive basis as conditions may require. For this purpose its arsenal must include a wide range of air, sea and land power based on both conventional and atomic weapons. These new weapons can be used not only for strategic purposes but also for tactical purposes.

The greatest deterrent to war is the ability of the free world

---

[30] Campaign address delivered Sept. 19, 1956, *New York Times* (Sept. 20, 1956).
[31] Henry A. Kissinger, *Nuclear Weapons and Foreign Policy* (1957), pp. 128, 177.

to respond by means best suited to the particular area or circumstance. There should be a capability for massive retaliation without delay.

But then the Secretary stated, with special emphasis: "I point out that the possession of that capacity does not impose the necessity of using it in every instance of attack. It is not our intention to turn every local war into a general war."[32]

By September 1957, research, production, and deployment of new and more manageable atomic weapons had advanced sufficiently to enable the architect of the strategy of massive retaliation virtually to renounce it publicly.

In the basic restatement of United States foreign policy embodied in his article, "Challenge and Response in United States Policy," Secretary Dulles reviewed the decade of experience in collective security and the evolution of the concept of the strategy of collective self-defense against the background of the continuing Soviet threat and the Soviet awareness of the significance of an evolving Western nuclear defense.

Referring to the years since 1950, he said:

The United States has not been content to rely upon a peace which could be preserved only by a capacity to destroy vast segments of the human race. Such a concept is acceptable only as a last alternative. In recent years there has been no other. But the resourcefulness of those who serve our nation in the field of science and weapon engineering now shows that it is possible to alter the character of nuclear weapons. It seems now that their use need not involve vast destruction and widespread harm to humanity.

[32] Foreign Policy and Its Relation to Military Programs, Hearings before the Senate Committee on Foreign Relations, 83 Cong. 2 sess., p. 4.

See also John Foster Dulles, "Policy for Security and Peace," Department of State Press Release 139 (March 16, 1954), p. 6. Quoted from article in Foreign Affairs (April 1954), p. 358. John Foster Dulles, "The New Phase of the Struggle with International Communism," Address made before Illinois Manufacturers' Association, Dec. 8, 1955, Department of State Bulletin, Vol. 33 (Dec. 19, 1955), pp. 1003-07.

Recent tests point to the possibility of possessing nuclear weapons, the destructiveness and radiation effects of which can be confined substantially to predetermined targets.

With the smaller atomic arms now in large-scale production and deployment,

In the future it may thus be feasible to place less reliance upon deterrence of vast retaliatory power. It may be possible to defend countries by nuclear weapons so mobile, or so placed, as to make military invasion with conventional forces a hazardous attempt. For example, terrain is often such that invasion routes can be decisively dominated by nuclear artillery. Thus, in contrast to the 1950 decade, it may be that by the 1960 decade the nations which are around the Sino-Soviet perimeter can possess an effective defense against full-scale conventional attack and thus confront any aggressor with the choice between failing or himself initiating nuclear war against the defending country. Thus the tables may be turned, in the sense that instead of those who are non-aggressive having to rely upon all-out nuclear retaliatory power for their protection, would-be aggressors will be unable to count on a successful conventional aggression, but must themselves weigh the consequences of invoking nuclear war.[33]

General Maxwell D. Taylor describes Dulles' position as the expression of a strong hope that some military solution would *eventually* be found to permit lessened dependence upon massive retaliation. He describes in some detail the debates in the National Security Council stemming from Dulles' statements. The Army, Navy, and Marine Corps representatives urged a change in the "basic national security policy" to reflect the changed conditions. To General Taylor's "disappointment," Secretary Dulles and his advisers "did not provide the strong support for a new strategy which I had hoped."[34] No change was made in the "basic national security policy."

[33] In *Foreign Affairs* (October 1957).
[34] Taylor, *op. cit.*, p. 65.

Thus, while the United States has in the disarmament negotiations revised its theoretical concept of deterrence, unfortunately our military establishments do not fully reflect the technological revolution. In many areas of the world, the West today would be unable to resist successfully an attack with conventional weapons except through resorting to massive retaliation.[35] In contrast, in the Soviet Union, the military establishments apparently have consistently kept in step with changing strategic concepts.

The Soviets have, if belatedly nonetheless intensively, prepared in recent years for warfare in the nuclear age. Literally each component of the military establishment has tremendously increased its capabilities in the period of post war modernization. It is significant and important that the Soviets have greatly increased their long-range sea and air offensive capabilities, and their air defense, with slackening attention to the improvement and maintenance of a large modernized ground force and supporting tactical aviation.[36]

THE SEARCH FOR PARTIAL,

CONFIDENCE-BUILDING MEASURES

The other major mutation born of the thermonuclear age also first emerged in the President's address of December 8, 1953. That address was the genesis of the concept that characterized the new approach in disarmament policy: the search among partial measures of arms control, including but not limited to those related to past disarmament proposals, for those which, though far short of the comprehensive limitations and reductions previously envisaged, could start to rebuild the confidence indispensable to a secure and lasting peace. Since major political settlements or major armaments reductions had not materialized within the prevailing negotiating environment, the

---

[35] Kissinger, op. cit., Chaps. 2, 6. Dr. Kissinger outlines the impact of thermonuclear weapons on our military establishments. See also Taylor, op. cit., p. 44.
[36] Raymond L. Garthoff, Soviet Strategy in the Nuclear Age (1958), Chap. 2, p. 58.

President announced that he was prepared to intervene actively to change the negotiating environment itself.

In the same speech that promised "swift and resolute retaliation" so great that an aggressor's land would be laid waste, the President declared:

> My country wants to be constructive, not destructive. It wants agreements, not wars, among nations. . . . I know that in a world divided, such as ours today, salvation cannot be attained by one dramatic act. I know that many steps will have to be taken over many months before the world can look at itself one day and truly realize that a new climate of mutually peaceful confidence is abroad in the world. But I know, above all else, that we must start to take these steps—NOW.[37]

The "new concept" of which the President spoke was not limited to the International Atomic Energy Agency:[38] and although it was not until August 1955 that the United States formally reserved its past positions on comprehensive disarmament, with the proposals on December 8, 1953, the policy of seeking immediately an agreement on comprehensive disarmament was in fact abandoned, and the search for partial immediately realizable measures began.

Thus, the perfection of thermonuclear weapons by both the Soviet Union and the United States immediately destroyed the concept of securing the elimination of nuclear weapons through accounting for all past production of nuclear materials. The margin of error in any system of accountability had become too great a risk.

A nuclear stalemate was emerging in which the state initiating an all-out nuclear strike would itself be annihilated through the second retaliatory strike. The possibility of a first strike of sufficient strength to annihilate the power of the recipient to retaliate was not yet an immediate problem.

[37] *Atomic Power for Peace*, p .7.
[38] Bernhard G. Bechhoefer, "Negotiating the Statute of the International Atomic Energy Agency," in *International Organization*, Vol. 12, No. 1 (1959). Detailed account of the origin and the relationship of the concept to disarmament.

The immediate problem for the Western military establishments was to revise strategic concepts in such a manner that the West might resist a conventional attack either with conventional weapons or with tactical nuclear weapons. The reappraisal of United States policy expressed itself positively in the arms control negotiations in a search for partial measures of disarmament that might improve the international atmosphere, and presumably lessen the danger of war.

The negative aspect of the reappraisal—the abandonment by the United States of the past proposals directed toward comprehensive disarmament—took place in August 1955. The complementary positive proposals for partial measures did not commence to emerge until late in 1956. As General Maxwell Taylor points out, the military establishments even today have not fully adapted themselves to the positive side of the reappraisal.

ORGANIZING THE NEW APPROACH

On March 19, 1955, President Eisenhower created a new position, that of Special Assistant to the President for Disarmament, and appointed Harold E. Stassen, former Governor of Minnesota and at the time director of the foreign aid agency, to fill the post. In his statement announcing this unprecedented step, the President mentioned as his primary reasons not only his "deep concern . . . for many years" over the "unprecedented destructive power of new weapons, and the international tensions which powerful armaments aggravate." He also stated a companion concern, in words reminiscent of President Franklin D. Roosevelt's wartime appraisal:

At the same time the tragic consequences of unilateral disarmament, the reckless moves of Hitler when the United States was weak, the Korean aggression when our armed strength had been rapidly diminished, and the vast extent of the armament now centered around the opposing ideology of communism, have been equally apparent to me.[39]

[39] White House Disarmament Staff, *Reference Documents on Disarmament Matters*, Background Series D1-D42, p. 43. Compare with ideas expressed in Robert E. Sherwood, *Roosevelt and Hopkins* (1948), p. 717.

The President outlined the functions of the new office as follows:

I have, therefore, established a position as Special Assistant to the President with responsibility for developing, on behalf of the President and the State Department, the broad studies, investigations and conclusions which, when concurred in by the National Security Council and approved by the President, will become basic policy toward the question of disarmament. The position will be of Cabinet rank. When indicated as desirable or appropriate under our Constitutional processes, concurrences will be secured from the Congress prior to specific action or pronouncement of policy.

I have appointed Harold Stassen as Special Assistant for discharge of this responsibility. He will be expected to take into account the full implications of new weapons in the possession of other nations as well as the United States, to consider future probabilities of armaments, and to weigh the views of the military, the civilians, and the officials of our government and of other governments.[40]

Up to this time Stassen had not been in a *negotiating* function; there was a separation in *negotiating* and *planning*. During the second session of the subcommittee in the spring of 1955, meeting at Lancaster House in London from February 25 to May 18, the United States was represented first by Ambassador Henry Cabot Lodge, Jr., and then by Ambassador James J. Wadsworth.[41]

On August 5, 1955, Stassen was also designated as:

Deputy United States Representative on the Disarmament Commission of the United Nations to sit for the United States in the Subcommittee of said Commission meetings.

In this phase of your work relating to the United Nations, you will serve under the direction of the United States Representative to the United Nations, Ambassador Henry Cabot Lodge, Jr., who

[40] *Ibid.*
[41] *United States Participation in the United Nations, Report by the President to the Congress for the Year 1955*, Department of State Publication 6318 (July 1956), p. 12.

in turn reports to the Secretary of State. In all other matters involving negotiations with other governments, you will be under the direction of and report to the Secretary of State.[42]

This placed Stassen, who was a member of the Cabinet and had direct access to the President in his capacity as Special Assistant on Disarmament, technically in a subordinate position to two other officers who were also members of the Cabinet, and who also had direct access to the President.

In the spring of 1957, however, this anomaly was partially corrected. Following the November 1956 policy decisions, on Stassen's recommendations and before he left for London as the head of the United States delegation to the United Nations subcommittee to undertake negotiations on this new policy, the Office of the Special Assistant to the President was physically transferred to the Department of State, and administrative changes were made that brought his activities under the formal jurisdiction of the Secretary of State. Although he retained the title "Special Assistant to the President," and the salaries of the staff continued to be paid from White House funds, his office became the "action office" within the Department of State for clearance and initiation of cables on disarmament. In June 1957, this action responsibility was transferred to the Office of the Special Assistant to the Secretary for Atomic Energy. This office later, in April 1958, inherited the function of disarmament policy formulation after Stassen's resignation on February 14, 1958, and the abolition of the Office of the Special Assistant to the President on Disarmament.

The White House Disarmament Staff and The President's Special Committee

Stassen began his task immediately. On March 20, 1955, he announced "as one of the first steps, the most thorough penetrating study

[42] Letter from President Eisenhower to Stassen, Aug. 5, 1955, released from the White House. Text in White House Disarmament Staff, *Reference Documents on Disarmament Matters*, p. 43.

that has ever been made on the relationship between armaments and disarmament" and invited "ideas, suggestions and comments" from everyone "because this is the search for the ideas by which mankind will have a better prospect for peace."[43]

He assembled a small staff consisting of eight experts loaned by the Departments of State, Army, Navy, and Air Force, the Atomic Energy Commission, the International Cooperation Administration, and the Central Intelligence Agency, and a research group of three analysts. Chief of staff for this group was Robert E. Matteson, who had been associated with Governor Stassen in the Foreign Operations Administration and earlier at the University of Pennsylvania. On January 13, 1956, Amos J. Peaslee, former American Ambassador to Australia, was designated as Deputy Special Assistant.[44]

In addition to the staff of officers on interdepartmental loan, Stassen also set up a small public relations team and created a large secretariat to record meetings, receive, reproduce, summarize, distribute, and file an impressive flow of materials from many sources—cables, United States and intergovernmental working papers, intelligence, press and periodicals, private studies, internal memoranda.[45] The secretariat, public relations officers, and secretarial staff accounted for nearly forty of an over-all personnel complement of fifty-two on the White House Disarmament Staff.

In order to expedite the review and coordination of disarmament matters within the Executive branch, a special interdepartmental committee on disarmament problems was established. Set up at the direction of the President in August 1955, the President's Special Committee on Disarmament was designed to serve as the principal channel of interdepartmental coordination in matters of disarmament. Proposals

---

[43] Transcript of a televised interview on "College Press Conference," ABC-TV (Mar. 20, 1955). During the two years that Stassen held this office he received about 3,000 communications in response to this invitation. A summary of one of the contributing background studies is found in White House Disarmament Staff, *Reference Documents on Disarmament Matters,* "Early Disarmament Chronology" and "Post-War Disarmament Chronology."
[44] White House press release, Jan. 13, 1956.
[45] The accumulated files in the secretariat alone totaled well over thirty cabinets when the White House office closed down in the spring of 1958.

originating in the Office of the Special Assistant on Disarmament that would otherwise have been reviewed in the Planning Board of the National Security Council, received their initial formal interdepartmental screening in the President's committee. It was composed of senior representatives (assistant secretaries or the equivalent) of the following departments and agencies: State, Defense, and Joint Chiefs of Staff, Atomic Energy Commission, Department of Justice, Central Intelligence Agency, and the United States Information Agency.[46]

The purpose, as stated in the letter from the President to Stassen, dated August 5, 1955, was to "provide maximum effectiveness in carrying forward a concentrated endeavor to reach a sound disarmament agreement under effective safeguards." It served as a device to keep the represented agencies informed of all aspects of United States disarmament policy planning.

Both the special staff and the President's committee were interdepartmental. In fact, the salaries of the officers loaned to the special staff were paid by their parent agencies. However, these men did not represent their agencies, as did the members of the President's special committee, for purposes of departmental approval or dissent. Comments, suggestions, or position papers drafted by members of the White House special staff were in the nature of services by personal staff assistants, and, for presidential decision, any proposals or positions so generated had to be fed through the formal coordination machinery of the President's special committee, and thereafter for major issues, through the National Security Council.

[46] See *The Executive Branch and Disarmament Policy,* Senate Foreign Relations Special Study No. 1 (February 20, 1956), pp. 1-9. The members of the President's Committee as therein listed were as of January 20, 1956, as follows: *State-Member:* David Wainhouse, Deputy Assistant-Secretary of State for International Organization Affairs; Alternate: Robert R. Bowie, Assistant Secretary of State, Director of the Policy Planning Staff, and State Department representative on the National Security Council Planning Board. *Defense-Member:* General Harper B. Loper; Alternate: Colonel Thomas W. Abbott (succeeding Colonel William B. Bailey); *United States Information Agency-Member:* Andrew H. Berding, Assistant Director of U.S.I.A. for Policy and Programs; Alternate: Orenn Stevens. *Justice-Member:* J. Lee Rankin, Assistant Attorney-General, Office of Legal Counsel; Alternate: Frederick W. Ford. *Central Intelligence Agency-Member:* Richard Bissell; Alternate: James Q. Reber. *Atomic Energy Commission-Member:* Dr. John von Neumann, member of commission; Alternate: Dr. Paul Fine.

Task Forces on Inspection

One of the more important organizational moves under the new arrangement was the creation of task forces on inspection. In August 1955, following the Summit Conference and the President's "open skies" proposal, Stassen asked a number of outstanding specialists to undertake a study of the methods and requirements of effective international inspection and control. Eight task forces were appointed to undertake a series of related studies.[47]

The inspection task forces were designated and their respective chairmen appointed in August 1955. Each task force leader in turn assembled a number of specialists for his field of inquiry. Public announcement concerning the appointment of these task forces was made by Stassen on October 7, 1955, during a session of the United Nations disarmament subcommittee.[48]

The composite task force effort, undertaken with the cooperation of several government agencies, constituted the first United States "operating manual" on disarmament inspection. It outlined in considerable detail the objects of control. It seemed to provide for the first time comprehensive guidance on "what to inspect, how and where it would be inspected, and a knowledge of what can and cannot be

[47] *Inspection and control of nuclear materials,* Chairman, Dr. Ernest Lawrence, Director of the University of California Radiation Laboratories, Livermore, California. *Aerial inspection and reporting,* Chairman, General James H. Doolittle (Retired), Vice President and Director of Shell Oil Company. *Inspection and reporting methods for army and ground units,* Chairman, Lt. Gen. Walter B. Smith (Retired), former Under Secretary of State and Ambassador to the Soviet Union, Vice Chairman of American Machine and Foundry Company, assisted by Lt. Gen. Lucien K. Truscott (Retired). *Navies and naval aircraft and missiles,* Chairman, Vice Adm. Oswald S. Colclough (Retired), Dean of Faculties, George Washington University. *Inspection and reporting methods for the steel industry,* Chairman, Benjamin Fairless, former Chairman, U.S. Steel Corporation. *Inspection and reporting methods for power and industry in general,* Chairman, Walker L. Cisler, President of the Detroit Edison Company. *Inspection and reporting of national budgets and finances,* Chairman, Dr. Harold G. Moulton, former President of the Brookings Institution. *Communications,* Chairman, Dr. James B. Fisk of the Bell Telephone Laboratories and member of the General Advisory Committee of the Atomic Energy Commission.

[48] U.N. Doc. DC/SC.1/PV.68 (Oct. 7, 1955), pp. 72-73.

profitably inspected if we seek to provide a safeguard against surprise attack and to supervise an international arms limitation agreement."[49]

The task forces presented their preliminary findings and recommendations on inspection at a joint meeting with the White House special staff at Quantico, Virginia, on October 22, 1955.[50] These initial reports were developed further during the next three months, and, following the submission of final reports with the cooperation of several departments in the government, the task forces disbanded. They continued, however, to be available as technical advisory groups. Although the extended, full-scale "brainstorming" exercise of the October 1955 Quantico sessions was not repeated, there were a few subsequent brief sessions of the task forces as a committee of the whole; and a number of additional special studies were undertaken at Stassen's and Secretary Dulles' request with reference to proposals considered during the London negotiations of 1957.

These reports remained highly classified. The findings of the reports were not made known outside the United States Government during Stassen's tenure as Special Assistant to the President on Disarmament, and were closely held within the government. Although Stassen had earlier told the Senate Subcommittee on Disarmament that "In due course and in the appropriate manner, we should be glad to discuss these projections with the subcommittee,"[51] he refused to release the results to any congressional members, for any reason, claiming the sanction of Executive privacy promised to the task force members at the outset of their services.[52]

The reports and the *expertise* of several of the members of the task forces who prepared them did, however, provide a substantive foundation for subsequent technical studies undertaken within and for the

[49] *Control and Reduction of Armaments*, Hearings before the Senate Committee on Foreign Relations, Pt. 1, 84 Cong. 2 sess., p. 12. See statement by Stassen.
[50] U.S. Department of State, *Disarmament: The Intensified Effort 1955-1958*, Publication 6676 (July 1958), p. 10.
[51] *Control and Reduction of Armaments*, Hearings, p. 8.
[52] *Congressional Record*, Vol. 104, No. 18, 85 Cong. 2 sess. (Feb. 4, 1958). Texts of exchange of letters between Senator Humphrey, Chairman of the Senate Subcommittee on Disarmament, and Stassen.

United States Government and the basis for working papers introduced into intergovernmental technical conferences on testing and on safeguards against surprise attack during the latter half of 1958.[53]

Significance of Organizational Changes

The significance of these organizational changes goes far beyond the realms of organization or procedure. Except for a brief period during 1946 and 1947 when Baruch represented the United States in the negotiations on atomic energy, all previous United States negotiators had suffered a number of handicaps.

The negotiators themselves never had easy access to the White House nor even to the Secretary of State. As a result, the channels for policy decisions were lengthy and complex. If occasions had arisen when speedy policy decisions would have been advantageous to the United States—no such occasion arose prior to 1955—it probably would have been impossible for the United States to secure the necessary authority in time to do any good. Stassen's position in the Cabinet helped to remedy this situation.

The United States negotiators had never received adequate support either in terms of finances or personnel to carry out their duties effectively. For example, the State Department personnel working full-time on disarmament during the period when Cohen was presenting basic proposals to the Disarmament Commission never numbered more than four.

When Patterson represented the United States in London, his staff consisted of five officers—two from the State Department, one from the United States Information Agency, and two from the armed services—and two stenographers.

[53] United Nations Nuclear Energy Commission, *Report of the Conference of Experts for the Study of the Methods of Detecting Violations of a Possible Agreement on the Suspension of Nuclear Tests*, Document EXP-NUC-28 (Aug. 20, 1958), and the subsequently released working documents of the conference; and U.N. General Assembly, *Report of the Conference of Experts for the study of Possible Measures which might be helpful in Preventing Surprise Attack and for the Preparation of a Report thereon to Governments*. Doc. A-4078 (Jan. 5, 1959).

Here again, Stassen's appointment was a mammoth stride in the right direction. During the 1957 intensive negotiations, approximately fifty officers from all interested United States agencies devoted their full time to the negotiations.

In an international negotiation with the Soviet Union, considerable leeway in both provision of personnel and expenditure of funds is essential to a successful result. The Soviet negotiators apparently as a matter of policy seek to protract and exacerbate the negotiations in order to exhaust the opposition and to obtain a favorable denouement as a result of sheer fatigue. Until Stassen's appointment, the United States negotiators never were in a position to build an organization adequate to oppose this Soviet tactic. An intense protracted negotiation such as took place in the spring and summer of 1957 would have been unthinkable either in the Disarmament Commission in 1952 or in the subcommittee in 1954. Neither the United States delegation nor any of the Western delegations was organized for such a contingency.

In a recent discussion of the methods and mechanics of diplomatic negotiating, Charles Thayer, a seasoned United States Foreign Service Officer, quotes a wise old German Socialist, Kurt Schumacher, who said, "The day you Americans are as patient as the Russians you will stop losing the cold war. And the day you learn to outsit them by a single minute you will start winning it."[54] In the 1957 negotiations on disarmament Stassen proved to be a prime exponent of the ability to outsit the Russians. In his determination to indicate this in definite behavior, he rented a large eighteenth century home on Grosvenor Square in London, wherein were lodged not only Stassen, but five members of his staff. In that atmosphere of permanence, much more than in hotel accommodations, the Americans served notice on the Russian delegation that they were prepared to dig in and negotiate for an indefinite length of time.

Stassen received the personnel resources and the policy directives to fill some of the glaring gaps in the substantive Western program. As a specific example, President Eisenhower had suggested as a part

[54] Charles W. Thayer, *Diplomat* (1959), p. 96.

of his program "a commitment by all nations to set an agreed limit upon that proportion of total production of certain strategic materials to be devoted to military purposes."[55]

This suggestion considerably enlarged certain ideas presented by the United States to the Conventional Armaments Commission in May 1950 in a brief paper dealing with the development of safeguards through industrial information.[56] Both the May 1950 paper and the President's proposal obviously required lengthy technical studies to determine their feasibility, and if they proved feasible, to convert the general ideas into precise programs. With the sole exception of an effective paper on the steel industry—produced in 1949 but never made public—the studies did not commence until Stassen set up his task forces.

This increased support within the United States Government lessened—but unfortunately did not eliminate—another handicap that had previously plagued United States negotiators—the lack of continuity in the operation. Partly because of lack of financial support, the subject of regulation of armaments had never been an attractive career either within the State Department or the armed services. Interest in the subject would rise in the presence of some specific fire that had to be extinguished and would lag as soon as the immediate urgency ebbed. As a result, in the main, with each new development within the field of regulation of armaments, new negotiators as well as untrained supporting staff had to start from the beginning. The appointment of Stassen raised hopes that the field might become sufficiently attractive to retain over a period of years the services of those who had developed some degree of *expertise*. In this way the United States would no longer be at a disadvantage in dealing with Soviet delegations in which several advisers had devoted themselves solely to this field since 1946, or the French, where Jules Moch remained "M. Désarmément" regardless of policy and government changes in his country.

Unfortunately, the advantages of continuity of tenure did not materialize until later, since Stassen deliberately sought fresh minds

[55] *The Chance for Peace*, p. 7.
[56] Senate Committee on Foreign Relations, *Disarmament and Security, A Collection of Documents, 1919-1955*, 84 Cong. 2 sess. (1956), p. 286.

that had not been exposed to the earlier negotiations and strove to create a completely new organization. Many of the problems that plagued Stassen during 1955 and 1956 may have arisen from inexperience—his own as well as that of his top advisers. It was not until 1957 that Stassen developed an experienced and smoothly functioning staff, some of whom continued to work on the problems after Stassen's departure from the scene.

Stassen used his special staff and the secretariat to the hilt, drawing from each of them ideas, intelligence collations, supporting briefs he needed to carry forward his tasks of negotiation within the United States Government, among the allies, and with the Soviet Union. He used his staff continuously and exhaustively, but he did not rely on their advice. As an administrator, as a statesman, and as a politician, his characteristic approach has almost invariably been to absorb omnivorously all the multitudinous data he has asked for, and to maintain an open mind, until the point of decision. Then, as he often phrased it himself, he "never looked back." The key decisions, including both the drafting of the major policy papers prepared during his tenure and the tactics of their use, he made alone, and carried forward alone, in several instances against the unanimous counsel of his staff, and even against the counsel of his task forces.

In the circumstances, the phenomenon of staff morale deserves particular mention, for it developed, grew, and was maintained until well after the 1957 negotiations ended in September. Despite—or, perhaps, as an integral part of—his lone hand method, Stassen was able to generate a sense of participation and an atmosphere of forward movement that provided the psychic momentum needed to keep long and painstaking and otherwise discouraging negotiations from grinding to a halt.

In his daily staff meetings, he invariably encouraged not only freedom but daring in the expression of views. Sometimes months later, ideas that in their initial expression resembled fantasy would turn into well-conceived proposals, after Stassen himself, to use his favorite expression, had "thought it through."

Liaison was one task he did delegate fully. During the six months of negotiations in London in 1957, before and especially after the new decisions of the United States on May 25, each officer of the delegation was assigned responsibility as a liaison officer to two or more allied and interested embassies, covering some twenty nations, keeping them up-to-date on the developments in the negotiations. The regular circulation of information does not solve the basic problem of achieving joint decisions, but it is essential to the cultivation of a continuing sense of partnership.

Some awareness—even as fragmentary as this—of Stassen's approach may be useful in understanding both the consequent course of negotiations and the effect of the subsequent transfer of the function back to the Department of State.

XII

The Soviet Reappraisal

A BASIC REAPPRAISAL of policy took place in the Kremlin almost simultaneously with the United States reappraisal, and the thermonuclear revolution played an important part in that reappraisal. The results were reflected in a rapid retailoring of military doctrine and strategy and in dramatic innovations in political doctrine and strategy.

Beginning in 1954, after a decade of domestic blackout on the subject of nuclear weapons, the Soviet Union embarked on a systematic campaign of informing the Soviet people of the possible effects of nuclear war and developed its own version of deterrence through massive retaliation, publicizing this at home and abroad.

On several occasions prior to 1955, the Soviet representatives had taken the position in the disarmament discussions that a nuclear war would destroy decadent capitalism, but that socialism would survive. When the Soviet leaders changed their approach, they were generally careful to avoid language that would estop them from continuing to adhere in international conferences to their old position. This is familiar Soviet bargaining technique.

However, particularly in statements outside the United Nations, the Soviet leaders stressed the mutual devastation that would result from a nuclear war. They brought home to their own people the idea that a nuclear war would virtually destroy both sides even though

270

after the initial thermonuclear strikes the socialist states might continue the war to a victorious conclusion. This admission of vast mutual devastation coupled with the new doctrinal claim that war is not fatalistically "inevitable," a deployment of weapons and forces that permit limited war and selective deterrence, and a marked shift to a diplomatic offensive, add up to a Soviet posture on mutual deterrence and nuclear stalemate not far from that held by the West.

It is hard to judge to what degree these visible evidences can be attributed specifically to the impact of the H-bomb and its implications for global annihilation.

The shift in Soviet position apparently commenced a little over a year after the death of Stalin in March 1953. This event released internal pressures for change in Soviet political and military strategy already in existence before the revolution in thermonuclear technology. The Soviet Union had, during the decade of domestic silence, raced feverishly to match the West's nuclear weapons position; the H-bomb in March 1954, with all its unexpected potential for mutual annihilation, occurred almost simultaneously with the climax of the Kremlin's race for nuclear parity with the West.

It would have been illogical for the Soviet Union to increase its emphasis on the importance of nuclear warfare, or for that matter to abandon its propaganda position of "ban the bomb" until it attained something close to nuclear parity with the West. Nor was a policy of "peaceful coexistence" new to the thermonuclear era; it had been preached with varying emphasis since 1917.[1]

However, the now familiar Soviet emphasis on tourism, cultural exchanges, and summit meetings commenced at this time. It would be a useless exercise to attempt to evaluate exactly the factors leading to this new emphasis on peaceful coexistence: the death of Stalin, the thermonuclear revolution, and probably also the West's conclusion of the treaties that brought Western European union—and, with it, Germany's postwar military forces—into existence.

It is difficult to estimate whether the shift in Soviet policy was

[1] Raymond L. Garthoff, *Soviet Strategy in the Nuclear Age* (1958), Chap. 4. See also H. S. Dinerstein, *War and the Soviet Union* (1959), Chap. 1, and Henry A. Kissinger, *Nuclear Weapons and Foreign Policy* (1957), Chaps. 5-6.

primarily a consequence of the thermonuclear revolution or had its origin in circumstances only remotely related to the arms race. In the context of the disarmament negotiations, the observable results of the Soviet reappraisal are consistent with either diagnosis. Leading Soviet officials may themselves genuinely fear the consequences of a thermonuclear war, or they may have appropriated its implications purely for purposes of diplomatic blackmail. In either case, the H-bomb has greatly enhanced both the usefulness and the desirability of nonmilitary means—including negotiations for disarmament—in pursuing the unchanged Communist goal of eventual Communist victory.

The boundaries of Soviet thinking on mutual nuclear destruction, and its alternative, lessening of tensions, mark precisely the limits of Soviet negotiations from 1955 through 1957 and therefore should be sketched in some detail.

THE INEVITABILITY OF WAR

The initial major doctrinal change resulting from the Soviet reappraisal after 1953 was the declaration that "there is no fatal inevitability of war."[2] This was accompanied by what was, for the Soviet Union, a new political concept: deterrence, expressed in its own threat of massive retaliation.

Khrushchev, in his first major theoretical pronouncement, before the Twentieth Communist Party Congress in Moscow in February 1956, set the stage for what has since governed Soviet tactics in the disarmament forum, as well as in the broader arena of the global cold war. The Marxist-Leninist precept on inevitability of war, he explained, had been correct for its time, but it no longer corresponded to contemporary conditions.

The principle of peaceful coexistence is gaining increasingly wider international recognition. And this is logical since there is no other way out in the present situation. Indeed, there are only two

[2] *New York Times*, Feb. 14, 1956. Excerpts from an official translation of speech by Khrushchev, as made available by the Soviet Information Bureau and TASS.

ways; either peaceful coexistence, or the most devastating war in history. There is no third alternative.

We presume that countries with differing social systems cannot just simply exist side by side. There must be progress to better relations, to stronger confidence among them, to cooperation.

As will be recalled, there is a Marxist-Leninist premise which says that while imperialism exists wars are inevitable. While capitalism remains on earth the reactionary forces representing the interests of the capitalist monopolies will continue to strive for war gambles and aggression, and may try to let loose war.

There is no fatal inevitability of war.

Now there are powerful social and political forces, commanding serious means capable of *preventing the unleashing of war by the imperialists and—should they try to start it—of delivering a smashing rebuff* to the aggressors and thwarting their adventuristic plans. . . . In view of the fundamental changes that have taken place in the world arena, new prospects have also opened up with regard to the transition of countries and nations to socialism. It is quite likely that the forms of the transition to socialism will become more and more variegated. Moreover, it is not obligatory for the implementation of those forms to be connected with civil war in all circumstances.[3]

This innovation in doctrine "provided the ideological basis for a strategy of indefinite continuation of the substitution of political for military forms of conflict."[4] Since war is no longer a useful course of national policy, it is no longer "inevitable."

MUTUAL DEVASTATION

A few unguarded Soviet statements admitting mutual annihilation occurred early in 1954 and during the Bulganin-Khrushchev tour of India in 1955. Thereafter, and until the Khrushchev visit to the United

---

[3] *Ibid.* Italics added.
[4] Garthoff, *op. cit.*, p. 7.

States in October 1959, however, the official line as formally laid down at the Twentieth Communist Party Congress in February 1956 was that thermonuclear war, while inflicting great losses, would destroy decadent capitalism but not communism: "Capitalism will find its grave in a new world war . . . the Socialist camp is invincible."[5]

Malenkov, who on March 12, 1954, denounced the "policy of the cold war because this policy is the policy of preparing a new world slaughter which, with the contemporary means of warfare, means the destruction of world civilization," was forced to revise this only six weeks later, on April 25, warning that if "the aggressive circles, trusting in the atomic bomb, were to decide on lunacy and would want to test the strength and might of the Soviet—there can be no doubt that the aggressor will be crushed with that same weapon and that such adventure will lead to the collapse of the capitalist social system." When Malenkov was compelled to resign the premiership in February 1955, Molotov, then Foreign Minister, declared in an obvious reprimand to Malenkov that "It is not 'world civilization' that will perish, however much it may suffer from new aggression, but the decaying social system of which bloodthirsty imperialism is the core."[6]

However, when Premier Bulganin and Khrushchev were in Bombay, India, being saluted by twenty-five trumpeting elephants, and having their first elephant ride, Khrushchev struck the theme of later pronouncements when he allowed that elephants were nice but no match for tractors when it came to usefulness.[7] More seriously, Bulganin declared that "Nehru is quite right in pointing out that coexistence is the only wise choice for all nations which would otherwise face but one alternative—mutual annihilation."[8] The important joint

---

[5] Khrushchev, address of Feb. 14, 1956, text as printed in *Komsomolskaya Pravda*, Feb. 15, 1956, p. 3. Cited by John S. Reshetar in testimony collected for Staff Study No. 8 of the Senate Committee on Foreign Relations, "Attitudes of Soviet Leaders Toward Disarmament," *Control and Reduction of Armaments*, S. Rept. 2501, 85 Cong. 2 sess., pp. 335 ff. This statement was omitted from the authorized excerpts released by TASS and published in the *New York Times*, Feb. 14, 1956.
[6] All quotations from *Pravda*, cited by Reshetar in S. Rept. 2501, pp. 90-91.
[7] *New York Times* (Nov. 24, 1955), p. 3.
[8] "Speech by N. A. Bulganin at a Bombay Meeting," *Soviet News* (Nov. 24, 1955), p. 7.

communiqué of Bulganin, Khrushchev, and Indian Prime Minister Nehru on Dec. 13, 1955, in New Delhi, included a statement regarding the "futility of war, which owing to the development of nuclear and thermonuclear weapons, could only bring disaster to mankind."[9] Bulganin's letter to President Eisenhower, of Jan. 23, 1956, said that "it is well known to everyone that the newest implements of war . . . place the peoples of all countries in an equally dangerous situation."[10]

On visiting Great Britain the Soviet leaders continued to emphasize their personal realization of the colossal destruction destined for both sides in the event of a third world war. Khrushchev dramatically spoke up at the first meeting of British and Soviet leaders at 10 Downing Street:

> What must be the way out? There is only one way out—peaceful co-existence. . . . Disputed questions cannot be settled by war. . . . We have tested the hydrogen weapon. You are preparing to test it. Both sides are aware of the power of that weapon. . . . To-day, as a result of the development of technology, war will not bring benefit to either side—it can only bring tremendous devastation.[11]

The conflict between these statements and the official Soviet line that only capitalism would perish in a nuclear war had begun to resolve itself.

On September 3, 1959, in his widely read article in *Foreign Affairs*, Khrushchev stated primarily for consumption abroad:

> What, then, remains to be done? There may be two ways out: either war—and war in the rocket and H-bomb age is fraught with the most dire consequences for all nations—or peaceful co-exist-

---

[9] *New York Times*, Dec. 14, 1955, p. 14.
[10] U.S. Department of State *Bulletin*, Vol. 24 (Feb. 6, 1956), p. 94.
[11] "Communiqué on First Meeting of British and Soviet Leaders": statement issued by the Foreign Office after the first meeting at 10 Downing Street between the Soviet leaders and the British Ministers on April 19, 1956, in *Soviet News*, No. 3375 (April 20, 1956), p. 2.

ence. Whether you like your neighbor or not, nothing can be done about it, you have to find some way of getting on with him, for you both live on one and the same planet.[12]

He enlarged this position in his September 18, 1959, address to the United Nations. "Is it possible to disregard the fact that the destructive potential of the means of warfare has reached such tremendous proportions, and can one forget that there is not one spot on the globe today that is inaccessible to nuclear and rocket weapons?"[13]

Khrushchev thus acknowledged to the world that a two-way nuclear strike would mean mutual devastation, though he remained silent on the question whether the devastation would be greater in the Soviet Union or in the West. An official Soviet statement in October 1960 moved some distance toward admitting the symmetrical destructiveness of nuclear warfare in both the East and West.[14]

A month later, however, an article in *Red Star*, Moscow, took the position that the Soviet Union could survive a nuclear first strike.

A number of bourgeois military theoreticians pay great attention to the length of a rocket-nuclear war. . . . Thus American General Lernay [Le May?] said that a universal rocket war will last no longer than two to three days. If it is a matter of conducting a war against great countries which comprise thousands of kilometers and which are well prepared militarily, a swift blitzkrieg cannot be relied upon. It must be made clear that the time a war will take cannot be planned in advance and in a categorical manner.

The article even expressed the hope that the Soviet defenses might avoid much of the devastation:

[12] *New York Times*, Sept. 3, 1959, p. 4. Reprint of Khrushchev's article "On Peaceful Coexistence" in *Foreign Affairs* (October 1959).
[13] *New York Times*, Sept. 18, 1959, p. 8. The primary purpose of this statement may have been to point out that there were no sanctuaries for the United States.
[14] Article by Talenski in *International Affairs* (Moscow).

In this connection the anti-aircraft and anti-rocket defenses which are called upon to protect the rear, as well as the troops, acquire extremely great significance. The crushing of the nuclear-rocket and rocket-carrying forces and the nuclear air force of the enemy will become one of the main tasks.

Now the rocket troops have become the main arms of our armed forces in general. This by no means signifies a curtailment in our land forces. Soviet military science holds the view that victory can be achieved only as a result of the correct utilization of rocket weapons in coordination with all the other means of armed combat.

Despite this emphasis on Soviet ability to survive a first nuclear strike, the author of the article never underestimates the devastation that would result from nuclear warfare.

At present a strategic rocket is capable of delivering a nuclear charge whose destructive power equals that of all the bombs dropped in the period 1940-1945 by Anglo-American Air Force on targets in Germany and the countries occupied by it. In a nuclear-rocket war, from the very first day, the deep rear will become a battlefield of fierce combat with all the terrible consequences resulting therefrom.[15]

It is clear that the Soviet leaders and military writers have moved away from the old position that an all-out nuclear war would destroy capitalism but leave the Communist states unscathed. They have conceded that such a war would produce mutual devastation, but probably not mutual annihilation. They have come close to admitting the existence of a "balance of terror" between East and West. They have brought this message to the Soviet people. In these circumstances, it would be of little consequence if some future Soviet negotiator at-

[15] Lt. General S. Krasilnikov, "On the Character of Modern War" *Red Star*, Nov. 18, 1960.

tempted to return to the old doctrine that a nuclear war would be harmful only to decadent capitalism.[16]

MASSIVE RETALIATION

In contrast with the evolution in the United States of the doctrine of deterrence through massive retaliation, the Soviet equivalent emerged *after* the Soviet Union achieved its counterpart of the United States March 1954 Bikini bomb. The concept of massive retaliation, stated in classical terms, was phrased by Khrushchev in one of his major addresses during the trip to India. There, on November 26, 1955, in Bangalore, laden with garlands as well as compliments from the Indian leaders, Khrushchev chose the occasion of his dramatic announcement of the Soviets' latest hydrogen bomb explosion to enunciate what has come to be characterized by the Russian proverb quoted in it: "If you live among wolves, you must howl like wolves."[17] He declared:

The latest H-bomb test explosion was the most powerful of the explosions thus far. Using a relatively small quantity of fissionable material, our scientists and engineers have managed to produce an explosion equal to that of several million tons of conventional explosives. But I want to tell you, friends, that the Soviet Union will never abuse its possession of this weapon, and we shall be happy if these bombs are destined never to be set off over towns and villages. Let these bombs lie and play on the nerves of those who would like to start a war. Let them know that war cannot be started for if they start it they will get a fitting reply.[18]

[16] The Chinese Communists continue to predict that "the United States or other imperialists" would be destroyed if they launched a nuclear war; but that "a civilization thousands of times higher than the capitalist system and a truly beautiful future" would be rapidly created on the debris of dead imperialism and would repay "the enormous sacrifices of a future imperialist war." . . . Quoted from *The Washington Post and Times-Herald*, April 20, 1960, Reuters report of an article in the Chinese Communist Party's official magazine, *Red Flag*.
[17] U.S. Department of State, *Soviet World Outlook, a Handbook of Communist Statements*, Publication 6836 (July 1959), p. 198.
[18] "Speech by Khrushchev in Bangalore," *Soviet News* (Nov. 30, 1955).

Other statements of the Soviet version of deterrence through massive retaliation have been offered periodically. For example:

We don't want to intimidate anyone; still less do we want to boast about the military technical achievements we have. But in order to cool the inflamed imaginations of the more zealous advocates of the arms drive, we have to recall the results of the recent tests of the latest Soviet hydrogen bomb:[19]

If war occurs, the countries of the socialist camp, united by common class and social-economic interests and a joint ideology will not only deal a smashing counter blow to the imperial aggressors but will achieve the latter's complete annihilation. Moreover, an attack of imperialist aggressors on any of the socialist countries will be regarded as an attack on the U.S.S.R. and the entire camp of socialism. . . . In the light of all this, the "theories" of some bourgeois military ideologists on so-called local, limited wars against the socialist countries look particularly foolish. . . .

If a new war occurs, it will be conducted primarily with new means of combat. These means have colossal destructive power, unlimited range, great speed, and great accuracy. It follows from this that from the very first moment this war would become a nuclear rocket war.[20]

These threats of "massive retaliation" are in as extreme language as any used by the United States when it alone possessed the atom bomb. The Soviet Union, in an era of nuclear stalemate, may be in a better position than the United States to make such a threat because of the genuine belief of its military leaders that the Soviet Union could carry on more easily than the West after reciprocal nuclear strikes. The experience of World War II when the Soviet Union carried on despite the loss of the major portion of its industry and apparently much of its natural resources may be convincing to the Soviet leadership. The fact that the Soviet leaders hedged their predictions of mu-

[19] "Speech by N. S. Khrushchev to the Session of the U.S.S.R. Supreme Soviet." *Soviet News* (Jan. 5, 1956), p. 6.
[20] Lt. Gen. S. Krasilnikov, "On the Character of Modern War," *op. cit.*

tual annihilation likewise has made it possible for the Soviet Union to rely on the nuclear threat much longer than the Western leaders, already on record as believing that a two-strike nuclear war would be mutual suicide.

Thus the impact of an impending nuclear stalemate on the theory of deterrence was equally profound for both the United States and the Soviet Union, but the results were not identical. For the West, the effectiveness of massive retaliation was undermined, and a theory of limited war and graduated nuclear deterrence had to be constructed and implemented to reinstate an effective deterrent. The Russians, on the other hand, suddenly gained and used a new political tool—the threat of massive retaliation—and moved rapidly in modernizing military doctrine and deployment of weapons and forces to produce a posture which did not *require* the exercise of massive retaliation, or even selective nuclear retaliation, in support of their own new strategic concept of deterrence.[21]

There is convincing evidence that although the Soviet Union has fully allowed for the *contingency* of nuclear war, the whole structure of its renovated military posture, in doctrine and deployment, has been in terms that increasingly place the burden of the initiation of nuclear war—including limited nuclear war—on the West.

The Soviet reliance on balanced forces, its retention of the old prenuclear Clausewitz objective of war as the destruction of the enemies' military forces, and the expectation of long wars[22] has produced a military posture that, ironically, fits the Western theory of selective deterrence as well as, if not better than, does the Western military posture.

President Eisenhower's statement after the 1955 Geneva conference that "there seems to be a growing realization by all that nuclear warfare, pursued to the ultimate, could be practically race suicide"[23] may not fully reflect the Soviet reappraisal, but its substantive corollary, the emergence of a situation of thermonuclear stalemate, has been

[21] Garthoff, *op. cit.*, pp. 101-03, 185.
[22] *Ibid.*, pp. 71-90.
[23] Radio-Television address by President Eisenhower, July 25, 1955. Text in *The Geneva Conference of Heads of Governments: (July 18-23, 1955)*, Department of State, Publication 6046 (October 1955), p. 84.

fully comprehended and well exploited by the Soviet Union. Under conditions of nuclear stalemate, the Soviet shift to an intensified diplomatic offensive, including its own set of disarmament proposals which it describes as "partial, confidence building measures," can be interpreted as a reflection of a deliberate decision for the moment to pursue its ultimate goals through negotiation. It follows that the Soviet tactic might suddenly change if, as a result of the missile gap or some other technological breakthrough, the situation of nuclear stalemate, in the judgment of the Soviet leaders, no longer prevailed.

THE SOVIET SHIFT TO

PARTIAL MEASURES

The first indication of the Soviet shift to a partial "confidence building" approach came on the heels of President Eisenhower's December 8, 1953 address. In a formal statement on December 21, 1953, the Soviet Union denounced the United States proposals for an international atomic energy agency to supervise and administer transfers of fissionable materials for peaceful uses and countered with its own separable, first step proposal: unconditional renunciation of use of "atomic, hydrogen or other weapons of mass destruction."

The proposal was presented in the context of "easing international tension and creating an atmosphere of mutual peace and confidence," and as "an important step toward achieving complete elimination of all nuclear weapons." It was formally introduced into the disarmament subcommittee discussions six months later, on June 1, 1954, and remained a primary and reiterated demand until 1958.[24]

The U.S.S.R. had on several previous occasions proposed the prohibition of the use of nuclear weapons. Indeed, this was one of the specific demands of the greatest Soviet propaganda campaign of the previous three years—the Stockholm Appeal.

However, the novel feature of the new proposal, particularly in the subcommittee forum, was that it was the first indication of the Soviet

[24] U.N. Doc. DC/SC.1/8 (June 8, 1954).

shift toward concentrating on alternatives other than comprehensive disarmament. It was the first indication that the Soviet Union might support partial measures that would reduce tensions in advance of a general and drastic disarmament program, the first substantive shift away from unconditional insistence on prohibition of nuclear weapons.

Meanwhile, the emphasis on peaceful coexistence was intensified along a broad front, marked by diplomatic and economic initiatives that stood in sharp contrast to the policies followed before the death of Stalin.

In November 1954, the Soviet Union joined in a unanimous vote in the United Nations approving an international conference on the peaceful uses of atomic energy, agreed to serve on an advisory preparatory commission,[25] and also agreed to engage in negotiations on the establishment of the International Atomic Energy Agency. In April 1955, the Soviet Union with Austria agreed on terms for the long-delayed treaty of peace, and in May joined in Four-Power signature of that treaty. A visit of conciliation to the Tito government in Yugoslavia, an invitation to Chancellor Adenauer to visit Moscow, unilateral reductions of armed forces beginning in August 1955, and an intensive campaign of economic and technical assistance in Asia and the Middle East[26]—all these punctuated a diplomatic offensive conducted on an accelerating scale. The campaign was such as to prompt an extraordinary statement by the United States delegation to the United Nations, addressed to the Secretary of State, and announced and discussed by him at a press conference on January 11, 1956:

The present period in history may one day be recognized as a major turning point in the struggle between Communism and freedom. It appears to be clearly a shift in the cold war, in which

---

[25] Res. 810 (IX), Dec. 4, 1954.

[26] Among these were the Soviet offer of a steel plant to India, sale of arms to Egypt, offers of assistance to Egypt in building the Aswan High Dam, Hungarian railway equipment for Egypt, Czech cement works and a sugar refinery for Syria, Polish capital equipment to various countries in the Middle East. See address by Deputy Under Secretary Murphy, "The New Soviet Diplomatic Offensive," in Department of State *Bulletin*, Vol. 34 (1956), pp. 168-71.

economic and social problems have moved to the forefront. . . . We [have been] conscious that the Soviet Union, elsewhere in the world, was using economic and social collaboration as a means for jumping military as well as political barriers.[27]

Reiteration of the role of "first step" measures in restoring confidence and trust, particularly among the great powers, became a common prelude to nearly all the separable, partial measures that beginning in 1955, were proposed and pressed on the West by the Soviet Union.[28]

Khrushchev's key address of February 14, 1956, to the Twentieth Communist Party Congress, further underlined the Soviet decision to make a major effort to secure agreement among the great powers on partial measures of disarmament.

For the first time since the war a certain détente has set in [in] international tension. In this atmosphere the Geneva Four Power Heads of Government conference became possible. The conference demonstrated the viability and correctness of the methods of negotiations between countries. . . .

And in this, absolutely necessary requisites in relations between great powers are equal efforts and mutual concessions. The method of negotiation must become the only method of resolving international issues.

Collective security in Europe, collective security in Asia and disarmament—these are the three major problems, whose solution

[27] Text of statement and transcript of Secretary Dulles' news conference of Jan. 11, 1956; *ibid.*, pp. 117-25.
[28] For example, the Soviet Government's May 10, 1955 proposals, usually remembered as marking Soviet acknowledgment that past nuclear production could not be controlled and suggesting ground control posts to guard against surprise attack, placed both of these, as well as other substantive, separable measures therein proposed, in a "confidence-building" context. (See Chap. 13.) The implication that execution of partial measures would precede the "execution of a broad disarmament program" is obvious. Soviet statements on its June 14, 1957 separable and controlled test cessation proposal invariably cite May 10, 1955 as its origin, even though its *separable* character was not delineated in the May 10 proposals.

can create a basis for a stable and lasting peace. . . . Pending agreement on the major questions of disarmament, we express readiness to agree to certain partial measures in this sphere, such as the cessation of tests of thermonuclear weapons, not to permit troops on the territory of Germany to have atomic weapons and the reduction of military budgets.[29]

This became the framework for the 1957 negotiations.

THE TWO PATHS

Following, as it did, the Soviet thermonuclear detonation of November 1955, Khrushchev's accompanying "two paths" theme carried a familiar echo of parallel United States pronouncements after Bikini:

The principle of peaceful coexistence is gaining increasingly wider international recognition. And this is logical, since there is no other way out in the present situation. Indeed, there are only two ways: either peaceful coexistence or the most devastating war in history. There is no third alternative.[30]

The "two paths" theme was repeated in the Soviet statement of November 17, 1956, which heralded the first break in Soviet opposition to aerial inspection:

The Soviet Government considers it necessary with all seriousness to underscore the fact that before the world at present are two paths: either the path for terminating the cold war . . . disarmament and the creation of all conditions for the peaceful coexistence of states with different economic and social systems, or the continuation of the armaments race, the continuation of the cold war—the path leading to an unprecedentedly burdensome and

[29] *New York Times*, Feb. 14, 1956.
[30] *Ibid.* Compare Khrushchev's language with that of President Eisenhower as given earlier in this study, Chap. 11, pp. 247-53.

destructive war which would bring to the entire world inestimable calamities and sufferings.[31]

By the end of 1956—but not until then—the readjustments of military theory and strategy to encompass the mutual restraints imposed by the thermonuclear age had proceeded far enough in both East and West to permit the opening of serious negotiations for the regulation of armaments on the new approach of partial, first step measures.

[31] White House Disarmament Staff, *Eisenhower-Bulganin Correspondence*, Secretariat Note 157, April 1, 1957, p. 80.

XIII

Interim Sparring

DURING 1955, the great powers considered the subject of the regulation of armaments on four separate occasions: (1) the second session of the Subcommittee of Five of the United Nations Disarmament Commission, which took place in London from February 25 to May 18; (2) the "Summit" Meeting of Geneva in late July and early August; (3) the third session of the Subcommittee of Five in New York from August 29 to October 7; and (4) the Geneva Meeting of Foreign Ministers from October 27 to November 16. In addition, the annual review of this subject by all states took place in the General Assembly in December 1955.

SETBACK

The Soviet attitudes in the General Assembly of 1954 had given some indication of change to a less rigid position. The most hopeful sign had been the proposal of Soviet representative Vyshinsky for the preparation of a draft treaty "on the basis of the British-French proposals."[1] In addition, Vyshinsky had shown slightly greater flexibility

[1] U.N. General Assembly, Ninth Session, *Verbatim Record*, Doc. A/2742 (Sept. 30, 1954), p. 2.

286

on the all-important problem of controls and had accepted the Western idea that armed forces should be reduced to fixed levels in lieu of a percentage reduction. While Vyshinsky had avoided committing the Soviet Union to a changed policy, nevertheless this show of flexibility had created some hope, which was strengthened when, for the first time since 1946, the General Assembly resolution suggesting that the disarmament subcommittee reconvene received unanimous support.[2]

On the day that the subcommittee reconvened, Andrei Gromyko on behalf of the Soviet Union introduced a resolution that in effect brought the Soviet Union back to its rigid pre-1954 position. The proposal called for (1) a freeze of armed forces, armaments, and arms expenditures at January 1, 1955 levels, (2) the immediate destruction of all nuclear weapons, and (3) "international control over the observance of the decision."[3] Furthermore, Gromyko in another Soviet resolution of March 8, 1955, insisted on the adoption of his proposal prior to any discussion of the British-French proposal.[4]

Thus, once again, the Soviet Union was insisting on a decision to disarm prior to the creation of machinery to ensure the observance of the decision. It was demanding the elimination of nuclear weapons, in which the West had superiority, prior to reduction of armed forces and conventional armaments in which the Soviet Union had superiority; and it was refusing to go ahead with negotiations on the basis of the British-French proposals until adoption of Soviet proposals that would in effect vitiate the British-French proposals.

This phenomenon of the Soviet Union first making a concession, then repudiating it, and later with a great fanfare of propaganda making the concession a second time as if it were new, is a familiar pattern in Soviet diplomatic negotiations. This time, however, the phenomenon seems to have been linked with broader political developments.

1. In the subcommittee discussions Ambassadors Lodge and Wadsworth were representing the United States. Simultaneously, Stassen,

---

[2] Res. 216 (IX), Nov. 5, 1954.

[3] U.N. Disarmament Commission, Subcommittee of the Disarmament Commission, *Second Report* (Oct. 7, 1955), Annex 1, Doc. DC/SC.1/12/Rev. 1 (Feb. 25, 1955). Cited hereafter by annex and document numbers.

[4] Annex 3, U.N. Doc. DC/SC.1/14 (March 8, 1955).

with cabinet rank, was recruiting a large staff and was inspiring a vast amount of well-publicized and much needed activity. The Soviet leaders may well have realized that at this point the United States was in no position to make the decisions that would be required as a part of any genuine negotiating. Therefore, it may have seemed untimely to offer concessions when counterconcessions were out of the question.

2. In fields outside of disarmament, despite the cessation of hostilities in Korea and Indochina, the developments did not indicate any appreciable thaw in the "cold war." This was the period of the Mutual Defense Treaty between the United States and the Republic of China; of the joint resolution of the Senate and House authorizing the President to employ the armed forces of the United States to protect Formosa; of the Baghdad Pact and SEATO; of the NATO agreement to share atomic information. At the same time, the Soviet Union had made what it must have regarded as a major concession in agreeing to the Austrian peace treaty. The Soviet leaders may well have concluded that a conciliatory position in the disarmament negotiations should await further evidences of a thaw in the cold war.

3. Moreover, this was the period of the great debate in the Soviet military establishment concerning "the laws of military science." Marshal Zhukov's editorial criticizing the military leaders who merely memorized Stalin's writings and calling for original thought in the study of military science was published in March 1955.[5] While this article reflected decisions that already had been made, it is reasonable to suppose that the application of the decisions in the military field to the disarmament negotiations followed rather than preceded the military decisions. Therefore, by March 1955, the Soviet reappraisal of position may not have proceeded far enough to permit even the reiteration of Vyshinsky's 1954 positions, let alone their development.

4. Vyshinsky's previous concessions were specifically directed to the British-French proposals, which in 1954 the United States had supported but *not* co-sponsored. The British-French proposals were an elaboration of past Western positions calling for "comprehensive dis-

[5] Raymond L. Garthoff, *Soviet Strategy in the Nuclear Age* (1958), p. 69.

armament." The Soviet Union may not have wished to go further into proposals for "comprehensive disarmament" without assurance that the United States was still moving in this direction.

This assurance soon materialized. On March 8, the United States and Canada joined with Great Britain and France in co-sponsoring a proposed United Nations resolution incorporating the entire substance of the British-French memorandum. On March 12, the Western powers introduced a further resolution reiterating some of the principles drawn from previous Western proposals that must govern any program of "comprehensive disarmament." In March and April, the Western powers introduced additional proposals generally restating past positions on reduction of armed forces, on nuclear weapons, and on a plan for supervising any disarmament program.[6] The United States and Canada did not join the United Kingdom and France in sponsoring the paper suggesting ceilings for armed forces.

On March 18, *after* the United States had indicated its continued interest in "comprehensive disarmament" through co-sponsoring the resolution incorporating the British-French memorandum, Gromyko suddenly returned in the main to Vyshinsky's September 1954 position accepting the Anglo-French plan as the basis of a disarmament treaty, but insisting that the discussion should proceed entirely on his version of the Anglo-French plan.[7]

Malik replaced Gromyko late in March, and thereafter the Soviet oratory was slightly less vituperative. However, until May 10, the discussions dragged on mainly in time-consuming and fruitless efforts to get the Soviet representative to explain the meaning of his proposals and to focus on specific issues. Meanwhile, the Western powers had made a good paper record by bringing their past proposals for "comprehensive disarmament" up to date.

The United States reaffirmation at this time of its support of the past comprehensive disarmament proposals was as incongruous as the

[6] Annex 4, U.N. Doc. DC/SC.1/15/Rev. 1 (March 8, 1955); Annex 6, U.N. Doc. DC/SC.1/17 (March 12, 1955); Annex 9, U.N. Doc. DC/SC.1/20 (March 20, 1955); Annex 12, U.N. Doc. DC/SC.1/23 (April 18, 1955); Annex 13, U.N. Doc. DC/SC.1/24 (April 19, 1955); Annex 14, U.N. Doc. DC/SC.1/25 (April 21, 1955).
[7] Annex 8, U.N. Doc. DC/SC.1/19/Rev. 1 (March 18, 1955)

Soviet return to complete rigidity. In the spring of 1954, when the reappraisal of United States positions was little more than a puff of smoke, the United States representative, Morehead Patterson, on at least two occasions had hedged the American support of previous positions because of weapons developments.[8] When the United States reappraisal had grown from a puff of smoke to a roaring flame, the United States in the spring of 1955 gave its unqualified support to the past programs, paying no attention to Stassen's operation. As a result, the reversal of United States positions, which was to take place four months later, was the more acute and startling.

The absence of coordination at this time within the United States Government probably had an administrative rather than a substantive foundation. Stassen was stressing the desirability of new minds and fresh viewpoints. Most of the political advisers of previous United States representatives in disarmament negotiations had moved on to new fields of activity. Lodge and Wadsworth, the United States representatives in London, with their backgrounds of representing the United States in the United Nations, reaffirmed positions in the subcommittee that in the past had proved politically attractive and had received almost unanimous support in the United Nations. Apparently, none of their immediate advisers was acutely aware of the implications of the pending United States reappraisal of policy. This episode vividly illustrated a great weakness in the United States approach toward the entire program of regulation of armaments—the absence of continuity, both of policy and of personnel.

MAY 10, 1955

On May 10, 1955, Malik introduced in the subcommittee without any advance warning a completely new proposal going far beyond any previous Soviet suggestions.[9] The proposal was long and rambling. The first part paralleled closely the program that year after year the Soviet Union was accustomed to introduce into the General Assembly

[8] See Chap. 10.
[9] Annex 15, U.N. Doc. DC/SC.1/26/Rev. 2 (May 10, 1955)

in its all-inclusive resolutions to get rid of the cold war: put an end to propaganda, settle outstanding problems through international negotiation, withdraw all troops from German territory, liquidate foreign military bases, foster the peaceful uses of the atom, settle Far Eastern problems, remove barriers to trade.

The second part of the resolution dealing with reduction of armaments and prohibition of atomic weapons called for a program far closer to the positions of the West than any previous Soviet proposals. The reductions and prohibitions were to take place in two stages (the West had suggested three stages and the Soviet Union had previously insisted that everything happen at once). In the first stage, there would be a freeze of levels of armed forces, conventional armaments, and military expenditures of the big five accompanied by an agreement on ceilings for armed forces. The figures for the ceilings for armed forces were those proposed by the Western powers. A world disarmament conference would fix the ceilings for other states. The reductions in armed forces and armaments from the existing levels to the agreed ceilings would take place in two stages: 50 per cent in the first stage and 50 per cent in the second stage. The elimination of nuclear weapons would not take place until the completion of 75 per cent of the reductions of armed forces and conventional armaments. This was fairly close to the Western position.

This part of the Soviet proposal contained other provisions that without much further negotiation and modification would be unacceptable to the West, such as the elimination of bases on foreign soil, a solemn pledge not to use nuclear weapons prior to setting up machinery to ensure the observance of the pledge, and a ridiculous time sequence cramming the entire process into the years of 1956 and 1957. Also for the first time, the Soviet Union dealt with nuclear tests, proposing their discontinuance under supervision of an international commission. Despite unsatisfactory features, this second part of the Soviet proposal marked a distinct advance toward an agreed program of comprehensive disarmament.

However, the Soviet Union reserved its startling changes of position for the third part of its resolution, entitled, "Concerning the Conclusion of an International Convention on the Reduction of Armaments and the Prohibition of Atomic Weapons."[10] This portion of the resolution commenced with a long preamble containing the following:

It is impossible to disregard the fact that there exists at present considerable international tension and mistrust in relations between States. It is this that accounts for the fact that, in the conditions of mistrust among States which have come into being, barriers of every sort are being erected even in regard to the interchange of industrial, agricultural, scientific, cultural and other delegations. Such a situation makes difficult the attainment of agreement regarding the admission by States to their enterprises, particularly those engaged in military production, of foreign control officials who might carry out the inspection of such enterprises.

In the existing situation, when many States are displaying legitimate anxiety for their security, it is difficult to expect that these States would trustingly provide other States with facilities for access to industrial and other resources of theirs which are vital to their security.

In so far as the necessary trust does not at the present time exist between States, a situation may arise in which the adoption of decisions on international control will in reality be reduced to a mere formality which does not achieve the objective. This is all the more inadmissible because, in present conditions, the greatest apprehensions exist among peace-loving peoples in connection with the existence of atomic and hydrogen weapons, in regard to which the institution of international control is particularly difficult.

This danger is inherent in the very nature of atomic production. It is well known that the production of atomic energy for peaceful purposes can be used for the accumulation of stocks of explosive atomic materials, and moreover, in ever greater quantities. This means that States having establishments for the production of atomic energy can accumulate, in violation of the relevant agreements, large quantities of explosive materials for the production of atomic weapons. The danger of this state of affairs becomes still

[10] *Ibid.*, p. 9.

more understandable if account is taken of the fact that where the corresponding quantities of explosive atomic materials exist production of actual atomic and hydrogen bombs is technically fully feasible and can be effected on a large scale.

Thus, there are possibilities beyond the reach of international control for evading this control and for organising the clandestine manufacture of atomic and hydrogen weapons, even if there is a formal agreement on international control. In such a situation, the security of the States signatories to the international convention cannot be guaranteed, since the possibility would be open to a potential aggressor to accumulate stocks of atomic and hydrogen weapons for a surprise atomic attack on peace-loving States.[11]

The resolution then outlined separately its system of controls during the first or preliminary stage of reduction of armaments and prohibition of weapons, and during the second stage, when greater confidence among nations had been achieved. In the first stage the control organ "shall establish on the territory of all the States concerned on a basis of reciprocity, control at large ports, at railway junctions, on main motor highways and in aerodromes."[12] In addition, the control organ would have the right to require states to furnish the necessary information on the execution of their measures for the reduction of armaments and armed forces, and would have unimpeded access to budgetary records of the various states. These powers were not very extensive, but they were far more than the Soviet Union had previously been willing to entrust to a control organ during the early stages of its program. At least the control organ would be able even at the outset to station some of its inspectors on the territory of the states that were to be inspected.

In the second stage, the international control organ would have far more extensive powers, including the power (a) "to exercise control, including inspection on a continuing basis to the extent necessary to insure implementation of the above-mentioned convention by all

[11] *Ibid.*, pp. 16-18.
[12] *Ibid.*, p. 20.

states"; and (b) "to have permanently in all States signatories to the convention its own staff of inspectors having within the bounds of the control function they exercise, unimpeded access at all times to all objects of control."[13]

These latter provisions came fairly close to an acceptance in principle of the Western position on international control. If in fact the Soviet Union had abandoned its previous position of limiting the international control organ to certain specified powers and now supported the general position that the control organ should have full power to exercise adequate control to ensure implementation of commitments, then on this important point the Western views and the Soviet views were identical.

On the equally important problem of detection of clandestine operations, the new Soviet position was somewhat more equivocal. If the phrase, "unimpeded access at all times to all objects of control," gave the control organization the right to inspect at any time any installation where it suspected a violation of commitments, then the new Soviet position in principle was again identical with the Western position. However, "objects of control" might have a narrower definition.

Of course, an agreement in principle did not mean that there would be agreement when attempts were made to translate the principles into a workable program. However, the Soviet Union in going a long distance toward agreement with the West on the principles of control was opening a path for meaningful discussion of what should be controlled. By combining in one paper a clear-cut statement that past production of fissionable materials could no longer be controlled and an agreement that controls should exist "to the extent necessary to insure implementation of the convention by all states," the Soviet Union was suggesting a disarmament program that no longer required the elimination of nuclear weapons. This was a clear invitation to the West to discuss partial measures of disarmament that might reduce tensions and might lead to a more complete program at some future time.

The Soviet Union, by dividing the May 10 proposals into three distinct parts, was in effect suggesting three separate paths for re-

[13] *Ibid.*, p. 21.

ducing world tensions. The first path was that of political settlements without proceeding to an armaments agreement. The second path was to go forward in the manner of the British-French proposals, now co-sponsored by the United States, and in principle to agree on the outlines of a program for radical reduction of armaments—in short, "comprehensive disarmament." Such an agreement in principle might reduce tensions even if the actual reductions in armaments were deferred. The third path pointed out that, in view of the impossibility of accounting for past production of fissionable material and in the existing state of world tensions, a comprehensive program of disarmament could not be achieved. As an alternative to outlining a broad and immediately unrealizable program for comprehensive disarmament, the Soviet Union was willing to proceed with partial measures that would improve world confidence and would permit more extensive agreements when confidence became greater.

Thus each ·part of this proposal suggested a distinct and separate path toward the same general objective. In all subsequent negotiations, the Soviet Union differentiated sharply between the second and third paths expressing its willingness to go ahead on either one. The Soviet Union also pursued the first path actively, but this was outside of the disarmament negotiations. The most visible results of the first path were the greatly increased contacts between East and West in cultural and economic fields.

All four Western representatives recognized the importance of the new Soviet proposals. Tuesday, May 10, suddenly became a significant date. Jules Moch of France in an immediate response, declared: "I would almost say that the whole thing looks too good to be true"; but with more than ordinary shrewdness he continued the comment: "I wish to be certain that this represents a well thought-out attitude and that tomorrow we will not have a surprise in the opposite direction; for it is indeed a surprise today to see practically all of our proposals accepted."[14] In the first Disarmament Commission meeting following the Soviet pronouncement, the British representative, Anthony

[14] U.N. Disarmament Commission, Subcommittee of the Disarmament Commission, *Verbatim Record*, Doc. DC/SC.1/PV.47 (May 10, 1955), pp. 56-57. Cited hereafter by document number and date.

Nutting, tagged the Soviet declaration as "an encouraging development and a significant advance"; he referred to it as "this welcome dividend" following two and a half months wherein there was "some success," but nothing like the advance that he had not dreamed possible "on Monday last, or even on Tuesday morning." David Johnson of Canada commented that the proposals "in several respects made a significant advance towards the Western position." Wadsworth, as chairman of the May 12 meeting where the new proposals were under discussion, speaking last of all, stated: "I should like to echo very generally the sentiments which have already been expressed by my three colleagues of the Western Powers."[15]

It was obvious that the Soviet proposal required careful study. Furthermore, the summit meeting was scheduled for the latter part of July and included the subject of regulation of armaments on its agenda. It was therefore logical for the subcommittee to adjourn on May 18 until the completion of the summit meeting.[16] ·

The eminent and devoted statesman and scholar, Philip Noel-Baker speaks of May 10, 1955, as "the moment of hope." This conclusion seems justified since the Soviet Union had now unequivocally abandoned its former intransigent positions, which had prevented any genuine negotiations ever since 1946. However, Noel-Baker's further conclusion that it would have been possible to move directly to a treaty for comprehensive disarmament along the lines of the Anglo-French proposal does not seem justified.[17] It is true that the Soviet Union continued to advocate a program of comprehensive disarmament. It could hardly have abandoned its close attachment to comprehensive disarmament in view of its past propaganda theme of "ban the bomb." However, its advocacy of "comprehensive disarmament," the second path forward, became more and more a statement of ultimate objectives rather than of immediately realizable measures.

The Soviet Union through admitting that past production of fissionable materials could no longer be controlled had invited a discussion of measures that could be controlled and had in the main ac-

[15] U.N. Doc. DC/SC.1/PV.48 (May 12, 1955), pp. 12, 21, 23.
[16] U.N. Doc. DC/SC.1/PV.49 (May 18, 1955), p. 13.
[17] Philip Noel-Baker, *The Arms Race* (1958), Chap. 2.

cepted the general principles of control advocated by the West. The Soviet Union was now calling for confidence-building measures that would permit increasingly complex systems of controls. May 10 marked the day when the Soviet Union recognized, as an alternative approach to the remote objective of comprehensive disarmament, the immediate objective of confidence-building measures that would reduce international tensions and diminish the likelihood of war. The future conduct of the Soviet Union in disarmament negotiations amply confirms this interpretation of the May 10 proposal.[18]

SUMMIT MEETING

At the meeting of the heads of government of the United States, the United Kingdom, the Soviet Union, and France held on July 21, 1955, the subject of disarmament was one of the most important items on the agenda. At the outset, President Eisenhower emphasized the importance of an adequate inspection system. He said:

The lessons of history teach us that disarmament agreements without adequate reciprocal inspection increase the dangers of war and do not brighten the prospects of peace. Thus it is my view that the priority attention of our combined study of disarmament should be upon the subject of inspection and reporting.[19]

Similarly, Sir Anthony Eden said that "No disarmament plan can be acceptable which does not contain a system of inspection and reporting which is adequate to support every phase of the plan."[20] The Prime Minister of France, M. Edgar Fauré, made similar statements,[21]

[18] Annex 18, U.N. Doc. DC/SC.1/29/Rev. 1 (Aug. 29, 1955), p. 4. See also, *New York Times*, Sept. 19, 1959, p. 9. Khrushchev's speech to the United Nations included this reference: "The Soviet Government deems it appropriate to recall its proposals of May 10, 1955, on disarmament which contains concrete considerations regarding partial steps in the field of disarmament."
[19] U.S. Department of State, *The Geneva Conference of Heads of Government, July 18-23, 1955*, Publication 6046 (October 1955), p. 57.
[20] "Speech by Sir Anthony Eden, Geneva, July 21, 1955," White House Disarmament Staff, *Reference Documents on Disarmament*, Background Series, D-1—D-42, p. 102.
[21] U.S. Department of State, *The Geneva Conference of Heads of Government*, p. 28.

and Marshal Bulganin in reporting to the Supreme Soviet on the Geneva meeting said on August 4, "As the United States President justly pointed out, every disarmament plan boils down to the question of control and inspection. This question is indeed very serious and we must find a solution to it which would be mutually acceptable."[22]

The specific programs brought forward by each of the four heads of government reflected to a greater or less degree the shift in emphasis to measures that might restore confidence and establish the basis for further progress.

On July 21, Bulganin said:

A broad disarmament programme can be carried out only if the "cold war" is brought to an end and the necessary confidence in relations between states, which unfortunately is now lacking, is established. It is to this very matter that our joint efforts should be primarily directed. . . . In our opinion it would be appropriate to make a joint recommendation that the United Nations should adopt this or a similar declaration designed to put an end to the cold war, reduce international tension and establish the necessary degree of trust in the relations between states, for unless this is achieved, we cannot seriously hope to settle the unsolved international problems.[23]

The measures Bulganin advocated "are those on which the positions of the States represented at this Meeting either fully coincide or have drawn much closer together." Bulganin then suggested an abbreviated version of the second part of the Soviet Union's May 10 proposals, also eliminating the close time schedule set forth in the proposals.[24] Bulganin's proposals were totally inadequate for a number of reasons. For example, they contained no provisions for effective international control beyond a general statement that there should be such controls. Likewise, Bulganin was again proposing a solemn obligation not to use

[22] "Geneva: Bulganin Report, Aug. 4, 1955," White House Disarmament Staff, *Reference Documents on Disarmament*, p. 88.
[23] Annex 18, U.N. Doc. DC/SC.1/29/Rev. 1, p. 4.
[24] *Ibid.*, p. 5.

nuclear weapons with no means of ensuring the observance of the obligation. If these proposals are regarded as long-range objectives rather than an immediately attainable program, however, they come a little closer to the Western positions than the May 10 resolution. The important point is that Bulganin was emphasizing at the summit the second rather than the third part of the May 10 resolution. The reason for this may have been that all of the Western suggestions in the subcommittee had been in this direction. It was only at the summit that the Western heads of government shifted to an approach more closely approximating the third part of the May 10 resolution.

Bulganin likewise proposed that:

Pending the conclusion of the International Convention on the reduction of armaments and the prohibition of atomic weapons, the Soviet Union, the United States of America, the United Kingdom, and France undertake not to be the first to use atomic and hydrogen weapons against any country and they call upon all other states to join this Declaration.[25]

Even though this was subject to the objection that it would leave to an aggressor the choice of his weapons, nevertheless it came closer to the Western position than previous Soviet contentions that it would be illegal for a state to use the nuclear weapon even in retaliation against use of such weapons by other states.

The programs and statements of the Western heads of government went further than the Soviet statements in shifting the emphasis from broad "comprehensive" disarmament to partial measures leading to the reduction of international tension. Anthony Eden said:

I therefore think the Soviet Government was right, if I may say so, in its proposals of 10 May to link disarmament with a reduction of international tension. The two are closely connected. If we are to make any practical progress towards disarmament, we have got

[25] U.S. Department of State, *The Geneva Conference of Heads of Government*, "Proposal by the Soviet Delegation," p. 56. Text from conference document CF/DOC/11 (July 21, 1955).

to find some way of breaking out of this vicious circle. We cannot wait until confidence between the nations is so strong that a plan of general disarmament can be adopted and brought into operation all in one move. This is essentially one of the international objectives which must be approved by stages, and we must make a start upon them now.[26]

Eden went on:

The United Kingdom delegation proposes that, as a means of increasing mutual confidence in Europe, consideration should be given to the establishment of a system of joint inspection of the forces now confronting each other in Europe. In specified areas of agreed extent on either side of the line dividing Eastern and Western Europe joint inspecting teams would operate by mutual consent.

This project would provide opportunity for the practical test on a limited scale of international inspection of forces in being and would provide valuable experience and lessons for use over a wider field in the future.

The willingness of the four Governments to accept such inspection would moreover demonstrate their determination to reduce international tension in Europe.[27]

In his accompanying address Eden explained that he conceived of the proposal as one which

. . . like the President's much bolder and more imaginative suggestion, it could be put into operation at once. I suggest that we should consider whether we cannot set up a simple, joint inspection of the forces now confronting one another in Europe. . . . This suggestion is not of course connected with the wider proposal for a possible limitation of forces which was connected with our dis-

[26] White House Disarmament Staff, *Reference Documents on Disarmament Matters*, p. 102.
[27] U.S. Department of State, *The Geneva Conference of Heads of Government*, "Memorandum by the United Kingdom Delegation," p. 59.

cussions for the unity of Germany. This suggestion could however be a practical experiment in the operative inspection of armaments, an experiment which if it were locally successful might extend outwards from the centre to the periphery. In this way, we might hope to establish a sense of security in Europe and begin the process of reducing tensions here.[28]

This was the first proposal for reducing the dangers of the outbreak of war by separating the antagonists in Central Europe. This underlying idea later became a part of all of the Russian programs, and the chief objectors were the Western powers rather than the Soviet Union.

Speaking for the government of France, Prime Minister Fauré proposed a step toward development of controls and sanctions in regard to disarmament based on financial and budgetary information. The French proposal called for an agreed reduction in the amount of military expenditures and the transfer of the funds thus released to an international fund for development and mutual assistance. Pointing out that the physical transfers of funds would constitute a type of self-enforcing mechanism for such an agreement, the French Prime Minister described its collateral functions, conceptually close to those envisaged by President Eisenhower in his atoms for peace plan:

In addition to its technical advantages, this system has a great moral advantage. It would stimulate the interest of world opinion in disarmament by appealing to sentiments other than those of fear and self preservation, and by creating international rivalry in human generosity.[29]

Suggestions along this line played some part in the 1957 negotiations—but not earlier. They will be discussed in Chapter 15.

President Eisenhower took the longest stride in shifting the emphasis to "a system . . . to develop the mutual confidence which will

[28] White House Disarmament Staff, *Reference Documents on Disarmament Matters*, p. 103.
[29] U.S. Department of State, *The Geneva Conference of Heads of Government*, "Statement by Premier Fauré," pp. 29-30.

open wide the avenues of progress for all our peoples." The President suggested as "a practical step" arrangements

> . . . to give to each other a complete blueprint of our military establishments . . . [and] to provide within our countries facilities for aerial photography to the other country—we to provide you the facilities within our country, ample facilities for aerial reconnaissance, where you can make all the pictures you choose and take them to your own country to study, you to provide exactly the same facilities for us, and we to make these examinations, and by this step to convince the world that we are providing as between ourselves against the possibility of great surprise attack, thus lessening danger and relaxing tension.[30]

This proposal along with the Soviet counterproposal to establish ground control posts[31] received extended debate prior to 1957, and therefore it seems appropriate at this point to go into greater detail in analyzing them and in discussing their relationship to the disarmament discussions.

THE UNITED STATES PROPOSAL

FOR "OPEN SKIES"

The first of the United States separable, first step "confidence-building" proposals to follow the initiative of the President's atoms for peace suggestions at the end of 1953 was offered by President Eisenhower, speaking directly to the then Premier Bulganin, at the summit meeting in Geneva.

He proposed what has come to be known as the "Open Skies" Plan —mutual exchange of blue prints "of our military establishments . . .

[30] Ibid., "Statement by President Eisenhower," pp. 57-58.
[31] U.N. General Assembly, Eleventh Session, U.S.S.R. Proposal, Doc. A/3366 (Nov. 17, 1956).

from one end of our countries to the other" and verification of these by reciprocal aerial inspection.

The predominant emphasis that subsequently has been placed on the function of this proposal as a safeguard against surprise attack has obscured the "confidence-building" function that originally was to be its prime contribution:

> Gentlemen, since I have been working on this memorandum to present to this conference, I have been searching my heart and mind for something that I could say here that could convince everyone of the great sincerity of the United States in approaching this problem of disarmament.

> I should address myself for a moment principally to the delegates from the Soviet Union, because our two great countries admittedly possess new and terrible weapons in quantities which do give rise in other parts of the world, or reciprocally, to the fears and dangers of surprise attack.

The President then made his proposal for exchange of complete blueprints of military establishments and aerial reconnaissance. He continued:

> Now from my statements I believe you will anticipate my suggestion. It is that we instruct our representatives in the Subcommittee on Disarmament in the discharge of their mandate from the United Nations to give priority effort to the study of inspection and reporting. Such a study could well include a step-by-step testing of inspection and reporting methods.

> The United States is ready to proceed in the study and testing of a reliable system of inspections and reporting, and when that system is proved, then to reduce armaments with all others to the extent that the system will provide assured results.

> The successful working out of such a system would do much *to develop the mutual confidence which will open wide the avenues of progress for all our peoples.*[32]

[32] U.S. Department of State, *The Geneva Conference of Heads of Government* (October 1955), pp. 58-59. Italics added.

That an earnest of good faith rather than unassailable security against surprise attack was the prime motivation seems clear by the fact that the same statement posed questions still to be answered by the technical studies not yet underway:

Questions suggest themselves. How effective an inspection system can be designed which would be mutually and reciprocally acceptable within our countries and the other nations of the world? How would such a system operate? What could it accomplish? Is certainty against surprise aggression attainable by inspection? Could violations be discovered promptly and effectively counteracted?[33]

Furthermore, in his opening statement on July 18, the President had not limited the problem to "sudden attack" but had included the alternative, albeit ambiguously stated, of "secret violation of agreed restrictions":

Surprise attack has a capacity for destruction far beyond anything which man has yet known. So each of us deems it vital that there should be means to deter such attack. Perhaps, therefore, we should consider whether the problem of limitation of armament may not best be approached by seeking—as a first step—dependable ways to supervise and inspect military establishments, so that there can be no frightful surprises, whether by sudden attack or by secret violation of agreed restrictions. In this field nothing is more important than that we explore together the challenging and central problem of effective mutual inspection. Such a system is the foundation for real disarmament.[34]

During the subcommittee meetings in the fall of 1955, the United States on August 30 submitted an Outline Plan[35] elaborating on the

[33] Ibid., p. 57.
[34] Ibid., p. 21.
[35] Annex 20, U.N. Doc. DC/SC.1/31 (Aug. 30, 1955).

elements of information to be exchanged and a procedure for the exchange of this information. Subsequently, during the 1956 subcommittee missions, the United States offered two proposals, neither of which was to be dependent on prior agreement on inspection or on the objects of inspection, to facilitate the exploration of inspection systems, particularly one to effectuate the Open Skies Plan: (a) Demonstration Test Areas—The United States and the Soviet Union to establish reciprocally pilot strips of roughly 30,000 square miles, containing prescribed military and industrial installations, for the purpose of testing and refining aerial and ground inspection techniques; and/or (b) Technical Exchange Missions—to be exchanged among the five subcommittee nations to study methods of control, inspection, and reporting.

Three years later, in May and July of 1958, but not until then, the Soviet Union at last agreed to technical discussions on the specific details of inspection systems in advance of agreement on their objectives.

THE SOVIET PROPOSAL FOR

"GROUND CONTROL POSTS"

The Soviet Union had also been considering the implications of the new weapons for great surprise attack. At Geneva, Premier Bulganin reiterated the Soviet interpretation, again submitting the May 10 proposals, which contained the following language:

It must also be borne in mind that *preparations for a new war,* the danger of which has been greatly increased by the development of atomic and hydrogen weapons, *inevitably necessitate the concentration of large military formations at certain points together with large quantities of conventional armaments*—aircraft, artillery, tanks, warships and so forth. Such concentration and the movement of large formations of land, sea and air forces cannot be effected except through important communication centres, ports and airfields. *Under conditions of modern military technique, the impor-*

tance of such points in the preparation of an aggressive war has not diminished, but is on the contrary increasing.

In addition to atomic and hydrogen weapons, for all their destructive capacity, armies of many millions and vast quantities of *conventional armaments, which are of decisive importance to the outcome of any* major war, would inevitably be involved in military operations in the event of the outbreak of war.

. . . In order to prevent a surprise attack by one State upon another, the International Control Organ shall establish on the territory of all the States concerned, on a basis of reciprocity, control posts at large ports, at railway junctions, on main motor highways and in aerodromes. *The task of these posts shall be to see to it that there is no dangerous concentration of military land forces or of air or naval forces.*[36]

It must be remembered that this was an opening bid, obviously not negotiable in its original form. The proposal for ground control posts acknowledged the existence of the problem of preventing surprise attack, whether prefaced by an atomic attack or confined to conventional armaments. In this sense, the Summit Conference succeeded in developing common ground for future negotiations.

This proposal, with its emphasis on concentrations of conventional forces, is unrealistic if measured against the United States concept of the role of surprise attack in initiating aggression—a role United States military strategists understandably conceive of as providing a probably decisive advantage to the aggressor if nuclear or thermonuclear weapons were employed.

But if the proposal is measured against the Soviet estimate of the role of surprise attack, a different evaluation is necessary. The Soviet proposal is fundamentally consistent with the new, post-Stalin Soviet military theory and its supporting strategy, described by Garthoff as follows:

The Soviet evaluation of strategic surprise as extremely important, but not in itself decisive, is quite pertinent to an understanding of So-

[36] Annex 15, U.N. Doc. DC/SC.1/26/Rev. 2 (May 10, 1955), pp. 18-20. Italics added.

viet offensive strategy. Surprise is considered an unreliable foundation upon which victory can be anticipated and hence not a sufficient
basis to justify launching a war against a vigilant major opponent.
It is recognized that under certain circumstances surprise may be a
necessary condition for success, but never a sufficient basis for
success in a war between prepared major powers. . . . Surprise,
then, is no recipe for blitzkrieg victory, even in the thermonuclear
era. And the Soviets are most unambiguous in their rejection of
the possibility of successful blitzkrieg between major powers.[37]

The Soviet strategic concept, in the thermonuclear era as before, is founded on the belief that the primary objective of military
operations is the destruction of hostile military forces, and not the
annihilation of the economic and population resources of the enemy.
. . . In keeping with the strategic concept, Soviet military doctrine
has consistently rejected any strategy based upon predominant
reliance on any particular weapons system. . . . Marshal Moskalenko
expressed this principle of Soviet military doctrine in the following
terms: ". . . *With the appearance of new technology, new more
powerful and more destructive weapons, the significance of men
on the battlefield not only does not decrease but increases all the
more.*" . . . Or, as Marshal of the Tank Troops Rotmistrov wrote
. . . "It is entirely clear that atomic and hydrogen weapons alone,
without the decisive operations of the ground forces with their
contemporary material, cannot decide the outcome of war."[38]

Soviet military strategists believe that the United States placed undue, and unwise, reliance on nuclear weapons, a deterrent power that
in any event is increasingly stalemated by comparable Soviet nuclear
capabilities. Consequently, the objects of control should more profitably be the capabilities for limited war—whether fought with conventional or tactical atomic weapons. This capability—rather than that for
great surprise attack—would be placed under surveillance by the control posts specified in the May 10 proposals.

The interpretation that Soviet "surprise attack" safeguards are
primarily designed to inhibit the use of forces in limited engagements

[37] Garthoff, *op. cit.*, pp. 85-86.
[38] *Ibid.*, pp. 71, 76, 77, 79.

is reinforced by the fact that, when the concept was reintroduced in March 1956, it was under the heading of a "Proposal for Agreement on the Reduction of Conventional Armaments and Armed Forces."[39]

The establishment of ground control posts, even in the first stage, was presented by the Soviets on May 10, 1955, in conjunction with a comprehensive agreement involving a "staged" reduction in two years to 1.5 million men for the United States and the Soviet Union, the discontinuance of tests, renunciation of use of nuclear weapons, liquidation of bases, cessation of production of nuclear weapons, and elimination of weapons during the second year. The definition of the rights of the control organ to "inspection on a continuing basis," with staff recruited "on an international basis permanently in all States signatories to the convention" was in turn circumscribed not only by required compliance with all the provisions of the "second stage" of the previously proposed convention for reduction of arms and prohibition of atomic weapons, but also compliance with the accompanying "declaration." The declaration additionally involved withdrawal of "armies of occupation from the territory of Germany inside their national frontiers . . . liquidation of foreign military bases on the territory of other states," the settlement of "outstanding questions in the Far East" and the elimination of "discrimination" in trade controls.[40]

Despite these conditions, which made nonsense out of the proposals as they stood, with their admission that it was no longer possible to account for past nuclear production, the Soviets implicitly recognized the emergence of a state of mutual thermonuclear deterrence.

UNITED STATES RESERVATION

OF POSITIONS

When the subcommittee of the United Nations Disarmament Commission resumed after the Summit Meeting, on August 29, 1955, the shift toward partial measures was self evident. The "first step" pro-

[39] U.N. Disarmament Commission Subcommittee of the Disarmament Commission, *Third Report*, Annex 5, Doc. DC/SC.1/41 (March 27, 1956), p. 1.
[40] *Ibid.*

posals of each of the heads of government of the four powers at the summit were immediately laid on the subcommittee table. The tactics of disentangling the discussion from the accumulation of positions on comprehensive disarmament were difficult but conceptually not insurmountable.

The issue was posed by a demand from the Soviet representative, Mr. Sobolev, for answers to five questions.[41] Three of these—on force levels and on phasing of prohibition and elimination of atomic weapons —reflected positions included in the Anglo-French proposals of June 11, 1954, which the U.S.S.R. had ostensibly accepted in September of 1954, and April 19, 1955, and two others represented Soviet proposals: renunciation of use of atomic and hydrogen weapons and discontinuance of tests.[42]

It was completely logical for the Soviet Union to raise these ques-

[41] Mr. Sobolev: "The first question which I should like to put is as follows: Are we all agreed that the levels of the armed forces of the United States of America, the Soviet Union and China should be fixed at one to one-and-a-half million men for each of these powers, and that the levels for the United Kingdom and France should be 650 thousand men each? Further, are we all agreed that the levels of armed forces for all other States should not exceed 150-200 thousand men?

"It would also be important to know whether the Western Powers agree that the complete prohibition of atomic and hydrogen weapons should enter into force when conventional armaments and armed forces have been reduced to the extent of 75 per cent of the agreed reductions and also that the elimination of these weapons from the armaments of States and their destruction should be completed during the process of the reduction of armaments by the final 25 percent of the agreed reductions. The Soviet delegation presumes that all the powers represented in this Sub-Committee agree that all atomic materials should thereafter be used exclusively for peaceful purposes.

"Further, the Soviet delegation would like a reply to the question whether the United States, the United Kingdom, France and Canada agree that simultaneously with the initiation of measures for the reduction of armaments and armed forces, States, before the entry into force of the agreement on the complete prohibition of atomic and hydrogen weapons, should assume a solemn obligation not to use nuclear weapons, which they should regard as prohibited to them, and that exceptions to this rule should be permissible for purposes of defence against aggression, when a decision to that effect is taken by the Security Council.

"It would also be important to clarify the question whether the United States, the United Kingdom, France and Canada agree that as one of the first measures for the execution of the programme for the reduction of armaments and the prohibition of atomic weapons, States possessing atomic and hydrogen weapons should undertake to discontinue tests of these weapons." U.N. Doc. DC/SC.1/PV.54 (Sept. 1, 1955), pp. 2-3.

[42] *Ibid.*, pp. 2-3.

tions. As we have seen, in the Disarmament Subcommittee in March and April 1955, all the Western powers had moved in the direction of a program of "comprehensive disarmament." At Geneva, the Western heads of government on the contrary had proceeded in the direction of "partial measures," and each of them had submitted a "partial measure" that had no particular relation to the former Western proposals. Sobolev must have anticipated a negative response to the fourth and fifth questions based on his own proposals. However, the responses to the questions as a whole would resolve the conflict between the summit positions and the subcommittee positions of the West.

The United Kingdom and France responded by reaffirming their adherence to the Anglo-French proposals, skillfully and gracefully reminding the Soviet representative that all their past proposals assumed the existence of "effective control":

To avoid all misunderstanding amongst ourselves—and I think Mr. Nutting will agree with me on this point, since he is as much responsible for the texts in question as I am myself—I should like to add that the Franco-British proposals of 19 April 1955 formed a whole and that when we referred, for example, to the abolition of atomic weapons we assumed in our proposals the existence of effective control. It is this effective control, therefore—a subject on which we are not at present in complete agreement with the Soviet delegation—that we must work out first. I apologize for returning to what might seem to be an obsession with me, but I think that if we could reach agreement on a system of control which we unanimously recognize to be completely effective we should have advanced our work considerably, and all the rest would become very much easier.[43]

The Canadian representative deferred answers on the basis of a continuing review within his government.[44]

In one of his first acts as deputy representative for the United

[43] Ibid., p. 16. See also statement by the representative of the United Kingdom, ibid., p. 17. See also, Nutting's extended reply at the next meeting of the subcommittee. U.N. Doc. DC/SC.1/PV.55 (Sept. 6, 1955), pp. 2-11.
[44] Ibid., pp. 31, 36

States, Stassen chose to place a "reservation" on all of the United States "pre-Geneva substantive positions" pending the outcome of the formal reappraisal of United States positions. Referring to the difficulties of inspecting for compliance with any agreements involving past nuclear production, he said:

> In view of these facts which have been set forth, the United States does now place a reservation upon all of its pre-Geneva substantive positions taken in this Sub-Committee or in the Disarmament Commission or in the United Nations on these questions in relationship to levels of armaments pending the outcome of our study jointly or separately of inspection methods and control arrangements and of review together of this important problem. In placing this reservation upon our pre-Geneva positions, may I make it perfectly clear that we are not withdrawing any of these positions, we are not disavowing any of them. But we are indicating clearly that we do not now reaffirm them, that we do turn our attention upon this essential factor of the inspection and control methods by which achievement could be obtained. Our aim to serve the cause of peace—a just and durable peace—and to improve security, reduce armaments, and lessen burdens remains the same. This reservation does affect the first three questions posed by the Soviet representative at our fifty-fourth meeting.
>
> In reference to the question put by the Soviet representative on the relationship to the Security Council, the further position of the United States is as follows. The United States will never use nuclear weapons or any other weapons in any other way than in accordance with our obligations under the United Nations Charter and in defense against aggression. We do not propose to expand the power of the veto in the Security Council in any new manner, as might be suggested in the Soviet question.
>
> In the matter of tests of nuclear weapons, the United States considers that this question is a part of the comprehensive disarmament question inter-related to the protection by effective inspection and control systems.[45]

[45] *Ibid.*, pp. 26-27.

While this reservation of positions was understandable and possibly was technically correct, politically it was an error. The United States might well have stressed its continuous adherence to the long-range objectives of comprehensive disarmament as set forth in the paper, "Essential Principles for a Disarmament Programme," submitted to the Disarmament Commission on April 24, 1952,[46] and as reaffirmed as late as April 18, 1955, in the Western proposal on nuclear disarmament.[47]

None of the principles of the 1952 proposal was inconsistent with the "open skies" proposal or any of the subsequent United States proposals. At the same time the United States could have pointed out that technical developments required vast changes in the measures for reaching that goal. This would have accomplished the purpose of the reservation of positions without exposing the United States to the charge that it repudiated its proposals as soon as the Soviet Union showed an interest in them. A more limited reservation of positions would also have been much closer to President Eisenhower's declaration of policy in his December 8, 1953, address to the United Nations: "So my country's purpose is to help us move out of the dark chamber of horrors into the light, to find a way by which the minds of men, the hopes of men, the souls of men everywhere can move forward towards peace and happiness and well being."[48]

Even a statement along the lines of one used by Stassen before the Senate Subcommittee on Disarmament would have preserved a negotiating posture more defensible from the heavy barrage of Soviet propaganda.[49] The United States had discarded unnecessarily the past

---

[46] Text in U.N. Disarmament Commission, *Official Records,* Special Supplement No. 1, *Second Report,* pp. 63-64.

[47] Annex 12, U.N. Doc. DC/SC.1/23 (April 18, 1955).

[48] President Eisenhower, "Atomic Power for Peace," Department of State *Bulletin,* Vol. 29 (Dec. 21, 1953), p. 849.

[49] "I come now to the important question of the actual reduction of armed forces and armaments.

"The United States remains pledged to work for, earnestly desires, and energetically seeks a comprehensive, progressive, enforceable agreement for the reduction of military expenditures, arms, armaments, and armed forces under effective international inspection and control.

"We are ready to consider any reasonable approach to that goal, including the method of limited approaches, each of which would foster an increase of confidence

positions that had received the greatest support and acclaim in the United Nations. It is noteworthy that Khrushchev in his statement to the United Nations in 1959 at times used almost the exact words of the 1952 proposals of the United States,[50] and Secretary of State Herter in effect, in 1960, reinstated the earlier United States objectives.[51]

The Soviet Union, for its part, found no forensic or moral difficulty in blandly proposing a comprehensive agreement encompassing a "major reduction of armaments" and "the complete prohibition of the use and production of atomic weapons"—and with the same breath acknowledging that ". . . there are possibilities beyond the reach of international control for evading this control and for organizing the clandestine manufacture of atomic and hydrogen weapons."[52]

It was characteristic of Stassen's approach that in his subsequent negotiations on new United States proposals he did not lift or remove the "reservation of positions" or reaffirm the old positions, even when in many instances the "new" proposals strongly echoed pre-Geneva conclusions. As noted in the preceding chapter, Stassen "never looked back." Consequently, rather than reaffirm past positions, he "moved beyond" the reserved position when new decisions were made.[53]

The reservation of positions may have been, as he has said, "honest and logical," but tactically it had the additional disadvantage of sug-

and narrow the disagreement so that the deadlock can be broken, and further reductions negotiated, provided always that the inspection system is proved and any arms cuts are reciprocal." *Control and Reduction of Armaments,* Hearings before the Senate Committee on Foreign Relations, 84 Cong. 2 sess., p. 16.

[50] U.N. General Assembly, Fourteenth Session, Plenary, *Official Records,* 799th meeting (Sept. 18, 1959).

[51] "National Security with Arms Limitation," Department of State *Bulletin,* Vol. 42 (March 7, 1960), pp. 354–58.

[52] Annex 15, U.N. Doc. DC/SC.1/26/Rev. 2 (May 10, 1955), p. 18.

[53] See the wording in his statement before the Senate Subcommittee on Disarmament:

"One measure which the United States has used to underscore its determination to launch the new approach has been to place a reservation upon the positions previously considered in the United Nations. We have not, for example, negotiated on the numerical ceilings on conventional forces, in the absence of a determination as to what could be done about nuclear weapons. We have neither rejected our past positions nor can we reaffirm them in blanket fashion. This has seemed to us an honest and logical course, especially while we are conducting the studies I have mentioned. The time has come to move beyond that reservation, under the new resolution passed by the United Nations General Assembly." *Control and Reduction of Armaments,* Hearings, p. 13.

gesting, as unavoidably it did, a breach in the Four Power unity. There was in fact no such substantive breach. Although there were, as indicated by the citations above, strong differences of view over the tactics of reserving past positions, differences of position among the allies did *not* center on whether or not comprehensive disarmament proposals as previously tabled—including inspected major reductions in force levels—were negotiable in the foreseeable future. All were agreed they were not. The problem was, rather, to determine the rate at which the new, partial measures approach could or should be negotiated, and the nature of the smaller measures and combinations of measures.

The result was that no coherent Western positions were possible during the remainder of 1955 and all of 1956. The Russians took full political advantage of this confusion by bringing forward a wide variety of proposed "first steps" with fairly good assurance that the Western response would have to be negative.

One reaction of a large share of the educated public to the Western indecision during this period was well expressed by Noel-Baker.

Has the thinking that inspired the U.S. policy of 1952-55 been eroded by the arms race? Have the U.S. Government reached the point reached by the British, French and Germans in 1914? Do they now believe that only armaments can make them safe, and that keeping the lead in weapons and in force is the only way to safeguard the national interest and uphold the peace?[54]

The answer of course is in the negative. Both the Soviet Union and the West, because of developments in military technology, were shifting their emphasis in the disarmament negotiations from "comprehensive disarmament," which became an ultimate objective rather than an immediate program, to "partial measures." The two main differences between the evolution of the Russian position and that of the West were:

1. The Russians moved faster and were ready with their program of partial measures a year before the West.

[54] Noel-Baker, *The Arms Race*, p. 30.

2. The West at this period forgot one of the fundamentals of all negotiations with the Soviet Union: that the Western proposals not only must be technically sound but must be politically attractive, since the Soviet Union will invariably interrupt any negotiation, however serious, to secure a propaganda advantage. The United States reservation of positions gave the Soviet Union the opportunity to reap such an advantage.

WESTERN PROPOSALS, 1956

The United States reservation of positions in August 1955 made it clear to all of the other negotiating states that little progress would be achieved until the United States had completed its reappraisal of policy. Nevertheless, the disarmament discussions continued, since pressure of world opinion would have prevented any long adjournment.

At the Geneva meeting of the heads of government in July 1955, the Foreign Ministers scheduled to meet in October were directed to seek solutions of the disarmament question. The sole progress at this meeting toward narrowing of differences was the statement of Molotov that the Soviet Union would accept aerial photography as one of the forms of control, "in the final stage of carrying out measures directed towards the reduction of armaments and the prohibition of atomic weapons."[55] Previously the Soviet Union had completely rejected the United States concept of aerial photography.

In December 1955, the tenth General Assembly debated disarmament extensively and adopted a resolution urging the states represented in the Subcommittee of Five to continue their endeavors to reach agreement on a comprehensive disarmament plan.[56] However, the General Assembly in addition suggested that priority be given to (1) such confidence building measures as Mr. Eisenhower's plan for

[55] U.S. Department of State, *The Geneva Meeting of Foreign Ministers, Oct. 27-Nov. 16, 1955*, Publication 6156 (December 1955), p. 183.
[56] U.N. General Assembly, Tenth Session, First Committee, *Official Records*, 559th Meeting (Dec. 16, 1955), p. 6.

exchanging military blueprints and mutual aerial inspection, Mr. Bulganin's plan for establishing control posts at strategic centers, and (2) all such measures of adequately safeguarded disarmament as are now feasible.

The General Assembly also showed its concern about the effect of atomic radiation on human health and established a fifteen nation United Nations scientific committee to collect and review information on this subject.[57]

Throughout 1956 the disarmament negotiations continued to be active. President Eisenhower and Premier Bulganin entered into an extensive exchange of correspondence. The letters were essential in setting the stage for the intensive 1957 negotiations.[58]

The Subcommittee of Five met in London for almost two months, March 19-May 4, 1956, and the Disarmament Commission met in New York for two weeks, July 3-16, 1956. The eleventh General Assembly, however, did not consider the report of the Disarmament Commission until January 1957[59] after the United States had completed its reappraisal of policy and had adopted new decisions.

The proposals both of the West and of the Soviet Union during the latter part of 1955 and all of 1956 were in the nature of interim sparring, groping for the positions that later emerged as the basis for the 1957 negotiations.[60]

The United States presented only one major proposal stemming from the December 8, 1953 atoms for peace address by the President. In the letter to Premier Bulganin dated March 1, 1956, President Eisenhower reassured the Soviet leader that adoption of the "open skies"

[57] *Ibid.,* p. 5.

[58] "The President to Premier Bulganin," March 1, 1956, Department of State *Bulletin,* Vol. 34 (March 26, 1956), pp. 514-15; "Premier Bulganin to the President," June 6, 1956, *ibid.,* Vol. 35 (Aug. 20, 1956), pp. 300-01; "The President to Premier Bulganin," Aug. 4, 1956, *ibid.,* pp. 299-300; "Premier Bulganin to the President," Nov. 17, 1956, *ibid.,* Vol. 36 (Jan. 21, 1957), pp. 89-90.

[59] U.N. General Assembly, Eleventh Session, First Committee, *Official Records,* 821st to 829th Meetings (Jan. 14-Jan. 25, 1957), p. 1.

[60] The numerous proposals of this period will be described only briefly at this time. Those 1956 proposals, which entered into the intensive negotiations in 1957, will be described in detail in the analysis of the 1957 period.

proposal, "combined with ground inspection teams which you proposed, . . . will in fact lead to a reduction of armaments."[61]

As substantive contributions toward such a reduction, the President then proposed, first, cessation of future production of fissionable material for explosive weapons under suitable and safeguarded arrangements:

> In my judgment, our efforts must be directed especially to bringing under control the nuclear threat. As an important step for this purpose and assuming the satisfactory operation of our air and ground inspection system, the United States would be prepared to work out, with other nations, suitable and safeguarded arrangements so that future production of fissionable materials anywhere in the world would no longer be used to increase the stockpiles of explosive weapons. With this could be combined my proposal of December 8, 1953, "to begin now and continue to make joint contributions" from existing stockpiles of normal uranium and fissionable materials to an international atomic agency. These measures, if carried out adequately, would reverse the present trend toward a constant increase in nuclear weapons overhanging the world. My ultimate hope is that all production of fissionable materials anywhere in the world will be devoted exclusively to peaceful purposes.

Second, he proposed agreement on "measures having a stabilizing effect, dealing with the control and limitation . . . of major types of armaments."

> In general, my feeling is that disarmament should be sought primarily, though not exclusively, in terms of limitations on armaments rather than on men. The former are more subject to supervision, regulation and control than the latter. In the present state of international affairs and especially in the absence of real peace in the Far East, I foresee that it may be difficult to agree on reduc-

[61] "The President to Premier Bulganin," March 1, 1956, Department of State *Bulletin*, Vol. 34 (March 26, 1956), pp. 514-15.

tions in the general level of armed forces at this time. It should, however, be possible now to agree on measures having a stabilizing effect, dealing with the control and limitation, under proper safeguards, of major types of armaments. These measures will be an essential part of the comprehensive system required to provide security to participating States.[62]

The concept of these proposals reflects a firm affirmation of the pre-Charter thinking on disarmament—maintenance of armed strength by the great powers. This was expressed, however, in terms of the thermonuclear age and the unresolved cold war.

During the early phases of such a programme, both the U.S.S.R. and the United States would have very extensive military strength, *including stocks of nuclear weapons.* I wish to make it clear that, so far as the United States is concerned, we would continue to hold such strength, not for aggression, nor for narrow national purposes, *but as a contribution toward world stability* in this transitional period.[63]

During the 1956 discussions, the United States also presented a tentative first stage package of "first steps": a control and inspection system capable of providing against surprise attack and verifying agreed levels of conventional armaments, to include aerial and ground inspection, mobile units, and a world-wide communications system; reduction of United States forces to 2.5 million men, with corresponding reductions in conventional armaments and expenditures even before major political settlements were reached on outstanding issues; a halt on nuclear production for explosive weapons purposes[64] combined with transfers from existing stockpiles to an international atomic energy agency for peaceful purposes (as proposed on December 8, 1953); and, given agreement to an inclusive inspection system covering all of the

[62] *Ibid.*, pp. 38-39.
[63] *Ibid.*, p. 39. Italics added.
[64] *Ibid.*, p. 38.

preceding measures, the testing of nuclear weapons to be limited and monitored in an agreed manner under international control.[65]

During both the August 1955 and the 1956 subcommittee meetings, France and the United Kingdom, separately and jointly, presented a number of additional working papers on phasing and on a control organ.[66]

The Anglo-French proposals of March 19, 1956, sought to adapt their original 1954 paper to the changed conditions through redefining the phases of a disarmament program. As heretofore, in the first stage there would be a freeze of existing levels of armed forces and military expenditures and the creation of an effective control organ. During the second stage, half of the agreed reductions of conventional forces would take place as previously proposed, but in the field of atomic energy the sole step would be to limit nuclear test explosions. In the third stage, nuclear test explosions for military uses and the manufacture of nuclear weapons would be prohibited, and the final reduction of conventional forces would take place. The effect of this amendment was to concentrate in the first two stages the type of actions where a control system could be effective.

By this time, in 1956, the Soviet Union was concentrating on partial measures that would limit the threat of a war and facilitate negotiated settlements, rather than on a comprehensive disarmament program, and these proposals therefore accomplished little toward further narrowing the differences between the Soviet Union and the West.

OTHER SOVIET PROPOSALS,

1955-1956

The shift to a partial, first step approach by the U.S.S.R. foreshadowed in 1954, became evident in the latter part of 1955 and 1956

[65] Annex 4, U.N. Doc. DC/SC.1/40 (March 21, 1956), pp. 1-3.
[66] Annex 16, U.N. Doc. DC/SC.1/27 (Aug. 29, 1955), and Annex 19, U.N. Doc. DC/ SC.1/30 (Aug. 29, 1955). Annex 2, U.N. Doc. DC/SC.1/38 (March 19, 1956), pp. 1-5.

when, in addition to the major shifts reflected in the May 10 proposals, not one but six separable, "first step" proposals were thrown into the hopper. This shift was the logical response to President Eisenhower's Geneva proposals and to Stassen's reservations of previous United States positions.

While several of these proposals had their counterparts in earlier years, for example, destroy stocks of nuclear weapons, freeze arms and "institute international control," and renounce use of atomic weapons, with the May 10 proposals the Soviet Union's separable steps became increasingly specific. More and more their proposals overlapped with political objectives which, especially in Europe, would eventually have to be negotiated without recourse to the use of military force, if the world was to avoid nuclear warfare. Bulganin at Geneva had proposed renunciation of "first use" of atomic and hydrogen weapons and also, as a first step, a freeze on foreign troops in Europe. At the Foreign Ministers Conference in October 1955, the Soviet Union, referring explicitly to Eden's earlier proposal at the summit, suggested a zone of limitation and "joint" inspection of armaments in Europe, "including Germany and certain bordering states."[67]

On March 27, 1956, the Soviet Union moved along this path when it introduced into the subcommittee of the Disarmament Commission its only resolution presented at that group of meetings. That resolution called for:

1. The reduction of conventional armaments and armed forces with an international control organization to ensure the fulfillment of obligations.

2. Creation in Europe of a zone where the location of atomic weapons could be prohibited and where ceilings would be placed on the forces of the United States, the Soviet Union, the United Kingdom and France, with joint inspection by the four states to ensure the observance of the obligations.

Part IV of the resolution read as follows:

Execution of Partial Measures in the Field of Disarmament. Independently of the attainment of agreement on the problems of

[67] U.S. Department of State, *The Geneva Meeting of Foreign Ministers*, pp. 37-38, 80-81.

disarmament, it is considered desirable that states should agree to carry out partial measures in this field, as follows: (1) To discontinue forthwith tests of thermonuclear weapons. (2) To insure that no atomic weapons are included in the armaments of troops in German territory. The States concerned shall take the necessary measures to carry out this provision within three months. (3) To reduce the military budgets of States by up to 15 per cent as against their military budgets for the previous year.[68]

This resolution, except for the paragraph quoted above, dealt only with conventional armaments, which were to be reduced independently of nuclear provisions. The Soviet Union followed up its May 10, 1955 "acceptance" of past Western force levels of 1 million to 1.5 million for the United States, the Soviet Union, and China, with lower figures stated for the United Kingdom and France, with another "acceptance," in July 1956, of the new Western force levels of 2.5 million.[69] In the intervening months, while Bulganin was writing to President Eisenhower, and while more and more emphasis was being directed toward nuclear weapons, Bulganin accused the United States of increasing its military bases in foreign territories, and increasing its military appropriations. The Soviet Union, on the other hand, according to Bulganin, announced:

. . . the reduction in the Soviet Union's armed forces in 1955 by 640,000 men; the reductions in the appropriations for military needs of the Soviet Union for 1956 by 9.6 billion rubles as compared to 1955; the Soviet Union's withdrawal from its last military base in . . . Finland-Porkkala-udd; and the initiative of the Soviet Union toward concluding a state treaty with Austria, which led to the withdrawal of all foreign troops from Austrian territory. . . .[70]

During this period these proposals, which merely confirmed the exist-

[68] Annex 5, U.N. Doc. DC/SC.1/41 (March 27, 1956), pp. 6-7.
[69] "Statement by Andrei Gromyko," U.N. Disarmament Commission, *Official Records,* 57th Meeting (July 12, 1956), pp. 1-16.
[70] "Premier Bulganin to the President," Feb. 1, 1956, Department of State *Bulletin,* Vol. 34 (March 26, 1956), p. 516.

ing status, were not considered serious negotiating offers, but merely tactical moves. In retrospect, however, they pointed the way to a new procedure for arms control: mutual unilateral reductions without formal agreement. In effect, both sides reduce armaments, without signing a paper.

When the Western representatives protested the absence of any provisions to control nuclear weapons, Gromyko made it clear on many occasions that nuclear weapons would be included in any comprehensive program, but that the March 27 resolution was directed toward partial disarmament.

> With this end in view, the Soviet Government has come to the conclusion that the cause of disarmament would be advanced if an initial agreement could be reached on conventional armaments. In other words, what is now needed is that agreement on conventional armaments should not be made conditional on agreements being reached on atomic weapons.[71]

Subsequently, Gromyko stressed:

> I think it must be clear from what I have said today that what we are proposing is a different approach to the solution of the disarmament problem, seeing that hitherto we have been unable to reach agreement on this important problem. In view of the fact that the linking of two questions—the question of conventional armaments and the question of atomic weapons—has been a serious obstacle on the way to agreement, the Soviet Government is proposing that agreement on the question of conventional armaments should not be tied to agreement on atomic weapons, thereby removing the serious obstacle which has been created in the course of our talks on the disarmament problem. As we know, the new Anglo-French proposals linked these two questions—conventional armaments and atomic weapons.[72]

[71] He pointed out that the "main difference . . . consists in the fact that in these proposals by the Soviet Government agreement on conventional armaments is not tied to agreement on atomic weapons."
[72] U.N. Doc. DC/SC.1/PV. 73 (March 27, 1956), p. 11.

Gromyko also protested with some vehemence that the United States in submitting its proposals in the subcommittee for aerial photography was veering away from the concept of partial confidence-building measures advanced by the President at the summit meeting in 1955. He said, "The proposal for aerial photography is in fact put forward as a basic—and indeed preliminary—condition for the execution of any measures whatsoever in the field of disarmament." He went on to observe that:

Even when President Eisenhower made the proposal regarding aerial photography, he did not envisage it as an integral part of some general disarmament programme, still less as a condition for the execution of some programme, but as a measure, so he said, for the creation of confidence between States and for the reduction of fear.

If we study the U.S. working paper more closely, we shall see that the focal point of that document is the question of control and that this question is presented in such a manner as in fact to divorce it from any concrete or practical measures of disarmament. I know that Mr. Stassen, and perhaps my other colleagues, will say that this is not so and that the United States working paper covers the entire field and provides for practical measures, including measures in the sphere of conventional armaments. But the point is that these measures are tied to a number of specific conditions which are impossible of fulfilment, which are not feasible.[73]

In his final statement on May 4, 1956, Gromyko reiterated that he had submitted the March 27 proposal on conventional armaments and armed forces for the reason "that the achievement of agreement on this important point would have made it easier to reach agreement on other questions relating both to conventional armaments and to the problem of the prohibition of atomic weapons." He referred specifically to a statement to the same effect by Macmillan at the summit meeting. He went on to observe:

[73] U.N. Doc. DC/SC.1/PV.82 (April 23, 1956), pp. 22-23.

The second feature of the Soviet proposal is that its introduction represents a new approach to the solution of the disarmament problem by means of agreement initially on those questions on which it is easier to reach the requisite accord, if, of course, there is a desire to do so. . . . The advantage of such an approach is obvious, since it enables agreements to be reached first of all on one of the two main questions relating to the disarmament problem, so that the ground may be prepared for agreement on the other question also.[74]

Gromyko stated frequently that the British and French papers presented at this meeting were still moving in the direction of "comprehensive disarmament" despite the positions supporting partial measures taken by the heads of government at Geneva. The same observations could have been made with equal force of the so-called declaration submitted by not only France and the United Kingdom but also by Canada and the United States on May 4, 1956, the last day of the session.[75] However, since this was the last day of the session, there was no time for such a comment.

After 1956, the Soviet Union never again concentrated solely on proposals for partial disarmament. Invariably the Soviet Union submitted two-pronged proposals—one prong sought the political advantages of advocating an idealistic program for comprehensive and drastic disarmament; the other prong was in the direction of partial measures that might be capable of immediate negotiation. This continued to be the Soviet technique when Khrushchev addressed the United Nations in September 1959.

While the Soviet suggestion of conventional disarmament as a separable proposal could not have produced any great reductions of armaments in view of the diminished importance of conventional weapons, the repetition and emphasis on three other separable measures—a ban on tests, renunciation of use of nuclear weapons, and a European zone of limitation of arms—were significant prologues to the major

[74] U.N. Doc. DC/SC.1/PV.86 (May 4, 1956), pp. 6-8.
[75] *Ibid.*, pp. 27-34, 52.

sparring during 1957. It is interesting that the campaign of the Soviet Union for a separable provision renouncing the use of atomic weapons slackened after 1957, when the incorporation of tactical atomic weapons into the armaments of defensive forces of both East and West had made substantial headway. Pressure for a test ban and some kind of an arms limitation zone in Europe, however, have continued as the most important first steps in the Soviet program down to the present.

The British Foreign Secretary in his report to the Parliament points out that "on two fundamental principles," the Soviet Union in 1956 had changed its position. The Soviet government no longer linked conventional and nuclear disarmament and also no longer linked disarmament and political settlements. During the negotiations on both disarmament and political settlements, "the first part of an agreed plan" could be carried out.[76]

It may seem presumptuous to treat as sparring almost two full years of meetings—at the Summit, of Foreign Ministers, in the Subcommittee, the Disarmament Commission and the General Assembly, plus an unprecedented flood of published diplomatic correspondence. The fact remains that until decisions emerged on the United States reappraisal, such meetings, no matter how numerous, could be only debates, even among our own allies, and not true negotiations.

This situation changed in mid-November 1956, when the first significant substantive United States policy decisions based on the reappraisal at last were made.

---

[76] Great Britain, *Report on the Proceedings of the Sub-Committee of the Disarmament Commission (March 19-May 4, 1956)*, Cmd. 9770, p. 6.

XIV

The Intensified Effort

IN NOVEMBER 1956, paradoxically, the Soviet Union and the United States almost simultaneously reached decisions that made possible the negotiations of 1957, which the State Department has described as the "intensified effort."[1] For the Soviet Union, these represented, given the lag in Soviet technology compounded by the period of theoretical and practical stagnation under Stalin, a phenomenally rapid readjustment to the thermonuclear age. The length of time it took for the United States to reach these decisions represented the unavoidable delays of democracy—interdepartmental clearance, periodic national elections—compounded in this case by two illnesses of a President whose decision was essential before any negotiations on the new approach could begin.

From the standpoint of the general international situation, November 1956 appeared to be the least likely month for United States and Soviet decisions to narrow differences. The last week of October witnessed both the ruthless Soviet suppression of the uprising of the Hungarian people and the Israeli and Anglo-French military action

[1] U.S. Department of State, *Disarmament: The Intensified Effort, 1955-1958*, Publication 6676 (July 1958).

326

against Egypt. In the United Nations, tensions between East and West reached a new peak, completely dispelling the so-called "Spirit of Geneva."

THE NEW UNITED STATES

DECISIONS

While the new United States decisions were reached in mid-November 1956, they were not made public until Ambassador Lodge outlined them before the First Committee of the General Assembly on January 14, 1957. They were introduced in the United Nations Disarmament Subcommittee in London by Representative Stassen on March 19, 1957.[2]

Lodge described the United States positions to the United Nations General Assembly as follows:

These new proposals will center upon five principal points. Before outlining these points, I wish to emphasize that the United States is ready and willing to take sound steps toward arms reductions, whether they are very small or whether they are large and extensive, provided, however, that any such steps must be subject to effective inspection. This insistence on adequate inspection is not a whim. It arises from the deep conviction after a thorough study that only an inspected agreement would serve the objective of a reliable peace....

We believe that renewed negotiations should strive towards these objectives:

1. To reverse the trend toward large stockpiles of nuclear weapons and to reduce the future nuclear threat.

2. To provide against great surprise attack and thus reduce the danger of major war.

[2] U.N. Disarmament Commission, Subcommittee of the Disarmament Commission, *Fourth Report*, Doc. DC/SC.1/PV.88 (March 19, 1957), pp. 21-30. Cited hereafter by annex and document numbers.

3. To lessen the burden of armaments and to make possible improved standards of living.

4. To insure that research and development activities concerning the propulsion of objects through outer space be devoted exclusively to scientific and peaceful purposes.

5. To ease tensions and to facilitate settlement of difficult political issues.[3]

After stating these objectives, Ambassador Lodge outlined the proposals of the United States to meet them:

[Nuclear Provisions.] *First:* The United States proposes that an agreement be reached under which, at an early date, under effective international inspection, all future production of fissionable materials shall be used or stockpiled exclusively for nonweapons purposes under international supervision. . . .

When such commitments are executed, it would then be possible to move reliably toward the reduction of existing stockpiles. When future production is controlled, it should be easier than with information now available to establish within a reasonable range of accuracy the approximate amount of fissionable materials previously produced, so that equitable and proportionate amounts in successive increments could be transferred from past production to internationally supervised national or international use for nonweapons purposes. . . .

[Testing.] *Second:* If such an arrangement to control the future production of fissionable material can be negotiated and put into effect it would then be possible, in a secure manner, to limit, and ultimately to eliminate, all nuclear test explosions. The United States proposes that this be done. Pending the negotiation of such an agreement, the United States is also willing to work out promptly methods for advance notice and registration of all nuclear tests, as has been suggested by the delegation of Norway, and to provide for limited international observations of such tests. . . .

[Force Levels and Conventional Armaments.] *Third:* The United States proposes that we move ahead toward the realization of a first

[3] U.S. Department of State *Bulletin,* Vol. 36 (Feb. 11, 1957), pp. 225-26.

stage reduction, under adequate inspection, of conventional armaments and armed forces using as a basis of measurement the figures of 2.5 million for the USSR and the United States, and 750,000 for France and the United Kingdom, upon which the countries represented on the Sub-Committee seem to agree. The United States proposes that we achieve this forward step through the progressive establishment of an effective inspection system concurrent with such reductions. An effective inspection system would require an appropriate aerial inspection component as well as ground units. The United States accepts the principle of establishing observers at key ground locations, as generally proposed by Marshal Bulganin, in addition to air inspection. . . . The United States does not believe that deeper reductions than those agreed for the first stage can be made unless some progress is made in settlement of the major political issues now dividing the world. . . .

[Missiles and Outer Space.] *Fourth:* . . . The United States proposes that the first step toward the objective of assuring that future developments in outer space would be devoted exclusively to peaceful and scientific purposes would be to bring the testing of such objects under international inspection and participation. . . .

[Safeguards against Surprise Attack.] *Fifth:* The United States continues to emphasize the importance of providing against the possibility of great surprise attack. This is not a minor or an ancillary proposal. The nature of modern weapons is such that if all nations are safeguarded against great surprise attack there is much less likelihood that a calculated major war would be initiated in the nuclear age. Likewise, such mutual assurances against great surprise attack would do much to prevent miscalculation by any nation regarding the intention of another. . . . The United States proposes therefore the progressive installation of inspection systems which will provide against the possibility of great surprise attack. The United States is willing to execute, either as an opening step or a later step, the complete proposal made in the summit conference at Geneva by President Eisenhower.

[A Control Organ.] It is clear that, whatever the first steps may be, a method of control, an organization of supervision, and a mechanism for regulation will be needed. The United States proposes that such an international agency for the regulation of armaments should be installed concurrently with the beginning of the program.[4]

Stassen in repeating these proposals to the subcommittee of the Disarmament Commission stressed that they were merely opening positions, which could be the basis for further negotiations.[5] The proposals presented four significant innovations, two of which bridged previously impassable ravines in the path of meaningful negotiation.

The first was the introduction of the concept of "progressive installation" of inspection systems. This concept was applied not only to systems to "provide against the possibility of great surprise attack" but also to those required to verify first stage man-power reductions, the proposed level of which remained, at this time, the same as suggested in 1956, 2.5 million for the United States, the Soviet Union, and China, and 750,000 for France and the United Kingdom.

The concept echoed the earlier United States proposals on progressive disclosure and verification, and even the Anglo-French approach to phasing. Now, however, separated from the substance of a comprehensive disarmament scheme and joined with the exploration of partial measures, it provided the essential ingredient for a mobile and flexible negotiating approach. Within obvious limits, the "progressiveness" might be applied geographically—to areas smaller than *all* of the United States and the Soviet Union; functionally—to one or a combination of objectives, such as man-power reductions, surprise attack safeguards, cessation of nuclear production; or by type of inspection—aerial or ground, mobile or static control posts.

The second innovation related to the new treatment of safeguards against surprise attack. As we have seen, Gromyko in March 1956 had protested bitterly that the United States proposals in the subcommittee on the subject of surprise attack were not a part of the group of measures of partial disarmament that might relieve international tensions. Instead they had become a precondition of an agreement for partial disarmament. Gromyko had claimed with considerable justification that

[4] *Ibid.*, pp. 226-28.
[5] U.N. Doc. DC/SC.1/PV.88 (March 19, 1957), p. 30.

this was a variation from the President's position at the summit meeting. In the new proposals, aerial overflight was incorporated into the paragraph on safeguards against surprise attack and became part of the package instead of a precondition, thus answering Gromyko's complaint. Indeed, it was in fifth place in the package.

The third and fourth innovations were equally important for the future negotiations. However, their effect was to expand the package of partial disarmament measures rather than to bring the negotiations closer together. The third innovation was the linking of a proposal "to limit and ultimately to eliminate all nuclear test explosions" to the previous suggestion for an inspected cutoff of nuclear production for weapons purposes and transfers from past production to nonweapons purposes. The November 1956 decisions permitted such a step to follow the installation of the cutoff. During the course of the 1957 negotiations, new United States decisions—in May and in August[6]— moved nuclear test cessation forward in the timetable to be *literally the first step* in an agreed series of first stage partial measures. The fourth innovation was a proposal to bring the testing of outer space objects "under international inspection and participation." The installation of a control system "concurrently with the beginning of the program" was assumed.

The Soviet Union had also made new decisions. Variants of previous proposals remained—reduction of military forces in Germany and in NATO and Warsaw Pact countries, liquidation of all foreign bases within two years, and a nonaggression pact between NATO and Warsaw Pact countries. But a declaration of November 17, 1956, sent to President Eisenhower, stated, for the first time, that the Soviet Government

. . . is prepared to consider the question of using aerial photography in the area in Europe where basic military forces of the North Atlantic Pact are located, and in countries participating in the Warsaw Pact to a depth of 800 kilometers to the East and West

[6] U.N. Doc. DC/SC.1/PV.112 (May 8, 1957), pp. 26-30; U.N. Doc. DC/SC.1/PV. 145 (Aug. 7, 1957), p. 5.

from the line of demarcation of the above-mentioned military forces, if there is agreement of the appropriate states.[7]

Thus the Soviet Union and the United States had almost simultaneously modified their initial positions on aerial overflight and defense against surprise attack sufficiently so that the negotiators were at least talking the same language.

The changes in position of both the United States and the Soviet Union on the question of defense against surprise attack, plus the United States recognition that the parts of the package of partial disarmament proposals could be considered and adopted separately rather than as a single indivisible scheme, laid the framework for the 1957 negotiations.

THE FIRST ROUND

LONDON 1957

On March 18, 1957, the United Nations Disarmament subcommittee opened its longest, most intensive—and last—series of negotiations. Three years of deliberations had taken place since the General Assembly had suggested the "Powers principally involved . . . seek in private an acceptable solution."[8] These deliberations had brought the five powers to a measure of accord on the technical difficulties of detection and control of nuclear weapons material and on the political difficulties of attempting to reach a comprehensive disarmament agreement in the current state of international tension and suspicion. The deliberations, however, had not brought agreement, even among the Western four, on the "initial . . . confidence building measures" which could launch a first stage partial agreement. Such was the task which faced the five powers in London.

Concurrent events of history added major difficulties to the laborious negotiating, affecting both the mood of the discussions and the content of the proposals and the counterproposals. Anglo-French-Ameri-

[7] Department of State *Bulletin*, Vol. 36 (Jan. 21, 1957), p. 92.
[8] Res. 715 (VIII), Nov. 28, 1953.

can relations had been severely strained by the crisis in Suez. Great Britain under the pressures of scarce budgetary and man-power resources had already made the decision to shift its defense strategy to primary reliance on the nuclear deterrent. The White Paper on Defense published on April 3 announced the armed services would be cut from 690,000 to 375,000 by the end of 1962; that the United Kingdom would withdraw 13,000 men from NATO, cut its aircraft contribution in half and make "further reductions later"; that the United Kingdom intended to test and stockpile megaton weapons.[9] Some 300,000 French troops were fighting in Algeria; and the French were again experiencing cabinet crises.

NATO as a whole faced decisions on nuclear stockpiles and the stationing in NATO territory of missile launching platforms, an issue with special political stress for the new partner, the Federal Republic of Germany, with fall elections just ahead and East Germany just across the border of "unnatural division." The fine-spun web of East-West communication had been abruptly cut by the tragic days of Hungary's fight for freedom.

Although the United States policy review had been completed, and the United States was now prepared to undertake the serious negotiations required to translate the general proposals into a plan, there was no real assurance at the outset of these meetings that the Soviet Union was equally prepared. The Soviet performance during January in the General Assembly debate did not lend itself to any solid hope. A new series of Soviet nuclear weapons tests had begun in August 1956 and the latest of six reported detonations occurred in March, on the eve of the opening of the sessions. The United Kingdom had announced plans to test and manufacture a megaton weapon between March and August of 1957.[10]

Furthermore, the events of the past autumn in Hungary and Suez had completely dissipated the temporary improvement in the international atmosphere following the summit meetings in July 1955.

Stassen had already let it be known that he would seek the Republi-

---

[9] Great Britain, *Defence: Outline of Future Policy*, Cmd.124 (April 1957).
[10] "AEC Announcement of the Soviet Detonation on March 8, 1957," *New York Times*, March 10, 1957.

can nomination for governor of Pennsylvania,[11] and within the United States delegation the prevailing prediction on the eve of departure for London was that the sessions would probably be over by Easter.

It is the more remarkable that in spite of these barriers, the London sessions, lasting through the summer until September 6, became a true negotiation, with substantive forward movement involving new and major policy decisions by both sides. This was new to the decade of arms control negotiations. The narrowing of differences took place in the course of and in consequence of the continuing negotiations.

None of the proposals before the subcommittee was dramatically new in substance. Earlier sessions of the subcommittee had debated similar versions of the Soviet and Anglo-French plans as well as many aspects of the new United States proposals. The "Fourth Country Problem"—the French had indicated that they were about to join the "nuclear club"—had been and continued to be an ever-present shadow. Nonetheless, from the beginning of the session, an atmosphere of expectation developed, almost unique in the long years of deadlock.

This was probably due in part to mutual recognition that nuclear warfare would be mutual suicide, to an awareness that a narrowing of differences on control, inspection, and force levels was not enough; that without some confirmed agreement between the East and West, however partial, the regrowth of confidence assumed essential to true security could not begin.

New Negotiating Techniques

This atmosphere of true negotiation was also helped, indeed developed, by the deliberate adoption of techniques that, though procedural in nature, opened up new substantive potential for agreement. The first of these was adoption of a separable, item-by-item agenda as the basis for subcommittee discussion, an approach urged by the French representative in May 1954 and again in April 1956, but only now adopted as an agreed technique: To consider the component

[11] *Ibid.*, March 14, 1957.

elements in an agreement "point by point rather than plan against plan."[12]

This approach had important advantages. It permitted the singling out of areas of agreement, and in so doing facilitated the serious and open exchange of views needed before further policy changes could be considered. Moreover, it gave time for frequent referral of new concepts to home governments without interrupting the continuity of negotiation; it cultivated the attitude of mind that could without prejudice consider a re-sorting and discarding of past elements in a new arrangement.

Selwyn Lloyd, referring to himself as a founder-member, or an "old boy" of the subcommittee, said in his opening statement:

It does seem doubtful to us whether much progress will be effected if each of us stands rigidly by his own plan. . . . it would be possible to investigate each of the important aspects of a disarmament agreement in turn without rigidly insisting at the outset on the manner in which particular issues . . . would . . . eventually be fitted into the framework of a disarmament treaty.

Stassen stated:

We come to this session not with rigid views of details, not in a straitjacket of precision on relatively minor points, but, rather, with firm fundamentals which we hope may be shared by others, and a wish to explore carefully the views of other delegations, to state our views openly and to endeavor to fit together a reciprocal, mutual, safeguarded agreement of benefit to each of our countries and to mankind.[13]

Also "we are more likely to move towards agreement if we start with

---

[12] U.N. Doc. DC/SC.1/PV.4 (May 19, 1954), p. 41; U.N. Doc. DC/SC.1/PV.78 (April 9, 1956), p. 9; U.N. Doc. DC/SC.1/PV.87 (March 18, 1957).
[13] U.N. Doc. DC/SC.1/PV.87 (March 18, 1957), pp. 9, 12.

areas of agreement and then gradually and carefully expand them, move by move, point by point."[14]

The Western four conceded to the Soviet insistence on placing cessation of nuclear tests at the head of the agenda. On March 28, 1957, accord was reached among the five on an order of discussion: nuclear test explosions, conventional disarmament, nuclear disarmament, international control organ, missiles and rockets, zones of limitation and inspection, and "other matters."[15]

A second main technique was the regular, systematic cultivation of informal sessions among the Western four and with the Soviet Union. These served to reinstate the original purpose envisaged for the subcommittee, private informal consultations among the principal powers. The use of regular four power consultation to concert Western tactics before the subcommittee meetings had been a common practice. It had, however, in fact served to isolate the Soviet representatives from the "private" consultations, and in the absence of an alternative forum, to encourage the use of the subcommittee meetings as a platform for Soviet polemics. Although the subcommittee sessions were secret, the formal verbatim recording of all that was said inhibited a free and frank interchange and the knowledge that at the end of the session all the "secret" verbatims would be released to the public largely negated their private character.

These disadvantages were in large measure overcome during the 1957 London negotiations by the deliberate cultivation of a complementary channel of informal communication with the Soviet delegation frequent enough to permit the fullest reciprocal exposition of the respective positions. In terms of time and frequency, these informal meetings, both with the Soviet Union and among the four, more than matched the 71 formal subcommittee meetings. Some of these private sessions were so informal that they could possibly have been termed "coffee hours." In the case of the United States and the Soviet Union, the talks took place in the casual settings of the American Embassy residence or in the Soviet Embassy. Stassen and Zorin were accompanied by no more than four or five members of each staff, which in-

[14] U.N. Doc. DC/SC.1/PV.88 (March 19, 1957), p. 17.
[15] U.N. Doc. DC/SC.1/PV.94 (March 28, 1957), pp. 6-38.

cluded interpreters. No verbatim records were taken, only informal notes by each side. There was no effort to pressure the Soviets for a quick response. On the contrary, repeatedly the United States delegate urged the Soviet delegate to take as much time as needed, to refer to his home government, if necessary; offered to answer at length all questions; and answered all questions, to ensure that the United States position was clearly understood before a firm Soviet response was formed.

The fact that six months later the Soviet response was decisively negative should not overshadow the equally significant fact that there was clearly a meeting of minds between East and West. The Soviet rejection could not be attributable to a misunderstanding of the West's position.

The apparent desire on the part of the Soviet Union seriously to seek some kind of agreement in the disarmament field undoubtedly influenced the modified tone of the formal presentations in the subcommittee. The habitual Soviet invective was singularly absent from the London sessions until the end—so much so that the violent attack on the Western position by the Soviet delegate on August 27,[16] although little different from the daily *Pravda* output, was unique to the sessions and clearly signaled the breakoff of Soviet participation in negotiations through the subcommittee.

Opening Positions, Soviet Union

While the United States at the opening of the 1957 session in London had launched immediately into its new approach of partial disarmament, this was not true for other members of the subcommittee. At the opening meeting, the Soviet Union again tabled proposals for a "comprehensive" disarmament plan, essentially repeating the terms of the November 17, 1956 proposals, but singling out the European area for special emphasis under two separate headings: The suggested "effective international control organ" was to be given as its primary task the establishment of and control over aerial inspection in an 800

[16] U.N. Doc. DC/SC.1/PV.151 (Aug. 27, 1957), pp. 2-32.

kilometer zone; and a "Zone of Limitation and Inspection of Armaments in Europe" was urged as "an important step toward the solution of the disarmament problem," reiterating almost verbatim the language of the earlier Soviet plan of March 17, 1956. The Soviet proposal for immediate suspension of nuclear tests, before the subcommittee in the form of a draft resolution on January 14, 1957, was not repeated in the March 18 paper, but the Soviet representative reaffirmed orally the fact that the Soviet Union was ready to proceed separately on that suggestion at any time.

This Soviet proposal, portions of which will be considered in detail in connection with the later negotiations, became known as the March 18 proposal. Its chief characteristics were:

1. It was a proposal for "comprehensive disarmament" rather than "partial measures." The British delegate pointed out that the proposal omitted any reference to the relationship between growing international confidence and the development of disarmament which had been recognized in the May 10, 1955, proposals and asked whether Zorin stood by previous Soviet statements of willingness to consider a partial plan in order to facilitate a practical start with disarmament. Zorin replied that he preferred to discuss the maximum range of measures to begin with; if this did not lead to agreement, the other possible approaches could be discussed at a later stage. This may have been a response to the confusing situation in 1956, when, despite the positions at the summit in 1955, the Western delegations veered back and forth between "comprehensive disarmament" and "partial measures."[17]

2. The representative of the Soviet Union, Kuznetsov, had previously laid these new Soviet proposals before Committee One of the General Assembly, on January 14, 1957. It can be seen by comparing the language with the United States position as outlined by Lodge, and repeated by Stassen in London in March, that despite the reciprocal innovations, the two positions would have to evolve much further before agreement on any of the items, singly or in a package, could be reached. Nor was the atmosphere in the General Assembly in January conducive to an optimistic estimate for the forthcoming

[17] U.N. Doc. DC/SC.1/PV.87 (March 18, 1957), p. 23.

negotiations. Kuznetsov had prefaced his exposition with a violent attack on United States and Western policy in the Middle East, necessitating the intervention and reprimand of the Chairman, Victor Belaunde of Peru, three times.[18] The repetition of the January 1957 position was an unfavorable omen.

3. The Soviet shift back to comprehensive disarmament proposals did not prevent the discussion of partial measures of disarmament from the outset. The first item on the agenda, nuclear test suspension, was conceded by the Soviet Union to be a subject for separate consideration.[19] Furthermore, all of the agenda items were relevant to both the comprehensive approach and the partial approach.

Thus, while the discussions could commence, they could not gather momentum until further decisions had been made.

Opening Positions, United Kingdom, France, and Others

The United Kingdom and France reintroduced the Anglo-French plan of June 11, 1954, as revised on March 19, 1956, and their working paper of May 3, 1956,[20] providing for comprehensive disarmament in both conventional and nuclear weapons in three stages, with limitations on testing and development of nuclear controls postponed to the second stage and prohibition of testing, manufacture, and use of nuclear weapons provided for in the third stage. This plan, like the Soviet March 18 proposals, moved in the direction of comprehensive disarmament.

Jointly with Japan and Norway, Canada had sponsored suggestions for advance registration of nuclear tests and, in the opening session of the subcommittee, these were reintroduced.[21] Proposals by

[18] U.N. General Assembly, Eleventh Session, First Committee, *Official Records*, 821st Meeting (Jan. 14, 1957), pp. 42-45.
[19] U.N. Doc. DC/SC.1/PV.87 (March 18, 1957), p. 23.
[20] U.N. Doc. DC/SC.1/PV.69 (March 19, 1956), p. 8; U.N. Doc. DC/SC.1/PV.85 (May 3, 1956), p. 2.
[21] U.N. Doc. DC/SC.1/PV.87 (March 18, 1957).

India and Yugoslavia calling for cessation of nuclear tests were also on the table.[22]

The papers sponsored by France and Canada at this time foreshadowed but did not fully reflect the positions of these countries during the negotiations. France literally became the "Fourth Country Problem," with its veteran representative, Jules Moch, as advocate.

This was clear from the outset. In his opening statement laying down the French position on cessation of tests—a position retained and reaffirmed down to and through the technical and diplomatic talks on testing begun in 1958—Moch spoke for all the countries soberly contemplating the grim requirements of effective national defense under conditions of an unchecked race in nuclear and thermonuclear weapons among the three great powers.

I further note that a considerable part of the [new Soviet] plan —several pages—deals with the cessation of atomic tests and that it calls for their cessation even in the absence of any agreement on disarmament. I must state very frankly that the French Government cannot agree to this. For France, the prohibition of tests is linked with the prohibition of manufacture. It is prepared to allow those Powers which have already built up stocks to retain them, at least during a transitional period. It is not prepared to allow those stocks to accumulate to an unduly high level while other Powers cannot form any. France does not wish to build atomic or hydrogen weapons, but would be compelled to do so if their production were continued throughout the world. It is ready to decide unwillingly to do so. We prefer the cessation of manufacture, and it is with the cessation of manufacture that we link the cessation of tests, though we do not wish to separate the two issues.[23]

This was the fundamental "opening position" of France—an attitude representing only the first of at least a half dozen "fourth countries" prepared, if necessary, to join the resource-devouring race.

[22] Annex 2, U.N. Doc. DC/SC.1/50 (April 8, 1957), pp. 1-2; Annex 4, U.N. Doc. DC/SC.1/52 (April 10, 1957), pp. 1-11; Annex 4, U.N. Doc. DC/SC.1/52/Add. 1 (June 24, 1957), pp. 1-5.
[23] U.N. Doc. DC/SC.1/PV.87 (March 18, 1957), pp. 44-45.

This basic attitude lent a vivid emphasis to Moch's warning in the same address:

Let us recall a suggestion which is now one year old. I said that we French still preferred comprehensive plans like the Franco-British plan. That is precisely what Mr. Selwyn Lloyd has just been saying. By isolating one element of this plan we are in danger of giving it a value very different from that which it has in a general context. But France desires above all that we should make progress. That is why I proposed in the Sub-Committee on 9 April, 1956, that we should renounce all our general plans, that we should divide them into their simple component elements, and that we should seek a specific agreement on each point—provided of course that the aggregate, the assembly of these isolated elements formed at the end of our study a whole which would be reasonable and acceptable to all. This method would constitute an important concession on our part, a concession hard and even painful to make because we are vain enough to cherish our plan and its comprehensiveness, which is twofold in that it embraces all aspects and all stages, and also reflects ideas which we have consistently affirmed since 1950.

... Today, as yesterday, I am convinced that we should study the points of the treaty one by one and achieve limited and secondary agreements in debate, provided that the result thus gradually achieved does not jeopardize the security of any of our States.[24]

The warning was also a prophecy, for in the course of the six months which followed, the relatively rapid progress made on issues separably considered was slowed and eventually halted when the inevitable day of reckoning arrived: their negotiated reassembly in the Western package of partial measures of August 29, 1957.[25]

If France was "The Fourth Country Problem," then Canada epitomized the "Other States." The legacy of the pre-Charter great power planning on disarmament, that concept under which the great powers,

[24] *Ibid.*, pp. 48-49.
[25] U.N. Disarmament Commission, Subcommittee of the Disarmament Commission, *Fifth Report*, Annex 5, Doc. DC/SC.1/66 (Aug. 29, 1957), pp. 1-10.

retaining their armed strength, would disarm the enemy and all other states, and, on their behalf, ensure collective security for all mankind, was never absent from the great powers forum, which, in fact, the subcommittee was, and was intended to be—"the Powers principally involved which should seek in private an acceptable solution. . . ."[26]

The "other states," on whose initiative the subcommittee had been formed, used Canada as their spokesman. In June 1957, after twenty-two years of control in the Canadian government by the Liberal Party, a Conservative government came into being. Lester B. Pearson, the Liberal leader who had been President of the United Nations General Assembly and had won a Nobel Peace Prize, became the leader of the opposition. The Conservatives under John G. Diefenbaker tended to stress the national interests of Canada and to follow less closely the views of the great powers. This changed role dovetailed with Canada's new place in the disarmament subcommittee meetings.

Actually, the roles of the fourth country and of other states had marked similarities. France was unwilling to abandon its nuclear weapons program, and Canada, along with many other states, was unwilling to agree to safeguards systems encroaching on its sovereignty in the absence of some palpable, verifiable evidence of voluntary self-restraint on the part of the three nuclear powers. It was therefore perhaps inevitable that the five-power forum should give way to three-power negotiation, as it did in 1958 with the technical talks on nuclear testing.

The United Kingdom realized and thereupon strongly urged the participants to go ahead with hammering out the technical details that were required to consolidate and confirm an agreement in whatever area a foothold could be found. When the British Secretary for Foreign Affairs chaired the opening session of the subcommittee in London, he made a brief and penetrating analysis of the areas of partial agreement. He pressed the representatives involved to consider the creation of technical working groups on each of the areas in which agreement in principle was being sought—such groups to work concurrently with the negotiations on the substance of the agreement.

[26] Res. 715 (VIII), Nov. 28, 1953.

I think much time might be saved in that way. There are many specific problems which such working groups might tackle.

The question to which I have already referred—that of the reduction of conventional armaments in relation to the reduction of military manpower—is obviously one of them because, obviously, unless levels of armaments are correctly related to permitted manpower then reductions in manpower are farcical because trained reserves could be equipped at short notice and thus bring the total of armed forces of a country well beyond the levels permitted by a disarmament convention. Therefore, there has to be control of armaments as well as of manpower.

Other specific matters which might be dealt with in a similar way by working groups include methods of inspection, in the air and on the ground, nuclear test explosions, the control of the production of nuclear material for weapons purposes, and other similar matters.[27]

THE MAIN EVENTS

Soviet acceptance of the new approaches of a separable item-by-item agenda and regular informal conferences made it possible for the sessions to move rapidly into a serious deliberation on the basic issues.

During the informal sessions and in the subcommittee, each of the possible elements of a plan was discussed in turn. The United States representative developed in detail the essentials of the United States proposals, explaining the relationship of the various parts and pressing the Soviet representative to state his government's ideas on a partial disarmament agreement. Before adjourning for the brief Easter recess beginning April 18, the delegates had dealt with four agenda items: nuclear testing, conventional armaments, nuclear disarmament, and the control organ; and they completed first-round discussion on the remaining items—missiles and zones of inspection and limitation—during the first days after the recess.

[27] U.N. Doc. DC/SC.1/PV.87 (March 18, 1957), pp. 10-11.

The Soviet delegate returned from Moscow with new instructions, and on April 30, 1957, he tabled new proposals, explaining that these represented the Soviet Union's genuine effort to reach partial agreement and that the more limited control provisions were related to the more limited nature of the measures contemplated.[28]

From this point on, the seriousness of the negotiations became evident. In May, immediately after the April 30 proposals of the Soviet Union, a further policy review was instituted in the United States. In response to a question on the new Soviet proposals, the President said that he thought they were "evidence that in this particular session of the Disarmament Committee, there is more honest and hard work being done than has been our experience in the past."[29]

I think that the reason that the Soviets are taking a different tone is because they, as well as all the rest of the world, are feeling the pinch of building, supporting, maintaining these tremendous military organizations. . . . And because they see, just as well as anybody else, where the world is really pushing, I believe they are now growing more serious.

Now this doesn't mean that they are not at the same time going to be very difficult, because they are going to want just as big an advantage out of the thing as they can get. They will want the scales tipped in their favor. We will try to insist it be a definite *quid pro quo* equality, and there will be so many arguments about that.

But I do believe that the seriousness comes about because of an awakening sense of responsibility everywhere; no matter how dictatorial or how arbitrary a government, you cannot escape the logic of world events as they are developing around us today.[30]

. . . So every word that indicates a desire to meet sensibly on a step-by-step basis, which is the only way, by the way, I think it can ever be done, I welcome it, and certainly don't reject it until it's been explored to the full.[31]

---

[28] U.N. Doc. DC/SC.1/PV.109 (April 30, 1957), pp. 2-30.
[29] *New York Times,* May 9, 1957, p. 18.
[30] *Ibid.,* May 16, 1957, p. 14.
[31] *Ibid.,* June 6, 1957.

During this period, a pattern was being established in the London talks that gave the participants a sense of genuine and serious negotiating response from the Soviet Union. A look at the calendar of the main events illustrates this strong though elusive evidence: a pattern of offer and response, of counteroffer and counterresponse, which is characteristic of and usually the unavoidable prelude to the few successful East-West negotiations that have occurred.

If the calendar is extended in time to include the main events of 1958, the character of the 1957 London sessions is even more apparent, as they were essentially an opening round in a continuing and probably prolonged series of negotiations leading to the thorough exploration of several of the substantive issues.

The London calendar was essentially as follows:

March 18: Opening positions outlined. Soviet Union presents comprehensive disarmament proposals. U.S. presents partial disarmament proposals.

March 18: U.K. suggests technical working groups.

April 30: New Soviet package of partial disarmament proposals.

May 25: New U.S. policy decisions following the May U.S. policy review.

June-July: NATO consultations.

June 14: U.S.S.R. offers to submit to control in connection with separate agreement for cessation of tests.

July 2: Western Four welcome Soviet offer, suggest technical talks.

July 2-3: U.S. outlines new position on testing and other nuclear controls.

July 8: U.S.S.R. outlines Soviet position on nuclear controls.

July 17: U.K. suggests technical talks.

August 2: Western Four present proposals for inspection zones to guard against great surprise attack, suggest technical talks on this.

August 21: Western Four present additional offers on testing and cessation of nuclear production.

August 26:   The U.S.S.R. rejects the Western position.

August 29:   Western Four present the package of partial disarmament proposals.

Close on the heels of the end of the subcommittee sessions, on September 6, came:

October 2:   Proposal by Polish Foreign Minister Rapacki for an "Atomic-Free" zone in Germany, Poland, and Czechoslovakia.

October 4:   The U.S.S.R. launches the first earth satellite.

October 10:   U.S. offers to begin technical talks on inspection for peaceful uses of outer space—the first fully separable step since "Open Skies" in 1955.

November 8:   Committee One of the United Nations General Assembly endorses the Four Power Proposals 57-9, with 15 abstentions, and suggests technical talks.

November 11: The U.S.S.R. announces that it would no longer take part in any negotiations in the Disarmament Commission and its subcommittee.

To see the pattern of offer and response in the 1957 negotiations, these main events should be read, not as a lineal progression in time, but as a series of equations. While the offer and response relationship is obvious for a number of these events, it is important to flag some of the equations that may be misinterpreted. The art of learning how to equate apples with apples, rather than with lemons, is indispensable in disarmament negotiations. In its absence, all formulas become unbalanced.

The most important of the equations is that of "The Soviet April 30th Proposals: Four Power August 29th Proposals."

Even so prominent a student of disarmament as Philip Noel-Baker has erred by matching the Soviet Union's March 18, 1957 proposals for *comprehensive* disarmament with the West's August 29th proposals for *partial measures.*[32]

[32] Philip Noel-Baker, *The Arms Race* (1958), pp. 25-27.

Actually, the United States response to the Soviet April 30 proposals came quite rapidly, in the new decisions by the President on May 25, following a full-scale interdepartmental review in Washington.[33] The August 29 four power proposals for partial disarmament measures represent—in a way perhaps unmatched since the translation of the language of the Four Freedoms into the Atlantic Charter—the negotiation of allied agreement to the substance and the language of a United States policy paper—the May 25 decisions. The process of negotiation, however, produced a greater rigidity in the August 29 proposals than in the earlier United States decisions.

The substance of the August 29 proposals had, with certain important exceptions, been laid before the Soviet Union privately and in the course of the formal subcommittee meetings between May 27, when the subcommittee resumed its sessions, and August 21, when the additional revisions on test cessation proposals were introduced, and had in large part been refused by the Soviet Union. The Soviet rejection two days prior to the tabling of the four power proposals on August 29 was not quite as unexpected as some of the contemporary comments may have suggested, nor was it quite as discouraging as the same comments may have claimed.

Well before the formal tabling of the August 29 proposals, the Western four and the Soviet Union had in fact begun to move away from the rigidity that the language of the August 29 proposals proclaimed and which the Soviet rejection of August 27 implied.

Illustrative of this—and of another important negotiating equation— is the Western inspection zones proposal of August 2,[34] presented personally by Secretary Dulles who flew to London for this purpose.

Detailed negotiations in NATO had preceded the presentation of these proposals. President Eisenhower described the role of consultation vividly and to the point early in July, when NATO consultations on those aspects of the May 25 decisions that particularly affected European states, in addition to the United Kingdom and France, were underway: The ABC correspondent (Edward P. Morgan) had suggested that certain administration moves (invitations to the Soviet

---

[33] U.S. Department of State, *Disarmament: the Intensified Effort, 1955-1958*, Publication 6676, pp. 50-51.
[34] U.N. Doc. DC/SC.1/PV.143 (Aug. 2, 1957), pp. 2-10.

Union and others to witness forthcoming nuclear explosions and increased distribution of U-235 for peaceful purposes) were efforts attempting "to refute the argument that we dare not be as sincere in disarmament as we would like to be. I am thinking in terms of the debate that has been going on as to what we would lose and what we would gain by suspending tests." The President answered:

For three long years, everybody in the Government, with the aid of task forces, on which we have had people like Dr. Lawrence and General Bedell Smith . . . have been working on this thing to develop a policy for the United States. You take that policy and you try to find out how it would affect other nations.

You don't want to go to the Soviets or to any other nation, for example, and make a proposal that affects a third country, without that third country's approval, because then you suddenly become like Napoleon and Alexander, on a raft in the Vistula, settling the fate of Europe.

We are not doing that. So you do have . . . the problem, after you make out a program that seems logical and decent to us as a country, to go and take up the problem with Germany, with France, with NATO, the whole NATO group, with Britain, with Canada, everybody that is affected by that proposal, in order that you don't just destroy the whole effort by sudden recalcitrance because someone believes their own sovereignty or their own rights have been ignored.[35]

The Soviet substantive negotiating response to the West's European inspection zone offer of a zone from "The Atlantic to the Urals" was not the August 27 rejection[36] but rather their endorsement of the Polish proposals for a more limited zone in Europe to be free of atomic weapons consisting of Germany—East and West—Poland and Czechoslovakia.[37] The delay in this instance, which involved Warsaw Pact

[35] New York Times, July 4, 1957.
[36] Annex 4, U.N. Doc. DC/SC.1/65/Rev. 1 (Aug. 27, 1957), pp. 1-31.
[37] "Premier Bulganin to the President," Dec. 10, 1957, Department of State Bulletin, Vol. 38 (Jan. 27, 1958), pp. 127-30.

partners, between the Western offer and a substantive response—about two months—is, interestingly enough, little less than the delay involved in negotiating a NATO offer on a European zone.

Similarly, the true "equation" on test cessation is probably the Soviet June 14 proposal for an inspected test suspension independent of other disarmament measures,[38] and the President's acceptance of this suggestion in principle, together with an offer to commence technical talks.[39] The abandonment by the United States of its insistence on the link of cessation of tests to the cutoff can be considered a negotiating equivalent to the earlier Soviet concession to agree to control posts to verify a test suspension for two or three years.

Thus, the London negotiations represented the opening round in a series of serious negotiating offers and responses extending beyond 1957. For both sides, the offers and responses may include a considerable number of communications extending over a period of time but not readily identifiable in black and white as "offers" and "responses."

[38] U.N. Doc. DC/SC.1/PV.121 (June 14, 1957), p. 10.
[39] "The President to Premier Bulganin," Jan. 12, 1958, Department of State *Bulletin*, Vol. 38 (Jan. 27, 1958), pp. 122-27.

XV

The Issues

The evolution of the negotiations on the substance of the various proposals is described in the following sections dealing with the main agenda items. The negotiations did not move logically from one agenda item to the next. After exhausting for the moment the discussions of, say, the first item, the negotiations would jump to another item and might return to the first item a month or six weeks later. As a result, a chronological narrative of the negotiations would be meaningless.

NUCLEAR TEST EXPLOSIONS

The first item on the subcommittee agenda was the subject of nuclear test explosions. This was logical for a number of reasons. The Soviet representative in his opening statement had stressed that action on nuclear testing should be taken independently of other disarmament measures. Thus the subcommittee was able to discuss this one measure of partial disarmament before the Soviet Union submitted its initial paper on partial steps on April 30, 1957.[1] The subcommittee al-

---

[1] U.N. Disarmament Commission, Subcommittee of the Disarmament Commission, *Verbatim Record*, U.N. Doc. DC/SC.1/PV.109 (April 30, 1957), pp. 2-30. Cited hereafter by document number and date.

ready had before it suggestions from Yugoslavia and from India[2] for the cessation of nuclear tests as the first step in a disarmament program. Likewise, the subcommittee had notice of a draft resolution of Canada, Japan, and Norway, introduced into the General Assembly.[3] The resolution recommended that the states concerned give urgent attention to the setting up of a system of nuclear test explosion registration with the United Nations as a preliminary step toward prohibition of nuclear weapons through progressive stages. It also requested the Secretary General and the United Nations Radiation Committee to cooperate with the states concerned in the operation of such a system with a view to keeping the total and expected radiation in the world under constant observation. The United States and the United Kingdom had supported this proposal. The Soviet bloc, India, and some other states had considered it inadequate.

In the early sessions of the subcommittee, the United States outlined its positions. Suspension or limitation of tests should commence after an inspection system to control the future production of fissionable materials had been installed and was operating successfully to ensure that all future production would be used or stockpiled exclusively for nonweapons purposes. Pending this, tests would be made subject to advance notice and registration with limited international observation. The limitation and prohibition of nuclear weapons testing should be part of a comprehensive disarmament program, and there should be no limitation on tests outside the context of such a program.

The United States restated the position presented to the United Nations General Assembly on January 14, 1957, that any eventual cessation of nuclear testing must be contingent on an agreement: (a) to divert all future production of fissionable materials to nonweapons uses, under international control, with appropriately planned measures to be undertaken to reduce existing nuclear weapons; and (b) to transfer the fissionable materials from such dismantled weapons to peace-

[2] U.N. Disarmament Commission, Subcommittee of the Disarmament Commission, *Fourth Report*, Annex 2, U.N. Doc. DC/SC.1/50 (April 8, 1957), pp. 1-2; Annex 4, U.N. Doc. DC/SC.1/52 (April 10, 1957), pp. 1-11; Annex 4, U.N. Doc. DC/SC.1/52/Add. 1 (June 24, 1957), pp. 1-5. Cited hereafter by annex and document numbers.
[3] U.N. General Assembly, Eleventh Session, First Committee, *Official Records*, 824th Meeting (Jan. 21, 1957), p. 57.

ful uses, also under international control and accountability.[4] The representatives of France, Canada, and the United Kingdom supported the United States in this position.

The Soviet representative continued to present the Soviet viewpoint that the hazards of nuclear test explosions made it wise to separate this problem from general disarmament and to treat it as a matter of particular importance. The Soviet representative, therefore, demanded prohibition *or* temporary cessation of tests as an immediate step, independent of disarmament and without control.[5]

On May 6, the British representative tabled in the subcommittee a memorandum calling for advance registration of tests as proposed by Canada, Japan, and Norway at the General Assembly and in addition asking for the establishment of a committee of technical experts to consider possible methods of limitation and control of tests.[6] The United Kingdom and United States representatives during this period pointed out that, on the basis of the scientific advice available to their governments, the detection of unauthorized tests could not be guaranteed without close control. Following their general policy that all disarmament measures must be controllable and subject to control prior to the measures taking effect, the Western four took the position that any suspension of tests must be under effective control.

The rationale behind the Western position that cessation of tests must be linked to the cessation of production of new fissionable materials for military purposes was that the cessation of tests in and of itself would in no way reduce the threat of nuclear war. The states with existing weapons could continue to stockpile new weapons. An agreement on cessation of tests standing alone would create an unjustifiable illusion of progress toward disarmament, which might lead the states to reduce their armaments without any lessening of the military threats from communism. The representative of each of the four powers stated the case as an advocate pleading before a jury. Jules Moch, in lucid oratory, pin-pointed the most important part of the case as "the undertaking to use all future production of fissionable ma-

[4] U.N. Doc. DC/SC.1/PV.88 (March 19, 1957), pp. 22-29.
[5] U.N. Doc. DC/SC.1/PV.112 (May 8, 1957), pp. 2-12.
[6] U.N. Doc. DC/SC.1/PV.110 (May 6, 1957), p. 10.

terials for nonweapons purposes, including stockpiling," going on with the statement: "We have made considerable concessions to the Soviet Union's case," in the matter of suspension of tests and later cessation of production.

It is no less a fallacy to say that a cessation of testing, adopted as a separate measure, would suffice to reduce the nuclear danger. Indeed, there would be nothing to prevent the testing States from carrying on production and commercializing the nuclear weapon by supplying it to other countries, as is unfortunately being done with submarines, tanks and aircraft.

There is therefore no doubt in our minds, just as there is none in Mr. Ritchie's [Canada], that the most effective way of halting the nuclear arms race would be the prohibition, not of testing, but of production for military purposes.[7]

The Western four recognized that the cessation of testing would make it virtually impossible for states other than the three possessing nuclear weapons to acquire them. This consideration vitally affected France, rapidly approaching the point where it would be the "fourth country" with nuclear weapons. France was unwilling to give up its prospect of becoming a nuclear power without an indication that the existing nuclear powers were moving in the direction of ultimate elimination of their arsenals of nuclear weapons.

In the latter part of April and in May, while the talks continued on a number of additional agenda items, policy reviews were taking place simultaneously in Washington and in Moscow. On May 16, the subcommittee recessed for ten days, and Governor Stassen returned to the United States to confer with the Secretary of State and other officials of the Executive branch of the government. On May 25 a conference was held with the President at the conclusion of which the Secretary of State announced that the President had taken decisions that would be embodied in further instructions to the United States representative at the subcommittee talks. After his return to London,

---

[7] U.N. Disarmament Commission, Subcommittee of the Disarmament Commission, *Fifth Report,* Annex 7, Doc. DC/SC.1/68 (Sept. 4, 1957), pp. 7-9.

Stassen in a statement to the subcommittee on May 27 recognized an improvement in the prospects of reaching an agreement between the Soviet Union and the West.[8]

On June 14, the Soviet representative announced that his government was willing to accept the Western contention that a cessation of tests should be subject to international control. Furthermore, he was willing to substitute "a two or three year moratorium" on tests for a complete suspension of the tests. His government would accept control posts in the territories of the United States, the United Kingdom, the Soviet Union, and in the Pacific area.[9]

The Western representatives immediately recognized that the Soviet Union had made a substantial concession and welcomed the move. A four-power written statement tabled in the subcommittee on July 2 noted that the Soviet acceptance of control posts "now brings within the realm of possibility a temporary suspension of nuclear testing as part of an agreement for a first step in disarmament." The statement noted that only three main differences remained between the Western position and the Soviet position. First, it was necessary to secure precise agreement on the duration and timing of the temporary suspension of tests. Second, it was necessary to define the precise controls that would be required. Third, it was necessary to establish the relationship of the suspension of tests to the other provisions of a partial disarmament agreement.[10] The Western powers suggested that a group of experts should be named to design the inspection system while the subcommittee itself considered the other two matters requiring agreement. The Soviet Union, however, declined to enter into technical discussions of the inspection system until the subcommittee resolved the other differences.

The United States representative at the same time agreed that test suspension would become "the first clause of the agreement that is operative."[11] In other words the test suspension could become effective prior to the installation of a controls system. This was the first occasion

---

[8] U.S. Department of State, *Disarmament: The Intensified Effort, 1955-1958*, Publication 6676 (July 1958), pp. 40-41.
[9] U.N. Doc. DC/SC.1/PV.121 (June 14, 1957), p. 13.
[10] Annex 11, U.N. Doc. DC/SC.1/59 (July 2, 1957), p. 1.
[11] U.N. Doc. DC/SC.1/PV.128 (July 2, 1957), p. 35.

when the United States relaxed its general position that before any disarmament commitment could take effect a control system must be in existence to ensure observance of the commitment.[12]

The United States on July 3 proposed a period of ten months suspension of tests as a time adequate for installation of inspection posts and to permit the agreement of other states. The temporary suspension could be extended for a longer period if the original agreement was working out successfully. As a part of the test cessation agreement, the nuclear powers would further agree to cooperate on the permanent design, installation, and maintenance of an inspection system to verify compliance with an agreement for cessation of production of fissionable materials for weapons purposes—"the cutoff." The cutoff itself, however, unlike test cessation would take place only after "installation of an inspection system adequate to verify compliance."[13]

Discussions with the Soviet Union of the remaining differences between their position and that of the West culminated in an offer on the part of the United States on August 21 (which had already been discussed informally with the Soviet representative) to extend the first suspension period from ten to twelve months, and to add a second suspension period also of twelve months—conditional only on "satisfactory progress in preparing an inspection system to supervise the nuclear production cutoff."[14] The Western and Soviet positions on the cutoff will be elaborated in the subsequent section dealing with the agenda item of nuclear disarmament.

The United States proposal on August 21 was the closest Western approach to the Soviet position. On the question of duration of tests, the Soviet Union was suggesting "two or three years." The West was replying with an unconditional offer of a one-year suspension and a conditional offer of an additional year. There was no discussion of when the suspension would commence, but presumably it could start almost immediately after an agreement had been reached.

The Soviet Union never accepted the Western position linking test suspensions to at least some preliminary steps in the direction of the

[12] About the same time, the United States made a similar concession in its proposals for reduction of armed forces.
[13] U.N. Doc. DC/SC.1/PV.129 (July 3, 1957), pp. 2-14.
[14] Annex 5, U.N. Doc. DC/SC.1/66 (Aug. 29, 1957).

cutoff. When the Western powers dropped this requirement early in 1958, sufficient agreement had been reached on the duration and timing of the suspension so that technical groups could undertake to resolve the last remaining difference—working out an adequate monitoring and inspection system. By that time, however, the terms of reference of the entire disarmament negotiation had radically changed.

NUCLEAR DISARMAMENT

The discussions of nuclear disarmament were closely related to nuclear testing. The United States proposed that all future production of fissionable materials be placed under international supervision and be used exclusively for nonweapons purposes. This proposal was undoubtedly the most important development emerging from the United States policy reappraisal. As stated previously, it was first made by Ambassador Lodge to the United Nations General Assembly in January 1957, and was reaffirmed by Stassen at the second meeting of the subcommittee on March 19. The proposal had two parts: first, the "cutoff" itself, the provision that all future production of fissionable materials should be used solely for nonweapons purposes; second, the suggestion that the producers of fissionable materials for weapons purposes (the United States, the United Kingdom, and the Soviet Union) should transfer to an international authority fissionable materials from previous production, thereby reducing the amounts of fissionable materials available to them for weapons uses. The immediate effect of such measures would be to assure that no states other than the three possessing weapons would ever secure them, and also to assure that the three countries with weapons programs would not increase their stocks of fissionable materials available for the manufacture of weapons. The proposal would ultimately lead to reductions of existing stockpiles and possibly in the distant future to the elimination of nuclear weapons.[15] The actual cutoff of production for weapons purposes would not take place until one month after the control system was functioning effectively.[16]

[15] U.N. Doc. DC/SC.1/PV.88 (March 19, 1957), pp. 22-29.
[16] U.N. Doc. DC/SC.1/PV.102 (April 12, 1957), p. 10.

This was the heart of the United States program to reduce international tensions and to lessen the menace of a nuclear holocaust. As we have seen, in the spring and summer of 1955, the Soviet Union and the United States almost simultaneously recognized that it would no longer be possible to account accurately for past production of fissionable materials. With the increased destructive potential of thermonuclear weapons, the concealment of even a small portion of past production of fissionable materials would pose a menace too great for any country to accept.

To meet the dilemma arising from this situation, the United States inaugurated a vast research project which established that a system of inspection could be devised that would permit accountability for *future* production of fissionable materials with an extremely high degree of accuracy. Part of the initiative for this research had come from the task forces Stassen had established.[17]

Concurrently with the United States effort, the United Kingdom had engaged in a research exercise using different methods but with the same objective and arriving at the same result as the United States operation.

During the exchange of correspondence between President Eisenhower and Premier Bulganin in relation to the proposed international atomic energy agency, the American President had suggested a meeting of scientists of the leading nuclear powers to follow immediately the International Conference on the Peaceful Uses of the Atom, which took place in Geneva in August 1955. The purpose of this meeting would be to exchange ideas on the design of a control system to ensure that nuclear materials arising from the production of power would be utilized solely for nonmilitary purposes. At this meeting, the Soviet scientists headed by Dr. Alexander Skobeltzyn were cooperative but skeptical of the possibility of designing any system that could accurately account for production of nuclear materials. The chief United States representative, the Nobel prize winner, Dr. Isadore Rabi, made a number of important and constructive technical suggestions which apparently had never previously occurred to the Russian scientists. They expressed not only interest but even enthusiasm at the idea of

[17] See Chap. 11.

"tagging fissile materials," and promised to make their own study of this problem.[18]

In the fall of 1957, the Soviet Union adhered to the statute of the International Atomic Energy Agency, which provided for the setting up of an international safeguards system to assure that fissionable materials made available by the agency to member states would be used solely for peaceful purposes. No member state, however, would be bound to submit to such a system of safeguards unless and until it requested and secured agency assistance on projects requiring fissionable materials. Since clearly neither the United States nor the Soviet Union would apply for assistance from the agency, the safeguards system to be established by the agency would not be applicable to their nuclear installations. However, the Soviet Union, through its adherence to the statute, had implicitly recognized the possibility of devising an effective inspection system to ensure that future production of fissionable materials would be used solely for peaceful purposes.

The statute provided a Preparatory Commission to consider various matters in connection with the establishment of the agency including its initial program.[19] During the discussions of the Preparatory Commission in February 1957, the United States representative, Richard Kirk of the Atomic Energy Commission, presented in some detail the outlines of the system that would be required to ensure against diversion of fissionable materials.[20] Though this system was directed primarily toward electric power reactors and not toward plutonium production reactors such as those at Hanford, Washington, the general principles of the safeguards would be the same. The Soviet representative in the Preparatory Commission generally approved of the position which Kirk explained, even though the Soviet Union might have reaped a propaganda advantage by associating itself with India, which

[18] *Proposed International Atomic Energy Agency Meeting of Six Governments* (Aug. 22-27, 1955) "to consider the problems of safeguarding or guaranteeing the peaceful uses of atomic energy against diversion of materials," U.N. Doc. S/PV.1/Rev. 1, pp. 2, 15; S/PV.5/Rev. 1, p. 5.
[19] *Report of the Preparatory Commission of the International Atomic Energy Agency,* GC.1/1, Gov. 1 (1957), p. 1.
[20] The published result of the system of safeguards appears in *Ibid.,* pp. 21–22.

regarded any restrictions on its use of nuclear materials as a new form of economic colonialism. Of course the system would never be applied within the borders of the Soviet Union. Nevertheless, this background gave some hope that the Soviet Union might be receptive to the design of an inspection system to police a nuclear cutoff.

Kirk repeated his description of the safeguards system in a public statement to the Senate Committee on Foreign Relations in May 1957 during the public hearings leading to the United States ratification of the statute.[21]

In July 1957, Jules Moch made a statement to the subcommittee which was similar in substance to Kirk's position. In addition, Moch attempted to estimate the total number of international inspectors that would be required to police the cutoff.[22] His estimate, while far too small, showed that the problem of inspection could be reduced to manageable proportions.

This United States proposal raised two separate issues: first, the merits of the proposal itself, and second, the question of linking this proposal to the proposals for suspension of testing. First let us consider the Soviet response to the proposal itself.

When the United States made this proposal the Soviet Union had not yet placed before the subcommittee its suggestions for partial measures of disarmament, dated April 30. Thus under familiar Soviet negotiating techniques, the Soviet response had to be in relation to its own proposals of March 18 for a comprehensive and complete disarmament program. In effect, to refer back to our metaphor, the Soviet Union was equating lemons with apples. The Soviet representative pointed out two conflicts between the United States proposal and the Soviet comprehensive proposal of March 18.

The first conflict rested on the fact that the Soviet program of March 18 required all states to renounce the use of nuclear weapons in the first stage of a disarmament program. The cutoff of nuclear

---

[21] "Statement of Richard L. Kirk, Assistant Director for International Organizations, Atomic Energy Commission," *Statute of the International Atomic Energy Agency,* Hearings before the Senate Committee on Foreign Relations, and Senate Members of the Joint Committee on Atomic Energy, 85 Cong., 1 sess., pp. 93-101.

[22] U.N. Doc. DC/SC.1/PV. 131 (July 5, 1957), p. 11.

production would not arise until the second stage. To meet this objection, the Western powers embarked on a frantic effort to discover some formula for limited renunciation of use of nuclear weapons that would be satisfactory to both the Soviet Union and the West. The Soviet Union had already rejected the formula proposed by Britain and France in 1955 and in 1956 that all states declare "that they regard themselves as prohibited, in accordance with the provisions of the Charter of the United Nations, from the use of nuclear weapons except in defence against aggression."[23] In rejecting this formula, however, the Soviet representatives had frequently cited with approval the Geneva protocols of 1925, outlawing the use of chemical and bacteriological weapons in war. The formula in these protocols provides merely a conditional renunciation of the use of chemical and bacteriological weapons, authorizing their use in retaliation.[24] The Western representatives hoped that a formula approximating as closely as possible the language of the Geneva protocols might be acceptable to the Soviet Union. This quest resulted ultimately in the strange language of the Western proposal on August 29: "Each party assumes an obligation not to use nuclear weapons if an armed attack has not placed the party in a situation of individual or collective self defense."[25] The language came fairly close to that of a Soviet reservation to the Geneva protocols. The use of the double negative, however, created great problems in English (though not in French or Russian). Stassen had his staff embark on an intensive search including Shakespeare and Bartlett's *Familiar Quotations* to find instances of literary use of the double negative. When the language of the August 29 proposals received final approval, during the visit of Secretary of State Dulles to London at the end of July, one of the assistant secretaries of state,[26] after hearing all the evidence in favor of this formula, expressed the consensus in the

[23] U.N. Disarmament Commission, Subcommittee of the Disarmament Commission, *Third Report*, Annex 2, Doc. DC/SC.1/38 (March 19, 1956) p. 1.
[24] "Protocol for the Pacific Settlement of International Disputes," *League of Nations: Index to the English Edition of the Fifth Assembly*, Geneva 1924, Annex 30a, pp. 498-502. Annex 26, on "Reduction of Armaments," contains section concerning Chemical Warfare, p. 468.
[25] Annex 5, U.N. Doc. DC/SC.1/66 (Aug. 29, 1957), p. 3.
[26] Andrew Berding.

conclusion that the use of the double negative in this circumstance "was not no good."

The second conflict between the United States proposals and the Soviet program of March 18 was that the United States proposal provided for a cutoff at an early stage of the disarmament agreements. The elimination of nuclear weapons would arise, if at all, only at a much later date and through the gradual process of joint contributions to an international organization from stockpiles of the states with nuclear weapons. In contrast, the Soviet proposals of March 18 provided for both the cessation of production of nuclear weapons and their elimination in a second stage—to be carried out in 1959. Nevertheless, since the discontinuance of production of nuclear weapons was in paragraph 2 of the second stage and their elimination was in paragraph 3, the Western states believed that the Soviet Union might be agreeable to a cutoff prior to complete elimination of weapons stockpiles.[27] If this were true, then the gap between the two positions might be bridged with some statement of intention to eliminate nuclear weapons as soon as a system of controls could be devised that would give reasonable assurance of observance of such a commitment. Other Soviet objections likewise might be negotiable. For example, since United States stockpiles of fissionable materials probably exceeded Soviet stockpiles, Stassen conceded that the contributions of the United States to an international stockpile from past production would exceed the Soviet contributions.[28]

In retrospect, the complete Soviet rejection of the United States proposal should have become apparent when the Soviet representative on April 30 introduced his proposal for partial disarmament measures. This proposal called for "a solemn undertaking to renounce the use for military purposes of atomic and hydrogen weapons of all types, including aerial bombs, rockets carrying atomic and hydrogen warheads," simultaneously with the conclusion of an agreement on measures for the reduction of armed forces, conventional armaments, and military expenditures. "The States parties to the agreement would give an

[27] U.N. Doc. DC/SC.1/PV.87 (March 18, 1957), pp. 34–35.
[28] U.N. Doc. DC/SC.1/PV.130 (July 5, 1957), p. 5.

undertaking to make every effort to conclude an agreement on the complete prohibition of atomic and hydrogen weapons, their elimination from the arsenals of States, the cessation of their production and the destruction of their stockpiles."[29] Thus it became apparent that the Soviet Union was unwilling to agree to the enforceable obligation of a cutoff operative at an earlier stage than the unenforceable obligation to eliminate nuclear weapons.

The Soviet rejection of the Western proposal became clear on July 8 when Zorin stated that a cessation of production of fissile material under international control involved a degree of control that no state could accept, unless there were general agreement on the complete elimination of nuclear weapons and the destruction of existing stockpiles.[30] This was a clear Soviet rejection of the entire concept of the nuclear cutoff as a part of a partial disarmament program. This position of the Soviet Union is understandable in view of its unwillingness to permit substantial breaches of the iron curtain. However, even when stated in clear terms, it was to receive little or no support from world public opinion and particularly from the segments of world opinion most concerned with ensuring future world peace.

Unfortunately, the conflict between the Soviet and the Western positions did not appear in public in these clear terms since two situations intervened that considerably muddied the waters. The first was the Western insistence on the provisions for transfer of nuclear weapons, which later became paragraph IV.C. of the August 29 proposals. The first paragraph of this section would permit states to transfer nuclear weapons to countries where their use would be in conformity with the obligation "not to use nuclear weapons if an armed attack has not placed the party in a situation of individual or collective self-defense."[31] In effect this would permit the United States and the United Kingdom to transfer nuclear weapons to the NATO countries including Germany. While the political factors leading to Western support of such a provision are obvious, it clearly ran contrary to the whole concept of nuclear disarmament—to prevent the spread of nuclear weapons. Furthermore, this made it possible for Germany to

[29] U.N. Doc. DC/SC.1/PV.109 (April 30, 1957), p. 22.
[30] U.N. Doc. DC/SC.1/PV.132 (July 8, 1957), pp. 3-28.
[31] Annex 5, U.N. Doc. DC/SC.1/66 (Aug. 29, 1957), p. 3.

secure nuclear weapons. It is difficult to imagine any suggestion more repugnant to the Soviet Union.

While Zorin's unfavorable reaction to this statement was immediate, the delayed responses of the Soviet Union even more clearly showed their dislike for a proposal that would permit nuclear weapons to come into possession of states not members of the nuclear "club." On September 4, at the end of the subcommittee meetings, Zorin reviewed this portion of the Western position in the following terms:

We often hear, in the statements of the Western representatives, the argument that the proposal for the cessation of production of fissionable materials for military purposes is designed to prevent other countries from acquiring atomic weapons. But how can we reconcile these statements with the measures being taken by the United States for the placing of atomic military formations and nuclear weapons in the territories of other States and especially in Western Germany and the other countries forming the North Atlantic military bloc? In many instances these plans or actions are contrary to the clearly-expressed will of the States concerned.[32]

This was further emphasized in Bulganin's letter to President Eisenhower December 10, 1957, after the Soviet Union had announced that it would no longer participate in the work of the Disarmament Commission or its subcommittee.

As for plans to transfer nuclear weapons to allies of the USA in Europe, such a step can only further aggravate an already complicated situation on that continent, initiating a race in atomic armaments among European states.

One likewise cannot fail to take into account, for example, the fact that the placing of nuclear weapons at the disposal of the Federal Republic of Germany may set in motion such forces in Europe and entail such consequences as even the NATO members may not contemplate.[33]

[32] Annex 12, U.N. Doc. DC/SC.1/73 (Sept. 5, 1957), pp. 10-11.
[33] "Premier Bulganin to the President," Dec. 10, 1957, Department of State *Bulletin*, Vol. 38 (Jan. 27, 1958), pp. 127-30.

The second situation that clouded the issues was the linking of the proposals for the cutoff to those concerned with nuclear testing. The initial arguments in favor of linking the two proposals were convincing enough. An agreement for the suspension of tests in and of itself would do little to reduce the menace of a nuclear holocaust, although it would make it difficult if not impossible for countries in addition to the United States, the United Kingdom, and the Soviet Union, to develop nuclear weapons. Despite the limited results obtainable from the suspension of tests, the Soviet Union was pouring forth a propaganda campaign which implied that if agreement were reached on test suspension, the entire threat of nuclear war would vanish. An agreement on test cessation might thus produce a degree of complacency among political leaders of Western states. This line of argumentation was sufficiently strong so that even the Japanese, who because of their own experiences were most violent in denouncing both nuclear weapons and nuclear tests, supported the link between test suspension and the cutoff.[34]

During the summer of 1957, world public opinion became far more aware of the true limitations of any test suspension program. The reasons for linking the cutoff to test suspension therefore became progressively weaker. On the other hand, the links between the two programs became stronger, largely because of the unwillingness of the French to give up their program for becoming the fourth nuclear power unless there were some assurance that the existing nuclear powers would ultimately give up their nuclear weapons. This tendency, which led in the August 29 proposals to a provision linking all of its parts as an inseparable package, will be considered subsequently.

Thus the intervention of these two lines of discussion obscured the basic fact that the Soviet Union had rejected the proposals for the cutoff because it was unwilling to submit to a control program adequate to ensure the observance of the cutoff. It would agree to a cutoff which could be enforced only if the West would agree to the complete elimination of nuclear weapons which could not be enforced under any known safeguards system.

[34] U.N. General Assembly, Twelfth Session, *Official Records*, Sept. 17-Dec. 14, 1957, Annexes, p. 10.

CONVENTIONAL DISARMAMENT

The United States proposals of March 18 for a first stage reduction of conventional armaments and armed forces went no further than to suggest that the levels of armed forces should be established at 2.5 million for the United States and the Soviet Union and 750,000 for France and the United Kingdom. Reductions beyond this first stage would depend on some progress toward the settlement of major political problems. Stassen called in general terms for the establishment of an effective inspection system including both air reconnaissance and ground units to ensure the observance of the conventional armaments commitments. The Soviet proposals of March 18 and also the Anglo-French proposals, directed as they were toward a comprehensive program of disarmament, went beyond the first stage and provided goals for subsequent stages.[35]

Except for agreement on the size of force levels for the great powers for the first stage, there was little common ground between the suggestions of the United States and those of the Soviet Union. In addition to calling for the reductions of force levels, the Russians in the first stage of their comprehensive program suggested the following: (1) Chinese forces in the first stage would be limited to somewhere between 1 million and 1.5 million men. This would bring the Chinese Communists into the negotiations from the outset. (2) Appropriations of states for armed forces and conventional armaments would be reduced correspondingly to the reductions in armed forces—with no suggested method for determining "corresponding reductions." (3) A world conference would determine the levels of the armed forces of states other than the great powers. The levels of the armed forces of such states would not exceed 150,000 to 200,000 men. (4) A supplementary agreement would designate military, naval, or air bases of the great powers in the territory of other states that would be abolished during the first stage. (5) The Soviet Union, the United Kingdom,

[35] U.N. Doc. DC/SC.1/PV.87 (March 18, 1957), pp. 18, 22-28, 48-49.

France, and the United States would reduce their armed forces stationed in Germany by one third in comparison to the level of the armed forces on December 31, 1956. (6) The United States, the United Kingdom, and France would make substantial reductions of their armed forces stationed in the territories of NATO members, and the Soviet Union would similarly reduce its armed forces stationed in the territories of the countries parties to the Warsaw Treaty.[36] In addition, as previously stated, states would make commitments not to use nuclear weapons, and states possessing nuclear weapons would assume the obligation not to allow the weapons to be stationed outside their national frontiers.

Obviously, despite superficial agreement between the Soviet Union and the West on the first stage levels of armed forces, the Soviet Union had introduced so many extraneous matters into its proposals that the discussion would have covered too much ground to be meaningful.

On the first day of the subcommittee talks, Stassen suggested early agreement on twelve months as the period within which the first stage of conventional disarmament should be completed. He then embarked on the problem of reductions of armaments, which he considered more important than the levels of armed forces. He suggested that the armaments eliminated under the agreement should be transferred to control depots under the jurisdiction of international inspectors. He also suggested that military expenditures should be reduced by 10 per cent. On the matter of procedures for working out the reduction of armaments, Stassen proposed a number of alternatives: (1) a system of reduction of major classes of armaments to specified quantitative levels; (2) a quota system based on definitions of man-power requirements and of the types of equipment appropriate for the reduced levels of man power; (3) a percentage reduction of major types of armaments. Stassen suggested that in the initial stage the reductions might be 10 per cent.[37]

During March and April, the discussions of conventional disarmament made little progress, primarily because there were too many divergences to permit focusing on any of them. On April 11, the

[36] *Ibid.*, pp. 32-36.
[37] *Ibid.*, pp. 18-19.

United Kingdom introduced a technical paper to solve the problem of finding a simple and convenient method of measuring the levels of armaments in terms of man power.[38] The paper, however, played no particular role in the later negotiations.

The Soviet proposals on April 30 for partial disarmament sufficiently narrowed the areas of divergence between the Soviet and Western positions so that the negotiations could go forward. First, the proposals omitted any reference to the level of forces of China during the first stage, thus avoiding the necessity of bringing the Chinese Communists immediately into the negotiations. Second, the Soviet government, while continuing to urge the abolition of military bases in foreign territories, merely called for an examination of the question and an agreement on which bases could be abolished within one or two years. Third, the Soviet Union, while continuing to press the desirability of reducing the forces of the great powers stationed in German territory and the forces of the United States, the United Kingdom, and France stationed in NATO countries as well as those of the Soviet Union stationed in the territory of the Warsaw Treaty countries, agreed that the details of any such reductions could be postponed to subsequent negotiations.

By making these concessions, the major differences between the Soviet position and the Western position were reduced to three. (1) The Soviet Union, while accepting the force levels for the first stage, advocated by the Western governments, insisted that there should be agreement on further reductions in a second stage. (2) The Soviet Union wished to achieve reductions in armaments by cutting military budgets by 15 per cent during the first stage. (3) The Soviet Union still insisted on a renunciation of the use of atomic weapons as part of its package of first stage measures.

In the last week of June and the first week of July, Stassen presented in considerable detail the United States position emerging from the May review of policy.[39] On the matter of armaments reduction, he suggested a concrete approach. The Soviet Union should submit a list

[38] U.N. Doc. DC/SC.1/PV.101 (April 11, 1957), pp. 6-9.
[39] U.N. Doc. DC/SC.1/PV.124 (June 25, 1957), pp. 2-5.

of arms that it would dispose of under its plan for 15 per cent reductions. The United States should submit a similar list. When agreement was obtained on the two lists, the items listed for reduction should be placed in disarmament depots under international supervision. This procedure bypassed the question whether armaments reductions should be 10 per cent or 15 per cent. Stassen pointed out that they might well exceed 15 per cent. The Soviet Union agreed in principle to this approach, thus eliminating one of the major differences.[40]

In response to the Soviet insistence that the first stage agreement must provide for greater reductions of armed forces than the levels the West had proposed,[41] Stassen said that under certain conditions the United States would accept new second and third force levels as follows: 2,100,000 for the United States and the Soviet Union at the end of the second stage and 1,700,000 for these countries at the end of the third stage.[42] The force levels of the United Kingdom and France should be reduced to 650,000 by the end of the third stage.[43] The Western four also suggested the formation of a working group to plan how the reductions would be implemented.[44]

On July 19, the Soviet representative declined to go into the question of implementing the reductions of armed forces unless the Western four would abandon their insistence that reductions beyond the first stage should await some progress in the settlement of political problems.[45] Stassen met this point by suggesting the provisions which later were incorporated into the August 29 proposals. The further reductions would be conditioned on several developments: (1) compliance with the provisions of the convention during the first stage, (2) expansion

[40] U.N. Doc. DC/SC.1/PV.125 (June 26, 1957), pp. 2-6.
[41] U.N. Doc. DC/SC.1/PV.124 (June 25, 1957), p. 11.
[42] Ibid., p. 9.
[43] U.N. Doc. DC/SC.1/PV.127 (June 28, 1957), pp. 3-4. Stassen's entire presentation can be found in the following Subcommittee Verbatim Records: 128th Meeting (July 2, 1957), pp. 28-43; 129th Meeting (July 3, 1957), pp. 3-14; 130th Meeting (July 5, 1957), pp. 2-14; 131st Meeting (July 5, 1957), pp. 22-26. Zorin's answer to the presentation followed in the 132nd Meeting, July 8, 1957.
[44] U.N. Doc. DC/SC.1/PV.137 (July 17, 1957). Presentation by Selwyn Lloyd, pp. 7-12.
[45] U.N. Doc. DC/SC.1/PV.138 (July 19, 1957), pp. 2-15.

of the inspection system to cover the second stage of reductions, (3) progress toward the solution of the political issues, and (4) adherence to the convention under acceptable terms of other essential states.[46]

This astute approach, which was characteristic of Stassen, tended to downgrade the importance of progress in settlement of political issues by making it merely one of four conditions, the other three of which would be acceptable to the Soviet Union. The Soviet Union gave the desired response—that it would accept the force goals suggested by the Western four provided the reductions "were in fact effected under the partial agreement and were not made contingent upon the settlement of political and other issues."[47]

Stassen's recitation of the four preconditions of achieving the second stage of reduction of armed forces highlighted an additional concession the Western four had made. Previously the Western four, and in particular the United States, had insisted that no reductions or limitations of armaments should take place until control machinery was in existence and in a position to ensure the observance of commitments. The United States, by insisting that the control machinery be in a position to police the reductions in the second stage, was in fact conceding that the first stage reductions might commence during the installation of such control machinery. The initial reductions in conventional forces would be taking place simultaneously with the establishment of the control machinery and before the machinery was in a position to verify the reductions. This position carried forward into the August 29 proposals. This was the second time the United States had indicated a willingness to diverge from its general position, the first instance being in connection with the suspension of nuclear testing. The explanation of this change of position probably is that the first stage reductions of forces by both the Western powers and the Soviet Union were not of sufficient consequence so that their violation would result in any catastrophe to the other side. Therefore, it was less important that ma-

[46] Ibid., pp. 16-25.
[47] Ibid., p. 10.

chinery be immediately available to verify the fact of the reductions.

After July 19, there was practically no further discussion in the subcommittee on the reduction of conventional armaments and armed forces. While the Soviet representative occasionally complained that the Western powers were imposing the precondition of political settlement to progress in disarmament, the Soviet Union did not attach too much importance to this precondition. The political precondition suggested by the Western four in fact had been downgraded to a point at which it was no longer of any consequence in the negotiation. The Soviet representative occasionally called on the United States to spell out further the method of armaments reduction and to give a further response to the Soviet recommendation of a 15 per cent reduction in military expenditures.

Nevertheless, it was clear that on the subject of the first stage reduction of armed forces and conventional armaments a high degree of agreement had been obtained between the Soviet and Western positions. If agreement had also been obtained on the matter of suspension of nuclear tests, there would have been little difficulty in extending that agreement to include the first stage of reduction of armed forces and conventional armaments. The failure to formalize the meeting of minds into a written agreement on this subject arose primarily from the insistence on the part of both the Soviet Union and the West on including in the package of first stage measures other subjects on which no agreement had been obtained. The Soviet Union insisted on a renunciation of the use of nuclear weapons. In the case of the West, the insistence was on a link between the suspension of nuclear tests and the cutoff.

It would be a mistake to attach too great importance to this agreement on reductions of armed forces and conventional weapons. With the development of more powerful nuclear weapons and more intricate missiles systems, it was inevitable that less stress would be placed on armies and conventional weapons. The reductions in armed forces and weapons contemplated in the 1957 negotiations have in fact taken place without an agreement largely as a result of technological changes in the methods of warfare.

SURPRISE ATTACK AND

INSPECTION ZONES

The next agenda item was entitled "Surprise Attack and Inspection Zones." As noted in a previous chapter, the impossibility of reconciling the approaches of the United States and the Soviet Union on this subject had been the greatest obstacle to meaningful negotiations in 1955 and 1956, and the most important concessions in both Soviet and United States policies at the end of 1956 were in this field.

While the 1957 negotiations went a long distance toward clarifying issues separating the Soviet Union and the West on this subject, they must be regarded only as a prelude to the much more thorough and penetrating exchanges of the technical meetings of 1958.

During the 1957 negotiations, the United States attached majoi importance to only the three topics: test suspension, cutoff, and measures to prevent surprise attack. As we have seen, the Soviet Union totally rejected the cutoff as a part of any scheme of partial disarmament. Its emphasis was on test suspension and measures to prevent surprise attack. If agreement had been obtained on either of these items without much difficulty, the agreement would have been extended to cover some measures of conventional disarmament. Without some agreement, however, on one or both of these major points, the 1957 negotiations were doomed to failure.

The position of the West on inspection zones developed late in the negotiations. The obvious reason for this was that the Western position could not be presented without the consent of all of the Western states that had come within the aerial and ground inspection zones. This clearance of positions lasted through June and early July, and the presentation of the final approved Western position did not take place until Dulles' visit to London on August 2. As a result, the full Soviet response did not take place during the subcommittee meetings.

Only in October, *after* the termination of the sessions of the subcommittee and after the Soviet Union had stated its intention to break away from the procedural framework of the subcommittee and the Disarmament Commission, did the Soviet Union come up with a response to the Western proposals for a European Zone. Therefore, it seems preferable to treat this response as the prelude to the technical discussions of 1958, confining the discussion in this chapter to the issues explored in the subcommittee.

The Initial Divergences

By the time the London negotiations began in 1957, proposals for safeguards against surprise attack and for inspection zones, particularly in Europe, had been well aired by both sides. The fundamental cleavage in objectives at the outset, in 1955, has already been suggested in an earlier chapter.

The original United States open skies proposal sought safeguards against surprise attack in proposals that combined confidence-building measures (based on an exchange of earnests of peaceful intent) with improved early warning measures (based on continued mistrust). The President's words bear repeating in this connection:

> I propose that we take a practical step. . . .
>
> To give to each other a complete blueprint of our military establishments, from beginning to end, from one end of our countries to the other, lay out the establishments and provide the blueprints to each other.
>
> Next, to provide within our countries facilities for aerial photography to the other country—we to provide you the facilities within our country, ample facilities for aerial reconnaissance, where you can make all the pictures you choose and take them to your own country to study, you to provide exactly the same facilities for us and we to make these examinations, and by this step to convince the world that we are providing as between ourselves against the possibility of great surprise attack, thus lessening danger and relaxing tension.[48]

[48] U.S. Department of State, *The Geneva Conference of Heads of Government, July 18-23, 1955*, Publication 6046 (October 1955), p. 58.

The United States objective in its succession of proposals for safeguards against surprise attack remained, as laid down in the Charter of the United Nations and in the statement in 1952 on "Essential Principles of Disarmament," not the regulation, but the *prevention* of war, through strengthening the deterrent to its initiation and reducing the risks of miscalculation.[49]

In contrast, the Soviet approach, although under the same label as the United States approach, was based on different premises and objectives. It seems increasingly clear that the Soviet Union is primarily interested in *avoiding* incidents that might set off a chain of events which would lead to nuclear war. As pointed out earlier, the new, post-Stalin Soviet military doctrine rejects the concept of successful blitzkrieg between major powers and does not conceive of surprise attack as having sufficient basis for success to risk its use against one of the great powers.[50] Given this view of surprise attack, Soviet arguments against the United States open skies proposal, whether as a means of guarding against surprise attack or as a means of reducing tension, are perhaps more straightforward and more soundly based than Western critics have been willing to admit. For example—Bulganin promptly reported his doubts on the efficiency of aerial photography in his report to the Supreme Soviet on August 4, 1955.

> With due respect to the striving to find a solution for the complicated problem of international control, which is contained in this proposal, one cannot but say at the same time, that the real effectiveness of such measures would not be great. During unofficial talks with the leaders of the United States Government we straightforwardly declared that aerophotography cannot give the expected results, because both countries stretch over vast territories in which, if desired, one can conceal anything. One must also take into consideration the fact that the proposed plan touches only the terri-

[49] The question can be raised whether all of the proposals that have been made by the United States in the course of negotiations on safeguards against great surprise attack would in fact strengthen the deterrent, or have the opposite effect. See, for example, the unpublished article by T. C. Schelling, "Meteors, Mischief and War," March 1960.

[50] Raymond L. Garthoff, *Soviet Strategy in the Nuclear Age* (1958), pp. 85-86.

tories belonging to the two countries, leaving out the armed forces and military constructions situated in the territories of other states.[51]

Khrushchev, then First Secretary of the Soviet Communist Party, later described the proposal, in the absence of accompanying reductions in arms, as "military reconnaissance" to gain information "for choosing the most convenient moment for sudden attack."[52]

The Soviet position that armaments and force levels must be reduced concurrently with installation of inspection systems in order to produce the relaxation of tensions was maintained down to and through the technical talks on safeguards in the fall of 1958.

. . . My colleagues and I have already had the opportunity to express their attitude on this proposal. It seems to us that in the present international situation and, moreover, under conditions of a completely unrestricted armaments race, the carrying out of such flights would not . . . free the peoples from the fear of a new war, but on the contrary would intensify that fear and mutual suspicion.

. . . Judge for yourself, Mr. President: What would the military leaders of your country do if it were reported to them that the aerophotography showed that your neighbor had more air fields? To be sure, they would order an immediate increase in the number of their own airfields. Naturally, our military leaders would do the same in a similar case. It is not difficult to understand that the result would be a further intensification of the armaments race.

It would be a different matter, if we could agree on a reduction of armaments and armed forces. Then, the carrying out of an appropriate control, the methods of which could be agreed upon, would be justified and necessary.[53]

Aerial inspection and aerial photographic surveys mean that information concerning the territory of given states as well as their

[51] *New York Times,* Aug. 5, 1955.
[52] *Ibid.,* Dec. 30, 1955. Address to the Supreme Soviet, Dec. 30, 1955. Excerpts as issued in English by TASS.
[53] "Premier Bulganin to the President," Feb. 1, 1956, Department of State *Bulletin,* Vol. 34 (March 26, 1956), p. 517.

industrial and other resources is placed at the disposal of other countries. In this connection, certainly, one cannot close his eyes to the fact that military and—it must be confessed—individual political personages in certain countries have more than once mentioned the desirability of obtaining more complete intelligence data on the military and industrial resources of the U.S.S.R. and they have not concealed the purposes for which they would like to have such data, emphasizing especially the importance of many foreign military bases situated in areas adjoining the boundaries of the Soviet Union. . . . mutual intelligence activity with the additional utilization of the latest achievements of technology would only increase the mutual fear of the danger of a sudden attack and would engender a war psychosis from which even now, as the facts prove, not all are free.

What I have said does not mean that we deny the importance of taking agreed measures to avert the danger of a sudden attack by one state upon another. By no means. We ourselves have proposed definite measures toward that end. I have in mind our proposal for the creation of control posts at the most important points (railroad junctions, airfields, highways, ports, etc.). The establishment of such posts, which is quite feasible even under the existing state of international trust, would exclude the dangerous secret concentration of armed forces by any state and, by the same token, would exclude the danger of a sudden attack. Of course, our proposal has value only if it is carried out as an integral part of the reduction of armaments and armed forces of nations. Without this, it loses its meaning, as do any other measures of control.[54]

Also:

In connection with the proposal of the 2 August (1957) of the United States, the United Kingdom, France and Canada on aerial photography, the Soviet Government stresses once again that no manner of inspection can shift the discussion of the disarmament

[54] Letter from Bulganin to Eisenhower, Sept. 11, 1956, *Soviet News*, Nos. 3471-3472, Sept. 17, 18, 1956.

problem out of deadlock. No kind of aerial photography can prevent surprise attacks by an aggressor possessing weapons of mass destruction together with the latest means of delivering them to the target, and armies numbering millions of men. A different way out must be sought.[55]

Thus it seems plausible that the Soviet Union meant exactly what it said when, on November 17, 1956 (and on March 18, 1957, April 30, 1957, and September 20, 1957) it accepted the concept of aerial inspection *"for the purpose of facilitating the quickest achievement of agreement"*[56] rather than as a means of guarding against surprise attack. Furthermore, to the extent that surprise attack safeguards *are* desired, the Soviet view appears to be to forestall buildups for attack in countries *other* than the great powers.

To summarize, the opposing concepts were, on the United States side, safeguards against great surprise attack through aerial and ground inspection; and on the Soviet side, safeguards against the outbreak of limited war (or safeguards against the exercise of the West's capacity for limited retaliation) through limitation and reduction of armaments in selected areas.

The argument over the method of safeguarding—aerial overflight or ground control posts—is obviously less important than the difference in the objective, particularly since the Soviet government conceived of the method itself as encompassing measures of partial disarmament. With objectives and premises as disparate as these, it is small wonder that many of the prolonged debates carried on under the heading of "surprise attack" appear to be little more than extended pairs of unilateral harangue. Yet, a rapprochement had begun.

Secretary Dulles, referring to the closely related problem of European security and German reunification, made the following statement at the very beginning of the exchanges on an inspection zone in Europe at the Foreign Ministers Conference which followed the summit meetings of 1955:

[55] Annex 4, U.N. Doc. DC/SC.1/65/Rev.1 (Aug. 27, 1957), p. 24.
[56] The phrase first appeared in the declaration of the Soviet government concerning the question of disarmament and reduction of international tension, Nov. 17, 1956, *Soviet News*, No. 3515, Nov. 19, 1956.

As I have examined, in parallel columns, the proposals which were put forward by the Western Powers . . . and compared them with the [Soviet] proposals . . . I found that there was a very considerable parallelism in our thinking. . . .

The idea that there should be a substantial zone within which special measures would be taken appears in Article 3 of the Western proposal and in the first proposition which Mr. Molotov outlined in his presentation on Monday.

The idea that within this zone there should be agreed limits of forces appeared in Article 3 of the Western proposal and in the second of the propositions which Mr. Molotov outlined in his presentation of Monday.

The idea that within this zone there should be reciprocal inspections to verify the agreed limitations appeared in Article 4 of the Western proposal and in the fourth proposition which Mr. Molotov outlined in his presentation of Monday.

Another special measure which the Western Powers suggested— that is, overlapping radar—does not have any counterpart in the Soviet proposals but this is a detailed proposal not touching on the substance. . . .

The concept that foreign forces, not forming part of agreed collective security, should be withdrawn on demand appears in Article 7 of the Western proposals and perhaps, although this is somewhat ambiguous, may be found within the context of the third of the propositions which Mr. Molotov made in his exposition of Monday when he speaks about the exercise of sovereignty.

The concept that there should be reaction against aggression appears in Article 8 of the Western Powers proposal and is also found in Article 2 of the draft Soviet treaty.[57]

The Shift Toward Common Ground

With the new policy decisions in November 1956 in the United States and the Soviet Union, the "parallel lines" to which the Secretary

[57] U.S. Department of State, *The Geneva Meeting of Foreign Ministers, Oct. 27-Nov. 16, 1955,* Publication 6158 (December 1955), pp. 85-86.

referred began to tend toward intersection. The American decisions as laid before the United Nations in January 1957, incorporated the Soviet insistence on some measures of limitation and reduction in armaments. The major innovation, "progressive installation of inspection systems which would provide against the possibility of surprise attack," was accompanied by proposals for inspected first stage reductions in armed forces and armaments to intermediate levels of 2.5 million for the Soviet Union and the United States, and 750,000 for France and the United Kingdom.[58] Aerial and ground inspection were methods prescribed for *both* objectives.

This United States shift toward common ground found its counterpart in the Soviet proposals of November 17, 1956, which included, for the first time, an offer to accept aerial inspection in a zone in Europe. Premier Bulganin's letter to the President of that date said the Soviet Union was "prepared to consider"[59] aerial inspection in a zone in Europe 800 kilometers on each side of the demarcation line between the opposing NATO and Warsaw Pact military forces. The same letter proposed a controlled one-third reduction in foreign armed forces stationed in the territory of Germany,[60] and this was followed by the restatement on March 18, 1957, of the proposal for a "Zone of Limitation and Inspection of Armaments in Europe" that would include a prohibition on "stationing of atomic military formations or any form of atomic and hydrogen weapons in the zone."[61] The language closely followed the first version of the proposal that was offered at the Foreign Ministers Conference of October-November 1955[62] following the summit. Secretary Dulles' prophecy was on the way to fulfillment.

The distinguished French representative on the United Nations subcommittee, Jules Moch, claims, and in large measure deserves,

[58] U.N. General Assembly, Eighth Session, First Committee *Official Records,* 821st Meeting (Jan. 14, 1957), pp. 41-42.
[59] "Premier Bulganin to the President," Nov. 17, 1956, Department of State *Bulletin,* Vol. 36 (Jan. 21, 1957), pp. 89-90.
[60] *Ibid.,* p. 77.
[61] U.N. Doc. DC/SC.1/PV.87 (March 18, 1957), p. 38.
[62] See statement by Molotov and proposal by the Soviet delegation, Oct. 31, 1955. Text in U.S. Department of State, *Geneva Meeting of Foreign Ministers, Oct. 27-Nov. 16, 1955,* p. 81.

credit for this initial break in the Soviet opposition to aerial inspection. His statement before the General Assembly in January 1957, recounted the history of his negotiating efforts to this end:

There remains aerial inspection, which has been the subject of so many discussions. I should like to examine this question quite dispassionately.

Having been present when President Eisenhower first presented his plan in Geneva, I recognize that this plan, separated at first from all disarmament measures, had as its ambition to restore international confidence by providing against surprise attacks, thus leaving the door open for future negotiations on disarmament. It did not, in its initial form, fit in with our concept, which was equally far removed from control without disarmament and disarmament without control. The Soviets, after careful consideration, categorically discarded this plan, as I had immediately foreseen would be the case and as I indicated right away to our American colleagues, who will, I am sure, remember that.

But the situation has changed considerably since Geneva. The aerial reconnaissance plan has been linked with Marshal Bulganin's plan for setting up fixed ground posts and incorporated in a disarmament plan of which—in the opinion of our United States colleagues—it has for a long time constituted the essential element. The Soviet Union, however, has remained adamant in its refusal.

On 10 July last [1956], before the Disarmament Commission, I made an attempt at compromise . . .

". . . So long as this method [of aerial inspection] remains effective, priority must be given to its application in the sensitive sectors where concentrations of conventional forces are normally to be effected. This amounts to proposing regular aerial reconnaissance over Western Europe and along the border between the two worlds in Scandinavia . . . and in the Middle East. If we add—for the sake of reciprocity rather than effectiveness—a zone in America equal in size to the . . . area of the Soviet Union which is included in the sensitive sectors, we can imagine a compromise between the 'all' proposed by one side and the 'nothing' proposed by the other, with possibilities of subsequently extending the photographed sector." . . .

I would add to the remark made by the United Kingdom Minister of State a comment on the technical inadequacy of these Soviet proposals. The important thing, in fact, is not to draw two lines at an equal distance from the dividing line, or to choose this distance in such a way as to include on one side the whole of Western Europe, except Spain, Portugal, Brittany, Cornwall and Scotland, and on the other side the people's democracies and, so far as the U.S.S.R. is concerned, only a narrow region of swamps. The problem, rather, is to include all the territories in which secret concentrations—whether of land forces or air power—might be dangerous, even though other more remote regions may be included, in order, as I have already indicated, to ensure a proper balance. That was my purpose in suggesting that the preliminary demarcation of these sectors should be entrusted to military experts with maps and coloured pencils. . . .

It matters little, however, that my compromise of a few months ago has been temporarily distorted. A certain advance is none the less being made as regards principles: we are no longer confronted with an absolute refusal on the part of the Soviet Union even to consider aerial inspection.

Similarly, Mr. Lodge told us, in his detailed statement of 14 January, that the United States proposes:

". . . the progressive installation of inspection systems which will provide against the possibility of great surprise attack. The United States is willing to execute, either as an opening step or as a later step, the complete proposal made in the summit conference at Geneva by President Eisenhower."

This proposal raises much hope, since it paves the way for progressive implementation.

Between the "all" and the "nothing" of last year, a way out of the deadlock is beginning to appear. Of course, we shall need a specific text, which will be drafted by the Sub-Committee. Once such an agreement has been drawn up, its signatories will have done much to advance the cause of peace.[63]

The new decisions on both sides launched the first stage of the negotiations on regional zones of inspection and limitation of armaments. The United States could in no circumstances agree to the Soviet proposal of November 17, 1956, which by its terms would tend to perpetuate the unnatural division of Germany, but it was prepared to consider a European zone if the Soviet Union would agree to a United States-Soviet aerial inspection zone.

Prior to the start of the subcommittee discussions, the United States decided to advance the concept of beginning aerial inspection by progressively expanding zones. During the opening weeks of the London negotiations, two initial zones, which could be expanded in successive stages to cover much wider areas, were informally discussed among the subcommittee delegations, including the Soviet delegation.

To facilitate discussion of this new concept, the United States delegation suggested for illustrative purposes: (a) a zone in Europe bounded on the west by 5° east longitude, in the east by 30° east longitude, and in the south by 45° north latitude; and (b) a United States-Soviet Union zone in the Bering Straits area extending from 140° west longitude to 160° east longitude, and south to 45° north latitude. Both zones converged on the North Pole.[64]

The Soviet Union responded with its proposals of April 30, 1957—urging a European zone to the west and south of the territory previously described, and for the first time suggesting a zone whose center line did not run on the demarcation line of Germany but instead ran

[63] U.N. General Assembly, Eleventh Session, First Committee, *Official Records,* 828th Meeting (Jan. 25, 1957), pp. 59-65. For diagrams illustrating the various proposed zones, see pp. 382-85.
[64] Secretary Dulles, in response to a question on the status of these proposals, emphasized at his press conference of May 14, 1957, that the initial proposals were official government proposals. U.S. Department of State *Bulletin,* Vol. 36 (June 3, 1957), p. 900. Note: Jules Moch had suggested the use of "specified parallels of latitude and specified meridians of longitude" in the subcommittee in London almost exactly a year earlier. U.N. Doc. DC/SC.1/PV.75 (April 3, 1956), p. 43.

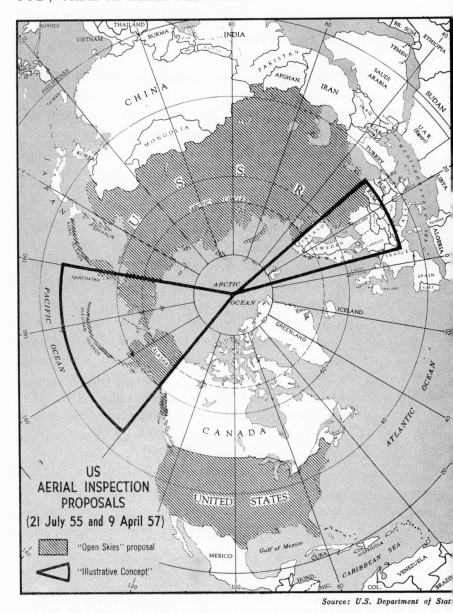

US
AERIAL INSPECTION
PROPOSALS
(21 July 55 and 9 April 57)

"Open Skies" proposal

"Illustrative Concept"

Source: U.S. Department of State

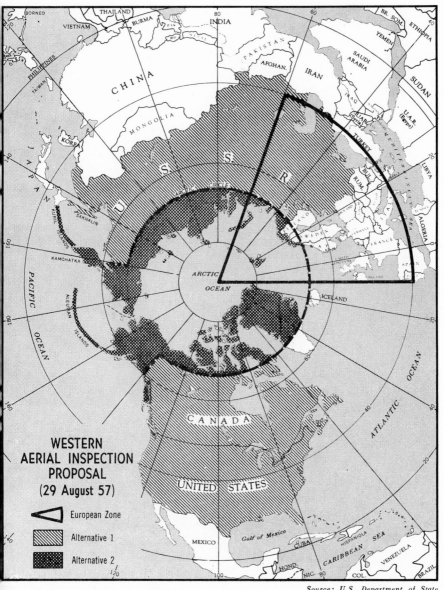

**WESTERN
AERIAL INSPECTION
PROPOSAL
(29 August 57)**

◁ European Zone

▨ Alternative 1

▨ Alternative 2

Source: U.S. Department of State

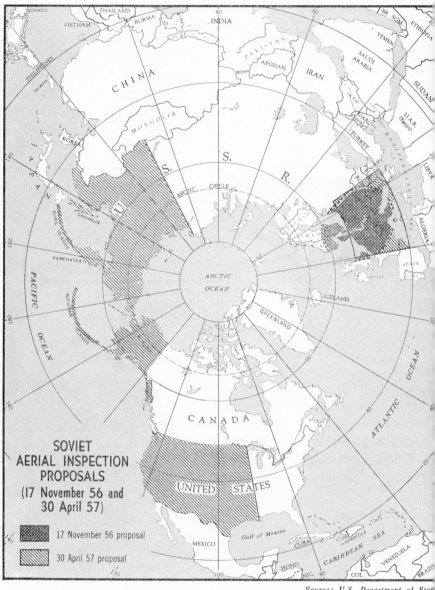

SOVIET
AERIAL INSPECTION
PROPOSALS
(17 November 56 and
30 April 57)

17 November 56 proposal

30 April 57 proposal

Source: U.S. Department of State

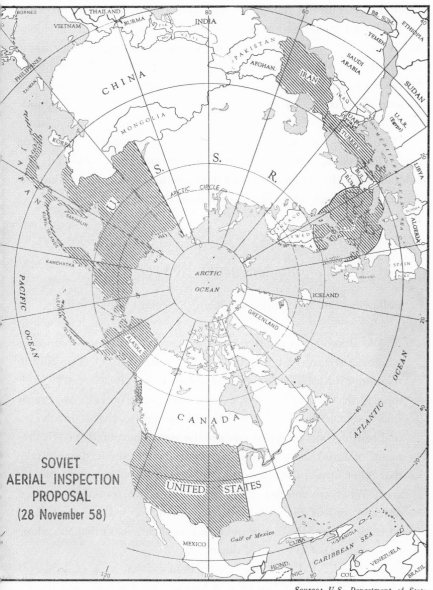

SOVIET
AERIAL INSPECTION
PROPOSAL
(28 November 58)

Source: U.S. Department of State

through the center of the Soviet zone in Germany. The zone proposed by the Soviet Union had as its boundaries: in the west, zero meridian; to the east, 25° east longitude; to the north, 54° north latitude; and in the south, 39° 38' north latitude. In response to the illustrative Bering Straits zone, the Soviet proposals of April 30 suggested an expansion to include the territory of the United States west of 90° west longitude and the territory of the Soviet Union east of longitude 108° east.[65]

With the appearance of this as a new Soviet negotiating position on aerial inspection zones, the United States undertook renewed consideration of the concept of initial inspection zones, converting the illustrative concept into a firm proposal in order to move rapidly ahead to an actual agreement.

The Consultations within NATO

Following the May policy decisions, Secretary Dulles stated:

We attach a top priority to getting a substantial inspection zone wherever we can get it quickly. Now, if we can get it quickly in relation to Europe, that is acceptable to us. If we can't get it quickly in relation to Europe but could get it quickly as regards some other area which is substantial enough so that it involves a real test of good faith and enables the significance and the requirements of aerial and ground inspection to be tested out, then we take that other area. In other words, we are not set upon any particular area. What we are set upon is trying to get something started quickly; and as far as we are concerned, we will take any area which is sufficiently free of political complications so that the whole process does not get bogged down. . . .

As I indicated two weeks ago, before I had this exchange of views on this with Chancellor Adenauer, we foresaw, and it took no great vision to do so, there would be quite a lot of complications in finding a European area where you could get quickly started. There are all sorts of problems in Europe. There is the prob-

[65] Annex 7, U.N. Doc. DC/SC.1/55 (April 30, 1957), p. 12.

lem of unification of Germany; there is the problem of NATO strategy. You have got quite a number of countries involved in that area. So you have a multiplicity of parties and for all these reasons I foresaw, and indicated, it might not prove to be the case that the European area would be included in the first step.

That is not because we don't want to have it included in the first step. It is merely a question whether that can be done quickly enough to stem the tide and to give the people faith to believe that something can come out of the disarmament talks. I don't think you can go on talking and talking for year after year and not get anywhere. I think there has got to be some progress made in order to keep these talks alive. I think if you made progress to some appreciable degree, that in itself would make it possible to make progress to a larger degree. . . . I see lots of troubles in including Europe in the first stage. But if the Europeans can clear up those troubles so they can get started there, we are happier.[66]

The consultations between Chancellor Adenauer and President Eisenhower, which had taken place the same week in Washington, resulted in a statement that:

If a beginning could be made toward effective measures of disarmament, this would create a degree of confidence which would facilitate further progress in the field of disarmament and in the settlement of outstanding major political problems, such as the reunification of Germany.[67]

At the same time the President officially invited the European nations to "take a leading role" in developing measures for disarmament "applicable to Europe."[68] Secretary Dulles confirmed this view at his press conference on May 29:

[66] Statement of Secretary Dulles in press conference, May 29, 1957, U.S. Department of State *Bulletin*, Vol. 36 (June 17, 1957), pp. 965–66.
[67] "Eisenhower-Adenauer Joint Declaration," White House Press Release (May 28, 1957).
[68] *Ibid.*

. . . Anything done with relation to Europe will only be done in accordance with the freely expressed will of the European countries concerned. We do not intend to put them in an awkward position by making proposals that involve them without their prior concurrence.[69]

The European countries including NATO had been kept informed of the major developments in the negotiations to date, but now it was clear that they must be drawn in for active, full, and complete consultation on the substance of further proposals affecting their territory.

During June and July the European governments, individually and collectively as members of the North Atlantic Council, studied, debated, and reached a decision on a European zone offer to the Soviet Union.

The Western Proposals

On July 22, before flying to London to participate personally in the final four power and NATO negotiations on the new proposals, Secretary Dulles publicly outlined the position of the United States on zones.

He said that the United States was not only prepared to accept reciprocal inspection of all its territory in North America, and was consulting with Canada on the possibility of enlarging this zone to include Canada, but that we were also ready to start with a less ambitious beginning, such as a zone in the Arctic Circle. He added that the United States was cooperating closely with its NATO allies on a European zone proposal.[70]

On August 2, in London, the Secretary, on behalf of the four powers presented to the subcommittee the agreed offer—an offer representing not alone concessions of the four powers but those of all seventeen NATO governments.[71] The four powers offered to the Soviet Union its choice of either broad or more limited inspection zones involving reciprocal inspection in the northern hemisphere and in Europe. The

[69] U.S. Department of State *Bulletin,* Vol. 36 (June 17, 1957), p. 967.
[70] "Radio and Television Report to the Nation by the Secretary of State," U.S. Department of State Press Release 430, July 22, 1957.
[71] Annex 1, U.N. Doc. DC/SC.1/62/Rev.1.

European zone offer was conditional on acceptance of at least a beginning in the Arctic Circle where United States–Soviet Union territory significantly adjoin. For the northern hemisphere zone, involving primarily United States–Soviet Union territory, the United States repeated its offer, now joined by Canada, of "All the territory of the continental United States, all Alaska including the Aleutian Islands, all the territory of Canada" in exchange for inspection of "all the territory of the Soviet Union." Alternatively, if this were not agreeable to the Soviet Union, the four powers with the consent of the governments of Denmark and Norway, offered:

All the territory north of the Arctic Circle of the Soviet Union, Canada, the United States (Alaska), Denmark (Greenland), and Norway; all the territory of Canada, the United States and the Soviet Union west of 140 degrees west longitude, east of 160 degrees east longitude and north of 50 degrees north latitude; all the remainder of Alaska; all the remainder of the Kamchatka peninsula; and all of the Aleutian and Kurile Islands will be open to inspection.[72]

With regard to Europe, the four powers offered "with the concurrence in principle of their European allies and in continuing consultation with them" to open to inspection "an area including all of Europe, bounded on the south by latitude 40 degrees north and in the west by 10 degrees west longitude and in the east by 60 degrees east longitude." Further, they offered, if the Soviet Union rejected this broad proposal, to discuss "a more limited zone of inspection in Europe . . . on the understanding that this would include a significant part of the territory of the Soviet Union, as well as the other countries of Eastern Europe."[73]

The character of the inspection system was described only in the broadest terms, but the Western powers urged that a working group of experts be set up to examine the technical problems:

With regard to the character of the inspection to safeguard

[72] *Ibid.*, pp. 1-2.
[73] *Ibid.*

against the possibility of surprise attack, it is understood that it would include in all cases aerial inspection, with ground observation posts at principal ports, railway junctions, main highways and important airfields, etc. as agreed. There would also, as agreed, be mobile ground teams with specifically defined authority. It is understood that ground posts may be established by agreement at points in the territories of the States concerned without being restricted to the limits of the above described areas, but the areas open to ground inspection shall not be less than the areas of aerial inspection. The mobility of the ground inspection would be specifically defined in the agreement with in all cases the concurrence of the countries directly concerned. There would also be all necessary means of communication.

Since the establishment of any inspection system is subject to agreement on the details of its installation, maintenance and operation, it is proposed, as a matter of urgency, that a working group of experts be set up at once to examine the technical problems and to report their conclusions which could form the basis for an Annex to the Agreement.[74]

These highly technical proposals—so technical that even the negotiators experienced difficulty describing them—were an attempt to steer through a narrow and tortuous channel bounded on either side by shoals. Among the more important problems that had to be resolved in connection with any European zone were the following:

1. The West could not consent to a European zone the center of which was the boundary between the NATO countries and the Warsaw Pact countries, since this would tend to perpetuate the artificial division of Europe.

2. For strategic reasons—in general the absence of depth of defense in Western Europe—a "neutral zone" in Central Europe would be unacceptable to the West. If the areas open to aerial inspection coincided with the areas where ground posts were located, this would tend to turn such areas into a "neutral zone."

[74] *Ibid.*, pp. 2-3.

3. The effectiveness of the ground posts would be to a large extent dependent on aerial inspection discovering the data that would be investigated by the ground posts.

4. An area of a given size west of the iron curtain would contain far more installations of strategic importance than an equal area east of the iron curtain because the vast area of the Soviet Union permitted defense in depth.

The difficulties of delineating an Arctic zone acceptable to all of the Western allies were much less. It should, however, be noted that any relatively small Arctic zone would for reasons of geography cover a large part of Canada but very little of the United States. The prospect of many inspection posts in Canada with few if any in the United States did not appeal to the newly elected Canadian Conservative government.

The Soviet Union denounced the Arctic proposal from the outset with Khrushchev's term "quite comical."[75]

Nevertheless, it was generally believed that until the Soviet Union should perfect intercontinental ballistic missiles capable of carrying nuclear warheads, its only means of delivering a nuclear attack on the United States would be from air bases in the Arctic zone. This almost certainly was a factor influencing the Soviet Union in its position.

Likewise, the Soviet Union was unwilling to discuss either of the alternative proposals for a European zone in the subcommittee forum. Although repeatedly pressed for some comment on "the more limited zone," Zorin ignored the subject, reserving the denunciations, in his August 27 and 29 speeches, for the subcommittee as a whole and for the Western package of partial proposals.

The technical nature of the Western proposals and the late date of their presentation precluded any Soviet response in August. Indeed, the Soviet response in October reflected rapid decision making. By October, however, the subcommittee meetings had terminated, and the further negotiation of this issue had to await the technical discussions of 1958.

[75] Excerpt from Khrushchev's Press Conference in Helsinki, Finland, June 13, 1957. Transcript in *New York Times,* June 14, 1957, p. 1.

INTERNATIONAL CONTROL ORGAN

When on May 8, 1957, the subcommittee reached the subject of an international control organ, Ambassador Zorin in the subcommittee meetings expressed his fears as follows:

> I am reminded of the course discussions of the disarmament question have taken throughout the period which has been under examination, both in the Subcommittee and before its establishment, in the United Nations. Let me remind you that, as soon as *rapprochement* seemed imminent and there was any possibility of agreement on the substance of any question, the issue of control was almost invariably raised and became an obstacle to the conclusion of any agreement.[76]

Ambassador Zorin's fears did not materialize in this series of meetings. On May 7, Governor Stassen went no further than to suggest two possible new functions for an international control organ. The first was

> . . . to establish a limitation upon the export and import of armaments which might include: (a) restrictions on types or items of armaments which might be exported or imported; (b) prohibitions of the export or import of armaments in certain areas or zones; and (c) requirements for notification to the organization of intention to export or import armaments and reports to the organization of the actual export or import of armaments.

Stassen's second suggestion was that the international control organ might devise means of notification of any significant movement of land forces over the soil of a foreign state, of sea forces over international waters, or of air forces flying either over the territory of a foreign state or over international waters.[77] Stassen never pressed these proposals any further, and the Soviet Union did not respond to them.

[76] U.N. Doc. DC/SC.1/PV.112 (May 8, 1957), p. 35.
[77] U.N. Doc. DC/SC.1/PV.111 (May 7, 1957), pp. 6-7.

Beginning June 27, the Western representatives developed the meager proposals that were later contained in the August 29 working paper. These proposals were: (1) that all the obligations contained in the convention would be conditional on the continued operation of an effective international control and inspection system, to verify compliance with its terms by all parties (in fact, two obligations in the same paper, the first period of test suspension and initial reductions of conventional forces, preceded an operating international control system); (2) that all control and inspection services be within the framework of an international control organization established under the aegis of the United Nations Security Council, which would include as its executive organ a board of control that strangely enough would have a voting formula requiring unanimity among the five members of the subcommittee—in other words a veto; (3) that all states make information available to the board of control and assist it in its operations; (4) that the functions of the international control organization would be expanded by agreement between the parties concerned as the measures provided for in the convention were progressively applied.[78] This language was sufficiently vague to be noncontroversial.

The Soviet proposals for international control contained in the March 18 paper calling for comprehensive disarmament were substantially the same as contained in the previous Soviet proposals of May 10, 1955 and November 17, 1956. The Soviet proposal of April 30 for partial disarmament eliminated control posts at airfields during the first stage. Zorin explained that the partial disarmament program would require fewer controls than the comprehensive program because there was less to be controlled. However, the Soviet representative did not at this time enter into any extensive development of its own program or criticism of the Western program.

Noel-Baker has criticized proposals of the Western four because of their meager control provisions.[79] In fact, the negotiations came closer to reaching some agreement than ever before largely because of the avoidance of this problem, which the Soviets had correctly described as "barriers" to agreement. It was possible for the West to avoid de-

[78] Annex 5, U.N. Doc. DC/SC.1/66 (Aug. 29, 1957).
[79] Noel-Baker, *The Arms Race*, p. 221.

tailed discussions of the problem of international controls for the reason that the Soviet Union in its proposals on May 10, 1955, had in principle accepted the Western position when it stated that the control organ should have the power "to exercise control including inspection on a continuing basis to the extent necessary to insure implementation of the above-mentioned convention by all States."[80]

When Zorin in 1957 proposed more restricted controls for a partial disarmament system than for comprehensive disarmament, this cast the shadow that the Soviet Union's position of May 10, 1955, of support for adequate controls applied only to its comprehensive proposals and not to the proposals for partial disarmament. However, at almost the same time, the Soviet Union's expressed willingness to accept a control system for test suspension created a contrary inference. Therefore the Western four were quite willing during these negotiations to rely on the general principles brought forward by the Soviet Union on May 10, 1955. The negotiations could thus take place on the *objects* of control rather than on the *methods* of control. This was the procedure for which the Soviet Union had always contended in the past. To repeat, however, it was not a possible negotiating procedure until the Soviet Union had supported a general principle of control which, if implemented, would protect the West.

The important Western suggestions on the subject of control were quite independent of the agenda item dealing with the international control organ. Whenever a substantive meeting of minds on any subject appeared close, the Western four—generally the British representative took the lead—called for the formation of a technical working group to devise a control system to police the specific measure on which agreement seemed within reach. Zorin invariably took the position that it was still premature to create a working group, since on each subject there were still outstanding substantive problems to be solved. However, in taking that position he was conceding that when a substantive meeting of minds was obtained, the proper procedure would be to set up such a technical group. The first two technical groups intended to devise inspection systems were not, however, set up until 1958.[81]

[80] Annex 15, U.N. Doc. DC/SC.1/26/Rev. 2 (May 10, 1955), pp. 16, 21.
[81] See Chap. 17.

During 1957, Secretary Dulles had pointed out on a number of occasions that the crucial test of Soviet willingness to enter into a meaningful agreement for the regulation of armaments would not be the agreement in principle but would be the accompanying detailed annexes.[82] Not until 1958 with the setting up of the working groups did the negotiations reach the stage of working out detailed annexes.

MISSILES AND ROCKETS

On January 14, 1957, Lodge in the United Nations General Assembly had called for international inspection of and participation in the testing of intercontinental missiles and other objects entering outer space. Stassen reaffirmed this suggestion in his opening statement to the subcommittee on March 19.[83]

In the Soviet proposals of March 18, Zorin called for international control of guided rockets to take place simultaneously with destruction of existing nuclear stocks—[84] in other words as the very last item in a comprehensive disarmament program. This reluctance to regulate missiles in an early stage of a disarmament program foreshadowed the sensational progress in the field of rockets which the Soviet Union was to announce later in the year. Since the Soviet Union intended to rely to such a great extent on missiles in its weapons systems, it logically postponed their regulation to the last stage of a comprehensive disarmament program. Along the same lines, the Soviet Union proposals for partial disarmament, on April 30, made no provision for regulation

[82] See "Secretary Dulles' News Conference of August 6, 1957," Department of State Bulletin, Vol. 37 (Aug. 26, 1957), p. 347. "Acceptance in principle is a long way off from gaining something that is satisfactory. Before you have anything concrete to put your teeth in here you have to find out what kind of inspection there is going to be." Again, "Secretary Dulles' News Conference of Dec. 10, 1957," ibid. (Dec. 30, 1957), p. 1024. Concerning the "agreement in principle" on military matters at the NATO Conference, Dulles stated that this was instead "an agreement which is highly specific and subject to a very well specified contingency. The ordinary use of the word 'agreement in principle' means that you accept the general idea but you reserve the right to frustrate that idea by a lot of detailed objections."
[83] U.N. Doc. DC/SC.1/PV.88 (March 19, 1957), p. 27.
[84] U.N. Doc. DC/SC.1/PV.87 (March 18, 1957), p. 33.

of missiles except to call for a solemn declaration renouncing the use of "all nuclear weapons including rockets."[85]

The discussions in the subcommittee of objects entering outer space did not commence until July 25 when the Western representatives made the modest proposal that a technical committee should study the design of an inspection system which would make it possible to ensure that the sending of objects through outer space would be exclusively for peaceful and scientific purposes. Stassen pointed out that it would be much easier to deal with armaments of this nature before they were perfected and became a real danger, just as it would have been easier to deal with atomic energy in 1946 before the commencement of an uncontrollable race.[86] Commander Noble, representing the United Kingdom, pointed out that the control of weapons entering outer space would assist in nuclear control, through policing the means of delivery of nuclear weapons. This might be a much easier task than eliminating existing nuclear stocks.[87]

Zorin's reply went no further than to repeat the relevant portions of the Soviet comprehensive disarmament proposals of March 18 and the provision in the April 30 proposals for renouncing the use of all nuclear weapons including rockets.[88]

In view of the successful launching of Sputnik less than three months after this discussion, it would have been unrealistic to anticipate any negotiation at this time by the Soviet Union. The Western representatives were generally aware of the tremendous volume of missile launchings that had taken place over the past year in the Soviet Union, and its refusal to discuss the problem merely confirmed their belief that it was about to announce technological achievements in the missiles fields. Therefore the discussion went no further.

The Western suggestions of July 25 were included as a part of their August 29 proposals.[89]

[85] Annex 7, U.N. Doc. DC/SC.1/55 (April 30, 1957), p. 9.
[86] U.N. Doc. DC/SC.1/PV.141 (July 25, 1957), p. 4.
[87] Ibid., p. 11.
[88] Ibid., pp. 15-16.
[89] U.N. Doc. DC/SC.1/PV.153 (Aug. 29, 1957), pp. 2-4.

"OTHER MATTERS"

The Soviet proposals to abolish military bases in foreign territory and to reduce the forces of the United States, the United Kingdom, and France stationed in NATO countries and the forces of the Soviet Union stationed in the Warsaw treaty countries come under the heading of "Other Matters."[90]

While the Soviet Union frequently reminded the Western powers of the existence of these proposals and of the failure of the West to reply to them, nevertheless one of the encouraging features of the Soviet approach toward partial disarmament was that the Soviet Union had not insisted on action on these suggestions as an indispensable part of its first partial disarmament program. Until the violent speech of August 27, which led almost immediately to the breakup of discussions, the Soviet Union had in effect acquiesced in the absence of discussion of these two issues.

Other items also included a memorandum from the Yugoslav government with certain suggestions concerning a program of partial disarmament.[91] Even though this memorandum received favorable comment from most of the Western delegates, it played no substantial part in the discussions.

After the Western representatives on August 21 had completed the presentation of their final positions in connection with the suspension of nuclear testing,[92] as set forth in a previous chapter, their sole remaining task was to gather together their positions in a single paper. This took place on August 29. However, the Soviet rejection of the entire Western approach preceded the August 29 proposals by two days.

[90] Annex 7, U.N. Doc. DC/SC.1/55 (April 30, 1957), pp. 10-11.
[91] Annex 4, U.N. Doc. DC/SC.1/52/Add.1 (June 24, 1957), pp. 2-3
[92] U.N. Doc. DC/SC.1/PV.149 (Aug. 21, 1957).

XVI

Détente

On May 17, when Governor Stassen returned from London to Washington to commence consultations on new United States proposals to respond to the Soviet proposals of April 30, he radiated optimism. He said that since his visit to Washington during Easter, the Soviet Union and the Western powers had moved "closer to agreement" on a first step arrangement that would involve aerial inspection and cuts in conventional military forces.[1] As we have seen in a previous chapter, the President was of the same opinion.

Yet, on August 27, three and one-half months later, Zorin broke the spirit of quiet negotiation which had generally prevailed throughout the conference with an unexpected and violent ninety-minute attack on the West—"the aggressive North Atlantic bloc . . . the fruitless disarmament talks . . . ruling circles . . . double game" and accused the United States of designing its inspection proposals "to contribute to the preparation of aggressive war."[2]

[1] *New York Times*, May 18, 1957. Report by Russell Baker on interview with Stassen on May 17, 1957, in Washington.

[2] This attack was the more shocking because it was presented as an official statement of the government of the Soviet Union and the phrases had been deliberately drafted, rather than being merely an oral extemporaneous outburst. U.N. Disarmament Commission, Subcommittee of the Disarmament Commission, *Verbatim Record*, 151st Meeting, U.N. Doc. DC/SC.1/PV.151 (Aug. 27, 1957), pp. 3-4. Cited hereafter by document number and date.

President Eisenhower voiced the shocked concern and disappointment of the free world in a statement made the following day:

It is deeply disappointing to all true lovers of peace that the Soviet Union should have already attacked, with such scornful words, the proposals which Canada, France, the United Kingdom and the United States are putting forward at the United Nations Disarmament Subcommittee in London. It is noteworthy that this attack coincides with the boastful statement by the Soviet Union that they have made advances in the development of means for bringing mass destruction to any part of the world. . . .

It would be tragic if these important first-stage proposals, fraught with such significance for the peace of the world, were rejected by the Soviet Union even before they could have been seriously studied and before the Western presentation is complete. Such a Soviet attitude would condemn humanity to an indefinite future of immeasurable danger.[3]

The rejection was abruptly confirmed on August 29 when, without the courtesy of even perfunctory reference to his home government, Zorin declared the Western proposals entirely unacceptable.

THE END OF THE

SUBCOMMITTEE

On September 6, after its 157th meeting, the subcommittee recessed, without reaching agreement on the timing or even the possibility of reconvening. This change did not burst forth like a thunderbolt from the clear skies. Cumulus clouds had appeared on the horizon as early as the last week of May and had reached menacing proportions before August 27. A series of events both within and outside the negotiations contributed to their failure. It is important to analyze

[3] Statement by President Eisenhower, White House Press Release, Aug. 28, 1957.

these events because of the insight they furnish into Soviet thinking. Let it be stated at the outset that no single simple formula explains all the Soviet attitudes and motivations. Any one or several of a number of overlapping and related events both within the negotiations and in the outside would have been sufficient to produce the détente. The Soviet leaders in their utterances relied on all of these events. When the time came to break off negotiations, the Soviet leaders acted neither mysteriously nor silently. On this occasion there were no silences but an abundance of shrieks. The problem is to cull the significant and sober statements from the shrieking.

The German Viewpoint

The first clouds appeared with the visit of Chancellor Adenauer to the United States at the end of May. The express purpose of the Chancellor's visit to the United States was to assure that no disarmament agreement might overlook or even prejudice the reunification of Germany. The Chancellor in the past had taken the even more extreme position that no serious negotiations on disarmament should take place until German reunification.

Chancellor Adenauer reported to the National Press Club in Washington that the United States and West German leaders were looking toward future international developments in four stages: (1) an initial disarmament agreement creating "a degree of confidence," (2) a big-four foreign ministers conference, (3) the reunification of Germany, (4) a comprehensive disarmament agreement. The decision over initial disarmament must be taken "between the United States and the Soviet Union." This would show whether the Soviet leaders were willing to move toward a relaxation of tension. If they are not, "then it doesn't serve any purpose to go further."

Specifically, the Chancellor stated that the United States had not proposed including Germany in a zone of mutual United States-Soviet aerial inspection in the initial stage. This would be left to the later "comprehensive" stage along with reductions in man power and arms.

Nor would initial disarmament arrangements in any way affect West Germany's armaments.[4] He did not, however, rule out Arctic inspection zones or the control of nuclear weapons and bombs.

Chancellor Adenauer was ruling out of the first stage negotiations two of the subjects in which the Soviet Union had shown the greatest interest—the separation of antagonists in Europe and conventional disarmament. The Soviet Union had shown no interest in a polar inspection zone, and the differences between the Soviet Union and the West on nuclear disarmament were so great that it was probable that they could not be bridged in this series of negotiations. Therefore, if reductions in conventional armaments and European inspection zones were eliminated from the package of partial measures, the only thing that would be left would be an agreement on suspension of nuclear tests.

Secretary Dulles recognized the implications of Adenauer's statements on the London negotiations. Following the Chancellor's statement, Dulles said that if the West Germans wanted to be excluded in the first stage that was up to them, but he observed, "I don't want to be the one that pronounced anything like a death-knell on including Europe in the initial stage."[5]

One other aspect of German-Russian relations apparently played a serious role in the disarmament negotiations. West Germany was approaching a national election in September. During the spring Adenauer, apparently with an eye to his electoral campaign, sought to create the appearance of activity in German-Russian relations. Early in April he had responded to a letter from Premier Bulganin by agreeing to send a delegation to Moscow to talk on trade and other matters. On April 25 he had a long talk with the Soviet ambassador. He made these conciliatory gestures simultaneously with his decision to rearm Germany and to request nuclear weapons in Germany.

The Soviet response, however, was to suggest in the subcommittee the Eden plan for a zone of controlled disarmament running down either side of the iron curtain and thus perpetuating the line between

[4] News Conference at the National Press Club, May 28, 1957, *New York Times*, May 29, 1957.
[5] *Ibid.*, May 30, 1957, p. 3.

East and West. At the same time, Bulganin issued the brutal warning that an atomic war would turn Germany into a cemetery.[6]

This series of developments probably created among the Soviet leaders the impression that an appearance of harmony between the Soviet Union and the West would increase the Chancellor's chances for an electoral victory, while the failure of the Chancellor to establish good relations with the Soviet Union would lead to the opposite result. Certainly the breakup of the disarmament negotiations occurring three weeks before the German elections would be a most dramatic signal of disharmony between East and West. It seems clear that the violent Soviet gestures had exactly the opposite result. Chancellor Adenauer was the victor in the German elections by the greatest majority that he had ever received. The Soviet policy stimulated a wave of patriotism in West Germany and rallied to the support of the Chancellor many voters who might otherwise have remained indifferent.

It should again be emphasized that during the summer of 1957 the relations between the Soviet Union and the West were generally tense as the obvious aftermath of the Hungarian and Suez incidents in the fall of 1956. The conciliatory tone of the disarmament negotiations was the exception. The breakup of the subcommittee discussions, therefore, placed the disarmament negotiations on the same tense basis

[6] "Dr. Adenauer in the Toils," *The Economist* (May 4, 1957). It is interesting to recall that, two years earlier, in the spring of 1955, disarmament negotiations were used by the British as an important aid to an election campaign. The British General Elections took place on May 26 and, during the weeks preceding, the Conservatives bally-hooed the "Peace of Eden" as of prime importance. ("The Hidden Hum," *The Economist*, May 7, 1955, p. 452.) In a discussion of the obvious speed-up of the negotiations, it was said that it was not surprising that excitement was in the air, but "in Britain there is clearly a tendency to over-excitement, which can be traced without doubt to electoral origins." ("Diplomacy on the Escalator," *The Economist*, April 30, 1955, p. 369.) Less than two weeks before the election the stress on heightened activity in the peace talks was increasingly blatant: "It is as peacemakers without peer that both Tory and Labour leaders present themselves to the electorate. By common consent the vote is to decide not who shall finger the trigger, but who shall thrust and parry with the olive branch. . . . Tory posters demand votes for 'the peace of Eden'; Tory canvassers recall Geneva. Mr. Bevan . . . has accused both the Government and, by implication, the Opposition, of 'playing' with the hydrogen bomb, in words so exactly similar to Marshal Zhukov's that he was lucky to escape the charge of plagiarism by a few hours." "Electing Peacemakers," *The Economist* (May 14, 1955), pp. 543-45.

as other issues between East and West. The threat to make Germany a cemetery was little different from threats and warnings directed at the same time at Norway, Denmark, Greece, and Iceland over the consequences of harboring Western troops and bases.[7]

Violent pronouncements during this period were not confined exclusively to the Soviet side. For example, on June 12, during one of the most crucial periods of the negotiation, the United States chose to make public the testimony of General Lauris Norstad, Supreme Allied Commander in Europe, to the United States Congress that his forces had the absolute power to destroy "anything that is of military significance in the Soviet Union at the present time."[8] Also during this crucial period the United Kingdom exploded its first thermonuclear device.

The Denigration of Stassen

Another factor leading to the breakup of the subcommittee negotiations was unquestionably the decline in prestige and authority of the United States negotiator, Harold Stassen. Stassen's personal prestige, both at the White House and at the State Department, because of the skill with which he conducted the London negotiations, apparently reached its peak during his consultations in Washington in the middle of May. During his stay in Washington, a high level conference took place at the White House that lasted approximately two hours and twenty minutes. In addition to Stassen, the participants were the President; Secretary Dulles; Admiral Strauss, chairman of the Atomic Energy Commission; Admiral Radford; Assistant Secretary of Defense Quarles; and Allen Dulles of the Central Intelligence Agency.[9] Stassen flew back to London on May 26 to resume the negotiations.

The substantive decisions that had been reached in Washington did not immediately become apparent. The Secretary of State, however, said, "that the new instructions for Mr. Stassen would be dis-

[7] Maxwell D. Taylor, *The Uncertain Trumpet* (1960), p. 48.
[8] *New York Times*, June 13, 1957, p. 23.
[9] *Ibid.*, May 18, 1957.

cussed with our allies insofar as they are involved." The new position, he added, is "flexible," and Stassen "has been given some limited authority for maneuver when he returns to the bargaining table."[10]

On June 7, Stassen flew back to the United States ostensibly to attend his son's graduation at the University of Virginia. However, he also consulted with officials in Washington concerning the negotiations. On June 12 the *New York Times* had the headline, "Dulles Concedes Rift With Allies on Disarmament." Dulles' press conference of June 11 mentioned a "procedural complication" which had caused some difficulty with the British and French. Dulles stated that he wanted it "perfectly clear" that "this is not a bi-lateral negotiation." To quote the *New York Times* on this interview, "Mr. Dulles did not confirm that Mr. Stassen was the 'procedural complication' that had caused friction among the Atlantic partners, but neither did his news conference dispel the reports."[11]

Two days later, the *New York Times* reported: "The U.S. is sending Dr. Konrad Adenauer a message indicating that Mr. Stassen exceeded his instructions in talking over certain disarmament issues with Valerian A. Zorin before the issues had been worked out among the Western Allies."[12]

At this point, a veteran career diplomat, Hon. Julius C. Holmes, was sent by the State Department to London to act as Stassen's deputy, and at the official level several additions were made to Stassen's staff of individuals who had experience in the field of disarmament but had not previously worked with Stassen. While Stassen remained optimistic and denied that he had been "reprimanded,"[13] the press reported that some high officials said privately this probably would be Stassen's last mission for President Eisenhower—a prediction that turned out to be true.

At his June 11 press conference Dulles was asked: "Is it correct . . . that the United States will be unable to propose any European zone or any proposal affecting troops, cutting troops or armaments in Europe

[10] *Ibid.*, May 26, 1957, p. 1.
[11] *Ibid.*, June 12, 1957.
[12] *Ibid.*, June 14, 1957, pp. 1 and 3.
[13] *Ibid.*

unless there is a unanimous agreement of all the NATO countries whose territory would be involved?" Dulles' answer was: "I don't know whether the word 'unable' is the correct word. Certainly we would not be disposed to present as an American program a program which involved Continental Europe and dealt with either inspection there or the positioning of forces there unless that was concurred in by all of the countries that were involved."[14]

It thus became apparent that Stassen would have to clear at least a portion of his positions far beyond the confines of the members of the subcommittee. This tied in directly with the conversations between the President and Chancellor Adenauer. It could be assumed that as a minimum, NATO clearance would be required of any aerial or ground inspection and of any reductions in conventional armaments.

At the same moment that Stassen's "free-wheeling" came under fire of criticism, Senator Knowland back home in Congress was guilty of similar behavior. He proposed to Dulles that Norway be withdrawn from the Atlantic Alliance in return for free elections in Hungary; the *raison d'être* of the offer was to test Soviet sincerity to negotiate a relaxation of tension in Europe. However, Norway was not consulted prior to the proposal. Senator Knowland simply suggested that Norway's consent would, "of course," be required, and later he insisted that he had proposed such an agreement with the Soviet Union only if Norway consented, but the damage had been done and the Norwegians were indignant.[15]

A recent biographer of Dulles explains these events as follows:

Contemporary accounts hinted that he [Stassen] had made a serious blunder, but its precise nature was never revealed.

What Stassen had done was to make the tactical mistake on June 11 of giving Zorin an informal preview, on paper, of the Western plan before it had been cleared by the Allies. Insiders to the negotiations say Stassen did not deviate more than a hair's breadth, if at all, from U.S. Government-confirmed policy. But his

[14] "Secretary Dulles' News Conference," June 11, 1957, Department of State *Bulletin*, Vol. 37 (July 1, 1957), p. 9.
[15] *New York Times*, June 12, 1957, p. 12.

act had two effects: it aroused the resentment of the Allies, who are always fearful of anything that smacks of an American attempt to negotiate over their heads with the Russians; and because of Stassen's known political ambitions, it aroused the suspicion of Government officials at home that in his eagerness to create a reputation as "the man who negotiated peace" he would commit the U.S. to some unsound position just for the sake of achieving an agreement with the Russians. . . . Stassen was called back to Washington and reprimanded.[16]

This episode profoundly affected the negotiations. We have seen that prior to Stassen, the United States representatives in the disarmament negotiations had lacked the prestige in the government and the easy access to the White House or even to the Secretary of State that was essential to a meaningful negotiation in this field. The Soviet leaders had accordingly reached the conclusion that the United States attached little importance to the subject of disarmament. The appointment of Stassen with Cabinet rank had at first appeared to remedy this situation, and to create the impression that he would be able to speak with authority for the United States. Now even Stassen could not negotiate with any assurance that his decisions would receive a government blessing. This inevitably led to Soviet disillusion with both the subcommittee and the Disarmament Commission as a forum of negotiation.

Since Khrushchev had reached a position of power, the desire of the Soviet Union to remove all East-West negotiations to the summit had never been far from the surface. While Stassen was consulting in Washington, Khrushchev, in an interview with the managing editor of the *New York Times*, had advocated settlement of East-West issues in a meeting of the heads of government. He even discarded the idea of a meeting of Foreign Ministers with the remark: "if it were a meeting between Gromyko and Dulles it might take a hundred years."[17] It was only a short step from this viewpoint to abandonment of the entire

[16] John Robinson Beal, *John Foster Dulles* (1959), p. 324.
[17] *New York Times*, May 11, 1957, pp. 1, 3. Khrushchev's interview with Turner Catledge in Moscow, on May 10, 1957.

structure of the Disarmament Commission and its subcommittee. Thus, the weaker Stassen's position became, the greater was the likelihood of the Soviet Union's discarding the subcommittee and the Disarmament Commission and insisting on a radically different approach.

A further consequence of the Washington consultations was the slowing down of the tempo of the negotiations. In June and July the subcommittee meetings were shorter and took place at less frequent intervals than in April and May. As stated in previous chapters, the Western positions on reductions in armed forces and conventional armaments were submitted to the subcommittee toward the end of June. Not until July 2 did the Western four officially acknowledge the Soviet concession of agreeing to inspection in connection with the suspension of nuclear testing.[18] New Western proposals in response to this Soviet concession were not forthcoming until August 21.[19] The Western response to the Soviet proposals on aerial and ground inspection zones took place on August 2, when Secretary of State Dulles joined the subcommittee and presented a working paper on behalf of the Western four.[20]

The appearance of Dulles in London to present the Western position in place of Stassen further emphasized Stassen's denigration. The London *Economist,* on August 3, at the conclusion of Dulles's visit, sounded the warning, "Enough damage has already been done by the backing and filling that has marred the record of these summary talks. Only the Russians who seem to be thoroughly enjoying the situation will benefit and not only in terms of propaganda, if this week of apparent drama is not followed by an early, if modest, denouement."[21]

Another factor that may have influenced Soviet attitudes was the situation within the Kremlin. In the first week of July, Khrushchev emerged the victor in a political clash, when the majority of the Presidium had originally opposed his positions. The majority of the Central Committee of the Communist party overruled the Presidium with the resultant disappearance from Soviet political life of Malenkov, Molotov,

[18] U.N. Doc. DC/SC.1/PV.128 (July 2, 1957), pp. 9, 11 and 29.
[19] U.N. Doc. DC/SC.1/PV.149 (Aug. 21, 1957), pp. 11-27.
[20] U.N. Doc. DC/SC.1/PV.143 (Aug. 2, 1957), pp. 2-10.
[21] "Drama Without Denouement," *The Economist* (Aug. 3, 1957).

Kaganovitch, and ultimately, Bulganin. Khrushchev had the full support of the Soviet military establishment in this contest. It is entirely possible that in order to achieve his victory, Khrushchev made some concessions in the field of disarmament to the more rigid views of the opposition. In any event, in the Soviet Union it has been common practice for the victors in an internecine struggle to adopt without attribution some of the policies of the defeated faction. In this instance, the defeated faction was known to be far less favorable to East-West negotiations than was Khrushchev.

An Inseparable Package

Despite all these storm warnings, the demeanor of the Soviet representative, Zorin, remained serene during most of August. While Zorin frequently protested the delays, his denunciation of the negotiations waited until August 27 after the West had presented all its positions informally and only two days before the August 29 written Western proposals, the contents of which had already been communicated to Zorin.

The final and only novel portion of the Western working paper of August 29 reads in part as follows:

"This working paper is offered for negotiation on the understanding that its provisions are inseparable."[22] Until the appearance of this provision, some hope had remained that the Soviet Union and the West might reach an agreement on the one subject of suspension of tests or even on the two subjects of suspension of tests and reductions in armed forces and conventional armaments.

The Soviet Union had moved in the direction of a limited agreement through conceding in its April 30 proposals that action on reduction of bases and on removal of troops from Germany need not be a part of the initial agreement for partial disarmament. The West was still insisting that the suspension of tests be linked with some progress

[22] U.N. Disarmament Commission, Subcommittee of the Disarmament Commission, *Fifth Report*, Annex 5, U.N. Doc. DC/SC.1/66 (Aug. 29, 1957), p. 10. Cited hereafter by annex and document numbers.

toward the broader objective of nuclear disarmament—the cutoff—but had not definitely linked test suspension to the remainder of its program. The importance of such a link was emphasized in Selwyn Lloyd's report to the House of Commons on July 23, 1957: "It is the linking of the suspension of tests with the cut-off in the manufacture of fissionable material for warlike purposes which is the great prize to be attained."[23] The link between test suspension and other disarmament measures was far less important:

> The reason why we say that the suspension of tests should also be linked with measures for a partial agreement about conventional disarmament is partly because we think that conventional and nuclear disarmament should go ahead *pari passu*, but also because we believe that we are within sight of agreement on a certain number of matters, and if there is a real urge to get agreement on suspension of tests, that should carry us through to agreement on these other matters to which I have already referred.[24]

The day before Lloyd's statement to Parliament, Secretary Dulles gave a major address in which he unequivocally came forth with the same idea.[25] The final paragraph made the suspension of nuclear testing conditional not only on an agreement for the cutoff but on the entire package of measures included in the August 29 proposals—reductions in armed forces and conventional armaments, control of objects entering outer space, safeguards against surprise attack, and many other provisions. This in the main may have reflected primarily the unwillingness of the French to give up their opportunity to become the fourth nuclear power unless it appeared that a fairly drastic disarmament agreement could be reached that would reduce the privileged military postures of the three existing nuclear powers.

On August 29, Zorin commented on this: "In other words, nothing in the document can be taken out; all these provisions are interlinked

---

[23] Great Britain, *Parliamentary Debates,* Commons, Vol. 574, Col. 266.
[24] *Ibid.,* Col. 267.
[25] "Disarmament and Peace" State Department *Bulletin,* Vol. 37 (Aug. 12, 1957), pp. 267-72.

and the rejection of any one of them would mean the shipwreck of the whole agreement."[26] Zorin immediately went on to note that the August 29 proposals contained no provisions concerning military bases in foreign territories and the reduction in the armed forces of the four powers stationed in Germany and in the NATO and Warsaw Treaty countries, thus emphasizing that the Soviet Union had made the concession of eliminating these items from its package of partial measures and obviously expected some concession in return. Instead, the August 29 proposals had increased rather than diminished the number of items the Western powers deemed essential to the package of partial disarmament measures.

Estimate

The complete impasse which had thus arisen within the negotiations would in itself have been sufficient to account for their termination. Nevertheless, it is probable that the prime causes of the Soviet change in attitude arose from events outside the negotiations rather than from the developments within them. One strong evidence of this is that when Zorin on August 27[27] and again in his final statement on September 4[28] violently denounced the West, using a propaganda approach heretofore absent from the subcommittee discussions, he was speaking from a previously prepared text. This differed from his usual custom of ad-libbing merely from notes. On the other hand, his statement of August 29 made without a previously prepared text was moderate and mild and fully in keeping with the atmosphere of reasonableness that had prevailed prior to August 27.

The Soviet propaganda blasts of August 27 and September 4 brought into the open all of the grievances that had accumulated during the months of negotiations. There were the delays in the negotiations:

[26] Annex 10, U.N. Doc. DC/SC.1/71 (Sept. 4, 1957), p. 10.
[27] U.N. Doc. DC/SC.1/PV.151 (Aug. 27, 1957), pp. 2-32. Zorin's specific remark: "That is the statement *I have been instructed by the Soviet Government* to make at today's meeting of the Subcommittee." Italics added.
[28] U.N. Doc. DC/SC.1/PV.155 (Sept. 4, 1957), pp. 2-8, 20.

While the Disarmament Subcommittee marks time the armaments race continues. . . . Despite energetic protests by the peoples of many lands, the United States Government has stationed its special atomic units in the territories of Western European states, members of NATO. All this has been taking place under cover of fruitless disarmament talks.[29]

Zorin paid his cynical respects to some of the Western leaders for their conduct during the negotiations.

In this connection, reference could be made to numerous statements made by General Norstad of the United States Army, the present Commander-in-Chief of the NATO forces, by Mr. Strauss, the Minister of Defense of Western Germany, and by other military chiefs of NATO who made no effort to conceal their plans of attack on the Soviet Union.[30]

The German political situation received great attention.

. . . But their action in establishing more and more military bases, in speeding up the remilitarization of Western Germany, and in the stationing of atomic units and nuclear weapons in the territory of Western Germany and other Western European Countries, speak very loudly. These actions provide irrefutable proof that the United States of America and the other Western Powers which have pledged their support to Adenauer do not desire a relaxation of tension in Europe. They need tension in order to preserve the division of Germany and inflame the mood of the revanchist elements, to which they look for help in reviving German militarism.[31]

Concerning the impaired role of the subcommittee,

Thus the Western powers have to all intents and purposes handed

[29] U.N. Doc. DC/SC.1/PV.151 (Aug. 27, 1957), p. 3.
[30] *Ibid.,* p. 19.
[31] Annex 12, U.N. Doc. DC/SC.1/73 (Sept. 5, 1957), p. 20.

disarmament over to NATO, their military organization. This fact causes particular alarm for the future of the disarmament talks. It is well known that the NATO leaders base all their calculations on the use of atomic weapons, the continuation of the armaments race, and preparations for a new war; and the transfer of the disarmament question to these people reflects the desire of ruling circles in the countries participating in the North Atlantic military alliance to doom the disarmament talks to failure.[32]

On this point, Zorin was not far from the mark if the recent biographer of Dulles is correct in his statement that "Before the proposal [of August 29] was formally submitted at London, Stassen was superseded in fact though not in name as head of the American delegation."[33] After all, it was Stassen who continued to deal with the Russians.

In summary, the chief elements contributing to the apparent Soviet change of positions and attitudes appeared to be the following:

1. As a result of the necessity of securing NATO clearance before the West could submit proposals to the subcommittee, the subcommitte had lost its usefulness. The objective of the subcommittee was to create a forum for speedy and informal consultation and negotiation. Its composition with four of the five members from the West reflected the fact that the Soviet Union was in a position to speak for the entire Soviet bloc while it took presumably four states to speak for the West. When it became apparent that the four could no longer speak for the West and that NATO clearance was required, the subcommittee had lost its usefulness.

2. The denigration of Stassen further emphasized that the subcommittee was no longer a forum where effective negotiations could take place. To the Soviet Union, the only useful forum for negotiations became the summit.

3. The August 29 proposals of the West, with the last paragraph requiring acceptance of the entire package of measures, eliminated the

---

[32] Annex 6, U.N. Doc. DC/SC.1/65/Rev. 1 (Aug. 27, 1957), p. 26.
[33] John Robinson Beal, *John Foster Dulles* (1957), p. 324.

last chance of early agreement and emphasized that the negotiations had reached a complete impasse.

4. This impasse conveniently coincided with the approach of the German election. Apparently, the Soviet leaders believed that this was the time for threats and violence rather than conciliation. The breakup of the disarmament negotiations was to the world the outstanding example of worsening of East-West relations.

5. Fortunately, a fifth and much more ominous element seemed to play no major role in the breakup of the negotiations. The simple and most usual explanation of the Soviet change given at the time was that with its scientific triumph in the development of outer space missiles— the ICBM on August 26 and the first satellite on October 2, 1957— the Soviet Union had no further interest in disarmament, and was reverting to its previous policy of utilizing the disarmament negotiations solely as a means of weakening the West. The developments after 1957 seem clearly to rule this out as the primary motive of Soviet policy. Otherwise the technical discussions commencing in 1958 and still continuing might not have been undertaken.

It therefore seems probable that the revived Soviet intransigence arose not from a change in substantive position but from its belief that the procedures and methods followed from 1952 to 1957 were no longer useful.

THE DISARMAMENT GENERAL

ASSEMBLY

The Disarmament Commission met on September 30, 1957, and almost without discussion voted to transmit the reports of its subcommittee to the General Assembly and the Security Council for their consideration.[34]

The Assembly had already convened two weeks earlier and quickly became known as the "Disarmament General Assembly." "At no time

[34] U.N. Disarmament Commission, *Official Records*, 64th Meeting (Sept. 30, 1957), pp. 1-17.

in recent years had Foreign Ministers and other heads of delegations given such prominence to disarmament in their opening remarks during the general debate."[35] Nor had the substance of the respective proposals received such a world-wide review.

This world-wide concern reflected the startling developments of the fortnight preceding the General Assembly. The sudden collapse of the subcommittee negotiations after the high hopes for a successful outcome stunned world opinion. This coincided with the Soviet announcement of the successful testing of an intercontinental ballistic missile and the successful launching of the first Sputnik on the eve of the General Assembly. The ominous shadow of these events resulted in a multitude of statements, informal proposals, and resolutions to solve the impasse.

The disarmament discussions in the Political Committee lasted almost a month, from October 11 to November 8, and the discussions continued in the plenary sessions of the Assembly from November 14 until November 18.

Three developments dominated the sessions and are the key to the numerous and confusing tactical steps and decisions.

1. The decision of the Western powers to seek a General Assembly endorsement of the August 29 proposals in the subcommittee.

2. The Soviet decision to refuse to participate in further negotiations in the Disarmament Commission or its subcommittee.

3. The diligent and sometimes frantic efforts of states other than the great powers to find a middle ground between the Soviet Union and the West which as a minimum would permit the continuance of negotiations.

Endorsement of the Western Proposals

Immediately following the opening of the disarmament discussions in the Political Committee, twenty-four states sponsored a resolution[36]

[35] U.S. Participation in the U.N., Report by the President to the Congress for the Year 1957, Department of State Publication 6654 (June 1958), p. 23.
[36] U.N. General Assembly, Twelfth Session, Official Records (Sept. 17-Dec. 14, 1957), Annexes, p. 12.

that in effect endorsed the Western proposals of August 29 in the sub-committee. The twenty-four sponsoring states included seven members of NATO, twelve Latin American countries, Australia, Laos, Liberia, the Philippines, and Tunisia. The resolution proposed that the subcommittee of the Disarmament Commission give priority to reaching a disarmament agreement which on its entry into force would provide for the following: (1) the immediate suspension of testing of nuclear weapons with prompt installation of effective international control including inspection posts equipped with appropriate scientific instruments; (2) the cessation of production of fissionable materials for weapons purposes and the complete devotion of future production of fissionable materials to nonweapons purposes under effective international control; (3) the reduction of stocks of nuclear weapons through a program of transfer on an equitable and reciprocal basis and under international supervision of stocks of fissionable materials from weapons uses to nonweapons uses; (4) the reduction of armed forces and armaments through adequate safe-guarded arrangements; (5) the progressive establishment of open inspection with ground and aerial components to guard against the possibility of surprise attack; (6) the joint study of an inspection system designed to ensure that the sending of objects through outer space would be exclusively for peaceful and scientific purposes.

It is true that the resolution merely indicated the fields for disarmament agreements rather than specifying the solutions for each field. For example, the resolution refers merely to "the progressive establishment of open inspection with ground and air components to guard against the possibility of surprise attack."[37] It did not, like the August 29 proposals, specify the inspection zones.

There were also two minor variations from the pattern of August 29. The General Assembly resolution did not refer to reduction in military expenditures and omitted the famous double negative provision of the August 29 proposals "not to use nuclear weapons if an armed attack has not placed the party in a situation of individual or collective self-defence."[38] However, the resolution made it clear that the first-step disarmament agreement must cover all six areas specified in the resolu-

[37] Ibid.
[38] Annex 5, U.N. Doc. DC/SC.1/66 (Aug. 29, 1957), p. 3.

tion. Like the August 29 proposal, it was a package proposal and had to be accepted in its entirety.

The unique feature of this resolution was not that it was offered but that the Western powers in spite of the violent opposition of the Soviet Union insisted that it be brought to a vote. In 1948, the Western powers with the support of the overwhelming majority in the General Assembly had secured a resolution approving the third report of the United Nations Atomic Energy Commission. The plan for control of atomic energy contained in this report, which was in its essentials the Baruch Plan, thereupon became the United Nations Plan.[39] Despite the unanimous approval of this resolution, excepting alone the Soviet Union and its satellites, the endorsement was a futile act because no disarmament resolution can be effective unless it receives the support of both the Western powers and the Soviet Union. After 1948 and until this twelfth General Assembly, with one exception so minor as to be negligible,[40] the Western powers never sought a United Nations endorsement of their substantive proposals against Soviet opposition. In each General Assembly when it appeared that the Soviet Union would oppose the Western proposals, the Western powers contented themselves with a resolution referring their proposals and also any proposals the Soviet Union might have made to the Disarmament Commission or its subcommittee or whatever other United Nations body was dealing with the problem.

The endorsement of the twenty-four power proposals was not the unanimous and enthusiastic acclaim that had greeted the Baruch proposals ten years earlier. Despite the strong and united support of all of the Western powers, the resolution endorsing this proposal was adopted by a vote of 56 to 9 with 15 abstentions. The opposing nine, of course, were the Soviet Union and its satellites. The 15 abstaining states included Nepal, Saudi Arabia, Sudan, Syria, Yemen, Yugoslavia, Afghanistan, Burma, Ceylon, Egypt, Finland, Ghana, India, Indonesia, and Japan. Thus practically all of the Asian and African states refused to support the resolution.[41]

[39] See Chap. 4.
[40] See Chap. 7.
[41] U.N. General Assembly, Twelfth Session, Plenary, *Official Records*, 716th Meeting (Nov. 14, 1957), p. 461.

Ambassador Lall of India explained his abstaining vote as follows:

I should like to say straight away that the delegation of India does not in any way impugn the motives or the sincerity of those delegations which sponsored this draft resolution. My delegation feels that there are certain aspects in the approach of these very delegations which would be more conducive to the progress of Disarmament discussions and to substantive achievements in this field than the pressing of this draft resolution to a vote.[42]

Ambassador de la Colina of Mexico who voted in favor of the resolution expressed the same fears:

My delegation will vote in favour on the clear understanding that as stated by a number of its sponsors, it is to be regarded not as an inflexible and rigid formula but merely as a step along the path of negotiation which will lead to disarmament. It seems doubtful, however, that this new parliamentary victory will serve to re-establish a basis on which negotiations can continue—and to negotiate means to compromise between the parties most directly concerned. I refer to the nuclear powers, whose cooperation is absolutely indispensable if the urgent task of disarmament is to be successfully completed.[43]

Ambassador Sandler, the representative of Sweden, likewise expressed doubts concerning the resolution.

It has generally been conceded that the policy of "all or nothing" with respect to disarmament has failed and that agreement on a more or less extensive programme of partial disarmament must be sought. However, there is still a danger that the "all or nothing" policy will be applied even to such partial disarmament measures by making the adoption of any one measure conditional upon acceptance of all the other measures. For its part, Sweden found the

[42] *Ibid.*, pp. 453-54.
[43] *Ibid.*, p. 460.

six points enumerated in the twenty-four-Power draft resolution acceptable, but it questions the necessity or wisdom of applying the "all or nothing" principle to them.[44]

Thus, the states other than the great powers who had made the most constructive contributions in the past toward mediation among the great powers feared the consequences of this action of the General Assembly. In such circumstances, the Assembly endorsement of the Western position was indeed a hollow victory.

Soviet Proposals

The Soviet Union made three main proposals in the General Assembly. The first of these was essentially a restatement of the paper the Soviet Union had introduced on April 30 in the subcommittee, calling for partial first-stage measures. The only new point was Gromyko's suggestion that "in view of the fact that the Western Powers are at present unwilling to agree to renouncing completely the use of atomic and hydrogen weapons, the Soviet Government proposes that the Powers possessing such weapons should assume a solemn undertaking not to use these weapons, say, for a period of five years."[45]

If in this General Assembly the Western powers had followed the precedents of previous years, this proposal would have been referred to the Disarmament Commission or its subcommittee for further consideration, thereby doing away with the necessity of a vote on the merits. Instead, the resolution was defeated by a vote of 45 to 11 with 25 abstentions. The number of abstentions made this also a hollow victory.[46]

The second Soviet proposal called for the discontinuance of all

[44] U.N. General Assembly, Twelfth Session, Committee One, *Official Records*, 884th Meeting (Oct. 29, 1957), p. 88.
[45] U.N. General Assembly, Twelfth Session, Plenary, *Official Records*, 681st Meeting (Sept. 20, 1957), p. 33.
[46] U.N. General Assembly, Twelfth Session, Committee One, *Official Records*, 893rd Meeting (Nov. 6, 1957), p. 140.

nuclear tests as of January 1, 1958, for a period of two or three years under the supervision of an international control commission. This proposal never came to a vote as the Soviet Union withdrew the resolution in favor of a resolution on the same subject submitted by India.[47]

The third Soviet proposal dealt with the procedural problem of enlarging the Disarmament Commission.[48]

Mediation

The factor that differentiated this discussion on disarmament from all previous discussions was the increased effort of states other than the great powers to mediate between East and West and to revive the negotiations among the great powers. A vast number of amendments were suggested for the twenty-four power resolution. Only three were accepted by the sponsors. One amendment by four Latin American countries, later co-sponsored by a fifth, recommended a study of the possibility of devoting additional resources made available as a result of disarmament to the improvement of living conditions in less developed countries.[49] A second, suggested by India, added a paragraph in the preamble recalling the General Assembly's 1954 resolution calling for efforts toward the eventual prohibition and destruction of all nuclear weapons. A third, proposed by Norway and Pakistan, suggested the establishment of groups of technical experts to study inspection systems for disarmament measures.[50]

Obviously none of these amendments affected the substance of the twenty-four power resolution. There were, however, three substantive proposals of great importance that sought to strike a midway position between the Soviet Union and the West. India and Japan submitted

[47] U.N. General Assembly, Twelfth Session, Plenary, *Official Records*, 681st Meeting (Sept. 20, 1957), p. 33, and 716th Plenary Meeting (Nov. 14, 1957), p. 453.
[48] *Ibid.*, 881st Plenary Meeting (Sept. 20, 1957), p. 34. Further discussion of this proposal on pp. 38-40.
[49] *Ibid.*, Annexes, Agenda Item 24 (Nov. 11, 1957), p. 15. Submitted by Bolivia, Costa Rica, El Salvador, and Uruguay; later co-sponsored by Mexico.
[50] *Ibid.*, p. 15.

their respective proposals in the form of resolutions.[51] The third proposal, a statement by the Polish delegate, was never turned into a resolution.[52]

The Indian resolution attempted to secure the immediate suspension of nuclear tests, prior to any agreement on the control machinery to ensure observance of the agreement. After describing the dangerous potentialities of further nuclear and thermonuclear explosions, under this resolution the General Assembly:

1. Requests the States concerned in view of the doubts expressed about the detectability of explosions and the need to dispel these doubts and also to provide against possible evasions, to agree forthwith to the nomination of a scientific technical Commission consisting of scientific technical experts representing the differing views together with eminent scientific technical participation to be agreed upon by the before mentioned representatives; 2. Requests the aforementioned commission to recommend to the Disarmament Commission an adequate system of inspection arrangements in all the territories of the world in which it might be necessary in order to supervise and render suspension of tests effective and to maintain the controls which will inspire the necessary confidence; 3. Appeals to the States concerned to agree without delay and to suspend tests of nuclear and thermonuclear weapons and to inform the Secretary-General of their willingness to do so.[53]

The resolution went on to call on all United Nations Member states to report any evidence they might detect of nuclear and thermonuclear explosions in any part of the world on land, air, or sea.

As previously noted, the Soviet Union withdrew its own resolution

[51] Ibid., pp. 10-11.
[52] U.N. General Assembly, Twelfth Session, Committee One, Official Records, 875th Meeting (Oct. 18, 1957), pp. 45-46. See also statement by Winiewicz of Poland in U.N. General Assembly, Twelfth Session, Plenary, Official Records, 716th Meeting (Nov. 14, 1957), pp. 454-55.
[53] U.N. General Assembly, Twelfth Session, Official Records, Annexes, Agenda Item 24 (Nov. 1, 1957), p. 11.

on test suspension to support the Indian resolution. The Indian resolution was rejected, receiving 22 affirmative votes as against 38 negative votes with 20 abstentions. The supporting votes included the Soviet Union and its satellites, the majority of the Asian and African countries and, in addition, Mexico. The abstentions included Sweden, Austria, Bolivia, Guatemala, Haiti, Iceland, Japan, and practically all of the Asian and African countries that had not voted in favor of the resolution. The opponents of the resolution consisted almost entirely of the NATO countries, a sprinkling of Latin American countries and some British Dominions. The only Asian and African countries to join the opposition were Pakistan and Tunisia.[54] Thus the Western powers achieved still another hollow victory.

The course of action proposed by the Indian resolution was in fact followed within less than three months after the adjournment of the Assembly, the sole important difference being in the constitution of the negotiating group.

The Japanese effort to bridge the gap between the East and West was considerably more ambitious. The Japanese resolution requested the Disarmament Commission:

(a) To re-convene its Subcommittee at an early date no later than January 1, 1958; (b) To recommend that the States members of the Subcommittee continue their endeavour to reach an agreement without delay on the unsettled points of the disarmament problem particularly on the initial measures of disarmament including the inspection system intended to ensure the prohibition of the manufacture of nuclear weapons and the devotion of fissionable materials only to peaceful purposes and to prevent surprise attack.

The resolution then called on the Member states concerned:

(a) To suspend all nuclear test explosions from the time an agreement is reached in principle on a supervision and inspection sys-

[54] *Ibid.* (Nov. 6, 1957), p. 139.

tem necessary to verify the suspension of tests until the discussion of the report of the Disarmament Commission at the next regular session of the General Assembly has been concluded; (b) To enter into negotiations immediately after the commencement of the suspension of tests in order to reach an agreement on the prompt installation of a supervision and inspection system necessary to verify the suspension of tests.[55]

Obviously the Japanese resolution went a long distance toward meeting the position the Western powers had supported in the disarmament discussions in June and July. It linked closely the provisions for suspension of tests with some progress in the direction of solving the larger problem of reducing and ultimately eliminating nuclear weapons from the arsenals of the great powers. This was in conformity with the West's position during most of the 1957 subcommittee negotiating actions. It had not been until August 29 that the Western powers proclaimed their entire proposal as an inseparable package. In short, the Japanese resolution, except for minor technical differences, apparently accepted the Western position as it stood at the end of July.

The Soviet Union was bound to oppose the Japanese draft resolution for the reason that it largely supported the approach of the Western powers. The intensity of the Soviet opposition was revealed in a note from the Soviet Union to the Japanese Foreign Ministry, subsequent to the General Assembly, containing the following indictment of the feature of the Japanese position emphasizing the close connection between the cessation of nuclear weapons tests and the cessation of the production of fissionable materials for military purposes:

. . . Such an attitude of Japan coincides with the attitude of the Western powers—the United States, Britain, and France, who resolutely oppose a cessation of atom and hydrogen weapon tests. . . .

The Japanese Government should know that the question of cessation of production of fissionable materials for military pur-

[55] *Ibid.* (Sept. 23, 1957), p. 10.

poses is an integral part of the question of the complete banning of atomic and hydrogen weapons, which includes first of all the banning of the use of atomic and hydrogen weapons as well as the cessation of the production of these types of weapons, their removal from the armaments of state, and the destruction of existing supplies of these weapons. . . .

The main object of putting forward such a proposal by the Western powers is the endeavor of the United States, Britain, and France not to allow agreement to be reached on the question of cessation of atomic and hydrogen weapon tests.[56] . . .

When the resolution was brought to a vote, the world witnessed the remarkable spectacle of its defeat through the *combined* opposition of the Western powers and the Soviet bloc. The thirty-two opposing votes —less than half of the membership of the United Nations—included the nine members of the Soviet bloc. It also included nine members of NATO, Canada, Australia, New Zealand, China, Spain, and nine Latin American countries. Practically all of the Asian and African countries and over half of the Latin American countries either supported the resolution or abstained. This was a far cry from the almost unanimous world opinion that had supported the Western positions against Soviet intransigence in earlier years.

The third attempt to find a midway position between the Soviet Union and the West was contained in a speech of the Polish Foreign Minister, Rapacki, in the general debate in which he proposed an atom-free zone in Central Europe.[57] The Polish Foreign Minister had made this proposal two years earlier, but it had never been integrated into the Soviet position. Perhaps the reason for this was that Anthony Eden's proposals at the summit in 1955 for a de-militarized zone in Central Europe were far more drastic and would probably have been far more welcome to the Soviet Union. At this time, Czechoslovakia as

[56] The President's Special Committee on Disarmament Problems, "USSR Note to Japanese Government," Dec. 5, 1957.
[57] U.N. General Assembly, Twelfth Session, Plenary, *Official Records,* 697th Meeting (Oct. 2, 1957), pp. 236-37.

well as Poland announced its willingness to agree to an atom-free zone in Central Europe, and both the Czechs and the Poles reported that the East Germans were also desirous of such an agreement. This proposal by the Polish Foreign Minister may properly be deemed as the Soviet reply to the proposals for zones made by Dulles when he appeared before the subcommittee during the last week of July and first week of August. The proposal was never introduced in the form of a draft resolution. However, since Rapacki's speech, it has become a part of the Soviet position presented in all subsequent sessions of the General Assembly.

Enlarging the Disarmament Commission

In his speech on September 20 at the opening of the General Assembly, the Soviet Foreign Minister, Andrei Gromyko, had expressed discontent with the "narrow and unrepresentative composition" of the disarmament subcommittee. He had asked: "How can one expect the Subcommittee to achieve positive results when four of its five members are countries of NATO," and when "whole continents like Asia and Africa are not represented?"[58] The Soviet Union proposed that the membership of the Disarmament Commission be enlarged to include the entire membership of the United Nations.

While the Soviet Union was calling for an enlarged membership of the Disarmament Commission, it did not at this time threaten to boycott future negotiations unless the General Assembly met its wishes. On November 11, after the Western powers had insisted on bringing the twenty-four power resolution to a vote in the Political Committee, and it became apparent that the resolution would also be brought to a vote in the General Assembly, the Soviet Union then announced that it would no longer participate in any negotiations either in the Disarmament Commission or the subcommittee.

A compromise resolution, sponsored by Sweden, India, Japan, Canada, Paraguay, and Yugoslavia, attempted to meet the Soviet com-

[58] *Ibid.*, 681st Meeting (Sept. 20, 1957), p. 34.

plaint that the commission was unrepresentative by raising the membership to twenty-five, including three members of the Soviet bloc.[59] The Soviet Union rejected this compromise but supported an amendment sponsored by Albania that further increased the membership to thirty-two. The Western powers rejected the Albanian amendment on the ground that a commission of thirty-two would be too unwieldly for serious negotiation.[60]

The resolution increasing the membership of the commission to twenty-five was adopted by a vote of sixty to nine (the Soviet bloc), with eleven abstentions.[61] The original Soviet proposal for a commission composed of all members of the General Assembly and the Albanian amendment had practically no support outside the Soviet bloc and were defeated. The Soviet representative thereupon repeated his statement that the Soviet Union would not participate in the future negotiations of the newly organized Disarmament Commission or of any subcommittee created by the commission. Thus, after more than eleven years, the negotiations within the framework of the United Nations to achieve some measure of disarmament had reached an impasse. The next steps took place outside the United Nations with only a tenuous link to the United Nations.

Western Motivation

The Soviet refusal to participate further in the work of the Disarmament Commission was a logical and foreseeable consequence of the Western insistence on securing the United Nations endorsement of their August 29 proposals. As previously suggested, this step was futile since no disarmament plan can possibly be carried out without the agreement and approval of the Soviet Union. Even the propaganda value of the General Assembly endorsement was reduced practically to zero in view of the half-hearted and lukewarm support of the Western

[59] *Ibid.*, 719th Meeting (Nov. 19, 1957), p. 491.
[60] *Ibid.*, p. 490.
[61] *Ibid.*, p. 491.

position by the states other than the great powers who over the years had been most concerned with disarmament problems—for example, Mexico, India, Japan, and Sweden. As a net result, several months later when the Western powers resumed arms control negotiations, they accepted arrangements far less favorable to the West than those that had been provided by the Albanian amendment. Why, then, did the Western powers reverse the practices of years of negotiations to follow a course of action the almost inevitable outcome of which could be foreseen—the disruption of the disarmament negotiations within the United Nations? There are a number of possible answers, or rather considerations, which may have led to this course of action.

In the first place, it became increasingly clear that any agreement that might have been reached between the Soviet Union and the West on the basis of the 1957 subcommittee discussions would have been highly distasteful to both France and West Germany. France on the threshold of achieving a nuclear weapons capability, was unwilling to give up this prospect through agreeing to the cessation of nuclear testing unless the other nuclear powers would at least take steps in the direction of eliminating their preferred status. West Germany strongly opposed any disarmament agreement that might perpetuate the artificial division of Germany or that might impose any restrictions on West German rearmament. Thus it is possible that France and Germany may even have welcomed the termination of negotiations. Yet it is difficult to believe that the French and German attitudes were decisive in influencing the United States and the United Kingdom to contend so strongly for the General Assembly endorsement of the August 29 proposals. Within three months after the termination of the General Assembly, the United States and United Kingdom had consented to renew negotiations outside the United Nations on the two subjects on which the French and Germans respectively were most sensitive—cessation of tests and defense against surprise attack.[62] In these renewed negotiations, the Western powers had expressly accepted the idea that agreements might be reached in either of these fields independent of agreements on other phases of a disarmament program. If the French and German opposition to separate agreements in these

[62] See Chap. 18.

areas had been the main factor in influencing the Western position in the General Assembly, it is hardly likely that a complete reversal of policy could have taken place in such a short period.

Noel-Baker has suggested that the British political situation may have played an important role in the decision to secure the endorsement of the August 29 proposals by the General Assembly. He has pointed out that Selwyn Lloyd placed great stress on the General Assembly endorsement in defending in Parliament the British position.[63] It was entirely logical for Lloyd to emphasize the Assembly endorsement in defending his position. Nevertheless, the full-fledged debate on the government's disarmament policy which took place in the House of Commons on July 23, two months prior to the General Assembly, makes it clear that the chief concern of Her Majesty's loyal opposition was that the channels of negotiation between East and West be maintained.[64]

It would have been far easier for the British government to support its position if the United Nations channels of negotiation had remained open, even though the government had not secured the formal endorsement of its position by the United Nations.

The decisive factor in this Western course of action may have been the attitude of the American Secretary of State, John Foster Dulles.

[63] Conversation with author.

[64] Great Britain, *Parliamentary Debates, op. cit.*, Statement by Mr. Henderson, Col. 273: "The real truth is that, lying behind all the efforts of Governments to reach agreement, is the background of mistrust and suspicion which has bedevilled disarmament negotiations since they were first initiated in 1946. Continued deadlock is no excuse for breaking off negotiations. The five Governments must persist in their task of getting a disarmament agreement." Col. 276: ". . . we believe that it is the first duty of the five Governments sitting at the Disarmament Subcommittee not to allow the present opportunity to pass, but to ensure that the first steps towards the goal of disarmament are now taken." Statement by Mr. Bevan, Col. 337: "It is not true to say that the Western Alliance would be weakened because no one here is arguing for unilateral disarmament. What we are arguing for is that there should be as much disarmament as can be mutually agreed and that that should be pursued even though it may not be accompanied by political settlements." Col. 338: "We in the Labour Party have said in other places that in our opinion there is not the slightest reason why we should not initiate discussions with the Russians about a European security system, and we cannot understand why the various overtures which have been made from the Russian side have not been met on our side. They could be probed. We could find out what Mr. Khrushchev means by some of his utterances. It may be that he means nothing at all except a rhetorical outburst, but let us find out."

On August 6, immediately after Dulles had presented to the Disarmament Commission the Western position in connection with inspection zones, in a news conference remarkable for its frankness and high seriousness, the Secretary made the following statement:

Q. Mr. Secretary, can you tell us something about the status of the disarmament talks in London? Are you optimistic of any possible value of the results?

A. Well, I try not to operate in terms of optimism or pessimism in this field. As I said several times, it is so important to arrive at a positive result that we have to accept that possibility as a working hypothesis and we have to keep working day by day plugging along in the faith, at least, that we will come to a positive result. I believe that the proposals made on behalf of the four Western Powers last week—and when I say the four Western Powers I should bring in that they were also concurred in by all of the NATO powers concerned—that represents perhaps the most significant proposal in terms of peace that I think has been made in recent history, perhaps ever. It embodies, of course, the basic concept of President Eisenhower's open skies proposal made at Geneva two years ago. It develops that by accepting the Bulganin proposal that there should also be ground posts and, indeed, we have come to the conclusion that any effective inspection should have the two components, air inspection and ground posts and either without the other is inadequate. . . .

In that atmosphere it will be possible, indeed inevitable, that we go ahead with reduction of armaments. Without that atmosphere I am dubious as to the possibility of making very much progress because the elements of military strength are so complex, so imponderable, that you cannot equate them in an atmosphere of fear and an atmosphere of danger. That has been proved, I think, particularly by the talks that took place between the allies after the First World War, eight years of discussions that took place at Geneva.[65]

[65] "Secretary Dulles' News Conference of August 6," Department of State *Bulletin*, Vol. 37 (Aug. 26, 1957), p. 346.

On September 10 after the disarmament subcommittee had adjourned, Dulles in commenting on the failure of the negotiations made the following statement:

I think it is an overstatement to say they have failed. If you will compare what was accomplished now as between what you might call the present allies, essentially the members of NATO with the results that attended the League of Nations disarmament talks at Geneva after the First World War, you will see that the achievement now is really quite monumental in comparison with the total inability at that time for the then allies to come to agreement among themselves.[66]

These statements show clearly that Dulles' main concern was to secure agreement among the Western powers. Secondly, his indoctrination into disarmament negotiations in the period between World Wars I and II had created a skepticism toward any constructive accomplishments in disarmament negotiations conducted in an atmosphere of mistrust. Therefore, he sincerely believed that some progress toward political settlement should precede any agreement in the field of disarmament.

Regardless of whether Dulles was justified in this latter belief, this clearly was not the policy the United States had followed ever since President Truman had resolved the issue in 1951 with his decision that political settlements and disarmament negotiations should proceed concurrently, with progress in either area facilitating progress in the other area.[67] Dulles' view was not the policy of President Eisenhower when on April 16, 1953, he stated, "As progress in all these areas [political settlements] strengthens world trust, we could proceed *concurrently* with the next great work—the reduction of the burden of armaments now weighing upon the world."[68] Dulles' view was not the

[66] "Secretary Dulles News Conference of September 10," *ibid.* (Sept. 30, 1957), p. 531.
[67] "A Plan for Reducing Armaments," address by President Truman, Nov. 7, 1951, *ibid.*, Vol. 25 (Nov. 19, 1951), p. 801.
[68] "The Chance for Peace," *ibid.*, Vol. 28 (April 27, 1953), pp. 601-02. Italics added.

policy which President Eisenhower set forth to the United Nations on December 8, 1953, when he said: "The United States, heeding the suggestion of the General Assembly of the United Nations, is instantly prepared to meet privately with such other countries as may be principally involved," to seek " 'an acceptable solution' to the atomic armaments race which overshadows not only the peace, but the very life of the world."[69] Dulles' view was not the policy of President Eisenhower when in his State of the Union message of January 9, 1958, he pointed out:

In the last analysis there is only one solution of the grim problems that lie ahead, the world must stop the present plunge toward more and more destructive weapons of war, and turn the corner that will start our steps firmly on the path toward lasting peace . . . Of all the works of peace, none is more needed now than a real first step toward disarmament.[70]

The most frequent explanation of this apparent policy conflict was in terms of the known differences between Dulles and Stassen, which in turn suggested two schools of thought within the United States government on the subject of negotiating with the Communists.

The first, or "relaxation of tension," policy is one which would recognize the strength of the Soviet Bloc and would do more to encourage the liberating tendencies within the Bloc. It would accept the Soviet [Union] as an equal power and would encourage the gradual evolution of the Soviet system toward freedom. The second, or "increased pressure policy," on the other hand, is one which would emphasize more the weakness of the Soviet Bloc, would look toward pressuring the Soviet leadership into agreements which represent concessions by the Soviets to their own interest, and would look toward striving to pressure the Soviet system into a collapse without a war.[71]

[69] "Atomic Power for Peace," ibid., Vol. 29 (Dec. 21, 1953), p. 849.
[70] Public Papers of the Presidents of the United States, Dwight D. Eisenhower, 1958, pp. 2-15 (Jan. 10, 1958).
[71] "The Disarmament Dilemma," Speech by Robert E. Matteson, Director of the White House Disarmament Staff, at the University of Minnesota Conference on "National Security in the Nuclear Age," (Feb. 18, 1958), p. 8.

The Soviet leaders have consistently associated Dulles with an "increased pressure" policy. Quoting an interview with Khrushchev, James Reston reports: "The impression has grown among the Soviet people that the United States does not want to come to an agreement. Of course, he added, he believes in the sincerity of President Eisenhower and of Harold E. Stassen, disarmament adviser, but he emphasized there were some people, for example Secretary of State Dulles, who did not want an agreement."[72]

This Soviet evaluation is oversimplified to such an extent that it conceals the truth. Dulles' tremendous achievements in welding the Western alliance, and simultaneously preventing the kindling of sparks which might have given rise to an international holocaust, were directed basically to the relaxation of East-West tensions and not to their augmentation. Even in the field of disarmament negotiations where Secretary Dulles was most skeptical, he had to his credit monumental achievements. For example, he had resisted the announced policy of Chancellor Adenauer to oppose any disarmament discussions until the unification of Germany. His personal efforts in securing a unified Western position in the subcommittee were certainly in the direction of relaxation of world tensions even though that position should have been regarded merely as a starting point for negotiations rather than as an inflexible doctrine. Finally, we must not forget that Dulles was the first American leader to realize that the development of thermonuclear weapons had destroyed the basis for the strategic doctrine of massive retaliation, and, far in advance of others, was supporting a change both in our military posture and in our disarmament position to reflect the new realities.

A more probable explanation of the motivations of the Secretary of State emerges from a study of the basic nature of his method of policymaking. In the summer of 1957, apparently there was no broad overall American policy that comprehended within itself both the unity of the West and a negotiable position toward armaments regulation. Rather, the American policy in all areas had emerged as a series of brilliantly conceived tactics to meet specific situations, to extinguish specific bonfires. When the Secretary of State was confronted in the

[72] *New York Times,* Oct. 8, 1957, p. 10.

summer and fall of 1957 with a negotiating situation where further progress in the disarmament negotiations cut across and conflicted with United States policies toward the NATO countries, it was logical, in view of Dulles' skepticism concerning armaments agreement, that the disarmament negotiations would have the lower priority.

This frame of mind was well illustrated in an interview between the Secretary of State and Christopher Siepell of the British Broadcasting Corporation on December 3, 1957. In response to a suggestion by Siepell for "talks with the Russians on some specific and limited issue, for instance, on the supply of arms to the Middle East," Dulles stated:

> Well, I think perhaps I am the world's greatest expert on conferences with the Russians, because, excluding meetings at the United Nations, I have attended myself no less than 12 such conferences beginning in 1945 and up to the last year. Now I am bound to say that very little has come out of these conferences, primarily because the Soviets cannot be relied upon to live up to their promises. And when you can't put faith and trust in a nation's promises, conferences produce very little.[73]

By the summer of 1957, the Secretary of State had reached the situation where as a result of years of brilliantly executed tactical maneuvers to meet specific situations, United States foreign policy had become the sum of the tactics and the Secretary of State was imprisoned by it. With the Secretary of State's skepticism concerning conferences with the Soviet Union, it was inevitable that the threat to the solidarity of the NATO alliance posed by the course of the disarmament negotiations should be resolved through reaffirmation of the solidarity of NATO. The General Assembly endorsement of the NATO position was merely the last step in that reaffirmation.

One result, however, was virtually to destroy years of painstaking efforts within the United Nations and in world public opinion to identify the West as the proponent of the policy of relaxing world tensions. The Western insistence on United Nations endorsement of a scheme that at best could be only one of many equally suitable

[73] Department of State *Bulletin,* Vol. 37 (Dec. 23, 1957), p. 989.

schemes created a shadow over Western sincerity that will take years to dissipate.

Noel-Baker contends, with much reason, that until a serious negotiation is tried, "Mr. Khrushchev can prove us insincere to the two-thirds of humanity who watch the arms race with growing fear and with a growing desperate feeling that there is nothing that they can do."[74]

THREE YEARS OF NEGOTIATION

Three years of intensified negotiations had apparently run the full circle from hopes of agreement to impasse. Yet the appearance of complete futility was misleading. Despite the optimism of the early months of 1955, and in contrast to the complete pessimism of December 1957, the Soviet and Western positions were measurably closer to each other at the end of 1957 than they had been at the beginning of 1955.

The constructive developments of the three years of negotiation could be summarized as follows:

1. By the end of 1957 both the Soviet Union and the West recognized that a nuclear war would devastate both sides.

2. They conceded that it was no longer possible to account for past production of fissionable materials, and therefore no known system of safeguards could give any reasonable assurance that both sides were observing a commitment to eliminate nuclear weapons.

3. This situation stimulated a search for measures that would reduce the threat of large-scale warfare. Both sides apparently recognized that the danger of an all-out nuclear war would be much greater if additional states possessed nuclear weapons. Both sides likewise recognized the necessity of avoiding international incidents or accidents that might set in motion a chain of events leading to a nuclear war.

4. The search for measures that would reduce the danger of a nuclear war inevitably led to a study of the safeguards systems that

[74] New York Times, Jan. 24, 1960. Address by Noel-Baker at the dedication dinner of the American Jewish Committee's Institute of Human Relations, in New York.

would accompany such measures. The most feasible measures would clearly be those that required the least complicated safeguards systems—the systems which could be installed with a minimum breach of the iron curtain. Any safeguards system operating behind the iron curtain as well as in the West would inevitably benefit the West more than it would benefit the Soviet Union. Therefore, the Soviet Union would expect a Western concession in return for its loss of secrecy through Soviet acceptance of international inspection behind the iron curtain. Both sides were proposing measures that might reduce tensions and lessen the chances of a nuclear war, and that at the same time would require relatively simple safeguards systems.

5. This search had singled out three promising fields: the cessation of nuclear testing, where at least large explosions in the atmosphere could readily be detected; defense against surprise attack, where a combination of aerial inspection and ground posts seemed to offer some security; and limitation of armed forces and conventional armaments. The Soviet Union and the West had already reached considerable agreement on first stage measures of conventional disarmament. However, the particular measures were of minor and diminishing importance, and an agreement on these measures without any agreement on nuclear weapons would at this time have been of little significance.

The disruption of the negotiations in August 1957 and the Soviet decision to boycott the Disarmament Commission did not arise because the substantive positions were growing further apart. The détente probably arose largely as a result of international events outside the field of the arms control negotiations. The one event within the negotiations that played a large role in ensuring their failure was the last-minute Western insistence that the entire Western program must be accepted in toto or not at all.

From the substantive standpoint, the most discouraging feature of the negotiations was that, commencing with July 1957 and more particularly during the General Assembly in the late fall of 1957, the West took a number of positions which called into question some of the most fundamental tenets underlying the negotiations.

One example of this was the last-minute Western insistence on the inseparability of its proposals. This position made its first appearance in the subcommittee in the latter part of August 1957, and by January 1958 this was no longer a part of the Western position.

A second Western departure from previous fundamental tenets was the suggestion in the August 29 proposals that the United States and the United Kingdom might be permitted to transfer nuclear weapons to its allies. Until this suggestion, the negotiations apparently had proceeded on the premise that both the Soviet Union and the West were firmly determined to do everything in their power to prevent additional countries from becoming nuclear powers. Such was the basic philosophy of President Eisenhower's atoms for peace program, on which the Soviet Union and the West had already reached some measure of agreement.

During the General Assembly, John Foster Dulles had called into question two fundamental tenets that President Truman had enunciated in 1949 and that thereafter had not been challenged. Dulles cast doubts on the desirability of further arms control negotiations until the international climate had improved. Ever since 1949, the Western position had been that any agreement on arms control in and of itself would improve the international climate, and therefore that arms control negotiations should proceed simultaneously with efforts to solve other outstanding political problems.

Even more important, the West, by insisting on a General Assembly endorsement of their August 29, 1957 proposals, despite Soviet opposition, had brought into question another fundamental tenet of the negotiations. Since 1948, the West had recognized that any measures for arms control would be futile without the approval of both the Soviet Union and the chief Western powers. Therefore, the West had refrained from obtaining United Nations endorsements of their positions. The disastrous consequence of this change of Western position was that from this point on, the Soviet Union declined to discuss disarmament or arms control except in a commission consisting of the entire membership of the General Assembly, which was far too large a group for negotiation, or in a group where representatives of the Soviet bloc equaled in number the representatives of the West.

The appointment of Harold Stassen in 1955 as the presidential aide on disarmament had inspired the highest hopes that at long last an organization would be established within the United States government adequate to deal with arms control problems. Stassen's close relationship with the President, his attendance at Cabinet meetings, and the location of his unit within the Executive Office of the President assured that arms control problems would receive speedy consideration at the top levels of government. For the first time since Baruch, the United States was allotting to arms control activities adequate funds and a sufficient number of skilled personnel. Stassen wisely decided to include on his staff personnel from the State Department, the Atomic Energy Commission, and each of the armed services who would be responsible directly to him, but who at the same time could contribute the skills and viewpoints of their respective agencies and services. Stassen immediately established able task forces to carry out the much needed studies to convert general principles into a technically precise program.

All this was to the good. Unfortunately, the results did not fully measure up to expectations. Stassen wished to start from scratch and therefore largely discarded the governmental organization that had preceded his appointment. This may have had advantages, but it almost certainly led to such ill-advised actions as the United States reservation of all its previous positions in August 1955. As Stassen and his staff gained in experience, the disadvantages of the break with the past largely disappeared. The separation of Stassen and his staff from the governmental agencies responsible for the development of United States policy in this field, created an administrative pattern readily leading to conflict and confusion within the government. Unfortunately, Stassen's personal relationships with the policy-making agencies—the State Department, Defense Department, and Atomic Energy Commission—were never sufficiently close to overcome this administrative handicap.

Moreover, although a number of Stassen's task forces made a considerable contribution to the study of the technical problems entrusted to them, this was not an especially satisfactory method for dealing with the problems. The task forces were *ad hoc* groups that dealt with the specific factual situations presented to them at the time of their appointment. When technological as well as political changes altered their terms of reference, they were no longer available to bring the reports up to date. Therefore, with one exception, the cutoff, the task force reports played little role in the negotiations.

In short, while the United States had moved a long distance in the direction of recognizing the importance of the arms control negotiations and providing a suitable structure, the operation still could not be described as effective and smoothly functioning.

The British and the French had the advantage of continuity of representation during the entire period. Jules Moch continued to represent France and on the most crucial occasions Selwyn Lloyd sat as the British representative. Selwyn Lloyd was ably assisted by a number of deputies whose tenures overlapped sufficiently to ensure their effective participation in the negotiations. These were Anthony Nutting, Commander Noble, and David Ormsby-Gore. Canada likewise had experienced and able representation. Neither the French, nor the British, nor the Canadians materially enlarged their staffs, and thus left to the United States the main duty of developing the technical ramifications of the new positions.

Since all of the negotiations until the General Assembly of 1957, took place in the Subcommittee of Five, the representatives of other states played less of a role in the negotiations than in earlier periods. After the subcommittee negotiations broke down in August 1957, the representatives of a number of states, in particular Mexico, India, Japan, and Yugoslavia, strove valiantly to prevent the complete collapse of arms control discussions.

During this period, the most dismal failures of the West were political. Apparently Stassen in the first year of his tenure had not yet learned the lesson that in any negotiation with the Soviet Union, the West must take a position that is not only sound but is also politically attractive—in other words, is good propaganda. Prior to 1955, over the years the Western powers had slowly and painfully evolved positions that had convinced the entire world that they were pursuing the highway to peace. The Western powers had advocated drastic but balanced limitations of armaments provided that the arms control agreements were accompanied by sufficient safeguards to ensure the observance of commitments.

Soviet intransigence during the last years of Stalin had undoubtedly assisted the West in obtaining overwhelming support for its position. When the Soviet leadership on May 10, 1955, gave its support to positions that ostensibly at least were much more attractive politically, it was essential for the Western leaders to reaffirm their devotion to the long-range objective of drastic limitations of armaments to ensure international peace. Unfortunately, the first important United States response to the more appealing Soviet stance was Stassen's reservation, which in effect was a rescinding of all previous United States positions. The United States thereby detached itself even from Cohen's non-controversial and universally applauded statement of the objectives of arms control. While technological advances in weapons required a reappraisal of United States positions, there was no change in United States objectives, but merely in the means of achieving the objectives. Stassen at no time related his later constructive and useful proposals to the long-range objectives of world peace. At a later date, he constantly stressed that his proposals were intended to lessen tensions immediately, thereby laying a foundation for further and more drastic limitations of armaments. However, he never re-created the image of a relatively disarmed and safe world which might ultimately result from arms control negotiations.

In 1955 and 1956 the Soviet Union followed the Western example of suggesting individual measures of arms control to lessen tensions without relating them to any long-range objectives. However, by 1957 the Soviet Union appreciated the political advantages of relating its position to the ideal of a disarmed world, even though the ideal might be unattainable. Thereafter, the Soviet approach had two prongs. The Soviet Union in the negotiations would initially advocate drastic and comprehensive disarmament. Somewhat later the Soviet leaders would say in effect: "if we cannot attain this drastic and comprehensive disarmament, we are willing to go along with partial confidence-building measures in the direction of the ultimate objective of total disarmament."

The events of the latter part of 1957 sufficiently clouded the world image of Western devotion to a genuine program of disarmament, so that in the General Assembly of 1957, the Western powers had lost the support for its positions of almost half of the Latin American countries and practically all of the Asian, African, and Middle Eastern countries. In the controversial votes in the 1957 General Assembly, most of these countries abstained from voting.

It may be significant that the most unpalatable Western positions —both Stassen's reservation of all previous positions in 1955 and in 1957 the Western combination of its positions into an inseparable package and its insistence on United Nations endorsement of the package —followed closely changes in the leadership of the United States delegation. The United States reservation of all previous positions in 1955 came within a month after the White House decision that Stassen, in addition to his function as Presidential Adviser, should be the negotiator. The 1957 decisions followed closely the denigration of Stassen and the assumption by Dulles of direct responsibility for the details of the negotiations as well as the broad over-all policy. In both instances, new brooms were sweeping clean. Also in both instances, but more particularly after 1957, world opinion forced the restoration of much that had been swept away—*after* substantial Western political losses.

Negotiations
1958-1960

PART SIX

Negotiations
1958-1960

XVII

New Procedures

On November 19, 1957, the General Assembly, over the opposition of the Soviet Union, enlarged the Disarmament Commission from 11 to 25 members.[1] The Soviet representative declared that this plan was unacceptable and that the Soviet Union would not participate in any future negotiations in either the old or the new Disarmament Commission or in the subcommittee of the Disarmament Commission. Thus the United Nations negotiations on arms control had come to a complete halt, accompanied by scathing denunciations of the United States by the Soviet Union. Despite Russian initiative in breaking up the negotiations and despite the doubts expressed during this period by the American Secretary of State concerning the value of arms control negotiations, the fact of no negotiations quickly became uncomfortable to both the Soviet Union and the West.

In less than ten days—on November 28—Foreign Minister Nehru of India, with his finger on the pulse of world opinion, "ventured" to appeal to the great leaders of the United States of America and the Soviet Union.

I do so in all humility but with great earnestness. We in India have grave problems to face, but I am overwhelmed by the thought

[1] Res. 1150 (XII), Nov. 19, 1957.

443

of the crisis in civilization which the world is facing today, the like of which it has not known ever before. . . .

. . . All the peoples of the world have the right to life and progress and fulfillment of their destiny. They have the right to peace and security. They can only preserve these rights now by living peacefully together and by solving their problems by peaceful methods. They differ in their creeds and beliefs and ideologies. They cannot convert each other by force or threats of force, for any such attempt will lead to catastrophe for all. The only way is to exist together peacefully in spite of differences and to give up the policy of hatred and violence.

The moral and the ethical approaches demand this. But even more so, practical commonsense points this way.

I have no doubt that this can be done. I have no doubt that America and Russia have it in their power to put an end to this horror that is enveloping the world and darkening our minds and our future.

. . . I appeal to them to stop all nuclear test explosions and thus to show to the world that they are determined to end this menace and to proceed also to bring about effective disarmament. . . .[2]

Whether influenced by world opinion or by an appraisal of their own self-interest, both the West and the Soviet Union soon started moving away from the positions that had caused the impasse.

MUTUAL CONCESSIONS

On December 15, Eisenhower in reply to Nehru, first paid his respects to the August 29 proposals, which offer "a meaningful opportunity for removing fear and gaining international trust. It is a source of great personal regret to me that these proposals have not so far

[2] "Prime Minister Nehru Statement November 28," Department of State *Bulletin*, Vol. 38 (Jan. 6, 1958), p. 18.

been found acceptable by the Soviet Union even as a basis for negotiations."[3]

He then in effect waved farewell to the proposals.

I know that the subject of testing of nuclear weapons is of understandable concern to many. I have given this matter long and prayerful thought. I am convinced that the cessation of nuclear weapons tests, if it is to alleviate rather than merely to conceal the threat of nuclear war, should be undertaken as a part of a meaningful program to reduce that threat. We are prepared to stop nuclear tests immediately in this context. However, I do not believe that we can accept a proposal to stop nuclear experiments as an isolated step, unaccompanied by any assurances that other measures—which would go to the heart of the problem—would follow. . . .[4]

The President then suggested that progress toward the goal of an agreement to devote all future production of fissionable material to peaceful uses must accompany an agreement for the cessation of nuclear tests. At the same time the states possessing nuclear weapons should begin to transfer to peaceful uses, on a fair and equitable basis, fissionable material presently tied up in stocks of nuclear weapons.

The President had started to untie the August 29 package by returning to the earlier United States positions under which an agreement for cessation of nuclear tests depended solely on progress toward the cutoff. He ended his communication as follows: ". . . I want to assure you with all the sincerity of which I am capable that we stand ready, unbound by the past, to continue our efforts to seek a disarmament agreement, including the cessation of nuclear testing, that will promote trust, security and understanding among all people."[5]

It seems probable that the three factors that were most instrumental in causing the breakup of the 1957 negotiations were the German elec-

[3] "Letter President Eisenhower to Prime Minister Nehru," *ibid.*, p. 17.
[4] *Ibid.*
[5] *Ibid.*, p. 18.

tion, the belated Western insistence that its proposals must be considered as a package, and the composition of the forum that would deal with arms control problems. The German election had taken place. Both the Soviet Union and the West now commenced to deal with the remaining two problems that had led to the impasse. This gave rise to two questions. First, in case of a resumption of negotiations, what would be the topics on which negotiations would take place? Second, what would be the forum for the negotiations?

In December, NATO gave its tentative answer to both problems. The heads of government conference of the North Atlantic Treaty Organization, which took place in Paris from December 16 to December 19, issued a declaration of principles including the following:

On the topics for negotiation, "We are also prepared to examine any proposal, from whatever source, for general or partial disarmament, and any proposal enabling agreement to be reached on the controlled reduction of armaments of all types."[6] Despite the inconsistency of the two parts of this sentence, it confirmed Eisenhower's willingness to go beyond the August 29 package.

On the forum for arms control discussions, "Should the Soviet Government refuse to participate in the work of the new Disarmament Commission, we would welcome a meeting at Foreign Ministers level to resolve the deadlock."[7] Thus NATO was suggesting that the arms control negotiations be raised to the Foreign Ministers level to resolve the deadlock.

The Soviet Union had started moving toward renewed negotiations even prior to the NATO action. On December 10, Bulganin wrote the first of a long series of letters to President Eisenhower dealing with crucial world problems. This letter placed greatest emphasis on the fears of the Soviet Union that nuclear weapons might be placed at the disposal of the Federal Republic of Germany. After noting that President Eisenhower was striving for peace and cooperation with other countries including the Soviet Union, Bulganin stated:

"A consciousness of the gravity of the present situation and concern

[6] Meeting of Heads of Government of NATO Countries, Department of State Bulletin, Vol. 38 (Jan. 6, 1958), p. 13.
[7] Ibid.

for the preservation of peace prompts us to address to you, Mr. President, an appeal to undertake joint efforts to put an end to the 'cold war,' to terminate the armaments race, and to enter resolutely upon the path of peaceful co-existence."[8] Bulganin then stressed the Soviet support for the Polish proposal to the General Assembly to create a zone free of atomic armaments in Central Europe. This Polish proposal, as we have seen, was the response to the Western proposals in the subcommittee for Arctic zones and European zones of inspection. Bulganin clearly showed that the Soviet Union deemed the Polish proposals an essential step in the East-West bargaining process, which had been going on during the previous summer. He did not go into any detailed elaboration of the Polish proposal. The process of elaboration took nine months.

Bulganin also included in his letter a number of the proposals the Soviet Union had been making year after year: a nonaggression pact between the NATO countries and the Warsaw Treaty countries; an agreement among the United States, Great Britain, and the Soviet Union to refrain from using nuclear weapons; an announcement of the suspension of all nuclear test explosions "if only for two or three years"; and increasing cultural and economic contacts between the Soviet Union and the West. Bulganin also suggested a forum for the negotiations, a meeting of heads of government.

At the session of the USSR Supreme Soviet on December 21, 1957, immediately following the NATO meetings, Gromyko went considerably further in the direction of outlining a basis for resumption of the arms control negotiations. He stated the two main obstacles to successful negotiations: "The United States and the United Kingdom, as they have done hitherto, are evading a solution of the disarmament problem, making an appropriate agreement dependent on a whole series of far-fetched and impracticable terms, especially with regard to control over disarmament."[9] In short, Gromyko was objecting to the fact that the August 29 proposals were to be considered as a package. The second obstacle was that:

[8] "Premier Bulganin to the President," Department of State *Bulletin*, Vol. 38 (Jan. 27, 1958), p. 130.
[9] *Soviet News*, No. 3749 (Dec. 23, 1957), p. 217.

The disarmament talks were held in recent years in an utterly abnormal situation. In the United Nations Disarmament Subcommittee where these talks have mainly been held in the last three years, the Soviet Union was opposed by four members of the North Atlantic bloc—the United States, the United Kingdom, France and Canada—which blocked any proposals that did not accord with the policy of this military bloc.

Gromyko went on to state that the Soviet Union would accept as a forum for disarmament negotiations a Disarmament Commission including all United Nations Member states, or alternatively "the establishment of a somewhat narrower Disarmament Commission in which the Socialist countries and the countries pursuing a neutral policy would account for at least half of the members"—the Albanian resolution in the 1957 General Assembly.[10]

Gromyko then confirmed Soviet support for partial confidence-building measures.

The Soviet government having analysed the course of many years of disarmament negotiations and the attitudes and proposals of the parties concerned, has arrived at the conclusion that in view of the present international situation, marked by tension in the relations between the states, the only realistic way to solve the disarmament problem would be to re-establish and strengthen international confidence. It is necessary to find common points of departure and, where the situation allows, to take the first, even if tentative, step towards disarmament. If the western powers are not prepared to agree to joint disarmament measures, what is there to prevent us from agreeing on mutual undertakings of a moral nature or on such individual measures as would contribute to the re-establishment of international confidence and help pave the way for the solution of the disarmament problem as a whole.[11]

[10] *Ibid.*
[11] *Ibid.*, p. 219.

At the same session, Khrushchev repeated Bulganin's suggestion that a meeting

of the heads of governments of socialist and capitalist countries be called to discuss in a businesslike way and on an equal footing the problems that have long been of deep concern to mankind, including the problem of disarmament, and to find mutually acceptable solutions. We consider that such a conference could be preceded by a meeting of representatives of the two strongest powers—the U.S.A. and the U.S.S.R.[12]

Bulganin conveyed the substance of the meetings of the Supreme Soviet to President Eisenhower in a letter dated January 8, 1958. This letter recited at great length the Soviet party line on most of the international episodes of recent years such as the Suez incident, the tensions in the Turkish-Syrian border area, and the German problem.

From the standpoint of disarmament negotiations, the only novelty in this letter was the Soviet rejection of the NATO idea of calling a conference of Foreign Ministers to precede a meeting at the highest level. Bulganin said:

To be frank, in this matter we share certain apprehensions which are expressed in many countries. If one takes into account the prejudiced position of certain possible participants in the Conference at this level with regard to the question of negotiations, there is no assurance that such negotiations would not at the present time meet with serious difficulties which would then create additional obstacles on the road to agreement on the questions which are subject to consideration, as well as on the road to the subsequent convening of a meeting at a high level with the participation of the Heads of Government.[13]

[12] "Text of Khrushchev Statement to Supreme Soviet," *ibid.*, p. 222.
[13] The White House, Disarmament Staff, Disarmament Background Series D-62, "Bulganin Letter to Eisenhower" (Jan. 8, 1958), p. 12.

This was a polite but scarcely concealed slap at John Foster Dulles. On January 12, Eisenhower wrote a significant letter to Bulganin. The responsibility for preparing this document rested in the Department of State.[14] This letter attempted the much-needed task of melding the United States policy toward disarmament into the over-all foreign policy of the United States. In view of the constant Soviet attacks on NATO, the letter went back to 1945 to explain the background of regional collective arrangements and their relatioaship to the provisions of the Charter of the United Nations for the maintenance of world peace.

Of course the United States would greatly prefer it if collective security could be obtained on the universal basis through the United Nations.

This was the hope when in 1945 our two governments and others signed the Charter of the United Nations conferring upon its Security Council primary responsibility for the maintenance of international peace and security. . . .[15]

The letter then pointed out that agreement had never been reached to provide the Security Council with the armed forces necessary to maintain peace and that the Soviet use of the veto had frustrated the work of the Security Council.

The possibility that the Security Council might become undependable was feared at the San Francisco Conference on World Organization, and accordingly the Charter recognized that in addition to reliance on the Security Council, the nations possessed and might exercise an inherent right of collective self-defense. It has therefore been found not only desirable but necessary if the free

---

[14] The Office of the Special Assistant to the President for Disarmament was physically and administratively transferred to the Department of State on March 1, 1957. While Governor Stassen had not formally resigned as Special Assistant to the President for Disarmament, he had already announced his intention to campaign for the governorship of Pennsylvania. See New York Times, March 2, 1957, p. 1.

[15] "The President to Premier Bulganin," Department of State Bulletin, Vol. 38 (Jan. 27, 1958), p. 123.

nations are to be secure and safe, to concert their defensive measures.

I can and do give you, Mr. Chairman, two solemn and categorical assurances.

1. *Never* will the United States lend its support to any aggressive action by any collective defense organization or any member thereof;

2. *Always* will the United States be ready to move towards the development of effective United Nations collective security measures in replacement of regional collective measures.[16]

The President went into considerable detail in outlining the objections to Bulganin's proposals, promising, however, that the NATO countries would study the question of de-nuclearizing an area in Central and Western Europe. The President then made some proposals of his own outside the disarmament field, which were probably as unnegotiable as the Soviet proposals: strengthening the United Nations by reducing the use of veto; proceeding with the reunification of Germany through free elections as agreed at Geneva in 1955; and international consultations on how to give the peoples of Eastern Europe opportunity to have governments of their own choosing as agreed at Yalta in 1945. This served the useful purpose of reminding the Soviet Union that the West as well as the Soviet Union could suggest problems incapable of immediate solution.

In the field of disarmament, the President in the main reiterated the August 29 proposals for partial measures of disarmament:

(a) I propose that we agree that outer space should be used only for peaceful purposes. . . .

(b) Let us also end the now unrestrained production of nuclear weapons. . . .

(c) I propose that as part of such a program which will reliably check and reverse the accumulation of nuclear weapons, we stop the testing of nuclear weapons, not just for two or three years, but indefinitely. . . .

[16] *Ibid.*

(d) Let us at the same time take steps to begin the controlled and progressive reduction of conventional weapons and military man-power.

(e) I also renew my proposal that we begin progressively to take measures to guarantee against the possibility of surprise attack. . . .[17]

Up to this point the President's suggestions were a little further away from the Soviet position than even the rejected August 29 proposals. The August 29 proposals had contemplated a temporary suspension of nuclear tests prior to any progress toward ending the unrestrained production of nuclear weapons. The President was now proposing that ending the unrestrained production of nuclear weapons should precede the cessation or the suspension of nuclear tests.

However, referring to the whole range of proposals, the President said:

The capacity to verify the fulfillment of commitments is of the essence in all these matters, including the reduction of conventional forces and weapons, and it will be surely useful for us to study together through technical groups what are the possibilities in this respect upon which we could build if we then decide to do so. These technical studies could if you wish be undertaken without commitment as to ultimate acceptance or as to the interdependence of the propositions involved. It is such technical studies of the possibilities of verification and supervision that the United States has proposed as a first step. I believe that this is a first step that would provoke hope in both of our countries and in the world, therefore, I urge that this first step be undertaken.[18]

There was nothing new about this United States position. It was in substance the same as Jules Moch's suggestions in 1954 for taking

[17] Ibid., p. 126.
[18] Ibid., pp. 126-27.

positions "sous reserve," which later made possible the serious negotiations in 1957. The position was likewise merely repeating the frequent suggestions of Selwyn Lloyd, propounded every time that any progress had been made toward limitations of armaments—that technical groups be set up to study the machinery necessary to monitor the limitations. At this time, however, and in this context, Eisenhower had moved one step further in separating the August 29 package of proposals.

The correspondence between Eisenhower and Bulganin continued. A bitter letter from Bulganin dated February 1 caused Eisenhower to "wonder . . . whether we shall get anywhere by continuing to write speeches to each other."[19] Private discussions in New York between the United States and Soviet representatives in the United Nations ended in a bitter exchange.

On March 31, however, the Supreme Soviet (after completing a series of nuclear tests) approved a decree abolishing nuclear tests in the Soviet Union but reserving the right to resume tests if other nations did not follow suit. Khrushchev informed President Eisenhower of this decree (Bulganin by this time having disappeared from the Soviet High Command). He proposed that the United States and the United Kingdom likewise "adopt a decision to renounce further tests."[20] Eisenhower in reply to Khrushchev repeated his offer to establish technical groups "to advise us as to what specific control measures are necessary if there is to be a dependable and agreed disarmament program."[21] Khrushchev was still not ready to agree to the technical talks.

The next step of the Soviet Government was to bring to the United Nations Security Council its claims of flights by American aircraft near Soviet territory. Ambassador Lodge after explaining the military necessity of the flights and the precautions lest any harm result, proposed an aerial inspection zone in the Arctic region, which would make the flights unnecessary. The Soviet Union vetoed the American pro-

[19] "The President to Premier Bulganin," *ibid.* (March 10, 1958), p. 373.
[20] United Nations General Assembly, "Decree of the Supreme Soviet Concerning the Discontinuance of Soviet Atomic and Hydrogen Weapons Tests, March 31, 1958," in U.N. Doc. A/3820 (April 8, 1958).
[21] "The President to Premier Khrushchev, April 8, 1958," Department of State *Bulletin,* Vol. 38 (April 28, 1958), p. 680.

posal. The Security Council thereupon rejected the Soviet resolution to end the flights.[22]

In a letter of April 22 to Eisenhower, Khrushchev repeated a Soviet proposal originally publicized on March 15, calling for a ban on the use of cosmic space for military purposes coupled with the elimination of foreign military bases; establishment of an international control machinery to ensure the observance of the agreements; and the creation of a United Nations agency for international cooperation in the study of cosmic space. The rationale for linking the liquidation of bases in foreign territories to prohibition of the use of outer space for military purposes was that both missiles and rockets and manned aircraft flying from foreign bases could be utilized to deliver hydrogen weapons on the Soviet Union. The Soviet Union had an advantage in missiles while the United States neutralized this advantage through its bases near the Soviet Union.[23]

On April 28, Eisenhower pointed out that Khrushchev's letter of April 22 was not an affirmative response to his proposal. He reiterated his suggestion that technical people get to work immediately on the practical problems of supervision and control, which would be indispensable to any dependable disarmament agreement. "The solution of these practical problems will take time. I am unhappy that valuable time is now being wasted." As an example he suggested "Why could not designated technical people agree on what would be required so that you would know if we violated any agreement to suspend testing and we would know if you should commit a violation?"[24]

On May 1, in a press conference explaining the suggestion for a technical conference, Dulles was asked the following question: "Mr. Secretary, the fact that you have offered this separately—does it mean that to an extent we have broken our own package?" The answer was: "Yes, it means to that extent, we have broken the package."[25] Dulles

[22] *United States Participation in the United Nations, Report by the President to the Congress for the Year 1958*, Department of State Publication 6852 (1958), pp. 14-15. Cited hereafter as *U.S. Participation in the U.N., Report* (with year).
[23] "Premier Khrushchev to the President," Department of State *Bulletin*, Vol. 38 (May 19, 1958), pp. 812-15.
[24] "The President to Premier Khrushchev," *ibid.*, p. 811.
[25] *Ibid.* (May 10, 1958), p. 806.

then established a possible line of retreat, which did not, however, contradict his main statement. Possibly Dulles' statement may have influenced Khrushchev to respond affirmatively. On May 9 he wrote:

> Your messages indicate that you attach great importance to having expert study of the technical details connected with the control of the execution of an agreement on the cessation of atomic and hydrogen weapons. Taking this into account, we are prepared in spite of the serious doubts on our part . . . to try even this course. The Soviet Government agrees to having both sides designate experts who would immediately begin a study of methods for detecting possible violations of an agreement on the cessation of nuclear tests with a view to having this work completed at the earliest possible date to be determined in advance.[26]

TECHNICAL CONFERENCES

Further correspondence resulted in agreement on the details of the technical discussions. The discussions would commence on July 1 at Geneva. The Soviet Union suggested that they be limited to three or four weeks with the United States agreeing that they should not last a long time but maintaining that they might stretch out slightly longer than three or four weeks. The experts designated to represent the West would include experts from the United Kingdom and France and possibly other countries as well as from the United States. Similarly, the Soviet Union intended to designate experts from Czechoslovakia and from Poland and perhaps from other states.[27] When the talks got under way, on July 1, the Soviet side and the West each had experts from four states.

On July 2, the day after the commencement of the technical meetings on test cessation, Khrushchev in a letter to Eisenhower agreed to a meeting of appropriate representatives including those of the military

---

[26] "Premier Khrushchev to the President," *ibid.* (June 9, 1958), pp. 940-41.
[27] See "The President to Premier Khrushchev," *ibid.*, p. 939; "Premier Khrushchev to the President," *ibid.*, pp. 1083-84; "Letter from President Eisenhower to the Soviet Premier (Khrushchev)," White House press release, June 10, 1958.

agencies of "both sides" at the level of experts for a joint study of the practical aspects of the problem of surprise attack.[28] After considerable correspondence, this conference also got under way on November 10. It included experts from ten countries, five from the West and five from the Soviet bloc. Thus a pattern was being established in arms control negotiations of Soviet representatives equal in number to the Western representatives.[29]

The experts meeting concerned with the detection of nuclear tests reached agreement that it is "technically feasible to set up a workable and effective control system for the detection of violations of possible agreement on the world-wide cessation of nuclear weapons tests."[30] On the next day, President Eisenhower welcomed the successful conclusion of the meetings and suggested a conference of the three nations that had tested nuclear weapons—the Soviet Union, the United Kingdom, and the United States—to negotiate an agreement for the suspension of nuclear weapons tests and the establishment of an international control system on the basis of the experts' report. At the same time, the President announced that the United States would suspend weapons tests for a period of one year from the beginning of the negotiations and might extend the suspension on a year-to-year basis depending on the progress of the negotiations. Khrushchev likewise accepted the report of the conference of experts, and after some correspondence, agreement was reached that a conference of the three powers with nuclear weapons should commence in Geneva on October 31, 1958, to prepare a treaty for the cessation of nuclear weapons tests.

The surprise attack conference of experts failed to achieve any agreement and recessed on December 18 "in view of the Christmas and New Year's holidays and to report to Governments on the work of the Conference." The participants expressed the hope that "discussions on the problem of preventing surprise attacks would be resumed as early

[28] "Premier Khrushchev's Letter to the President," Department of State *Bulletin*, Vol. 39 (Aug. 18, 1958), pp. 279-81.
[29] Since this chapter deals only with procedures, we shall not at this point consider the substantive content of the two sets of meetings.
[30] See Chap. 20.

as possible."[31] They never have resumed, though the subject was included in the ten power meetings in 1960.

The conferences to achieve cessation of nuclear testing are continuing and are by all odds the most important developments in the field of arms control since World War II. Before turning to the substantive developments in the conferences, it seems desirable to continue the narrative of the gradual evolution of procedures that permitted in 1960 the resumption of East-West arms control negotiations.

THE 1958 GENERAL ASSEMBLY

AND ITS AFTERMATH

The 1958 General Assembly debated disarmament for 27 days with a greater number of states participating in the drafting of resolutions than ever before in the history of the United Nations.[32]

While the technical conference on the suspension of nuclear tests had met with some success, and the Tripartite Conference on Nuclear Tests as well as the Technical Conference on Surprise Attack were actually in session during the General Assembly, the limited objectives of all of these meetings were only too obvious. The vast majority of the membership of the United Nations wished to get the disarmament negotiations started once more on a broader basis and, if possible, in a framework that would improve the chance of agreement. The numerous draft resolutions introduced into the meetings all had that objective in view.

Three General Assembly agenda items raised the question of disarmament. The first was a memorandum of the Secretary-General of the United Nations, which after noting that the disarmament machinery of the United Nations had become inoperative, but that the technical conferences then under way provided possibilities for further progress, suggested that the General Assembly might wish to "define

[31] See Chap. 18.
[32] U.S. Participation in the U.N., Report 1958, p. 26.

its attitude . . . toward the results of the Conference of Experts" and to consider the primary objective of "balanced world-wide disarmament."[33] In addition, the Soviet Union placed on the agenda two items: the first called for the immediate unconditional discontinuance of nuclear tests with emphasis on the danger of atomic radiation.[34] The Soviet Union made this suggestion even though it was participating in a conference that would achieve the result of cessation of nuclear tests with the development of adequate control machinery. The second Soviet item called for reduction of military budgets "as an important practical step towards halting the arms race"[35] and for channeling the savings into developing peaceful sectors of the economy. This was a return to one of the specific proposals the Subcommittee of Five had debated in 1957 with particularly unpromising results. It would obviously have appeal for underdeveloped countries. Despite Soviet objections, all three agenda items were taken up simultaneously.

The long discussion in the Political Committee of the General Assembly centered on three issues: test cessation, surprise attack, and machinery in and outside the United Nations to permit the resumption of broader discussions of disarmament.

Nuclear Test Cessation

The greatest differences developed on test cessation. The Soviet Union had introduced a resolution calling for the discontinuance of tests regardless of whether agreement could be reached on machinery to monitor the discontinuance.[36] In the Political Committee, India sub-

[33] U.N. General Assembly, Thirteenth Session, *Official Records*, Agenda Item 64, Annexes, "Memorandum by the Secretary-General" (Sept. 30, 1958), pp. 18-19.

[34] U.N. General Assembly, Thirteenth Session, *Official Records*, Agenda Item 70, Annexes, "Letter dated 15 September 1958 from the Chairman of the Delegation of the USSR to the Secretary-General" (Sept. 15, 1958), p. 12.

[35] U.N. General Assembly, Thirteenth Session, *Official Records*, Agenda Item 72, Annexes, "Letter dated 18 September 1958 from the Chairman of the Delegation of the USSR to the President of the General Assembly" (Sept. 18, 1958), p. 13.

[36] U.N. General Assembly, Thirteenth Session, *Official Records*, "Soviet Draft Resolution Introduced in the First Committee of the General Assembly; Cessation

mitted a draft resolution that in substance reached the same result as the Soviet resolution. It called for immediate suspension of weapons tests pending agreement at the Geneva Conference, but the resolution would require the suspension to continue indefinitely even though no agreement were reached on the monitoring system.[37]

The view of the Western powers on all of the issues was presented in a resolution sponsored by seventeen countries urging the parties to the Geneva talks to make every effort to reach early agreement on the suspension of nuclear tests under effective international control and not to undertake further testing; calling attention to the importance and urgency of reaching the widest possible measure of agreement against the possibility of surprise attack; and asking for continued efforts to secure a "balanced and effectively controlled world-wide system of disarmament."[38] The resolution also sought to minimize any propaganda value which the Soviet Union might have obtained from its suggestion for reductions in military budgets by inviting states to increase, out of any disarmament savings, their investment in economic development, especially in the less developed countries.

Austria, Japan, and Sweden submitted a resolution on the subject of nuclear tests which covered much of the same ground as the seventeen state resolution. It expressed the hope that the forthcoming conference on nuclear tests would succeed and would lead to an acceptable agreement, and requested the three parties to that conference to report to the General Assembly the results of their negotiations.[39]

Finally, Ireland introduced a resolution calling attention to the

---

of Atomic and Hydrogen Weapons Tests, Oct. 5, 1958," Doc. A/C.1/L.203 (Oct. 9, 1958) and Corr. 1 (Oct. 21, 1958).

[37] U.N. General Assembly, Thirteenth Session, *Official Records*, "Revised Indian Draft Resolution Introduced in the First Committee of the General Assembly: The Discontinuance of Atomic and Hydrogen Weapons Tests, Oct. 14, 1958" (Oct. 14, 1958). The original Indian resolution was introduced Oct. 5.

[38] U.N. General Assembly, Thirteenth Session, *Official Records*, Agenda Items 64, 70, and 72, Annexes, "Argentina, Australia, Belgium, Brazil, Canada, Denmark, Ecuador, Iran, Italy, Laos, Netherlands, New Zealand, Norway, Pakistan, Thailand, United Kingdom of Great Britain and Northern Ireland, and the United States of America: draft resolution" (Oct. 10, 1958), p. 21.

[39] U.N. General Assembly, Thirteenth Session, *Official Records*, Agenda Item 64, Annexes, "Austria, Japan and Sweden: draft resolution" (Oct. 31, 1958).

danger of an increase in the number of states possessing nuclear weapons and providing for establishment of a committee to study the dangers inherent in the future dissemination of nuclear weapons.[40]

During the debates, the Indian and Yugoslav delegations made valiant efforts to secure a compromise formula acceptable both to the Soviet Union and the West. However, this failed since India would not move away from its stand that nuclear tests should cease even if no agreement were reached on a safeguards system to monitor the cessation of tests. Ultimately, the seventeen power draft resolution and the resolution of Austria, Japan, and Sweden were adopted with only the Soviet bloc voting in opposition. There were, however, a great number of abstentions, chiefly among the African and Asian nations.[41]

The Indian resolution—which by this time had fourteen sponsors all from Asian and African countries—calling for what would amount to a permanent ban on nuclear tests was rejected in the General Assembly by a vote of 41 to 27 with 13 abstentions. It is significant that this resolution received the support of practically all the African and Asian states in addition to the Soviet bloc and that the 13 abstaining states included some of the best friends of the Western governments, Austria, Iceland, Iran, Ireland, Japan, Jordan, Lebanon, Liberia, Malaya, Mexico, New Zealand, Sweden, and Tunisia.[42]

The Political Committee likewise adopted the Irish resolution by a vote of 37 to 0. However, there were 44 abstentions including both the United States and the Soviet Union, and therefore the Irish representative withdrew the resolution.[43]

[40] U.N. General Assembly, Thirteenth Session, *Official Records*, Agenda Item 64, Annexes, "Ireland: draft resolution" (Oct. 17, 1958), p. 22.

[41] U.N. General Assembly, Thirteenth Session, *Official Records*, Agenda Item 64, Annexes, "India and Yugoslavia: revised draft resolution," Doc. A/C.1/L.210/Rev. 1 (Oct. 31, 1958), p. 22. Also Doc. A/C.1/L.210/Rev. 2 (Nov. 3, 1958), p. 23. See also "Report of the First Committee," Doc. A/3974 and Add. 1 and 2 (Nov. 3 and 4, 1958), pp. 25-26.

[42] U.N. General Assembly, Thirteenth Session, *Official Records*, "Revised Indian Draft Resolution Introduced in the First Committee of the General Assembly: The Discontinuance of Atomic and Hydrogen Weapons Tests, Oct. 14, 1958," Doc. A/C.1/L.202/Rev. 1 (Oct. 14, 1958). The original Indian resolution (A/L.246) was introduced Oct. 5. The rejection by the General Assembly was on Nov. 4.

[43] U.N. General Assembly, Thirteenth Session, *Official Records*, Annexes, "Report of the First Committee," Doc. A/3974 and Add. 1 and 2 (Nov. 3 and 4, 1958), p. 27.

Enlargement of the Disarmament Commission

The other two main subjects of the disarmament debate were less controversial. A resolution sponsored by India and Yugoslavia, which merely noted the scheduled technical meeting on surprise attack and expressed the hope that agreement would be achieved, was adopted unanimously.[44] India and Yugoslavia also took the initiative in calling for the enlargement of the Disarmament Commission to include all the members of the General Assembly, as requested by the Soviet Union a year earlier. Although some Members of the United Nations would have preferred further discussion of the composition of the Disarmament Commission in the hope that a different formula would be reached, the Indian-Yugoslav resolution was passed unanimously with a series of French amendments,[45] clarifying the terms of reference of the newly constituted commission. Thus, the General Assembly expressed its continued interest and concern in disarmament, even though the only active discussions were taking place outside the United Nations, and provided a commission to which the participants in the technical conferences could refer their agreements. In this manner, the United Nations had reasserted its interest in disarmament and moved a short distance toward establishing a framework for future United Nations negotiations.

Aftermath

One year later, a four-power communiqué following a meeting of the Foreign Ministers of the United States, France, the United Kingdom, and the Soviet Union, pronounced that agreement had been reached among these four governments "to set up a committee to consider disarmament matters."[46] The committee consisted of five Western

[44] *Ibid.,* Indian-Yugoslav draft resolution. U.N. Doc. A/C.1/211, Nov. 3, 1958, p. 27.
[45] *Ibid.,* U. N. Doc. A/C.1/L.212 (Oct. 27, 1958).
[46] "Four-Power Communiqué on Disarmament Negotiations," Department of State *Bulletin,* Vol. 41 (Sept. 28, 1959), pp. 438-39.

powers—the United States, France, the United Kingdom, Canada, and Italy—and five members of the Soviet bloc—the Soviet Union, Bulgaria, Czechoslovakia, Poland, and Rumania. The communiqué acknowledged the primary responsibility of the United Nations for general disarmament measures. The committee would explore reductions of all types of armaments and armed forces under effective international controls. The United Nations would be kept informed of the results of the deliberations, which would provide "a useful basis for consideration in the U.N." Thus a negotiating procedure to deal with all phases of disarmament, not within the United Nations but linked to it, had come into existence. This brings the narrative of procedures to September 1959.

It had taken almost two years to re-establish the shattered negotiating machinery. The seemingly sterile maneuvers of this two-year period served to sharpen and highlight some basic features inherent in the arms control negotiations.

First, world opinion would not permit the negotiations to end. Within a month after the stalemate of 1957, both the Soviet Union and the United States became uncomfortable and sought ways to resume negotiating.

Second, both in the Bulganin-Eisenhower correspondence and later in the 1958 General Assembly, the Soviet Union showed its preference for broad statements of principles (which might unilaterally disarm the West) rather than precise, detailed safeguarded agreements. Even after the Soviet Union as a last resort, after months of note-writing, had consented to negotiate a precise treaty providing for test cessation with international machinery to ensure the observance of the treaty, in the General Assembly of 1958, it turned around and supported the Indian initiative in favor of a simple ban of tests regardless of safeguards.

Third, the Soviet Union was willing to proceed with detailed negotiations for a safeguarded agreement when it could not achieve its goal in any other way.

Fourth, the agreement for the resumption of negotiations arose as a result of patient negotiations accompanied by mutual concessions. The West gave up its insistence on treating its August 29, 1957 proposals as an inseparable package. It may be a coincidence that the Soviet acceptance of technical negotiations followed by eight days the Dulles' admission that the package had been separated. The Soviet Union thereby gave up its previous objection to technical negotiations on a safeguards system prior to complete agreement on the objects of control. The West bowed to the Soviet insistence that the negotiating group should consist either of the entire membership of the General Assembly or of a more limited group where the representatives of the Soviet bloc equaled in number the representatives of the West.[47]

Fifth, the votes in the General Assembly showed the declining prestige of the West in the field of arms control. On the only substantive issue—the Indian resolution for unconditional cessation of nuclear testing regardless of agreement on the monitoring system—the Western support came almost entirely from NATO countries and from Latin America.

In short, the two years of procedures largely predetermined the direction and underlying conditions of the substantive deliberations that followed.

[47] The Tripartite Conference on Test Cessation was an exception. The group consisted of the only three states which at the time had nuclear weapons.

XVIII

The Technical Conference to Prevent Surprise Attack

THE TWO technical conferences in 1958, "The Conference of Experts for the Study of Possible Measures Which Might be Helpful in Preventing Surprise Attack" and "The Conference of Experts to Study the Possibility of Detecting Violations of a Possible Agreement on the Suspension of Nuclear Tests," marked a change in direction. The conference dealing with test cessation started four months ahead of the surprise attack conference. However, the surprise attack conference lasted only six weeks, from November 10 to December 18, and thereupon recessed without ever reconvening. The technical conference on suspension of nuclear tests, lasting from July 1 until August 21, reached agreed conclusions. Its work was continued by "The Conference on the Discontinuance of Nuclear Weapons Tests," which convened on October 31, 1958 and which still continues in session. Therefore, even though the technical negotiations on test cessation got started first, in the interests of clarity, this study deals first with the shorter and less significant conference on surprise attack. The meetings on nuclear test cessation will be discussed in the following chapter.

The chief factor that differentiates these technical conferences from all previous negotiations in the field of arms control is that for the first time since World War II the negotiating parties were talking in terms that in their precision, at least, approached the requirements of a treaty. All previous negotiations dealt with general principles, which would have required vast elaboration and some change before they could be incorporated into a meaningful treaty. In the technical conferences that commenced in 1958, more particularly those dealing with test cessation, both sides finally got down to the precise discussion of the contents of a treaty.

This change in the nature of the conferences necessitates a corresponding change in historical treatment. The main importance of all the previous negotiations rested in their political implications. Therefore a narration of such conferences could reproduce their flavor and their results with comparatively scant attention to technical details. The detail could be limited to what is essential to an understanding of the political implications of the negotiations.

The same pattern will hold true if these technical negotiations likewise turn out to be abortive. If, on the other hand, the positions that first burgeoned in the technical conferences ripen into agreements between East and West, these positions must be examined, figuratively speaking with a magnifying glass, to show not only political but also technical implications. For example, an agreement allowing a specified number of on-site inspections to determine whether a seismic disturbance arises from an earthquake or an explosion has both political and technical implications. The political implications are susceptible of explanation with background information confined to three or four sentences describing the extremes of the divergent estimates as to the effectiveness of such a provision. A technical description of the data underlying the extreme estimates and an attempt to evaluate the extreme estimates at a minimum might be a hundred times as long.

This study will continue the pattern of brief description as in the case of the earlier negotiations and will include only sufficient technical data to permit an estimate of political implications. The reasons for thus limiting the scope of this study are twofold: first, it would be premature to attempt the larger and more technical study while the test cessation negotiations are still pending and while it still seems probable that much of the data submitted to the surprise attack negotiations will find their way into the broader disarmament negotiations that may emerge in the near future. Second, highly technical studies in general are beyond the objectives of this book.[1]

THE CONFLICTING

VIEWPOINTS

The conference to study measures to prevent surprise attack convened in Geneva on November 10, 1958 with ten participating states: five Western powers and five members of the Soviet bloc. The terms of reference of the conference had emerged from the long series of communications between Eisenhower and Bulganin and Eisenhower and Khrushchev. Eisenhower had suggested as early as January 12 that "it would surely be useful for us to study together through technical groups. . . . These technical studies could, if you wish, be undertaken without commitment as to ultimate acceptance, or as to the interdependence, of the propositions involved."[2] Eisenhower had several times renewed this suggestion and had specifically mentioned the subject of defense against surprise attack for such technical talks.

On July 2, the day after the opening of the conference on nuclear tests, Khrushchev wrote to President Eisenhower:

> Mindful of the importance that agreement on joint measures for the prevention of surprise attack by one state against another would have for the preservation of universal peace, I should like to propose to you . . . that the governments of our countries show practical initiative in this important matter. In the opinion of the Soviet Government, it would be useful if in the near future the appropriate representatives—including those of the mili-

[1] A technical study of the test cessation negotiations (probably at a somewhat later date than the present) would be exceedingly useful to supplement the primarily political treatment contained in this study.

[2] "The President to Premier Bulganin," Department of State *Bulletin*, Vol. 38 (Jan. 27, 1958), p. 126.

tary agencies on both sides, e.g., at the level of experts—designated by the Governments of the USSR, the USA, and possibly by the governments of certain other states, met for a joint study of the practical aspects of this problem and developed within a definite period of time, to be determined in advance, recommendations regarding measures for the prevention of the possibility of surprise attack. . . .

Khrushchev stated: "However, it appears to me that agreement on this point is also fully possible, if only all parties would base their position on the necessity of taking into account the security interests of each of the parties to the agreement and refrain from actions that would aggravate the situation and increase the danger of war." Khrushchev claimed that past Western proposals for inspection zones did not "consider equally the legitimate interests of the security of all the states concerned."[3]

The American Embassy in Moscow on July 31 sent a note to the Soviet Foreign Ministry suggesting certain details of the forthcoming conference and indicating disagreement with Khrushchev's statement that the Western proposals relating to zones of inspection against surprise attack "failed to strike a balance between the interests of both sides." The United States then suggested "technical discussions of measures to reduce the possibility of surprise attack even though made without reference to particular areas."[4]

In Khrushchev's reply of September 15, he suggested that:

Such a meeting would be fruitful if its work is directed toward the working out of practical recommendations concerning measures to prevent surprise attack *in combination with definite steps in the field of disarmament.* . . . Moreover, it is clear that the experts will

[3] "Premier Khrushchev's Letter to the President," *ibid.,* Vol. 39 (Aug. 18, 1958), p. 280.
[4] "Note from the American Embassy to the Soviet Foreign Ministry: Prevention of Surprise Attack, July 31, 1958," *ibid.,* pp. 278-79.

have to give serious attention also to such technical questions as means and objects of control and the results which might be secured by these measures.[5]

The reply of the American Embassy on October 10 defined the purpose of the meeting:

To examine the methods and objects of control and to assess the results that might be obtained from the adoption of those methods in lessening the danger of surprise military attack. The study should be undertaken with a view to the preparation of a technical report which could be recommended for consideration by governments. . . . The discussions should take place without prejudice to the respective positions of the two Governments as to the de-limitation of areas within which measures might be established, or as to the timing or inter-dependence of various aspects of disarmament.[6]

On November 1, just ten days before the convening of the conference, the Soviet Foreign Ministry on the subject of the conference "confirms its position on this question set forth in the note of 15 September and considers that the work of the forthcoming conference of experts should be directed to working out practical recommendations on measures for prevention of surprise attack in conjunction with definite steps in the field of disarmament."[7]

This detailed description of the correspondence leading to the conference is important because of the later complete lack of agreement between the Soviet and Western delegates as to its objectives.

Over the years the United States could frequently be accused of failure to attach proper importance to arms control negotiations and failure to give the representatives the administrative and financial sup-

[5] "Note from the Soviet Foreign Ministry to the American Embassy Regarding Surprise Attack Negotiations, September 15, 1958," *ibid.* (Oct. 27, 1958), pp. 648-49. Italics added.
[6] "Note from the American Embassy to the Soviet Foreign Ministry Regarding Surprise Attack Negotiations, October 10, 1958," *ibid.*, p. 648.
[7] "Note from the Soviet Foreign Ministry to the American Embassy Regarding Surprise Attack Negotiations," *ibid.* (Nov. 24, 1958), p. 816.

port required for a meaningful negotiation. For this conference the administrative and financial arrangements of the United States were more than ample. The United States delegation consisted of fifty experts and advisers. It included eminent scientists such as Dr. G. B. Kistiakowsky and Dr. J. B. Wiesner and high ranking military officers such as General O. P. Weyland of the United States Air Force and Rear Admiral P. L. Dudley of the United States Navy. The chief of the delegation, William C. Foster,[8] had an outstanding record both in business and in the United States Government, with no previous exposure to the subject of disarmament. Furthermore, he was appointed to the position less than thirty days prior to the convening of the meeting. The senior political adviser, an experienced Foreign Service Officer, Julius Holmes, had served ten weeks in London in the summer of 1957 as a deputy to Governor Stassen. The only other members of the delegation with substantial previous experience in the field of arms control negotiations were three capable assistants who played a relatively minor role in the decisions of the delegation.

Two days before the meeting, the United States handed to the Soviet Government in Moscow a proposed agenda, the chief headings of which were as follows:

I. Identification of the objects of control: The instruments of surprise attack.

II. Means of control: The technology of observation and inspection.

III. The application of inspection and observation techniques to the problem of surprise attack and the evaluation of the results of such application.

IV. General technical characteristics of systems to reduce the threat of surprise attack.[9]

[8] U.S. Department of State, "Official Report of the United States Delegation to the Conference of Experts for the Study of Possible Measures Which Might be Helpful in Preventing Surprise Attack and for the Preparation of a Report Thereon to Governments" (Feb. 14, 1958), Annex A, pp. 6-7.

[9] U.N. General Assembly, "Report of the Conference of Experts for the Study of Possible Measures Which Might be Helpful in Preventing Surprise Attack. . . ." U.N. Doc. A/4078, S/4145 (Jan. 5, 1959). Annex 1 cited hereafter by document and annex numbers.

The Soviet draft agenda consisted of three items:

1. Exchange of opinions on practical steps that can be taken now with a view to preventing the danger of a surprise attack and on partial disarmament measures to be carried out in conjunction with these steps.
2. Consideration of the tasks of ground control posts and aerial photography.
3. Preparation of the experts' report to the governments of the countries represented at the conference, containing conclusions and recommendations and measures for prevention of a surprise attack in conjunction with certain steps regarding disarmament.[10]

The conflict between the two agendas is so great that it is difficult to understand how they could have been drafted for the same conference. The immediate problem of an agenda was solved by going into the conference without an agenda. However, the conflict in ideas continued through the conference. The Western governments and the Soviet bloc each presented their separate positions with little attempt to reconcile them, and the report of the conference was little more than a statement of the two sets of positions.

The difference in viewpoint carried into the composition of the delegations. The delegations of the Soviet bloc, amounting to forty-two experts and advisers (as compared to one hundred and eight experts and advisers from the West), apparently included no scientists, but consisted entirely of personnel of foreign offices and of military establishments.

During the conference, the Western powers went ahead with the submission of their technical papers, and the Soviet Union proceeded to submit its "practical steps" to prevent the danger of a surprise attack. After all the documents were submitted, Foster in his final statement commented:

[10] Ibid., Annex 2, Nov. 11, 1958.

The contrast between these two sets of documents is self-evident. We have sought to promote technical discussion and understanding. You have sought discussion of a selection of political proposals, for the most part not susceptible of technical assessment. We have, in the later stages of our discussion, been able to achieve, in a fragmentary and restricted way, some critical discussion of various aspects of control. The difference in our approach has, however, remained so wide that it cannot be overcome in this session. The only practical course to follow is to refer to governments the task of reconciling this difference in the hope that future discussions may deal with the problem to better effect. . . .[11]

THE WESTERN POSITIONS

Despite this basic conflict, the conference produced some useful results. The Western experts submitted six technical papers which are likely to ease the path of any future conference that comes to grips with the problem of reducing the danger of surprise attack. Foster expressed as follows an important accomplishment:

. . . The U.S. Government now has a conceptual foundation and a store of expert talent for dealing with this problem which it has never had before.[12]

The first of these technical papers was a "Survey of the Relevant Technical Aspects of Possible Instruments of Surprise Attack as a Prerequisite for Examining Means of Detection and Systems of Inspection and Control."[13] This survey in tabular form listed the various possible means of delivery of surprise attack, both missiles and manned aircraft. As to each of the instruments that might be used for delivering

[11] *Ibid.*, Annex 14, Dec. 18, 1958, p. 2.
[12] U.S. Department of State, "Official Report of the United States Delegation to the Conference of Experts . . ." p. 14.
[13] U.N. Doc. A/4078, S/4145, Annex 5, Nov. 11, 1958, pp. 2-12.

a surprise attack, it noted the range of the instrument, the general characteristics pertinent to the problem of surveillance and observation and some of the types of evidence that might indicate the imminence of a surprise attack.

The Western experts having described the instruments of surprise attack, proceeded in the second paper, to "a survey of some of the techniques which the Western Experts believe would be effective in the observation and inspection of the instruments of surprise attacks."[14] These techniques were divided into three classes, aerial and satellite techniques, ground techniques, and underwater techniques. The first two corresponded in a general way to the suggestions of both the Soviet Union and the West in 1957 for a combination of aerial reconnaissance and ground posts to lessen the danger of surprise attack. The third and novel technique was far less important. However, this study went far beyond anything that had been broached in 1957. It described each of the techniques in great detail, indicating their potential as well as their limitations.

The third Western paper was preceded by the following description:

This paper is intended to illustrate a method of work. It must not be taken as a substantive proposal or as a specific proposal. Nor does this paper discuss the actual implementation of a practical system. Any actual system which might arise from international discussion could clearly be implemented gradually, if so desired, by gradual installation and increase of inspection effort.[15]

With this "caveat," the paper then described a system for observation and inspection of long-range aircraft. The system included a complete aerial survey of any country subject to inspection. It also included ground observation and inspection at all military airfields. The paper went into some detail in describing the means of communicating the observations to a data-processing center and the method of central evaluation of the data.

[14] *Ibid.*, Annex 6, Nov. 19, 1958, pp. 2-14.
[15] *Ibid.*, Annex 7, Nov. 24, 1958, p. 1.

The fourth Western paper used the same method as the third paper in connection with a possible system for observation and inspection of ballistic missiles, and the fifth paper applied the techniques to outline a possible system for observation and inspection of ground forces.[16]

The sixth and final Western paper, which sought to link the preceding papers, was entitled "An explanatory statement regarding certain factors involved in the planning of an integrated observation and inspection system for reducing the possibility of a surprise attack." This paper sought to correlate the technical papers to the entire problem of arms control. It traced the past efforts of the United Nations to meet the dangers of surprise attack through elimination of nuclear weapons, pointing out that both the Soviet Union and the West since 1955 had agreed that this approach was not feasible.

It follows that the only practical step to reduce the danger of surprise attack by nuclear weapons is to monitor the vehicles of delivery. . . . Studies undertaken by the Western Experts prior to this conference have indicated that in contra-distinction to the monitoring of nuclear weapons, the monitoring of complete weapon systems important as instruments of surprise attack is still feasible.[17]

The previous Western papers had outlined a system to accomplish that objective.

The first purpose is to keep each side informed when there are no preparations for an attack on the other side, so that the present state of uncertainty and tension could be replaced by a feeling of greater security. The second purpose—of equal importance—of such systems is to provide reliable warning of preparations for an attack and the quickest possible warning of an attack that has actually been launched. An inspection system, by providing better warning, assures a more certain defensive response by the victim of aggression and hence deters a potential aggressor if he is aware of the consequences of his actions and is not willing to accept a near-total devastation of his own country as a sequel to his own attack.

[16] *Ibid.*, Annex 10, Dec. 3, 1958, pp. 1-14; Annex 11, Dec. 5, 1958, pp. 1-15.
[17] *Ibid.*, Annex 13, Dec. 17, 1958, pp. 1, 5.

The first function of the inspection system—that of informing of an absence of preparations for a surprise attack—reduces the possibility of accidents developing into pre-emptive attacks, thus it reduces the danger of attacks through misunderstanding. The net result is a relaxation of tensions.[18]

After summarizing the general principles and features of the previous papers, this paper reaches certain general conclusions as follows:

The Western Experts fully realize that effective integrated systems are rather complex organizations involving thousands, but probably not tens of thousands of personnel. Such systems cannot be put into effect over night, both because of technical and of political factors. Although a step-by-step implementation appears, therefore, unavoidable in practice, and the selection of particular steps and their timing is a matter for political negotiations, the Western Experts have already drawn some tentative technical conclusions on these matters based on their preliminary studies.

While it is very clear that comprehensive inspection systems, especially if complemented by controlled disarmament measures, reduce the danger of surprise attacks, the same is not always true of partial inspection measures which may be thought of as suitable steps in the implementation of an integrated system. If partial implementation of the desired system is not very carefully carried out according to mutually agreed programs, there might be such a temporary advantage to one side or the other as to be dangerous. Clearly, methods of step-by-step implementation of a system which had been agreed upon as desirable would have to be the subject of detailed negotiation which would make allowance for the several important instruments of surprise attack, each with different characteristics and ranges of action. The Western Experts believe that with proper planning and timing of the successive steps, a mutually acceptable procedure can be devised.

The Western Experts believe that co-operative inspection and

[18] *Ibid.*

observation systems can reduce the danger of surprise attacks by (i) providing earlier and more certain warning, (ii) more importantly giving reassurance that no surprise attack is in preparation and thus reducing the danger of unwarranted pre-emptive attacks, (iii) through both the preceding actions reducing tensions and thus reducing incentives for an arms race. The gains thus anticipated for participating parties are substantial in themselves. They also will have a most important collateral effect in making agreements on controlled disarmament easier and more certain because of increased mutual confidence and reduced tensions. By themselves co-operative inspection systems can only reduce, not eliminate the danger of surprise attack, but they are a safe and sure road to its further reduction through controlled disarmament.[19]

Despite the fact that no agreements ever emerged from the surprise attack conference, these United States position papers have already played an important role in the negotiations and may in the future play a still more essential part. The papers suggested for the first time that the elimination of nuclear warfare might take place through a drastic control of the means of delivery of nuclear weapons. The Soviet Union and the United States had been in agreement ever since 1955 that it was no longer possible to eliminate nuclear warfare through control of fissionable materials since it was impossible to account for all past production of fissionable materials. In the later negotiations, Jules Moch and the French delegation have seized on this alternative and have supported it strongly.[20] In May 1960, the Soviet Union likewise shifted to this approach. Meanwhile the United States apparently has had some second thoughts, and its recent statements and positions have never gone as far as the portions of the paper quoted above.

[19] *Ibid.*, pp. 11, 12. It is interesting that the final conclusion referred to "cooperative inspection and observation systems." This was a new concept for the arms control negotiations. Previous Western papers had always spoken of inspection conducted by an international agency. Cooperative inspection seems to imply a situation in which the Soviet Union and the United States would inspect each other.

[20] See Chap. 20.

More important, these papers along with the corresponding papers in the technical conference on test cessation were the first indications of great progress within the United States Government in translating into a precise program the general principles which had developed in twelve years of negotiations. In 1954 the United States proposals for an international control organ had not gone beyond a check-list of problems. This faithfully reflected the stage of preparation within the United States Government.

The task forces organized by Stassen made a good start in the direction of placing some flesh on the bare bones of the United States position. However, even in the summer of 1957, except on the one subject of nuclear cutoff, there was no indication that the United States had thought through the numerous problems involved in setting up a safeguards system. The surprise attack papers in contrast will almost certainly be a starting point in future negotiations.

THE SOVIET PROPOSALS

The Soviet proposals in their essence were an expansion of the Polish proposals for a zone in central Europe, free of atomic weapons, first submitted to the General Assembly of 1957.[21] These proposals were incorporated in the December 1957 round of letters that Premier Bulganin sent to the Western heads of government after the conclusion of the 1957 Assembly.

Immediately prior to the opening of the experts' conference on surprise attack Adam Rapacki, the Polish Foreign Minister, revised his previous proposals and presented them in a news conference, which placed the proposals in their political context. He recalled a "memorandum of February 14, 1958, which had," he said, "developed the principles of a broad control system of the implementation of the obligations proposed by us." Now, as the West and the East made ready for the conference, he proposed "the maximum step possible." He was

[21] U.N. General Assembly, Twelfth Session, Plenary, *Official Records*, 697th Meeting (Oct. 2, 1957), pp. 235-38.

ready to implement the plan for an atom-free zone in Central Europe in two stages:

In the first stage a ban would be introduced on the production of nuclear weapons on the territories of Poland, Czechoslovakia, the German Democratic Republic, and the German Federal Republic. An obligation would also be undertaken within the proposed zone to renounce the equipping with nuclear weapons of the armies which do not yet possess them as well as the building of relevant installations for them. At the same time, appropriate measures of control would be introduced. This would amount therefore, one may say, to the freezing of nuclear armaments in the proposed zone.

The implementation of the second stage would be preceded by talks on the appropriate reduction of conventional forces. Such a reduction would be effected simultaneously with the complete denuclearization of the zone. Again it would be accompanied by the introduction of appropriate control measures. . . .

Such a modification, however, would meet the suggestions and conclusions resulting from the attitude of many Western politicians, who expressed their opinions in connection with our initiative. . . . This concerns the fears, without considering here whether they are well founded or not, of "upsetting the existing military equilibrium" between the two groups in Europe, and weakening the defenses of the West, fears about the withdrawal of American forces from Europe, and so forth. . . .

Therefore, since many and serious voices have been raised asking for the linking of the denuclearization with reduction of other armaments in Central Europe, we are ready to consider such voices favorably, but under one condition: that the discussions on the two joint subjects will not be protracted endlessly while nuclear armaments come to be included in the arsenals of new armies.[22]

[22] "News Conference Remarks by the Polish Foreign Minister (Rapacki) Regarding an Atom-free Zone in Central Europe (Extracts), Nov. 4, 1958," U.S. Department of State, *Documents on Disarmament, 1945-1959*, Vol. II, Publication 7008 (August 1960), pp. 1217-1219.

When the Soviet Union produced its plan for prevention of surprise attack,[23] the proposals covered the ground of the earlier Soviet suggestions of November 17, 1956,[24] for aerial and ground inspection within a zone in Central Europe, as well as an aerial photography zone in eastern Siberia and the western half of the United States. An aerial photography zone over Iran, Japan, and Okinawa was added. The distinctive feature of this new proposal was that it specifically outlined the tasks, functions, and numbers of ground control posts and the procedures for aerial photography. The initial objective of the new proposals was to achieve an agreement to keep modern types of weapons of mass destruction out of the territory of Germany.

The Soviet Union agrees that within the zone for the establishment of control posts [at railway junctions, major ports, and on main roads] there should be 28 control posts in the territory of countries parties to the Warsaw Treaty (assuming of course that these countries consent), including 6 posts on the territory of the U.S.S.R., provided that there be established 54 posts on the territory of countries parties to the North Atlantic Treaty and the Baghdad Pact including 6 posts on United States territory. . . .

The Soviet Government believes that ground control posts and aerial photography cannot of themselves reduce the danger of surprise attack, particularly with the present types of weapons. This becomes all the more clear if one takes into account the fact that the establishment of ground control posts and the taking of aerial photographs do not affect existing means of surprise attack and would neither lead to a reduction in the number of such means nor to the removal of these devices from certain potentially most dangerous regions.

Ground control posts and aerial photography cannot become effective means of reducing the danger of surprise attack if they are not linked up with steps designed to reduce concentrations of armies of the two opposing politico-military groupings in the potentially most dangerous regions of Europe and to prohibit the sit-

[23] U.N. Doc. A/4078, S/4145, Annex 8, Nov. 28, 1958.
[24] See Chap. 13.

ing of the most dangerous types of weapons of mass destruction, at least to begin with, in part of Central Europe, that is, in both parts of Germany.

Consequently, the Soviet Government proposes that an agreement be reached on: (a) a reduction in the size of foreign armed forces on the territories of European States, and (b) not keeping modern types of weapons of mass destruction in the territories of the Federal Republic of Germany and the German Democratic Republic. . . .

If we adopt as our polestar the desire to work out practical measures for reducing the danger of surprise attack instead of indulging all the time in empty discussions about this danger, then, in the opinion of the Soviet Government, these measures should be accompanied by an undertaking on the part of States possessing nuclear weapons and rockets not to keep atomic, hydrogen and rocket weapons in either part of Germany where the principal armed forces of the North Atlantic Treaty and the Warsaw Treaty come into contact and where even a minor incident carries within it the danger of grave consequences for the world.[25]

During this conference, as previously noted, for the first time, the Soviet Union described the ground control posts and the provisions for aerial inspection which it had been advocating ever since 1956.[26] The Soviet ideas of an inspection system turned out to be considerably narrower than might have been anticipated from the language of the less detailed past proposals commencing with those of June 11, 1946, advanced during the discussions of the Baruch Plan. The ground posts in Central Europe would contain six to eight control officers equally divided in nationality between the NATO-Baghdad-Pact countries and the Warsaw Treaty countries and serviced by the nationals of the country to be inspected. The chief of the post was to be a national of the country that was being inspected. The inspectors were to keep "direct visual watch," assisted by optical and photographic equipment, on the movements of troops and equipment by land and by sea. Local

[25] U.N. Doc. A/4078, S/4145, Annex 8, Nov. 28, 1958, pp. 3-7.
[26] *Ibid.*, pp. 1-9.

communication facilities were to be used, with reports in a "mutually agreed code" to which both sides had access. The air groups, with "representatives of the opposite side" would take pictures of their own territory, which pictures would be processed, interpreted, and studied by a photography centre on which both sides were equally represented.

In effect this was little more than self-inspection. However, it paralleled the proposals the Soviet Union was making in the Tripartite Conference on Test Cessation, and, like them, might have been a base for extended discussions with possible modifications of the initial positions. This detailed system of inspection bore little resemblance to the Soviet broadside of May 10, 1955, calling for an adequate inspection system.[27]

Finally, the Soviet proposals reiterated the completely different Soviet ideas as to the most probable origin of a surprise attack. The West conceived of a surprise attack arising from long-range missiles or manned aircraft carrying thermonuclear weapons flying over the polar areas. The Soviet Union considered that the danger arose from the "fact that there are concentrated in Europe and the Middle East in close proximity to each other the main armed forces of the countries which are parties to the North Atlantic Treaty, the Baghdad Pact, and the Warsaw Treaty and because of that the danger of an armed conflict beginning is especially great." Therefore, the agreement on measures aimed at the prevention of surprise attack should be arrived at as regards that region.[28] In short, the Soviet Union seems to be more interested in avoiding the outbreak of limited war that might flare into general war than protection against massive surprise attack.

By the end of the conference, Foster conceded that "a step-by-step implementation appears, therefore, unavoidable in practice and the selection of particular steps and their timing is a matter for political negotiations."[29] This was drawing close to the Soviet contention that the initial steps to prevent surprise attack should be taken in a single region. The Soviet advocacy of stages in installing the surprise attack measures was drawing toward long-standing Western positions.

[27] See Chap. 12.
[28] U.N. Doc. A/4078, S/4145, Annex 9, Nov. 28, 1958, pp. 1-2.
[29] Ibid., Annex 13, Dec. 17, 1958, p. 11.

The Soviet proposals whether deliberately or by coincidence paralleled in form the Western inspection zone proposals of August 29, 1957.[30] The Soviet Union proposed a big and a little zone in Europe just as the West had proposed a big and a little zone in the Arctic area. The West in 1957 had made agreement on a European inspection zone conditional on Soviet prior acceptance of a polar zone. The Soviet Union now stated "the establishment of an aerial photography zone in the Far East and in the United States of America is only possible if an agreement is reached on establishing ground control posts and an aerial photography zone in Europe and the Middle East."[31] Regardless of whether any agreement might have emerged, this symmetry set the stage for efforts to reach a middle ground between the Western surprise-attack positions of August 29, 1957 and the new Soviet proposals. However, the Western negotiators had no authority to discuss the August 29 proposals, which were deemed political rather than technical.

The Soviet proposals again showed the Soviet concern lest Germany receive nuclear weapons. The Soviet Union was willing to pay a price, though not a high one, in terms of penetration of the iron curtain for some assurance that Germany would not become a nuclear power.[32]

In short, the Soviet Union apparently came to this conference prepared to take steps in the direction of the previous Western proposals only to find that the West was approaching the talks from a completely new angle, paying no attention to the past.

RECESS

Despite the solid accomplishments of these studies from the political standpoint, the Western approach left much to be desired. Foster constantly emphasized the wide difference in approaches between the Soviet Union and the West.[33]

In the intergovernmental communications setting up the conference,

[30] See Chap. 15.
[31] U.N. Doc. A/4078, S/4145, Annex 8, Nov. 28, 1958, p. 5.
[32] *Ibid.*, p. 7.
[33] *Ibid.*, Annex 14, Dec. 18, 1958, pp. 1-9.

the Soviet Union had made it amply clear that it would deal with certain specific measures for arms control and reduction and, at the same time, would discuss the specific safeguards systems required to enforce these measures of reduction. The Western papers in contrast presented a complete safeguards system suitable for a drastic program of disarmament. It is abundantly clear that the Western program would have resulted in a massive breach of Soviet secrecy—so vast a penetration of the Communist world that it might easily have imperiled the continued existence of the Communist regimes. The establishment of such a system would clearly benefit the West far more than the Soviet Union. It is scarcely necessary to repeat that a large portion of the data that the safeguards system would develop in the free world is already known to the Soviet Union. On the other hand, because of the effectiveness of the iron curtain, the West does not have the equivalent knowledge of Soviet installations. In the intergovernmental communications setting up this conference, the Soviet Union had stressed that "settlement of the problem of the prevention of surprise attack is possible, of course, only if the interests of all parties are taken into account in an equitable manner, wherein no single state will be placed in an unequal position from the standpoint of ensuring the interests of its security."[34] Nevertheless, the West was proposing a system that would result in tremendous advantages to the West through the destruction of Soviet secrecy, without the slightest indication of the price the West would be willing to pay for such advantages. The sole answer to this problem of the price the West would pay was the United States suggestion that "at some future date" the Soviet Government might wish to advance its proposals again "in some suitable political forum."[35]

This Western position flouted the experience of twelve years of negotiations on arms control. At the start of the postwar negotiations, the most reasonable Soviet objection to the Baruch Plan ostensibly had been that, while providing international control, it was silent on how

[34] "Premier Khrushchev's Letter to the President," July 2, 1958, Department of State Bulletin, Vol. 39 (Aug. 18, 1958), p. 280.
[35] U.N. Doc. A/4078, S/4145, Annex 14, Dec. 18, 1958, p. 2.

and when international control would lead to the elimination of nuclear weapons. The Soviet leaders constantly expressed the fear that after the establishment of international control, the West might never go ahead with the elimination of nuclear weapons. In 1952, the initial paper submitted by the United States to the United Nations Disarmament Commission, the paper on disclosure and verification of armed forces and armaments, was quite analogous to, though far less technical than, the studies presented to the surprise attack conference. Like these studies, it provided for a safeguards system and postponed the problem of the limitations and reductions of armaments which the safeguards system would seek to enforce. To be sure, Cohen promised future papers on reductions of armed forces and armaments and the Western powers actually submitted such papers to the Disarmament Commission within two months after the disclosure and verification paper. Nevertheless, the prior submission of the paper on safeguards had helped to poison the atmosphere of the Disarmament Commission negotiations.

When in 1954 the Soviet Union abated somewhat its propaganda program and introduced a measure of sanity into the arms control negotiations, Malik effectively and with considerable humor made the point that the West was insisting on safeguards first and reductions and prohibitions at a later date, claiming that the specific date was the Grecian Kalends, which meant the day after doomsday. Within two weeks after the Anglo-French memorandum of June 1954, which first attempted to establish a relationship in time between the installation of a safeguards system and the effective dates of measures for arms limitations, the West had informal notice that the Soviet Union was reconsidering its positions.

All the negotiations from the fall of 1954 through 1957, whether for a program of comprehensive disarmament or for partial confidence building measures of disarmament rested firmly on the concept of a gradual and step-by-step installation of the safeguards system accompanied by specific measures of arms reduction. As Moch phrased this compromise formula, "no disarmament without control; no control without disarmament." In the surprise attack conference the West had in fact reversed itself and gone back to proposing control without disarmament.

This raises the inference that the United States did not have a prepared position prior to the conference. The three chief United States experts had not had any previous experience in the field of political negotiation of arms control. This was also true of the vast army of high-ranking military officers, scientists, and theoretical strategists from the Rand Corporation and elsewhere.

In his official report on the conference, Foster points out: "The Western Experts prepared for the conference in the course of two series of meetings; the first being in Washington, D.C., from 20 October to 25 October, and the second, in Geneva from 6 November to 9 November."[36] It is a testimony to the ability and industry of Foster and his delegation that they were able to do as well as they did without any United States position in advance of the negotiations, and with only twenty days of advance exposure to the problems of a disarmament negotiation.

Foster himself apparently learned the political lesson quickly, but not soon enough to rescue the conference. On January 30, 1959, a month after the end of the conference, in testimony before the Senate Subcommittee on Disarmament, Foster made the following statements:

We also have now a much more precise notion of the difficulty of separating the technical from the political in analyzing the problems of surprise attack and of the need, in pursuing technical discussions on the subject, to have agreement all around on what questions should be answered. . . . We were much impressed by the importance which Soviet representatives attached to secrecy as a military asset. In effect, they seem to believe it enables them to possess a form of "hardening" of their bases which we do not have. Thus they regard any encroachment upon this secrecy as a unilateral disarmament step . . . on their part which must be com-

[36] U.S. Department of State, "Official Report of the United States Delegation to the Conference of Experts . . ." p. 3.

pensated for by other measures. The technical argument which the Soviets used to give respectability to their opposition to measures limited to observation and inspection was that merely to disclose location of all the possible targets and the state of military activity to a would-be aggressor would improve the chances for a successful surprise attack. . . . As you know, the USSR has consistently taken the position that surprise attack measures should include measures of disarmament.[37]

One of Foster's most brilliant and knowledgeable scientific advisers was Dr. Jerome B. Wiesner of Massachusetts Institute of Technology, whose interest in arms control negotiations has continued to the present.[38] The surprise attack negotiations represented his first experience on the firing line. In August 1960, in a publication of *Daedalus*, Dr. Wiesner suggests that Western disarmament proposals generally call on the Soviet Union to accept more inspection than it is prepared to receive without extensive disarmament, while Soviet proposals require the West to accept arms limitation without adequate inspection.

These asymmetrical views are the natural consequence of the security problems faced by each group. . . . If progress is to be made in the future, the negotiating groups will have to be much better prepared and they will have to be determined to respect and consider fairly the actual, and possibly even the imagined, security needs of the other side. Furthermore, both groups must be realistic in their security objectives. That is, each must be prepared to accept some risks in implementing arms-control systems. The objective should be to find security systems less dangerous than the accelerating arms race rather than to achieve a system capable of providing absolute security, an obviously unobtainable goal.[39]

[37] *Disarmament and Foreign Policy*, Hearings before the Senate Committee on Foreign Relations, 86 Cong. 1 sess., pp. 61-63.
[38] Dr. Wiesner was appointed as Science Adviser to President Kennedy on Jan. 11, 1961. *New York Times*, Jan. 12, 1961.
[39] *Daedalus*, Journal of the American Academy of Arts and Sciences (Fall 1960), pp. 916-21.

Clearly, Dr. Wiesner also had second thoughts on the United States approach to the surprise attack conference.

Perhaps the most remarkable feature of this conference was that it did not end with a violent Soviet propaganda blast. Foster must receive much of the credit for this favorable denouement. The final statement of the Soviet delegate, V. V. Kuznetsov, while containing many elements of propaganda, in general was moderate.

One does not have to be experienced in politics or military matters to see that, in view of the mistrust and suspicion among the Governments, the establishment of a control and inspection system, particularly only over the types of weapons the West is interested in, without the parallel application of disarmament measures, cannot be otherwise regarded than as an attempt to take advantage of the control for purposes of reconnaissance. In present conditions, control alone, without measures for increasing confidence and developing co-operation, can only render the situation more acute and contribute to the arms race. In actual fact, a Power, learning in the course of such "universal" control that it is behind its rival, and receiving definite military technical-information, would do everything in its power to catch up. And judging by the policy of the Western Powers this dangerous rivalry can only end in a catastrophe.

It goes without saying that the socialist countries, striving, not for an arms race, but to reach an agreement on disarmament and for the consolidation of world peace, cannot agree with such so-called "control," which can only help a would-be aggressor and which would increase the danger of a surprise attack.

. . . The tactics of concentrating on gathering military information and establishing a control system which would facilitate the gathering of such information, are by no means new, although the Western representatives did try to put them forward as a "fresh" approach to the problem of preventing a surprise attack.

The problem of preventing a surprise attack is the problem of the preservation of peace. Its solution is in the interests of all peoples.

As regards the socialist countries, they will from now on strive with might and main to see that the problem of preventing a surprise attack finds a positive solution.[40]

Instead of terminating the conference as a result of the impasse "the participants at the Conference agreed to suspend the meetings of the Conference in view of the Christmas and New Year holidays and to report to Governments on the work of the Conference. The participants express the hope that discussion on the problem of preventing surprise attacks would be resumed as early as possible."[41]

This Soviet attitude was a vast improvement on all previous Soviet responses to Western proposals dealing solely with safeguards and controls. The unaccustomed Soviet moderation leads to the surmise that the West may have lost an opportunity for clarifying and narrowing East-West differences.

[40] U.N. Doc. A/4078, S/4145, Annex 15, Dec. 18, 1958, pp. 11-13.
[41] *Ibid.*, p. 3.

XIX

The Nuclear Test
Cessation Conferences

THE SERIES OF MEETINGS dealing with the problem of cessation of
nuclear testing commencing in July 1958 and still continuing represent
by far the most important development in the field of international arms
control negotiations since World War II. For the first time, the Soviet
Union and the West have embarked on the precise task of drafting a
treaty. For the first time, apparently unresolved differences did not
disrupt the meetings but resulted in changes of approach permitting
further progress. To a greater degree than heretofore, the negotiations
proceeded independently of the outside temperature of East-West
relationships. Even if the conferences never result in any East-West
agreement, they have already produced a greater understanding between Soviet and Western scientists and a fuller appreciation all over
the world of the technical problems of arms control. They have
spawned a vast amount of extra-governmental activity to help solve the
technical problems of arms control, including the useful "Pugwash"
conferences of Soviet and Western scientists[1] and the great array of

[1] The "Pugwash Conferences" refer to a series of meetings attended by scientists
from the West and from the Soviet Union. The first meeting took place in July
1957, in Pugwash, Nova Scotia, at the estate of Mr. Cyrus Eaton, who has financed
three out of the five conferences held up to this time in Austria and Canada. The
sixth took place in Moscow in November 1960. According to three leading Ameri-

488

technical studies undertaken under the auspices of United States educational foundations. Most important, the prognosis for the ultimate success of the conferences remains good.

More than four hundred meetings have taken place to date in these conferences. The official records, which are now declassified, run to many thousands of pages. It is impossible at this time to distill the essentials from this vast record since the determination of what is essential will depend on the direction of future negotiations.

It would likewise be brash and probably impossible to suggest an answer to the complex question of whether the discontinuance of nuclear testing is in the security interests of the United States. The conflicting arguments have been forcefully presented both in technical and popular form. As Dr. Leo Szilard points out: "Because of the prevailing secrecy, it is impossible to appraise the disadvantages of the cessation of bomb tests."[2] Without such an appraisal, it is impossible to attempt the correlation of political and technical considerations essential to any meaningful opinion on the best Western position in the negotiations.

This study can be useful in pointing out (1) the extent to which the issues and attitudes of past negotiations persisted in the far more extensive and detailed test cessation negotiations; (2) the changes in past positions and attitudes that appeared when the negotiators found themselves confronted with specific treaty language; (3) the applicability of the experience in the test cessation negotiations to other arms control negotiations.

It is also possible to make *suggestions,* based on *assumptions* con-

---

can scientists, Harrison Brown, Bentley Glass and Eugene Rabinowitch, members of the "U.S. Pugwash Continuing Committee," the name "Pugwash Conference" has become "widely known in America, Europe and the Soviet Union as designating a spontaneous, independent, and nonpartisan activity of scientists concerned with the survival of mankind in the atomic age." However, the scientists, while grateful for Mr. Eaton's financial aid, make it clear that Mr. Eaton's involvement in these scientific conferences can be only that of one of the guests, and "not of a sponsor or active participant." Excerpts from a letter to the editor of the *Washington Post and Times-Herald* (Sept. 24, 1960).
[2] Leo Szilard, "To Stop or Not to Stop," *Bulletin of Atomic Scientists,* Vol. 16 (March 1960), p. 83.

cerning presently unanswerable issues, the validity of which will depend entirely on the correctness of the assumptions.[3]

CHIEF EVENTS

This sketch of the chief events of the long and complicated series of conferences is merely the prelude to a more detailed treatment of the most important issues with political implications.

The Conference of Experts to Study the Possibility of Detecting Violations of a Possible Agreement on Suspension of Nuclear Tests met at Geneva on July 1, 1958, and completed its work on the United States and the Soviet Union, each government named a principal expert to serve as chairman of the delegation: Dr. James B. Fisk, Executive Vice President of Bell Telephone Laboratories, served for the United States and Dr. Evgeny Fedorov, a distinguished Soviet geophysicist, served for the Soviet Union. Both delegations included experts and advisers from a number of states. The Western delegation had advisers from Canada, France, and the United Kingdom, and the Soviet delegation had advisers from Czechoslovakia, Poland, and Rumania. The conference reached agreement on the technical feasibility of monitoring an agreement for the suspension of nuclear weapons testing.[4] The report described in detail the effects of nuclear explosions in the atmosphere, at high altitudes, under water, and under ground, and the methods of detecting with existing technology such explosions and distinguishing them from natural phenomena.[5]

[3] For a more complete narrative of the negotiations see "Geneva Conference on the Discontinuance of Nuclear Weapons Tests," by William J. Gehron, U.S. Department of State Bulletin, Vol. 43 (Sept. 26, 1960), pp. 482-97. For a thorough analysis of Soviet and Western positions see U.S. Senate Committee on Foreign Relations, Conference on the Discontinuance of Nuclear Weapons Tests, Analysis of Progress and Positions of the Participating Parties, October 1958-August 1960, 86 Cong. 2 sess.
[4] United States Participation in the United Nations, Report by the President to the Congress for the Year 1958, Department of State Publication 6852 (1959), pp. 3-10. Cited hereafter as U.S. Participation in the U.N., Report (with year).
[5] "Report of the Conference of Experts to Study the Possibility of Detecting Violations of a Possible Agreement on the Suspension of Nuclear Tests, Aug. 21, 1958," Department of State Bulletin, Vol. 39 (Sept. 22, 1958), pp. 453-62.

After analysis of the statistical data, the Western and Soviet dele-gations each outlined a system designed to identify nuclear explosions exceeding 1 kiloton (TNT equivalent energy). The Hiroshima explo-sion had a force of 20 kilotons. The detection of explosions of this intensity in the atmosphere or under water presented no problem. There were difficulties in detecting such explosions at high altitudes and far greater problems of underground detection. Because of these latter problems, the conference determined to work out a system under which a five kiloton explosion (one fourth of Hiroshima) would in some circumstances be the minimum detectable yield.

Accordingly, the conference recommended a network of 170 land-based control posts and ten ship-based control posts. The land-based control posts would be distributed as follows: North America, 24; Europe, 6; Asia, 37; Australia, 7; South America, 16; Africa, 16; Ant-arctica, 4; islands 60. These posts would be supplemented by regular flights of air-sampling aircraft along the peripheries of the oceans and by special flights to investigate suspicious events. This system would probably detect and identify explosions of one kiloton yield on the surface of the earth, in the open ocean, and at altitudes up to ten kilometers. It would detect explosions of this yield at higher altitudes but would not always distinguish them from natural phenomena.

The problem arose in connection with underground explosions. The system would probably record seismic signals from explosions of one kiloton yield, but would not identify whether the signals arose from earthquakes or explosions. However, for signals of five kiloton equiva-lent energy, the system in 90 per cent of the cases could identify whether the source of the seismic wave was an earthquake or an ex-plosion. For the remaining 10 per cent of such seismic signals—varying from 20 to 100 natural events annually, on-site inspection would be required to determine whether a nuclear explosion had taken place.

The conference then made certain general suggestions for an inter-national control organ to carry out the necessary activities on a world-wide scale.

The United States and the Soviet Union accepted the report of the experts and on August 22, the day after the submission of the report, President Eisenhower suggested a meeting of the three states with nuclear weapons to negotiate an agreement to suspend nuclear weapons testing and to establish an international control system on the basis of the experts' report. At the same time, the President expressed the willingness of the United States to suspend testing "on a basis of reciprocity" on a year-by-year basis, provided that: (a) "the agreed inspection system is installed and working effectively"; and provided further that (b) "satisfactory progress is being made in reaching agreement on and implementing major and substantial arms control measures such as the United States has long sought."[6]

After some intergovernmental correspondence, it was agreed that the conference should convene at Geneva on October 31, 1958. The conference started badly as a result of detection of three Soviet nuclear tests during its first week. A White House statement deplored this situation and noted that the United States thereby considered itself relieved of its self-imposed obligation not to test.[7] Apparently, however, these Soviet tests were last-minute efforts to beat the deadline of October 31, which for unexplained technical reasons were delayed. Since the first week of November 1958, none of the parties to the conference apparently have made further nuclear tests.

The United States named as its chief delegate to this conference one of its ablest and most experienced negotiators, the Honorable James J. Wadsworth, Deputy United States Representative to the United Nations. The relatively small delegation included representatives of the State Department, the Atomic Energy Commission, and the military services with long experience in arms control negotiations as well as high technical qualifications. The British and Soviet delegations also utilized some of their ablest and most experienced negotiators. The British delegate was the Minister of State for Foreign Affairs, David Ormsby-Gore, who had represented the United Kingdom in the subcommittee of the Disarmament Commission in the summer of 1957. The experience of the chief Soviet delegate, Semyon Tsarapkin, went back to the 1946 meetings which considered the Baruch Plan. Tsarapkin was assisted by Usachev, who for many years has acted as an adviser

[6] U.S. Participation in the U.N., Report 1958, p. 11.
[7] Ibid., p. 12.

to the Soviet delegations dealing with arms control. The relative success of the negotiations may stem in part from the fact that in this negotiation, all the participants appointed chief delegates with vast experience in this field.

The tripartite conference, except for occasional recesses, has been in continuous session since October 31, 1958. The recesses generally come at times when further progress of the negotiations seems hopeless without shifts in position. At least until the summer of 1960, sooner or later the shifts have materialized that permitted further forward movement with a slight change in direction.[8]

The first month of meetings reproduced the by now familiar East-West debate on agenda. The Soviet Union once again sought an agenda, the first item of which was to prohibit nuclear tests. After agreement on the first item, under the second item, a "protocol" could set up the international control system.[9] This was the familiar technique of all Soviet negotiations, asserted with slight variations, from

[8] Chronologically, the periods of meetings and recess were as follows:

Meetings	Recess
1. Oct. 31 to Dec. 19, 1958	Dec. 20, 1958 to Jan. 4, 1959
2. Jan. 5 to March 19, 1959	March 20 to April 12, 1959
3. April 13 to May 8, 1959	May 9 to June 7, 1959
4. June 8 to Aug. 26, 1959	Aug. 27 to Oct. 26, 1959
5. Oct. 27 to Dec. 19, 1959	Dec. 20, 1959 to Jan. 11, 1960
6. Jan. 12 to April 14, 1960	April 15 to April 24, 1960
7. April 25 to May 12, 1960	May 13 to May 26, 1960
8. May 27 to Aug. 22, 1960	Aug. 23 to Sept. 26, 1960
9. Sept. 27 to Dec. 5, 1960	Dec. 6, 1960 to March 20, 1961

The meetings of the conference itself have been supplemented by three meetings of "experts" of the three participating states. (1) meeting of experts on high altitude detection problem—June 22 to July 10, 1959; (2) meeting of experts on underground detection—November 25 to December 18, 1959; (3) meeting of experts to make plans for underground test research program—May 11 to May 27, 1960.

U.S. Department of State, "Key Issues and Background Geneva Negotiations on the Discontinuance of Nuclear Weapons Tests" (published periodically from March 10, 1959 to June 1, 1960). See also William J. Gehron, "Geneva Conference on the Discontinuance of Nuclear Weapons Tests," Department of State Bulletin, Vol. 43 (Sept. 26, 1960), pp. 482-97.

[9] Ibid., p. 483.

1946 through 1952. The prohibitions and limitations must precede the controls. The agenda should be used to predetermine the substantive result. After a month, the Soviet Union agreed to enter into an immediate discussion of the control system and the conference began to discuss specific treaty provisions. Before the Christmas recess, it reached agreement on four relatively noncontroversial treaty provisions.

The next set of obstacles appeared at the first meeting after the Christmas recess. Data from underground explosions carried out in Nevada in the fall of 1958 disclosed that the method of distinguishing earthquakes from underground explosions recommended in the experts' report was much less effective than previously estimated. This would mean that a greater number of earthquakes would be indistinguishable from explosions and either a greater number of on-site inspections or a greater number of inspection posts or both would be necessary for an effective system. At this time, the Soviet Union was unwilling to convene a new session of experts to discuss the technical problem.

At the same time, the discussion of treaty provisions reached an impasse over three issues:

1. *The veto.* The Soviet Union insisted that the three initial parties to the treaty (the United States, the United Kingdom, and the Soviet Union) should have a veto over all substantive decisions.

2. *On-site inspections.* The Soviet Union insisted on a right of veto over a decision to conduct an on-site inspection and also that the teams to conduct such inspections be organized on an *ad hoc* basis and composed of nationals of the country to be inspected.

3. *Control post staffing.* The Soviet Union demanded that personnel of the control posts be composed of nationals of the country to be inspected with one or two "observers" from the outside. This was virtually self-inspection.[10] These three Soviet demands obviously would reduce to zero the value of the control machinery. On all of these matters, shifts took place that permitted the continuance of discussions.

The first significant modification came from the West. On January 19, 1959 the United States and United Kingdom announced that con-

[10] *Ibid.*, pp. 486-87.

tinued suspension of nuclear tests was no longer dependent on progress on other disarmament measures but was conditional only on the installation and satisfactory operation of a controls system.[11] Thus the cessation of nuclear testing was separated from the Western "package" disarmament proposals of August 29, 1957.

On April 13, in order to break the impasse, President Eisenhower in a letter to Premier Khrushchev suggested a ban solely of tests in the atmosphere which could be maintained by a simplified detection system not requiring most of the controversial controls that had created the impasse. This limited agreement would allay "the fears of unrestricted resumption of nuclear testing with attendant additions to levels of radioactivity."[12]

On April 23, Khrushchev rejected this suggestion but suggested that "the possibility of concluding an agreement on the cessation of nuclear tests would be brought closer if we reached an understanding to determine in advance for each side the number of annual trips of inspection teams to the site."[13]

This opened a door to discussion to resolve not only the problem of on-site inspections but also to incorporate into the controls system the new data on detection of underground explosions. On May 14, after some further prodding, Khrushchev made some vague suggestions to relax the veto on other questions relating to the operation of the control organization. At the same time, Khrushchev consented to a further technical conference on detection of explosions at high altitudes.[14] Khrushchev's initiative, to repeat, merely opened the door to some progress. By the time of the recess at the end of August, the conference had moved slightly forward.

The meeting of experts on detection of high altitude explosions had recommended placing in orbit some six earth satellites equipped with counters that could detect the radiation from nuclear explosions in

[11] *Ibid.*, pp. 483-84.
[12] "The President to Premier Khrushchev," Department of State *Bulletin*, Vol. 40 (May 18, 1959), pp. 704-05.
[13] "Premier Khrushchev to the President," *ibid.*, p. 705.
[14] "Premier Khrushchev to the President," *ibid.* (June 8, 1959), pp. 826-27.

outer space.[15] The United States accepted the experts' recommendations as a correct technical assessment at that time. The Soviet Union accepted the conclusions of the experts.

The Soviet Union had reduced the number of issues in the control organization where it insisted on a veto, but approval of the budget would still require a Soviet affirmative vote. The Soviet Union would raise the number of foreigners at control posts to ten or eleven, thus coming closer to a compromise Western formula for staffing the posts with one third Soviet personnel, one third United Kingdom and United States personnel, and one third from other countries.[16]

The United States had submitted on June 12 the findings of a United States "Panel on Seismic Improvement," which suggested modifications of the original technical conference report to permit improved detection of underground explosions in the light of the new data. The original safeguards system, even when supplemented in accordance with the Soviet suggestion by a small agreed quota of on-site inspections not subject to Soviet veto, would go only a short distance toward solving this impasse on methods of detecting underground explosions. The Soviet Union still refused further technical discussions on detecting underground explosions.

During the discussions in the winter and spring of 1959, agreement had been reached on the texts of thirteen additional noncontroversial articles of the treaty, making a total of seventeen agreed articles.

In summary, by October 27, 1959, when the meetings resumed after a late summer recess, the control system had been expanded to permit better detection of high-altitude explosions; also the differences on the subjects of the veto and the composition of the control posts were narrowing. On the basic problem of detecting underground tests with its related issue of on-site inspections, the differences had also narrowed

[15] Gehron, "Geneva Conference on the Discontinuance of Nuclear Weapons Tests," ibid., Vol. 43 (Sept. 26, 1960), pp. 482-97.
[16] U.S. Department of State, "Background on Geneva Negotiations for the Discontinuance of Nuclear Weapons Tests," Addendum, Aug. 28, 1959. See also Gehron, "Geneva Conference on the Discontinuance of Nuclear Weapon Tests," Department of State Bulletin, pp. 487-88; U.S. Senate Committee on Foreign Relations, Conference on the Discontinuance of Nuclear Weapons Tests, p. 42.

slightly with the Soviet agreement to permit a specified quota.[17] However, the gap was still too wide to be readily bridged.

The meetings from October 27 until the Christmas recess produced two significant developments. The Soviet Union at last consented to a meeting of experts to analyze the problems involved in the detection of underground tests. The meeting resulted in a few agreed improvements in the detection machinery. In the main, however, the political overtones of the meeting prevented any extensive revision of the 1958 Geneva technical conference conclusions. The Soviet scientists were almost entirely negative in their approach and on the surface paid no attention even to authenticated data. This attitude was anticipated. The Western data necessarily involved some shift in the Soviet political position, a shift that was far beyond the authority of the scientists. The technical conference at least succeeded in conveying to Soviet scientists the Western data and the justification for Western conclusions from the data, a necessary step in the mysterious process of Soviet policy making. The second development at this time was the so-called Soviet "package proposal" of December 13, 1959, which consolidated the piecemeal concessions the Soviet Union had made up to this time on the issues of the veto, the composition of the control commission and control posts, on-site inspections and several less important matters.[18]

On the composition of the control commission, the United States and the United Kingdom had expressed a preference for a control commission—the body that would oversee the work of the entire control system—comprised of the three original parties and four others selected by the general conference. Specifically, this would mean adding one ally of the United States and the United Kingdom, one ally of the Soviet Union, and two neutrals (3-2-2). The new Soviet formula called for a commission comprised of the United States and the United Kingdom plus an ally, the Soviet Union plus two allies, and one neutral nation (3-3-1).

[17] U.S. Department of State, "Background on the October-December 1959 Sessions of the Geneva Negotiations for the Discontinuance of Nuclear Weapons Tests," Jan. 15, 1960.
[18] U.S. Senate Committee on Foreign Relations, *Conference on the Discontinuance of Nuclear Weapons Tests,* p. 5.

The Soviet Union's package was presented on the basis that, if the United States and the United Kingdom would accept its formula for the composition of the control commission, it would accept the Western control post staffing pattern (1/3-1/3-1/3) and would also give up its demand for a veto over budget matters.[19]

This "concession" must be interpreted in connection with a previous three-power agreement that a two-thirds vote would be required for decisions on the budget. Acceptance of the Soviet 3-3-1 formula would mean that one member of either the Soviet bloc or the Western group would have to join with the other to muster the necessary two-thirds vote. Therefore, this aspect of the Soviet proposal would turn an unqualified veto into a "hidden" veto. Thus, the Soviet "package" did not solve the problem of the veto.

Furthermore, on decisions requiring only a majority vote, the neutral member of the commission would continuously be in the unenviable position of casting the deciding vote between East and West. Also, a control commission with only one out of seven members independent of the Western allies and the Soviet bloc would scarcely be a representative group to govern a world-wide control system.[20] The package proposal, by indicating the Soviet willingness to consider the Western formula for staffing of control posts, somewhat narrowed the differences on that problem that had caused the impasse.

When the conference reconvened on January 12, 1960 after the Christmas recess, the United States sought to center the discussion on the technical data concerning detection of underground explosions developed at the conference of experts. The Soviet Union on the other hand focused attention on its package proposal probably because no political decisions had as yet emerged from the Kremlin in connection with the new technical data.[21]

On February 11, the United States, supported by the United King-

[19] *Ibid.*, pp. 21, 22, 46.
[20] The Soviet proposal was also unsatisfactory in regard to the staffing pattern in that it called for subdivision of the one third of the staff not furnished by the original parties to the treaty into ninths—one ninth, allies of the United States and the United Kingdom; one ninth, allies of the Soviet Union; and one ninth unaligned.
[21] U.S. Department of State, "Background on Geneva Negotiations for the Discontinuance of Nuclear Weapons Tests," Addendum III, June 1, 1960, p. 1.

dom, proposed a phased treaty that would bypass many of the problems creating the impasse in the negotiations. In its essence, the treaty would end immediately all nuclear weapons tests where effective controls could be readily established. This would include all tests in the atmosphere, the only type of tests involving possible major health perils; all tests in the oceans; all tests in space to the greatest height at which effective controls are possible; and all underground tests above a seismic magnitude of 4.75 (corresponding to a yield of 19 kilotons under Ranier coupling—an explosion tamped in dirt). The threshold was expressed in terms of signal strength rather than yield as a result of agreement between Soviet and Western scientists.[22]

The United States further suggested a research program to improve detection machinery and a gradual lowering of the threshold with improvements in detection methods. The United States estimated that the 4.75 threshold would require twenty on-site inspections annually in the Soviet Union to provide adequate deterrence against deliberate violations. The Soviet Union immediately rejected this approach, but in its response, broadened its criteria for determining events that would automatically entitle the West to utilize its quota of on-site inspections with the Soviet Union.[23]

On March 19, however, the Soviet Union radically shifted its position. In the main, it accepted the United States proposal for a phased treaty, specifying, however, that the treaty itself must in addition to prohibiting tests above the threshold call for a moratorium of "four to five years" on tests below the threshold. The results of the joint research program undertaken in the meantime would determine whether the moratorium should continue.[24] The ending of tests above the threshold under the proposal had depended on resolution of several of the key divergences that had created the original impasse. The new Soviet suggestions unfortunately did not deal with these matters.

President Eisenhower and Prime Minister Macmillan after their Camp David meeting on March 29 moved one step toward the new Soviet position. They announced that the United States and the United

---

[22] Gehron "Geneva Conference on the Discontinuance of Nuclear Weapons Tests." Department of State *Bulletin*, p. 485.
[23] *Ibid.*
[24] *Ibid.*

Kingdom would agree that as soon as the phased treaty had been signed and arrangements had been made for a coordinated research program to improve control methods for events below seismic magnitude 4.75, they would be ready to institute a voluntary moratorium of agreed duration on nuclear tests below 4.75. However, the moratorium would not be instituted until settlement of the other outstanding divergences.[25]

As a result of this announcement and a favorable Soviet reply, a third session of the experts of the three powers convened on May 11 to exchange information on the research programs. The conference itself recessed on May 12 for the duration of the disastrous summit conference in Paris.

The meetings of the conference in June and July, after the summit debacle, achieved some minor progress. The Soviet government accepted a British proposal dealing with certain details of staffing the central organization. Also, the Soviet representative for the first time suggested a specific number of veto-free on-site inspections—three annually, a preposterously low figure. Tsarapkin rejected the United States proposals that the out-of-date nuclear devices that would be used in the research program should be open for safeguards inspection so as to assure that they would not be used clandestinely for weapons development. Since the Soviet Union was not interested in any further underground tests, it would not contribute to the pool. However, Tsarapkin saw a positive factor in United States recognition that the nuclear devices should be open to inspection.[26] In general, after the summit upheaval, the Soviet representatives did not make even minor shifts to bridge any of the remaining gaps between the positions; nor did they recede from previous positions nor perceptibly stiffen their stands. Most important, the Soviet Union did not break up this particular negotiation.

This sketchy narrative of the complicated principal events is a necessary prelude to the more thorough analysis of the most important issues with political overtones.

[25] *Ibid.*, pp. 485-86.
[26] U.S. Senate Committee on Foreign Relations, *Conference on the Discontinuance of Nuclear Weapons Tests*, pp. 36-48.

CHIEF ISSUES WITH

POLITICAL IMPLICATIONS

The Subcommittee on Disarmament of the Senate Foreign Relations Committee lists twenty-five unresolved issues.[27] An analysis of the past arms control negotiations is particularly relevant to problems raised by one issue that has already been resolved and by five that are unresolved. The first broad issue that emerged in the test cessation negotiations was whether there should be technical discussions at all. Even though the convening of the original technical conference apparently answered the question in the affirmative, the Soviet Union on several occasions attempted to reverse that answer. The next three issues that emerged simultaneously in the tripartite conference were the combined technical and political issues of the composition of the control commission and control posts, the veto, and the matter of on-site inspections. A fifth important issue stemmed from the necessity of including within the conference the newly discovered data showing added difficulties in detecting underground explosions. A large portion of the conference was devoted to the various efforts to surmount this problem. A sixth major issue has arisen in connection with a joint research program of underground nuclear explosions to improve methods of detection. This issue has emerged too recently to permit political evaluation.

The discussion of these specific issues makes possible a consideration of the broader problems implicit in this and all other negotiations with the Soviet Union—the Soviet and Western motivations. These in turn raise the questions of greatest importance to the United States. Should the United States support a test ban? Does the United States today support a test ban? These questions are unanswerable on the basis of present information. However, an analysis of the negotiations does shed light on some of the considerations to be included in any answer.

[27] *Ibid.,* p. 3.

Technical Negotiations

The initial technical conference had reached agreed conclusions with comparative ease. The first broad issue confronting the tripartite discussions was whether the negotiations to end nuclear tests should proceed through technical discussions. The very existence of the conference on its face required an affirmative answer to this problem. Nevertheless, it must be pointed out that Khrushchev accepted technical discussions only as a last resort.[28]

In the General Assembly of 1958, the Soviet Union gave full support to an Indian resolution that would have ended nuclear tests regardless of whether a satisfactory system could be evolved to monitor the obligation. If the Soviet Union had been successful in its efforts to obtain passage of such a resolution by the General Assembly, it is naive to suppose that this series of negotiations would have gone any further. At the opening of the tripartite conference, the Soviet Union again showed its preference for securing the ending of nuclear tests without a monitoring system. Its agenda had as its first item "Agreement on the Ending of Nuclear Tests." Only after such an agreement had been reached, would it have been possible to proceed to the second item, which called for a protocol to the initial agreement ending tests which would provide a monitoring system.[29] Again, it is improbable that the Soviet Union would have taken any interest in setting up the monitoring system if it could have achieved its objective of ending the tests without a monitoring system.

This Soviet tactic harked back to the original negotiations in 1946 in connection with the Baruch Plan for the international control of atomic energy. At that time, the Soviet Union insisted that control must come through treaties. The initial treaty would provide for the prohibition of nuclear weapons. A subsequent treaty would provide the control system. The Soviet Union at that time had specifically stated

[28] "Premier Khrushchev to the President," April 23, 1959, Department of State Bulletin, Vol. 40 (June 8, 1959), pp. 826-27.
[29] U.S. Participation in the U.N., Report 1958, pp. 13, 23.

that the prohibition of nuclear weapons must continue even though no agreement was ever reached on the later treaty for the control system. This tactic also recalled the procedure in arms control negotiations followed consistently by the Soviet Union from 1946 through 1952 of attempting to secure a substantive decision through a procedural device. The Soviet Union in this case was attempting to secure an end of nuclear testing through an agenda that permitted discussion of the monitoring system only after agreement that nuclear testing must end.

The outcome of this controversy forcefully reiterates certain patterns of Soviet policy that have carried through all the years of arms control negotiations. In broadest terms the pattern can be described as follows: the preferred position of the Soviet Union is to secure in arms control negotiations the unilateral disarmament of the West. This could best be achieved by a paper agreement for disarmament unaccompanied by the safeguards machinery to ensure observance of the commitment. If the Soviet Union could not secure its preferred position of disarmament without safeguards, it was ready to proceed toward safeguarded disarmament and seemed to prefer an arms control agreement containing safeguards to an unrestricted armaments race. Applying the pattern to this specific issue, the Soviet Union's preference was to end tests without control machinery. However, it was ready to go forward toward an agreement with control machinery and preferred such an agreement to the resumption of testing.

The first road block of vast dimensions appeared in three overlapping Soviet suggestions submitted simultaneously in the discussions of the structure and methods of operation of the control commission: the composition of the control commission and control posts, the voting formula in the control commission and the problem of on-site inspections. Much of the background material is the same for all three issues. Nevertheless, the issues are sufficiently distinct so that they must be discussed separately. The reason for simultaneous emergence of all three issues lies in the fact that for the first time the Soviet Union was moving from generalities into specifics of writing a treaty.

Composition of Control Commission and
Control Posts

The Soviet Union almost at the outset of the discussions proposed that all supervisory, technical, and service personnel at control posts be nationals of the country in which the post is located. One or two foreign observers would be permitted at the control post with no authority over the operation of the post. This in effect was self-inspection and was an apparent reversal of Soviet positions. As early as June 11, 1947, the Soviet Union during the discussions of the Baruch Plan had proposed "an international commission for atomic energy control" which would "have its own inspectorial apparatus."

Terms and organizational principles of international control of atomic energy, and also composition, rights and obligations of the International Control Commission, as well as provisions on the basis of which it shall carry out its activities, shall be determined by a special international convention on atomic energy control, which is to be concluded in accordance with the convention on the prohibition of atomic weapons.[30]

The Soviet Union had on several occasions in later years reaffirmed its support for its June 11 proposals and indeed had gone beyond these proposals at later dates. Yet when confronted with the task of drafting a specific treaty, the Soviet Union was proposing a machinery that could scarcely be described under the rubric "international control." The closest parallel in past negotiations to this type of machinery was Gromyko's statement in the summer of 1946 in the United Nations Atomic Energy Commission that the only way to ensure a convention prohibiting atomic weapons was for the individual states to pass domestic legislation.[31] The Soviet Union had almost immediately altered this earlier position as a result of the meeting of Foreign Ministers in November 1946. Now it was back again.

[30] U.N. Doc. AEC/24 (June 11, 1947).
[31] See Chap. 4.

On May 10, 1955, the Soviet Union, in principle at least, had gone considerably further in the direction of a truly international safeguards system by suggesting the establishment of an "international control organ" that should have the right and power "to exercise supervision, including inspection on a continuing basis, to the extent necessary to ensure implementation of the convention by all states."[32] This was certainly an even further cry from the limited and spineless machinery the Soviet Union was now suggesting.

During one of the Pugwash conferences of Soviet and Western scientists, Dr. E. K. Fedorov, the chief Soviet expert in the test cessation conferences, explained the background for the Soviet control proposals:

The complete absurdity of putting the control organization in the position of a super-government, acting on the territories of sovereign states irrespective of their will and desire, is obvious. It is hardly necessary to mention the obvious fact that any kind of activity of the control organization on the territory of any country may be conducted only so far as the governments of these countries agree to it, and more than that, actively support it.[33]

This philosophy as well as the Soviet proposal was inconsistent with the declared policies of the Soviet Government in support of international control. This inconsistency could have only two explanations —either the change in top policy was not genuine or the change at the top did not penetrate very far into the monolithic structure of Soviet bureaucracy. The experience of this negotiation seems to support the latter explanation. On this and other issues, Khrushchev himself moved slowly but steadily into positions more consistent with the later Soviet policy positions.

The Western compromise formula for staffing the control posts with one third United States or United Kingdom personnel, one third Soviet personnel and one third from other countries could itself

---

[32] *Soviet News*, No. 3162 (May 11, 1955).
[33] Dr. E. K. Fedorov, "The Agreement on the Cessation of Nuclear Tests must be Concluded without Delay!" *Bulletin of Atomic Scientists*, Vol. 15 (October 1959), p. 332.

scarcely be decribed as "international control." Likewise both the Soviet and the Western proposals for the composition of the control commission are far from the United Nations concept of an international control organ. The Soviet Union proposed a commission of seven, consisting of the United States, the United Kingdom, and one ally; the Soviet Union plus two allies; and one neutral nation. The United States and the United Kingdom had also suggested a commission of seven members: The United States, the United Kingdom, and one ally; the Soviet Union and one ally; and two neutrals.[34] The experience in the negotiation of the statute of the International Atomic Energy Agency in 1955 and 1956 made it amply clear that an international conference would never willingly accept either of these formulas for a control commission.

Thus, the Soviet Union and, to a lesser extent, the United States and the United Kingdom were coming close to the original Roosevelt-Churchill-Stalin concept of the "Four Policemen" who would maintain order in the postwar world. The Soviet Union had wholeheartedly accepted this concept during World War II, and had reluctantly moved toward the broader concept of a United Nations. Despite apparent changes in Soviet policy, the detailed program was still facing in the direction of the earlier concept which once again emerged into daylight when, for the first time, the Soviet leaders began discussing a precise program rather than general principles.

The Veto

The Soviet Union originally insisted on a veto in the control commission for the United States, the United Kingdom, and the Soviet Union on all decisions on matters of substance. On the surface, it was no longer adhering to the concession originally made in February 1947, that the control commission to supervise the international control of atomic energy could act by majority vote. In fact, the Soviet position in 1959 was substantially identical to its 1947 position. The Soviet

[34] U.S. Department of State, "Key Issues and Background, Geneva Negotiations on the Discontinuance of Nuclear Weapons Tests," March 10, 1959, p. 1.

position in 1947 was presented in the form of amendments and additions to the first report of the United Nations Atomic Energy Commission.[35] Essentially, the Soviet 1947 proposal was that the international control commission should possess powers and be charged "with responsibility necessary for the effective implementation of the terms of the convention and for the prompt discharge of its day-to-day duties. Its rights, powers and responsibilities should be clearly established and defined by the convention." The convention would act by majority vote "in appropriate cases."[36] Although these 1947 proposals were never very clear, they could probably be interpreted to permit more decisions without a right of veto than the initial bargaining proposals in 1959. However, in 1959, it did not take long for the Soviet Union to modify its opening position.[37] Most of the argumentation over the next few months arose not over whether the Soviet Union should have a general right of veto, but whether the right of veto should extend to decisions concerning the budget and decisions to dispatch teams to investigate events that could be nuclear explosions. On the latter point, the Soviet positions in 1947 and 1959 were identical. The Soviet Union in 1947 never conceded that the control commission would have the right to investigate clandestine or unreported facilities.[38]

Any deterioration of the Soviet position on the veto between 1947 and 1959 was confined to the question of a decision concerning the budget. The Soviet Union had a precedent for this position. In the International Atomic Energy Agency negotiations in 1955 and 1956, the Soviet Union had initially insisted that decisions on the budget should require a three-fourths majority of both the membership of the International Agency and the board of governors.[39] Under the formula for

[35] See Chap. 4.
[36] U.N. Security Council, First Year, *Official Records*, "Soviet Proposal Introduced in the Security Council: Draft Amendments and Additions to the First Report of the United Nations Atomic Energy Commission, Feb. 18, 1947," Supplement No. 7, pp. 63-68.
[37] U.S. Senate Committee on Foreign Relations, *Conference on the Discontinuance of Nuclear Weapons Tests*, p. 51.
[38] See Chap. 4.
[39] "Note from Soviet Minister of Foreign Affairs to American Embassy, Oct. 1, 1955," U.S. Department of State, Press Release 527 (Oct. 6, 1956), pp. 22-24.

composition of the board of governors, this in fact would have ensured a Soviet veto. In the negotiations on the International Atomic Energy Agency, the Soviet Union modified its original position after much negotiation, and the pattern of the negotiations apparently repeated itself in the negotiations on test cessation.

While the Soviet Union was thus taking a slightly more rigid position on the veto than twelve years earlier, the Western powers had also on occasions modified their positions on the veto. In 1957 the Western powers had proposed that all control and inspection services for the entire Western program of disarmament be within the framework of an international control organization established under the aegis of the United Nations Security Council, which would include as its executive organ a board of control having a voting formula requiring unanimity among the five members of the subcommittee—in other words, a veto. This position strangely enough found its way into the August 29, 1957 package proposals.[40] It never received much discussion during the subcommittee meetings and in retrospect should be viewed as an abberation of Western policy. It may have influenced the Soviet Union in its decision to press for a veto.

In the light of the historical background, the Soviet position on the veto was not too discouraging. The Soviet Union had consistently contended that the Western powers through their control of the majority of votes in the United Nations have their own veto. It was willing to accept majority decisions in the United Nations on matters that it did not regard as fundamental to its security. However, it has always fallen back on the right of veto in matters that it deemed fundamental to its security. This is a problem inherent in all arms control negotiations with the Soviet Union, and the Soviet attitude in the test cessation conferences was neither more encouraging nor more discouraging than in previous negotiations. Ever since the San Francisco Conference of 1945, the solution of this problem has been to specify decisions both when a veto is permitted and when it is enjoined. The conference on test cessation has followed the same procedure.

[40] U.N. Doc. DC/SC.1/66 (Aug. 29, 1957). See Chap. 15.

On-Site Inspections

As pointed out in the discussion of the veto, the Soviet insistence on a veto in connection with the dispatch of inspection teams to determine whether suspicious events were in fact nuclear explosions, was in full conformity with previous Soviet positions. Thus the later Soviet offer to accept an annual quota of inspections that might be undertaken despite Soviet opposition was an advance beyond previous Soviet positions. To be sure, the quota of three veto-free inspections was ridiculously small, and the Soviet offer was couched in terms that made it uncertain whether the control commission would have complete freedom in deciding on the events it wished to investigate. Nevertheless, the very offer of such a quota was a breach of the iron curtain, however slight, and moved into new ground in arms control negotiations. The most urgent task now of the conference is to attempt to get the Soviet Union to raise its offer.[41]

THE NEW DATA ON

UNDERGROUND EXPLOSIONS

An event that profoundly influenced the course of the negotiations on arms control was the discovery by the United States, as a result of the series of underground nuclear explosions carried out in Nevada in the fall of 1958,[42] that it is more difficult to distinguish between earthquakes and explosions than had previously been estimated. Therefore a short time after the meeting of technical experts had reached a limited agreement, it became necessary for the United States to suggest modification of the agreement. This was most unfortunate since any agreement with the Soviet Union in the field of arms control is extremely rare and difficult to obtain.

[41] Ibid., pp. 25-26.
[42] U. S. Participation in the U.N., Report 1959, Department of State Publication 7016 (1960), p. 7. This series of underground explosions was known as "Hardtack II." See Fortune Magazine (March 1959), p. 124.

Unquestionably the United States followed the only proper course when it brought the new data to the attention of the negotiators on January 5, 1959. The fact that the Soviet delegation at the outset paid no attention to this new data could be anticipated. No positive reactions by the Soviet Union could be expected prior to the completion of the mysterious and time-consuming bureaucratic processes of policy formation in the Kremlin, which have never taken less than three months. The first indication that it was in fact considering the new data came in the form of Khrushchev's letter to the President on April 23, 1959, approximately three months after the Soviet negotiators learned of the data.

President Eisenhower's letter of April 13, 1959 to Khrushchev had suggested an immediate agreement on the discontinuance of all nuclear weapons tests in environments where the agreed control system would clearly show violations.[43] This was an appropriate approach. Officially, the United States was indicating its continued support of an agreement to end nuclear testing.

However, outside the official channel of negotiation, events were transpiring that might well create the impression among the Russians that the United States was reversing its position and wished to resume testing, regardless of whether adequate control machinery could be established. It was clear that many individuals in high places of the United States Government had opposed the original decision of the President to support the ending of nuclear tests and welcomed the new data as an opportunity to reverse the original decision. At this time, the movement to resume testing, spearheaded by Dr. Edward Teller, began to gather momentum. The most dramatic expression of this movement was an article by Charles J. V. Murphy, appearing in the March 1959 issue of *Fortune Magazine*, entitled "Nuclear Inspection: A Near Miss." This article went into detail in describing the controversy within the United States Government over the problem of ending nuclear tests, an issue that "split the Administration, and set the scientists, including the members of the President's own Science Advisory

[43] "The President to Premier Khrushchev," Department of State *Bulletin*, Vol. 40 (May 18, 1959), pp. 704-05.

Committee, in opposing camps." Those who opposed the decision to suspend testing were specifically listed: Admiral Strauss (Chairman of the United States Atomic Energy Commission), other members of the Atomic Energy Commission, and the Joint Chiefs of Staff. The conclusion was: "Dulles has stated categorically that the U.S. would not bind itself to a total suspension that could not be safely enforced. That would seem to close the door on an agreement within the original context of the Geneva discussions."[44] The article then advocated an agreement to stop all atmospheric tests, but to permit continued underground testing.

The detailed material for these ideas could not have been assembled without the active cooperation of certain sectors of the United States Government. The motivation clearly was to build popular sentiment to reverse the previous presidential decision to support the ending of tests. The Soviet leaders, with some reason, concluded that the true ground for the reversal of United States policy would be not that a test cessation ban was unenforceable but that the United States in the interest of its security should resume tests.

The campaign in the United States to reverse the American position could reasonably create doubt whether the United States representative in the negotiations could in fact speak for the United States Government. Two years before, Stassen, despite his White House position, turned out not to be speaking for his government. This impression of lack of unity and leadership within the United States Government at a minimum added to the difficulties of negotiating.

The Soviet actions in the light of their justified suspicions of United States motives, seem quite moderate. By the end of the summer, the additional data on explosions at high altitudes had been incorporated into the control system. In December 1959, the Soviet technical experts got down to considering the new data on the underground tests, and in February 1960, the Soviet Union came forward with a suggestion that took account of the new data, but at the same time would for a period of five years prevent the resumption of underground testing. While many of the details of the Soviet proposal were unsatis-

[44] Pp. 155, 162.

factory, the Soviet moves showed signs of increasing flexibility rather than of rigidity. The signs of flexibility became fewer after the U-2 incident, but the Soviet Union did not recede from its previous positions.

APPARENT SOVIET MOTIVATION

In the General Assembly in 1958, the Soviet Union had strongly supported the initiative of India in proposing a cessation of nuclear tests even though no machinery was set up to ensure the observance of the commitments.[45] India was concerned primarily with the impending menace to world health arising from the growing levels of radiation in the atmosphere and from the increase in strontium 90 resulting from fall-out.

In the 1959 General Assembly, the Soviet Union had likewise supported the Asian and African states in their opposition to the forthcoming French nuclear tests in the Sahara.[46] Ostensibly, at least, the African states based this opposition to the French tests solely on the ground of the danger of fall-out in the adjoining territories.

In view of Russian support for these positions, it would be logical to deduce that one important Soviet motivation in advocating so strongly the ending of tests was fear of the consequences of excessive radiation in the atmosphere. The negotiations in the tripartite conference, however, proved that this was not a major Soviet motivation. On April 13, 1959, President Eisenhower had suggested to Khrushchev the immediate discontinuance of nuclear tests within the atmosphere and under water. Such an agreement would completely eliminate the hazards of radioactivity resulting from testing. Khrushchev initially rejected this approach in its entirety in his note of April 23.[47] When the Soviet Union on March 19, 1960, modified its original rejections and agreed to a phased treaty along the general lines suggested by the United States, it attached as a condition to its agreement a moratorium

[45] U.S. Participation in the U.N., Report 1958, p. 23.
[46] Ibid., Report 1959, pp. 16-17.
[47] "The President to Premier Khrushchev," Department of State Bulletin, Vol. 40 (May 18, 1959), pp. 704-05. "Premier Khrushchev to the President," ibid., p. 705.

of four or five years on the underground tests not covered by the initial ban.[48] This demonstrated clearly that concern for mounting levels of atmosphere contamination was not the major motive behind the Soviet advocacy of a test ban.

Two other possible motives presumably played a role in the Soviet decisions: (1) The so-called "Fourth Country" or "N[th] Country" problem—the danger that a large number of states would obtain nuclear weapons, increasing the danger of outbreak of nuclear war; (2) a Soviet desire to prevent improvement in existing United States nuclear weapons that might result from further testing by the United States. It is important to attempt to weigh the relative importance of these motives to the Soviet Union.

If the primary objective of the Soviet Union in the test cessation negotiations was to hinder the United States in developing small nuclear warheads for an antimissile missile with nuclear warhead, this would strongly support the position of many United States scientists and military leaders advocating an immediate resumption of testing by the United States. Their position would be even more justifiable if the Soviet motive were more devious and visualized a situation in which the United States would be prevented from testing under ground, but the Soviet Union, because of its iron curtain, could "cheat" with fairly good assurance that it would not be caught.

On the other hand, if the prime Soviet motive was to prevent additional countries from securing nuclear weapons, then the self-interest of the Soviet Union to this extent would coincide with the self-interest of the United States and the United Kingdom, and an agreement beneficial to both the Soviet Union and the West would become a possibility.

Both the past negotiations in the general field of arms control and the present test cessation negotiations indicate Soviet concern that more states will secure nuclear weapons and Soviet willingness to pay a price—though not a large one—in terms of an international in-

[48] "Significant Progress in the Test Ban Negotiations." Remarks in the Senate by Senator Hubert H. Humphrey, *Congressional Record,* daily ed., March 23, 1960, pp. 5903-11. For further discussion see the *New York Times,* Special article by A. M. Rosenthal, from Geneva (March 19, 1960).

spection system operating within its territories, for an agreement to cease testing.

The record of the Soviet Union in negotiating the statute of the International Atomic Energy Agency, and until very recently, in the establishment of safeguards systems within that agency, reveals apparent concern over the possible spread of nuclear weapons systems.[49] India has always taken the lead in opposing the rather stringent provisions for safeguards contained in the statute of the agency and has continued to oppose the establishment of any extensive system of safeguards to implement the provisions of the statute. The Soviet Union might have reaped considerable political advantages by giving full support to the Indian position. Nevertheless, it has until recently gone along with the position of the United States in insisting on a fairly rigid safeguards system.

The safeguards system of the international agency, to be sure, would apply only to countries seeking assistance from the agency and therefore would not apply to the Soviet Union or to the United States. Quite logically, the Soviet Union was willing to consent to more extensive safeguards systems outside the Soviet Union than within it. Its recent shift of position in the agency in the direction of the Indian position in all probability reflects the Soviet view that the agency will not dispose of significant quantities of fissionable material. Therefore the agency system of safeguards will not, as originally anticipated, become the prototype for the more extensive safeguards systems required to deal with limitations on nuclear weapons. Emelyanov, the Soviet director in the agency, specifically linked his recent opposition to extensive agency safeguards with the absence of progress toward nuclear disarmament. The prototype system is much more likely to develop from the control posts that might be established to monitor the cessation of nuclear testing.

The general Soviet attitude on whether additional states should secure nuclear weapons can best be described by the term "coy." Obviously, it is not popular to take the lead in supporting a position whereby three countries could have perpetual military superiority

[49] Bernhard G. Bechhoefer, "Negotiating the Statute of the International Atomic Energy Agency," *International Organization,* Vol. 13 (Winter 1959), pp. 38-59.

through their monopoly of the most effective military weapon. Such a position is offensive to a number of countries, especially France and Communist China. Therefore, in its public utterances, the Soviet Union has always supported the presently unattainable end of elimination of all nuclear weapons. Nevertheless, in general the Soviet Union has seldom sought to obtain propaganda advantages when the United States and the United Kingdom advocated the unpopular position of continuing the three-state monopoly of nuclear weapons.

When the Irish Foreign Minister raised the question directly in the 1958 and 1959 General Assemblies, by asking the Assembly to support urgent steps to prevent further dissemination of nuclear weapons, the Soviet Union, in 1958, along with the United States, abstained on the essential paragraph of the resolution, which obtained 37 affirmative votes with 44 abstentions. There were no negative votes. The Irish representative immediately withdrew the resolution, expressing gratification that no negative votes had been cast against his resolution.[50] In 1959, the Irish representative recast the resolution so that it merely called for a study of the problem by the recently formed Ten-Nation Disarmament Committee. In this form the resolution received the support of both the Soviet Union and the United States.[51]

The Soviet opposition to the United States proposals that all further production of fissionable material be utilized solely for peaceful purposes, the cutoff, is not inconsistent with Soviet opposition to the spread of nuclear weapons to additional countries. The cutoff would, of course, be far more effective than test cessation in ensuring that no additional countries would develop nuclear armaments. The Soviet opposition to the cutoff rests firmly on the proposition that in the early stages of a disarmament agreement, the machinery to police the cutoff would cause too great a breach of its secrecy to be acceptable to the Soviet Union.

[50] U.N. General Assembly, Thirteenth Session, First Committee, *Official Records*, Agenda Item 64 (Oct. 17, 1958). The resolution was withdrawn on Nov. 3, 1958, p. 11.
[51] U.N. General Assembly, Fourteenth Session, Plenary, *Official Records*, 805th Meeting (Sept. 23, 1959), pp. 130-33.

Thus, while the Soviet Union still seems committed to support proposals that will prevent the spread of nuclear weapons, it will nevertheless pay only a limited price for a resolution for cessation of nuclear tests. The negotiations themselves are the best evidences of the price the Soviet Union is willing to pay.

One of the reasons for the unwillingness of the Soviet Union to pay a higher price could well be its doubt as to the effectiveness of a test cessation ban in preventing additional countries from developing nuclear weapons. Dr. Teller has frequently pointed out that a state might develop a weapons capability without exploding any weapons. He acknowledges, however, that this would be much more difficult to accomplish than if the state were in a position to make weapons tests.[52] A far more significant loophole in world efforts to prevent the spread of nuclear weapons is the possibility of the transfer of completed weapons by nuclear powers to their allies. The Western proposals in the subcommittee in the summer of 1957, which were incorporated into the August 29 proposals, specifically left this door open.[53] If the door had been closed, the French with their stated policy of becoming a fourth nuclear power, and possibly the NATO countries, might not have supported the Western proposals. Many of Zorin's bitterest denunciations of the Western proposals arose from this feature. It is conceivable that the Soviet Union would permit a far greater breach of its iron curtain if the proposals for test cessation were accompanied by other proposals the combination of which would ensure that Germany and possibly Communist China would not in the near future obtain nuclear weapons.

In this connection, it should be recalled that in the summer of 1958 the Soviet Union consented to two technical discussions: one on test cessation and one on methods of reducing the danger of surprise attack. In the surprise attack conference, the Soviet Union had stressed a nuclear-free zone in Central Europe. The initial Soviet suggestions for a safeguards system in connection with measures to reduce the

[52] Edward Teller, "The Feasibility of Arms Controls and the Principle of Openness," in *Daedalus* (Fall 1960), pp. 781-99.
[53] See Chap. 15.

danger of surprise attack were quite similar to the safeguards system for monitoring nuclear tests. If the East-West negotiations had moved simultaneously toward agreement on test cessation and a nuclear-free zone in Central Europe, the question arises whether the Soviet Union might not have been willing to pay a greater price in terms of penetration of the iron curtain than the price it was willing to pay merely for test cessation alone on the ground of its greater assurance against an increase in the number of countries with nuclear weapons. This discussion leads to the conclusion that the Soviet desire to prevent the spread of nuclear weapons to other countries continues to play a substantial role in the Soviet decisions.

It is much more difficult to estimate the extent to which Soviet thinking is governed by a desire to place obstacles in the path of the improvement of Western nuclear weapons, and even more to create a situation whereby the West would be prevented from making nuclear tests but the Soviet Union could cheat with reasonable assurance that its tests would remain undetected. There is one shred of circumstantial evidence to support a conclusion that the Soviet Union may not be planning to cheat. The type of nuclear tests the Soviet Union might be able to conceal would have a relatively low kiloton yield. This type of test would be more useful in developing tactical weapons than strategic weapons. There are indications that the Soviet Union, unlike the United States, has not geared its military system to tactical nuclear weapons.[54]

A vivid discussion of the question whether the Soviet Union intends to "cheat" is contained in an exchange of letters between Senator Humphrey and John McCone, Chairman of the Atomic Energy Commission. Apropos of two newspaper articles written by the columnist, Joseph Alsop, who indicated that Mr. McCone was convinced that the Soviet Union had been testing nuclear weapons secretly underground, Senator Humphrey asked whether such allegations had been made. McCone's answer was a reiteration of an answer he had previously

[54] Raymond L. Garthoff, *Soviet Strategy in the Nuclear Age* (1958), pp. 156-66. Also see Herbert S. Dinerstein, "The Soviet Military Posture as a Reflection of Soviet Strategy," The Rand Corporation (Jan. 15, 1958), pp. 18-20.

given to the question: "Is there any reason to believe that the Russians are clandestinely testing despite their unilateral announcement of a moratorium?"

McCone's response was: "There is no information on this subject whatever. However, my personal views are that the opportunities are great and it is relatively easy to do and there is no possible means of detection. Therefore I feel that they would be tempted to carry on in the absence of any possibility of getting caught." McCone continued:

> . . . The reference to detection in my response was, of course, made in the context of underground nuclear detonations of a magnitude below the capabilities of existing instrumentation.
>
> In summary, I am not aware of the existence of technical evidence which would support a finding that the Soviets have been testing secretly during the moratorium. However, there is no reasonable assurance to the contrary. It is possible to conduct underground tests without detection and the gains to be made are very considerable. Therefore, the temptation is great and the risk of discovery is small.[55]

Wadsworth in his "farewell" news conference prior to his resignation as United States representative to the United Nations expressed the view "that the Russian Government has every intention of living up to any agreement they make from the standpoint of nuclear tests or the larger areas of disarmament. Nobody in the world, including ourselves, can guarantee what a successor government might do."[56]

The Soviet Union throughout the years of negotiations apparently always had as its preferred position the unilateral disarmament of the West. Such a motive can hardly be absent from the Soviet calculations in connection with the proposals for test cessation. Therefore the Western negotiations must realistically continue to seek agreements that will be as beneficial to the West as to the Soviet Union.

[55] *Disarmament Developments Spring 1960*, Hearing before the Senate Committee on Foreign Relations, 86 Cong. 2 sess. (June 10, 1960), p. 49.
[56] *New York Times*, Jan. 18, 1961.

WESTERN MOTIVATION

From the moment that the United States advocated modifying the technical conclusions of the first meeting of experts, the Soviet Union has contended that the true motivation of the United States is its desire to resume testing. This issue has sometimes been in the foreground but invariably has been a background refrain during all the tripartite negotiations. The basic questions are: Does the United States continue to support the ending of tests? Should the United States continue to support the ending of tests?

Dr. Teller and Dr. Hans Bethe have respectively on several occasions admirably summarized the tactical and military arguments in support of and in opposition to the resumption of testing.[57] This study can merely add some political comments.

The political factors clearly point to the desirability of the United States continuing to seek a safeguarded agreement to cease testing. Important political factors are the desirability of postponing the day when more states will have substantial nuclear weapons systems, world sentiment for cessation of testing, and the possibility that United States-Soviet cooperation in the monitoring system will be the first step in the direction of genuine accomplishment.

The only reliable indication that cessation of nuclear testing was in accord with the security interests of the United States was the original decision of President Eisenhower to support the cessation of tests. Presumably, the President had the full knowledge, both technical and political, which is available to only a very few officials of the United States Government. Teller's strong reliance on political arguments of doubtful validity to justify resumption of testing may indicate that the technical arguments are inconclusive, or in the alternative may be a distorted response to the equally distorted attacks on his position.

As Dr. Szilard has pointed out, it is impossible to construct an equation of advantages and disadvantages of resuming tests since one

[57] Teller in *Daedalus*, pp. 781-99, and many other articles. Hans Bethe, "The Detection of Underground Explosions," in *Bulletin of Atomic Scientists*, Vol. 15 (June 1959), p. 257.

important element in the equation—the military advantages of resuming tests—is and must remain secret.[58] The equation, however, should contain political as well as military factors. The question the United States must decide is not: Will the monitoring machinery give full assurance of the detection of all attempted nuclear tests? The proper question is: Will the danger of a nuclear war be greater or less than it is today if the United States agrees with the Soviet Union on a cessation of tests with a system of safeguards along the general lines developed up to this point in the negotiations?

One of the major tasks of President Kennedy will be to answer this question. The important consideration is that the answer, once it is made, shall receive the loyal and unified support of the entire United States Government, legislative as well as executive.

[58] Szilard, op. cit.

XX

The General Disarmament Negotiations

THE UNITED NATIONS GENERAL ASSEMBLY in 1958 had expressed its determination that initiatives should continue for a "balanced and effective world-wide system of disarmament," and had unanimously voted to enlarge the Disarmament Commission to include all the Members of the United Nations.[1] This latter resolution further requested the commission to make every effort to reach agreement in the field of disarmament.

The meeting of the Foreign Ministers of the United States, the United Kingdom, France, and the Soviet Union in August 1959, two years after the break-up of the Disarmament Commission subcommittee, reached agreement on procedures for resuming general disarmament negotiations. The four powers agreed to form a Ten-Power Disarmament Committee.

The four governments conceive of this committee as a useful means of exploring through mutual consultations avenues of possible progress towards such agreements and recommendations on the limitation and reduction of all types of armaments and armed forces under effective international control as may, in the first

[1] See Chap. 17, p. 461.

521

instance, be of particular relevance to the countries participating in these deliberations. Furthermore, it is the hope of the four governments that the results achieved in these deliberations will provide a useful basis for the consideration of disarmament in the United Nations.[2]

Immediately thereafter both the Soviet Union and the United States embarked on steps in the direction of renewed disarmament negotiations. Khrushchev submitted to the American periodical *Foreign Affairs* a lengthy article entitled "On Peaceful Coexistence," which explored the entire field of coexistence of states with different social systems and the possibilities of reducing East-West tensions. Two paragraphs of this article were of particular interest in specifying the Soviet attitude toward disarmament. "There may be two ways out: either war—and war in the rocket and H-bomb age is fraught with the most dire consequences for all nations—or peaceful coexistence."[3]

At a later point in the article after pointing out the difficulties of reaching agreement on a drastic solution to the disarmament problem, he stated:

When it became clear that it was very difficult under these conditions to solve the complex disarmament problem, immediately we proposed another concrete idea to our partners; let us concentrate our attention on those problems which lend themselves most easily to a solution; let us undertake initial partial steps on matters concerning which the views of the different parties have been brought closer together.

Khrushchev then went on to repeat that one of these questions "is the question of discontinuing atomic and hydrogen weapon tests."[4] Khrushchev was smiling, not scowling.

[2] *United States Participation in the United Nations, Report by the President to the Congress for the Year 1959*, Department of State Publication 7016 (1960) p. 11. Cited hereafter as *U.S. Participation in the U.N., Report* (with year). The Four Powers issued a joint communiqué on Sept. 7, 1959.
[3] "On Peaceful Coexistence," in *Foreign Affairs*, Vol. 38 (October 1959), pp. 1-18.
[4] *Ibid.*

Eisenhower's first step toward a renewal of general disarmament negotiations, taken a week before the meeting of the Foreign Ministers, was the appointment of a Boston attorney, Charles A. Coolidge, former Assistant Secretary of Defense, to conduct a broad review of America's disarmament policies in the hope that it would help reduce "the burden of armaments" and contribute to a "just and durable peace."[5]

The enlarged Disarmament Commission of the United Nations met on September 10 and unanimously welcomed the resumption of negotiations on general disarmament; reiterated the hope "that the results achieved in these deliberations will provide a useful basis for the consideration of disarmament in the United Nations"; and requested the Secretary-General to provide appropriate facilities for the proposed consultations.[6]

The General Assembly convened a week later, and the addresses by both Secretary of State Christian Herter and British Foreign Secretary Selwyn Lloyd on September 17 dealt with disarmament. Herter went no further than to describe in some detail the current negotiations for a cessation of tests and to hope for "general limitation and control of armaments and armed forces. The degree to which we succeed may determine Man's future. . . . We must use all of our imagination and ingenuity to devise a way of controlling this race to prevent it from exploding into nuclear conflict."[7]

On the same day, Selwyn Lloyd brought forward a revised and up-to-date version of the Anglo-French program introduced originally in 1954. The United Kingdom wished "to move forward by balanced stages towards the abolition of all nuclear weapons and all weapons of mass destruction and towards the reduction of other weapons and armed forces to levels which rule out the possibility of aggressive war."[8] He then outlined in some detail the three stages of the program. The first stage was roughly the equivalent of the previous Western proposal for partial measures of disarmament, which would increase

[5] *Washington Post and Times-Herald* (June 30, 1959), p. 86.
[6] *U.S. Participation in the U.N., Report 1959*, p. 12.
[7] "Peaceful Change," Department of State *Bulletin*, Vol. 41 (Oct. 5, 1959), p. 472.
[8] U.N. General Assembly, Fourteenth Session, Plenary, *Official Records*, 798th Meeting (Sept. 17, 1959), pp. 24-26.

national confidence and would make possible the more drastic measures of disarmament proposed for the second and third stages. The specific measures suggested for the first stage need not be considered in detail since they were superseded by the Western paper presented to the Ten-Power Disarmament Committee negotiations in March 1960.[9] These first stage measures, however, did eliminate some parts of the August 29, 1957, package proposals that had been most objectionable to the Soviet Union. Furthermore, in the first stage, technical conferences parallel to those already taking place on the problem of cessation of nuclear tests would be convened immediately to work out the technical details both of the armaments limitations and of the controls. In the second and third stages, Selwyn Lloyd recreated the ideal of a relatively disarmed world, which had been the basis for all Western proposals prior to 1955. Figuratively speaking, the shade of the tree of total disarmament was a refreshing and comfortable atmosphere in which to rest. Twenty-four hours later, Khrushchev in his personal appearance before the General Assembly revealed that the Soviet Union had decided to enjoy the shade of the same tree.

GENERAL AND COMPLETE

DISARMAMENT

On September 18, 1959, Khrushchev in person addressed the United Nations General Assembly in New York. He launched immediately into a description of the disaster to the world in the event of nuclear warfare.

It is difficult to imagine the consequences, for mankind, of a war in which these monstrous means of destruction and annihilation were used. If such a war were allowed to break out, the number of

[9] U.S. Department of State, "Official Report of the United Nations Delegation to the Conference of the Ten-Nation Committee on Disarmament" (March 15-June 28, 1960), submitted by Frederick M. Eaton, Chairman of the delegation. Cited hereafter as *Eaton Report.*

victims would be counted, not in millions, but in many tens, and even hundreds of millions of human lives. It would be a war in which there was no difference between the front and the rear, between soldiers and children. It would result in the laying in ruin of many large cities and centres of industry, and in the irrevocable loss of the greatest cultural monuments, created over the centuries by the efforts of human genius. Nor would such a war spare future generations. Its poisonous trail in the form of radio-active contamination would long continue to maim people and claim many lives.

And can it be forgotten that there is now not a single place on the globe that is out of the reach of nuclear and rocket weapons?[10]

In the 1959 United Nations speech, Khrushchev had brought home to the Communist world as well as to the West the message that a nuclear holocaust was unthinkable. It would no longer be possible for the Communists to assert with any conviction in arms control negotiations the Soviet doctrine of 1954, which continues to be the doctrine of the Chinese Communists, that a nuclear war would destroy decadent capitalism but that communism would survive.

After a discussion of the obstacles which up to that point had prevented international disarmament agreements, Khrushchev came to his main theme:

The Soviet Government, after examining from all angles the situa-

---

[10] U.N. General Assembly, Fourteenth Session, Plenary, *Official Records*, 799th Meeting (Sept. 18, 1959), p. 34.

Khrushchev's outspoken statements have finally been confirmed by the Soviet military. In Moscow's monthly magazine *International Life* Major General Nikolai Talensky of the Soviet General Staff writes as follows:

"There is no practical way to repulse a nuclear rocket attack."

"A nuclear war will destroy whole countries and populations. . . . The loss would be no less than 500 to 600 million people."

"Surprise attack undoubtedly has its advantages. . . . However, the opportunity of an answering blow remains. [Thus] nuclear war is not only extraordinarily dangerous for the victim, but it is also suicide for the aggressor himself."

"The process of development of the technique of destroying peoples makes it impossible now to use weapons for the solution of political tasks. . . . War as an instrument of policy is becoming outdated. . . ." *Time Magazine* (Oct. 24, 1960).

tion which has arisen, has reached the firm conclusion that the way out of the impasse must be sought through general and complete disarmament. This approach completely eliminates the possibility of any State gaining military advantages of any kind. General and complete disarmament will remove all the obstacles that have arisen during the discussions of the questions involved by partial disarmament, and will clear the way for the institution of universal and complete control.[11]

Khrushchev proceeded to paint a vivid and appealing picture of a disarmed world. He borrowed liberally from past Western positions— from ideas of Jules Moch in 1954 and ever since: "We are in favour of genuine disarmament under control but we are against control without disarmament;" from Benjamin Cohen: "The essence of our proposals is that all States should carry out complete disarmament and should divest themselves of the means of waging war. . . . States should be allowed to retain only strictly limited police [militia] contingents— on a strength agreed upon for each country—equipped with light firearms and intended solely for the maintenance of international order and the protection of the citizens' personal safety." "Agreement among States to undertake general, complete disarmament would afford convincing practical confirmation of the absence of any aggressive designs on their part and the presence of a sincere desire to build their relations with other countries on a foundation of friendship and cooperation. With the destruction of weapons and the disbanding of armed forces, States would be left without the material capacity to pursue any policy but a peaceful one."

Khrushchev then made his appeal to the underdeveloped areas.

General and complete disarmament would also create completely new opportunities for the assistance of States whose economies are at present still underdeveloped and stand in need of cooperation from more advanced countries. Even if only a small part of the resources released by the cessation of military expenditure on the part

[11] U.N. General Assembly, Fourteenth Session, Plenary, *Official Records*, 799th Meeting (Sept. 18, 1959), p. 36.

of the Great Powers were devoted to assisting such States, this could literally usher in a new epoch in the economic development of Asia, Africa and Latin-America.

Having enjoyed the refreshing shade of the tree of "general and complete disarmament," Khrushchev plainly and succinctly suggested a program of partial measures of disarmament.

It goes without saying that, if at present the Western Powers do not, for one reason or another, express their readiness to embark upon general and complete disarmament, the Soviet Government is prepared to come to terms with other States on appropriate partial measures relating to disarmament and the strengthening of security. In the view of the Soviet Government, the most important steps are the following:

(1) The establishment of a control and inspection zone, and the reduction of foreign troops in the territories of the Western European countries concerned;

(2) The establishment of an "atom-free" zone in Central Europe;

(3) The withdrawal of all foreign troops from the territories of European States and the abolition of military bases on the territories of foreign States;

(4) The conclusion of a non-aggression pact between the member States of NATO and the member States of the Warsaw Treaty;

(5) The conclusion of an agreement on the prevention of surprise attack by one State upon another.

The Soviet Government considers it appropriate to recall its disarmament proposals of 10 May 1955, which outlined a specific scheme for partial measures in the field of disarmament. It is convinced that these proposals constitute a sound basis for agreement on this vitally important issue.[12]

The day after Khrushchev's speech, the Soviet Government filed in the General Assembly a declaration following the main lines of his

[12] *Ibid.*, p. 37.

speech, but considerably longer, and providing for the achievement of general and complete disarmament in three stages.[13] The short section of the declaration dealing with partial measures of disarmament was substantially identical with Khrushchev's speech.

The Western reaction to the events in New York is vividly described in the London *Economist* of September 26. *The Economist* first dealt with Lloyd's speech:

. . . Mr. Selwyn Lloyd's speech was unfortunately buried by Mr. Khrushchev's more publicized oration, but it deserves some attention for its painstaking attempt to get somewhere on disarmament. . . .

For those who really understand the technicalities of disarmament (there must be nearly a hundred such in the world, and all except Mr. Anthony Nutting are at the United Nations) Mr. Lloyd's speech was highly significant, and it may yet be the basis on which further negotiations are carried on at the forthcoming ten-power disarmament talks. But it failed to make any impact on the public or even on the average small-power foreign minister (there are some fifty here).

As to Khrushchev's speech,

. . . Second thoughts are showing that his proposals cannot be so summarily dismissed. On the propaganda front, in spite of their naivety, they did have an appeal to a large section of the Assembly —not simply because the small powers are against war (at least amongst great powers), but also because there appeared to be some logic in the thesis that if nuclear weapons make war too horrible to contemplate, it is war which must be abolished, not just nuclear weapons. Consequently the Russian plan will certainly be debated at the Assembly, where it will have the great merit of putting Russia on the side of the angels—idealist, extremist perhaps, but extremist for peace.

[13] U.N. General Assembly, Fourteenth Session, "Declaration of the Soviet Government on General and Complete Disarmament," U.N. Doc. A/4219 (Sept. 19, 1959).

Secondly, a more careful reading of the speech has shown that in fact it was not all propaganda. In a brief paragraph or two, Mr. Khrushchev outlined a second Russian proposal for *partial* disarmament. This proposal which contains ideas about a nuclear-free zone in Europe as well as the usual demand for abolition of overseas bases, is presumably what Mr. Khrushchev intends to raise with President Eisenhower this week-end....[14]

In its lead article that same week, *The Economist* comments shrewdly on the American reaction. "Mr. Khrushchev has spent a whole week among Americans just after giving the United Nations Assembly his latest proposals on disarmament; and only Mr. Adlai Stevenson (and Mr. Garst, the maize expert) seem to have made any serious attempt to find out what he really means."[15]

The General Assembly discussion of the Soviet item that was labeled "General and Complete Disarmament" occupied seventeen meetings from October 9 until November 2. The United States belatedly pulled back part way to its 1952 positions, favoring drastic reductions of armaments, which Khrushchev had now appropriated, and supported "the greatest possible amount of controlled disarmament." Jules Moch was the author of the only novel Western position, suggesting that a high priority be given to measures prohibiting the development, manufacture, and possession of all means for the delivery of nuclear devices. The United States experts in the surprise attack conference a year earlier had expressed the view that this was a feasible method of controlling nuclear devices.

The General Assembly unanimously adopted the inevitable resolution calling on the Ten-Power Disarmament Committee to consider all of the proposals and suggestions made during the session of the Assembly, including both Khrushchev's proposals and those of Selwyn Lloyd.[16] The crucial debates would of necessity take place in the smaller group. Unfortunately, the title of the resolution was "general and complete disarmament," a phrasing which permitted the Soviet

[14] "Wooing 'The Fifth Great Power,'" *The Economist* (Sept. 26, 1959), p. 1031.
[15] "Arms and the Russian," *ibid.*, p. 995.
[16] Res. 1378 (XIV), Nov. 20, 1959.

leaders to claim in the later meetings that the General Assembly had endorsed the Soviet proposals and that the Western proposals did not conform to the resolution.[17] In the General Assembly, Khrushchev had succeeded admirably in transferring from the West to the Soviet Union the garlands of peace.

The Soviet leaders graciously accepted the garlands. The Soviet representative, Kuznetsov, in his final statement to the Political Committee of the General Assembly on October 27, 1959, stated:

The wide response which the proposal of the Soviet Union on general and complete disarmament has met, testified to the fact that the idea of complete disarmament had been "enthusiastically acclaimed by the people in all countries." The peoples looked to the States to proceed without delay to work out measures for the implementation of general and complete disarmament. The consent of States in that field would be interpreted throughout the world as a convincing proof of the sincere desire of States to conduct international relations on the basis of friendship and cooperation.[18]

Four days later, Khrushchev in his address to the Supreme Soviet once again stressed the second road to a disarmament agreement.

. . . But we are prepared to consider other proposals so as to reach mutually acceptable solutions on the disarmament problem. . . . We have more than once proposed measures to make the European atmosphere less tense, to safeguard the security of all the peoples living in the area. We are prepared both for far-reaching steps in this direction and for any sensible partial measures. We only wish this matter to progress, the situation in Europe to be im-

[17] For example, see Ten-Power Disarmament Committee, *Verbatim Records*, Third Meeting (March 17, 1960): statement of Mezincescu (Rumania), Great Britain Cmd. 1152, p. 59; Fifth Meeting (March 21, 1960): statement of Nosek (Czechoslovakia), p. 87.
[18] U.N. General Assembly, Fourteenth Session, First Committee, *Official Records* (Oct. 27, 1959), p. 40.

proved so that the European tangle does not remain so closely entangled.

In the same address Khrushchev expressed his confidence in President Eisenhower.

During my United States visit I met and talked with President Dwight Eisenhower, with other statesmen, representatives of various circles and the ordinary people of America. I gained the conviction that an overwhelming majority of the American peoples does not want war and wants relations between our countries to improve.

Many outstanding American personalities with the President at their head, understand this attitude of the American people, are perturbed by the situation arising from the arms race and the cold war and want to march along the path of consolidating peace.[19]

Khrushchev was still smiling.

SEARCHING FOR A POSITION

On December 21, the Western powers invited the Communist powers to disarmament discussions in Geneva on March 15, and the invitation was accepted.[20] It now became essential for the West to prepare a position for this conference. In the previous General Assembly, Selwyn Lloyd had produced a useful though somewhat technical program. Jules Moch had made an interesting suggestion to eliminate in an early stage the systems for delivering nuclear weapons on their targets. The United States had confined itself to generalities and to its promise to study the Soviet proposals, a grossly inadequate position for a serious negotiation.

If the review of Western policy on disarmament made by Charles

[19] Moscow Radio broadcast (Oct. 31, 1959), *Pravda* (Nov. 1, 1959).
[20] *U.S. Participation in the U.N., Report 1959*, p. 22.

A. Coolidge had produced any tangible results by the time of the General Assembly, they were not apparent. On December 16, the *New York Times* in a dispatch from London noted:

> . . . The British are disappointed at the failure of President Eisenhower's special Commission to move more quickly in its review of the disarmament question . . . the original date for the Commission's Report was January 1st, but the Report is not expected now until February.
>
> The British view, it was learned today, is that there can be no firm Western policy on disarmament until the United States decides its policy. That decision, it is said, will not be made until after the Coolidge Commission Report.

When the Western powers issued their invitation to the Soviet bloc to commence the disarmament talks in Geneva in March, they also decided that the disarmament specialists of the Western countries should meet in Washington on January 25 to work out an agreed set of disarmament proposals to be presented at Geneva.

Sometime in January 1960, the long-awaited Coolidge report finally made its appearance. While the report has never been published officially, there is ample evidence that it was unsatisfactory. One of the experienced "disarmament reporters" for the *New York Times* wrote that "the Report suggested general lines of approach and principles but no fully worked out program . . . State and Defense Department officials therefore have started from scratch in working out a new program."[21] The London *Economist* commented:

> The proposals which Mr. Charles Coolidge's study group made to the President at the beginning of the year have been thrust under the cushion as hastily as an improper novel. It seems that Mr. Coolidge drew most of his assistants from among the sceptics who think that general disarmament would be not only impracticable

[21] Dana Adams Schmidt, *New York Times*, Feb. 11, 1960,

but positively dangerous. He appears therefore to have confined his report to a few suggestions for limiting conventional forces and preventing surprise attacks.[22]

The Washington *Evening Star* on April 22 published what purported to be a portion of the Coolidge Report. Without going into any detail in discussing the specific recommendations, it is apparent that the estimate by *The Economist* was sound. Fundamentally, the Coolidge Committee recommendations were for further armaments rather than disarmament. The report apparently opposed any cutback either in conventional or nuclear weapons or any agreement to ban underground nuclear testing without regard to safeguards. It is true that a strong defense position can not only be consistent with arms control but also can facilitate arms control. However, the Coolidge report, as far as is known, made no attempt to develop arms control proposals in harmony with a strong defense posture. The report again demonstrated that even an individual of ability and good will cannot, in a period of sixty or ninety days, master the subject of international arms control sufficiently to produce any significant contribution. Despite this experience, President Eisenhower in January 1960 appointed as the head of the United States delegation to the ten-power consultations, Frederick Eaton of New York,[23] who had little experience in diplomatic negotiations and no experience in the field of arms control. Because of Eaton's outstanding ability as an advocate, his lack of experience in the new environment did not handicap him in the day-to-day conduct of the negotiations. It did handicap him in securing from his government a realistic position from which to negotiate.

Eaton found himself confronted immediately with the conference of the five Western nations to develop a position for the March 15 Geneva meetings, a preparation period of barely two months. Immediately "Western officials expressed concern over the slowness with which the United States had evolved a new disarmament plan to meet

[22] "American Survey: Divided on Disarmament," *The Economist* (Feb. 20, 1960), p. 712.
[23] *New York Times*, March 16, 1960.

Premier Khrushchev's proposal for total disarmament."[24] *The Economist* made the comment:

> . . . The United States is the only nuclear power that by mid-week had not made public a general disarmament plan to lay before the ten-power talks which open in Geneva next month. It is in the extraordinary position of having invited its allies to Washington and then having kept them talking about peripheral matters, such as the chairmanship and the tactics the Russians are likely to follow.[25] . . .

A general United States position finally emerged in an address by Secretary of State Herter to the National Press Club in Washington on February 18, which should be considered as the United States response to Khrushchev's United Nations speech. On the American purpose in the disarmament negotiations Herter said:

> Speaking generally, we will have two major goals in the forthcoming negotiations:
> *Urgently,* to try to create a more stable military environment, which will curtail the risk of war and permit reductions in national armed forces and armaments.
> *Subsequently,* to cut national armed forces and armaments further, and to build up international peace-keeping machinery, to the point where aggression will be deterred by international rather than national force. . . .
> A more stable military environment will require measures to control the two types of dangers of a continuing arms race to which I referred. *First,* to meet the danger of miscalculation, there is need for safeguards against surprise attack . . . These safeguards could include zones for aerial and mobile ground inspection.

The Secretary then referred to the August 1957 proposals for inspection "in Europe, the Arctic area and equivalent areas of North America and the U.S.S.R."

[24] *Ibid.,* Feb. 11, 1960.
[25] *The Economist* (Feb. 20, 1960), p. 712.

The second danger—that of the promiscuous spread of production of nuclear weapons—is one that we, our major allies, and the Soviet Union should all view with real concern.

To guard against this danger, the testing of nuclear weapons and eventually the production of fissionable material for weapons purposes must be prohibited under effective inspection. We are trying to make a first step to this end in the Geneva Test Suspension negotiations.[26]

All of this was a solid basis for a position on the initial steps in a disarmament program. However, it must be emphasized that it was only *a basis for a position,* not a position.

The Secretary of State went on to the subject of general disarmament—the ultimate objective of any disarmament program.

To assure a world of peaceful change, we should project a second stage of general disarmament. Our objective in this second stage should be two-fold: *First,* to create universally accepted rules of law, which if followed would prevent all nations from attacking other nations. Such rules of law should be backed by a World Court and by effective means of enforcement—that is, by international armed force. *Second,* to reduce national armed forces, under safeguarded and verified arrangements to the point where no single nation or group of nations could effectively oppose this enforcement of international law by international machinery.[27]

The Secretary of State had virtually restated the original objectives of the United Nations and had even brought back into the picture the necessity of an international armed force to maintain peace in a relatively disarmed world. The new negotiations would deal with the ultimate objectives of a disarmament program and at the same time suggest as the first stage of the program immediately realizable par-

[26] "National Security With Arms Limitation," Department of State *Bulletin,* Vol. 42 (March 7, 1960), pp. 355-56.
[27] *Ibid.,* p. 357.

tial measures of disarmament, which would "create a more stable military environment." The United States had thus accepted the general frame of reference of the Soviet proposals. The problem was to translate this into specific proposals for the conference.

THE TEN-POWER CONFERENCE

At the opening of the Ten-Power Conference on March 15, the Soviet Union re-submitted the proposals it had made to the General Assembly the previous September.[28] Khrushchev sent a greeting to the conference, stating that he had instructed the Soviet representatives "to strive for the earliest working out of a treaty on general and complete disarmament."[29] It said nothing about partial measures of disarmament.

The Western powers submitted a Five Power Working Paper on General Disarmament. The paper commenced with the statement that:

(A) The ultimate goal is a secure, free, and peaceful world in which there shall be general disarmament under effective international control and agreed procedures for the settlement of disputes in accordance with the principles of the United Nations Charter.
(B) The task of the Ten Nation Disarmament Conference should be to work out measures leading toward general disarmament which can only be attained by balanced, phased and safe-guarded agreements.
(C) All measures of disarmament must be observed and verified by an appropriate international organization.[30]

The Western powers had thus accepted the same ultimate objectives as the Soviet Union. The immediate task of the negotiations was expressed as follows by the United States representative, Frederick Eaton:

[28] *Eaton Report,* p. 3.
[29] *New York Times,* March 16, 1960.
[30] Department of State *Bulletin,* Vol. 42 (April 4, 1960), p. 511.

We must design a plan broad and promising in scope and yet realistic in conception, a plan which moves by measured safeguarded steps toward an attainable goal. Not one which raises false hopes of a sudden and easy solution to one of mankind's oldest problems—the problem of abolishing war among nations—but a plan which will bring to a halt this frightening race to create even more massive means of destruction.[31]

Stated in more specific terms, "The Allies . . . noted that the Soviet bloc, while having stated its willingness to embark upon a program of complete and general disarmament, omitted any reference to specific measures by which this objective could be reached."[32] The Western plan, however, was also ill-suited to accomplish this objective.

The Western paper suggested certain measures that should "be undertaken forthwith." The Soviet bloc delegations immediately complained that these measures "concentrated on studying disarmament instead of carrying out disarmament."[33]

The first of the measures to be undertaken immediately was "the establishment of an International Disarmament Organization (IDO) by progressive steps, following a joint study of the composition and functions of such an organization and its relationship to the United Nations."[34] This would be a logical step if it were coupled with specific measures of arms limitation. Otherwise, it was merely a repetition of the original Western positions in 1946 and 1947 that control must precede disarmament, positions which had been modified beginning in 1954 with the Western suggestions for phasing the institution of controls and the various prohibitions and limitations.

The second measure to be undertaken immediately was "prior notification to the International Disarmament Organization of proposed

[31]Ten-Power Disarmament Committee, *Verbatim Records*, First Meeting (March 15, 1960), p. 24.
[32] *Eaton Report*, p. 4.
[33] *New York Times*, March 16, 1960, p. 1, report by A. M. Rosenthal. Most of the *New York Times* articles on disarmament, subsequently quoted, are reported by Rosenthal.
[34] Ten-Power Disarmament Committee, *Verbatim Records*, Annex 7 (March 16, 1960), p. 921, par. A.

launchings of space vehicles and the establishment of cooperative arrangements for communicating to the International Disarmament Organization data obtained from available tracking facilities."[35] This was a distinct retrogression from the Western proposals of August 29, 1957, that "within three months after the entry into effect of the convention, they will co-operate in the establishment of a technical committee to study the design of an inspection system which would make it possible to assure that the sending of objects through outer space will be exclusively for peaceful and scientific purposes."[36] The earlier proposal dealt with all missile launchings, while this one limited itself in the first stage to launchings of space vehicles.

The third measure was for "the collection of information on present force levels and on armaments."[37] The Soviet bloc could justifiably complain that this measure was to study disarmament rather than to carry out disarmament.

The fourth measure was "the coordinated reduction or limitation of force levels" of the Soviet Union and the United States to 2,500,000 and the reduction of armaments through placing in storage for international supervision, agreed types and quantities of conventional armaments.[38] This was in substance the same proposal concerning conventional reductions contained in the August 29, 1957, proposals. In 1957 substantial agreement had been reached between the Soviet Union and the West on this proposal, which in 1957, as in 1960, was accompanied by provisions for further reductions in later stages. Even in 1957, the increased importance of nuclear weapons and of missiles greatly reduced the significance of this first stage limitation. The Soviet Union had emphasized this by unilaterally announcing on January 15, 1960, a domestic law reducing the level of its forces to 2,423,000. The United States had in fact reduced its forces to the 2,500,000 level. Therefore, this proposal for a first-stage limitation was not a reduction.

The fifth Western measure for the first stage called for the submis-

[35] *Ibid.*, par. B.
[36] See Chap. 15.
[37] Ten-Power Disarmament Committee, *Verbatim Records,* Annex 7, p. 921, par. C.
[38] *Ibid.*, par. D.

sion, by various states of certain information on their expenditures, to the international disarmament organization. Again the West was calling for a study of disarmament.[39]

The sixth and last proposal for the first stage suggested that joint studies be undertaken immediately on eight subjects relating to disarmament.[40]

Even more significant than the Western suggestions for first-stage measures were the omissions. The Soviet paper had expressed Soviet willingness to come to agreement on appropriate partial measures of disarmament, the most important of which were:

1. Establishment of a control and inspection zone with a reduction of foreign troops in the territories of the corresponding countries of Western Europe; 2. Establishment of a denuclearized zone in Central Europe; 3. Withdrawal of all foreign troops from the territories of European States and liquidation of military bases in foreign territories; 4. Conclusion of a non-aggression pact between NATO members and the Warsaw Treaty States; 5. Agreement on the prevention of surprise attack by one State against another.[41]

The first, second, and fifth of these suggestions dealt with topics included in the Western August 29, 1957, proposals for partial measures of disarmament (even though the Soviet Union had rejected the Western proposals). The first stage of the new Western paper—the equivalent of proposals for partial measures of disarmament—did not include any of these topics.[42] Therefore, in this respect also, the March 15 Western paper was a retrogression from Western positions of August 1957. The unsubstantial first stage of the Western plan would scarcely encourage the Soviet Union to shift from broad propaganda discussions of general disarmament to the practical but politically less attractive negotiations on partial measures. It encouraged the Soviet

[39] *Ibid.*, par. E.
[40] *Ibid.*, par. F.
[41] *New York Times*, Sept. 19, 1959, p. 10 L.
[42] *Eaton Report*, p. 3.

bloc constantly to reiterate that "not one of the measures proposed by the Western Powers can be regarded as a realistic and serious disarmament measure."[43]

The first ten days of discussions witnessed a considerable amount of inconclusive probing on both sides. The Soviet satellite delegations requested the West to furnish greater detail concerning its proposals. The West sought to focus the issue on controls and to secure precise statements as to the types of controls the Soviet plan contemplated and how they would be installed. The Soviet Union altered its timetable on disarmament stages but not in such a manner as to permit the conference to come to grips with the precise problem of the measures to be included in the first stage.[44] Zorin made the interesting suggestion that international verification of the reduction of armed forces and armaments would be permitted but that "if inspectors are sent to verify armed forces and armaments which are not subject to reduction or abolition, . . . that cannot be regarded as other than military intelligence or, to use a coarser word, spying."[45]

On March 24, Zorin moved a little closer toward discussion of first stage measures. He stated that the Soviet Union would not permit aerial inspection of all its territory until the world was completely disarmed. However, the Soviet Union would consider negotiating on a limited aerial inspection to check up on specific measures of disarmament. This was obviously an invitation to renew the discussion of a European and possibly a Polar inspection zone.[46] The reply of the West was to "start talking right away—next Monday—" on an organization to enforce the reductions in armed forces and conventional weapons. Zorin felt that this would be a "useless job" unless agreement was reached on all the stages and principles of the Soviet plan for total disarmament in four years.[47] This stand made even the most optimistic

[43] Ten-Power Disarmament Committee, *Verbatim Records*, Twenty-seventh Meeting (April 22, 1960), p. 502.
[44] *Eaton Report*, pp. 3-4.
[45] Ten-Power Disarmament Committee, *Verbatim Records*, Seventh Meeting (March 23, 1960), p. 141.
[46] *Ibid.*, Eighth Meeting (March 24, 1960), p. 152.
[47] *New York Times*, March 26, 1960.

of the Western delegates, Jules Moch, a little gloomy about the fu, ture.[48]

On March 28 the West submitted the outlines of an international disarmament organization associated with the United Nations, but the Soviet bloc declined even to discuss the subject until agreement would be reached on its program of general and complete disarmament. The Soviet bloc also refused to discuss partial disarmament measures.[49]

In the same meeting, Moch suggested alternatively that the conference should "leave aside for the moment this goal [general and complete disarmament] . . . in order to see what we could do in a first stage toward that goal, then in a second stage, and so on." Zorin agreed.[50]

At the next meeting, the Bulgarian delegate sought to shift the discussion to the broad question whether the Soviet plan or the Western plan came closer to achieving general and complete disarmament.[51] This approach permitted the Soviet bloc to reap full propaganda advantages from the absence of arms reductions in the first stage of the Western proposals.

On April 5, the Western delegates formally turned down Khrushchev's proposals for general and complete disarmament: "It was a decision based on the growing conviction of Western delegations that the Soviet Union was blocking a decision to move on to specific disarmament steps in an attempt to get the maximum out of the negotiations." On April 7, Zorin in turn rejected the Western plan.[52]

On April 8 the Soviet bloc took a new line and submitted a statement of principles to govern the implementation of "General and Complete Disarmament." Purporting to follow the General Assembly resolution

[48] Ten-Power Disarmament Committee, *Verbatim Record,* Fourth Meeting (March 25, 1960), speech by Mr. Eaton (USA), p. 171; speech by Mr. Zorin (USSR), p. 175; speech by M. Moch (France), p. 182.
[49] *Ibid.,* speech by Mr. Cavalletti (Italy), Tenth Meeting, p. 184; speech by Mr. Mezincescu (Rumania), pp. 189, 191, 193. Discussion in *New York Times,* March 29, 1960, p. 1.
[50] Ten-Power Disarmament Committee, *Verbatim Records,* Tenth Meeting, pp. 200, 202. This was the closest point to specific negotiations.
[51] *Ibid.,* Eleventh Meeting (March 29, 1960), p. 208.
[52] *Ibid.,* speech by Mr. Eaton, Sixteenth Meeting (April 5, 1960), p. 290; speech by Mr. Zorin (USSR), Eighteenth Meeting (April 7, 1960), pp. 349, 357. See also *New York Times,* April 6, 1960, p. 1.

of November 20, 1959, which had called on the conference to "accept as an urgent practical task the implementation of the general and complete disarmament of all States," this Soviet bloc suggestion had five paragraphs. The first defined general and complete disarmament. The second paragraph stated that general and complete disarmament is to be carried out according to an agreed sequence by stages and is to be completed within a strictly defined time limit of four years. The third paragraph provided that implementation of all measures envisaged by the program of general and complete disarmament be carried out under international control whose scope should correspond "to the scope and nature of disarmament measures implemented at each stage." An international control organization would be set up as a part of the treaty. The fourth paragraph recited that after the completion of the program, states would retain at their disposal only limited contingents of police to maintain internal order. The fifth and most devious paragraph stated: "Implementation by States of the programme of general and complete disarmament may not be interrupted or made dependent on the fulfillment of any conditions not stipulated in the treaty."[53] This in effect assured that the program of disarmament would go on even though no agreement be reached on the methods of international control. The paragraph stated that violations of the treaty would be submitted to the Security Council and the United Nations General Assembly "for the institution of measures against the violator in accordance with the provisions of the United Nations Charter."[54] This would be the only safeguard until agreement was reached on an international control organ.

This was a propaganda proposal since it would commit the West to general and complete disarmament within four years without any assurance of safeguards. It was a more subtle version of the traditional Soviet proposals that a treaty for disarmament must precede the treaty providing for international control. For good measure the Soviets in addition were insisting on the West's immediately agreeing not to use

[53] Ten-Power Disarmament Committee, *Verbatim Records*, Nineteenth Meeting (April 8, 1960), pp. 369-70. "Text of Soviet Bloc's Arms Statement," *New York Times*, April 9, 1960.
[54] Ten-Power Disarmament Committee, *Verbatim Records*, Nineteenth Meeting (April 8, 1960), p. 370.

any nuclear weapons to resist an attack with conventional weapons. Obviously, the negotiations were getting further and further away from practical issues with each of the Soviet bloc delegations delivering long statements suitable for later publication. The next day Eaton and Zorin agreed that the talks should adjourn from April 29, when the summit conference was to commence in Paris, until June 6.

Before adjournment on April 26, the Western powers presented their own version of the general principles governing disarmament entitled "statement on conditions" for disarmament.[55] The statement declared that the disarmament process and any agreement finally reached must fulfill the following conditions: disarmament must be carried out in stages and as rapidly as possible, but with no fixed timetable; nuclear and conventional measures must be balanced in the interest of equal security for all countries; disarmament measures must be effectively controlled to ensure full compliance; and disarmament measures must be negotiated progressively according to the possibility of their early implementation and effective control. The final goal of a program of general and complete disarmament under effective international control must be to achieve the elimination of weapons of mass destruction and their means of delivery and the reduction and limitation of all types of forces and weapons to levels required only for internal security and the fulfillment of obligations under the United Nations Charter. The Western powers had at last returned to Cohen's 1952 statements of the objectives of a disarmament program. Six weeks of negotiation, however, had merely served to move the two sides further away from a discussion of specific measures.

The long recess from April 29 to June 6 reflected the view that the Ten-Power Conference was unlikely to make any progress in the absence of some decision at the summit conference in Paris to modify initial positions. The U-2 episode and the disruption of the summit conference even before it commenced destroyed this hope. With Khrushchev moving around Paris constantly accompanied by General Malinowsky and losing no opportunity to insult the President of the United States, it was doubtful whether the Ten-Power Conference would ever reconvene. However, five days before June 7, the date set

[55] *Ibid.*, Twenty-ninth Meeting (April 26, 1960), pp. 536-37.

for reconvening, the Soviet Union submitted a new plan to the Western delegates.[56]

As a background for this new Soviet proposal, it should be recalled that the only first-stage Western proposal for any limitation of the novel weapons of mass destruction called for prior notification to the international disarmament organization of proposed launchings of space vehicles. The Soviet deputy representative, Eleksei Roschin, one of the most capable and experienced of Soviet advisers, had stated in a press conference on March 21 that the Soviet Union could not agree to this provision "in a vacuum" as it touched on Soviet security. Roschin was then asked whether that would imply that the Soviet Union considered itself ahead in space propulsion. He answered "Why, of course."[57]

In an apparent reversal of this attitude, the Soviet Union underlined the following paragraph, which was a part of the long introduction explaining the Soviet motives for introducing a new proposal.

The Soviet Government, since it fervently believes that mankind must be freed as quickly as possible from the threat of the outbreak of a nuclear-rocket war, proposes that agreement should be reached to begin the process of general and complete disarmament with the prohibition and destruction under international control from the very first stage of all means of delivering nuclear weapons to their targets and the simultaneous liquidation of military bases in the territories of other States.[58]

The Soviet memorandum recalled that:

In the course of the negotiations, some Powers, among them France, expressed the view that disarmament should begin with the prohibition and destruction of vehicles for the delivery of nuclear, chemical and biological weapons, such as military rockets,

[56] *Ibid.*, Annex 10, pp. 925-32.
[57] *New York Times*, March 22, 1960.
[58] U.N. General Assembly, "Letter dated 2 June 1960 from the Permanent Representative of the Union of Soviet Socialist Republics to the United Nations addressed to the Secretary General," Doc. A/4374 (June 2, 1960), p. 5.

military aircraft, warships and the like, due regard being had to the need for the simultaneous liquidation by States of such military bases as they may possess in foreign territories.[59]

By this time the negotiations had reached a point at which the only significant feature of any proposals would be the first stage measures. This new Soviet proposal suggested a mammoth first stage.

1. Nuclear weapons shall be eliminated from the arsenals of States, their manufacture shall be discontinued and all means of delivering such weapons shall be destroyed. . . .

2. All foreign troops shall be withdrawn from the territories of other States to within their own national boundaries. . . .

3. From the very beginning of the first stage until the final destruction of all means of delivering nuclear weapons, the launching into orbit or the placing in outer space of special devices, the penetration of warships beyond the limits of territorial waters and the flight beyond the limits of their national territory of military aircraft capable of carrying weapons of mass destruction shall be prohibited.

4. Rockets shall be launched exclusively for peaceful purposes in accordance with predetermined and agreed criteria and subject to agreed verification measures, including on-the-spot inspection of the launching sites for such rockets.

5. States possessing nuclear weapons shall undertake not to transmit such weapons or information necessary for their manufacture to States which do not possess such weapons. At the same time, States which do not possess nuclear weapons shall undertake to refrain from manufacturing them.

6. States shall correspondingly reduce their expenditures for military purposes.

7. During the first stage the following control measures shall be carried out:

This paragraph of the proposal then elaborated an extensive system of

[59] *Ibid.*

inspection which included the broadest suggestions ever made by the Soviet Union for the detection of clandestine installations.

    8. During the first stage, a joint study shall be made of measures to effect the cessation of the production of nuclear, chemical and biological weapons and the destruction of stockpiles of such weapons, such measures to be carried out during the second stage.

    9. The first stage shall be completed in approximately one year to eighteen months. . . .[60]

One of the purposes of this proposal obviously was to attempt to create a rift between the French position and that of the other Western powers. While the United States in the surprise attack conference had originally suggested the idea that nuclear disarmament should be achieved through regulation of the means of delivery, it was Jules Moch who had enthusiastically carried the idea forward. The determination of France to become a fourth nuclear power in recent years has always been a source of possible friction between France and the other Western powers. The basis for the French decision to become a nuclear power was its determination to avoid the perpetuation of a position of inequality vis-à-vis the nuclear powers. In simplest terms, either all states should abandon nuclear weapons or the French should possess them. Thus the French in 1957 were unwilling to join in proposals for the cessation of nuclear testing, which would prevent France from becoming a nuclear power, unless such proposals were accompanied by a program that would ultimately eliminate all nuclear weapons. The French position became especially difficult with the recognition by both the Soviet Union and the United States that it was no longer possible to trace past production of fissionable materials and therefore ensure the total elimination of nuclear weapons from national arsenals. As a part of this policy of lessening its inequality, in 1957 Jules Moch had taken the lead in setting out the specific provisions of a safeguards system to ensure that all future production of nuclear materials would be used for purposes of peace.[61] General

[60] *Ibid.*, pp. 9-11.
[61] See Chap. 15.

de Gaulle was even more insistent than his predecessors either that France should become a member of the nuclear club or that nuclear weapons be eliminated. Therefore, it was only natural for Jules Moch and the French Government to embrace enthusiastically the possibility of eliminating nuclear weapons through controlling the means of delivery. Moch praised the Soviet Union for changing many of its positions; at the same time he felt it necessary to warn the Russian delegates that any idea of splitting the West would be a serious error as nothing would shake the French solidarity with its allies.[62]

The main Western response to the Soviet proposals was technical and colorless. The Western effort to obtain clarification of the Soviet proposals of June 2 was made by a series of questions which were put to the Soviet delegation.[63] Eaton characterized the Soviet answers as follows:

In spite of the evasiveness of many Soviet answers to questions, it became clear that the new Soviet paper was primarily a change in format from the earlier September 18 proposals, and that most of the unrealistic and unacceptable concepts of that earlier document remained.

Thus, for example, the Soviet Delegation maintained that moving a proposal for elimination of nuclear delivery vehicles from the last to the first stage of a disarmament program was in response to views expressed by the French Delegation, whereas in fact the Soviet proposal would have required the free world to commit itself as a first step to destroy within a matter of months its essential means of collective self-defense.

With regard to the critical question of control and inspection, there appeared to be little change in the Soviet position even though the Soviet paper of June 2 devoted more space to the subject than did the Soviet paper of September 18. The discussions showed that the Soviet delegation was unwilling to accept even in

[62] Ten-Power Disarmament Committee, *Verbatim Records*, Thirty-seventh Meeting (June 13, 1960), pp. 689-90. Also see *New York Times*, June 14, 1960, pp. 1 and 12.
[63] Ten-Power Disarmament Committee, *Verbatim Records*, Thirty-seventh Meeting (June 13, 1960), pp. 700-03.

principle that international inspectors would have the right to determine if clandestine installations existed in excess of agreed amounts; the Soviet position would limit the inspectors merely to counting those particular installations or forces that a government declared it was eliminating.[64]

By June 16 it had become apparent that regardless of the merits of the Western position, the West was losing the propaganda battle at Geneva and would have to present some new proposal of its own to redress the balance. On June 17, Eaton left by jet plane for Washington and David Ormsby-Gore, the British delegate, flew back to London.

ANOTHER IMPASSE

While the United States in recent years has rarely had the advantage of continuity of representation for any long period of time, in arms control discussions, the American press has been under no such handicap. Thomas J. Hamilton and A. M. Rosenthal have been the *New York Times* correspondents at these meetings for many years. Hamilton admirably summed up the progress of the Geneva negotiations:

Certain Soviet actions in the post-Stalin era, in particular the ruthless suppression of the uprisings in East Berlin and Hungary, have been a decided propaganda handicap. Moreover, Mr. Khrushchev probably overplayed his hand with the U-2 plane incident.

President Eisenhower's Atoms for Peace program captured the imagination of the world, but there was no satisfactory follow-through. And the blunders committed by the Eisenhower Administration in dealing with the U-2 counterbalanced Soviet errors. Above all, the United States has produced nothing approaching an effective answer to Mr. Khrushchev's proposal for total disarmament which was a propaganda triumph when he submitted it to the General Assembly last September.

[64] *Eaton Report*, pp. 6, 7.

General Disarmament / 549

After wringing the original proposal dry, Mr. Khrushchev recently submitted a revision even better calculated to win popular support: It accepts the French proposal that disarmament start with the prohibition of the means of delivering nuclear weapons and it calls for a quite complete inspection system. . . .

Naturally it would be helpful for the United States and its Allies to keep hammering away at the obscurities and the defects of the Khrushchev plan. But it is even more essential to get to work on a Western proposal in the hope of producing one that once again would capture the imagination of the world.[65]

It is difficult to disagree with any portion of this statement.

At this time, Senator Hubert Humphrey of Minnesota sounded a warning. Since 1955 Senator Humphrey had been the Chairman of the Disarmament Subcommittee of the Senate Foreign Relations Committee. By diligent and persistent study he had acquired a profound knowledge of all aspects of the arms control problem. On June 24, 1960 Senator Humphrey made a farsighted address to the United States Senate on the status of the disarmament negotiations. He summed up the situation before the summit negotiations.

The essence of the Soviet plan was lots of talk about disarmament, little control, and no study. The essence of the Western plan was lots of study, a bit of control and an uncertain and indefinite amount of disarmament. I believe that that is just about as capsule a kind of explanation as can be given on this complicated subject.[66]

Senator Humphrey then analyzed in some detail the new Soviet proposals. He concluded:

The six points I have cited convey a general impression of conciliation. On reading the total proposal, one is at least tempted to the conclusion that the Soviets have in this proposal moved closer to the position of the Western Powers. There is an inconsistency.

[65] "Arms and Propaganda," New York Times, June 19, 1960, p. E 9.
[66] Congressional Record, Vol. 106, No. 117, 86 Cong., 2 sess. (June 24, 1960), p. 2.

The Soviets do not combine a tabling of their proposals with words: "Let's get down to business." They do almost the opposite . . . one does not know whether the Soviet Union has submitted a proposal for the purpose of serious negotiation or for the purpose of breaking off talks. . . . As a result of these various discussions and study, I wrote to the President offering certain suggestions. I hesitate to offer suggestions to the President during the course of negotiations. He presumably has so many experts and officials on which to call. Yet we witnessed within the past months and years a great lack of ideas and proposals in the field of foreign policy, and particularly with respect to the matter of arms control.

It disturbs and perplexes me that in view of the crucial nature of the arms control problem, the Administration consistently fails to take the initiative. Probably one of the explanations is that this question has not been taken seriously enough throughout the national security structure. Therefore, no matter how much the President may desire to seek progress toward disarmament, his subordinates do not follow through with the kind of dedication, study, and thoroughness which the situation requires.

Senator Humphrey then suggested a four-point program: That all future production of long-range bombers be prohibited under effective inspection and control safeguards; that international observers be stationed at all military air bases; that we conduct with the Soviet bloc a study of the ways and means to stop the production of fissionable materials for weapons purposes; and that the Chinese Communists be included in the disarmament negotiations.[67]

Regardless of the soundness of this program, something equally dramatic was required to regain some of the political initiative the West had lost. Senator Humphrey had prophetically sounded the warning that the Soviet bloc might be about to disrupt the negotiations.

The West received warning from another source. Prime Minister Nehru of India, speaking in New Delhi, strongly supported the revised Soviet disarmament plan. He said that the new proposals were "just,

[67] *Ibid.*, pp. 2, 3.

constructive, straightforward and helpful and undoubtedly exhibit the Soviet Union's desire to bring about disarmament and not play about with it."[68] Nehru made no reference to the Western position on disarmament. Surely, the hurricane flags were flying.

Eaton returned to Geneva, and, before the meeting of June 27, informed Zorin that as a result of the discussions in Washington, the United States delegation would table a new paper within the next few days following consultations with the allied delegations.[69] When the Ten-Power Conference met on June 27, the Polish delegate was in the chair. He recognized each of the five communist delegates who announced their intention to walk out from the conference. Zorin, certainly expressing a premeditated Soviet decision, prefaced his speech with the remark that "the Government of the Soviet Union has instructed the Soviet delegation to make the . . . statement today."

The record then reads as follows:

Naszkowski (the Polish delegate). After the statements made by the Representatives of the Five Socialist States, the work of the Ten Nation Committee is discontinued, and it is quite clear that the role of the chairman has been exhausted.

The Representatives of Bulgaria, Czechoslovakia, Poland, Rumania and the Union of Soviet Socialist Republics started to withdraw from the meeting.

M. Moch (France) Point of order. Mr. Chairman, I ask you to recognize me. I ask to speak, Mr. Chairman. Do you know the rules of procedure? What a scandal!

Mr. Ormsby-Gore (United Kingdom) Point of order, Mr. Chairman.

Mr. Eaton (United States) Point of Order.

M. Moch (France) I ask for the floor, I ask that this meeting continue and that the next representative in alphabetical order should take the chair. Mr. Ormsby-Gore, please take the chair. The meeting is going on. This is a scandal. It is hooliganism. What

[68] *New York Times,* June 25, 1960.
[69] *Eaton Report,* p. 8.

a shameful performance! If this is your kind of democracy I can only say that it is a fine one! The representatives of Bulgaria, Czechoslovakia, Poland, Rumania and the Union of Soviet Socialist Republics withdrew from the meeting.[70]

Eaton then tabled the United States proposals even though the Soviet bloc representatives were absent. The new proposals were indeed less innocuous than the March proposals. The crux of all the proposals was the first stage, and in its latest initiative, the United States, like the Soviet Union, was suggesting a large first stage.

The eight measures now included in the first stage were: 1. As in the March proposals, establishment of an international control organization. 2. Prohibition of the placing into orbit or stationing in outer space of vehicles carrying weapons capable of mass destruction. The March proposals had merely provided for prior notification to the control organization of all launchings of space vehicles. This paragraph did not deal with missile launchings. 3. "Prior notification to the International Disarmament Control Organization of all proposed launchings of space vehicles and missiles and their planned tracks" coupled with the "establishment of a zone of aerial and ground inspection in agreed areas including the United States and the USSR;" and "an exchange of observers on a reciprocal basis at agreed military bases, domestic and foreign." The first part of this section calling for prior notification of all proposed launchings of space vehicles and missiles might have been an appropriate subject for further discussion if it had not been coupled with the extensive aerial and ground inspection provisions, which were more suitable to enforce prohibition of missile launchings than merely to detect them. 4. "Declaration of and institution of on-site inspection at mutually agreed operational air-bases, missile launching pads, submarine and naval bases, in order to establish a basis for controls over nuclear delivery systems in sub-

[70] "Arms Parley at Geneva Ends in an Uproar," *New York Times*, June 28, 1960, p. 1. The corrected *Verbatim Records* softened some of the above statements. See Ten-Power Disarmament Committee, *Verbatim Records*, Forty-seventh Meeting (June 27, 1960), p. 887.

sequent stages." It was suggested that this type of safeguard is also more suitable for an agreement eliminating the use of missiles in warfare than for agreement merely prohibiting the stationing of space vehicles in outer space and requiring advance notification of missile launchings. 5. Slightly expanded provisions (in comparison to the March proposals) for initial force level ceilings. 6. Provisions for placing agreed quantities of conventional armaments in storage depots under supervision of the international control organization, the same as the provisions in the March proposals. 7. "The production of fissionable materials for use in weapons shall be stopped upon installation and effective operation of the control system found necessary to verify this step . . . and agreed quantities of fissionable materials from past production shall be transferred to non-weapons uses, including stockpiling for peaceful purposes, conditioned upon satisfactory progress in the field of conventional disarmament." This was the cutoff which the Soviet Union had rejected for any early stage of disarmament negotiations because of the massive breach of the iron curtain required in order to have an effective control system. In one minor respect, this proposal would presumably have been even more objectionable to the Soviet Union than the 1957 proposals. The transfer of fissionable materials from past production in these proposals was conditioned "upon satisfactory progress in the field of conventional disarmament." There was no such limitation in the August 29, 1957, proposals. 8. Provisions on financial data substantially similar to those contained in the March proposals.[71]

This first and crucial stage, described in capsule form, provided for slightly more disarmament and much more international control than the March proposals. In many respects, it was even less suitable for serious negotiation with the Soviet Union than the March proposals. The illogical linking of measures of limitation and reduction with control systems unsuitable for those measures seems to testify to hasty preparation and liberal use of paste and scissors. Furthermore, the restoration of the cutoff to the first stage would have militated against any genuine negotiations.

[71] *Ibid.*, pp. 934-35.

The Soviet Union might easily have gained propaganda advantages from a thorough and reasonable discussion of the new Western proposals. Furthermore, the crude disruption of the proceedings recalled some of the worst episodes of the Stalin era: Gromyko's boycott of the Security Council during the discussions of the presence of Soviet troops in Iran almost at the beginning of the United Nations in 1946, and the repeated Soviet walk-outs from each United Nations organ in 1950 as the organ defeated the Soviet resolution to unseat the "Representative of the Comintern." This Soviet tactic, calculated to outrage the intellectual élite who represent most states in the United Nations, was particularly untimely in view of Nehru's endorsement of the Soviet position less than a week earlier.

It is also difficult to reconcile the Soviet insult to international organizations with the later tactic of seeking to turn the 1960 General Assembly into a summit meeting of the heads of all states Members of the United Nations. As the London *Economist* pointed out, the Soviet action seemed consistent with a propaganda appeal that it alone had proposed anything in the negotiations. "The Russians felt they must escape from Geneva before the tabling of new Western proposals spoilt the nice simplicity of their claim."[72] Likewise the walk-out might be part of the new pattern of toughness.

On July 3 in a speech at Linz, Austria, Khrushchev gave another possible explanation for Soviet actions: He was convinced that there was no use in talking with the United States on disarmament until after the elections and inauguration of a new administration.[73]

The July walk-out was in all likelihood linked with the broader decision of Khrushchev to appear in New York at the General Assembly, but was not calculated to create an atmosphere favorable to Khrushchev in that body. The full motivation of that broader decision remains obscure.

Eisenhower speedily and effectively protested to Khrushchev.

The withdrawal of the Soviet delegation stands in sharp contrast

[72] "Arguing with their Feet," *The Economist* (July 2, 1960), p. 13.
[73] *New York Times,* July 4, 1960, p. A 6. Actually, Khrushchev had made the same statement in private conversations at least six months earlier.

to the repeated Soviet official declarations of intent to settle by peaceful means through negotiation all outstanding international issues, among which, it would have been expected, would be the question of disarmament, acknowledged by the Soviet Government to be the most important question facing the world today. . . .

The goal of disarmament is an aspiration common to all mankind and an objective which all governments must relentlessly strive to achieve. For its part, the United States Government remains determined to spare no effort to arrive at mutually acceptable agreements on concrete measures, the implementation of which would represent a solid advance toward the goal of complete and general disarmament under reliable and effective international control.[74]

On July 22, Henry Cabot Lodge called for a meeting of the entire Disarmament Commission including representatives of all states Members of the United Nations. The Soviet Union countered by calling for a United Nations summit talk on disarmament in which the heads of government of all the Members of the United Nations would participate. The Soviet delegate to the United Nations, Plato D. Morozov, told Dr. Luis Padilla Nervo, of Mexico, the chairman of the Disarmament Commission, that a Disarmament Commission meeting "on the eve of the General Assembly Session" would only "aggravate the situation."[75] This probably meant that the meeting of the Disarmament Commission might interfere with the build-up of the Khrushchev appearance in the General Assembly.

When the commission met on August 16, all of the representatives of the Soviet bloc were in their chairs despite rumors that they might boycott the session. Henry Cabot Lodge, in a thoroughly professional and brilliant farewell speech to the United Nations reviewed briefly the entire discouraging history of arms control negotiations beginning with 1946 and ending in the Geneva impasse of the previous month.[76]

[74] "Text of U.S. Reply to Soviet on Arms," *ibid.*, July 3, 1960, p. 2.
[75] *Ibid.*, Aug. 2, 1960, pp. 1 and 3.
[76] *Ibid.*, Aug. 17, 1960, p. 4 C. This was termed a "farewell speech" because Lodge was withdrawing from the United Nations as a result of having been

He re-submitted the proposals which the United States had tabled in Geneva on June 27 with a minimum of detailed description. He listed the concessions to the Soviet view, which as described by Lodge, were accurate but certainly meager, in sharp contrast to Eaton's claims.[77]

1. We included a definition of general and complete disarmament, in terms not very different from the Soviet definition.

2. We accepted the principle that each measure of a disarmament program would be carried out in an agreed and strictly defined period of time.

3. We adopted a provision based on the Soviet plan of June 2 for a review by the Security Council of the progress of disarmament at the end of each disarmament stage. This is something they wanted.

4. We agreed to a figure of 1.7 million for the armed forces of the USSR and the United States in the second stage of the disarmament program. That is a real thing to agree to.

5. We accepted a technical examination of measures necessary to control, reduce and eliminate agreed categories of nuclear delivery systems, including missiles, aircraft, surface ships, submarines and artillery. This concerned a measure to which the Soviet Union had given first place in its disarmament program. And this, Mr. Chairman, we accepted.

As rapidly as possible Lodge moved into territory where his position was stronger and launched into a description of the dangers of the arms race and the necessity of moving toward disarmament.

He added two new proposals that were calculated to have great world appeal. The first was the United States declaration of its readiness on a reciprocal basis "to set aside 30,000 kilograms of weapons grade U235, as the amount which the United States and the Soviet Union would each initially transfer to an international agency." The second proposal was that:

nominated by the Republican party as its candidate for the Vice-Presidency in the presidential election.
[77] *Eaton Report*, p. 8.

The United States is ready to join the Soviet Union in halting, by successive steps, the production of fissionable materials for weapons use. . . . We are prepared to shut down, one by one, under international inspection, our major plants producing enriched uranium and plutonium if the Soviet Union will shut down equivalent facilities. We are prepared to do this now—with no delay at all.[78]

While these new proposals were attractive, they were not calculated to bring on any serious negotiations, since they were elaborations of the United States proposals for a cutoff, which the Soviet Union had decisively rejected as a first-stage measure of disarmament.

Lodge's speech indicated, however, that he at least had relearned the lesson, which the United States had twice forgotten, that in arms control negotiations the United States position must be both sound and politically attractive. If it is unsound, the Soviet negotiators with their skill developed through years of experience will easily reveal the flaws. If it is unattractive, the Soviet Union will abandon the most serious of negotiations to score a propaganda victory.

It is difficult to come to an end of the narrative of the arms control negotiations since the events move on steadily and relentlessly. The importance of the subject is so great that the pauses to refresh are few and short. The appraisal of the most recent period of arms control negotiations can best be undertaken as a part of the broader review of the entire fifteen years of almost constant movement.

[78] United States Mission to the United Nations, Press Release 3457, Aug. 16, 1960, pp. 8, 9, 11 and 12.

PART SEVEN

An Appraisal

XXI

Highway With Signs

BEFORE ATTEMPTING to estimate where the arms control negotiations now stand and the direction of their movement, it may be helpful to look back briefly over the highway of fifteen years of international negotiations.

When the Charter of the United Nations was signed in 1945, it was not foreseen that the subject of arms control would assume such a dominant role in the United Nations during the early years of its existence. The United Nations Charter emphasized saving succeeding generations from the scourge of war, primarily through the establishment of an effective collective security system. While the Covenant of the League of Nations had looked to disarmament as one of the first and principal steps toward peace, the Charter used the word "disarmament" only twice and in those two instances implied that extensive disarmament of the great powers was to be an eventual rather than an immediate objective.

Immediately after the signing of the Charter at San Francisco, the explosion of the atomic bomb over Hiroshima in August 1945 brought to the fore the entire problem of the regulation of armaments. The negotiations for regulation of armaments could not and did not go forward in an atmosphere of friendly cooperation.

Roosevelt, Churchill, and Stalin had visualized a postwar world in

561

which the united action of the great powers for the prosecution of the war against Hitler would be continued for the organization and maintenance of international peace and security. Soviet attempts to enlarge the area of Communist domination in Europe, commencing almost immediately after the defeat of Germany, had destroyed the possibility of such collaboration. The rapid demobilization of the Western armed forces after the war may well have encouraged the Soviet leaders to believe that their aggressive policies would succeed. As one result of the Soviet policies, however, the arms control negotiations almost from their inception took place under conditions of distrust rather than of collaboration.

For the purposes of this study, arms control negotiations have been divided into five periods.

In the first period, lasting from January 1946 till December 1948, the United States submitted to the United Nations Atomic Energy Commission the Baruch Plan for complete international control of atomic energy at all stages from the uranium mines to the completed weapons. The United Nations discussion of the Baruch Plan at the outset was relatively detailed and precise and generally free of propaganda broadsides, a type of negotiation never thereafter repeated until the summer of 1957.

The Soviet Union submitted counter proposals for the prohibition of nuclear weapons with safeguards that the United Nations found to be inadequate protection against violations. This became a familiar pattern for arms control negotiations. The West could not take the risk of accepting proposals with inadequate safeguards. The West, however, was making proposals that would have destroyed Soviet secrecy, a large element in Soviet military strength. Furthermore, the Western proposals never explained in any detail when and in what manner the world-wide installation of control machinery would bring about the elimination of nuclear weapons. Therefore, the West was offering little of value in return for the destruction of Soviet secrecy. This also became a familiar pattern for arms control negotiations.

During this period, the Soviet Union brought before the United Nations the problem of the reduction of conventional armaments, an initiative resulting in the establishment of the United Nations Commission on Conventional Armaments. The discussions in this commission never passed the stage of propaganda. The Soviet Union concentrated on a demand for a one-third reduction of all armaments and armed forces, but resisted all efforts to establish the figures from which the one-third reduction would take place. Furthermore, in view of the admitted superiority of the Soviet bloc in conventional armaments, the effect of any such reduction, even if faithfully observed, would have widened the imbalance already favoring the Soviet Union in the field of conventional armaments. The West made no proposals of any consequence during this period in the Conventional Armaments Commission. In retrospect this seems shortsighted since the West was placing its full emphasis on the elimination of atomic weapons, the only weapons in which it had superiority.

The second period extending from the conclusion of the General Assembly of 1948 until the establishment of the Disarmament Commission in the winter of 1951-1952 can best be described as "complete frustration." Discussions took place each year in the General Assembly and in both of the United Nations commissions dealing with arms control. However, no programs or proposals of any consequence were submitted by either the Soviet Union or the West.

Outside the negotiations, the Soviet Union conducted two intensive propaganda programs directed toward producing world sentiment for disarmament without controls. The first of these propaganda moves was the Stockholm Appeal, a petition circulated by the Communists throughout the world and receiving millions of signatures. Its message can be summarized by the three words "ban the bomb." The second and later propaganda campaign centered on the accusation that the United States had engaged in bacteriological warfare in Korea.

During this period the Soviet Union withdrew for a time from participation in all organs of the United Nations including the two commissions dealing with arms control because of the failure to seat the Chinese Communist representative. After the return of the Soviet representatives, they continued to use the United Nations organs largely as forums for propaganda, and no serious negotiation was possible. During these years, the Western powers likewise made no serious detailed proposals, but did succeed in developing a general approach to the problems of arms control that met with the unanimous approval of all Members of the United Nations except the Soviet bloc. It was in this phase that the Western powers developed their system of alliances to contain Soviet aggression.

The third period commenced with the establishment of the United Nations Disarmament Commission in January 1952 and lasted until the end of 1954. In 1952 and 1954 the Western powers, with the United States taking the leadership, developed the outline of a comprehensive program for drastic but safeguarded disarmament in both the atomic and conventional fields. Until the final days of the London sessions of the subcommittee of the Disarmament Commission in June 1954, the Soviet response continued to be primarily negative. In 1952, the Soviet negative responses to the United States proposals took the form of propaganda blasts, which only rarely sought even to discuss the issues of the negotiations. After the death of Stalin, the Soviet language was less vituperative, and the lengthy speeches at least purported to deal with the issues under discussion. In the fall of 1954, the Soviet Union indicated its willingness to go forward in the negotiations on the basis of some of the proposals which the Western powers had submitted, thus foreshadowing the changed Soviet position that prevailed in the next phase of the negotiations.

The fourth period, lasting from January 1955 until December 1957, commenced with an almost simultaneous reappraisal of policies by the Soviet Union and the West. The development of thermonuclear weapons and the approach of a nuclear stalemate made a reappraisal inevitable. The Soviet reappraisal could not take place until the death of Stalin. One sign of the reappraisal in the United States was the appointment of Harold Stassen, with Cabinet rank, as the United States negotiator, and the provision of a staff with adequate numbers to carry out an important and complex international negotiation.

In August 1955, Stassen "reserved" and, in effect, rescinded the United States position on all former proposals, announcing that the quantities of fissionable materials already produced were so great that it would no longer be possible to devise a system that would account for all past production of fissionable materials. The elimination of nuclear weapons with adequate safeguards to assure compliance—the crux of all earlier plans for control of atomic energy—was no longer possible.

Three months before the United States reservation of positions, the Soviet Union on May 10, 1955, proposed three separate paths for decreasing international tensions and reducing the danger of war. The first path called for increasing economic and cultural contacts together with a settlement of political issues. The second path called for drastic and comprehensive disarmament on the general lines of the Western proposals of the previous three years. The third path called for partial measures of disarmament, which would reduce tension and lessen the danger of war and might lead to more drastic future measures of disarmament.

For the first time, the Soviet Union conceded in principle that reductions and limitations of armaments need not precede the establishment and operation of the machinery of a control plan adequate to ensure that the reductions and limitations in fact take place. The Soviet Union at the same time publicly agreed with the Western position that it was no longer possible to devise a control system that could account for all past production of fissionable materials. Likewise the Soviet Union began to inform its people that as a result of the increase in power and number of nuclear weapons, an all-out nuclear war might devastate the Soviet Union as well as the West. Previously the Soviet position had been that nuclear warfare would destroy decadent capitalism but somehow would leave the Communist world unscathed.

It took from 1955 until November 1956 for the revised viewpoints of the Soviet Union and the West to crystallize sufficiently to permit any genuine negotiation. In the spring and summer of 1957, both sides submitted proposals that ostensibly considerably narrowed the differences. Three months of intensified negotiations resulted in some further narrowing of differences, but no formal agreement on any measures either of comprehensive or partial disarmament. At the end of August 1957, the Soviet Union, probably motivated largely by international developments outside the arms control negotiations, rejected the Western proposals and terminated the negotiations. The impasse became even greater during the General Assembly of 1957 and ended with the Soviet Union's refusing to participate in any future discussions in the Disarmament Commission as then constituted or in its sub-committee.

The fifth period commenced in January 1958 and still continues. With the Soviet refusal to participate in the established United Nations organs for discussion of arms control, the first efforts not only of the Soviet Union and the Western powers but also of other states were directed to establishing new methods of negotiation. These efforts led to the convening of two technical conferences in 1958, one to study possible measures to prevent surprise attack, and the other to consider the problem of nuclear test cessation. The first recessed after approximately three months without even reaching agreement on the scope of the discussion. The second reached sufficient agreement to permit the convening of another conference of the nuclear powers—the United States, the United Kingdom, and the Soviet Union—to draft a treaty providing for the cessation of nuclear tests with appropriate controls. This conference still continues. Despite some agreement, a substantial number of important problems remain to be resolved before a treaty emerges.

In the fall of 1959, Khrushchev appeared before the United Nations in New York to advocate a resumption of general disarmament negotiations and to propose a program for "General and Complete Disarmament." He conceded, however, the possibility of agreement on partial disarmament if it were impossible to obtain agreement on general and total disarmament. A Ten-Power Conference, five Western powers and five members of the Soviet bloc, was convened in the spring of 1960 to resume the broader negotiations. It lasted from March until June when the Soviet delegate broke up the conference just as the West was about to submit revised proposals. A sage capsule comment on the positions in this conference was that the Soviet plan amounted to "Lots of talk about disarmament, little control and no study"; the Western plan, "Lots of study, a bit of control and an indefinite amount of disarmament."[1] As of the present, the Nuclear Test Cessation Conference continues with little progress; the Soviet Union and the West both express the desire for further negotiations on the broader problems of arms control but have reached no agreement

[1] See Chap. 20, statement of Senator Hubert Humphrey.

either on the forum for the negotiations or on the subjects or approach
when negotiations resume.

Thus, on the surface, the fifteen years of negotiations have resulted
in a total impasse with no formal agreements of any nature. Except in
the field of nuclear test cessation, the great powers cannot even decide
on procedures for resuming negotiations.

EMERGENCE OF A CONSENSUS

Although fifteen years of almost constant negotiation failed to produce a formal agreement on any phase of arms control, an implicit and
more subtle accord or consensus seems to have emerged. Mainly this
consensus is merely an agreed framework for negotiations. It goes
somewhat further, however, and includes some substantive ideas. It
rests on the fundamental recognition by both the Soviet Union and
the West that a two-way nuclear strike would create such devastation
that both sides must pursue policies designed to avoid such an eventuality. It rests also on the realization that, regardless of the wishes of
the Soviet Union and of the West, world public opinion has not
allowed and apparently will not allow arms control negotiations to
lapse.

From time to time during the narrative of the events of the past
fifteen years, we have sought to sketch segments of an apparently
inevitable framework for arms control negotiations. The end of the
narrative is the appropriate place to assemble and evaluate these areas
of accord.

1. Both the Soviet Union and the West have recognized that an
uncontrolled arms race increases the likelihood of a disastrous nuclear
war.

2. Both the Soviet Union and the West seem to recognize that one
path they must follow to reduce the likelihood of a nuclear war is the
path of negotiations for arms control. Furthermore, no matter how
hopeless the outlook may be, both within and outside the United
Nations, world public opinion strongly favors the continuance of arms
control negotiations. It may well be that limitations of armaments can-

not be achieved in the present tense international atmosphere. But when either the Soviet Union or the West shows some inclination to permit the negotiations to lapse pending improvement in the international atmosphere, the General Assembly of the United Nations invariably takes the position that some measure of agreement on arms control would in and of itself improve the international atmosphere and facilitate the settlement of other outstanding international controversies. Generally, both the Soviet Union and the West have concurred, and the negotiations continue. One element in this position has been that a limited agreement on arms control has seemed no more difficult to achieve than the settlement of other major political differences between the East and the West, such as the problem of Berlin or the status of the Chinese Communists. Therefore, unless either the Soviet Union or the West determines deliberately to flout world public opinion and is prepared to accept the penalties of such a course of action, the negotiations are likely to continue for many years. The position that arms control negotiations should be suspended pending an improvement in the international atmosphere is no longer available for either the United States or the Soviet Union.

3. Any progress toward arms control will depend on agreement among the great powers, primarily the United States and the Soviet Union. An attempt such as that made by the West in 1957 to obtain, over the objections of the Soviet Union, an overwhelming endorsement of the United Nations General Assembly for its position is futile and damaging to the states that make the attempt. The United Nations General Assembly may pass judgment on the attitudes of the great powers in the arms control negotiations and may exert its influence through suggesting means of reconciling differences among the great powers. The great powers may hesitate to disregard United Nations recommendations receiving adequate support. However, an important substantive agreement to control arms depends on prior great power agreement.

4. The stated ultimate objective of any arms control agreement must be a drastic limitation and reduction of armaments. This objective may be expressed in the words of Khrushchev as "general and total disarmament"; in the words of the United Nations Charter, as

saving "succeeding generations from the scourge of war," or maintaining "international peace and security with the least diversion for armaments of the world's human and economic resources"; or even in the more technical terms developed by the Disarmament Commission as "regulation and limitation of all armed forces and armaments, and elimination of weapons of mass destruction under international control."[2] The negotiations might be much easier if the parties could limit themselves to a consideration of partial confidence-building measures of disarmament, which would improve the international atmosphere and set the groundwork for later and more drastic measures. This was the approach of both the Soviet Union and the West in 1955 and 1956, and with slight modifications in the intensified negotiations of 1957. Partial measures of disarmament, however, have far less popular appeal than broadsides calling for general and total disarmament. From 1955 to 1957, the leaders of both the Soviet Union and the West on occasions attempted to obtain propaganda advantages through advocating drastic disarmament whenever the negotiations for partial disarmament reached an apparent impasse. This experience seems for the present to foreclose the possibility of negotiating for partial disarmament except as the first stage of a broader program of total disarmament.

5. Both the Soviet Union and the West have agreed that the ultimate objective will not be achieved immediately and that any program will provide for disarmament in stages. In recent years, both sides have suggested three stages. The crucial portion of the negotiations will, of course, deal with the first stage. This framework of calling for total disarmament and negotiating only on the first stage may seem awkward and indeed hypocritical in view of the almost insuperable obstacles in going beyond the first stage.

6. The Soviet Union will agree to almost any measure of arms control not involving a control system that extensively penetrates the iron curtain. This may be an enlargement and expansion of its postwar position of seeking to utilize the arms control negotiations to secure the unilateral disarmament of the West. The Soviet Union has shown that it is always willing to interrupt the complicated negotiations for

[2] These objectives are not identical, but may be equivalent in terms of popular appeal.

controlled disarmament in order to obtain the limitations without the control. The Soviet leaders, as they claim, may be genuinely appalled at the difficulty of setting up a control system, and might genuinely go through with a thorough program of disarmament even without controls if the West would do the same. Certainly the West cannot take any serious chance. Therefore, for the foreseeable future the West must continue to require that negotiations for controls proceed simultaneously with negotiations, and perhaps some action, looking toward limitations and reductions. The Soviet Union has shown its willingness to proceed along these lines.

7. Just as the West cannot consent to negotiations on limitations and reductions without negotiations on controls, the Soviet Union will never negotiate on the controls without negotiating on the reductions and limitations to which the controls will apply. An example of Western failure to appreciate this basic requirement was the surprise attack conference, which took place in November and December 1958. The understandable reason behind this Soviet position is that the installation of any control system will benefit the West more than it will benefit the Soviet Union, because most of the information that the control system will develop in the West is probably known to the Soviet Union. The converse is definitely not true. Therefore the Soviet Union will always insist that the West pay a price for the penetration of the iron curtain resulting from any international control system. For this reason, the negotiation of the price the West will have to pay must proceed simultaneously with the negotiation of the control system.

8. The crux of any arms control negotiations for the foreseeable future will be the development of the first stage. In the selection of measures for the first stage, two criteria have logically emerged: (a) measures of limitation and reduction where the self-interest of the Soviet Union coincides with that of the West, (b) measures requiring a comparatively simple safeguards system in order to ensure observance of commitments. It will be obvious that if the safeguards system does not require an extensive penetration of the iron curtain, the concessions the West will have to make to obtain an adequate control system behind the iron curtain will be smaller.

9. The Soviet Union and the West seem to be in agreement that some measures should be undertaken to prevent the accidental outbreak of a nuclear war—either through a misreading of signals that might launch the great powers into a push-button war, or through the outbreak of a conventional war in a tinderbox area that might spread into a nuclear holocaust.

10. At various times during the negotiations, both the Soviet Union and the West seemed to have recognized that the danger of outbreak of a nuclear war would be greater in the event of an increase in the number of states possessing nuclear weapons systems.[3]

This was the basis for the United States positions in support of an elaborate system of safeguards in the International Atomic Energy Agency. The Soviet Union likewise supported a strict safeguards system whenever the negotiations were genuinely secret, and in public negotiations[4] never obstructed the unpopular United States efforts to obtain an extensive safeguards system. It seems probable that one important factor influencing the Soviet Union to support a convention calling for the cessation of nuclear testing is that such a convention might measurably delay the development of dangerous nuclear weapons systems by countries other than the United States, the Soviet Union, and the United Kingdom. Additional states could nevertheless obtain nuclear weapons without testing through transfer by states now possessing them. The Western proposals in the subcommittee of the Disarmament Commission during the summer of 1957, culminating in

---

[3] See Thomas C. Schelling, "Reciprocal Measures for Arms Stabilization," *Daedalus*, Vol. 89, p. 901n. "It seems a current interpretation that there is still some element of implicit understanding about not transferring nuclear weapons to other countries. Its status is presently a great deal more ambiguous than the author expected a couple of years ago; nevertheless there must be a general awareness on both sides that the restraint of either will be weakened or dissolved by promiscuousness on the other's part."

[4] See Meeting of Six Governments "to consider the problems of safeguarding or guaranteeing the peaceful uses of atomic energy against diversion of materials," Geneva (August 22-27, 1955), S/P/V 5 Rev. 1, p. 5 and S/P/V 1 Rev. 1, pp. 2 and 15. (The minutes of these meetings are now declassified.) The Soviet Union supported the safeguards even more strongly in a technical meeting in February 1957 in connection with the work of the Preparatory Commission of the International Atomic Energy Agency.

the August 29 proposals, left open the possibility of transfer of nuclear weapons by the United States to NATO, which since 1957 has become a probability. This raised doubts in the Soviet Union whether the United States was adhering to its policy of preventing additional states from obtaining nuclear weapons capabilities. It also raised "the bogey of Germany," the fear that Germany "may have nuclear weapons put at her disposal."[5] Despite these doubts, the past accord still seems to be a factor in the negotiations.

11. In recent years, both the Soviet Union and the West seem to be exercising a degree of restraint in avoiding one-sided proposals. It is not possible to dismiss lightly the most recent Soviet proposal to eliminate all delivery systems for nuclear weapons in the first stage of disarmament with an avowal that such a measure, even if fully enforced on both sides, would benefit the Soviet Union more than the West. Similarly, it is not possible to reject brusquely the series of overlapping Soviet proposals for a zone in Central Europe free of nuclear weapons coupled with some aerial inspection. The West began to avoid one-sided proposals at an earlier date. Of course the Western proposals as originally introduced are unduly favorable to their proponents in the recognition that any negotiation with the Soviet Union involves difficult bargaining. The West has constantly emphasized that its initial positions are not necessarily its final positions. While the Soviet leaders have not been equally forthright, nevertheless, in the three serious negotiations of recent years—the negotiations for the International Atomic Energy Agency, the disarmament subcommittee negotiations in 1957, and the present test cessation negotiations—the initial positions of the Soviet Union have not turned out to be its final positions. Most of the present Soviet proposals could be quite reasonable, *provided* that the Soviet Union were willing to permit an adequate control system to ensure the observance of the agreements to carry its proposals into effect. The only way to determine whether the Soviet Union is serious about its proposals is to attempt to draft the detailed annexes that will accompany any agreements in principle. This is the procedure of the test cessation conference.

12. Quite recently the Soviet Union seems to be facing a problem

[5] Jules Moch, "Man's Folly Today Will Pass," *New York Times Magazine,* Aug. 14, 1960, pp. 79, 80.

that has always confronted the Western powers. For the first time, the Soviet Union may not be able to speak with authority for the entire Soviet bloc. The Soviet leaders cannot be sure that the Chinese Communists will accept their decisions. Furthermore, the Soviet Union cannot forge links with the so-called neutralist bloc and at the same time disregard their views. The first impact of such a development logically enough appears in the forums of international negotiation. An initial indication of this changed viewpoint is the Soviet suggestion that the Ten-Power Conference to consider general problems of disarmament be raised to include five members of the neutral bloc, and thus become a fifteen power conference. Expansion in the numbers of the technical group will obviously complicate the negotiations. The presence of states not irrevocably committed to the Communist position and whose friendship the Soviet Union is cultivating would, however, furnish some assurance that the Soviet Union does not plan to return to outrageously propagandistic proposals. But this situation has not yet resulted in East-West accord.

13. With the exception of the Baruch Plan, all the Western proposals prior to 1952 were too general to permit extensive progress toward an arms control convention. Beginning in 1952, the Western proposals became progressively more precise reflecting the increased consideration given to arms control problems within the governments of the Western powers, and particularly within the Government of the United States. Some Western proposals in 1958 and subsequent years attained the precision required for an international convention. The Soviet proposals correspondingly became more precise after 1954 but have invariably been less detailed and have reflected a less thorough analysis of problems than the Western proposals.[6]

ALARM SIGNALS

It is not possible to assert with conviction that the arms control negotiations have moved consistently toward the emergence of explicit or tacit accords. While the general trend seems to be in that direction,

[6] Professor T. C. Schelling *op. cit.*, deals in detail with the emergence of informal arms understandings outside the field of the arms control negotiations.

a number of developments during the past two years may run counter to this pattern:

1. From May 1955 through 1959, the Soviet Union was willing to discuss either a program of comprehensive disarmament or partial first-stage measures of disarmament. The Soviet statement of May 10, 1955, contained completely separate proposals setting forth these two alternative approaches. In the 1957 intensive negotiations, the Soviet Union started out with proposals for comprehensive disarmament, but after about six weeks produced alternative proposals for partial measures of disarmament. When Khrushchev addressed the United Nations General Assembly in 1959, he devoted most of his speech to general and total disarmament, but also emphasized that if general and total disarmament could not presently be achieved, the Soviet Union would consider measures for partial disarmament, and enumerated a number of the measures on which negotiations could immediately commence. On the other hand, in the ten-power discussions, all efforts of the Western representatives to focus the discussions on the first stage of a program of general and total disarmament—which was the equivalent of partial measures of disarmament—failed. This could mean that the Soviet Union has again shifted its course away from the precise and detailed discussions that have made possible the progress in the test cessation negotiations, and back toward the general enunciation of propaganda slogans that thwarted all the negotiations from 1947 until 1955. On the other hand, this shift might be a temporary one, to reap immediate propaganda benefits, perhaps induced by the Soviet belief that during the year of an American presidential election, no progress toward agreement on arms control was possible.

In view of this Soviet posture, it would appear to be advantageous for the West to take some steps in the 1961 reconvened General Assembly to assure that the next stage of the negotiations will deal from the outset with first-stage measures. The Assembly will inevitably pass a resolution calling for a renewed discussion. A provision recommending immediate negotiation of a detailed first stage of disarmament, comprehending reductions and limitations of armaments as well as the control machinery to ensure their enforcement would almost certainly receive such broad support that the Soviet Union could not readily oppose it. Such a provision might eliminate days of futile debate in the next stage of the negotiations during which the Soviet delegate would follow the typical Soviet tactic—"You [the West] make a substantive concession and we [the Soviet bloc] will agree to talk."

2. The Soviet Union has set more precise limitations than hitherto on the degree of inspection and international control it will permit prior to a realization of general and complete disarmament.

> The extent of the control and inspection exercised shall correspond to the stage reached in the phased disarmament of States. Upon the completion of general and complete disarmament which shall include the disbandment of all services of the armed forces and the destruction of all types of weapons including weapons of mass destruction (nuclear, rocket, chemical, bacteriological), the International Control Organ shall have free access to all objects of control.[7]

Both in its proposals of September 1959 and June 1960, the Soviet Union has ruled out unrestricted access of international inspection machinery to Soviet territory and unlimited aerial overflight of Soviet territory in the early stages of a disarmament program. Presumably, it would not rule out limited overflight or limited ground inspection directly related to specific commitments. A more rigid Soviet position on controls would lessen if not destroy the possibility of meaningful negotiations. Perhaps this is merely an opening position, which might be changed in the course of detailed discussions. It may go no further than to constitute Soviet notice to the West that if the West insists on establishment of an international control system in the initial stage of the disarmament program, the objects of control must be limited to those where the control system would not require ground access to or overflight of the entire Soviet territory.

3. The inordinate length of the nuclear test cessation conference leads to the suspicion that the Soviet Union may be deliberately prolonging the negotiations in order partially to paralyze the defense

---

[7] "Declaration of the Soviet Government on General and Complete Disarmament, Sept. 19, 1959" U.N. Doc. A/4219 (Sept. 19, 1959).

efforts of the West. Other interpretations are possible.[8] For example, the Soviet Union may today place little value on nuclear test cessation unless accompanied by further agreements to ensure that Germany will never become a nuclear power. The Soviet dilatory tactics, however, underline the necessity of the West's maintaining its military strength during negotiations. There is no inconsistency between simultaneous rearmament and negotiation for disarmament, and past Soviet attempts in the United Nations to reap propaganda benefits from any Western posture of strength have failed.

4. The movements away from an accord have not been confined to the Soviet Union. We have seen how the United States on occasions has taken positions completely at variance with its longest established policies. The August 29, 1957, Western proposals cast doubts on the previously expressed determination of the United States and United Kingdom to prevent the spread of nuclear weapons to other countries. In the General Assembly of 1957, the Western powers reversed their precedent of ten years standing that they would refrain from seeking approval of their substantive positions over Soviet opposition. Also in 1957, Secretary of State Dulles had called into question the position originally taken by President Truman nine years earlier and confirmed by President Eisenhower that disarmament discussions should proceed simultaneously with efforts to resolve other outstanding political issues. Similarly, the United States proposals in the surprise attack conference in 1958 as well as the Western proposals at the outset of the Ten-Power Conference in 1960 must have appeared to the Soviet Union as a retrogression on the part of the West to their pre-1954 positions that controls must precede limitations. The Western concept that controls and limitations might be phased, first developed in 1954, had encouraged the initial Soviet relaxations of its earlier intransigent positions.

It must be well-nigh incomprehensible to the Soviet leaders that the Western states, and in particular the United States, can lightly move away from well-established positions and can equally lightly move back to them. Any such changes in Soviet policy would have implied a basic shift that might last for years.

[8] See above Chap. 18.

Despite these meanderings it is suggested that in general the direction of the highway of arms control negotiations has been toward increasing accord.

DIRECTION POSTS

This analysis of fifteen years of negotiations has now reached the point where it is possible to make suggestions for the future. These suggestions rest on certain basic assumptions, the most vital of which is that arms control negotiations are important and can materially affect East-West relationships. The present Soviet policy of "peaceful coexistence" comprehends within it negotiations on arms control and possibly, though not certainly, agreements that are not one-sided. The policy also contemplates the unacceptable Soviet goal of the ultimate world-wide triumph of communism. If negotiations are to be of long-term value, the Western assumption must be that an extended period of world peace accompanied by reduction of tensions and some reciprocal limitations of armaments may eventually lead to Communist acquiescence in an indefinite postponement of aggressive Communist expansionism.

The assumption that arms control negotiations are important includes a corollary that the West can continue to negotiate and at the same time maintain its military strength. This study does not question the supreme importance of Western deterrent capability in preventing the outbreak of war, and assumes that negotiations can be conducted in a manner that will avoid the weakening of the deterrent.

A further assumption is that even with the rapid changes in military technology, an accord resulting from arms control negotiations can be reduced to writing in such a manner that it will contribute to world peace and security. If the accords cannot be reduced to a formal written agreement, then they need not be achieved by formal negotiation.[9]

Finally, an assumption underlying all arms control negotiations is

[9] One alternative to the negotiating technique would be unilateral but presumably related announcements by the West and the Soviet Union of voluntarily assumed limitations.

that increased East-West contacts can create better understanding and produce a climate in which war is less likely.

CONDITIONS OF NEGOTIATIONS

1. For better or for worse, the great powers seem to be embarking on long and protracted technical negotiations for a disarmament or an arms control program. The prototype for these negotiations may well be the present conference to achieve cessation of nuclear testing.[10]

For the immediate future, it seems probable that the only convincing objection to most proposals of the Soviet Union for arms control will be that it is unwilling to permit a sufficient breach of its iron curtain to give any assurance to the world that the Soviet Union is observing its own commitments. The only method of establishing the inadequacy of Soviet control proposals is to go through the difficult and tedious detailed negotiations on the control machinery required to ensure observance of any and all first-stage measures mutually acceptable to the Soviet Union and the West. Too often in the past, the shortcomings of the Western performance have permitted the Soviet Union to reject Western moves for the wrong reason—for a reason which did not disclose to the entire world that the sole issue of consequence was *Soviet* insistence on maintaining its own iron curtain. Detailed negotiations furnish the most effective measure of the merits and failings of the Soviet approach.

2. The Western guide to any such negotiation must be nothing less than a strategic plan for disarmament. General Maxwell Taylor points out that Western strategic planning today deals with the problem of all-out war but does not adequately take into consideration the more likely eventuality of a limited nuclear war or a war with conventional weapons.[11] Almost certainly the strategic planning likewise does not

[10] Statement of Philip D. Farley, Special Assistant to the Secretary of State for Disarmament and Atomic Energy, in *Technical Problems and the Geneva Test Ban Negotiations,* Hearing before the Senate Committee on Foreign Relations, 86 Cong. 2 sess.

[11] Maxwell D. Taylor, *The Uncertain Trumpet* (1960), Chap. 4, pp. 57-79.

take into account the possibilities of limitations and reductions of armaments. The West could profitably have four strategic plans: for all-out war, for limited nuclear war, for war with conventional armaments, and for disarmament. The strategic plan for disarmament should cover the problem of conversion of United States industry to nonmilitary uses in the event of an agreement for drastic reductions of armaments.[12]

3. It is fundamental that all Western proposals shall be both politically attractive and sound. If they are unsound, the skilled Soviet negotiators will inevitably expose their weaknesses; if they are politically unattractive, the Soviet Union continues to be willing to interrupt the most serious of negotiations in order to secure a cheap propaganda advantage. Arms control proposals are directed to two separate audiences: the delegations of the United Nations and world public opinion. With the vast increase in membership of the United Nations through the admission of the newly formed states of Asia and Africa, the Western powers should more than ever seek to address their proposals to the United Nations delegates with the realization that in perhaps the majority of the Members of the United Nations, there is no coherent public opinion apart from the intellectual and social elite that dominates the life of these states and generally furnishes the United Nations delegates.

4. On the crucial question of adequacy of safeguards, the West should not hold out for an ideal system of safeguards but should ordinarily look with favor on a safeguarded agreement providing considerably more security than a situation of no agreement and no safeguards. The application of this standard to a specific situation such as the nuclear test cessation negotiations is very difficult and requires full knowledge and understanding of security considerations.

5. While the United States should continue to seek a unified posi-

[12] The Soviet Union seems to be much further away from a strategic plan for disarmament than the United States. The broad "Communist line" on arms control is reasonably clear and consistent, and changes are infrequent and slow. However, except on nuclear test cessation and to a less extent on surprise attack, the negotiations reveal little Soviet thinking in the direction of transforming the broad line into a practical program.

tion with its allies, it should nevertheless recognize that a point may come in the negotiations when a unified position is no longer possible. The United States has witnessed French opposition to inclusion of test cessation in the first stage of disarmament negotiations unless it is linked to other measures requiring too vast a breach of the iron curtain to be acceptable in a first stage to the Soviet Union. The United States has in the past seen German opposition to any provisions for inspection zones within Central Europe to lessen the likelihood of the outbreak of hostilities in that tinder-box area which might spread into a world conflagration. The United States may well witness in the near future Chinese Communist opposition to first-stage provisions deemed essential by both the Soviet Union and the West. It is entirely possible that the nuclear powers of today might reach agreement on measures that would receive the support of neither their Western allies nor of Communist China. It is possible that in the event of such an agreement, world peace and security would be better served through going forward with the agreement than through maintaining complete Western unity in the arms control negotiations. Expressed in another way, the time may fast be approaching when a unified Western position obtained figuratively through determining the lowest common denominator of all separate Western positions will no longer be adequate.

6. The Western powers should not oppose in principle inclusion of representatives of neutral powers in the negotiating groups reporting to the Disarmament Commission. The presence of neutral states is some assurance against extreme Soviet proposals. This does not necessarily mean that the West should support the specific Soviet move to add five designated neutral states to the Ten-Power Conference. If the negotiating group is thus enlarged, the West should make it clearly understood that certain portions of the negotiations may have to be undertaken by a considerably smaller group—perhaps only the Soviet Union and the United States—and that in effect the enlargement of the Ten-Power Conference will mean one additional step in the already slow process of negotiation.

7. The United States, and if possible other Western powers, should maintain and increase their military strength during the arms control negotiations and until the world has incontrovertible evidence that

the efforts to limit armaments under international safeguards will be at least partially successful. This may involve a type of central planning and direction and public discipline, which the American public in the past has accepted only in times of "hot" war. The planning and discipline may be necessary not only to meet the present Soviet challenge, but also to convert the American economy in the unlikely event of an agreed program for vast reductions in armaments. The very existence of central planning and direction, however, would go some distance in convincing the Soviet Union that the United States is seriously interested in disarmament, and in refuting the Communist line that the United States can never disarm extensively because of the destructive effects on its capitalist economy.

FEASIBLE FIRST STAGE

MEASURES

The negotiations have evolved in such a manner that any and all first-stage measures must be linked to the ultimate objective of drastic reductions and limitations of armaments. However, the most important and most detailed negotiations must of necessity deal with the first stage. It is suggested that five areas have emerged where negotiations for a first stage might result in accords.

1. Nuclear test cessation. This is the only area in the field of arms control where the Soviet Union and the West have come to grips with the problem of devising specific treaty language. This subject is especially suitable for a first-stage agreement, because the control machinery required to detect underground explosions with a yield of twenty kilotons or more and other explosions of considerably less magnitude, would be much less extensive and oppressive than for most other forms of arms control.

Also, a test cessation agreement might delay the spread of nuclear weapons to fifth, sixth, and "n'th" countries and is therefore in an area where the self-interest of the Soviet Union seems to coincide with that of the United States.

The dilatory tactics of the Soviet Union in the long negotiations commencing in 1958 raise the question whether the Soviet Union is utilizing the device of protracted discussions accompanied by an unsafeguarded moratorium on testing to secure a military advantage. In the absence of a finding by the President of the United States that the immediate resumption of nuclear testing is essential to the security of the United States, the United States and the United Kingdom should seek as rapidly as possible to resolve their remaining differences with the Soviet Union and to achieve agreement expressed in a convention for the cessation of nuclear testing. One reason for early agreement is that the experience in installing and operating the control machinery required by such a treaty should materially expedite the implementation of additional conventions requiring more complex control machinery. The remaining differences with the Soviet Union might be more readily resolved if simultaneous negotiations were instituted which would ensure that Germany and perhaps Communist China would never become nuclear powers as a result of transfer of weapons from existing nuclear powers.

2. Establishment of zones free of nuclear weapons. The Western powers should seek to resume negotiations with the Soviet Union on measures to prevent surprise attack including zones in Europe and perhaps elsewhere free of nuclear weapons and zones of aerial overflight. The crux of the Soviet proposals of 1958 in the surprise attack conference was the establishment of a zone in Central Europe—including Germany—that would be free of nuclear weapons. The control system to ensure observance of the commitments involved in any such agreement would be extensive in the zones, but might not be objectionable to the Soviet Union as only a relatively small portion of the Soviet Union need be located either in the "nuclear-free" zone or in the zone of aerial overflight.

The establishment of a nuclear-free zone in Central Europe, with an international inspection system, would presumably lessen the danger of outbreaks of local hostilities that might spread into a third world war. An agreement on a nuclear-free zone in Central Europe would also give reasonable assurance that in the foreseeable future,

Western Germany would not become a nuclear power. On many occasions, the Soviet Union has indicated the importance it attaches to this objective and presumably it would be willing to pay a high price to ensure its achievement. Part of that price might be outside the field of arms control negotiations and might include the settlement of the Berlin problem.

Thus, the establishment of a nuclear-free zone in Central Europe is probably at the moment inextricably intertwined with more general political settlements, and could not proceed any distance prior to a decision of a summit conference. However, an immediate indication of Western willingness to negotiate in this area might facilitate both a meaningful summit conference and the resolution of the remaining differences in the test cessation conference. Admittedly, any move in the direction of changing the status quo in Germany involves grave risks, which must be balanced against the risks inherent in the maintenance of an unsatisfactory status quo in Germany over a long period of years.

3. Control of missiles and missile delivery systems. The Western powers should enter into negotiations with the Soviet Union on the control of missile and other systems for the long-range delivery of weapons of mass destruction. The Soviet proposals of May 1960 should be discussed in detail to determine whether the Soviet Union is ready to accept in the first stage of a disarmament program an international control system adequate to ensure against violations. The United States should renew its proposals of June 1960 for prior notification to an international disarmament control organization of all proposed launchings of space vehicles and missiles and their tracks. The United States proposals should be linked, however, to a safeguards system required to detect violations rather than to the more extensive systems necessary to prevent violations.

The Ten-Power Conference produced two radically different approaches to the problem of control of missiles and missile delivery systems. The Western proposals of June 29, 1960, called merely for (1) a prior notification to an international disarmament control organization of all proposed launchings of space vehicles and missiles and their tracks and (2) an agreement that such launchings should be solely for peaceful purposes. While the technical difficulties of a system to ensure detection of unauthorized missile launchings should not be minimized,[13] such a system would not require land access to or overflight of the entire area of the Soviet Union. Indeed the monitoring system might involve less of a breach of the iron curtain than the system contemplated in the test cessation negotiations.

The safeguards system included in the Western proposals of June 1960 is far more extensive and seems more suitable for preventing unauthorized missile tests than for detecting them after they have taken place. It is inconceivable that the Soviet Union would agree to the installation of this more extensive system except as a part of an agreement eliminating missile delivery systems.

The Soviet proposals for elimination in the first stage of all missile launching systems as well as all other methods of long-range delivery of nuclear weapons would require a vast inspection system, encompassing the entire Soviet Union. It is most unlikely that the Soviet Union would agree to such an inspection system and thus sacrifice fully its secrecy in the first stage of a disarmament negotiation. However, if the Soviet Union would accept and install an adequate control system as a part of the first stage, it is difficult to envisage how this Soviet proposal could affect adversely the security of the West. Therefore, a detailed discussion of the Soviet proposal becomes essential.

4. Agreed reduction of armed forces and conventional weapons. The West should seek to enter into technical negotiations for some limitations of armed forces and conventional armaments. The distance between the stated Western and Soviet positions for first-stage limitations is narrow, and the required controls are not sufficiently extensive to furnish a major obstacle to agreement. Indeed, as early as 1957, it probably would have been possible to reach agreement in this area.

The contemplated first-stage levels of armed forces for both the Soviet Union and the United States under current proposals would not, however, require substantial reductions beyond those that are likely to take place in any event because of technological change.

[13] D. G. Brennan, D. E. Dustin, and H. G. White, *The Use of Radar for Monitoring International Agreements on Missile and Space Flights* (April 27, 1960).

Therefore, the first-stage agreement, standing alone, would have little significance. The great defect of the Western proposals of March 16, 1960, was that, with one insignificant exception, they called for no limitation or reductions in the first stage beyond those insubstantial reductions in armed forces and conventional armaments. The remaining first-stage measures called for studies of disarmament rather than actual disarmament.

Despite the diminished importance of a first-stage agreement on reduction of armed forces and conventional armaments along the lines of current Soviet and Western proposals, this is an area urgently requiring study and negotiation. With growing realization of the mutual devastation that would result from nuclear warfare, the probabilities are increasing that future wars may be waged with conventional forces and weapons. With both the Soviet Union and the United States possessing sufficient nuclear weapons to destroy each other, the arms race of the future may be in the field of conventional weapons. Furthermore, any significant limitation of armed forces and conventional weapons must necessarily, from the outset, apply to Communist China, with its mass armies, which must be brought into the negotiations at the earliest possible date.[14]

Thus, the negotiations for first-stage limitations and reductions of armed forces and armaments are likely to raise the most important issues inherent in proceeding from the first to later stages.

5. Development of an accord limiting the use of nuclear weapons. With the increasing devastation that would result from nuclear warfare, it is inconceivable that either the Soviet Union or the West would play the aggressor and initiate the first nuclear strike unless the aggressor were reasonably certain that the first strike would eliminate the retaliatory capacity of the victim. This is the situation of nuclear stalemate.

For many years the Soviet Union, as a part of its "ban the bomb" propaganda campaign, completely disregarded the gradual emergence of a nuclear stalemate. The Communist line, which received consider-

[14] Effective conventions relating to nuclear testing and missiles would require the adherence of Communist China within a relatively short period after their entry into force.

able neutralist support,[15] was that any use of a nuclear weapon was contrary to international law, even if in retaliation, and would brand the country utilizing such weapons as a war criminal. The Soviet Union has gradually receded from this extreme position, and in its 1960 proposals conceded that the use of nuclear weapons in retaliation against nuclear attack would be permissible. The Soviet Union has also suggested a renunciation of the use of nuclear weapons for a limited time, say three years.

At present, the West might not be in a position to renounce completely the use of nuclear weapons to defend against an attack pursued with conventional weapons without exposing large areas of the world to certain military defeat in the event of a Communist attack. In many areas, the Western disadvantage might be as great or greater if a war commenced with conventional weapons developed into a limited nuclear war. In the future, however, the Western military establishments may be reconstituted in such a manner that aggression with conventional weapons could be successfully resisted with conventional weapons.

Any accord that may already have developed between the Soviet Union and the West limiting the use of nuclear weapons as a result of mutual recognition of the devastation of nuclear warfare is probably at this moment confined to the utilization of the most destructive weapons. It may be in the interests of both the Soviet Union and the West to express this accord in terms of mutual renunciations. This involves two problems.

The first relates to the value of formal renunciations that are no better than the word of the renouncing states. Despite this limited value, both the Soviet Union and the West in the United Nations Charter renounced the use of force in international relations. The Soviet Union seems to attach greater significance to verbal affirmations than the West,[16] possibly because the Soviet Union seems to have little difficulty in avoiding its affirmations. It is suggested that the formalization of an existing accord might in fact enhance the possibility of prog-

---

[15] For example, Nagendra Singh, *Nuclear Weapons and International Law* (1959).
[16] Ten-Power Disarmament Committee, *Verbatim Records*, Twenty-third Meeting (April 14, 1960), Great Britain Cmd. 1152, pp. 432-33.

ress toward significant safeguarded arms control, and that the Western powers should explore the possibility of agreeing on some formula of renunciation.

The second major problem would be to work out a suitable formula. One possibility would be renunciation of the use of the most destructive nuclear weapons except in retaliation, yet permitting limited nuclear warfare to resist aggression commenced with conventional weapons. It would be very difficult to delineate boundaries between the renounced weapons and those that could still be used to defend against an attack with conventional weapons. Another possibility would be a renunciation for a limited period of time, as suggested by the Soviet Union. This also creates great problems. It is suggested, however, that this is a field worthy of exploration.

U.S. GOVERNMENT

ORGANIZATION OF ARMS CONTROL

The United States is almost certain to bear the main burden in future arms control negotiations within the framework heretofore suggested. Therefore, the development and maintenance of a suitable organization within the United States Government may be comparable in importance to the initiation of sound substantive proposals.

When Governor Harold Stassen resigned as the White House Adviser on Disarmament in March 1958, the larger portion of the skilled staff he had built up over three years had already dispersed. Over the next two years, a few members of Stassen's staff found their way into the office of the Special Assistant to the Secretary of State on Disarmament and Atomic Energy Affairs, where they joined several State Department officers to form a small group devoting its full time to the subject of arms control.

When, in 1958, negotiations were once more renewed in the two technical conferences dealing respectively with test cessation and measures to prevent surprise attack, the patterns of staffing the two sets of negotiations were in sharp contrast. The chief United States delegate in the test cessation conference was Ambassador James J. Wadsworth, the Deputy United States Representative to the United Nations, who for five years had been negotiating almost constantly with the Russians and had on many occasions represented the United States in arms control negotiations. Ambassador Wadsworth was assisted by a relatively small staff of advisers, also with considerable experience in arms control negotiations, taken from the State Department, the military services, and scientific organizations. Perhaps as a result, the test cessation conference has continued to this day with some narrowing of the differences between Soviet and Western positions.

In sharp contrast, the chief United States delegate to the surprise attack conference, William Foster, was thrust into the negotiations with approximately a month's notice. His large supporting staff of highly competent scientists and military advisers and a few high-ranking Foreign Service officers included only one officer, of comparatively low rank, with substantial experience in the field of negotiating arms control.

Foster and his staff not only had to conduct the negotiations but also had to create a United States position. The position, which he presented, faithfully reflected the skills and experience and also the limitations of his top advisers. In general, the position was technically brilliant and politically inadequate. Foster himself soon recognized the political shortcomings of the United States position and skillfully guided the conference to an agreed recess after six weeks, avoiding the East-West antagonisms that ordinarily accompany the breakup of a negotiation. As pointed out in an earlier chapter, Foster's testimony before Congress two months after the recess of the conference showed his own realization of the shortcomings of the United States effort.[17]

When the great powers decided in 1959 to resume discussion of the broader issues of arms control and disarmament, the United States Government followed the pattern of the surprise attack conference rather than that of the test cessation conference. As we have seen, the President first determined to have a complete review of all previous United States positions and appointed Charles Coolidge to conduct this review. Coolidge had no experience in arms control negotiations and

[17] See Chap. 18.

his top-ranking State Department advisers also had no such experience. Coolidge had the difficult task of learning the entire field and producing a report in four months. It would have been a miracle if the Coolidge report had produced a position that could be immediately used in arms control negotiations, and the miracle did not take place.

In January 1960, with the renewed negotiations in the Ten-Power Conference less than three months distant, the President appointed Frederick Eaton to represent the United States. Eaton also had had no experience either in negotiating with the Russians or in the field of arms control and, with the sole exception of his deputy, Charles Stelle, Eaton's top political advisers lacked such experience. As pointed out in an earlier chapter[18] Eaton, like Foster, was handicapped by a rigid and inadequate position. While Eaton's ability as a negotiator somewhat compensated in the day-to-day discussions for his lack of experience in the arms control field, he was unable to convince the United States Government of the necessity of bringing forward creative and politically realistic positions.

The United States governmental machinery dealing with problems of arms control has four main tasks: first, to conduct the basic studies essential to the development of a United States policy; second, to formulate recommendations for the United States policy; third, to translate the policy into a position suitable for presentation in an international negotiation; fourth, to conduct the international negotiations.

The first requisite for a successful governmental operation is to secure and retain an adequate staff. Prior to the appointment of Governor Stassen in 1955, except for the brief period when Baruch represented the United States in the atomic energy negotiations, the number of personnel assigned to arms control work within the United States Government was grossly inadequate. Any negotiation with the Soviet Union requires considerable luxury in the provision of personnel because of the well-established Soviet tactics of seeking to win the negotiation through exhausting the opposing negotiators.[19] From the standpoint of numbers, Stassen's staff was adequate for the arms control

---

[18] See Chap. 20.
[19] It is difficult to estimate the size of Soviet delegations, since some Soviet advisers never appear in public meetings. It is certain, however, that a large number of individuals within the Soviet Government deal with problems of arms control.

negotiations in which he participated. After Stassen's resignation, the personnel within the United States Government devoting full time to arms control activities became fewer—too few to continue with the greatest efficiency all phases of the program that commenced in 1958.

The provisions for staffing the surprise attack conference in 1958 were more than ample. However, this was a one-time operation, and the vast majority of the personnel ceased to operate in the field of arms control after the recess. Furthermore, their skills mainly related to the technical as opposed to the political aspects of arms control. Since 1958, the number of personnel assigned to arms control has been barely sufficient to keep up with the day-to-day operations and has been insufficient to permit the long-range planning and background studies essential to an efficient negotiation.

A mere increase in the number of personnel would not fully meet the problem of securing an effective organization. Arms control over the years has come to involve a wide variety of skills. It requires *expertise* in atomic energy and in military strategy and weapons systems, and also in political negotiations with the Soviet Union, in international organization and, indeed, in the background and the ritual of the arms control negotiations themselves. The experts in a particular skill must also have some aptitude for comprehension of the remaining skills that enter into the successful conduct of an arms control negotiation. For example, an atomic energy expert must have a comprehensive knowledge of his field of specialization. In addition, in order to direct his specialized knowledge into channels that can be useful in the negotiations, he must have some aptitude for international political negotiations, or at least the ability to appreciate the political requirements of such negotiations. An officer whose primary experience is in the field of international negotiations cannot be blind to fundamental scientific advances and development of new weapons systems. Thus, effective personnel must not only be flexible in their thinking and possess the ability to comprehend a variety of viewpoints, but must also combine specialized training with some broad general training.

During the period from 1946 through 1960, the conditions within the United States Government were not very propitious for attracting highly qualified personnel to the arms control negotiations. Arms control experience has not been a road for advancement in rank in either the military services or the Foreign Service. As a consequence, Foreign Service officers and military officers, after serving for two or three years in the field of arms control, were glad to obtain assignments to other activities, often just as they began to acquire the skills that would make them most useful in arms control activities. This apparently reflected the failure of individuals in both the State Department and the military services to attach great importance to the arms control negotiations.[20]

Too frequently, officials of both the State Department and the military services have failed to appreciate the importance of the negotiations and have underestimated the skills required at the official level in arms control work. As an example of recent lack of awareness, the National Planning Association has pointed out[21] that a high ranking State Department official in April 1960 acquiesced in the statement before the Appropriations Committee of the House of Representatives that the Department of State did not have or need people on its staff who were familiar with atomic energy and the technical problems of disarmament, and that its activity at disarmament conferences was confined to "protocol and arrangements and things of that kind." As a result of this performance, the Congress denied the State Department an appropriation of $500,000 for additional studies in this field, an item that had been approved by the Bureau of the Budget.

[20] The assertion has been made that the representatives of the military services and the Atomic Energy Commission have with rare exception tended to emphasize the obstacles to arms control rather than the possibilities of finding a common ground with the Soviet Union. (Saville Davis, "Recent Policy Making in the United States Government," *Daedalus*, Vol. 89, p. 957.) It is suggested that this is an overstatement. The great problem in relation to military personnel has been that the assignments have been too short to permit the officers to operate effectively. A number of officers of the Atomic Energy Commission have been engaged in arms control work for many years, one of them having been a member of Baruch's staff. The contribution of these experienced scientists, as well as of many members of the armed services whose assignments lasted for several years, has been of tremendous value.

[21] *Strengthening the Government for Arms Control,* a Report by the National Planning Association, Pamphlet 109 (1960).

Despite the difficulties of attracting adequate numbers of skilled personnel to arms control activities in the United States Government, the progress in the period from 1958 to 1960 has been great. One feature of this progress deserving special notation is the contribution of the President's Scientific Advisory Committee under Dr. James Killian and Dr. G. B. Kistiakowsky. The State Department in October 1960 set up a new unit to deal solely with problems of arms control. The Acting Deputy Director, Edmund Gullion, is a high ranking Foreign Service officer who participated actively in arms control negotiations as far back as 1947 and served three years on Stassen's staff. He has added to the previous State Department unit a group of officers from several branches of the government with notable experience in this field.

Securing suitable personnel in adequate numbers at the official level is only one phase of the problem of conducting an effective governmental operation. A second problem relates to the selection and training of a suitable negotiator. All of the Soviet negotiators have had years of training in this field. Tsarapkin and Gromyko were participating in the original 1946 negotiations. Jules Moch has represented France almost continuously since 1951; David Ormsby-Gore has represented the United Kingdom since 1957. From 1958 through the summer of 1960, Wadsworth, who since 1954 had participated in the United Nations discussions on arms control, represented the United States in the test cessation negotiations. His effective conduct of the negotiations may be in part attributable to his long experience. We have pointed out, however, that lack of an adequate United States position handicapped Foster and Eaton even more than their limited experience in international negotiations for arms control.

This points to a fundamental flaw in the organization of arms control within the United States Government. The highest officials of the Government—the President, the Secretaries of State and Defense—burdened by a multitude of problems both domestic and foreign, cannot develop sufficient familiarity with arms control problems to formulate a United States policy. The negotiator himself must have sufficient standing within the United States Government so that he can readily present the problems and his views at the highest levels of government, and must have sufficient experience and knowledge of his subject so that his presentation will be convincing. David Ormsby-Gore, as Minister of State in the United Kingdom, has sufficient rank, and with his many years of experience, carries sufficient weight in the councils of the British Government. Since the resignation of Harold Stassen and especially since the death of John Foster Dulles, no one in the United States Government with detailed understanding of arms control problems has been in a position to play a similar role. This has complicated not only the task of developing an adequate United States policy, but also of adapting the policy to the rapidly changing situations developing within the negotiations.

The difficulties of communication since 1958 between the negotiator and the highest echelons of government seem to be one key to the lack of continuity of United States policy which we have frequently noted over the years.

In summary, a sound organization within the United States Government for arms control requires:

1. A supporting staff adequate in numbers, proficient in a variety of skills and with some training in all of the major fields contributing to arms control.

2. Procedures within the government permitting the ranking official dealing on a full-time basis with arms control rapid access to the highest levels of government and facilitating the necessary interdepartmental clearances of positions.

3. An official in charge of arms control negotiations with sufficient rank to permit expeditious decisions at top levels of government, and with sufficient experience to make a convincing presentation both within the government and in the international negotiations of the problems of arms control.

In 1959 and 1960, considerable study and public discussion have taken place of the necessity for a more effective organization within the United States Government. Senator Hubert Humphrey and others have suggested the establishment of a new peace agency. The National Planning Association has made a careful review of the entire problem. During the presidential campaign, both Senator Kennedy and Vice President Nixon supported an expanded effort.

It is suggested that the following general organizational pattern seems most suitable for a successful effort by the United States in the field of arms control:

1. A separate arms control unit should be set up within the United States Government with responsibility for all of the main functions that are part of an arms control program: research and background studies, preparation and presentation within the United States Government of proposed United States policies; transformation of United States policies into negotiating positions; and conduct of the international negotiations. The most important factor of a successful organizational pattern in this field is that the same unit shall both prepare the groundwork and conduct the negotiations.

2. This unit should contain personnel with technical knowledge in the fields of atomic energy and other sciences; in weapons systems and other military problems; in international negotiations; and in the specific and highly technical field of arms control negotiations themselves. The technical personnel should have some training in the chief disciplines, other than their specialities, that enter into an arms control negotiation. Much of this training can take place through cross fertilization of ideas as a result of joint efforts to come to grips with the problems of arms control from varying viewpoints. Past experience in dealing with political-military problems outside the field of arms control, and training in the educational institutions conducting advanced political and strategic studies should be helpful.

3. The chief of the unit should be the principal United States negotiator, and his rank should permit him direct access to the President. If the unit is located within the State Department, the chief might well have the rank of Undersecretary. The chief should have a deputy who would be his alter ego in Washington on the many occasions when the chief negotiator is abroad. Because of the highly technical nature of the subject, it would be advantageous for the tenure of the chief and his deputy to be for a substantial period.

4. Because of the great interest of the Atomic Energy Commission, the Department of Defense and military services, and some other agencies in the subject of arms control, interdepartmental machinery should ensure rapid communication of ideas to and from the arms control unit, and facilitate rapid clearance of proposed positions by inter-

ested departments and agencies. The initial development of positions and background material reflecting the viewpoint of the Atomic Energy Commission, the military services, and other agencies, might better be achieved through the detail of personnel with the requisite specialized skills to the unit for assignments of several years.

5. The unit should preferably be located within the Department of State. The most important function of the unit is to conduct international negotiations, and this is within the domain of the Department of State.[22] The viewpoints of other interested agencies can be expressed through detail of personnel of such agencies to the arms control unit and through the interdepartmental machinery for clearance of positions. In the past the State Department has frequently failed to provide the necessary support for this activity, and as pointed out has often shown scant awareness of its importance. Some critics of the Department of State have doubted its ability to organize the vast technical research effort required to furnish sufficient support for the negotiations. Recent developments within the department indicate that the situation may be changing. If it should turn out, however, that the department is not in a position or is unwilling to provide adequate support for the activity, it would be preferable to station the unit in the Executive Offices of the President where the approach to the White House is easiest, rather than to split the unit into a negotiating group within the State Department and a research group in some other area of the government.

6. Many of the personnel in the unit would be on detail from the military services, or from the Atomic Energy Commission. The question arises whether the State Department officers assigned to this work should be incorporated within the Foreign Service of the United States. It is suggested that most of the work of the unit is so technical and requires such a degree of training, that assignments to the unit do not

---

[22] While all of the negotiations are conducted under the rubric of the United Nations, it seems preferable for the chief of the unit to report directly to the Secretary of State rather than to the chief of the United States mission to the United Nations. The reasons for this are the dissimilarity of the problems of arms control negotiations from other problems coming before the United Nations together with the fact that the bulk of the negotiations today take place outside the United Nations. Close liaison should be maintained between the arms control unit and the United States delegation to the United Nations.

fit readily either into the recruitment program or the program of rotation of personnel of the Foreign Service. Therefore, the positions in the unit requiring primarily a political or State Department orientation, should probably not be classified as Foreign Service positions, though suitably qualified Foreign Service officers might be assigned to them. It is suggested that a decision to classify the positions as Foreign Service positions would be justifiable only in the event of a solution of certain broader problems related to rotation of Foreign Service assignments and establishment of channels of promotion to make the Foreign Service as attractive to "specialists" as to "generalists." In the absence of these changes in existing Foreign Service programs, the unit would probably be unable to attract and retain in Foreign Service positions, personnel with the required skills and training.

This description of the organizational shortcomings of the United States efforts tends to focus emphasis on the failures of the United States and to disregard its successes. It should be reiterated that, despite all the shortcomings, the United States has made the major contribution to any progress in this field that may have taken place. The United States has gone much further than any other country in developing the detailed programs both for arms limitations and for international control systems, that is, a strategic plan for disarmament. It is necessary to reiterate that except in the two fields of surprise attack and nuclear test cessation, there is practically no evidence of serious Soviet studies such as those that have taken place in the United States, both within and outside the government, especially in 1959 and 1960.

Furthermore, from the standpoint of world public opinion, Soviet moves have frequently been far more blundering than Western moves. For example, it is probable that the Soviet Union would have stood to gain from exposing the weaknesses of the Western proposals in the Ten-Power Conference in June 1960 instead of disrupting the conference. It is especially noteworthy that Zorin's experience of many years did not prevent the ill-advised actions of his government; and that Zorin both in 1957 and in 1960 made it clear that his government had instructed him to make the statements breaking up the negotiations.

While an improvement of the United States organizational pattern should assist in maintaining and enhancing United States prestige, this would not be the prime objective. Despite some erratic performance, United States prestige in this field remains relatively high, partly because of Soviet blundering. The most important reason for an expansion and improvement of the United States organization for arms control is to ensure that the United States will be technically prepared to grasp effectively an opportunity for an East-West arms control agreement that would improve world security when and if that opportunity arises. It is highly unlikely that any other state will make the technical efforts required to transform an agreement in principle on safeguarded limitations of armaments into an operative treaty.

THE OUTLOOK

Jules Moch has expressed the view that the Soviet Union required immediate reduction in armed forces and armaments in order to maintain and increase its civilian production. A further motive is Soviet realization that even a triumphant war would shatter all Soviet economic progress.[23] Nevertheless, it is suggested that the record of fifteen years of negotiations does not yet support the proposition that controlled disarmament is an urgent Soviet objective. The Soviet Union apparently still hopes to achieve its preferred alternatives of disarmament of the West or of disarmament without controls. It has not yet shown a desire to sacrifice any of the strength that it derives from its secrecy in an early stage of a disarmament program.

There is no present indication that maintenance of relative Soviet military strength vis-à-vis the West is incompatible with betterment of the Soviet standard of living. There is even some indication that Soviet hopes of avoiding some of the devastation of a two-strike nuclear war have slightly increased. In these circumstances, it is difficult to find a Soviet motivation for speeding the achievement of controlled disarmament.

On the other hand, many possible developments could change Soviet motivation and Soviet positions. The years of negotiation seem to show that no single event or single motivation determines the course of

[23] Moch, op. cit., pp. 79, 80.

Soviet policy. The Soviet decisions seem to result from weighing many factors in order to achieve a balance. A comparatively slight variation in any of the numerous weights on either side of the scales might upset a precariously balanced decision and result in a changed decision. It seems unlikely that entirely new ideas will suddenly transform divergences into accords. The approach of the "new broom" has not been productive in the field of arms control.

The experience of past negotiations has shown that more probably a breakthrough to agreement on controlled disarmament would arise from each side submitting a number of technical programs, the differences in which might be coherent only to a small corps of experts on each side. A Soviet plan and a Western plan might draw sufficiently close to permit construction of a bridge between them. The West has not yet pursued such a course sufficiently resolutely and consistently to assert with conviction that further negotiations will be futile.

This process of attaining new accords may require extended and patient negotiations lasting for years. The tribulations of such negotiations, however, are more than justified if they help to avoid the outbreak of nuclear war. It is possible that arms control negotiations may be one of the roads or even the main road leading to significant future East-West accords. In that event, the negotiations would truly be a highway to peace and increased security. The West should remain in a position to travel speedily over that highway if and when its direction and destination become apparent.

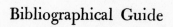

Bibliographical Guide

Bibliographical Guide

In view of the ready availability of bibliographical material, the objective of this "bibliographical guide" is to indicate the most important available materials in connection with the specific approach of this book, which might be described as an analysis of the negotiations and their relation to the chief events of the period. No attempt is made to list the materials following technical or strategic approaches to the subject. This bibliography also excludes writings dealing primarily with the general political attitudes of the Soviet Union and the West and material on the disarmament negotiations between World War I and World War II. These fields are covered in the three bibliographies listed below.

American Academy of Arts and Sciences. *Daedalus. Special Issue on Arms Control,* Vol. 89, No. 4, Fall, 1960. The most important publications since 1956 are listed in the bibliography, pp. 1055-70.

U.S. Congress, Senate. Committee on Foreign Relations. *Disarmament and Security: A Collection of Documents 1919-55.* Washington: Government Printing Office, 1956. Contains a list of "Selected References," pp. 1002-26, including references to previous bibliographies.

U.S. Department of State is presently preparing a comprehensive bibliography that should be available by the summer of 1961.

BASIC MATERIAL

The basic material for study of the postwar negotiations on arms control is found in the verbatim and summary records and in the reports of

601

the organs, commissions, and committees of the United Nations, or acting under the auspices of the United Nations, which have dealt with aspects of the arms control problem.

The Security Council dealt extensively with arms control problems in 1946-1947. The General Assembly and its political committee have dealt with aspects of arms control in all sessions since 1946. The Security Council and the General Assembly established the United Nations Atomic Energy Commission, which dealt with phases of the arms control problem in 1946, 1947, 1948, and 1949. They also established the Commission for Conventional Armaments, which dealt with other phases of the disarmament problem in each year from 1946 through 1950.

In 1946 and 1947, the Military Staff Committee, established under Article 45 of the Charter of the United Nations, dealt significantly with problems related to arms control. In 1949 and 1950, pursuant to a General Assembly resolution, the six sponsoring powers of the United Nations Atomic Energy Commission engaged in consultations to determine whether a basis existed for international control of atomic energy. In 1950, the General Assembly established the so-called Committee of Twelve to determine the possibility of combining the work of the United Nations Atomic Energy Commission and the Commission for Conventional Armaments. The committee met and issued a report in 1951. In 1951, the General Assembly established the Disarmament Commission to replace both the United Nations Atomic Energy Commission and the Conventional Armaments Commission. The Disarmament Commission continues in existence and has had sessions each year commencing in 1952. The membership of the commission was enlarged in 1957, and further enlarged in 1958 to include all the Members of the United Nations. The Subcommittee of Five of the Disarmament Commission was established by the commission pursuant to a suggestion in a General Assembly resolution in 1953, and was the most important negotiating group during 1954, 1955, 1956, and 1957.

The negotiations leading to the International Atomic Energy Agency dealt with problems closely related to arms control, and took place in several stages during the years 1954, 1955, and 1956. "The Conference of Experts for the study of Possible Measures which might be helpful in Preventing Surprise Attack" met pursuant to agreement among the great powers, with the approval of the United Nations, in 1958. The "Conference of Experts to Study the Possibility of Detecting Violations of a Possible Agreement on the Suspension of Nuclear Tests" likewise took place in 1958 and was immediately followed by the "Conference on the Discontinuance of Nuclear Weapons Tests," which continues in session (April 1961). The

Ten-Power Disarmament Committee was established as a result of an exchange of notes between the Soviet Union and the United States in the summer of 1959 and was in session in 1960.

Verbatim records of all these meetings and conferences are available at the headquarters of the United Nations and in United Nations depository libraries with the following exceptions:

1. Some of the most important developments in the United Nations Atomic Energy Commission in 1946 and in 1947 took place in subsidiary groups where no verbatim records were kept.

2. Some of the important developments in the Disarmament Commission in 1952 took place in the committees of the commission where only summary records were kept. Since these developments in all instances were in the form of statements of the United States delegate, they are available in verbatim press releases of the United States delegation to the United Nations.

3. The verbatim records of meetings of the Subcommittee of Five of the Disarmament Commission are generally unavailable in United Nations depository libraries. There were no summary records.

4. In the United Nations depository libraries, the summary records of the First Committee of the General Assembly on disarmament matters are available, but generally the verbatim records are unavailable. The verbatim records are available at the United Nations Headquarters.

5. The verbatim records of the Ten-Power Disarmament Committee have not been published officially, but a few copies are available. These records, however, have been published by the British Government. (Cmd. 1152, 1961.)

6. The extensive verbatim records of the Conference on the Discontinuance of Nuclear Weapons Tests and the short verbatim records of the surprise attack conference have not been published. They are available at the Department of State, at the British Foreign Office, and at United Nations Headquarters.

7. There are neither summary nor verbatim records of the negotiations leading to the adoption of the Statute of the International Atomic Energy Agency except for the international conference in September 1956.

8. The records of the Military Staff Committee are technically classified but add nothing to the records of the Security Council in considering the committee reports.

All committees and commissions dealing with arms control problems have issued reports of their operations that include proposals submitted to them, certain auxiliary material placed before them, and verbatim texts of some important statements. With a few exceptions, the reports do not contain conclusions or recommendations.

The most significant documents relating to the negotiations have been assembled by the United States Department of State in:

Documents on Disarmament 1945-1959, 2 vols. Publication 7008. Washington: Government Printing Office, 1960.

Two collections of documents made for the Senate Committee on Foreign Relations contain some important materials not included in the Department of State publication.

U.S. Congress, Senate. Committee on Foreign Relations. *Atoms for Peace Manual.* S. Doc. 55. 84 Cong. 1 sess. 1955.

————. ————. *Disarmament and Security: A Collection of Documents 1919-55.* 84 Cong. 2 sess. 1956.

OFFICIAL ACCOUNTS

The most complete official account of the negotiations is contained in the series of annual reports of the President of the United States to the Congress:

U.S. Participation in the U.N., Report by the President to the Congress. Annual volumes since 1945. Washington: Government Printing Office, annually beginning with 1946. Each report after 1945 dealt in some detail with arms control negotiations.

The limitations of this narrative are:

1. It reflects the official position of one government—the United States.

2. The intent of the reports is to focus attention on the sum total of activities of the United Nations in all fields each year. Therefore, the emphasis is on the relationship of the arms control negotiations to other events of the year rather than on any continuity from year to year.

3. The methods of treatment of the arms control negotiations vary considerably from year to year.

A less complete but probably more illuminating official narrative covering most of the negotiations is found in the series of "White Papers" issued by the United States Government from time to time. These include:

U.S. Department of State. *Disarmament: The Intensified Effort 1955-1958.* Publication 6676. Washington: Government Printing Office, 1958, 65 pp.

―――. *Geneva Conference on the Discontinuance of Nuclear Weapon Tests.* Publication 7090. Washington: Government Printing Office, 1960, 16 pp.
―――. *The International Control of Atomic Energy: Growth of a Policy.* Publication 2702. Washington: Government Printing Office, 1946, 281 pp.
―――. *The International Control of Atomic Energy: Policy at the Crossroads.* Publication 3161. Washington: Government Printing Office, 1948, 251 pp.
―――. *The Record on Disarmament.* Report of U.S. Deputy Representative to Disarmament Commission on London Meeting of Subcommittee of Five and on Disarmament Commission Meetings—July 1954. Publication 5581. 1954, 20 pp.
―――. *United States Efforts toward Disarmament.* Report to the President by the Deputy U.S. Representative on the United Nations Disarmament Commission. Publication 4902. 1953, 42 pp.

At least three of these reports, *Growth of a Policy, Policy at the Crossroads,* and *United States Efforts toward Disarmament,* are superb performances. The limitations of these reports are:

1. As in the case of the reports of the President, they reflect the official view of the United States.

2. There are several portions of the negotiations with which the reports do not deal.

Useful but abbreviated narratives of the negotiations from the official British point of view are:

Central Office of Information. *The Disarmament Question 1945-56.* R.F.P. 3408. London: H. M. Stationery Office, 1956, 54 pp.
Great Britain. Foreign Office. *The Search for Disarmament. A Summary.* London: H.M. Stationery Office, 1960, 46 pp.

A Soviet official account of the negotiations is contained in:

Khvostov, V. Disarmament Negotiations, History of the Problem. *International Affairs,* No. 1. Moscow, 1961, pp. 92-97. This article covers the period to 1955. A second article covering the period since 1955 has been promised.

Selected Books and Articles

The following books and articles contribute significantly to the narrative and interpretation of the negotiations:

American Academy of Arts and Sciences. *Daedalus. Special Issue on Arms Control,* Vol. 89, No. 4, Fall, 1960. Articles by the following authors deal, to a material degree, with negotiations: A. D. Barnet, Kenneth E. Boulding, Robert R. Bowie, Donald G. Brennan, Saville Davis, Paul M. Doty, William T. R. Fox, William R. Frye, Hubert H. Humphrey, Thomas C. Schelling, Jerome B. Wiesner.

L'Atome pour ou contre L'Homme. Paris: Pax Christi, 1958, 356 pp. The best account of the Stockholm Appeal.

Barnet, Richard J. *Who Wants Disarmament?* Boston: Beacon Press, 1961, 140 pp. Good description of the Baruch era and of Soviet goals.

Baruch, Bernard M. *The Public Years.* New York: Holt, Rinehart & Winston, 1960, 431 pp. Chapter XIX, "Control of Atomic Energy."

Bechhoefer, Bernhard G. "Negotiating the Statute of the International Atomic Energy Agency," *International Organizations,* Vol. XIII, No. 1, Winter 1959. An account of the negotiations leading to the formation of the agency.

Biorklund, Admiral E. *International Atomic Policy during a Decade.* London: Allen & Unwin Ltd., 1956, 135 pp. Brief chronicle of most important events with some conclusions.

Blackett, P. M. S. *Atomic Weapons and East-West Relations.* London: Cambridge University Press, 1956, 107 pp. Analysis of the background of Western decisions in the 1952-55 period.

Brodie, Bernard. *Strategy in the Missile Age.* Princeton, N.J.: Princeton University Press, 1959, 423 pp.

Byrnes, James F. *Speaking Frankly.* New York: Harper & Brothers, 1947, 316 pp. Essential background material for periods prior to 1947.

Coit, Margaret L. *Mr. Baruch.* Boston: Houghton Mifflin & Co., 1957, 784 pp. Chapter 20 deals with international control of atomic energy.

Cornides, Wilhelm. "Abrustungsverhandlungen und Deutschlandfrage seit der Genfer Gipfelkonferenz von 1955," *Europe Archives,* 1960, Folge 4, p. 103; Folge 7/8, p. 213; Folge 9, p. 281. Best narrative of German view towards arms control.

Dinerstein, H. S. *War and the Soviet Union.* New York: Frederick A. Praeger, 1959, 268 pp. Outstanding analysis of Soviet attitudes.

Dzelpy, E. N. *Désatomisea l'Europe? La Verité sur le "Plan Rapacki."* Bruxelles: Ed. Politiques, 1958, 165 pp.

Feis, Herbert. *Between War and Peace.* Princeton, N.J.: Princeton University Press, 1960, 867 pp. Chapter 23 contains the best account of the notification of the Soviet Union on the first explosion of a nuclear device.

Garthoff, Raymond L. *Soviet Strategy in the Nuclear Age.* New York: Frederick A. Praeger, 1958, 283 pp. All phases of Soviet strategy as related to arms control negotiations.

Goodrich, Leland M. and Simons, Anne P. *The United Nations and the Maintenance of International Peace and Security.* Washington: The Brookings Institution, 1955, 709 pp. Part Five deals with the United Nations program for regulation of armaments and negotiations through 1953.

Hinterhoff, Eugene. *Disengagement.* London: Stevens & Sons Ltd., 1959, 433 pp.

Kissinger, Henry A. *The Necessity for Choice.* New York: Harper & Brothers, 1961, 372 pp. Chapters IV, V, and VII take a primarily political approach and refer extensively to the negotiations.

———. *Nuclear Weapons and Foreign Policy.* New York: Harper & Brothers, 1957, 463 pp. Chapter 7 deals with political factors.

Krylov, S. B. *Materials for the History of the United Nations,* Vol. 1, "Framing of the Text of the Charter of the United Nations." Academy of Sciences of the U.S.S.R., 1949. Unpublished translation by H. Bartlett Wells (undated), 338 pp. Account from Soviet point of view of anticipated framework for world peace.

Millis, Walter, ed. *The Forrestal Diaries*. New York: The Viking Press, 1951, 581 pp. Indispensable material on United States decisions on arms control in 1946 and 1947.

Moch, Jules. *En Retard de la Paix*. Paris: Robert Laffont, 1958, 287 pp. Continues the narrative of the negotiations until 1958.

———. *La Folie des Hommes*. Paris: Robert Laffont, 1954, 285 pp. Fine statement of the emerging nuclear peril and of the negotiations from 1952 to 1954.

Murphy, Charles J. V. "The Case for Resuming Nuclear Tests," *Fortune*, Vol. LX, April 1960, p. 148. Article influenced the negotiations.

———. "Nuclear Inspection: A Near Miss," *Fortune*, Vol. LIX, March 1959, p. 122. Article influenced the negotiations.

National Planning Association. *Strengthening the Government for Arms Control*. National Planning Pamphlet 109, 1960, 28 pp. Best analysis of organizational problems within the United States Government.

Noel-Baker, Philip. *The Arms Race: A Programme for World Disarmament*. London: Stevens & Sons, 1958, 578 pp. An outstanding description of portions of the arms control negotiations combined with a brilliant exposition of the author's viewpoint.

Nogee, Joseph Lippman. "Soviet Policy Toward International Control of Atomic Energy." Unpublished dissertation, Yale University, 1958. The most comprehensive narrative of the international atomic energy negotiations.

Nutting, Anthony. *Disarmament: An Outline of the Negotiations*. London: Oxford University Press, 1959, 52 pp. Seeks to present a coherent picture of the negotiations as a whole. Only an outline.

Oppenheimer, J. Robert. "Atomic Weapons and American Policy," *Foreign Affairs*, Vol. 31, July 1953. The first indication of the probable political impact of thermonuclear weapons.

Osborn, Frederick. "Negotiating on Atomic Energy 1946-47," in Raymond Dennett and Joseph E. Johnson, eds. *Negotiating with the Russians*, Chap. 7. Boston: World Peace Foundation, 1951, 310 pp. Outstanding description of Soviet negotiating techniques.

Pokrobsky, Major General G. I. *Science and Technology in Contemporary War*. Translated and annotated by Raymond L. Garthoff. New York: Frederick A. Praeger, 1959, 180 pp. A statement of Soviet strategy by a Soviet General.

Russell, Ruth B. assisted by Muther, Jeannette E. *A History of the United Nations Charter: The Role of the United States 1940-1945*. Washington: The Brookings Institution, 1958, 1140 pp. The authoritative account of the development of the arms control provisions of the United Nations Charter.

Schelling, Thomas C. *The Strategy of Conflict*. Cambridge: Harvard University Press, 1960, 309 pp. While not primarily concerned with the negotiations or the political approach, this book is the main source of many ideas likely to appear in future negotiations.

Sherwood, Robert B. *Roosevelt and Hopkins: An Intimate History*. New York:

Harper & Brothers, 1948, 980 pp. Best account from United States viewpoint of anticipated postwar framework for world peace.

Stimson, Henry L. "The Decision to Use the Bomb," *Harper's Magazine*, April 1947.

U.S. Atomic Energy Commission. *In the Matter of J. Robert Oppenheimer; Transcript of Hearing before Personnel Security Board, April 12, 1954 through May 6, 1954*. Washington: Government Printing Office, 1954, 993 pp. Contains account of background of important United States Government decisions particularly in 1952 and 1953.

U.S. Congress. Senate. Committee on Foreign Relations. *Conference on the Discontinuance of Nuclear Weapons Tests: Analysis of Progress and Positions of the Participating Parties, October 1958-August 1960*, 86 Cong. 2 sess. Washington: Government Printing Office, 1960, 110 pp.

———. *Control and Reduction of Armaments: Final Report of the Subcommittee on Disarmament*, 85 Cong. 2 sess. S. Rept. 2501. Washington: Government Printing Office, 1958, 663 pp. A wealth of material on many phases of arms control.

Index

countries. *See under* Nuclear weapons

Suggestion for control of means of delivery of nuclear weapons, and French and Soviet support, 473, 475, 544, 545, 546-47

Support of proposals for comprehensive disarmament, incongruity of, 288-90; abandonment of, 258

Task forces appointed to study problems of control, and reports of, 263-65

Theory of deterrence through massive retaliation, revision, 250-56, 278-80

Thermonuclear device, successful tests. *See* Thermonuclear weapons

Three Nation Agreed Declaration on Atomic Energy, 33, 43

To be one of postwar powers, 16

Views on procedure of safeguards system for arms control, 162

Wadsworth, James J., 232-34, 259, 287, 290, 296, 492, 588, 592

United States Information Agency, 262

Uranium, 42-43, 64, 556

Urey, Harold C., 38

Usachev, I. G., 121, 492

Vandenberg, Sen. Arthur, 112

Vandenberg resolution, 99-101, 151

Varga, E. S., 49, 113, 149-50

Versailles Treaty limits German rearmament, 12

Veto, great-power. *See* Security Council: Voting

Veto in control commission for nuclear test ban and over on-site inspections, negotiations on in nuclear test ban conference, 494-98 *passim*, 500, 501, 506-508

von Neumann, John, 262 n

von Rauch, Georg, 150

Voznesensky, N. A., 114

Vyshinsky, Andrei, 121, 130, 141, 150, 165, 168, 207:

Attacks and claims in U.N., 144-45

Discussion of arms control in 9th General Assembly, 232-34

Reaction to tripartite proposals for arms control, 164

Statement of Soviet position on arms reduction control system, 137

Statement on Soviet nuclear explosion, 134

Support for British-French arms control proposals, withdrawal, 286-89

Wadsworth, James J., 232-34, 259, 287, 290, 296, 492, 588, 592

Wainhouse, David, 262 n

Wallace, Henry, attacks on U.S. policy toward U.S.S.R., 35, 38, 92, 113

War Department, U.S., 30, 42

Warsaw Congress, 146, 147

Warsaw pact, 331, 348

Warsaw pact countries, Soviet proposals for removal of military bases and forces of other countries in, 397, 410

Wei, Hsio-ren, 70-71

Welles, Sumner, 16

West (*see also individual countries*):

Answer to Soviet proposal in Subcommittee of Five corresponding to Stockholm appeal, 223-24

Areas of agreement and divergence with U.S.S.R. on arms control, 46, 567-76; *see also* Atomic Energy Commission, U.N.: Divergences

Chances of agreement with U.S.S.R., 5, 112-17

Concept of origin of surprise attack, 480

Concession to Soviet insistence on arms control negotiations by entire membership of General Assembly, 463

Continued military strength seen necessary, 160-61, 576, 577, 580-81

Declining prestige in arms control field, 416, 460, 463

Failure to respond to Soviet proposals for removal of military bases and forces in foreign countries, 397, 410

Military posture of, 6

Motivations in seeking nuclear test ban, 519-20

Need for arms control proposal to capture world imagination, 549

Negotiations for general arms control measures:

Future steps in, suggestions for, 574, 577-87

Positions and policies in, 7, 164, 215, 216; based on Anglo-French memorandum on phasing and timing of disarmament,

after, 5; disarmament talks after, 11-14, 22, 428, 429
World War II planning for future arms reduction, 14-24

Yalta Conference, role in planning international organization, 19, 20, 23
Yugoslavia:
Active participation in Political Committee discussions of arms control, 207
Efforts to prevent collapse of arms control negotiations, 437
Efforts to secure compromise in 13th General Assembly, 460
Proposal for cessation of nuclear tests, 340, 351
Proposals for program of partial disarmament, 397

Resolutions for increasing membership of Disarmament Commission, 424-25, 461
Soviet relations with, 150, 282

Zhdanov, Andrei, theories of, effect on Soviet ideology, 113-15, 116, 130, 149-50
Zorin, Valerian, 121, 168, 204-06, 336, 338, 392-96 *passim*, 404, 405, 596: attack on West in 1957 Subcommittee session, and rejection of proposals of, 391, 398, 398 n, 399, 409-10; reasons, 400-413; negotiations in ten-power disarmament conference, 540, 541, 543; walkout, 551-52; reaction to U.S. proposal to transfer nuclear weapons to other countries, 363